you can have a challenging career and a life too. when we were named one of *FORTUNE* Magazine's 100 best companies to work for, smart staff development and our vacation policy were cited. we believe in building challenging careers and giving you the support to lead a fulfilling life inside and outside of work. those are our priorities. what are yours? visit pwc.com/mypriorities

life-friendly*

*connectedthinking

PRICEWATERHOUSECOOPERS 🅿

you can have a challenging career and a life too. when we were named one of *FORTUNE* Magazine's 100 best companies to work for® smart staff development and our vacation policy were cited. we believe in building challenging careers and giving you the support to lead a fulfilling life inside and outside of work. those are our priorities. what are yours? visit pwc.com/mypriorities

life-friendly*

*connectedthinking

PRICEWATERHOUSECOPERS

SPECIAL
ADVERTISING
SECTION

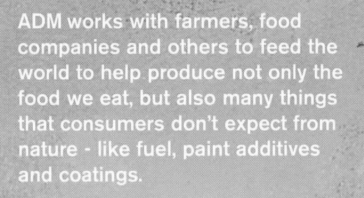

ADM works with farmers, food companies and others to feed the world to help produce not only the food we eat, but also many things that consumers don't expect from nature - like fuel, paint additives and coatings.

Whether we're finding new markets or new uses for farmers' crops, or whether we're working to meet the changing customer demands in existing markets, ADM is *Resourceful by Nature*™.

ADM®

RESOURCEFUL BY NATURE™

A family of hospitals.
For families everywhere.

The HCA Family has been providing quality healthcare since 1968. Today we are a national leader in innovative healthcare technology, providing Patient Safety initiatives which are helping to improve the future of healthcare for families across the country. Our HCA family includes 190 hospitals and more than 180,000 dedicated employees, all working together to provide the best in healthcare. It's an ongoing commitment to families, renewed daily by our family.

HCA
Hospital Corporation of America℠

NOT ON
MY WATCH.

HOMELAND SECURITY.
IT'S STAYING ONE STEP AHEAD OF THE ENEMY.

WE COMB THE DATA. RUN POSSIBLE SCENARIOS.
BECAUSE ANTICIPATING A THREAT MEANS WE CAN STOP IT.

Developing advanced surveillance systems. Providing leading-edge
infrastructure protection. The latest modeling and simulation
facilities. Northrop Grumman is committed to making sure America
is a step ahead of terrorism. It's a career defining challenge where
only the best and the brightest will succeed. Making it perfect for
someone like you.

Achievement never ends.

For current opportunities, please visit our website:
careers.northropgrumman.com

NORTHROP GRUMMAN
DEFINING THE FUTURE™

careers.northropgrumman.com

The Vault/INROADS Guide to Diversity Internship, Co-op and Entry-Level Programs is made possible through the generous support of the following sponsors:

Abercrombie & Fitch

AMERICAN FAMILY INSURANCE

AMERICAN EXPRESS

ARAMARK

ADM

ASIAN DIVERSITY CAREER EXPO

Bayer

Bristol-Myers Squibb
Hope, Triumph and the Miracle of Medicine™

CIT

citigroup

CSC
EXPERIENCE. RESULTS.

CONVERGYS
Outthinking Outdoing

Duke
REALTY CORPORATION

ERNST & YOUNG

The Vault/INROADS Guide to Diversity Internship,
Co-op and Entry-Level Programs
is made possible through the generous support
of the following sponsors:

Fifth Third Bank
Working Hard To Be The Only Bank You'll Ever Need.
Fifth Third Bank is an Equal Opportunity Employer.

imagination at work

HCA
Hospital Corporation of America

IBM

NORTHROP GRUMMAN
DEFINING THE FUTURE

Johnson & Johnson

Northwestern Mutual
FINANCIAL NETWORK

Liberty Mutual

Limited brands

OSRAM SYLVANIA

**The Vault/INROADS Guide to Diversity Internship,
Co-op and Entry-Level Programs
is made possible through the generous support
of the following sponsors:**

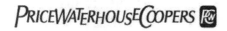

TimeWarner

XEROX.

American Express
Tax and Business Services Inc.

REACH IMAGINE FOCUS PURSUE REACH IMAGINE FOCUS PURSUE
REACH IMAGINE FOCUS PURSUE REACH IMAGINE FOCUS PURSUE
REACH IMAGINE FOCUS PURSUE REACH IMAGINE FOCUS PURSUE
REACH IMAGINE FOCUS PURSUE REACH IMAGINE FOCUS PURSUE
REACH IMAGINE FOCUS PURSUE REACH IMAGINE FOCUS PURSUE
REACH IMAGINE FOCUS PURSUE REACH IMAGINE FOCUS PURSUE
REACH IMAGINE FOCUS PURSUE REACH IMAGINE FOCUS PURSUE

One Firm, Many Pathways

American Express Tax and Business Services offers exciting careers for CPAs and Consultants who aspire to be the best in their field. Our vision, to be "The Premier Accounting and Consulting Firm Serving Mid-Market and High-Net Worth Individuals" means that we are focused on helping our clients achieve financial success through long-term relationships based on trust and superb client service.

If you are looking for a place where there is endless opportunity to grow and develop, where each day you will face new challenges, where your passion and intelligence will be rewarded then we encourage you to visit *www.americanexpress.com/tbs* to learn more about our firm!

American Express Tax and Business Services Inc. has a professional services relationship with the New York public accounting firm of Goldstein Golub Kessler LLP ("GGK LLP"), which is a separate and independently owned and operated entity. GGK LLP is a practice 100% owned by CPAs, and through our relationship with GGK LLP, our staff can acquire the experience to meet the requirements for CPA licensure. American Express Tax and Business Services Inc. is a wholly owned subsidiary of American Express, a publicly owned company. American Express employs CPAs but is not a licensed CPA firm.

We currently have the following positions available across our different practice areas:

Senior Accountant
Accounting Manager
Tax Accountant

Please visit us online at *www.americanexpress.com/jobs* where you can find detailed position descriptions and instructions on how to submit your resume as well as information about our comprehensive benefits.

The media's watching Vault!
Here's a sampling of our coverage.

"For those hoping to climb the ladder of success, [Vault's] insights are priceless."
– *Money magazine*

"The best place on the web to prepare for a job search."
– *Fortune*

"[Vault guides] make for excellent starting points for job hunters and should be purchased by academic libraries for their career sections [and] university career centers."
– *Library Journal*

"The granddaddy of worker sites."
– *US News and World Report*

"A killer app."
– *The New York Times*

One of Forbes' 33 "Favorite Sites"
– *Forbes*

"To get the unvarnished scoop, check out Vault."
– *Smart Money Magazine*

"Vault has a wealth of information about major employers and job-searching strategies as well as comments from workers about their experiences at specific companies."
– *The Washington Post*

"Vault has become the go-to source for career preparation."
– *Crain's New York*

"Vault [provides] the skinny on working conditions at all kinds of companies from current and former employees."
– *USA Today*

EXPERIENCE Success

$14.3 billion: CSC's annual revenues for the 12 months ending July 1, 2005.

853,924,175: Number of miles Space Shuttles have traveled with support from CSC.

78,000: Number of CSC employees worldwide.

5,200: Number of financial institutions worldwide that use CSC software.

221: Number of Fortune 500 companies CSC has worked with in the past 10 years.

80: Number of countries where CSC serves clients.

34: Number of languages in which CSC conducts business worldwide.

19: Number of CSC Global Centers of Excellence.

15: Number of industries CSC serves.

1: The ranking of Team CSC — CSC's world-famous cycling team — in the 2003 Tour de France Team Championship.

Based in El Segundo, California, Computer Sciences Corporation is among the world's largest providers of global IT services. Our talented staff of 78,000 professionals is testimonial to CSC's open, dynamic culture and our deep commitment to diversity.

We invite you to visit **http://careers.csc.com** to explore open positions across the global CSC. And discover for yourself why CSC is a great place to grow.

We have opportunities for candidates with skills in IT infrastructure and applications, project management, finance, and accounting. Submit your resume today (reference Job Code VR05) at **http://careers.csc.com.**

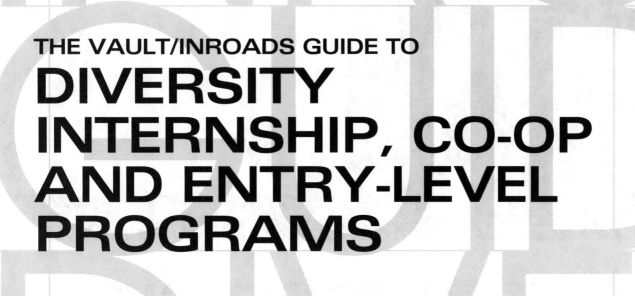

THE VAULT/INROADS GUIDE TO
DIVERSITY INTERNSHIP, CO-OP AND ENTRY-LEVEL PROGRAMS

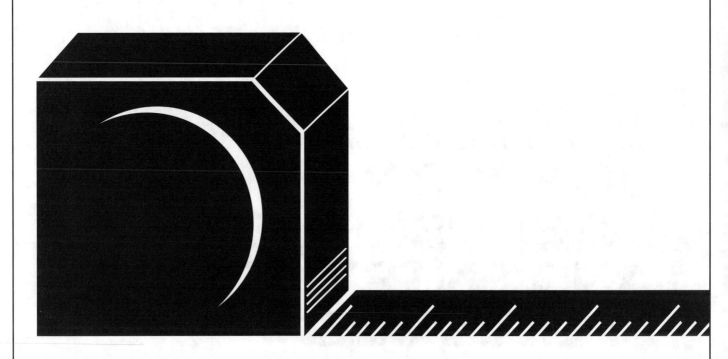

The positive effect of beginning your career with Ernst & Young is too great to measure.

A great start can take you further. At Ernst & Young we've created an environment that's conducive to personal and professional growth and success. And what we're offering is an opportunity to learn from some of the best talent in the industry. Become a benchmark for success. Visit us on the Web at ey.com/us/careers, or look for us on campus.

Audit · Tax · Transaction Advisory Services

ERNST & YOUNG

Quality In Everything We Do

©2005 ERNST & YOUNG LLP

THE VAULT/INROADS GUIDE TO

DIVERSITY INTERNSHIP, CO-OP AND ENTRY-LEVEL PROGRAMS

VAULT EDITORS

Acknowledgments

Acknowledgments from Vault

We are extremely grateful to Vault's entire staff for all their help in the editorial, production and marketing processes. Vault also would like to acknowledge the support of our investors, clients, employees, family, and friends. Thank you!

Acknowledgments from INROADS

INROADS would like to thank the entire staff of Vault for their work in completing this very useful resource. In addition, a warm thank you goes to our former CEO, Charles I. Story, for his vision in leading this effort, Wilson Martinez del Rio, Tanza Pride, Mercedes Lytle, Jacquelyne Bailey, Tina Marie Bradley, Thomas Powell, Patricia Merritt, INROADS Managing Directors and their staff, and all of our corporate sponsors who so willingly donated time, funding, and efforts to support this publication.

Special thanks also from Vault and INROADS to the committee members who helped finalize the survey: Steve Canale of GE, Shannon Thrasher-Bynes of IBM, Carin Kaiser of Kraft, Shaneen Tatum of Lockheed Martin and Kim Washington-Barr of PricewaterhouseCoopers.

Diversity

is a source of strength for our people and our businesses.

At Citigroup, we have worked hard to create a workplace with an emphasis on inclusion, innovation and merit, rooted in our shared values and respect for our colleagues and the millions of people we serve. We aspire to be a company where the best people want to work; a company dedicated to empowering individuals and families around the world; and a company that provides opportunity for all.

citigroup͡

Table of Contents

Employers highlighted above provided generous underwriting support for the Vault/INROADS Guide to Diversity Internship, Co-op & Entry-Level Programs.

Employers highlighted above provided generous underwriting support for the Vault/INROADS Guide to Diversity Internship, Co-op & Entry-Level Programs.

INROADS®

UNLEASH YOUR POTENTIAL

TEREX, the third largest equipment manufacturer in the world, strives to recruit, employ and develop highly talented and motivated individuals.

We believe that having a diverse group of employees stimulates ideas and creative thinking, a key to both our success and yours.

For more information about TEREX internships and career opportunities, please visit us at www.terex.com.

THE STRENGTH OF MANY. THE POWER OF ONE.

TEREX is an Equal Opportunity Employer / Affirmative Action Employer M/F/D/V

 TEREX

Employers highlighted above provided generous underwriting support for the Vault/INROADS Guide to Diversity Internship, Co-op & Entry-Level Programs.

Our differences
make our community stronger.

We embrace all the things that
make us different. We support
an environment that respects
every person's heritage . . .
every person's dreams.

Exelon.

Employers highlighted above provided generous underwriting support for the Vault/INROADS Guide to Diversity Internship, Co-op & Entry-Level Programs.

CIT is a leading commercial and consumer finance company and a leader in the financial industry. We are committed to the development of our employees and invite you to explore the opportunities we have available. Whether you are just beginning your career or are a seasoned professional, there are a variety of current opportunities that could be right for you. We offer competitive salaries and comprehensive benefits as well as programs for educational assistance, Work/Life and internal training. For more information about a career at CIT, visit us at www.cit.com.

1 CIT Drive
Livingston, NJ 07039

It is the policy of CIT to be an Equal Opportunity Employer. CIT maintains a policy of nondiscrimination with employees and applicants for employment. No aspect of employment with CIT will be influenced in any manner by race, color, religion, age, sex, national origin, marital status, disability, citizenship, veteran status, sexual orientation or any other basis prohibited by applicable law.

CIT

Introduction

Vault is proud to partner with INROADS, a top non-profit organization that trains and develops talented minority youth for professional careers in business and industry, on the first annual edition of the *Vault/INROADS Guide to Diversity Internship, Co-op & Entry-Level Programs*. Vault and INROADS make ideal partners to bring students, young professionals and educators the most recent, accurate and up-to-date information on corporate diversity planning, representation, strategies and programs.

For this first annual Guide, 129 top companies and organizations shared their actions and goals in the crucial area of corporate diversity in self-reported profiles. By participating in the Guide, companies are not endorsing Vault or INROADS, and there is no requirement that they be, have been or plan to be an INROADS partner. Rather, they are expressing their commitment to, and appreciation of, the importance of diversity in the 21st century workplace.

We thank all the participants in the first annual *Vault/INROADS Guide to Diversity Internship, Co-op & Entry-Level Programs* and we hope that its readers will find it instructive and useful in evaluating potential employers and partners.

The Editors
Vault, Inc.

Letter from Charles I. Story

Dear Reader,

We are proud to have been invited by Vault, the nation's premier career guide publisher, to participate in the inaugural issue of the *Vault/INROADS Guide to Diversity Internship, Co-op and Entry-Level Programs*. Working with Samer Hamadeh, Vault President and CEO, and his staff has been a pleasure. We now have a guide to assist talented, qualified students with resource information to aid them in their search for opportunities. In addition, corporations now have a source with which to benchmark their pipeline programs. As more young people of color pursue corporate opportunities, there inevitably will be more diversity on the executive floors of corporations across the country.

Having worked with corporations for 25 years, it is readily apparent that, despite much progress, there is still a dearth of diversity at executive levels. The Guide will enable corporations to demonstrate their commitment to diversity and its benefits.

Until diversity at all levels is no longer an issue, partnerships and resource guides such as this one, will continue to be a requisite ingredient in doing business. INROADS is pleased to be a part of the solution for corporations who believe in the imperative of building diverse workforces, yet struggle with developing a pool of hirable, trainable, and promotable professionals who can, over time, shape the direction of business and industry.

Creating these opportunities for students and businesses is what INROADS does, it's what we believe in, and it's what gets us out of bed every morning. INROADS identifies and develops a consistent flow of future executive talent through an intense internship process that includes training, mentoring and coaching.

I am very excited about the possible impact this guide will have on our communities and schools and expect it to positively affect the future workplace. I challenge students and new graduates to evaluate the opportunities listed in this book and to learn more about INROADS. Opportunities are there for the taking. It's up to you to take advantage of them. If you are reading this letter as a corporate leader, I challenge you to make a difference in your workplace and continue to nurture diversity. Become a partner with INROADS and sponsor a Next Level Opportunity!

Mission Led,

Charles I. Story,
President and CEO

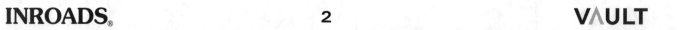

Letter from Chris Simmons

PricewaterhouseCoopers (PwC) is honored to be among the top organizations that stand out as leaders in diversity. Diversity is not just a feel-good proposition; it is about finding the best talent, hiring them, coaching and developing them, keeping them motivated, and retaining them for many years to come.

Why should companies focus energy on diversity? For one, the demographics of the population, as well as the population mix on college campuses, are changing. We understand that in order to be competitive in this new talent world, your reputation and competency in the area of diversity must be first-class.

A top inclusion strategy is not about treating everyone the same. It's about doing what is appropriate based upon individual differences-where people come from, their background and their experiences-to make everyone feel welcome, valued and supported. We acknowledge that while special standards are never acceptable, special efforts are often required. National diversity programs should be geared toward closing some of the gaps in terms of recruiting, retention and leadership representation among women and minorities. While companies have made significant progress, there is much more work to be done.

Much of PwC's success in the area of diversity recruiting has resulted from our partnership with INROADS, which has provided us with some of the best minority talent this country has to offer. In fact, in 2005 PwC was the largest employer of INROADS interns, sponsoring over 200 interns. In 2004, the firm offered jobs to 93% of the graduating seniors, 91% of which were accepted.

PwC is a proud supporter of the mission and objective of the INROADS program and this guide, and we congratulate INROADS and Vault on this extraordinary project. This annual directory will provide minority students the information they need to get their start at some of the world's greatest organizations.

I wish each of you the best.

Sincerely,

Chris Simmons
Chief Diversity Officer
PricewaterhouseCoopers

IT REALLY IS ALL ABOUT YOU.

We know, you've heard that before. But at INROADS® it's true. Apply for the Internship that gets you into America's top companies. You're a high achiever. Have good grades. And a burning desire to rock the corporate world. So why wait until you graduate? You can be there NOW.

INROADS Interns work for companies like **GE, Pfizer, Lockheed Martin and other Fortune 500s.** Take the opportunity to lead and grow. Get training from executive mentors. Get the inside track to a great career and a great future. *And get paid.*

INROADS is listed by the Princeton Review as one of America's Top Ten Internships. So, if you've got what it takes, take the first step.

To apply online, visit us at **www.INROADS.org.**

The mission of INROADS is to develop and place talented minority youth in business and industry and prepare them for corporate and community leadership.

INROADS®

How to Use this Guide

Over the past few years, most U.S. companies have devoted increasing resources to diversity initiatives as well as to the management and administration of these efforts. Nearly all have developed their own unique cultural approach and methods of administration. The *Vault/INROADS Guide to Diversity Internship, Co-op and Entry-Level Programs* was developed to provide students with the essential objective information necessary to meaningfully evaluate corporate diversity initiatives and programs. We hope that the information contained within this guide will enable students to match their interests and career objectives with an appropriate company.

The guide format presents the same information for all companies in a user-friendly way, addressing the degree to which several widely-recognized "best practices" are being incorporated into the company's diversity program.

The complete survey sent to the company is printed in the guide. In cases where a company did not respond to a question, the unanswered question is not reprinted in their profile; it is simply left out. For questions where companies had the option of choosing one or more options to answer a question, we listed the choices the company chose; to see which answers the company did not choose, you can refer to the full text of the survey.

We encourage you to use the information in the guide as a springboard to ask constructive questions and open a dialogue that will empower you to define your relationship with the company. In the case of students evaluating potential employers, it may be whether the company's efforts measure up to your personal goals and developmental needs.

The survey upon which the *Vault/INROADS Guide to Diversity Internships, Co-ops and Entry-Level Programs* is based was finalized by the efforts of a committee composed of representatives from top companies in fall 2004. Participants included Steve Canale of GE, Shannon Thrasher-Bynes of IBM, Carin Kaiser of Kraft, Shaneen Tatum of Lockheed Martin and Kim Washington Barr of PricewaterhouseCoopers.

Definitions

The survey refers to full-time or permanent exempt employees in the U.S. Entry-level college graduate hires are new full-time, professional or white-collar hires made directly from undergraduate institutions. The survey also covers interns, who typically work during the summer months, and co-ops, who typically work for more extended periods of time during the school year.

For this survey, diversity is defined as male and female minorities and white women but does not include gay and lesbian employees.

For this survey, minorities are defined as those whose ethnic background is other than White/Caucasian (e.g., African-American/Black, Latino/Hispanic, Asian and Native American).

Firm Contact Info

This section contains basic information, including the contact person for diversity hiring. Offices and revenues, also in this section, give a sense of the size of the company.

Recruitment

Here's where you find out how to get hired at the company of your choice. This section contains useful information on schools at which the company recruits (for new hires) as well as other outreach efforts, including participation in conferences, career panels and scholarship programs. Similar info is available for professional hires, as well as insight on whether the company uses women and/or minority-owned executive search firms to make hires.

Internships and Co-ops

Internships and co-op programs are a key way to be hired by any top company. This section describes the type of internship and co-op programs (there may be more than one) offered by the company, as well as contact information.

Scholarships

Many companies offer special scholarship programs for qualified minority students. You'll find the details, including the amount, the deadline to apply and contact information in this section for companies that offer scholarships.

Affinity Groups/Employee Networks

If you're thinking of joining a company you may wish to join an affinity group or employee network, which is an internal organization that addresses the needs and interests of specific minority groups. and other employee groups

Entry-Level Programs/Full-Time Opportunities/Training Programs

Looking for a place to work after graduation that may differ from the place where you did your internship? This section gives an overview of the type of entry-level positions at the company, including training and any kind of educational perks, like tuition reimbursement.

Strategic Plan and Diversity Leadership

Once a company has committed to work at being more diverse, there are various ways in which the company can advance that commitment. It may be helpful for the reader to pay attention to what steps the company's management has taken to communicate its diversity commitment widely and to develop a clear action plan for progress. Is diversity progress a goal that has been set with company-wide responsibility and accountability? Do diversity leaders have a voice on management issues? You can begin to explore some of those issues in this section.

Demographics

Find out how large your potential employer is, and see its revenue growth. Companies may choose to add additional information on minority and male/female demographics if they choose.

Retention and Professional Development

This section covers retention rates of women and minorities, as well as the steps the company is taking to reduce attrition.

Diversity Statement

Many companies have a kind of guiding credo that shapes their approach to employment diversity issues; you'll find it in this section (if the company has one.)

Additional Information

This section of the diversity profile is comprised of a narrative composed by the company. There were no requirements regarding what had to be addressed (although we admit to having made a few suggestions). For example, some companies chose to list diversity awards. This section offers a great place for the company to elaborate on some of its answers to the survey question and discuss things they are doing that we may have failed to cover.

In conclusion, we hope that this book assists you in identifying companies that are a good match to your diversity values and needs. Remember: although you can get a quick impression by flipping through these pages and looking at diversity program overviews, and yes/no responses, the most important factor is the commitment of the company to diversity goals. We hope you find what you're looking for in the *Vault/INROADS Guide to Diversity Internship, Co-op and Entry-Level Programs*.

Survey Invitation Letter from Vault and INROADS

Dear Employer,

We are writing to invite you to participate in an exciting project and to ask for your involvement in what promises to be an effective means to explore corporate performance in the critical area of diversity.

INROADS, a non-profit organization that trains and develops talented minority youth for professional careers in business and industry, and Vault Inc., a premier source of employment information for MBAs, JDs, college students and grad students, have partnered to develop the attached Corporate Diversity Survey. We finalized the survey with the advice and assistance of a committee of representatives from top employers (GE, IBM, Kraft Foods, Lockheed Martin and PricewaterhouseCoopers – all among the INROADS Top 10 in terms of number of interns). We are requesting that all firms listed below complete the survey, which we believe represents the best way to stimulate diversity progress and achieve a measure of consistency in how diversity information is reported.

Vault will compile all of the completed surveys into a directory called the *Vault/INROADS Guide to Diversity Internship, Co-op & Entry-Level Programs*. The guide's purpose is to educate the business and career center communities, as well as interested students and recent graduates, on the commitment and types of diversity programs in place at approximately 600 major corporations (see list below). The objectives of publishing the guide are:

- To provide a consistent profile of current corporate diversity planning, implementation and representation;

- To identify the best practices for the design and implementation of diversity initiatives in companies; and

- To outline the strategies, programs, and metrics that top companies use to increase the recruitment, retention and promotion of minority and women employees.

This guide differs from some of Vault's other publications, such as the *Vault Guide to the Top 100 Law Firms* and the *Vault Guide to the Top 50 Banking Employers*, in two significant ways:

- **There are no rankings.** Rather, Vault is simply gathering and presenting information about each company's diversity efforts. Firm profiles will appear in alphabetical order.

- **All information is self-reported by each firm.** Each employer's data will be published virtually as submitted, with only minor editing from Vault for clarity and length, and all edits will be reviewed <u>and approved by the employer prior to publication</u>.

The *Vault/INROADS Guide to Diversity Internship, Co-op & Entry-Level Programs* will be distributed in print and electronic form free of charge to every firm that submits a completed survey, to 10,000 current and recent INROADS Interns, and to the career center offices at approximately 500 colleges and universities in the United States.

We hope that you will join us in this effort by completing and returning the attached survey in a timely manner.

If you have any questions, please direct them to Vault VP of Content, Marcy Lerner, at (212) 366-3724 or mlerner@vault.com, or INROADS New Media Manager, Tanza Pride, at TPride@INROADS.org.

Best regards,

Charles Story
President & CEO
INROADS
www.INROADS.org

Samer Hamadeh
Co-founder & CEO
Vault
www.vault.com

Vault/INROADS Diversity Survey

Survey Introduction

Thank you for taking the Vault/INROADS Diversity Survey (2006 edition). Following are a few pointers on completing the survey. If you have any questions about the survey or how to answer a question, please contact Marcy Lerner, Vault VP of Content, at marcy@staff.vault.com or at (212) 366-3724, or Tanza Pride, INROADS New Media Manager, at tpride@INROADS.org. We thank you for your understanding and welcome comments and feedback as we seek to improve the survey for future editions.

The Process

Participation is entirely free of charge. We ask that a representative or group of representatives from your firm complete the attached questionnaire (in MS Word format) within the next five weeks. Please note that each firm should complete and return only one questionnaire. Do not handwrite or PDF survey responses. Please e-mail the completed questionnaire to editor Woodwyn Koons at wkoons@vault.com.

Distribution

The *Vault/INROADS Guide to Diversity Internship, Co-op and Entry-Level Programs* (15,000 total print copies) will be distributed free of charge to every employer that submits a completed survey, to over 10,000 former and current INROADS interns, and to the undergraduate career office of approximately 500 colleges and universities in the United States. The guide will also be sold through college and university bookstores and on the Internet. Excerpts from the Guide will also be available free at www.vault.com. At no additional charge, moreover, the entire Guide will be available to Vault Gold subscribers and to the 500-plus colleges and universities worldwide that have subscribed to the Vault Online Career Library. (1,000,000 total PDF copies.)

Instructions

1. You may opt to skip any question. If you skip a question, we will not publish the question in your completed entry.

2. The survey covers only U.S. internship, co-op and entry-level hiring, although we do ask for your worldwide locations, employee numbers and revenue figures.

3. The survey refers to full-time exempt employees in the U.S.

   - Entry-level college graduate hires are new full-time, professional or white-collar hires made directly from undergraduate institutions.

   - Exempt employees are employees who are not temporary, hourly or contract.

4. Under section I, Diversity Team Leader/Diversity Campus Recruiting Team Leader, please list the person or persons heading the diversity recruiting efforts at your organization.

5. Under section I, Office Locations, feel free to list the exact locations or supply the number of locations, to list your headquarters plus the number of offices, or to use any other method you prefer of listing locations.

6. Under section XII, Additional Information, points you may wish to address in the narrative include:

- More detail on diversity scholarships for interns, co-ops or entry-level college hires

- More detail on part-time/flex-time programs

- More detail on the workings of your diversity committee

- The names of minority associations with which you have relationships

- A list and description of diversity awards and honors

- Any financial support or service donated to minority public interest organizations and the name of such organizations.

We very much appreciate your participation and look forward to your response.

Instructions

I. Firm Info

Contact Person: _____ Title: _____

Diversity Team Leader/Diversity Campus Recruiting Team Leader: (name & title):

_____

Firm Name: _____

Address: _____

City: _____ State: _____ Zip: _____

Phone: _____ Fax: _____ E-mail: _____

Office Locations (worldwide): _____

_____

2004 Revenues (U.S.) _____ Total (Worldwide) _____

Web site address for diversity _____

II. Recruitment of Interns, Co-ops and Entry-level College Graduate Hires

1. Does your firm annually recruit at any of the following types of institutions? (Check all that apply and list the schools).

- ☐ Ivy League schools: _____

- ☐ Other private schools: _____

- ☐ Public state schools: _____

- ☐ Historically Black Colleges and Universities (HBCUs): _____

- ☐ Hispanic Serving Institutions (HSIs): _____

☐ Native American Tribal Universities: _____

☐ Other predominantly minority and/or women's colleges: _____

2. Of the schools that you listed above, do you have any special outreach efforts directed to encourage minority students to consider your firm?

☐ Hold a reception for minority students

☐ Conferences.   Please list: _____

☐ Advertise in minority student association publication(s)

☐ Participate in/host minority student job fair(s)

☐ Sponsor minority student association events

☐ Firm's employees participate on career panels at school

☐ Outreach to leadership of minority student organizations

☐ Scholarships or intern/fellowships for minority students

☐ Other. Please specify: _____

3. What activities does the firm undertake to attract minority and women employees?

☐ Partner programs with women and minority associations

☐ Conferences. Please list: _____

☐ Participate at minority job fairs

☐ Seek referrals from other employees

☐ Utilize online job services

☐ Other, please specify: _____

(a) Do you use executive recruiting/search firms to seek to identify new diversity hires? Yes ☐ No ☐

(b) If yes, list all women- and/or minority-owned executive search/recruiting firms to which the firm paid a fee for placement services in the past 12 months: _____

_____

II. Internships and Co-ops

For the following section, please repeat this template as necessary for all of your U.S.-based internships and co-ops, including those aimed at minority undergraduate students and non-minority undergraduate students (i.e., INROADS)

Name of internship/co-op program: _____

Deadline for application: _____

Number of interns in the program in summer 2004 (internship) or 2004 (co-op): _____

Pay ($US) _____ (indicate if by week, by month, or for entire program)

Length of the program (in weeks): _____

Percentage of interns/co-ops in the program who receive offers of full-time employment

_____

Web site for internship/co-op information

_____

Please describe the internship program or co-op, including departments hiring, intern/co-op responsibilities, qualifications for the program and any other details you feel are relevant.

IV. Scholarships

For the following section, please repeat this template as necessary if you have more than one scholarship aimed at minority undergraduate students.

Name of scholarship program: _____

Deadline for application for the scholarship program: _____

Scholarship award amount ($US) _____ (indicate if by week, by month, or for entire scholarship)

Web site or other contact information for scholarship

_____

Please describe the scholarship program, including basic requirements, eligibility, length of program and any other details you feel are relevant.

V. Affinity Groups/Employee Networks

For the following section, please repeat this template as necessary if you have more than one affinity group at your organization.

Name of affinity group/employee network

Please describe the affinity group/employee network, including its purpose, how often it meets, web site, etc.

VI. Entry-level Programs/Full-time Opportunities/Training Programs

For the following section, please repeat this template as necessary if you have more than one full-time, entry-level program, training program or management/leadership program at your organization.

Name of program: _____

Length of program _____

Geographic location(s) of program _____

Please describe the training/training component of this program _____

Please describe any other educational components of this program (i.e., tuition reimbursement)

_____

VII. Strategic Plan and Diversity Leadership

How does the firm's leadership communicate the importance of diversity to everyone at the firm? (e.g., e-mails, web site, newsletters, meetings, etc.)

1. Who has primary responsibility for leading diversity initiatives at your firm? Name of person and his/her title:

_____

2. (a) Does your firm currently have a diversity committee? Yes ☐ No ☐

If yes, please describe how the committee is structured, how often it meets, etc.

_____

(b) If yes, does the committee's representation include one or more members of the firm's management/executive committee (or the equivalent)? Yes ☐ No ☐

(c) If yes, how many executives are on the committee, and in 2004, what was the total number of hours collectively spent by the committee in furtherance of the firm's diversity initiatives? How many employees are on the committee, and how often does the committee convene in furtherance of the firm's diversity initiatives?

Total Executives on Committee: _____

3. Does the committee and/or diversity leader establish and set goals or objectives consistent with management's priorities?

Yes ☐ No ☐ Partially (explain): ☐ _____

Please elaborate, if you wish.

4. Has the firm undertaken a formal or informal diversity program or set of initiatives aimed at increasing the diversity of the firm?

Yes, formal ☐ Yes, informal ☐ No ☐

Please elaborate, if you wish.

5. (a) How often does the firm's management review the firm's diversity progress/results?

☐ Monthly

☐ Quarterly

☐ Twice a year

☐ Annually

☐ Does not review/measure progress/results

☐ Other, please specify_____

(b) How is the firm's diversity committee and/or firm management held accountable for achieving results?

VIII. Demographic Profile

(Numbers requested are firm totals for U.S. and international offices on 12/31/04 and on 12/31/03.)

	Total in the U.S.		Total outside the U.S.		Total worldwide	
	2004/2003		2004/2003		2004/2003	
1. Number of employees						
2. Revenues						

Please elaborate on your firm's demographic profile, including the percentage of minorities in the U.S., number of minorities in the U.S., percentage of male/female employees, percentage of minorities and/or women on the executive team, and any other figures you may wish to reveal.

IX. Retention & Professional Development

1. How do 2004 minority and female attrition rates generally compare to those experienced in the prior year period?

☐ Higher than in prior years

☐ Lower than in prior years

☐ About the same as in prior years

☐ Please elaborate if you wish.

2. Please identify the specific steps you are taking to reduce the attrition rate of minority and women employees. (It is suggested that you elaborate on this issue in the final question of this survey.)

☐ Develop and/or support internal employee affinity groups (e.g., minority or women networks within the firm)

☐ Increase/review compensation relative to competition

☐ Increase/improve current work/life programs

☐ Adopt dispute resolution process

☐ Succession plan includes emphasis on diversity

☐ Work with minority and women employees to develop career advancement plans

☐ Review work assignments and hours billed to key client matters to make sure minority and women employees are not being excluded

☐ Strengthen mentoring program for all employees, including minorities and women

☐ Professional skills development program, including minority and women employees

☐ Other. Please specify

XI. Diversity Mission Statement

Please state your organization's diversity mission statement if applicable.

XII. Additional Information

In a narrative of 500 words or less, please provide any additional information regarding your firm's diversity initiatives that you wish to share. See instructions for details and suggestions.

Firms invited to participate in the Vault/INROADS Diversity Survey

3M

A.G. Edwards, Inc.

AAA Automotive Club

Abbott Laboratories

Abercrombie & Fitch

ABN AMRO Holding N.V.

Accenture

Advance Auto Parts

Advanced Micro Devices (AMD)

AdvancePCS

AES

Aetna Inc

Affiliated Computer Services

AFLAC, Inc.

AGCO

Agilent Technologies, Inc.

AIG

Air Products & Chemical

AK Steel Holdings

Albertsons

Alcoa, Inc.

Allegheny Energy, Inc.

Allergan, Inc.

Allied Waste Industries

Allmerica Financial

Allstate Insurance

Alltel

Altria Group, Inc.

Amazon.com

Amerada Hess

Ameren Corporation

American Axle & Mfg.

American Cast Iron Pipe Co.

American Electric Power

American Express Company

American Family

American Financial Grp.

American Greetings

American Red Cross

American Standard

AmerisourceBergen

Ametek

Amgen

AMR

AmSouth Bancorporation

Anadarko Petroleum

Anheuser-Busch Companies, Inc.

Aon Corporation

Apache

Apple Computer

Applied Materials, Inc.

Aramark

Archer Daniels Midland

Armstrong Holdings

Arrow Electronics

ArvinMeritor

Asbury Automotive Group

Asea Brown Boveri Inc.

Ashland Inc

AstraZeneca PLC

AT&T

AT&T Wireless Services

Aurora Health Care Inc.

Autoliv

Automatic Data Processing (ADP)

AutoNation

Auto-Owners Insurance

AutoZone

Avaya Inc.

Avery Dennison

Avon Products

BAE Systems

Baker Hughes

Ball

BancWest Corporation

Bank of America

Bank of New York

Barnes & Noble

BASF Corporation

Baxter International

Bay State Medical Center

Bayer AG

BB&T Corporation

BE&K, Inc

Becton, Dickinson, and Company

Bed Bath & Beyond

BellSouth

Berkshire Hathaway

Best Buy

Big Lots

BJC Health System

BJs Wholesale Club

Black & Decker

Blue Cross and Blue Shield Association

Boeing Company, The

Boise Cascade

Bonneville Power Administration

Borders Group

Boston Scientific Corporation

Briggs & Stratton

Brinker International, Inc.

Brinks

Bristol Myers Squibb

Brunswick

Bunzl PLC

Burlington Northern Santa Fe Railway Co.

Burlington Resources

C. R. Bard, Inc.

C.H. Robinson Worldwide

Cablevision Systems

Caesars Entertainment

Calpine

Campbell Soup Co.

Capgemini

Capital One Financial Corporation

Cardinal Health Inc

Caremark Rx

CarMax

Caterpillar

CDW Computer Centers, Inc.

Cendant Corporation

CenterPoint Energy, Inc.

Centex Homes

Central Parking Corporation

Cerner Corporation

Charles Schwab

Charter Communications

ChevronTexaco

CHS

Chubb Corporation, The

Cigna

Cinergy Corporation

Cintas Corporation

Circuit City Stores

Cisco Systems

CIT

Citigroup Inc.

City National

Clarian Health

Clear Channel Communications

Clorox Corporation

CNA Insurance

CNF

Coca-Cola

Coca-Cola Bottling Company

Coca-Cola Enterprises

Colgate-Palmolive

Collins & Aikman

Colorado Springs Utilities

Columbia Hospital of Milwaukee

Comcast

Comerica, Inc.

Compass Bancshares, Inc.

Computer Associates Internation

Computer Sciences Corporation

Conagra

ConocoPhillips

Conseco

Consolidated Edison

Constellation Energy

Consumers Energy Corporation

Continental Airlines

Convergys

Cooper Tire & Rubber

Coors Brewing Company (Adolph Coors)

Corn Products International Inc

Corning Incorporated

Costco Companies

Countrywide Financial

Coventry Health Care

Cox Enterprises

Crown Holdings

CSX Corporation

Cummins

CVS

D&K Healthcare Resources Inc

D.R. Horton

DaimlerChrysler AG

Dana Corporation

Danaher

Darden Restaurants

Daymon Worldwide

Dell

Deloitte

Delphi Automotive

Delta Air Lines

Deluxe Corporation

DENTSPLY International

Deutsche Financial

Devon Energy Corporation

Dial Corporation

Dillards

Dole Foods

Dollar General

Dominion Resources

Dominion Resources Services Company

Dominos Pizza, Inc.

Donaldson Company

Dover

Dow Chemical Company

DTE Energy

Duke Energy Corporation

Duke Realty Corporation

Dun & Bradstreet

Dynegy

E.I. Dupont

E.W. Scripps Company, The

Eastman Chemical

Eastman Kodak Company

Eaton Corporation

eBay Inc.

Echostar Communications

Ecolab

Edison International

El Paso Corporation

El Paso Electric

Electronic Data Systems

Eli Lilly

EMC Corporation

Emcor Group

Emerson Electric

Energy East

Engelhard

Entergy Corporation

Enterprise Rent-A-Car Company

Equitable Life Assurance Society of the

Equity Office Properties Trust

Erie Insurance

Ernst & Young

Estee Lauder

Exelon Corporation

Express Scripts

Exxon Corporation

Family Dollar Stores

Fannie Mae Foundation

Federal Aviation Administration

Federal Reserve Bank of NY

Federal-Mogul Corporation

Federated Department Stores

FedEx Corporation

Fidelity Investments

Fidelity National Financial

Fifth Third Bancorp

First American Corp.

First Data Corporation

First Energy Corp.

First National Bancshares, Inc.

Fisher Scientific

Fluor

FMC Corporation

Foot Locker Inc

Ford Motor

Fortune Brands, Inc.

FPL Group

Frank Russell & Company

Freeport-McMoRan Copper & Gold Inc.

Gannett Corporation

Gap Inc.

Gateway

General Dynamics Land Systems

General Electric

General Growth Companies

General Mills Inc.

General Motors Corporation

Genuine Parts

Georgia-Pacific Corporation

Gillette

GlaxoSmithKline plc

Golden West Financial Corporation

Goldman Sachs

Goodrich Corporation

Goodyear Tire & Rubber

Graybar Electric

Great Plains Energy, Inc.

Group 1 Automotive

Guardian Life of America

Guradian Life Insurance Company of America

H&R Block

H.J Heinz

Halliburton

Hallmark Cards

Harley-Davidson

Harleysville Group, Inc.

Harrahs Entertainment

Hartford Financial Services Group Inc.

HCA

Health Insurance Plan of Greater New York

Health Net

Hearst Corporation

Henry Schein

Hershey Foods

Hewlett-Packard

Hibernia

Hilton Hotels

Hitachi

Home Depot

Honeywell International Inc.

Hormel Foods

Host Marriott

Household International

HSBC

Hughes Supply

Humana

Huntington Bancshares

IAC/InterActiveCorp

IBM

IKON Office Solutions

Illinois Tool Works

IMS Health Incorporated

ING Americas

Ingram Industries

Intel Corp.

International Council of Shopping Center

International Paper

International Steel Group

Interpublic Group of Companies

Interstate Bakeries

ITT Industries, Inc.

J.C. Penney

Jabil Circuit

Jacobs Engineering Grp.

JEA Technology Services

Jefferson-Pilot

JM Family Enterprises

Jo-Ann Stores Inc

John Deere

John Hancock

Johnson & Johnson

Johnson Controls Inc.

Jones Apparel Group

JPMorgan Chase

Kaiser Permanente

KB Home

Kellogg

Kelly Services

Kerr McGee Corporation

KeyCorp

KeySpan

Kiewit Corporation

Kimberly-Clark

Kindred Healthcare

Kmart Holding

Knight Ridder

Kohl's Corporation

KPMG L.L.P.

Kraft Foods

Kroger Company

L-3 Communications

Laidlaw International

Land OLakes Inc.

LandAmerica Financial

Lear Corporation

Leggett & Platt

Lehman Brothers Holdings

Level 3 Communications, Inc.

Levi Strauss

Lexmark International

Liberty Mutual Insurance

Limited Brands

Lincoln Financial Group

Liz Claiborne

Lockheed Martin Corporation

Loews Corporation

Longs Drug Stores

L'OREAL USA, Inc.

Lowes Companies, Inc.

Lucent Technologies, Inc.

Lyondell Chemical

Manpower

Marathon Oil

Marriott International Inc.

Marsh & McLennan Companies, Inc.

Marshall & Ilsley Corporation

Masco

Massachusetts Mutual Life

Mattel Inc.

Maxtor

Mayo Foundation

Maytag

MBNA Corporation

McDonald's Corporation

McGraw-Hill

McKesson Corporation

MeadWestvaco Corporation

Medco Health Solutions

Medtronic, Inc.

Mellon Financial

Merck

Merrill Lynch & Co Inc

METLIFE

MGIC Investment Corporation

MGM Mirage

Michelin North America

Microsoft

Middle Tennessee State University

Minnesota Mutual Life Insurance

Mirant

Mohawk Industries

Monsanto Co.

MONY-Mutual of New York

Moodys Corporation

Motorola

Murphy Oil

Mutual of Omaha Insurance

Nash Finch

National City Corporation

National Fuel Gas

Nationwide Insurance

Navistar Corporation

NBC Universal

NCR Corp

NetBank

New York Life Insurance Company

New York Times

Newell Rubbermaid

Newmont Mining

Nextel Communications, Inc.

Nike Inc.

NiSource

Nordstrom, Inc.

Norfolk Southern

Nortel Networks Corporation

North Carolina State Government

Northeast Utilities

Northern Trust Company (The)

Northrop Grumman Corporation

Northwest Airlines

Northwestern Mutual Financial Network

Nucor

NVR

Office Depot

OGE Energy

Ohio State University Hospitals

Olin Corporation

OM Group

Omaha Public Schools

Omnicare

Omnicom Group

Oracle

Owens & Minor

Owens Corning

Owens-Illinois

Oxford Health Plans, Inc.

Paccar

Pacific Life Insurance Company

PacifiCare Health Sys.

Parker Hannifin Corp.

Pathmark Stores

Pearson Education, Inc.

Pepco Holdings

Pepsi Bottling (PBG)

Pepsi North America

PepsiAmericas

PepsiCo Inc.

Performance Food Group

PETsMART Inc

Pfizer Inc

PG&E Corp.

Phelps Dodge Corporation

Philip Morris Companies, Inc.

Phillips-Van Heusen

Pinnacle West Capital

Pitney Bowes

Plains All American Pipeline

PNC Financial Corp.

PPG Industries

PPL Corporation

Praxair

Premcor

PricewaterhouseCoopers

Principal Financial Group

Procter & Gamble

Progress Energy, Inc.

Progressive

Protective Life Corp.

Prudential Financial

Public Service Enterprise Group

Publix Super Markets

Pulte Homes

Qualcomm

Quest Diagnostics

Qwest Communications International

R. J. Reynolds Tobacco Holdings, Inc.

R.J. Reynolds Tobacco

R.R. Donnelley & Sons

RadioShack Corporation

Raytheon

Reebok International

Regions Financial Corporation

Reliant Energy

Rite Aid

Roche Pharmaceuticals

Rockwell Automation Inc.

Rockwell Collins

Ross Stores

Roundys

Royal Bank Of Canada

Royal Dutch/Shell group of Companies

Russell Corporation

Ryder Systems Inc.

Ryland Group

Safeco Corp.

Safeway Stores

Saks Incorporated

Sanmina-SCI

Sara Lee Corporation

SBC Communications, Inc.

SC Johnson & Son

SCANA

Schering-Plough Corporation

Schlumberger

Science Applications International Corp.

Sealed Air

Sears Roebuck

SEI Investments

Sempra Energy

ServiceMaster

Shaw Group

Shell Oil

Sherwin-Williams Co.

Siemens

Simmons Company

SLM Corporation

Smith International

Smithfield Foods

Smurfit-Stone Container

Sodexho

Solectron Corporation

Sonic Automotive

Southern Company

Southwest Airlines

Southwest Gas Corporation

Spartan Stores

Sprint Corporation

SPX

St. Paul Companies (The)

Staples Inc.

Starbucks Coffee Company

Starwood Hotels & Resorts Worldwide

State Farm Insurance

State Street Corporation

Steelcase Inc.

Storage Technology Corporation

Stryker

Sun MicroSystems

Sunoco Inc

SunTrust Banks

SUNY Upstate Med Univ

SUPERVALU Inc

Symbol Technology

Synovus Financial Corp.

Sysco

T. Rowe Price

Target Corporation

Teachers Insurance & Annuity (TIAA-CREF)

Tech Data Corporation

TECO Energy

Telephone & Data Sys.

Temple-Inland

Tenet Healthcare

Tenneco Automotive

Terex Corporation

Tesoro Petroleum

Texas Instruments

Textron

The Williams Companies

Thrivent Financial for Lutherans

Time Warner, Inc.

Timken

TJX Companies, The

Toyota Motor Corp.

Toys 'R' Us

TransMontaigne

Travelers Corporation (The)

Triad Hospitals

Tribune Company

Turner Corporation (The)

TXU

Tyco International

Tyson Foods

UAL

Unilever US Inc.

Union Bank of California

Union Pacific Corporation

Union Planters Corporation

UNISYS

United Auto Group

United Defense Industries Inc

United HealthCare Corp.

United Parcel Service

United Rentals, Inc

United States Steel

United Stationers

United Technologies Corporation

UnitedHealth Group

Universal Health Services

University Hospitals/Cleveland

UnumProvident

US Airways Group

US Bancorp

USAA

USG Corporation

USX

Valero Energy

Verizon Communications

Verizon Wireless

VF Corporation

Viacom

Visteon

Vulcan Materials Co.

W.R. Berkley

W.W. Grainger, Inc.

Wachovia Corporation

Walgreens

Wal-Mart Stores

Walt Disney

Washington Mutual Savings Bank

Waste Management Inc

WellChoice

Wellpoint Health Networks Inc.

Wells Fargo & Company

Wesco International

Western & Southern Financial

Weyerhaeuser

Whirlpool Corporation

Winn-Dixie Stores

Wisconsin Energy

WPS Resources

Wyeth

Xcel Energy

Xerox Corporation

YMCA

Yum! Brands

Zions Bancorporation

Zurich Financial Services Group

VAULT'S
DIVERSITY CENTRAL

The hub for workplace diversity information on Vault

Vault Corporate Diversity Profiles
Read about diversity initiatives at 100s of top employers

Vault Guides

- *Vault/INROADS Guide to Diversity Entry-Level, Internship and Co-Op Programs*

- *Vault/SEO Guide to Investment Bank Diversity Programs*

- *Vault/MCCA Guide to Law Firm Diversity Programs*

- *Vault Guide Conquering Corporate America for Women and Minorities*

Vault Employee Surveys
See what employees say about diversity at their employers

Expert career advice articles about corporate diversity issues

Go to www.vault.com/diversity

VAULT
> the most trusted name in career information™

DIVERSITY ORGANIZATION SPONSORS

Job Fair ▪ Seminars ▪ Networking Reception

5th Annual
ASIAN DIVERSITY
CAREER EXPO

The Largest Career Event For Asian Americans in the United States.

May 5, 2006
New York City
Madison Square Garden

EVENT HIGHLIGHTS:
- Speak with recruiters from prestigious companies, attend an onsite interview, FIND A JOB!
- Corporate cultural training session by Cross Cultural Connections
- Get FREE resume critiquing and attend FREE workshops on "Targeting the Job You Want", "Leadership Development in Today's Competitive Corporate Climate" and "Turning Your Interviews Into Offers/Acing Your Meetings" by the Five O'Clock Club
- Attend FREE seminars on "Jobs in Asia" and "Asian Americans in the Workplace" hosted by the Asian Pacific Islander American Corporate Leadership Network (ACLN)
- Utilize DELL'S FREE CYBERCAFE!

Confirmed Exhibitors

Memorial Sloan Kettering Cancer Center	Oxford Health Plans A United Healthcare Co.	Bank of America
Dell	The New York State Education Department	Milton Hershey School
MedUSInt	DaimlerChrysler Services	The Intelligence Community
Primerica Financial Services	New York Life	Enterprise Rent-A-Car
Bear Stearns & Co., Inc.	Internal Revenue Service	Federal Bureau of Prisons
Pepsi Co.	HSBC Bank USA, NA	BP America
AT&T	Department of Defense – Recruitment Assistance Division	Intel Corporation
United States Secret Service	The Procter & Gamble Company	Starbucks Coffe Company
Kao Products, Inc.	Johnson & Johnson Family Of Companies	Merck & Co.
Mercedes-Benz USA, LLC	Central Intelligence Agency	New York City Police
USAREC MOPS Army-Starcom Worldwide	MasterCard International	Metro Recruiting Station
National Instruments	U.S. Postal Service	LG Electronics
Time Warner Cable	U.S. Department of Labor	
Federal Bureau of Prisons Metropolitan Correctional Center	The Hershey Company	
National Geospatial Intelligence Agency	The U.S. Department of Commerce	
New Jersey Judiciary Administrative Office of The Courts	School District of Philadelphia	
U.S. Federal Bureau Of Investigation	Department of Energy	
U.S. Department of Justice Drug Enforcement Administration	Colgate-Palmolive Co.	
Sandia National Laboratories	MetLife Auto & Home	
State Farm Insurance	DaimlerChrysler Corporation	
US Dept of State/Diplomatic Security Recruitment	ARAMARK	
Choice Hotels International, Inc.	International Broadcasting Bureau/Voice of America	
National Credit Union Administration	New York State Police	
Talbert	American International Group (AIG)	
Social Security Administration	Stryker Orthopaedics	

REGISTER NOW by visiting www.asiandiversity.com/event
- Online Pre Registration **Free**
- On Site Registration **$10**

Presented By: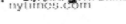

Platinum sponsor:    **Silver Sponsor:**

Media Sponsor:

EXCEL... IMPACT... SUCCEED

325 EXHIBITORS
10,000 ATTENDEES
TECHNICAL PROFESSIONAL CONFERENCE
GRADUATE SCHOOL CONFERENCE
BLACK ENGINEERING FACULTY NETWORK
INTERNATIONAL CONTINGENT

33rd Annual National Convention
Columbus, Ohio
March 28 - April 1, 2007

NSBE

NATIONAL SOCIETY of BLACK ENGINEERS
www.nsbe.org   (703) 549-2207

Mission: to increase the number of culturally responsible Black engineers who **excel** academically, **succeed** professionally and positively **impact** the community.

DIVERSITY
PROFILES

Diversity is about who we are as individuals – what is seen and unseen

Abercrombie & Fitch

601 New Fitch Path New Albany, OH 43054 Phone: 614-283-6500 www.abercrombie.com/careers	**Diversity Leadership** Todd Corley, VP Diversity 6301 Fitch Path New Albany, OH 43054

Recruiting

Please list the schools/types of schools at which you recruit.

• Ivy League schools

• Other private schools

• Public state schools

• Historically Black Colleges and Universities (HBCUs)

• Hispanic Serving Institutions (HSIs)

Do you have any special outreach efforts directed to encourage minority students to consider your firm?

• Hold a reception for minority students

• Conferences

• Advertise in minority student association publication(s)

• Participate in/host minority student job fair(s)

• Sponsor minority student association events

• Outreach to leadership of minority student organizations

• Scholarships or intern/fellowships for minority students

What activities does the firm undertake to attract minority and women employees?

• Partner programs with women and minority associations

• Conferences

• Participate at minority job fairs

• Utilize online job services

Do you use executive recruiting/search firms to seek to identify new diversity hires?

Yes

If yes, list all women- and/or minority-owned executive search/recruiting firms to which the firm paid a fee for placement services in the past 12 months:

The McMillian Group

Internships and Co-ops

INROADS

Length of the program: 10 weeks

Scholarships

UNCF/Abercrombie & Fitch Scholarship Program

Scholarship award amount: $3,000

Applicants should have a minimum GPA of 3.0 and be enrolled in a four-year institution. Please contact UNCF (United Negro College Fund) for additional details.

Entry-Level Programs/Full-Time Opportunities

Manager in Training (MIT) Program

The program is designed to build a diverse pipeline of highly skilled store managers, who exhibit strong leadership skills and business acumen.

Length of program: 90 days (approximately)
Geographic location(s) of program: Various

A Bachelor's degree is required

Strategic Plan and Diversity Leadership

How does the firm's leadership communicate the importance of diversity to everyone at the firm?

E-mails, our web site, newsletters, district-wide meetings, all-store conference calls

Does your firm currently have a diversity committee?

No

Has the firm undertaken a formal or informal diversity program or set of initiatives aimed at increasing the diversity of the firm?

Yes, formal

How often does the firm's management review the firm's diversity progress/results?

Weekly, via conference calls with all store recruiters in which we review diversity scorecard data on applications and hires, offers made, etc.

Diversity Mission Statement

The following statement on diversity and inclusion can also be found in our annual report.

At Abercrombie & Fitch we are committed to increasing and leveraging the diversity of our associates and management across the organization. We support those differences through a culture of inclusion, so that we understand our customers, enhance organizational effectiveness, capitalize on the talents of our workforce and represent the communities in which we do business.

The Employer Says

In order to keep our associates, customers, vendors and the broader community informed of our progress and efforts in creating a world class organization, which is focused on our people, we created a section on diversity and inclusion on our website (which is accessible from the home page) that openly lists our strategic partners, inclusion initiatives and efforts in the communities in which we do business.

Accenture

1345 Avenue of the Americas
New York, NY 10105
Phone: (917) 452-4400
www.accenture.com
uscareers.accenture.com

Locations (worldwide)
More than 110 offices in 48 countries

Diversity Leadership
Felix J. Martinez, U.S. Diversity Recruiting
161 N Clark, Chicago IL 60601
Phone: (312) 693-2616
Fax: (312) 652-2616
E-mail: felix.j.martinez@accenture.com

Recruiting

Please list the schools/types of schools at which you recruit.

• We recruit at public, private and Ivy League schools. We've highlighted the HBCUs and HSIs that we recruit with.
• *Historically Black Colleges and Universities (HBCUs):* Howard, Morehouse, Spelman, FAMU, NC A&T, Prairie View A&M, Clark Atlanta, North Carolina A&T
• *Hispanic Serving Institutions (HSIs):* UPR – Rio Piedras, UPR – Mayaguez

Do you have any special outreach efforts that are directed to encourage minority students to consider your firm?

• We hold a diversity-focused open house in Atlanta, Chicago & D.C. and hold receptions at all our targeted schools
• Conferences: National Black MBA Association, National Society of Black Engineers, National Society of Hispanic MBAs, Society of Hispanic Professional Engineers, Society of Women Engineers
• Participate in/host minority student job fair(s): National Black MBA Association, National Society of Black Engineers, National Society of Hispanic MBAs, Society of Hispanic Professional Engineers, Society of Women Engineers
• Sponsor minority student association events
• Accenture's employees participate on career panels at school
• Outreach to leadership of minority student organizations
• Scholarships or intern/fellowships for minority students
• Other: Accenture has created several programs aimed at attracting and retaining ethnic minority and women employees, including Accenture's Women's Networking Forum, Accenture's Commitment to Empower Successful Students and Student Leadership Conference.

What activities does the firm undertake to attract minority and women employees?

• Partner programs with women and minority associations: Catalyst, INROADS, National Black MBA Association, National Society of Black Engineers, National Society of Hispanic MBAs, Society of Hispanic Professional Engineers, Society of Women Engineers
• Conferences: See above
• Participate at minority job fairs: National Black MBA Association, National Society of Black Engineers, National Society of Hispanic MBAs, Society of Hispanic Professional Engineers, Society of Women Engineers
• Seek referrals from other employees
• Leverage online job services
• Other: Accenture hosts exclusive Open House & Networking Events for minority and women employees.

Do you use executive recruiting/search firms to seek to identify new diversity hires?

Yes

Internships and Co-ops

Accenture Internship Program

> *Deadline for application:* Applications are due in early winter
> *Pay:* Accenture offers competitive wages for interns.
> *Length of the program:* They last for a period of at least 10 weeks – typically from late May/early June and ending in mid- August/early September.
> *Percentage of interns/co-ops in the program who receive offers of full-time employment:* Approximately 90-95% of interns receive offers for employment
> *Web site for internship/co-op information:* campusconnection.accenture.com

Other Programs

Aside from our overall internship program, Accenture has been a strong supporter of INROADS interns since the organization began in 1970 in Chicago and was one of the original 17 corporate sponsors. We also have a limited number of internships available through the National Action Council for Minorities in Engineering (NACME) and the Accenture On-Campus Internship program. Interesting Fact: Accenture partner Andrew Jackson from the Cleveland office was the first inductee into the INROADS Alumni Hall of Fame.

We also provide internship opportunities to students participating in Accenture's Commitment to Empower Successful Students Program and Accenture's Women's Networking Forum.

Intern Responsibilities

Intern analysts participate in a variety of roles, including those of an actual full-time analyst. As an intern, you may participate in client or internal engagements with an emphasis on the planning, design and installation of management information systems. Assignments may include:

• Defining user requirements
• Programming
• Coding and testing applications
• Analyzing, designing and implementing business process improvements
• Project administration
• Researching work on a proposal
• Developing an array of technology-based solutions to improve business performance-from interactive, virtual technologies to object-oriented, client/server and Internet applications
• Developing training and human performance management programs

Additionally, all interns attend a three-day leadership conference during the summer. The agenda for the conference includes team building exercises, meeting our executives, diversity presentations, networking opportunities, motivational speakers and a showcase of our clients..

Scholarships

Accenture American Indian Scholarship Fund

Deadline for application for the scholarship program: Application process is held during the May/June timeframe each year

Scholarship award amount: Three types of scholarships are awarded for various amounts (see below).

Web site or other contact information for scholarship:

careers3.accenture.com/Careers/US/DiversityInclusion/AIGC.htm

Three types of scholarships will be awarded to high-achieving American Indian students seeking degrees and careers in the technology and business fields:

• Accenture Scholars – three undergraduate scholarships of $20,000 each will be awarded to high school seniors pursuing a four-year undergraduate program in technology or business at a U.S. university or college.

• Accenture Fellows – three graduate scholarships of $10,000 each will be awarded to undergraduate students pursuing a two-year graduate program with an emphasis on business or technology at an accredited U.S. university or college.

• Finalist Scholarships – two undergraduate scholarships of $2,000 per year for four years and one graduate scholarship of $1,000 per year for two years will be awarded to candidates for the Accenture Scholars and Fellows scholarships.

Minority Scholarship Program

Scholarship award amount: $2,000 per recipient.

Web site or other contact information for scholarship:

careers3.accenture.com/Careers/US/DiversityInclusion/Charitable_Contributions/

The Minority Scholarship Program is administered by the Accenture Foundation and is targeted toward African American, Hispanic, Asian American and Native American undergraduate and graduate students. Applicants must attend one of the Accenture source schools and must have at least a B average. Winners are selected based on merit, with individual award amounts of $2000.

United Negro College Fund

Scholarship award amount: $2,000 per recipient

Web site or other contact information for scholarship:

careers3.accenture.com/Careers/US/DiversityInclusion/Charitable_Contributions/

United Negro College Fund is a minority higher education assistance organization, which meets the needs of 40 selected HBCUs through comprehensive educational assistance for fund raising, educational programs and technical assistance. Accenture funds one merit-based scholarships of $2,000 each across the six key national HBCUs – Morehouse, Howard, Spelman, Prairie View A&M, Florida A&M University and North Carolina A&T University.

Matching Contributions Program

Deadline for application for the scholarship program: Ongoing

Scholarship award amount: Matching contributions to provide various scholarships

Web site or other contact information for scholarship:

careers3.accenture.com/Careers/US/DiversityInclusion/Charitable_Contributions/

The Matching Contributions Program pays $2 for every $1 donated by Accenture to Historically Black Colleges and Universities (HBCU) and Hispanic Serving Institutions (HIS). The funding is used to provide scholarships to deserving students at the participating HBCUs and HSIs in the name of Accenture.

Affinity Groups/Employee Networks

Through a National Networking Program, Accenture provides the structure and guidance necessary to develop, maintain and grow the following local networking groups in each office location:

• African American
• Asian American
• Gay and Lesbian
• Hispanic American/Latino
• Multicultural
• Women
• Work/Life Strategy

These groups provide individuals who share a common purpose an opportunity to come together to discuss specific issues related to workplace diversity. They:

• Present members with networking opportunities
• Foster a means for individuals with similar backgrounds to discuss similar challenges and opportunities
• Offer professional direction
• Promote diversity throughout the company
• Support national and local recruiting activities
• Provide employees with heritage packets that highlight various cultural celebrations throughout the year

We currently have 32 U.S. offices with active Local Office Diversity Programs. In locations that lack critical mass of the demographic groups above, or where the location does not have formalized interest groups, Multicultural Groups have been put in place.

Entry-Level Programs/Full-Time Opportunities

Our professionals are encouraged to understand the value in differences. Diversity training programs are available to all Accenture employees to raise their awareness of cultural diversity and help them more fully appreciate the differences in each of us.

Here are just some of the diversity training programs we offer.

Appreciating Gender Differences: This three-hour instructor-led course heightens the awareness of gender differences and demonstrates the importance of appreciating and valuing the dynamics between men and women. This helps create an inclusive workplace which increases team innovation and productivity. The course is available to all U.S. employees at Accenture.

Cultural Awareness Guides: These information briefs (available for individual study) provide information to help our employees increase their cultural awareness and provide insight on work styles and behaviors across specific cultures, including appropriate salutations, communications etiquette, preferred modes of communications, meeting styles and respect.

The Diversity Principle: This one-hour course is designed to empower each individual to have a positive impact on Accenture through diversity awareness. Employees learn how they can create a work environment rich in diversity that celebrates the valuable contributions of every team member. The presentation defines diversity at Accenture, establishes diversity as a key company priority and demonstrates how negative stereotypes and related situations can contribute to a non-productive working environment.

The Diversity Principle in Motion: Presented in a group setting, this workshop takes a further in-depth examination of people's perceptions and behaviors regarding individuals who are different from them. It helps participants recognize inappropriate behaviors related to differences in the workplace and become fully aware of the vehicles in place to address these behaviors, presents Accenture's commitment to the diversity initiatives, and makes participants aware of relevant Accenture policies related to diversity.

We also offer other training resources for teams to use at a local or organizational level.

Diversity Ice Breakers: Fun, education activities that teams and communities can use to demonstrate the importance of diversity at Accenture.

Mentoring Toolkit: Accenture has developed a 'mentoring toolkit' to help individuals foster their own mentoring rela tionships on a formal or informal and on-going basis. These mentoring relationships are in addition to mentoring activ ities established through our two national programs, the Mentoring Program for Women and the Minority Mentoring Program.

Strategic Plan and Diversity Leadership

How does the firm's leadership communicate the importance of diversity to everyone at the firm?

Accenture communicates regularly with employees through our global inclusion program. Some of the vehicles we leverage are:

• Executive memos
• Internal website
• Local memos
• U.S.-wide newsletter
• Networking meetings
• Conference calls

Who has primary responsibility for leading diversity initiatives at your firm?

Accenture's leadership regards diversity as one of the most important priorities for our company. Given how importantly we value diversity for our business and our people, we have a Chief Diversity Officer, Kedrick Adkins, who reports directly to the CEO.

Kedrick's role encompasses creating and implementing a broad strategy for diversity within Accenture, including the following:

• Develop a strategy to increase and effectively manage diversity among all of our global workforces
• Implement training programs to increase our awareness of and sensitivity to diversity issues
• Create appropriate internal and external communication
• Increase diversity among our supplier base
• Monitor and measure performance against plan objectives

Does your firm currently have a diversity committee?

Yes

Accenture's diversity initiatives are led by three primary groups:

U.S. Diversity Advisory Council
The U.S. Diversity Advisory Council is a group of leadership partners with representation from several of the Operating Units and Capability Groups. The Diversity Advisory Council confirms priorities, helps set strategic direction and takes a leadership role in implementing key initiatives.

U.S. Women's Steering Group
The U.S. Women's Steering Group is comprised of a committee of Accenture female partners. The U.S. Women's Steering Group manages, implements and leads different women's initiatives across the U.S.

Workforce Diversity Leads
Within each of the Accenture entities there is a lead dedicated to ensuring that diversity is embraced by all Accenture employees.

If yes, does the committee's representation include one or more members of the firm's management/executive committee (or the equivalent)?

Yes

Does the committee and/or diversity leader establish and set goals or objectives consistent with management's priorities?

Yes

Has the firm undertaken a formal or informal diversity program or set of initiatives aimed at increasing the diversity of the firm?

Yes, formal

How often does the firm's management review the firm's diversity progress/results?

Quarterly

The Stats

Employees: 103,000 (Approximate total headcount at end of fiscal year 2004 – August 31, 2004)
Revenue: U.S. $13.67 billion (fiscal 2004 – 12 months ended August 31, 2004)

Retention and Professional Development

Please identify the specific steps you are taking to reduce the attrition rate of minority and women employees.
• Develop and/or support internal employee affinity groups (e.g., minority or women networks within the firm)
• Increase/improve current work/life programs
• Work with minority and women employees to develop career advancement plans
• Strengthen mentoring program for all employees, including minorities and women
• Professional skills development program, including minority and women employees

Diversity Mission Statement

Accenture is a global management consulting, technology services and outsourcing company. With more than 115,000 people in 48 countries, we bring together the unique experiences and perspectives of a diverse workforce to deliver cutting-edge technologies and solutions to companies around the world to help them become high-performance businesses. Accenture strives to attract and retain the best people and provide an environment where they can all develop professionally and build a rewarding career. As a result, we have an environment rich in diversity that acknowledges each individual's uniqueness, values his or her skills and contributions, and promotes respect, personal achievement and stewardship. Learn more about our diversity efforts at diversity.accenture.com.

The Employer Says

Accenture is committed to helping build tomorrow's leaders. We sponsor various workshops and forums for minorities and women to help foster their growth and development. The events also serve as an excellent opportunity for college students of similar background to get to know each other and learn more about a career in consulting.

Here are three of Accenture's key programs:

1. Accenture's Commitment to Empower Successful Students

This three-year program is targeted toward diverse, rising sophomores with majors in Business, Computer Science and Engineering. Participating students will:

• Shadow Accenture personnel for a day at a local office
• Attend networking lunches to help establish a mentoring relationship
• Participate in the End of Year Forum to understand how to meet long-term career goals
• Attend the Leadership Conference the summer following their second mentoring year
• Gain valuable exposure to the business world, explore the consulting career path and understand what companies are looking for!

2. Accenture Student Leadership Conference

This three-day conference is held for a limited number of outstanding seniors at our education center in St. Charles, IL (near Chicago). This helps participants further develop and refine leadership skills and experience the same learning environment as full-time employees.

3. Accenture's Women's Networking Forum

This program is a series of one-day networking events at Accenture local offices for top female students in their junior or senior year. Selected women will attend a one-day event at the local Accenture office closest to their university and:

• Network and build relationships with top Accenture female employees, along with women from other universities
• Gain valuable exposure to the business world and build leadership skills to use in any business setting
• Get a realistic preview of what it's like to be an Accenture employee
• Explore career paths within Accenture and understand what we are seeking in future employees
• Learn how to successfully overcome challenges women face in the workplace

AETNA

151 Farmington Avenue
Hartford, CT 06156
Phone: (860) 273-0123
Fax: (860) 273-3971
www.aetna.com

Diversity Leadership
Carlos Figueroa, Director, University Relations
151 Farmington Avenue
Hartford, CT 06156
Phone: (860) 273-7831
Fax: (860) 273-1757
E-mail: figueroac1@aetna.com

Recruiting

Please list the schools/types of schools at which you recruit.

• Ivy League schools
• Other private schools
• Public state schools
• Historically Black Colleges and Universities (HBCUs)

Do you have any special outreach efforts that are directed to encourage minority students to consider your firm?

• Hold a reception for minority students
• Conferences (NSHMBA, ALPFA, NABA, NBMBAA)
• Advertise in minority student association publication(s)
• Participate in/host minority student job fair(s)
• Sponsor minority student association events
• Firm's employees participate on career panels at school
• Outreach to leadership of minority student organizations
• Scholarships or intern/fellowships for minority students
• What activities does the firm undertake to attract minority and women employees?
• Partner programs with women and minority associations
• Participate at minority job fairs
• Utilize online job services

Do you use executive recruiting/search firms to seek to identify new diversity hires?

Yes

Internships and Co-ops

Aetna's Summer Internship Program

Deadline for application: We post new dates every year
Number of interns in the program: In 2005, there were 121 interns and 12 co-op students.
Pay: $10-16 per hour
Length of the program: 12-14 weeks
Web site for internship/co-op information: www.aetna.com

Aetna's internship and cooperative education programs offer college students the experience of a lifetime. As an intern, students will have the opportunity to use their creativity and fresh perspectives in a health care company that thrives on change. Students will be able to formally integrate their academic knowledge and explore career interest through productive and exciting work assignments.

An intern is a student who has completed at least 45 credit hours and is employed full-time throughout the summer months (10-12 weeks).

A co-op is a student who has completed at least 45 credit hours and is employed full-time in six month work blocks (January through June or July through December).

Scholarships

Aetna Information Services (AIS) Scholarship

Scholarship award amount: Four scholarships in the amount of $2,500 each
The Scholarship Program is run in partnership with the following schools: University of Connecticut, Bay Path College and Temple University (these scholarships are focused on providing financial assistance to Women and Students of Color)

Affinity Groups/Employee Networks

Aetna African-American Employee Network (AAEN)

Mission: To provide opportunities for members to develop and enhance their professionalism through programs, workshops and network opportunities, and to develop a strong partnership between Aetna and AAEN that supports strategic business initiatives.

Aetna Hispanic Network (AHN)

Mission: To support Aetna's diversity initiatives and programs by assisting with Aetna's strategic goals in Hispanic emerging markets, and providing AHN members with professional and career development.

Aetna Network of Gay, Lesbian, Bisexual and Transgender Employees (Angle)

Mission: To contribute to Aetna's business and diversity strategies by providing networking support to our members and resources to the corporation.

Aetna Women's Network (AWN)

Mission: To bring women together to help develop the "new Aetna" by offering skill development tools, breaking down geographic and functional barriers to career growth, and developing leadership and exposure.

Aetna Working Mothers' Network (AWMN)

Mission: To bring working parents together to help support, develop and retain talent for Aetna.

Asian-American Network (AsiANet)

Mission: To support Aetna's diversity initiatives and programs, assist Aetna in achieving its goals in the global and Asian-American markets, and assist network members with their personal and career development.

Please visit our website for details of each:
www.aetna.com/diversity/networks.htm

Entry-Level Programs/Full-Time Opportunities

The Aetna Information Services Leadership Development Program

This program is a three-year, fast track program where talented new graduates are recruited, hired and developed into the future technology leaders at Aetna. LDP participants work on a series of challenging assignments within Aetna Information Services, Aetna Project Services and other selected Aetna business areas in the Pennsylvania and Connecticut offices. These positions last approximately 8 months each with one required rotation outside the participants' home office location.

The E.E. Cammack Group School

The E.E. Cammack Group School is a national college recruitment program that provides extensive sales, service and product training in the Middle Market, National Accounts and Aetna Global Benefits sales organization. The Group School is a premier one-year, fast track program where talented new graduates are recruited, hired and developed into the future sales leaders at Aetna.

Actuarial Training Program

Aetna's Actuarial Training program offers a strong management development component with targeted rotational assignments. The program is managed by a committee comprised of Fellows of the Society of Actuaries, which ensures growth in the skills and knowledge necessary to become a financial leader.

Strategic Plan and Diversity Leadership

How does the firm's leadership communicate the importance of diversity to everyone at the firm?
A combination of e-mails, web site, newsletters and meetings

Who has primary responsibility for leading diversity initiatives at your firm?
Raymond J. Arroyo, Chief Diversity Officer

Does your firm currently have a diversity committee?

Yes. Diversity Alliance Team is a multi-disciplinary team that leverages and integrates members' resources to maximize Aetna's diversity-related presence and reach, internally and externally. The goal is to help Aetna earn the distinction, financially and by reputation, of being the preferred benefits company for all of our constituents.

Does the committee's representation include one or more members of the firm's management/executive committee (or the equivalent)?

Yes

How many executives are on the committee, and in 2004, what was the total number of hours collectively spent by the committee in furtherance of the firm's diversity initiatives? How many employees are on the committee, and how often does the committee convene in furtherance of the firm's diversity initiatives?

• We have executives from the businesses represented at all times.
• We have several diversity committees organized by business segment, and each committee has at least one executive. We also have two enterprise-wide diversity committees with several active executive members.

Does the committee and/or diversity leader establish and set goals or objectives consistent with management's priorities?

Yes

Has the firm undertaken a formal or informal diversity program or set of initiatives aimed at increasing the diversity of the firm?

Yes, formal

• Annual Diversity Milestones (initiatives) are established by each business segment and progress is reported quarterly
• The staffing organization has a comprehensive outreach and recruitment strategy
• Employee engagement and inclusiveness are promoted as an organizational value and are measured by an annual employee surey examining our workplace culture
• Enterprise-wide diversity training is updated annually and provided for various levels and segments of the organization
• The focus on diversity goes beyond our workforce – it's woven into the fabric of providing quality service to our consumers in multi-cultural markets

How often does the firm's management review the firm's diversity progress/results?

Quarterly

How is the firm's diversity committee and/or firm management held accountable for achieving results?

By individual and departmental scorecards

The Stats

Employees: 26,848 (2004, U.S.)
Employees: 26,819 (2003, U.S.)

Retention and Professional Development

Please identify the specific steps you are taking to reduce the attrition rate of minority and women employees.

• Develop and/or support internal employee affinity groups

• Increase/improve current work/life programs

• Succession plan includes emphasis on diversity

• Work with minority and women employees to develop career advancement plans

• Strengthen mentoring program for all employees, including minorities and women

• Professional skills development program, including minority and women employees

Diversity Mission Statement

We foster an inclusive work environment through collaboration and partnerships to increase employee engagement, strengthen business relationships, encourage innovation, influence multicultural markets and ultimately enhance Aetna's business results.

The Employer Says

Diversity is a brand imperative that helps to bring Aetna's health and related benefits to the attention of the fastest-growing segments of the U.S. population – the African-American and Hispanic/Latino markets, as well as the Asian market. In addition, Aetna's ongoing commitment to diversity builds greater competency among Aetna's employees. As a result, diversity is an important element of Aetna's strategic initiatives.

We will deliver on Aetna's brand promise by valuing and respecting the strengths and differences among our employees, customers and communities because they reflect our continued future success. Our customers, suppliers and strategic partners are increasingly diverse and multicultural. We must be positioned to understand, interface, relate to and meet their needs. Our challenge is to seek out and use our diversity in ways that bring new and richer perspectives to our jobs and to our business.

We are currently focused on the following:

• Recognizing diversity as a business imperative in increasing our business opportunities and partnerships with key external marets, communities and suppliers

• Creating a work environment that engages, enables and empowers people to do their best work

• Focusing specifically on recruitment, retention and development of diverse talent at all levels in the organization

• Establishing and supporting programs that increase the understanding and appreciation of cultural differences through the Aetna Foundation and charitable giving

• Providing diversity education to all employees

Agilent Technologies

395 Page Mill Rd.
Palo Alto, CA 94306
Phone: (650) 752-5000
Fax: (650) 752-5633
Toll Free: (877) 424-4536
www.jobs.agilent.com

Locations (worldwide)

U.S.: Alabama • Arizona • California •
Colorado • Connecticut • District of
Columbia • Florida • Illinois • Indiana;
Iowa; Louisana • Maryland •
Massachusetts • Minnesota • Mississippi •
Missouri • New Jersey • New Mexico •
New York • North Carolina • Ohio •
Oklahoma • Oregon • Pennsylvania •
Tennessee • Texas • Vermont •
Washington • West Virginia • Wisconsin

ASIA PACIFIC: Australia • China • India •
Japan • Korea • Malaysia • Singapore

EUROPE: Belgium • France • Germany •
Netherlands • United Kingdom

Diversity Leadership

Lakiba Pittman, Diversity Sourcing and
Recruiting Program Manager
395 Page Mill Road
Palo Alto, CA 94306
Phone: (650) 752-5219
Fax: (650) 752-5900
E-mail: lakiba_pittman@agilent.com

Recruiting

Please list the schools/types of schools at which you recruit.

• *Ivy League schools:* Cornell
• *Other private schools:* Stanford University, Santa Clara University
• *Public state schools:* UC Berkeley, UC Santa Barbara, UC Davis, CalPoly San Luis Obispo, Colorado State, University of Colorado at Boulder
• *Historically Black Colleges and Universities (HBCUs):* NCA&T
• *Hispanic Serving Institutions (HSIs):* New Mexico State

Do you have any special outreach efforts that are directed to encourage minority students to consider your firm?

• Conferences: CGSM, SWE, NSBE, SHPE
• Advertise in minority student association publication(s) (sometimes)
• Participate in/host minority student job fair(s)
• Sponsor minority student association events
• Firm's employees participate on career panels at school
• Outreach to leadership of minority student organizations
• Scholarships or intern/fellowships for minority students

What activities does the firm undertake to attract minority and women employees?

• Partner programs with women and minority associations
• Conferences: SWE, WITI
• Participate at minority job fairs yes
• Seek referrals from other employees yes
• Utilize online job services yes

Do you use executive recruiting/search firms to seek to identify new diversity hires?

No (rarely)

Internships and Co-ops

INROADS is one of our sourcing channels for the U.S. Internship Program. Students from INROADS are incorporated into the company-wide Internship Program.

> *Deadline for application:* Applications for the U.S. Internship Program are accepted throughout the year. Most of our offers for internship assignments are presented to candidates during the months of January through May, and often into June.
>
> *Number of interns in the program in summer 2004 (internship) or 2004 (co-op):* In 2004 there were 118 U.S. interns employed by Agilent. Seven of those interns were hired from the INROADS Program.
>
> *Pay:* Varies, based on year in school and physical work location. Average salary for an undergrad technical intern is $3800 per month. Average salary for an undergrad non-technical intern is $3600 per month.
>
> *Length of the program:* Varies. Minimum length is 10 weeks, but some assignments could last as long as six months.
>
> *Percentage of interns/co-ops in the program who receive offers of full-time employment:* Percentage of eligible interns who receive offers from Agilent is approximately 70%. Eligible interns are those who are scheduled to graduate and who have received favorable performance evaluations by their managers.
>
> *Web site for internship/co-op information:* www.jobs.agilent.com/students/usa.html

Agilent's U.S. Internship Program is designed for those who really want to contribute and gain practical experience in their area of interest. The goal of this program is to hire students into regular jobs after graduation. To qualify, a student must:

• Have completed his/her freshman year in college
• Have strong academic achievement in a technical or business curriculum pursuing a BS, BA, MS, MBA or Ph.D.
• Be majoring in:
    • Electrical Engineering
    • Mechanical Engineering
    • Industrial Engineering
    • Computer Science
    • Computer Engineering
    • Chemical Engineering
    • Chemistry
    • Bio Science
    • Materials Science
    • Physics
    • Management Information Systems
    • Computer Information Systems
    • Information Technology
    • Masters in Business Administration

Affinity Groups/Employee Networks

Asian Employee Network (AEN) – Bay Area

Mission – to help create a company in which all members of a diverse, global workforce can contribute to their highest potential in meeting the business needs of Agilent, its partners and customers. We seek to actively involve Asian American employees in this ongoing process. AEN has an executive sponsor, an internal website and monthly and quarterly events. The group also hosts some events with other similar network groups from other local companies.

Bay Area Women's Network (BAWN)

Mission:

• To exemplify and celebrate the strength, citizenship and diversity of Agilent's women
• To promote professional development and personal/life skills development for Agilent women
• To advocate for the growth and development of women leaders within Agilent

BAWN is an employee network group that works to achieve its mission statement via public forums, video viewings, roundtable discussions, communications programs and attending events of interest together. While we are focused on issues that impact women, our forums provide skills and knowledge development for all Agilent employees. Having men join our organization and participate in our forums encourages an open dialogue and better learning for all. The group has an internal website and quarterly events.

Black Employee Network Forum (BEF) – Bay Area

Purpose and direction:

• To be at the forefront of helping Agilent meet its high-performance, high-growth goals.
• To assist Bay Area African-Americans assume leadership roles within Agilent.
• To assist Bay Area African-American employees in achieving their personal and professional development goals.
• To promote a sense of belonging and unity within the Agilent environment

The BEF has monthly meetings and an executive sponsor.

Gay & Lesbian Employee Network (GLEN) – Sonoma County

Agilent Technologies' GLEN vision is an outgrowth of Agilent Technologies' organizational values and corporate objectives.

Agilent Technologies is a safe and pleasant work environment free of harassment and discrimination where all employees, regardless of their sexual orientation, are recognized for their individual achievements, gain a sense of satisfaction and accomplishment, are rewarded and promoted equally and receive equal opportunities and benefits.

Agilent Technologies is a supportive environment for gay, lesbian, bisexual and transgender employees. At work, they feel comfortable to be open about their sexual orientation, and employees treat their families like they treat all other employees' families.

Glen has quarterly meetings and an executive sponsor.

(East) Indian Employee Network Group (INET) – Bay Area

INET envisions Agilent to be an organization that helps attract and retain a diverse workforce including people from different nations. The employees of Indian origin are organized to:

• Support, Develop and Grow as members of this organization to achieve their full professional potential.

• Offer a competitive advantage for Agilent through a diverse perspective on future challenges.
• Bring together employees of Indian origin in order to make meaningful contribution to Agilent by increasing
• knowledge of the global and multicultural market place.
• Make Agilent a diverse and a better place to work for everyone.

INET has monthly meetings and occasional forums.

Management of Development and Advancement (MDA) – Sonoma County

Mission:

To lead diversity initiatives across all Sonoma County Employee Network Groups and increase management's understanding of diversity as a critical and necessary factor for Agilent's long term business success. The vision is to achieve strategic alignment and cooperation across all Sonoma County Employee Network Groups and foster an environment where all employees feel valued.

Women's Leadership Development (WLD) – Sonoma County

To provide a forum that gives women opportunities to practice leadership skills by coordinating various projects such as educating girls about careers in technology and science, professional skills development workshops and resolving workplace issues related to women.

The Physical Informational Emotional (PIE) Networking Group – Colorado

To provide information and support for all employees, and to help them enhance their physical and emotional capabilities by offering opportunities to:

• Increase functionality, productivity and happiness
• Improve personal development
• Maximize their contributions to Agilent's success

PIE is a great example of a successful grass roots effort.

PIE formed in May 1989 as a result of a group of non-management people who felt there was a need for a networking group for employees with physical and/or emotional disabilities.

Diversity is a critical area of focus for Agilent. In partnership with Agilent's Diversity Made Real Program, PIE's goals include informing and supporting all employees experiencing physical and/or emotional limitations.

Others

• Abilities Network
• La Voz (Hispanic Network Group)
• Native American Employee Network
• Northern Colorado Diversity Team
• Celebrating Our Differences Group
• Spokane Inclusivity Taskforce

Entry-Level Programs/Full-Time Opportunities

Agilent has a long history of hiring diverse college students from leading universities all over the world. In the U.S. alone, we hire between 50-100 college grads every year. We encourage summer internships, and convert nearly 50% of our interns to regular, full time positions after graduation. We strongly believe that college students bring the latest in technology to Agilent and are the future leaders of our company.

Agilent is in the midst of a pilot entry-level program for one of our businesses. It is a robust and sustainable engineering rotation program that adds long-term value to Agilent and its business by accelerating individual entry-level capability and technical breadth.

Agilent has a year-long global Next Generation Leadership Program which has two strategic corporate programs designed to accelerate the readiness of Agilent's leadership pipeline by identifying and developing a pool of top talent capable of managing world-class emerging, growth and mature businesses. Participants in this program are nominated by management and selected by their respective businesses, and as such the programs are not open for general enrollment:

LEAD is a strategic leadership development process designed to accelerate the readiness of high potential Operating Managers and Individual Contributors for Integrating Manager or expanded leadership roles.

AIM is a strategic leadership development process designed to accelerate the readiness of high potential Integrating Managers for senior or expanded leadership roles.

Program objectives and benefits: increase leadership effectiveness, gain self and strategic business insights, establish global network, expand circle of influence and develop strategic business skills.

Program components include: 360 degree assessment, workshops, global leadership forums, leadership in action series, coaching, mentoring, networking and business project teamwork

Both programs feature a proven accelerated development process which provides 1) opportunities to build leadership skill & confidence in own abilities through involvement in action learning with peers in high potential cross-functional, cross-business and cross-geographic teams, networking and virtual learning events, 2) a feedback-rich environment based on Agilent's Leadership Framework and 3) alignment with a continuous leadership pipeline.

Strategic Plan and Diversity Leadership

How does the firm's leadership communicate the importance of diversity to everyone at the firm?

Agilent has several means to communicate the importance of diversity to everyone at the firm: internal website, internal newsgram (INFOSPARK), coffee talks, forums, brown bags, employee network group sessions and more.

Who has primary responsibility for leading diversity initiatives at your firm?

In the U.S. – Trish Jamieson, HR Management Services & Diversity Manager. We also have a Diversity Council led by the Sr. VP of HR and one of the executive team – the Sr. VP of one of our businesses.

Does your firm currently have a diversity committee?

Yes. This is a new council that is in the prep stages.

If yes, does the committee's representation include one or more members of the firm's management/executive committee (or the equivalent)?

Yes

If yes, how many executives are on the committee, and in 2004, what was the total number of hours collectively spent by the committee in furtherance of the firm's diversity initiatives? How

many employees are on the committee, and how often does the committee convene in furtherance of the firm's diversity initiatives?

Total Executives on Committee: 2

Does the committee and/or diversity leader establish and set goals or objectives consistent with management's priorities?

Yes (once committee is established).

Has the firm undertaken a formal or informal diversity program or set of initiatives aimed at increasing the diversity of the firm?

Yes, formal and informal. Agilent has, since its inception, included diversity initiatives in its overall staffing plans; currently we are also developing a formal Diversity Recruiting and Sourcing Program.

How often does the firm's management review the firm's diversity progress/results?

Monthly – managers with diversity responsibility monitor monthly

Quarterly – executives review quarterly

The Stats

Employees: 28,000 (2004, U.S.)
Revenue: $7.2 billion (2004)

At the end of FY 2004, the ethnic/racial composition of the U.S. workforce is as follows – executives and senior managers only:

• Caucasian: 86.9%
• Asian/Pacific Islander: 8%
• Hispanic/Latin : 2.8%
• African American : 2%
• Native American/Alaskan : .3%

Retention and Professional Development

How do 2004 minority and female attrition rates generally compare to those experienced in the prior year period?

About the same as in prior years

Please identify the specific steps you are taking to reduce the attrition rate of minority and women employees.

• Develop and/or support internal employee affinity groups (e.g., minority or women networks within the firm)
• Work with minority and women employees to develop career advancement plans (some mentoring)
• Strengthen mentoring program for all employees, including minorities and women
• Professional skills development program, including minority and women employees

Diversity Mission Statement

Harness Global Diversity as Agilent's competitive advantage

At Agilent, we believe that our global competitiveness will be accomplished not only by designing, manufacturing, marketing and selling superior products, but also by leveraging the diversity of our customers, stakeholders, employees and partners all around the world.

Our success is achieved through:

• An environment that enables all to develop and contribute to their full potential
• Leaders that engage, focus, mobilize and leverage all cultures
• Strategies that direct our diverse, collective intelligence to solve urgent business challenges
• Excellent resources and tools that enable our people to excel
• Systems and processes that align and support our vision for success

The Employer Says

At Agilent, we recognize the business value of integrating diversity and inclusion into our normal business practices. While we maintain a distinct Diversity Compliance/AA program, beyond that, diversity and inclusion is everyone's responsibility and thus, you will find aspects of it throughout the company. For example, there is a diversity component in the staffing organization where we work to increase the diversity of our pipeline; there is a diversity component to our Corporate Affairs activities where we work in diverse communities around the world with our Agilent After School Initiative; and there is a diversity component in our Global Leadership and Learning Function where we have tools and resources to help our employees, managers and leaders work more effectively across cultural boundaries. Also, within each business there is the focus on how to unleash and focus the diverse ideas of all of our global population to contribute to innovation and business success for our company.

Here is a statement from our CEO:

"Agilent's inclusive environment and workforce, and our acceptance of diverse ideas, help us achieve global success in several ways: we attract and retain top talent; we create an environment of diversity of thought and insight, which will only improve our ability to be innovative in everything we do. The bottom line is that diversity and inclusion give us a powerful business advantage, and we want to make sure they remain a part of our business philosophy, planning and practice.

Bill Sullivan, President and CEO

Air Products and Chemicals, Inc.

7201 Hamilton Blvd.
Allentown, PA 18195
(610) 481-4911
Fax: (610) 481-5900
www.airproducts.com/careers

Diversity Leadership:
Stacy Halliday, Recruiter, Engineering and IT
7201 Hamilton Blvd.
Allentown, PA 18195
E-mail: hallidsb@airproducts.com

Recruiting

Please list the schools/types of schools at which you recruit.

• Ivy League schools
• Other private schools
• Public state schools

Do you have any special outreach efforts that are directed to encourage minority students to consider your firm?

• Hold a reception for minority students
• Conferences (NSBE, SWE, Consortium)
• Participate in/host minority student job fair(s)
• Sponsor minority student association events
• Scholarships or intern/fellowships for minority students

What activities does the firm undertake to attract minority and women employees?

• Partner programs with women and minority associations
• Participate at minority job fairs

Do you use executive recruiting/search firms to seek to identify new diversity hires?

No

Internships and Co-ops

INROADS, GEM, Air Products

Deadline for application: Varies based on assignment
Number of interns in the program in summer 2004 (internship) or 2004 (co-op): 125 total
Pay: Varies based on experience
Length of the program: 10-26 weeks

Percentage of interns/co-ops in the program who receive offers of full-time employment: approximately 67% of the interns who are returning to school for their senior years

Web site for internship/co-op information:
www.airproducts.com/Careers/NorthAmerica/UniversityRecruiting/Co-OpInternProgram.htm

Affinity Groups/Employee Networks

Employee Networks are part of an overall diversity program intended to make Air Products a more inclusive, creative, responsive and efficient organization-one that recognizes and captures all the potential of its people.

Air Products has four employee networks:

Ethnically Diverse Employee Network
Gay and Lesbian Empowered Employees
Parents Association
Women in Business

Web site for more information:
www.airproducts.com/Careers/NorthAmerica/Diversity/EmployeeNetworks.htm

Entry-Level Programs/Full-Time Opportunities

Career Development Program

The Career Development Program (CDP) is a strategic investment in the future of Air Products. Since this program began in 1959, it has provided a steady flow of talent including B.S. and M.S. Engineers, Ph.D. Engineers and Scientists, B.S. and M.S. Information Technology (IT) Specialists, and Financial and Commercial MBAs into our company.

On this program participants are given an opportunity to develop their skills and interests through various positions in different areas of the company. This normally involves the completion of three different assignments during the first two to three years of employment. Every individual is encouraged to take an active role in influencing his or her career path.

Over the years, many past and current leaders of Air Products including our current Chief Executive Officer, John P. Jones, have joined the company through the Career Development Program. We're looking for people who will help shape the future of Air Products.

Engineering Career Development Program

The Engineering Career Development Program (CDP) is designed for entry-level chemical and mechanical engineers (0-2 years of experience). The program provides entry-level chemical and mechanical engineers with experience in various areas of the company in various types of positions. While on the program, participants are able to develop their engineering and professional skills while achieving a better understanding of their interests and strengths.

The program consists of three rotations that include different locations and assignments with durations of 10 to 12 months. Typical assignments for chemical engineers on the program may include manufacturing, environmental health and safety, operations, process, production, project, research and start-up roles. Typical assignments for mechanical engineers on the program may include manufacturing, safety, operations, maintenance, reliability and design roles.

Program Requirements

Academic Record: Air Products hires candidates with outstanding academic records. A baseline GPA is one of the factors we consider in addition to work experience and activity involvement.

Disciplines: Recent graduates or rising seniors who have received or are pursing a B.S. or M.S. in the following majors will be considered:Chemical Engineering; Mechanical Engineering

Assignment Descriptions

Air Products offers you a world of engineering opportunities on our Career Development Program (CDP). Numerous engineering positions are available in both our world headquarters in the Lehigh Valley, Pennsylvania area and in our many field locations throughout the United States. Typical engineering roles are discussed below.

Design Engineers: Responsible for the design, analysis, specification and troubleshooting of mechanical equipment for use by various operating groups. Typical equipment items are valves, piping, pressure vessels, heat exchangers and packaged process units. Other specialty items such as blend panels, burners, food freezers and gas cabinets are also within the scope of design engineers.

Machinery Engineers: Involved with the design, application, selection and long-term operation of compressors, turbines, pumps and expanded systems, including auxiliaries such as lubrication and seal systems, heat exchangers, piping and instrumentation and control systems.

Maintenance Engineers: Provide a variety of support services to our production facilities. Preventive and predictive maintenance programs, troubleshooting, work order systems, planning and scheduling, lubrication programs and work sampling are among their responsibilities.

Manufacturing and Operations Engineers: Involved in all phases of manufacturing and plant operations. Assignments for chemical and mechanical engineers are found in Air Products' Maintenance, Process, Production, Project Engineering and Quality Assurance functions. Their assignments are either at our corporate headquarters or domestic plants.

Process Engineers: Responsible for optimum process design and improvement of our facilities. This includes not only the development of a thermodynamically efficient process, but also the economic design of each piece of equipment. Process engineers apply engineering principles to the design, development and operation of chemical and gas separation plants across a wide range of businesses-specialty chemicals, cryogenic air separation, high-temperature process for the production of hydrogen and carbon monoxide, electronic specialty gases (ESG), liquefied natural gas (LNG) and hydrocarbon separation processes.

Process Control Engineers: Ensure that the production plants we build can be monitored and controlled to optimum efficiency. Depending on its size and complexity, a plant may employ a simple PLC (programmable logic controller) or more sophisticated DCS (distributed control system), each of which must be configured to perform appropriate control and monitor display functions. Advanced control applications such as MPC (model predictive control) also fall within their realm of responsibility.

Process Systems Engineers: Responsible for developing P&IDs (process and instrumentation diagrams) that provide the definitive scope of equipment, valves, flowmeters, safety devices, etc., for a new facility. They also ensure that all start-up, shutdown and other operational and maintenance requirements are included in the facility's design.

Product Development Engineers: Responsible for the technical, economic and business aspects of new market development from conception through commercialization and, ultimately, to customer acceptance. They become involved in equipment design and testing, process development, economic and market studies, and sales and profit forecasts.

Production Engineers: Responsible for monitoring the production process to ensure sound operation and the efficient use of raw materials and energy. Their work typically includes resolving technical operating problems to minimize production costs and to improve on-stream time.

Project Engineers: Manage and coordinate the efforts of our various engineering groups and other departments in the design and construction of a facility. As a project engineer, you must be both a capable engineer and administrator, using critical path methods and computer cost control as tools in taking the facility or equipment from the contract signing to start-up.

Project Development Engineers: Responsible for capital cost estimates and profitability analyses for major capital expenditures. They are involved throughout the project cycle, coordinating all engineering input for the initial bid to the customer, preparing a detailed project budget and managing final execution of the project's cost.

Research and Development Engineers: Support a broad spectrum of research activities from long-range fundamental programs to more market-driven applied R&D efforts. Significant resources of the company are committed to numerous areas, including cryogenic and noncryogenic gas separation technologies, wastewater treatment, liquid natural gas processing, polymers, industrial and specialty chemicals and environmental controls.

Safety Engineers: Ensure that we are applying the highest degree of technology to maximize safety in the laboratory and field environments. Responsibilities include leading HazOp reviews for specific projects, developing fault trees for safety-relief scenarios and analyzing incidents for root cause failures.

Start-Up Engineers: Responsible for the start-up and commissioning of all new production facilities. They inspect all equipment, perform operational readiness inspections, commission equipment and conduct performance testing of the entire facility.

The Information Technology Career Development Program

The Information Technology Career Development Program (CDP) is designed for entry-level IT specialists (0-2 years of experience) joining Air Products. The program provides entry-level IT specialists with experience in various areas of the company in various types of positions. While in the program, participants are able to develop their technical and professional skills while achieving a better understanding of their areas of interests and strengths.

The program consists of three rotations that include different assignments with durations of approximately 10 months. Typical assignments for IT specialists on the program may include business process, e-business, infrastructure, data and regional execution services.

Program Requirements

Academic Record: Air Products hires candidates with outstanding academic records. A baseline GPA is one of the factors we consider in addition to work experience and activity involvement.

Disciplines: Recent graduates or rising seniors who have received or are pursing a B.S. or M.S. in the following areas will be considered:

- Computer Science
- Computer Engineering
- Information Systems
- Information Technology
- Management Sciences and Information Systems

Assignment Descriptions

Air Products' Global Information Technology Group is dedicated to serving the company's worldwide businesses, and plays a key role in achieving strategic objectives. IT products and services cover the spectrum of business functions, allowing participants of the IT Career Development Program to gain a broad knowledge of company activities. Typical roles for IT CDP participants are discussed below.

IT Business Process Services: incorporates the application development and support activities for our global Gases and Chemicals businesses and provides liaison and support to the enterprise business process activities, as well as applied engineering, modeling and computer aided engineering services for Engineering. Business Process Services consist of four primary process groups with three supporting centers of expertise: Offering and Customer Relationship Management (CRM); Supply Chain Management (SCM); Asset Creation and Improvement; and Enabling Processes. The centers of expertise include the ERP/SAP (Enterprise Resource Planning/Systems and Applications in Data Processing) program management office; Decision Sciences; and Application Delivery Services across the Global IT organization.

E-Business IT Services: includes such diverse activities as APDirect™, our online ordering system, as well as solutions services, value-added services, web business, business-to-business applications, application technical standards, and systems integrity support and testing-all with a global focus and all aimed at enhancing the way business is done. By understanding the needs and capabilities of its customers, Air Products is creating applications that deliver value, strengthen businesses, and ultimately strengthen the industries in which it participates. Several years in a row, Air Products E-Business initiatives have been recognized by InternetWeek as one of the top 100 e-business programs in the U.S.

IT Infrastructure Services: is responsible for Global Telecommunications and Network Services, the Service Operations center and the Client Server organizations. Consolidated infrastructure services standardize the desktop, the server environment and mainframe services, and provide focused, rapid advancement in telecommunications and data networks. IT Infrastructure Services organization provides an ideal opportunity to develop and apply in-depth technical knowledge across a variety of technologies.

IT Planning, Business Relationship, and Data Services: includes the office of the Chief Information Technologist, which is responsible for planning the IT Architecture, managing the introduction of new computer technology into Air Products and creating the architecture design for new applications. In addition, this office runs projects to evaluate and introduce step-out computer technology, which has a high potential to deliver business value to Air Products. IT Planning, Business Relationship and Data Services also includes Data Resource Management Services; Decision Support Services; IT Strategy Development, Operational Planning, Budgeting, and Forecasting; IT Work Portfolio and Process Management; Change Management; Communications and Resource Management; and Strategic Alliance Management. Knowledge Management Services is also a part of this function and addresses the expanding requirements for best practices sharing, team collaboration and self-help through an effective, responsive intranet.

IT Country Clusters and Regional Execution: provides development and business analysis resources as well as functional leadership of IT personnel in key global regions, including Asia, Latin America, Eastern Europe and South Africa for all Gases, Chemicals and Corporate functions in those geographies.

Web site for more information

www.airproducts.com/Careers/NorthAmerica/UniversityRecruiting/WelcomeAndOverview.htm

Strategic Plan and Diversity Leadership

Who has primary responsibility for leading diversity initiatives at your firm?

Victoria Boyd, Director of Diversity

Does your firm currently have a diversity committee?

Yes

If yes, does the committee's representation include one or more members of the firm's management/executive committee (or the equivalent)?

Yes

If yes, how many executives are on the committee, and in 2004, what was the total number of hours collectively spent by the committee in furtherance of the firm's diversity initiatives?

Total executives on the committee: 5

Does the committee and/or diversity leader establish and set goals or objectives consistent with management's priorities?

Yes

Has the firm undertaken a formal or informal diversity program or set of initiatives aimed at increasing the diversity of the firm?

Yes, formal

How often does the firm's management review the firm's diversity progress/results?

Quarterly

The Stats

Employees: 10,000 (2004, U.S.)
Employees: 10,000 (2004, outside U.S.)
Employees: 20,000 (2004, worldwide)

Allstate Insurance Co.

2775 Sanders Rd.
Northbrook, IL 60062
(847) 402-5000
Fax: (847) 836-3998
www.allstate.com

Locations (worldwide)

Nationwide

Diversity Leadership
Monika Kim, HR Sr. Consultant
2775 Sanders Road
Northbrook, IL 60062

Recruiting

Please list the schools/types of schools at which you recruit.

• Ivy League schools
• Other private schools
• Public state schools
• Historically Black Colleges and Universities (HBCUs)
• Hispanic Serving Institutions (HSIs)

Do you have any special outreach efforts that are directed to encourage minority students to consider your firm?

• Advertise in minority student association publication(s)
• Participate in/host minority student job fair(s)
• Sponsor minority student association events
• Firm's employees participate on career panels at school

What activities does the firm undertake to attract minority and women employees?

• Partner programs with women and minority associations
• Participate at minority job fairs
• Seek referrals from other employees

Do you use executive recruiting/search firms to seek to identify new diversity hires?

No

Internships and Co-ops

Allstate Internship Program

Deadline for application: Rolling

Number of interns in the program in summer 2004 (internship): 107

Pay: Weekly

Length of the program: 12 weeks

Percentage of interns/co-ops in the program who receive offers of full-time employment: For 2004, 23%

Web site for internship/co-op information: www.allstatecareers.com

Applicants must be current college students.

Scholarships

Education Support Programs

Through a partnership with the ConSern Education Program, Allstate offers assistance to any employee or family member in securing a loan for private (K-12), undergraduate, graduate and professional education. A total of 2,974 employees utilized the ConSern program in 2004 for education loans or assistance, and $96,000 was given out to employees in the form of educational loans. In addition, employees and family members are also eligible to obtain a $1,000 scholarship through the ConSern program; two Allstate employees were recently awarded free scholarships from the program.

Allstate never ceases to try new approaches to support and counsel its employees and their families. In 2004, the company piloted a program with College Coach to address the growing needs of the "tween" age group. The leading source of educational advisory services to school-age students and their families, College Coach offers employees training workshops, one-on-one counseling and an on-demand help desk to coach them through all aspects of the college process. In 2004, pilot programs were conducted at Allstate's corporate headquarters as well as its locations in Charlotte, NC, Hudson, OH and in Dallas, TX. The programs drew 175 workshop attendees, 109 individuals seeking counseling, and over 700 Help Desk inquiries.

Entry-Level Programs/Full-Time Opportunities

Learning & Development

A high-performance work environment requires continuous learning. Allstate invested more than $14.8 million in 2004, helping employees cultivate new skills leading to new job opportunities through a variety of programs:

• The Learning Resource Network (LRN) – an e-learning platform for interpersonal, technical and leadership development courses – available 24/7 at virtually every employee's workstation. The LRN total usage for 2004 was 843,238 hours.

• Professional Education programs that offer industry and professional designations as well as tuition reimbursement for undergraduate and graduate degree programs.

• Onsite open enrollment undergraduate and MBA programs at the corporate headquarters in Northbrook, as well as online undergraduate and graduate degree programs supported by tuition reimbursement and available to all eligible employees through the University of Phoenix.

Professional Education – At a Glance

2004 Results

• Industry designation expenditures: $ 6.6 million
• Tuition reimbursement: $ 8.2 million

Onsite Executive MBA

• 68 Current Participants
• 121 Graduates (program-to-date)
• 36.8% Women

Onsite Open Enrollment MBA (established 2001)

• 115 Current Participants
• 36 % Women

Onsite Undergraduate Program (established 2001)

• 70 Current Participants
• 74% Women

Online University of Phoenix Program (established 2002)

• 171 Undergraduate Participants
• 58 Graduate Participants
• 76% Women

Workshops

Instructor-led workshops account for the other 50% of Allstate's job-related education. In addition to its corporate headquarters, instructional facilities are located in all regional offices, call centers, processing centers and other facilities. Workshops are by Allstate facilitators as well as outside vendors in order to provide a full range of topic coverage and a variety of viewpoints.

Strategic Plan and Diversity Leadership

How does the firm's leadership communicate the importance of diversity to everyone at the firm?

For Allstate's corporate culture, a commitment to communication is fundamental, and it begins at the top. Edward M. Liddy, Allstate Chairman and Chief Executive Officer, describes a deceptively simple modus operandi: "At Allstate, we invest in truthful communication in a multitude of ways, through our people and through our processes. The result is a culture in which people are free to express their opinions, challenge the status quo and help guide the company with a sound moral compass."

Liddy believes that open, honest, two-way communication is the bedrock of ethical standards. "How much time you invest in communication is equally important," he notes. "An independent study showed that Allstate annually devotes an estimated two million man-hours to communication in all forms – face-to-face, electronic and print. These hours not only reflect corporate and departmental communications, but also local communication efforts throughout the company by individual units and offices that dedicate resources to communication."

• The flow of information from Allstate's senior management to all employees is ongoing, and it is accomplished through a mulitude of vehicles and media.
• Quarterly Communication Meetings hosted by Ed Liddy
• Town Hall Meetings Conducted by Ed Liddy and Fellow Senior Leaders
• Allstate NOW: This popular company communications vehicle has been published continually since the 1970s, and is now an online publication directed to all employees vand agents. Allstate NOW features news, information and interviews designed to

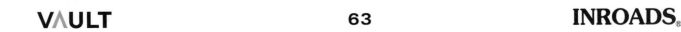

inform and align employees and agencies behind company strategies and key initiatives, and also to foster pride in working for Allstate. The site recorded more than 1.2 million visits in 2004, which attests to its popularity and value as a communications source.

- "Helping Hands" Volunteer Opportunities: This ongoing schedule of events is posted prominently near each cafeteria.
- Broadcast Bulletins: From weekly Allstate NOW broadcast emails – providing employees with updates on everything from company and industry news, upcoming programs, events and volunteer opportunities – to voicemail broadcasts communicating messages around safety security and stability, Allstate believes in using all mediums to communicate thoroughly, honestly and frequently with employees.
- Intranet Website
- Company Management & Department Leader Communications: These individuals disseminate information on an ongoing basis via departmental/group meetings, e-mail and video messages, memoranda and publication articles.
- External Company Communications: These include press releases and media/trade publication articles, as well as speeches delivered by company leaders to a variety of audiences.

Liddy is convinced of the value of employee communications in fostering understanding, enthusiasm and a sense of belonging. "I believe that when employees are well-informed and understand the business and their roles," he notes, "it shows in their performance – and in their commitment to the company and its standards."

Mr. Liddy is a champion for diversity and uses all of the above venues to discuss the importance of diversity and work/life.

Who has primary responsibility for leading diversity initiatives at your firm?

- Anise Wiley-Little, Director of Diversity & Work/Life.

Does your firm currently have a diversity committee?

Yes. To further expand on the company's commitment and great strides with regard to diversity, Allstate recently formed a Corporate Diversity Council to ensure that Allstate continues to meet the changing demographic needs of both customers and employees.

The Diversity Council consists of 14 senior-level decision-makers – including representatives from the diversity team, supplier diversity, marketing, corporate relations, selection and leadership – dedicated to integrating diversity with Allstate business strategy. Chairman and CEO Ed Liddy is the executive sponsor of the council.

The Diversity Council's will strive to assess all of the diversity initiatives throughout the company with a futuristic focus on two or three long-term initiatives that will strengthen our unified approach to diversity and the measurement behind it.

Allstate also has a Diversity & Work/Life team dedicated to improving diversity and work/life, meeting affirmative action goals, ergonomics, equal pay and external recognition. The team is comprised of seven full-time staff members reporting in to a director.

If yes, does the committee's representation include one or more members of the firm's management/executive committee (or the equivalent)?

Yes.

The council includes 14 senior level decision-makers – including representatives from the diversity team, supplier diversity, marketing, corporate relations, selection and leadership. Chairman and CEO Ed Liddy is the executive sponsor of the council.

Does the committee and/or diversity leader establish and set goals or objectives consistent with management's priorities?

Yes. The mission of the Corporate Diversity Council is to identify, recommend and champion the implementation of strategies and initiatives to effectively drive high performance for all, maximizing productivity of Allstate's Workforce. At Allstate, managing diversity is a strategy for leveraging differences in the workplace and marketplace to gain a competitive advantage.

Has the firm undertaken a formal or informal diversity program or set of initiatives aimed at increasing the diversity of the firm?

Yes, formal. A primary element in Allstate's diversity strategy is effective, mandatory education for all employees. Since its inception in 1993, Allstate's "best practice" level diversity education program has reached more than 40,000 employees. Allstate's employee composition reflects this focus, as 60 percent are female and 28.5 percent are minorities.

• All Allstate employees with 6 – 12 months of service must complete a curriculum called Diversity – Allstate's Competitive Edge (ACE) that includes a facilitated four-hour workshop and a one-hour follow-up online course, both of which stress the importance of diversity in contributing to an environment of workplace success. Program components include case studies addressing diversity in the workplace and customer scenarios involving diversity issues.

• Allstate leadership regularly reinforces our commitment to diversity. To emphasize the importance of such knowledge among leaders, Allstate recently rolled out a new diversity training curriculum for new managers called "Creating an Environment for Success." During this facilitated workshop participants develop specific actions to increase their effectiveness through self-assessment, shared best practices and an increased understanding of the importance of differences and their implications on management/leadership style. This course is also available as an optional refresher for existing managers with direct reports who have previously completed other diversity training.

• A video used in the training feature three leaders sharing their vision of diversity: Ed Liddy, Chairman and CEO, Tom Wilson, President and COO, Allstate Protection and Casey Sylla, President, Allstate Financial.

• During 2004, a total of 2,378 new employees attended the interactive diversity training at Allstate.

How often does the firm's management review the firm's diversity progress/results?

Annually

How is the firm's diversity committee and/or firm management held accountable for achieving results?

All leaders at Allstate who have direct reports and/or hiring responsibilities are held accountable to create a supportive and inclusive environment, and to develop and promote minorities and women through a leadership development process. Leadership regarding diversity results is evaluated on their job performance reviews. Finally, achievement of the diversity objectives are measured and linked to their merit increases.

From the beginning, Allstate's Diversity Initiative has recognized that a keystone of an effective and viable diversity effort is leaders consistently modeling desired behaviors. As a result, leaders have been held accountable for passing along the diversity message and ensuring that these behaviors are not just present, but publicly valued and acknowledged in their area.

The Diversity Initiative is top down. Beginning at the top, the Senior Management Team oversees that diversity objectives are understood and implemented by ensuring that the necessary training, development and support for those objectives are in place. Managing a diverse work force is a major company responsibility, and in order for the responsibility to be realized, performance standards were established, including:

• Achievement of affirmative action objectives
• Completion of diversity education for all 35,000 non-agent employees by year-end 1996 and the requirement that new employees complete training within their first year
• Completion of skill assessment and development of a learning agreement to close skills gaps for each employee
• Inclusion of a diverse slate of qualified candidates in every selection pool
• A requirement to manage a supportive work environment where all employees are able to contribute to their full potential
• Compensation tied to achieving key diversity objectives
• Since 1995, under Allstate's Performance Management process, all leaders with employee accountability shared common major responsibility to increase individual, team and organizational performance by creating a productive and supportive work environment

The Stats

Employees: 37,236 (2004, U.S.)
Employees: 37,671 (2004, U.S.)
Employees: 1,186 (2004, outside U.S.)
Employees: 38,857 (2004, worldwide)

Retention and Professional Development

How do 2004 minority and female attrition rates generally compare to those experienced in the prior year period?

About the same as in prior years

Please identify the specific steps you are taking to reduce the attrition rate of minority and women employees.

Develop and/or support internal employee affinity groups (e.g., minority or women networks within the firm)

• Increase/review compensation relative to competition
• Increase/improve current work/life programs
• Adopt dispute resolution process
• Succession plan includes emphasis on diversity
• Work with minority and women employees to develop career advancement plans
• Review work assignments and hours billed to key client matters to make sure minority and women employees are not being excluded
• Strengthen mentoring program for all employees, including minorities and women
• Professional skills development program, including minority and women employees

Diversity Mission Statement

At Allstate, Diversity is a strategy for leveraging differences in the workplace and marketplace to gain a competitive advantage.

American Airlines

4333 Amon Carter Blvd.
Forth Worth, TX 76155
(817) 963-1234
Fax: (817) 967-9641
www.aacareers.com

Diversity Leadership

John Igoe, Workforce Strategy Consultant
4333 Amon Carter
Ft. Worth, TX 76155
Phone: (817) 963-9441
E-mail: john.igoe@aa.com

Recruiting

Please list the schools/types of schools at which you recruit.

- *Ivy League schools:* Harvard
- *Other private schools:* Duke, Southern Methodist University, Texas Christian University, Baylor, Northwestern, Georgetown, MIT, Carnegie, Kellogg, Chicago
- *Public state schools:* University of Northern Texas, University of Texas-Austin, Baylor, Arizona State University, University of Oklahoma, Ohio State University, Penn State, Texas A&M
- *Historically Black Colleges and Universities (HBCUs):* Howard, Clark, Prairie View
- *Hispanic Serving Institutions (HSIs):* University of Texas at El Paso

Do you have any special outreach efforts that are directed to encourage minority students to consider your firm?

- Conferences. NSBE, SHPE, NABA, NSHMBA, BMBA, ALPFA, SWE, AISES, Reaching Out, BDPA
- Participate in/host minority student job fair(s)

What activities does the firm undertake to attract minority and women employees?

- Partner programs with women and minority associations
- Conferences. WITI, WIA, NWMBA
- Participate at minority job fairs
- Seek referrals from other employees

Do you use executive recruiting/search firms to seek to identify new diversity hires?

No

Internships and Co-ops

INROADS

Number of interns in the program in summer 2004 (internship) or 2004 (co-op): 1
Length of the program: 8 weeks

Affinity Groups/Employee Networks

Names of affinity groups:

- African-American Employee Resource Group
- Asian Cultural Association
- Caribbean Employees
- Christian Resource Group
- Employees with Disabilities
- Gay, Lesbian, Transgender and Bisexual Employees
- Indian Employees
- Jewish Resource Group
- Latin Employee Resource Group
- Muslim Resource Group
- Native American Employee Resource Group
- Women in AAviation
- Work and Family Balance
- 40 Plus/Senior Employees

Strategic Plan and Diversity Leadership

How does the firm's leadership communicate the importance of diversity to everyone at the firm?
E-mails, web site, newsletters and meetings

Who has primary responsibility for leading diversity initiatives at your firm?
Debra Hunter Johnson, VP, Diversity and Corporate Leadership

Does your firm currently have a diversity committee?

Yes

Does the committee's representation include one or more members of the firm's management/executive committee (or the equivalent)?

Yes

Does the committee and/or diversity leader establish and set goals or objectives consistent with management's priorities?

Yes

Has the firm undertaken a formal or informal diversity program or set of initiatives aimed at increasing the diversity of the firm?

Yes, formal

How often does the firm's management review the firm's diversity progress/results?

Monthly

Retention and Professional Development

How do 2004 minority and female attrition rates generally compare to those experienced in the prior year period?

About the same as in prior years

Please identify the specific steps you are taking to reduce the attrition rate of minority and women employees.

• Develop and/or support internal employee affinity groups
• Increase/improve current work/life programs
• Succession plan includes emphasis on diversity

American Electric Power (AEP)

1 Riverside Plaza
Columbus, OH 43215-2372
Phone: (614) 716-1000
Fax: (614) 716-1823
www.AEP.com/careers

Locations
Arkansas • Indiana • Kentucky •
Louisiana • Michigan • Ohio • Oklahoma,
Tennessee • Texas, Virginia • West
Virginia

Diversity Leadership
Mary Cofer, Director, Personnel Services &
EEO

Employment Contact
Peggy Sibila Buck, College
Relations Coordinator
1 Riverside Plaza
Columbus, OH 43215
Phone: (614) 716-1856
Fax: (614) 716-1864
E-mail: psbuck@AEP.com

Recruiting

Please list the schools/types of schools at which you recruit.

• Ivy League schools
• Other private schools
• Public state schools
• Historically Black Colleges and Universities (HBCUs)
• Hispanic Serving Institutions (HSIs)
• Other predominantly minority and/or women's colleges

Do you have any special outreach efforts that are directed to encourage minority students to consider your firm?

• Conferences
• Participate in/host minority student job fair(s)
• Firm's employees participate on career panels at school
• Outreach to leadership of minority student organizations
• Scholarships or intern/fellowships for minority students

What activities does the firm undertake to attract minority and women employees?

• Partner programs with women and minority associations
• Conferences
• Participate at minority job fairs
• Seek referrals from other employees
• Utilize online job services

Do you use executive recruiting/search firms to seek to identify new diversity hires?

Yes

Internships and Co-ops

> *Number of interns in the program in summer 2004 (internship) or 2004 (co-op):* 45 total
> *Length of the program:* 12 weeks
> *Percentage of interns/co-ops in the program who receive offers of full-time employment:* 25-85%
> *Web site for internship/co-op information:* www.AEP.com/careers

Co-op Participants

- Must be in their sophomore year at college (a minimum of 50 credit hours) and preferably have completed at least one core class
- Are available to co-op for a minimum of two non-consecutive terms
- Are willing to possibly rotate to different work sites to expand knowledge and experience with differing projects
- 3.0 GPA or better
- Preferably U.S. citizens or permanent residents

Interns

- Must be in their junior or senior year of college
- Work one or two sessions, typically only during the summer
- 3.0 GPA or better
- Preferably U.S. citizens or permanent residents

Scholarships

AEP scholarships are awarded annually on a competitive basis to children of AEP employees who are high school seniors planning to pursue a baccalaureate degree. AEP does not offer college scholarships to our customers or their children. However, AEP does have a long history of support for K-12 education, as well as for colleges and universities, including grants for teachers and workshops. Read more about it on our website at www.aep.com under the "About Us" tab.

Entry-Level Programs/Full-Time Opportunities

Analysts

- Must have completed their undergraduate degree in a business-related area
- Prefer 1-3 years of related experience
- Are willing to rotate to different work assignments for a more complete understanding of the business for a duration of approximately one to two years

Strategic Plan and Diversity Leadership

How does the firm's leadership communicate the importance of diversity to everyone at the firm?

E-mails, web site, newsletters, meetings and mandatory training

Who has primary responsibility for leading diversity initiatives at your firm?

Mary Cofer, Dir Personnel Svcs & EEO. (Please contact her for diversity-related specifics.)

Does your firm currently have a diversity committee?

Yes

The Stats

Employees: 20,000 (2004, U.S.)
Employees: 17,000 (2003, U.S.)
Revenue: $14.7 billion (2004, U.S.)
Revenue: $14.1 billion (2003, U.S.)

Diversity Mission Statement

AEP is committed to providing and fostering an inclusive business environment that leverages the unique talents, perspectives and experiences of each employee.

Additional Information

Our Commitment to Diversity

Like fingerprints, every human being is different. Beyond obvious differences such as race, gender, age, height and weight, there are more subtle dissimilarities: personality, motivation, education, work ethic and goals.

At AEP, we recognize and respect the differences among those who contribute to the success of our company: our investors, our shareholders, our customers and our employees. We know that together, we make up one, great organization – a company that produces a product that allows each and every one of us to pursue success in life and in business and in everything that we do.

Recently, we launched a series of diversity initiatives under the theme "Everyone Counts." These initiatives are ongoing and dedicated to the philosophy that each of us has something valuable to contribute to the good of the organization. We encourage different points of view, all working together toward AEP's common goals. We value unique thinking within the context of teamwork.

We understand that to truly succeed, all of us must stretch beyond our own personal comfort zones of the familiar and embrace the similarities and differences of others who contribute to the success of our company.

American Family Insurance

6000 American Pkwy.
Madison, WI 53783
(608) 249-2111
Fax: (608) 243-4921
www.amfam.com

Locations (worldwide):
17 States

Diversity Leadership
Jeff Close, Technical Staffing Specialist
6000 American Parkway
Madison, WI 53783
Phone: (608) 249-2111
Fax: (608) 243-6529
E-mail: jclose@amfam.com

Recruiting

Please list the schools/types of schools at which you recruit.

• *Private schools:* Edgewood College in Madison and all other Wisconsin private colleges
• *Public state schools:* University of Wisconsin-Madison and University of Wisconsin System Schools, Madison Area Technical College and Technical Colleges throughout Wisconsin, Herzing College, Northern Illinois University, University of Illinois, Illinois State University., Drake University, Iowa State University, Northern Iowa University

Do you have any special outreach efforts that are directed to encourage minority students to consider your firm?

• Conferences: NEON – National Economic Opportunity Network, MSLC – Multicultural Student Leadership Conference
• Advertise in minority student association publication(s)
• Participate in/host minority student job fair(s)
• Sponsor minority student association events
• Firm's employees participate on career panels at school
• Outreach to leadership of minority student organizations
• Scholarships or intern/fellowships for minority students

What activities does the firm undertake to attract minority and women employees?

• Partner programs with women and minority associations
• Participate at minority job fairs
• Seek referrals from other employees
• Utilize online job services

Do you use executive recruiting/search firms to seek to identify new diversity hires?

Yes

List all women- and/or minority-owned executive search/recruiting firms to which the firm paid a fee for placement services in the past 12 months.

Consultis, New Directions and several other firms.

Internships and Co-ops

I/S Summer Internship Program

Deadline for application: March 1
Number of interns in the program in summer 2004 (internship) or 2004 (co-op): 10 interns
Pay: $15.81/hr. (2004), $16.10/hr (2005)
Length of the program: 12 weeks
Percentage of interns/co-ops in the program who receive offers of full-time employment: 10% of 2004 interns
Web site for internship/co-op information: www.amfam.com/careers

Those who intern in Applications Development work side-by-side with a mentor and other full-time technologists to provide application planning, design, development, enhancements and maintenance. We work with a variety of web, client server and mainframe development tools. We provide professional and technical services for the development and ongoing support of both our end users and the I/S Division. In this developmental position, interns gain experience as they program, test and debug applications and subroutines under the leadership of our mentor and senior technologists. Other possible opportunities may be available in Base Technology support areas such as Database Administration, Networking, Security, Peripheral Components, Customer Support, Desktop Platforms, Server Support and End User Computing.

Actuarial Internship Program

Deadline for application: March 1
Number of interns in the program in summer 2004 (internship) or 2004 (co-op): 5 Interns (2004), 4 Interns (2005)
Pay: $15.81/hr. (2004), $16.10/hr (2005)
Length of the program: 12 weeks. There may be opportunities to work part-time during the school year and to work over the semester break as well.
Percentage of interns/co-ops in the program who receive offers of full-time employment: 25% of 2004 interns.
Web site for internship/co-op information: www.amfam.com/careers

The American Family Property/Casualty and Life/Health actuarial summer internship programs are designed to involve the student in a variety of actuarial activities, including assistance in modeling projects and development of rate indications. These activities will provide the student with valuable experience in the type of work they could be involved with in their future career.

Requirements

• Pursuit of a bachelor's degree in Actuarial Science, Math or a related field such as Risk Management, Statistics or Computer Science
• Depending on the position, there may be a requirement that the candidate has sat for at least one of the Actuarial exams.
• The candidate should be at least in their second year of school at a University.
• Depending on the position, courses in Interest Theory and/or Actuarial Mathematics may be required.
• Experience with Microsoft Office and programming languages such as Visual Basic is considered a plus.

INROADS

Deadline for application: Ongoing
Number of interns in the program in summer 2004 (internship) or 2004 (co-op): 6 Interns (2004)
Pay: Hourly rate varies depending on year in school
Length of the program: 12 weeks in the summer. There may be opportunities to work part-time during the school year and to work over the semester break as well.
Web site for internship/co-op information: www.amfam.com/careers

INROADS interns at American Family are placed in paid positions related to their majors or career goals. We strive to match their interests and skills with the needs of our internal divisions. Most INROADS interns work at American Family during summers between academic sessions. But in some cases these summer opportunities can turn into a continuous engagement during the school year based on manager needs and intern availability.

Corporate Internship Program

Deadline for application: Ongoing
Number of interns in the program in summer 2004 (internship) or 2004 (co-op): 77 Interns (summer 2004)
Pay: Hourly rate varies depending on year in school
Length of the program: 12 weeks in the summer. There may be opportunities to work part-time during the school year and to work over the semester break as well.
Percentage of interns/co-ops in the program who receive offers of full-time employment: 4% overall
Web site for internship/co-op information: www.amfam.com/careers

All of the above programs fall under the umbrella of the Corporate internship program at American Family Insurance. In addition to matching students to positions aligned with their majors and career goals, each student is assigned a mentor, provided meaningful work, opportunities to interact with fellow interns, a performance appraisal and the opportunity to provide feedback on their internship experience with American Family.

Entry-Level Programs/Full-Time Opportunities

EXCEL Claims Training Program

Length of program: 6 weeks
Geographic location(s) of program: Training takes place at our corporate headquarters in Madison and though out our 17 operating states.

Please describe the training/training component of this program: Classroom training, hands-on training in our education center, and on-the-job training & mentoring.

Strategic Plan and Diversity Leadership

How does the firm's leadership communicate the importance of diversity to everyone at the firm?
All new employees participate in a diversity workshop. New managers receive more in-depth training. There are numerous e-mails, presentations, etc. promoting diversity throughout the year.

Who has primary responsibility for leading diversity initiatives at your firm?
Director of Strategic Staffing

Does your firm currently have a diversity committee?

Yes

Please describe how the committee is structured, how often it meets, etc.:
Committees are located at our major offices. The teams consist of HR representatives, employees and managers.

Does the committee's representation include one or more members of the firm's management/executive committee (or the equivalent)?

No

Does the committee and/or diversity leader establish and set goals or objectives consistent with management's priorities?

Yes. At the core of our diversity efforts is the PEOPLE Plan. To us, "PEOPLE" stands for "Partnership in Equal Opportunity Producing Leadership Excellence." Included within the PEOPLE Plan are initiatives that enrich and support not only our employees but also the communities we serve. These initiatives include internships, educational programs, scholarships, neighborhood and community involvement activities, support of emerging market development and active participation in cultural celebrations.

Has the firm undertaken a formal or informal diversity program or set of initiatives aimed at increasing the diversity of the firm?

Yes, formal and informal. The firm's goal is for our workforce to reflect the population of the communities in which we do business. On a less formal level, the Strategic Staffing area of HR has developed a community outreach program to offer job seeking and career planning services to our local minority communities.

How often does the firm's management review the firm's diversity progress/results?

Quarterly

Retention and Professional Development

Please identify the specific steps you are taking to reduce the attrition rate of minority and women employees.

- Increase/review compensation relative to competition
- Increase/improve current work/life programs
- Succession plan includes emphasis on diversity
- Strengthen mentoring program for all employees, including minorities and women
- Professional skills development program, including minority and women employees
- Other: The advancement of women and minorities is a major corporate goal.

Diversity Mission Statement

American Family Insurance is dedicated to fostering a culture that is welcoming, diverse and inclusive – a culture that supports our goal of attracting and retaining "the best and the brightest."

The Employer Says

We promote a culture of diversity and inclusion through ongoing efforts that include a variety of initiatives designed to promote awareness and understanding of the value that inclusion and diversity bring to us all:

- Our commitment to inclusion and diversity enables our employees to contribute to our business in a way that enhances their performance and helps them provide world-class service to our diverse customers. And by ensuring that inclusion and diversity are woven throughout our culture and business practices, we are creating the foundation for future success.

- We strive to build the most talented workforce possible – one that mirrors the communities we serve. We believe it is motivating for employees to work in an inclusive environment where they feel respected and valued for their individuality. That's why we embrace and celebrate our unique differences and similarities.

- At American Family, inclusion and diversity are a part of our very foundation. From a strong foundation, there are no limits to what we can achieve.

- American Family Insurance is an equal opportunity employer.

American Red Cross

2025 E St., NW
Washington, DC 20006
Phone: (202) 303-4498
Fax: (202) 942-2024
Toll Free: (800) 435-7669
www.redcross.org

Diversity Leadership

David G. Wilkins, Esq., Chief Diversity Officer
20205 E Street, NW
Washington, DC 20006
Phone: (202) 303-7565
Fax: (202) 303-0200
E-mail: Wilkinsdg@usa.redcross.org

Recruiting

What activities does the firm undertake to attract minority and women employees?

• Partner programs with women and minority associations
• Conferences:
• National Urban League
• National Minority Supplier Development Council
• Congressional Black Caucus
• U.S. Pan Asian Chamber of Commerce
• NAFEO
• Participate at minority job fairs
• Seek referrals from other employees
• Utilize online job services

Internships and Co-ops

Presidential Internship

Deadline for application: March
Number of interns in the program in summer 2004 (internship) or 2004 (co-op): 25
Pay: $400.00/week
Length of the program: 10 weeks
Web site for internship/co-op information: www.redcross.org

Scholarships

The Presidential Intern Program brings diverse undergraduate and graduate college students into the Red Cross in key professional areas by providing paid internships. The relationships fostered between the interns and Red Cross often results in future employees, donors and volunteers.

Entry-Level Programs/Full-Time Opportunities

STAR TRACK

Length of program: Two years
Geographic location(s) of program: National in scope

Please describe the training/training component of this program:

StarTrack III is a two-year (2002 through 2004), self-directed executive development program sponsored and funded by National Headquarters. The program's goal is to develop a diverse, highly qualified pool of up to 30 high-potential candidates who are competitive for chapter executive vacancies in the top 150 chapters within six years of entering the program. Participants, with the guidance of experienced coaches, create and execute a competency-based Individual Development Plan that includes chapter-based experiential activities and training, both internal and external to the American Red Cross.

Please describe any other educational components of this program (i.e., tuition reimbursement):

Participation in Star Track III will necessitate periodic, program-sponsored travel throughout the United States, ranging from 1 day for various meetings, to up to 4 weeks for interim assignments. The cumulative time commitment away from the office is a minimum of seven weeks spread over the 24-month program.

Specific program components include:

• Individual Development Plan – Using feedback from a 360-degree assessment process, participants compare their current mastery of skills and competencies with those required of a high-performing chapter executive, to create an Individual Development Plan. This plan forms the road map for self-directed learning activities during the program.
• Coaching – An experienced chapter executive will be matched with the participant to assist in creating the Individual Development Plan. This coach will work with the participant for the duration of the program, checking progress and assessing competency development, through regularly scheduled telephone conversations and meetings.
• Individual Chapter-Based Assignments – A 4-week interim chapter executive assignment and a 1-week Audit Services team chapter assignment are arranged for each participant during the program. These two "hands-on" assignments have been consistently rated the most valuable aspects of StarTrack by past participants.
• Workshops – Three group workshops will be conducted during program.
  • A 3-day workshop in April 2002 will introduce participants and coaches to StarTrack Program III, their roles and responsibilities, coaching models, strategies for forming and maintaining a coaching relationship, the results of the participant's 360-degree assessment, and creation of the Individual Development Plan.
  • A 2-day workshop, to be held midway through the two-year program in April 2003, will be designed and developed to meet the evolving needs of participants. Includes meeting with coaches to complete the 12-month progress assessment.
  • A final workshop is held in the last month of the program involving both participants and coaches to assess participants' competency development during the program.
• Panel Review Team Interview – Participants attend a Panel Review Team interview at the 18th month of the program to demonstrate and receive feedback on their competency mastery. Interviews are conducted by teams of two experienced chapter executives and one chapter chair, who use real-life scenarios to objectively assess participants on their mastery of critical chapter executive competencies and provide constructive feedback.

Strategic Plan and Diversity Leadership

How does the firm's leadership communicate the importance of diversity to everyone at the firm?

Corporate Diversity Department works closely with Communications & Marketing and their staff, using broadcast emails, internal and external websites, "The Diversity Works" newsletter and various other media to promote the strategy and plans for increasing the diversity of the organization.

Who has primary responsibility for leading diversity initiatives at your firm?

David G. Wilkins, Esq., VP and Chief Diversity Officer

Does your firm currently have a diversity committee?

Yes

If yes, please describe how the committee is structured, how often it meets, etc.

The National Diversity Council is composed of volunteer leaders from any Red Cross Chapter or Blood Region, appointed by the National Board of Governors, and charged to provide advice to the Board on diversity matters. Each member serves for one-three year term, with the potential to be reappointed for an additional term. The Council meet three times per year.

If yes, does the committee's representation include one or more members of the firm's management/executive committee (or the equivalent)?

Yes

If yes, how many executives are on the committee?

Total executives on the committee: 1

Does the committee and/or diversity leader establish and set goals or objectives consistent with management's priorities?

Yes

Please elaborate, if you wish.

Diversity strategy and goals are set as a component of the corporate business planning process

Has the firm undertaken a formal or informal diversity program or set of initiatives aimed at increasing the diversity of the firm?

Yes, formal. The overall focus of the Corporate Diversity Department is to increase the diversity of Red Cross staff and volunteers and to ensure the organization increasingly represents the diverse communities its serves. Specifically, we pursue explicit market segment approaches to the African-American, Asian Pacific Islander, and Hispanic/Latino communities, as well as our Youth and Young Adult and Supplier Diversity programs.

How often does the firm's management review the firm's diversity progress/results?

Annually

How is the firm's diversity committee and/or firm management held accountable for achieving results?

The President and CEO sets performance goals, including diversity goals for her direct reports and evaluates their performance against all of these goals in determining merit increases.

The Stats

Employees: 30,000 (2004, U.S.)
Revenue: $3 billion (2004, U.S.)

Red Cross headquarters demographic profile: approximately 80/20 majority/minority; 60/40 female/male; 2/12 minorities/majorities on the executive team.

Retention and Professional Development

How do 2004 minority and female attrition rates generally compare to those experienced in the prior year period?

About the same as in prior years

Please identify the specific steps you are taking to reduce the attrition rate of minority and women employees.

• Develop and/or support internal employee affinity groups (e.g., minority or women networks within the firm)

• Adopt dispute resolution process

• Succession plan includes emphasis on diversity

Diversity Mission Statement

By 2008, every household in America will be involved with the Red Cross as volunteers, employees, blood donors, financial donors, customers and/or suppliers assuring that we are representative of America and recognized for our commitment to diversity and inclusiveness.

The Employer Says

All great organizations are built on great foundations. The American Red Cross is built on a foundation based on diversity-positive leadership throughout all its operations making it an inclusive organization fostering inclusive service to all Americans and our international neighbors in need.

The Red Cross has a solid foundation of commitment to diversity and we are building upon it every day. Valuing the diversity among people- diversity of thinking, backgrounds and culture- helps the Red Cross better meet the needs of the communities we serve. The diversity among Red Cross workers is vital to developing and delivering life-saving services to the American public. Drawing upon those similarities and learning about the differences enhances our human experience and helps make us one of the most relied upon and recognized humanitarian organizations in the world.

Through our national network of Red Cross units in every community in the country, we build relationships and run programs working towards our goals:

• To integrate diversity into every Red Cross unit's strategic and business planning processes;

• To increase understanding of how diversity impacts the mission of the American Red Cross;

• To help units use diversity as a strategy to enhance their regular business activities.

To achieve the broadest possible success from our organizational investment in diversity, the Red Cross has established programs, both locally and nationally. We also have Diversity Consultants who are trained in the use of our Strategic & Tactical Model for Diversity Business Planning. The Red Cross also established partnerships with organizations that share our diversity goals and help us reach diverse audiences. The programs, consultants and partnerships are what help us work towards realizing our full potential and strive towards the total diversity of our people, programs and services.

Anheuser-Busch Companies, Inc.

1 Busch Place
St. Louis, MO 63118
(800) 342-5283
Fax: (314) 577-2900
www.anheuser-busch.com

Locations (worldwide)

St. Louis (Corporate Office), Offices
Worldwide

Diversity Leadership

John Auer, Director
One Busch Place, 181-1
St. Louis, MO 63118
Phone: (314) 577-2261
Fax: (314) 577-0719
E-mail: john.auer@anheuser-busch.com

Recruiting

Please list the schools/types of schools at which you recruit.

- Public state schools
- Historically Black Colleges and Universities (HBCUs)
- Hispanic Serving Institutions (HSIs)

Do you have any special outreach efforts that are directed to encourage minority students to consider your firm?

- Participate in/host minority student job fair(s)
- Firm's employees participate on career panels at school
- Outreach to leadership of minority student organizations
- Scholarships or intern/fellowships for minority students

What activities does the firm undertake to attract minority and women employees?

- Participate at minority job fairs
- Seek referrals from other employees
- Utilize online job services

Do you use executive recruiting/search firms to seek to identify new diversity hires?

Yes

Internships and Co-ops

INROADS

Number of interns in the program in summer 2004 (internship) or 2004 (co-op): 40+
Pay: Varies
Length of the program: Varies
Web site for internship/co-op information: www.buschjobs.com

Scholarships

Hispanic Scholarship Fund and Urban Scholarship Fund

Scholarship award amount: Varies

Web site or other contact information for scholarship: www.anheuser-busch.com

Entry-Level Programs/Full-Time Opportunities

The company has a wide variety of training programs available to all employees.

Strategic Plan and Diversity Leadership

How does the firm's leadership communicate the importance of diversity to everyone at the firm?

We have communication meetings across the country where diversity is one of the many topics discussed with employees. Also, a diversity page is now available through our company's Intranet.

Who has primary responsibility for leading diversity initiatives at your firm?

Arturo Corral, Director of Diversity

Does your firm currently have a diversity committee?

Yes

Please describe how the committee is structured, how often it meets, etc.:

We have a corporate committee that is structured by representation across business units with Human Resource Generalists and Specialists. This group meets on a monthly basis and is lead by the diversity team.

Does the committee's representation include one or more members of the firm's management/executive committee (or the equivalent)?

Yes, the committee includes a number of executives.

Please describe the committee.

There are about 12 members total and the total time devoted, including planning, meeting and follow-up is approximately 10-20 hours per month.

Does the committee and/or diversity leader establish and set goals or objectives consistent with management's priorities?

Yes. The committee aligns its activities to goals and objectives of HR as well as the company's vision and mission.

Diversity Mission Statement

A Diversity Workforce is made up of individuals with a variety of backgrounds and ethnic make-up and experiences which translate into different perspectives.

Applied Materials

3050 Bowers Avenue
Santa Clara, CA 95054
www.appliedmaterials.com/careers/index.html

Locations (worldwide)
US
Asia
Japan
Europe
India
Israel

Diversity Leadership
Terri Sligh, Director Global Diversity

Employment Contact
Dana Pulliam, College Programs Manager
2881 Scott Blvd.
Santa Clara, CA 95050
Phone: (408) 633.9514
Fax: (408) 563.7743
E-mail: Dana_Pulliam@amat.com

Recruiting

Please list the schools/types of schools at which you recruit.

• *Ivy League schools:* Cornell
• *Other private schools:* Stanford, MIT, Cal Tech
• *Public state schools:* Berkeley, University of Texas-Austin, Texas A&M, University of Illinois, Purdue University, Georgia Tech, Arizona State University, University of Texas-El Paso, Michigan State University

Do you have any special outreach efforts that are directed to encourage minority students to consider your firm?

• Participate in/host minority student job fair(s)
• Outreach to leadership of minority student organizations

What activities does the firm undertake to attract minority and women employees?

• Partner programs with women and minority associations
• Conferences: SWE, NSBE, NABA and SHPE
• Participate at minority job fairs
• Seek referrals from other employees
• Utilize online job services

Do you use executive recruiting/search firms to seek to identify new diversity hires?

No

Internships and Co-ops

College Programs Intern/Co-Op Program

Deadline for application: Open
Number of interns in the program in summer 2004 (internship) or 2004 (co-op): 160
Pay: Pay is by the hour and varies
Length of the program: Varies
Percentage of interns/co-ops in the program who receive offers of full-time employment: 30-40%
Web site for internship/co-op information: www.appliedmaterials.com/careers/college_intern.html

Applied Materials offers various internship and co-op programs designed to provide students with hands-on experience, an opportunity to develop skills in an area of interest and the ability to gain knowledge about the company and the semiconductor industry while enhancing their education. Paid internships and co-ops are offered throughout the company, in multiple divisions and vary in both duration and location.

Students seeking an internship or co-op assignment must:

• Be enrolled in a degree-seeking program.
• Be enrolled in a minimum 9-hour class load or three-quarters of the full-time load during the fall and spring semesters. (Course requirements do not apply to summer internships or co-op assignments.)
• Possess a 2.5 GPA or above on a 4.0 scale and a 4.0 on a 5.0 scale.
• Students who wish to be considered for a co-op assignment must register through their university co-op office.

Affinity Groups/Employee Networks

LEAD (Leadership Encouraging Achievement through Diversity)

LEAD provides the opportunity for the corporation and its African American employee base in Austin to team up to create a general sense of community and emphasize corporate citizenship among all employees, ultimately reinforcing Applied Materials' standing as an employer of choice.HIP (Hispanics in Partnership)

HIP (Hispanics in Partnership)

HIP's mission is to create networking opportunities for employees, to cultivate leadership and to promote career growth, thus enabling a corporate partnership for diversity. The group's members aim to serve as role models by promoting educational opportunities within the Hispanic population, while also encouraging all AMAT employees to participate in the opportunities provided by Hispanics in Partnership.

WPDN (Womens Professional Development Network)

The mission of the Austin WPDN is to inspire and enable a community of women to reach their full potential while strengthening Applied Materials' goal to be an employer of choice.

Entry-Level Programs/Full-Time Opportunities

Global College Hire Program

Length of program: Varies
Geographic location(s) of program: U.S., Europe and Asia

Applied Materials' Global College Program (GCP) is a specialized full-time paid opportunity for new college graduates. It is designed to train and develop new graduates in all fields, enabling them to make a significant contribution to the company while learning information valuable in their full time position.

The Global College Program leverages the success of the new college graduates to meet the changing business needs globally. The program is designed to aid in the assimilation of all new college hires in the company globally and provide training and assimilation resources for all hires from Support to Business to Engineering. Whether the new hire is a Financial Analyst in Santa Clara , a planner in Austin or a support engineer in Europe or Asia – or any other position in any other location – this program will provide the tools to enable the new college hire to make an impact quickly. Customized training and assignments, along with activities designed to provide networking, team building and technical learning are incorporated into the program.

Training: This new hire program includes training courses and project assignments designed to help with the transition from academia to the corporate environment. The assignments can be in a variety of functional areas relevant to the background and job position of the new college graduate. Networking, leadership and team building opportunities are available to provide the global college hires with valuable contacts and skills. Each employee will receive a customized training plan. Participants will receive technical and professional development training specific to their full-time employment or general to Applied Materials' culture. To learn more about the program, please visit our web site: www.appliedmaterials.com/careers/global_college_program.html

Strategic Plan and Diversity Leadership

Who has primary responsibility for leading diversity initiatives at your firm?
Terri Sligh, Director, Global Diversity

If you believe
in the power
of potential,
you're in.

You're
in great
company.

At ARAMARK, we go beyond embracing diversity as a corporate guideline.
We live it through the individual perspectives, varied backgrounds, and the myriad of cultures and talents our people bring to the company. We believe that as we move forward in the global marketplace, our commitment to value and leverage diversity as a people and business strategy is key to our success.

ARAMARK is a world leader in providing award-winning food and facilities management services to health care institutions, universities and school districts, stadiums and arenas, international and domestic corporations, as well as providing uniform and career apparel. ARAMARK was ranked number one in its industry in the 2005 FORTUNE 500 survey and was also named one of "America's Most Admired Companies" by FORTUNE magazine in 2005, consistently ranking since 1998 as one of the top three most admired companies in its industry as evaluated by peers. ARAMARK was also named one of the best companies for diversity by Black Enterprise magazine, one of the nation's leading business publications. Headquartered in Philadelphia, ARAMARK has approximately 242,500 employees serving clients in 20 countries.

For more information about ARAMARK, professional opportunities available, and application procedures, please visit www.aramark.com

www.aramark.com
An equal opportunity/affirmative action employer committed to workforce diversity.

ARAMARK

ARAMARK

Aramark Tower
1101 Market St.
Philadelphia, PA 19107
www.ARAMARK.com

Locations (worldwide)
Headquartered in Philadelphia, ARAMARK has approximately 242,500 employees serving clients in 20 countries.

Diversity Leadership
Elizabeth Campbell, Vice President, Employment Practices & Services, FSS, and Corporate Diversity Officer

Employment Contact
Jessica Park, Senior Manager of College Relations
1101 Market Street
Philadelphia, PA 19107
Phone: (800) 999-8989
Fax: (215) 413-4132
E-mail: park-jessica@aramark.com

Recruiting

Please list the schools/types of schools at which you recruit.

- *Ivy League schools:* Cornell
- *Other private schools:* J & W Providence, Villanova, Widener, Brigham Young University
- *Public state schools:* Penn State, Texas Tech, University of Texas-Austin, University of Southern California, University of Missouri, University of Massachusetts, University of Houston, University of Illinois, Rutgers, Ohio State
- Historically Black Colleges and Universities (HBCUs)
- Hispanic Serving Institutions (HSIs)
- Native American Tribal Universities
- Other predominantly minority and/or women's colleges

Do you have any special outreach efforts that are directed to encourage minority students to consider your firm?

- Hold a reception for minority students
- Conferences: National Society of Minorities in Hospitality, NABA, NSBE, NAACP, National Urban League, National Urban League Black Executive Exchange Program, National Black MBA Association, National Society of Hispanic MBAs, Society of Women Engineers, Thurgood Marshall Scholarship Fund
- Advertise in minority student association publication(s)
- Participate in/host minority student job fair(s)
- Sponsor minority student association events
- Firm's employees participate on career panels at school
- Outreach to leadership of minority student organizations
- Scholarships or intern/fellowships for minority students

What activities does the firm undertake to attract minority and women employees?

- Partner programs with women and minority associations
- Conferences: See above
- Participate at minority job fairs
- Seek referrals from other employees

• Utilize online job services

Do you use executive recruiting/search firms to seek to identify new diversity hires?
Yes

Internships and Co-ops

Accounting Co-op Program, Hospitality Internship Program, Mission One Internship Program, Engineering Internship Program

Deadline for application: In March every year
Number of interns in the program in summer 2004 (internship) or 2004 (co-op): 164 Interns in fiscal year 2004
Pay: An average of $10 per hour
Length of the program: 10-12 weeks
Percentage of interns/co-ops in the program who receive offers of full-time employment: 35%
Web site for internship/co-op information: www.aramark.com/careers

Scholarships

The scholarship is provided through Thurgood Marshall Scholarship Fund and National Society of Minorities in Hospitality organization. There are numerous scholarships and awards contributed by lines of businesses in their local communities.

Deadline for application for the scholarship program: Deadlines determined by the organizations
Scholarship award amount: Varies
Web site or other contact information for scholarship: Go to www.NSMH.org and www.thurgoodmarshallfund.org

Affinity Groups/Employee Networks

Women's Summit, Kaleidoscope Summit and additional summits within divisions

Entry-Level Programs/Full-Time Opportunities

Pathways to Leadership, LEAD (Leadership Excellence and Development), Accounting Representatives, Human Resource Representatives

Length of program: 12-17 weeks
Geographic location(s) of program: Major metropolitan areas

Pathways to Leadership is not a traditional training program. Instead, it is a learning program designed to provide new managers with information on ARAMARK's operations and culture in a more structured format. Throughout the learning experience, new managers will partner with an on-site or remote coach who will provide direction with training plans and feedback on the learner's progress. Also included are opportunities to build a network with other managers and access to other resources.

Pathways to Leadership is a comprehensive learning experience created by our talented leaders who shared their knowledge, experiences and best practices for demonstrating success at ARAMARK.

LEAD

Leadership, Excellence and Development is a fast track management on-boarding program to provide an opportunity to succeed in ARAMARK Uniform Services. The three phase process includes orientation, services and offerings, production, merchandise, office training, sales and account installation, hands-on training focused on sales representative training and more.

Building Leadership Skills (BLS)

This workshop is for the first-line supervisor and manager of today whose responsibilities are ever-increasing and constantly changing. BLS addresses how to handle increasing responsibilities in an efficient, effective and legal way. The workshop includes: Introduction to Leadership, Understanding Diversity, Understanding Behavior, Interactive Communication, Coaching for Performance, Leveling, Time Challenged, Conflict Resolution, and Managing Change.

Tuition Reimbursement

In addition to the leadership programs offered by ARAMARK, there is a Tuition Reimbursement Program available to pursue further education.

Strategic Plan and Diversity Leadership

How does the firm's leadership communicate the importance of diversity to everyone at the firm?

The firm has a commitment to diversity called Kaleidoscope which is detailed on their intranet site. Other communication vehicles include Diversity Tool Kit, Annual Report, recruitment advertisements, website postings, internal communications, on-line diversity training module, other diversity training included as part of the leadership development series, executive speeches and presentations both internally and externally, publication of diversity-focused awards and recognition.

One of the highlights of diversity best practices is distribution of over 5000 Customized English-to-Spanish dictionaries for ARAMARK managers.

Who has primary responsibility for leading diversity initiatives at your firm?

Elizabeth Campbell, Vice President, Employment Practices & Services, FSS, and Corporate Diversity Officer

Does your firm currently have a diversity committee?

Yes

Please describe how the committee is structured, how often it meets, etc.

The Diversity Leadership Council is comprised of the Chairman and CEO, the senior operational leadership and representatives of the key functional areas with responsibility for aspects of diversity, specifically: corporate affairs (with respect to branding and marketing), human resources (with respect to employee retention, recruitment and training) and supply chain management (with respect to supplier diversity).

The Diversity Leadership Council was formed by our Chairman and CEO in 2002 to drive the strategies and deliverables regarding the implementation of Kaleidoscope: ARAMARK's Commitment to Diversity. The Council meets periodically to approve specific strategies and review progress made. The Corporate Diversity Officer provides monthly updates on Kaleidoscope to the EVP of Human Resources, a member of the DLC.

Does the committee's representation include one or more members of the firm's management/executive committee (or the equivalent)?

Yes

How many executives are on the committee, and in 2004, what was the total number of hours collectively spent by the committee in furtherance of the firm's diversity initiatives? How many employees are on the committee, and how often does the committee convene in furtherance of the firm's diversity initiatives?

The regular membership of the DLC includes over ten executives. However, the work of the DLC is supported by numerous professionals within the functional areas of responsibility identified above (i.e. corporate affairs, human resources and supply chain management). Because the development of more specific strategies and the implementation thereof from a tactical perspective is fully integrated into the on-going work of these functional departments, we cannot calculate the number of hours spent by specific individuals on such matters. For example, we sponsored numerous diversity-related events and career fairs during 2004, and involved not only human resources professionals but operations and other functional professionals to support to these activities throughout the country.

Does the committee and/or diversity leader establish and set goals or objectives consistent with management's priorities?

Yes. ARAMARK's Kaleidoscope Business Case: "Key to maximizing the success of our Mission One business strategy is our ability to understand and mirror the diversity of our clients and customers. When we do so, we are able to create more innovative solutions, provide superior service offerings, effectively utilize diverse suppliers, and differentiate ourselves from our competitors – thereby achieving our overall growth objectives. Through Kaleidoscope, we provide the tools and resources necessary for us to retain, develop and recruit the diverse, high-performing team required to meet the complex needs of our clients and to exceed their expectations."

Has the firm undertaken a formal or informal diversity program or set of initiatives aimed at increasing the diversity of the firm?

Yes, formal

ARAMARK's Diversity Leadership Council (DLC) was formed in 2002 to drive strategies and deliverables for Kaleidoscope. The team has three principal goals:

• To retain, develop, and recruit a diverse, high-performing workforce – the One Best Team – that enables us to achieve our growth objectives, and

• To create an environment that allows all employees to contribute to their fullest potential and increases our organizational capabilities.

• To enable ARAMARK to enhance our client and customer partnerships by better serving their diverse needs

How often does the firm's management review the firm's diversity progress/results?

Monthly

How is the firm's diversity committee and/or firm management held accountable for achieving results?

ARAMARK's corporate leadership and functional leadership are held accountable for the success of the implementation of programs within their respective areas of responsibility. For example, ARAMARK keeps managers accountable in the Career Management Process through the highly regarded dimensions for "Selecting strong and diverse talent" and "Developing strong and diverse talent." The Career Management Process is followed by our Management Development Review to evaluate progress and performance. The Management Development Review (MDR) includes opportunities for ARAMARK, on a business-by-business, and on a function-by-function basis, to identify specific goals and objectives (and related accomplishments) for increasing workforce diversity, implementing diversity training programs and otherwise driving diversity within the applicable line of business and/or function. These MDRs are presented to the Chairman and CEO and to other members of senior management.

The Stats

DEMOGRAPHIC PROFILE	TOTAL IN THE U.S.		TOTAL OUTSIDE THE U.S		TOTAL WORLDWIDE	
	2004	2003	2004	2003	2004	2003
Number of employees	178,500	N/A	64,000	N/A	242,500	N/A
Revenues	$8.4 billion	N/A	$1.8 billion	N/A	$10.2 billion	N/A

Both the Board of Directors and the Executive Management Committee include female and minority representation. Our 2004 Employer Report indicates 77.5% of overall employees are minorities including females.

Retention and Professional Development

Please identify the specific steps you are taking to reduce the attrition rate of minority and women employees.

- Develop and/or support internal employee affinity groups (e.g., minority or women networks within the firm)
- Increase/review compensation relative to competition
- Increase/improve current work/life programs
- Succession plan includes emphasis on diversity
- Work with minority and women employees to develop career advancement plans
- Professional skills development program, including minority and women employees
- Other: We have a broad and inclusive employee retention strategy that includes compensation and benefit programs, training and development programs, internal and external professional development opportunities, etc. Specifically, we work with a number of "strategic alliances," including Catalyst, Women's Foodservice Forum, Multicultural Foodservice and Hospitality Alliance, National Black MBA Association, National Hispanic MBA Association and other organizations that give our employees professional developmental opportunities as well as demonstrate ARAMARK's commitment to diversity.

Diversity Mission Statement

Definition of Diversity

The mosaic of people who bring a variety of backgrounds, styles, perspectives, values and beliefs as assets to ARAMARK and our partners.

Kaleidoscope Vision

ARAMARK is comprised of unique individuals who, together, make the Company what it is and what it can be in the future. Only when all individuals contribute fully can the strength and vision of ARAMARK be realized.

Principles for Valuing Diversity

- Because we are committed to being a company where the best people want to work, we champion a comprehensive diversity initiative.
- Because we thrive on growth, we recruit, retain and develop a diverse workforce.
- Because we succeed through performance, we create an environment that allows all employees to contribute to their fullest potential.

The Employer Says

"ARAMARK's senior leadership knows that it takes a diverse team to best serve our clients and customers, which in turn helps us grow our business. We're fully committed to Kaleidoscope as an important people and business strategy."

— Joe Neubauer, Chairman and Chief Executive Officer

ARAMARK is a world leader in providing award-winning food and facilities management services to health care institutions, universities and school districts, stadiums and arenas, international and domestic corporations, as well as providing uniform and career apparel.

Recognitions include:

• ARAMARK was ranked number one in its industry in the 2005 *Fortune* 500 survey and was also
• Named one of "America's Most Admired Companies" by *Fortune* magazine in 2005
• Consistently ranking since 1998 as one of the top three most admired companies in its industry as evaluated by peers.

95

ADM works with farmers, food companies and others to feed the world to help produce not only the food we eat, but also many things that consumers don't expect from nature - like fuel, paint additives and coatings.

Whether we're finding new markets or new uses for farmers' crops, or whether we're working to meet the changing customer demands in existing markets, ADM is *Resourceful by Nature*™.

ADM

RESOURCEFUL BY NATURE™

Archer Daniels Midland Company

P.O. Box 1470
Decatur, IL 62525
Phone: (800) 637-5843 ext.4814
or ext. 5249
Fax: (217) 451-4383

Diversity Leadership

John Taylor; Director, Corporate and Supplier
Michael Marty, Manager College Relations

Employment Contact

www.admworld.com/naen/careers/college.asp
careers.admworld.com

Recruiting

Please list the schools/types of schools at which you recruit.

- *Ivy League schools: –* University of Chicago, Tufts, Emory
- *Other private schools:* Rose-Hulman Institute of Technology, Millikin University, Bradley University, Illinois Weslyan University, Illinois College, Culver-Stockton College, University of Dayton;
- *Public state schools:* University of Illinois, Illinois State University, Southern Illinois University, Eastern Illinois University, Western Illinois University, University of Missouri Columbia, Texas A&M, University of Missouri Rolla, Iowa State, Kansas State, Purdue University, Oklahoma State, University of Iowa, University of Nebraska, University of Minnesota, University of North Dakota, North Dakota State, South Dakota School of Mines, Florida State University, Florida A&M, Ohio State University, Michigan Tech University, University of Michigan, University of Wisconsin; New Mexico State; Northern Iowa University; Vincennes University; Montana State University; University of Idaho; Michigan State University;
- *Historically Black Colleges and Universities (HBCUs):* North Carolina A&T; Clark Atlanta University;
- *Hispanic Serving Institutions (HSIs):* New Mexico State; Texas A&M
- Native American Tribal Universities
- Other predominantly minority and/or women's colleges

Do you have any special outreach efforts that are directed to encourage minority students to consider your firm?

- Hold a reception for minority students
- Conferences
- Advertise in minority student association publication(s)
- Participate in/host minority student job fair(s)
- Sponsor minority student association events
- Firm's employees participate on career panels at school
- Outreach to leadership of minority student organizations
- Scholarships or intern/fellowships for minority students

What activities does the firm undertake to attract minority and women employees?

- Partner programs with women and minority associations
- Conferences
- Bradley Morris Inc.
- Advancing Minorities Interest in Engineering (AMIE)

• Minorities in Agriculture, Natural Resources and Related Sciences (MANRRS)
• Society for Women Engineers
• Women for Hire
• National Society of Black Engineers
• Urban League Diversity Job Fair
• National Association of Black Accountants
• Kappa Alpha Psi Diversity Job Fair
• Institute of Food Technologist
• Congressional Black Caucus
• National Black MBA Association
• Latinos for Hire
• Society of Women Engineers
• Participate at minority job fairs
• Seek referrals from other employees
• Utilize online job services

Do you use executive recruiting/search firms to seek to identify new diversity hires?

Yes

Internships and Co-ops

ADM Internship Program

Deadline for application: We will accept students until April, but complete most recruiting by the end of fall semester
Number of interns in the program in summer: 2004 (internship) or 2004 (co-op) 98 summer interns; 1 co-op (just starting this program)
Pay: Monthly salary dependent upon division where intern works
Length of the program: 10-12 weeks
Percentage of interns/co-ops in the program who receive offers of full-time employment: 60%
Web site for internship/co-op information: www.admworld.com

An internship with ADM allows students to work in a variety of different areas within the company; Accounting, Internal Audit, Engineering, IT, Elevator Management, Grain Terminal Operations Management, Commodity Trading and other Specialty areas. Students can find themselves in a variety of different locations across the Midwest. They can range from working in a manufacturing environment to a country grain elevator or even in a corporate setting. Our program promotes the development of the student while providing a training ground for potential employees. Our internship provides many benefits; including a monthly salary, housing arrangements and a structured orientation and wrap-up ceremony. Students are required to have a minimum GPA of 2.8, be of junior status and be legally authorized to work in the United States.

Our co-op program is new in existence and mirrors our summer internship program. Of course the major difference is the amount of time the student works for us. Most students have the opportunity to work from May-December and will return to school at the beginning of their spring semester.

Scholarships

Kansas State ADM Scholarship

The recipient of this scholarship will be a student properly enrolled in the College of Agriculture at Kansas State University from a diverse background pursing degrees in grain science, agriculture economics / agricultural engineering or food science at Kansas State University. Successful applicants will have 60 hours of college credit with a GPA of 3.0/4.0 or better. Each scholarship award is valued at $10,000. There may be additional qualification criteria and interested students should contact the College Relations Department at ADM for full details.

Illinois State ADM Scholarship

The recipient of this scholarship will be a minority student who is interested in the food and agribusiness industries and enrolled in the Department of Agriculture at Illinois State University. In addition, applicants must be U.S. citizens and classified as new beginning freshmen or new transfer students with a transfer degree who have applied for and been admitted to the fall term with a major and sequence offered by the Department of Agriculture. Each scholarship is valued at $5,000 per year (at $2,500 per semester following certification of qualification) and is renewable for up to eight consecutive semesters (four semesters for transfer students). The total potential value of the scholarship is $20,000. Each scholarship recipient is required to maintain at least a 2.8 cumulative GPA. There may be additional qualification criteria and interested students should contact the College Relations Department at ADM for full details.

Affinity Groups/Employee Networks

ADMWIN; ADM Women's Initiative Network

The ADM Women's Initiative Network (WIN) exists to facilitate the professional development of women at ADM, while helping them reach their individual goals and potential. One part networking, one part professional development, one part mentoring, WIN draws on the most important resource we have: each other. Working together, with the support of top ADM management, we'll help enhance the positive impact of women in our company through recruitment, retention and development efforts.

Entry-Level Programs/Full-Time Opportunities/Training Programs

Training Program for Engineering (referred to as a Production Assistant)

Recent engineer graduates are assigned to a production unit where they gain first hand exposure to leadership of employees, equipment trouble-shooting and dealing with the myriad of challenges faced routinely in a facility that operates around the clock, 365 days a year. The experience begins with on-the-job training through observation and typically progresses to full responsibility for a work group working rotating shifts during the first year. Production Assistants experience very a "hands-on" environment and are placed at one of our processing facilities through the United States, primarily within the Midwest.

Training Program for Commodity Training (referred to as a Commodity Trader Trainee)

The position of Commodity Trader Trainee is one of buying and selling commodities in the cash market, as well as making and coordinating arrangements for the transportation of the product. Our commodity traders learn the fundamentals of the business

by embarking on an intense two-month training curriculum, which involves thorough classroom and on site learning. Training occurs at our corporate headquarters, river terminals, country elevators and processing plants.

Training Program for Grain Terminal Operations Management (referred to as a Grain Terminal Operations Management Trainee)

This position is a three-stage position. The employee will be stationed at one of approximately 50 elevators across the Midwest United States. The trainee then moves into stage two of their training program and will be relocated to a different elevator/terminal for further training. Stage three of this program is the continuous career advancement. Positions in stage three will include supervisors, superintendents, multiple location management, middle management, and corporate careers.

The Stats

DEMOGRAPHIC PROFILE	TOTAL IN THE U.S.		TOTAL OUTSIDE THE U.S		TOTAL WORLDWIDE	
	2005	2004	2005	2004	2005	2004
Number of employees	16,146	16,450	9,465	9,867	25,641	26,317
Revenues	N/A	N/A	N/A	N/A	$35.943 billion	$36.151 billion

Retention and Professional Development

Please identify the specific steps you are taking to reduce the attrition rate of minority and women employees.

• Develop and/or support internal employee affinity groups (e.g., minority or women networks within the firm)
• Increase/improve current work/life programs

Diversity Mission Statement

ADM remains committed to unlocking the potential of all of its people. To this end, we seek to recruit talent wherever it exists. This is an inclusive policy that recognizes the need for concerted efforts to tap into a diverse pool of human resources as we continue to serve and thrive in an increasingly diverse society. In this way, we can provide our suppliers, customers, Shareholders and global community with maximum value now and into the future.

We interpret diversity in its broadest sense. While we are, of course, an equal opportunity employer, ADM also welcomes a broad mix of attitudes, approaches, perceptions and backgrounds

Additional Information

Supplier Diversity

ADM places a high priority on its commitment to Supplier Diversity, in which we have significantly expanded our utilization of minority-owned, women-owned, disabled veteran-owned and HUBZone-located enterprises to provide products and services to ADM. We work with such groups as the National Minority Supplier Development Council (NMSDC) and the Women's Business Enterprise National Council (WBENC) in order to meet this commitment.

Aurora Health Care

www.Aurorahealthcare.org

Locations (worldwide)

Aurora Health Care is a health care provider in Wisconsin. Our corporate office is located in Milwaukee.

Diversity Leadership

Rhonda Taylor-Parris, Director, Workforce Planning
2920 W. Dakota Avenue
Milwaukee, WI 53234-3910
Phone: (414) 647-3346
Fax: (414) 647-4878
E-mail: Rhonda.Taylor-Parris@Aurora.org

Recruiting

Please list the schools/types of schools at which you recruit.

• Private schools
• Public state schools

Do you have any special outreach efforts that are directed to encourage minority students to consider your firm?

• Participate in/host minority student job fair(s)
• Firm's employees participate on career panels at school
• Scholarships or intern/fellowships for minority students

What activities does the firm undertake to attract minority and women employees?

• Participate at minority job fairs
• Seek referrals from other employees
• Utilize online job services

Do you use executive recruiting/search firms to seek to identify new diversity hires?

Yes

Internships and Co-ops

INROADS-Wisconsin

Deadline for application: Based on the INROADS program requirements

Number of interns in the program in summer 2004 (internship) or 2004 (co-op): 19 interns in summer 2004 and 26 interns in summer 2005

Pay: Pay is bi-weekly; rate depends on field and standing in school (range: $10.30 – $18.75)

Length of the program: 10-week minimum commitment

Percentage of interns/co-ops in the program who receive offers of full-time employment: over 50% receive offers

Web site for internship/co-op information: www.inroads.org

Internships are offered in the following career fields:

- **Business:** Finance, Accounting, HR, Marketing
- **Information Service/Technology:** MIS, IS, IT, Computer Science
- **Engineering:** Biomedical Engineering
- **Medical:** Pre-med, Physical Therapy, Occupational Therapy, Athletic training, Nursing, Pharmacy

All students must meet all INROADS program qualifications. (Many students who attend school in-state work throughout the school year.)

Scholarships

Justene McCord INROADS Intern Scholarship

Deadline for application for the scholarship program: Mid-July

Scholarship award amount: $1,000/per year awarded

This scholarship is only offered to returning Aurora INROADS interns who meet the requirements and are nominated for it.

Stanley Kritzik Innovation and Technology Scholarship

Deadline for application for the scholarship program: None

Scholarship award amount: $1,000/per year awarded

This scholarship is only offered to Information Technology Aurora INROADS interns who meet the requirements.

Aurora Health Care INROADS Intern Book Scholarship

Deadline for application for the scholarship program: None

Scholarship award amount: 10 $200 scholarships awarded per year

This scholarship is offered to 10 Aurora INROADS interns who meet the requirements.

Entry-Level Programs/Full-Time Opportunities

Aurora Leadership Academy

Length of program: 15 months
Geographic location(s) of program: Milwaukee, WI

Please describe the training/training component of this program: This program prepares employees with high potential for first line management positions. Employees are nominated by their immediate supervisor and are paired up with a leader that serves as a mentor.

Strategic Plan and Diversity Leadership

How does the firm's leadership communicate the importance of diversity to everyone at the firm?

The importance of diversity and Aurora's commitment to diversity is captured in our values. Aurora's values consist of accountability, teamwork and respect, setting the standard for service, continually improving our quality, controlling our costs, and "The Power of Diversity." We communicate the commitment to diversity in our management bulletin, the Aurora Today (employee newsletter), and the Aurora Diversity Plan.

Who has primary responsibility for leading diversity initiatives at your firm?

Rhonda Taylor-Parris, Director of Workforce Planning

Does your firm currently have a diversity committee?

Yes

Please describe how the committee is structured, how often it meets, etc.

The committee members consists of Aurora's seven senior leaders of the organization and they meet on a quarterly basis.

Does the committee's representation include one or more members of the firm's management/executive committee (or the equivalent)?

Yes

Please describe the committee.

The committee members consist of Aurora's seven senior leaders of the organization and they meet on a quarterly basis. Meetings are held more frequently if needed.

Does the committee and/or diversity leader establish and set goals or objectives consistent with management's priorities?

Yes. Goals and objectives are set annually and added to the annual strategic plan. Departments throughout the organization draft their business plans according to the goals and objectives set forth in the strategic plan.

Has the firm undertaken a formal or informal diversity program or set of initiatives aimed at increasing the diversity of the firm?

Yes, formal. Diversity education modules are placed on our internal diversity website for managers to facilitate with their staff. The diversity modules are resources that provide an opportunity for employees to learn more about diversity and provide a forum for the expression of concerns and the sharing of experiences. Aurora also provides classes in the "Managing Diversity Education Series" for managers to learn how to effectively manage in a diverse environment.

How often does the firm's management review the firm's diversity progress/results?

Quarterly

INROADS®

How is the firm's diversity committee and/or firm management held accountable for achieving results?

Employee's attitudes around diversity are captured in an annual survey that Aurora conducts. The results of the survey determine our diversity index, which is what leaders are held accountable for improving/maintaining. Achievement of outcomes is included in the incentive and merit increases as a part of the annual performance review process.

The Stats

Employees: 25,000 (2004, U.S.)
Revenue: $2.5 billion (2004, U.S.)

Retention and Professional Development

How do 2004 minority and female attrition rates generally compare to those experienced in the prior year period?

About the same as in prior years

Please identify the specific steps you are taking to reduce the attrition rate of minority and women employees.

The attrition for rate of minority and women employees is not a critical issue for us.

Diversity Mission Statement

In order to provide the best health care and achieve the desired health outcomes for all that we serve, a diverse and culturally competent workforce is essential.

Avaya Inc.

211 Mt. Airy Rd.
Basking Ridge, NJ 07920
www.avaya.com/careers

Locations (worldwide)

Corporate Headquarters are in Basking Ridge, NJ.

Avaya has multiple locations throughout the United States and over 90 locations worldwide.

Diversity Leadership

Campus Recruiter, University Recruitment

Recruiting

Please list the schools/types of schools at which you recruit.

• Ivy League schools
• Other private schools
• Public state schools

We currently recruit at a number of schools; go to www.avaya.com/careers to see a complete listing.

Do you have any special outreach efforts that are directed to encourage minority students to consider your firm?

• Outreach to leadership of minority student organizations

What activities does the firm undertake to attract minority and women employees?

• Partner programs with women and minority associations
• Utilize online job services

Do you use executive recruiting/search firms to seek to identify new diversity hires?

Avaya has a strong commitment to diversity, and the firms with which we partner understand the importance of identifying the best talent for the opportunities that we have available.

Internships and Co-ops

Avaya Summer Internship Program

Number of interns in the program in summer 2004 (internship) or 2004 (co-op): approximately 20 but varies annually
Pay: Competitive
Length of the program: 10-12 weeks

The majority of internships at Avaya consist of 10-12 weeks in the summer. Depending on the needs of the business, summer interns are often offered part-time internships during the school year. All departments generally hire interns in the summer and

responsibilities vary. Interns are generally expected to provide value at the same level of a full-time associate. We provide networking events for interns nationally with various scopes.

Affinity Groups/Employee Networks

Employee business partner groups are open to all employees (EBPGs). By supporting the unique needs of their communities, EBPGs enable the company to maximize the talents of their members to achieve the company's objectives.

4A – Asian/Pacific American Association for Advancement at Avaya
ABL – Alliance of Black Leaders at Avaya
EQUAL! – Supporting Gay, Lesbian, Bisexual, and Transgendered Employees at Avaya
HISPA – Hispanic Association of Avaya
IDEAL – Individuals with Disabilities Enabling Advocacy Link
NOVA – Natives Offering Value at Avaya
WAVE – Women at Avaya Valuing Excellence

Entry-Level Programs/Full-Time Opportunities

MBA Rotation Programs in each of our businesses that include Finance, Operations, IT, Services, Sales & Marketing

Length of program: Full-time only for 2-3 years
Geographic location(s) of program: Worldwide opportunities, but primarily at our headquarters in Basking Ridge, NJ

Please describe the training/training component of this program: Each business has a specific training module for the rotation program.

All full-time associates are eligible for tuition reimbursement. Avaya supports training at every level. The first of our six strategic outcomes as outlined by our leadership is "Avaya is known for its performance-based culture." This outcome underlines the importance of improving the capabilities of our people and encouraging higher levels of performance. Accordingly, Avaya has launched a training curriculum designed to build the skills needed to deliver optimal business results. Each employee is entitled to education offered through Avaya University. Avaya University offers a myriad of skills-based courses, management courses and diversity training for continued learning.

Strategic Plan and Diversity Leadership

How does the firm's leadership communicate the importance of diversity to everyone at the firm?

Diversity is at the center of our values. Avaya's diversity initiatives are strategically tied to our business objectives and observe corporate measures: revenue, cost, people and process. Our support for diversity has evolved far beyond legal compliance. We not only value diversity, we purposefully acknowledge and support the diversity of individuals as a competitive advantage within the context of our business environment.

New employees learn of Avaya's environment of inclusion through the New Hire Orientation program. Additionally, specific training is available for Equal Opportunity/Affirmative Action.

Diversity Mission Statement

Our value as a company is realized by recognizing the value of each individual. Our strategic intent is to create a culture of unity and global community, where every employee feels included, supported and respected.

We align around common business objectives – revenue, cost, people and process – and within that framework, we acknowledge and support diverse groups. We are a global company in every sense – geographically, strategically and culturally.

We embrace diversity as a competitive advantage. Harmonizing and leveraging the diversity of our people will realize our full potential. In the spirit of global community, our diversity will unite us, and it will enhance the quality of our work and our work-lives.

HealthCare   CropScience   MaterialScience

BayerUS.com

Bayer CropScience

100 Bayer Rd.
Pittsburgh, PA 15205-9741
Phone: (412) 777-2000
Fax: (412) 777-2034
www.bayerjobs.com

Employment Contact
Summer Busto, Manager, Talent Acquisition
& Domestic Relocation
P.O. Box 12014
Research Triangle Park, NC 27709
Phone: (919) 549-2437
E-mail: summer.busto@bayercropscience.com

Recruiting

Please list the schools/types of schools at which you recruit.

• Public state schools

Do you have any special outreach efforts that are directed to encourage minority students to consider your firm?

• Other: INROADS Program

What activities does the firm undertake to attract minority and women employees?

• Seek referrals from other employees
• Utilize online job services

Do you use executive recruiting/search firms to seek to identify new diversity hires?

No

Internships and Co-ops

INROADS

Number of interns in the program in summer 2004 (internship) or 2004 (co-op): 6
Length of the program: 14
Web site for internship/co-op information: www.bayerjobs.com

We hire interns in various departments based on need and availability of projects. For the past 2 summers we've had interns in O&I, Supply Chain, Marketing, HR, Government Regulatory Affairs and Accounts Payable.

BNSF Railway

2500 Lou Menk Drive
Fort Worth, TX 76131-2828
www.bnsf.com

Locations (worldwide):

Fort Worth, TX (Corporate Office)
Operations in a total of 26 states and 2
Canadian provinces

Diversity Leadership:

Contact Person: Susan Hutchison

Warren Davis, Director Staffing
Phone: (817) 352-1667
Fax: (817) 352-7108
E-mail: warren.davis@bnsf.com

Ed McFalls, AVP,
Human Resources & Diversity
Phone: (817) 352-1690
Fax: (817) 352-7108
E-mail: ed.mcfalls@bnsf.com

Recruiting

Please list the schools/types of schools at which you recruit.

• Private schools
• Public state schools
• Historically Black Colleges and Universities (HBCUs)

Do you have any special outreach efforts that are directed to encourage minority students to consider your firm?

• Conferences: NSBE, NSHBA, NBMBA, NACE (local, regional and national)
• Participate in/host minority student job fair(s)
• Outreach to leadership of minority student organizations
• Scholarships or intern/fellowships for minority students

What activities does the firm undertake to attract minority and women employees?

• *Conferences:* NSBE, NSHBA, NBMBA, NACE
• *Other:* BOLD Initiative

Do you use executive recruiting/search firms to seek to identify new diversity hires?

No – No recent need

Internships and Co-ops

BNSF Railway Internship Program

Deadline for application: Early spring
Number of interns in the program in summer 2004 (internship) or 2004 (co-op): 99
Pay: Varies
Length of the program: Varies; typically eight to ten weeks
Web site for internship/co-op information: www.bnsf.com/jobs

The BNSF internship program gives college students practical, on-the-job experience in a business environment.

Candidates for internships are typically full-time students currently enrolled at a college or university who are pursuing an undergraduate degree or a graduate degree in a field of study that supports BNSF's business objectives. BNSF recruits candidates from college campuses, minority student referral programs, the Internet, employee referrals and unsolicited resumes.

Interns are assigned to a department which will then direct the intern's activities on a specific projects and work assignments.

BNSF Departments that seek interns include: Accounting/Finance, Corporate Audit Services, Engineering, Human Resources, Marketing, Mechanical, Safety, Technology Services, Transportation/Operations and other support departments. While most assignments are at BNSF's corporate headquarters (Fort Worth, Texas), some interns are placed in field locations across the BNSF system. Field assignments are predominantly for the Transportation/Operations, Engineering and Mechanical departments.

The program includes an orientation with an overview of corporate policies and appropriate conduct. Interns participate in several key activities throughout their program, including:

• Presentations by various department leaders;
• Midterm and final activity status reports prepared by the intern;
• Intern team presentations at the end of the program;
• Midterm and final performance evaluations by supervisors;
• Exposure to some BNSF Management Trainee Program activities;
• Networking opportunities

Scholarships

BNSF Diversity Scholarships

Deadline for application for the scholarship program: Students apply through their universities by March of each year.
Scholarship award amount: Honored recipients receive $5,000 (payable in two annual installments of $2,500 for students' Junior and Senior years).

Five scholarships are established at four pre-designated universities. Students must have at least a 3.00 GPA, be well-rounded and pass a skills assessment exam. A facility review panel recommends top two to three sophomore students. Students all receive two summer internships with BNSF.

Affinity Groups/Employee Networks

Native American, Hispanic, Women's, African-American and Asian American groups. Their purpose is to promote the professional and personal development of its members. Meet at least monthly. All have internal websites.

Entry-Level Programs/Full-Time Opportunities

BNSF Railway Management Trainee Program

BNSF recruits candidates from college campuses, the Internet, BNSF's former interns and internal job postings. As part of the selection process, a potential candidate visits BNSF's corporate headquarters to participate in panel interviews and a comprehensive skills assessment. Candidates for the Program must be team players who value diversity and who drive for results. They should also have a good scholastic record, a history of leadership roles in school or the community, previous internship experience, ability to analyze problems logically, and excellent oral and written communication skills.

> *Length of program:* 6-12 months
> *Geographic location(s) of program:* Across BNSF system, with large number at corporate headquarters

Please describe the training/training component of this program: Management trainees receive cross-functional, departmental training during their 6-or 12-month training period, as well as exposure to all departments through an initial 1-month corporate orientation. Each trainee can request a BNSF mentor for career and personal guidance. The training itself is tailored to the individual and monitored by the sponsoring business group and Human Resources department.

Strategic Plan and Diversity Leadership

How does the firm's leadership communicate the importance of diversity to everyone at the firm?
BNSF communicates through internal diversity conferences, diversity councils, affinity groups, newsletters, departmental meetings, awareness training sessions and various written forms of communication

Who has primary responsibility for leading diversity initiatives at your firm?
Ed McFalls – Assistant Vice President, Human Resources and Diversity

Does your firm currently have a diversity committee?

Yes

If yes, please describe how the committee is structured, how often it meets, etc.

There are two types of diversity committees:

- **Executive Diversity Council:** consists of BNSF's CEO, his six direct reports and the AVP of Human Resources and Diversity. Group meets quarterly to review diversity successes and opportunities. In 2004, this group spent at least eight hours as a council, but they address initiatives throughout the year during weekly executive meetings.

- **Regional Diversity Councils** (across our system): consist of both union and management employees that are responsible for resolving diversity tensions in their respective locations. In 2004, each council spent approximately 36 hours furthering diversity initiatives (monthly meetings of approximately 3 hours each).

If yes, does the committee's representation include one or more members of the firm's management/executive committee (or the equivalent)?

Yes

Does the committee and/or diversity leader establish and set goals or objectives consistent with management's priorities?
Yes. Each committee's goals are established based upon BNSF's overall diversity strategy.

Has the firm undertaken a formal or informal diversity program or set of initiatives aimed at increasing the diversity of the firm?

Yes, formal. BNSF has a robust formal diversity strategy that addresses Executive/Leadership support, recruiting and enhancing talent, community involvement and continual education and awareness.

How often does the firm's management review the firm's diversity progress/results?

• Quarterly   (CEO & Sr. VPs perform a detailed review quarterly.)

• Annually   (VP and AVP are provided an overview/update at annual management meeting.)

The Stats

Employees: 40,000 (2004, U.S.)
Revenue: $10.9 billion (2004, U.S.)
Employees: 40,000 (2003, U.S.)
Revenue: $9.4 billion (2003, U.S.)

2004: Exempt employees 4,868 (844 (17.3%) women; 688 (14.1%) minorities)

Retention and Professional Development

How do 2004 minority and female attrition rates generally compare to those experienced in the prior year period?

About the same as in prior years

Diversity Mission Statement

We view diversity as a business necessity, a business opportunity and a moral imperative. To achieve diversity, BNSF has undertaken strategies and actions that recognize, accept, value and utilize the differences and similarities among all applicants, employees, customers, suppliers and the community.

To advance our vision, we have a Diversity Business Purpose. Embracing diversity helps BNSF to: recruit, hire and promote the best diverse talent; create a collaborative workforce that functions as a team; understand and market to a diverse customer base; procure from a diverse supplier base; and provide quality service that meets our customers' needs and requirements.

Additional Information

By design, BNSF's Diversity Definition is simple: respecting and valuing the differences and similarities of people. Too often, diversity is defined by the traditional terms of race, gender, age, religion and culture. At BNSF, we have expanded the definition to include diversity of mind, experience, education, skills and thought.

BNSF Affinity Groups share a vision to advance the personal and professional development of their members, expose their members to increased leadership opportunities, provide support and networking for members, participate in community service, and work with Corporate Diversity to achieve other BNSF People initiatives, including employee recruitment and retention. Nevertheless, they are unique when they address the particular needs of their group. Currently, there are five active Affinity Groups at BNSF: BNSF Asian American Network; Hispanic Leadership Council; African-American Networking Group; Women's Network; and the Council of Native Americans.

Hundreds of BNSF people throughout the railway have volunteered for the Regional Diversity Councils, and they work tirelessly to educate co-workers about different cultures and backgrounds. They are also responsible for identifying and resolving local

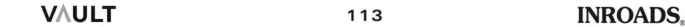

diversity tensions, before formal resolutions have to be implemented. They host diversity celebrations such as Martin Luther King, Jr. Day, Veteran's Day, Cinco de Mayo and Women's Month, among others. Lastly, they promote community advocacy initiatives by getting involved with the communities in which they live and work.

BNSF has hosted annual Diversity Forums and summits to bring together 200 to 300 employees and the leadership team to share ideas and identify ways for BNSF to enhance its diversity efforts. Invitees include a broad representation of BNSF departments and are randomly selected to allow opportunity for more BNSF people to participate in the conferences. At each event, participants have the opportunity to talk with BNSF leaders, brainstorm ideas on how to make BNSF a more diverse community, listen to experts' insights and perspectives on success in corporate America, network with employees from throughout the company, and participate in experiential learning.

BNSF offers a variety of alternative work arrangements on a limited basis, informally administered by each department, for certain positions including traditional flextime, daily flextime, compressed workweek and telecommuting/working from home.

Boeing Company, The

www.boeing.com/employment/college

Diversity Leadership
Tammy Shilipetar, College Recruiter and
Boeing Intern Coordinator
P.O. BOX 3707 MC 1F-69
Seattle, WA 98124

Recruiting

Please list the schools/types of schools at which you recruit.

• Ivy League schools
• Other private schools
• Public state schools
• Historically Black Colleges and Universities (HBCUs)
• Hispanic Serving Institutions (HSIs)
• Native American Tribal Universities
• Other predominantly minority and/or women's colleges

Do you have any special outreach efforts that are directed to encourage minority students to consider your firm?

• Advertise in minority student association publication(s)
• Sponsor minority student association events
• Firm's employees participate on career panels at school
• Outreach to leadership of minority student organizations
• Scholarships or intern/fellowships for minority students

What activities does the firm undertake to attract minority and women employees?

• Partner programs with women and minority associations
• Participate at minority job fairs
• Utilize online job services
• **Other:** Work with INROADS

Internships and Co-ops

The Boeing Company Student Development Program

Deadline for application: Positions are open from early fall through late spring

Number of interns in the program in summer 2004 (internship) or 2004 (co-op): 800 interns and co-ops across the U.S. in 2004

Pay: Paid internships, based on the discipline and year in school

Length of the program: 12-14 weeks for internships, six months for co-ops

Percentage of interns/co-ops in the program who receive offers of full-time employment: 50-60 %

Web site for internship/co-op information: www.boeing.com/employment

Scholarships

Boeing Scholarship

Deadline for application for the scholarship program: Money is given to selected colleges and universities, and the colleges and universities select the students on Boeing's behalf.

Scholarship award amount: Varies from school to school

Web site or other contact information for scholarship: Please obtain information from individual schools

Affinity Groups/Employee Networks

Boeing Asian American Association

BRANCH – Boeing Regional Association Network for New College Hires

Boeing Black Employees Association

Boeing Employee Association for Sexual Minorities

Boeing Hispanic Employees Network

Boeing Employees Association for Gays and Lesbians

Boeing Employee Ability Awareness Association

Each affinity group meets based on the individual affinity group charter. Information about Boeing's affinity groups can be found on the external

Web site: www.boeing.com/special/globaldiversity/. Each affinity group has a web site on Boeing's internal web.

Entry-Level Programs/Full-Time Opportunities

BCFP (Boeing Career Foundation Program) and ISCFP (Information Systems Career Foundation Program)

Length of program: 2 years

Geographic location(s) of program: Across the U.S. in various sites

Please describe the training/training component of this program: Rotation every four months to six different business or IS related fields, such as accounting business analysts, financial analysts or IS specific rotations.

Please describe any other educational components of this program: All Boeing employees are entitled to tuition reimbursement.

Strategic Plan and Diversity Leadership

How does the firm's leadership communicate the importance of diversity to everyone at the firm?

Every year we receive a reaffirmation letter from the CEO on Affirmative Action and EEO stating that the Company sees Affirmative Action, EEO and diversity as three distinct commitments.

Who has primary responsibility for leading diversity initiatives at your firm?

Beverly Pizzano, Director, Cultural Diversity

Does your firm currently have a diversity committee?

Yes

If yes, please describe how the committee is structured, how often it meets, etc.

The frequency of Boeing's diversity steering committee meetings are governed by their charter.

If yes, does the committee's representation include one or more members of the firm's management/executive committee (or the equivalent)?

Yes

Retention and Professional Development

Please identify the specific steps you are taking to reduce the attrition rate of minority and women employees.

• Develop and/or support internal employee affinity groups (e.g., minority or women networks within the firm)
• Increase/review compensation relative to competition
• Increase/improve current work/life programs
• Adopt dispute resolution process
• Succession plan includes emphasis on diversity
• Work with minority and women employees to develop career advancement plans
• Strengthen mentoring program for all employees, including minorities and women
• Professional skills development program, including minority and women employees

Diversity Mission Statement

Boeing's mission is to value and leverage multiple perspectives, experiences and capabilities by driving the integration of diversity, equity and fairness principles into all practices and processes to achieve enterprise objectives.

Bonneville Power Administration

905 NE 11th Ave.
Portland, OR 97208
www.jobs.bpa.gov

Locations
HQ Office is in Portland OR; various jobs located in Oregon, Washington, Idaho and Montana

Diversity Leadership
Godfrey Beckett, Manager, Diversity and EEO

Employment Contact
Employment & Benefits
P.O. Box 3621
Portland, OR 97208
Phone: (503) 230-3055
Fax: (503) 230-3816

Recruiting

Please list the schools/types of schools at which you recruit.

• Ivy League schools
• Other private schools
• Public state schools
• Historically Black Colleges and Universities (HBCUs)
• Hispanic Serving Institutions (HSIs)
• Native American Tribal Universities
• Other predominantly minority and/or women's colleges

Do you have any special outreach efforts that are directed to encourage minority students to consider your firm?

• Advertise in minority student association publication(s)
• Participate in/host minority student job fair(s)
• Sponsor minority student association events
• Firm's employees participate on career panels at school
• Outreach to leadership of minority student organizations
• Scholarships or intern/fellowships for minority students

What activities does the firm undertake to attract minority and women employees?

• Partner programs with women and minority associations
• Participate at minority job fairs
• Seek referrals from other employees
• Utilize online job services

Do you use executive recruiting/search firms to seek to identify new diversity hires?

Yes

Internships and Co-ops

STEP (student temporary employee program) and SCEP (student career experience program)

Deadline for application: rolling

Number of interns in the program in summer 2004 (internship) or 2004 (co-op): at the end of Fiscal Year 2004 we had 72 students (including both STEP and SCEP)

Pay: Range is from $10 to $25 per hour, dependent on type of position

Length of the program: STEP participants generally work in one-year increments but could work during the summer only. For SCEP, if program requirements are met and FTE (manpower authorization) and budget are available, a participant can be eligible for a permanent position upon graduation.

Percentage of interns/co-ops in the program who receive offers of full-time employment: SCEP participants only are eligible for possible conversion to full-time employment. At the end of Fiscal Year 2004 43 students were offered full-time career positions.

Web site for internship/co-op information: www.jobs.bpa.gov (Click on "student" and you will get info on our two programs.)

Any organization within BPA can recruit students if they have the FTE (manpower authorization) and budget to fund the position

Entry-Level Programs/Full-Time Opportunities

High Voltage Power System Electrician, Line Worker and Substation Operator Apprentice Program

Length of program: 3½ to 4 years

Geographic location(s) of program: Washington, Oregon, Montana & Idaho

Please describe the training/training component of this program: Intensive classroom study, homework and on-the-job-training. End-of-Step presentations, exams and reviews are required every six months and if successful, the apprentice will be promoted to the next step of the apprenticeship program, and finally to journeyman.

Please describe any other educational components of this program: Pay starts out at $20.91 per hour. To join the company as a SCEP, you must meet all the student eligibility requirements, be enrolled in a two-year college in a course of study leading to a degree or certificate related to the electric utility industry, such as electrical theory, electronics, industrial arts or industrial technology. Watch for the vacancy announcements at our web site each fall for complete details.

Strategic Plan and Diversity Leadership

Who has primary responsibility for leading diversity initiatives at your firm?

Currently, Godfrey Beckett, Manager Diversity and EEO

Does your firm currently have a diversity committee?

Yes

If yes, does the committee's representation include one or more members of the firm's management/executive committee (or the equivalent)?

Yes

Does the committee and/or diversity leader establish and set goals or objectives consistent with management's priorities?

Yes

Has the firm undertaken a formal or informal diversity program or set of initiatives aimed at increasing the diversity of the firm?

Yes, formal and informal

The Stats

At this time we have 3,035 government employees at BPA.

Diversity Mission Statement

The Office of Human Resources, Diversity and EEO provides leadership and serves as a principal advisor to the Senior Vice President, Employee and Business Resources, the BPA Administrator and Chief Executive Officer and Executive Committee members on the impact and use of policies, proposals and programs related to human capital management, diversity management, equal employment opportunity and achievement of a high performing organization.

Office staff develops, facilitates, administers and oversees and evaluates effective strategies, programs, policies and reports that support the BPA mission through:

• Strategic agency-wide Human Capital Management program, which includes alignment of BPA mission and people; measurement of management accountability and organizational improvements; and, semi-annual reports to DOE Headquarters

• Human Resources, Diversity and Equal Employment Opportunity policy development, evaluation and oversight

• Legislative proposal development and analysis

• Labor Relations, including technical assistance to, and coordination of, the Partnership Council

• EEO Title VI and VII compliance and resolution programs, which includes affirmative employment planning and reporting

• Alternative Dispute Resolution programs

• Diversity management strategy and program support, including technical assistance to, and support of, the Pluralism Council

• Workforce Statistics and Analysis

Borders Group

---

100 Phoenix Dr.
Ann Arbor, MI 48108
(734) 477-1100
Fax: (734) 477-1965
www.bordersgroupinc.com

Locations (worldwide)
Ann Arbor, MI (corporate headquarters)

Diversity Leadership
Suzann Trevisan, Senior Manager, Specialty Recruiting
100 Phoenix Drive
Ann Arbor, MI 48108
Phone: (800) 243-7510
Fax: (734) 477-1127

Recruiting

Please list the schools/types of schools at which you recruit.

• Public state schools

Do you have any special outreach efforts that are directed to encourage minority students to consider your firm?

• Participate in/host minority student job fair(s)
• Other: We sponsor the minority career fairs at UofM and MSU.

What activities does the firm undertake to attract minority and women employees?

• Participate at minority job fairs
• Seek referrals from other employees
• Utilize online job services

Do you use executive recruiting/search firms to seek to identify new diversity hires?

No

Internships and Co-ops

Borders Group Summer Intern Program

Deadline for application: January 1
Number of interns in the program in summer 2004 (internship) or 2004 (co-op): 6
Length of the program: 12 weeks
Percentage of interns/co-ops in the program who receive offers of full-time employment: It depends on the year. Last year was 100 percent.
Web site for internship/co-op information: www.bordersgroupinc.com

We continue to build upon the success of our Summer Internship Training Program. The program is intended to provide meaningful work experience to rising college seniors who would then become candidates for our College Graduate Training Program after graduation. Interns are placed in positions in finance, marketing/merchandising, information technology and human resources for a 12- to 14-week summer experience with Borders Group. In addition, our summer interns participate in an informative and interactive training program that is designed to help prepare them for their career.

Affinity Groups/Employee Networks

African American Employee Action Group, Women's Employee Action Group, GLBT Employee Action Group

Employee Action Groups are a vehicle to better understand and support the complexity of varying employee and customer cultures and backgrounds. EAGs represent the diversity of and within a unique constituency, and are employee-driven teams composed of individuals at varying levels and with different functions. The purpose of the Employee Action Groups is to explore and construct meaning on a range of issues that support diversity efforts in the workplace, marketplace, and the local community. These groups meet on a monthly basis.

Entry-Level Programs/Full-Time Opportunities

College Grad Training Program

Length of program: 6 months
Geographic location(s) of program: Ann Arbor, MI

We have had great success with our College Graduate Training Program. The goal of the program is to hire and develop college graduates in order to build a strong foundation of future leaders within Borders Group. College grads are placed in meaningful roles throughout our organization in the following functional areas: finance, marketing/merchandising, information technology and human resources. In addition, participants go through an informative and interactive training program that is designed to help prepare them for success at Borders Group. The College Graduate Training Program consists of the following elements:

• Mentorship Guidance-College grads are partnered with a mentor who is a leadership team member.
• Cross-Functional College Grad Team Project-College grads work together in cross-functional group projects that provide the company with predetermined deliverables at the end of the training period.
• Operational Activities-College grads spend time training in our stores and distribution centers in order to see how our internal customers operate.
• Professional Development Series-College grads participate in a number of training sessions that are designed to build their professional skills.
• Functional Learning Lessons-College grads participate in a number of meetings with departmental leaders who share more specific information on how Borders Group operates.

Strategic Plan and Diversity Leadership

How does the firm's leadership communicate the importance of diversity to everyone at the firm?

Web site, Electronic Newsletters, Quarterly Scoop and Value of Employment newsletters, Intranet, Meetings, Training Programs

Who has primary responsibility for leading diversity initiatives at your firm?

Dan Smith, Senior Vice President of HR and Suzann Trevisan, Senior Manager of Specialty Recruiting and Retention

Does your firm currently have a diversity committee?

Yes

The committee meets monthly. Borders Group has developed a diversity task force to focus on building strategic initiatives that drive diversity awareness throughout the organization. The diversity task force is made up of a wide variety of Borders Group employees from each level of the company. The task force establishes the focus for diversity efforts throughout our business units, and develops strategies with the help of advisory committees made up of employees from the corporate offices, the field and the distribution facilities.

Using various methods like those listed below, the diversity task force and the advisory committees have improved our overall business and nurtured Borders Group's commitment to diversity. The Diversity Task Force focuses on the areas of employee awareness, customer outreach, supplier diversity and recruiting/retention.

If yes, does the committee's representation include one or more members of the firm's management/executive committee (or the equivalent)?

Yes

> **Total executives on the committee:** Varies between three to six each year

Does the committee and/or diversity leader establish and set goals or objectives consistent with management's priorities?

Yes

Has the firm undertaken a formal or informal diversity program or set of initiatives aimed at increasing the diversity of the firm?

Yes, formal

How often does the firm's management review the firm's diversity progress/results?

Monthly

Retention and Professional Development

Please identify the specific steps you are taking to reduce the attrition rate of minority and women employees.

• Develop and/or support internal employee affinity groups (e.g., minority or women networks within the firm)
• Increase/improve current work/life programs
• Succession plan includes emphasis on diversity
• Work with minority and women employees to develop career advancement plans
• Professional skills development program, including minority and women employees
• Other: We have our Pacesetters Programs at the corporate level and in the field which are specifically dedicated to employee development. Both divisions of the program place an emphasis on minority recruitment and retention initiatives.

Diversity Mission Statement

At Borders Group, diversity is who we are. Our commitment to diversity extends to progressive policies, which uphold the right to personal dignity and fairness.

Every person has the right to be treated with respect and dignity, regardless of race, religion, color, creed, national origin, age, gender, gender identity, sexual orientation, disability, veteran or military status, marital status or citizenship status, and other categories protected by applicable federal, state and local laws.

Borders Group supports the individualism of each employee and encourages all who wish to grow to explore their talents and seek expanded opportunities. This deep-rooted enthusiasm for diversity of people and perspectives extends far beyond the walls of our stores. It reaches from our corporate office into our stores, distribution centers and into every community we serve around the world.

Life.
Enhanced.

New Breakthroughs, New Opportunities.

If you're looking for an exciting place to work with a future full of opportunities, consider Bristol-Myers Squibb. We recently launched four major medicines in just over two years. And we have a robust pipeline of investigational products to treat serious diseases with unmet needs, including diabetes, rheumatoid arthritis and related medical disorders. Help us fulfill our mission *to extend and enhance human life*. You'll not only enrich the lives of others, but also have the opportunity for a rewarding career with personal and professional advancement in a high-caliber, team-oriented environment.

Find out more at
www.bms.com/career/

Bristol-Myers Squibb

345 Park Ave.
New York, NY 10154-0037
Phone: (212) 546-4000
Fax: (212) 546-4020
www.bms.com

The Employer Says

Different perspectives make it possible. At Bristol-Myers Squibb, we're a diverse team of talented and creative people — each with a different perspective. We value each person's unique contributions and inspire each other to develop the innovative solutions that extend and enhance the lives of our patients around the world.

Flexibility makes it possible. At Bristol-Myers Squibb, our people find fulfillment in their work, extending and enhancing the lives of patients around the world. And they have fulfilling lives at home too. Bristol-Myers Squibb offers a flexible range of work/life programs that help our employees at each stage of their lives. We're proud to be ranked in the top 100 of Working Mother Magazine's "Best Companies for Working Mothers."

Opportunities make your growth possible. Ask yourself – how far do you want to go? At Bristol-Myers Squibb, we're determined to be the company where our employees can achieve their career goals. We offer a range of opportunities to help you get there. It's simple. Your growth helps us to better extend and enhance the lives of patients around the world.

Bunzl Distribution

Bunzl Corporate Office
701 Emerson Road, Ste. 500
St. Louis, MO 63141
Ph: (314) 997-5959
Fax: (314) 997-1405
www.bunzldistribution.com

Locations (worldwide)

Offices worldwide. In the U.S.: New Jersey • Philadelphia • Atlanta • St. Louis • Dallas • California • Kansas City

Diversity Leadership

Monique Bowens
701 Emerson Road Suite 500
St. Louis, MO 63141
Phone: (314) 997-5959
Fax: (314) 228-0002
E-mail: monique.bowens@bunzlusa.com

Recruiting

Please list the schools/types of schools at which you recruit.

• Participate in/host minority student job fair(s)
• Sponsor minority student association events
• Outreach to leadership of minority student organizations
• Scholarships or intern/fellowships for minority students

What activities does the firm undertake to attract minority and women employees?

• Participate at minority job fairs
• Seek referrals from other employees

Do you use executive recruiting/search firms to seek to identify new diversity hires?

Yes

If yes, list all women- and/or minority-owned executive search/recruiting firms to which the firm paid a fee for placement services in the past 12 months:

We haven't placed any candidates as of yet

Internships and Co-ops

INROADS

Number of interns in the program in summer 2004 (internship) or 2004 (co-op): 7
Pay: Varies according to grade level; range is from $10-$14 per hour
Length of the program: Summer, winter and spring breaks
Percentage of interns/co-ops in the program who receive offers of full-time employment: 100%

Entry-Level Programs/Full-Time Opportunities

Management Trainee Program (i.e. Sales, Sales Management, Warehouse, Distribution, Logistics)

Length of program: 6-12 months
Geographic location(s) of program: Worldwide

Please describe the training/training component of this program: We customize and diversify our business in all segments with highly skilled and self-driven candidates in the above core areas. Also, we make sure our candidates understand our entire business scope.

Please describe any other educational components of this program: We offer tuition reimbursement for undergraduate and graduate degrees. Also we offer 4 year scholarships for all Bunzl employee dependents.

Strategic Plan and Diversity Leadership

How does the firm's leadership communicate the importance of diversity to everyone at the firm?

We conduct diversity training along with communicating the diversity initiatives to the employees through our intranet.

Who has primary responsibility for leading diversity initiatives at your firm?

Robin Pokoik, V.P. HR & Benefits

Does your firm currently have a diversity committee?

No

Has the firm undertaken a formal or informal diversity program or set of initiatives aimed at increasing the diversity of the firm?

We are in the process of creating a diversity program within our organization.

The Stats

Employees: 2,240 (2004, worldwide)
Employees: 2,432 (2003, worldwide)

Calpine Corporation

50 West San Fernando Street
San Jose, CA 95113
www.Calpine.com/careers

Locations (worldwide)
Folsom, CA; Houston, TX; Boston, MA;
Jupiter FL; Atlanta, GA; Tampa, FL;
Lincolnshire, IL; Rheden, The Netherlands;
Hull, UK

Diversity Leadership
Ruth Gaccetta, Director, HR & Diversity
2 Atlantic Avenue
Boston, MA 02110
Phone: (617) 557-5321
Fax: (617)557-5356
E-mail: rgaccetta@calpine.com

Recruiting

Please list the schools/types of schools at which you recruit.

• *Ivy League schools:* Princeton
• *Public state schools:* San Jose State University, Texas A&M, UT at Austin, Rice University, etc.

Do you have any special outreach efforts that are directed to encourage minority students to consider your firm?

• INROADS Program

What activities does the firm undertake to attract minority and women employees?

• Partner programs with women and minority associations
• Conferences. Please list: NSBE, AABE, NSBA, Lat-Pro, ASW
• Participate at minority job fairs
• Seek referrals from other employees
• Utilize online job services

Do you use executive recruiting/search firms to seek to identify new diversity hires?

Yes

If yes, list all women- and/or minority-owned executive search/recruiting firms to which the firm paid a fee for placement services in the past 12 months:

Wesley, Bartles & Brown

Internships and Co-ops

Calpine Corporation Internship/Co-Op Program (implemented in 2005)

Deadline for application: 5/27/2005
Pay: $10-$15/hour
Length of the program: 10-12 weeks
Web site for internship/co-op information: www. Calpine.com (under construction)

Scholarships

Calpine Scholarship Program

Deadline for application for the scholarship program: March 1st
Scholarship award amount: $1,000-$5,000

Calpine Scholarships will be applied to educational expenses at any accredited, non-profit college or university in the United States or Canada. A student may transfer from one college to another and retain the award. The selection of the recipients of Calpine Scholarships will be based on a combination pf academic merit, leadership activities and involvement in community activities. Heaviest weight is placed on academic merit as evidenced by grades, class rank and standardized test scores. Evidence of leadership activities, involvement in community activities (including part-time work) is also important in ranking the applicants, but does not comprise more than 30% of the total weight. If an applicant is already enrolled in college, the college GPA will also be considered.

Strategic Plan and Diversity Leadership

Who has primary responsibility for leading diversity initiatives at your firm? Name of person and his/her title:

Ruth Gaccetta, Director, Diversity

Does your firm currently have a diversity committee?

No

Does the committee and/or diversity leader establish and set goals or objectives consistent with management's priorities?

Yes

Has the firm undertaken a formal or informal diversity program or set of initiatives aimed at increasing the diversity of the firm?

Yes, formal. We've increased recruiting for diverse schools, associations, etc., and we've instituted an awareness campaign for employees to create employee referrals.

How often does the firm's management review the firm's diversity progress/results?

Twice a year

The Stats

Employees: 3,250 (2004, U.S.)
Employees: 250 (2004, outside U.S.)
Employees: 3,500 (2004, worldwide)
Revenue: $9 billion (2004, worldwide)

23% Female
16.5% Minority

Retention and Professional Development

How do 2004 minority and female attrition rates generally compare to those experienced in the prior year period?

About the same as in prior years

Please identify the specific steps you are taking to reduce the attrition rate of minority and women employees.

• Work with minority and women employees to develop career advancement plans
• Professional skills development program, including minority and women employees

Diversity Mission Statement

Calpine is committed to having a workplace in which every person and every group is respected, feels accepted, has value and contributes. Employment decisions are made on the basis of merit. We want to have the best available person in every job. Calpine policy prohibits discrimination on the basis of race, color, creed, sex, religion, marital status, age, national origin or ancestry, physical or mental disability or sexual orientation. We recognize that a diverse workforce is necessary for the continuing success of our company.

Capital One

1680 Capital One Dr.
McLean, VA 22012
(703) 720-1000
www.capitalone.com/careers

Locations (worldwide)
United States (Virginia, Washington D.C., California, Florida, Idaho, Massachusetts, Texas), Canada, United Kingdom, France

Diversity Leadership
Rob Keeling, Director of Diversity
Hilary Knox, Campus Recruiting Manager
Contact person:
Kim Hodges, Diversity Consultant
15000 Capital One Drive
Richmond, VA 23238
(804) 967-1000
E-mail: kimberly.hodges@capitalone.com

Recruiting

Please list the schools/types of schools at which you recruit.

- *Ivy League schools:* Cornell, Harvard, University of Pennsylvania
- *Other private schools:* Duke, Notre Dame, University of Richmond, Rensselaer, Carnegie Mellon
- *Public state schools:* University of Virginia, Virginia Tech, Georgia Tech, University of Texas, University of Michigan, University of Maryland, Penn State, Ohio State, Rutgers, University of Illinois, NC State, Purdue, William & Mary, University of Florida, University of Wisconsin, University of Minnesota and James Madison University
- Other predominantly minority and/or women's colleges: Wellesley

Do you have any special outreach efforts that are directed to encourage minority students to consider your firm?

Advertise in minority student association publication(s)
Sponsor minority student association events
Firm's employees participate on career panels at school

What activities does the firm undertake to attract minority and women employees?

- *Conferences:* Simmon's School of Management Leadership Conference, Linkage Women in Leadership
- *Participate at minority job fairs:* NSBE, NBMBAA, NSHMBA, National Association of Women MBAs, Reaching Out   MBA, MEAC/SWAC job fair, SWE
- Seek referrals from other employees
- Utilize online job services

Do you use executive recruiting/search firms to seek to identify new diversity hires?

No

Internships and Co-ops

Capital One Summer Intern Program

Deadline for application: March 10
Number of interns in the program in summer 2004 (internship) or 2004 (co-op): 26
Pay: $23 per hour
Length of the program: 11 weeks
Percentage of interns/co-ops in the program who receive offers of full-time employment: 90%
Web site for internship/co-op information:
www.capitalone.com/careers/campusrecruiting.shtml

If you're looking to put your education to the test in real business situations, beef up your resume, add to your skills, and have fun too, then our Summer Intern Program may be perfect for you! As an intern, you'll get involved in and be responsible for challenging projects that can have a significant impact on our business-no making coffee or picking up dry cleaning here! Your projects will typically be team-oriented, and you'll gain new skills in a positive learning environment. Other great benefits of our intern program include the following: executive speaker series, team building events, intern-specific training class.

Scholarships

Capital One NSBE Scholarship

This scholarship is offered each year in conjunction with the NSBE National Conference. You may view details for applying in the NSBE scholarship guidelines.

Capital One NSHMBA Scholarship

This scholarship is offered each year in conjunction with the NSHMBA National Conference. You may view details for applying in the NSHMBA scholarship guidelines.

Affinity Groups/Employee Networks

Five Associate Networks:

African American Network, Asian Pacific Network, Hispanic Network, LGBT (Lesbian, Gay, Bisexual and Transgender) Network, Women's Network

Capital One's Associate Networks were created to support Capital One's growing diverse population. These networks provide support in the form of programs, resources and tools that enable Capital One's diverse associates to achieve their full potential in an environment that values the differences we bring to the workplace.

The networks also support the organization's diversity strategy. Their objectives are closely linked to Capital One's goals of recruiting, retaining and developing diverse talent and leveraging their differences to contribute to the success of the organization.

Diversity Mission Statement

"At Capital One, diversity means finding associates with different backgrounds, life and work experiences, beliefs and communication styles. Diversity means seeking and embracing our differences because of the richness those differences add to our lives and the many advantages they provide to our business."

– Rich Fairbank
Chairman and Chief Executive Officer

CenterPoint Energy, Inc.

1111 Louisiana St.
Houston, TX 77002
(713) 207-1111
Fax: (713) 207-3169
www.centerpointenergy.com

Locations (worldwide)

Texas (HQ), Arkansas, Illinois, Indiana, Louisiana, Minnesota, Mississippi, Missouri, Ohio, Oklahoma and Wisconsin,

Diversity Leadership

Toni Green, EEO/Diversity Analyst
1111 Louisiana St. #4071A
Houston, TX 77002
Phone: (713) 207-7409
Fax: (713) 207-9566
E-mail: toni.green@centerpointenergy.com
Contact person: Alice B. Otchere, Sr. Director, Human Resources

Recruiting

Please list the schools/types of schools at which you recruit.

• *Private schools:* Rice University, South Texas College of Law
• *Public state schools:* Texas A&M, Oklahoma State University, Oklahoma University, Sam Houston State University, University of Arkansas, University of Houston, University of Texas at Austin, Louisiana State University, Louisiana Tech, Mississippi State
• *Historically Black Colleges and Universities (HBCUs):* Texas Southern University, Prairie View A&M University
• *Native American Tribal Universities:* University of Oklahoma

Do you have any special outreach efforts that are directed to encourage minority students to consider your firm?

• Participate in/host minority student job fair(s)
• Sponsor minority student association events
• Participate on career panels at school
• Outreach to leadership of minority student organizations
• Provide scholarships or intern/fellowships for minority students

What activities does the firm undertake to attract minority and women employees?

• Partner programs with women and minority associations
• Participate at minority job fairs

Do you use executive recruiting/search firms to seek to identify new diversity hires?

Yes

Internships and Co-ops

Number of interns in the program in summer 2004 (internship) or 2004 (co-op): Spring 2004 co-ops: 8; Summer 2004 interns: 32; Fall 2004 co-ops: 10

Pay: Varies

Length of the program: Varies due to assignment(s)

Percentage of interns/co-ops in the program who receive offers of full-time employment: 65%

Web site for internship/co-op information: www.centerpointenergy.com

The CenterPoint Energy intern/co-op program is comprised of undergraduate and graduate interns. These interns report to different areas within the organization such as Strategic Planning, Legal, Accounting/Finance and Gas Engineering as well as engineering groups within electric operations. The intern/co-op responsibilities vary depending on a student's field of study and classification within that field. To be considered for the CenterPoint Energy intern/co-op program, the student must be enrolled at an accredited college/university and have an overall GPA of 3.0 or above.

Strategic Plan and Diversity Leadership

How does the firm's leadership communicate the importance of diversity to everyone at the firm?

The importance of diversity is communicated via e-mail, company Internet/Intranet web site, newsletters, brochures, literature, meetings and training.

Who has primary responsibility for leading diversity initiatives at your firm?

Alice B. Otchere, Senior Director, Human Resources

Does your firm currently have a diversity committee?

Yes.

The committee members include a cross-section of management representing the various business and functional units. CenterPoint Energy's Workplace Diversity Council conducts regular quarterly meetings where diversity initiatives are discussed and planned. Additionally, the Council's standing committees meet as needed.

If yes, does the committee's representation include one or more members of the firm's management/executive committee (or the equivalent)?

Yes

Please describe the committee.

There are eight executives on the Workplace Diversity Council. The Workplace Diversity Council also includes six members of senior management and one non-management employee. The Workplace Diversity Council meets quarterly. Also, seven of CenterPoint Energy's Senior Executives sit on an Executive Diversity Steering Committee. The Executive Committee, along with the Workplace Diversity Council, direct the strategy for the company's three elements of diversity-Workplace Diversity, Supplier Diversity and Community Relations.

Does the committee and/or diversity leader establish and set goals or objectives consistent with management's priorities?

Yes. The Workplace Diversity Council will:

- Provide advice and consultation regarding effective implementation of our strategic plan for diversity;
- Provide ideas and recommendations for future promotion of diversity awareness throughout the workplace;
- Serve as ambassadors, both internally and externally, for the increased emphasis and focus surrounding corporate workforce diversity initiatives;
- Review, evaluate, advise and monitor progress and results of workforce diversity and inclusion initiatives; and

• Advise executive leadership and our Executive Diversity Steering Committee regarding enterprise-wide activities and issues in the diversity arena.

Has the firm undertaken a formal or informal diversity program or set of initiatives aimed at increasing the diversity of the firm?

Yes, a formal diversity program is in place. CenterPoint Energy's Workplace Diversity Counsel reviews people management processes to determine how to more effectively incorporate diversity and inclusion awareness via workforce recruiting/staffing, employee development, performance management, leadership development and corporate policies and procedures. In addition, CenterPoint Energy has implemented the BOLD Initiative (Building Opportunities for Leadership Diversity), a Leadership Development Program and the Workforce Diversity Initiative.

How often does the firm's management review the firm's diversity progress/results?

Twice a year

How is the firm's diversity committee and/or firm management held accountable for achieving results?

Semi-annual meetings between the CEO and business unit executives are scheduled to assess areas of opportunity and monitor progress of the plan(s) to address opportunities.

The Stats

Employees: 10,648 (2004, U.S.)
Revenue: $8.510 billion (2004, U.S.)
Employees: 11,043 (2003, U.S.)
Revenue: $7.790 billion (2003, U.S.)

As of Q1/2005 the following demographics are noted:

Total Employees: 9,058
Total Females: 2,204 or 24%
Total Males: 6,854 or 76%
Total Minorities: 2,693 or 30%

Executive Team Minorities: 10%
Executive Team Females: 10%

Retention and Professional Development

How do 2004 minority and female attrition rates generally compare to those experienced in the prior year period?

The 2004 Female attrition rates were 30.3%, reflecting a decrease from the previous years (2002-2003). The 2004 attrition rate for minorities was 36.7%, increasing from 34.1% in 2003 and 25.5% in 2002.

Please identify the specific steps you are taking to reduce the attrition rate of minority and women employees.

• Succession plan includes emphasis on diversity
• Strengthen mentoring program for all employees, including minorities and women
• Professional skills development program, including minority and women employees
• Other: Implemented CNP University, an online resource that affords all employees developmental opportunities to increase their knowledge and skills.

Diversity Mission Statement

At CenterPoint Energy, every employee counts. Our company is committed to creating an inclusive work environment where business results are achieved through the skills, abilities and talents of our diverse workforce.

We foster:

• A culture in which mutual respect is the standard and where different backgrounds and viewpoints are considered competitive advantages;

• An environment where all employees have opportunities for personal and professional development; and

• Recognition that diversity and inclusion are key components of our business competencies.

• Diversity at CenterPoint Energy has three elements: workplace diversity and inclusion, supplier diversity and community relations. All three are an important part of our vision to be America's leading energy delivery company ... and more.

The Employer Says

At CenterPoint Energy we are guided by a set of core values that define who we are and what we believe in. We're committed to doing business with integrity, accountability, initiative and respect-respect for our employees, business partners, shareholders, customers and our communities.

We incorporate diversity messages into new and existing training programs including new employee orientation. All new employees will complete the training as a part of the CNP University core curriculum. A three-part online training course has been developed for managers and was implemented in 2004. In the fourth quarter of 2004, an employee version was introduced. In addition to our stand-alone training tool, a Diversity Knowledge Map has been added as a component of a new supervisory training course introduced in January 2005.

The Workplace Diversity Council partnered with Human Resources representatives to deliver diversity presentations and present current statistics for business and functional unit management. To ensure management has a broader understanding of diversity, an electronic workplace demographic tool keeps real time reports available.

CenterPoint Energy's strategy is clear: to create a high performance culture characterized by an open, inclusive and diverse work environment. CenterPoint Energy believes that it is vital to have a workforce that reflects the diversity of our customers and the communities we serve. We believe that diversity plays a key role in helping us achieve our vision to be recognized as America's leading energy delivery company...and more.

Cinergy Services

139 E. 4th St.
Cincinnati, OH 45202
Phone: (513) 421-9500
Fax: (513) 287-1088
Toll Free: (800) 262-3000
www.cinergy.com/careers

Diversity Leadership
General Manager, Inclusion Strategies

Employment Contact
Bernadette Toebbe, Supervisor, Recruitment
139 E. Fourth St. EY100
Cincinnati, OH45201
Phone: (513) 287-3628
Fax: (513) 287-2482
E-mail: Bernadette.Toebbe@cinergy.com

Recruiting

Please list the schools/types of schools at which you recruit.

• *Private schools:* Rose Hulman Institute of Technology, University of Evansville
• *Public state schools:* University of Cincinnati, Purdue, Kentucky, Ball State, Xavier (OH), Ohio U, Louisville

Do you have any special outreach efforts that are directed to encourage minority students to consider your firm?

• Advertise in minority student association publication(s)
• Participate in/host minority student job fair(s)
• Sponsor minority student association events
• Firm's employees participate on career panels at school
• Outreach to leadership of minority student organizations

What activities does the firm undertake to attract minority and women employees?

• Partner programs with women and minority associations
• Participate at minority job fairs
• Seek referrals from other employees
• Utilize online job services

Do you use executive recruiting/search firms to seek to identify new diversity hires?

Yes

If yes, list all women- and/or minority-owned executive search/recruiting firms to which the firm paid a fee for placement services in the past 12 months:

None over the last 18 months.

Internships and Co-ops

Cinergy Co-op/Internship Program

Deadline for application: January and May (for spring and fall co-op program); January for summer internship
Pay: An hourly rate based on class year and major
Length of the program: Approximately 12 weeks
Web site for internship/co-op information: www.cinergy.com/careers

The company's co-op/intern program is designed to provide students with an opportunity to work in a variety of departments in order to gain a broad experience. Our co-op/intern recruiting needs are primarily focused on students pursuing undergraduate degrees in accounting, finance, electrical, mechanical and chemical engineering. On occasion, a limited number of co-op/intern opportunities may be available for business and information technology majors.

INROADS

Deadline for application: Determined by INROADS
Number of interns in the program in summer 2004 (internship) or 2004 (co-op): Three interns during summer 2004
Pay: An hourly rate based on class year and major
Length of the program: Approximately 12 weeks
Percentage of interns/co-ops in the program who receive offers of full-time employment: Not applicable at this time
Web site for internship/co-op information: www.cinergy.com/careers

INROADS internships are designed to provide students with an opportunity to work in a variety of departments to gain a broad experience, or a specific area aligned with their career interests and goals. Our INROADS recruiting needs are primarily focused on students pursuing undergraduate degrees in accounting, finance, electrical, mechanical and chemical engineering. On occasion, a limited number of co-op/intern opportunities may be available for business and information technology majors.

Next Level

Deadline for application: Open
Number of interns in the program in summer 2004 (internship) or 2004 (co-op): Five interns during summer 2004
Pay: An hourly rate based on class year and major
Length of the program: Approximately 10 weeks
Percentage of interns/co-ops in the program who receive offers of full-time employment: Not applicable at this time
Web site for internship/co-op information: www.cinergy.com/careers

The Next Level is an internship program targetedtowards students of color in the Greater Cincinnati area. This summer internship experience is designed to provide students with an opportunity to work in a variety of departments to gain a broad experience and to prepare them for life in corporate America. Students pursuing undergraduate degrees in accounting, finance, electrical, mechanical and chemical engineering are highly desired; however, business and information technology majors are eligible for this program.

Affinity Groups/Employee Networks

The Collaborative for Positive Change (CPC)

The mission of the CPC is to establish and maintain a support system that focuses on the empowerment of African-American employees while contributing to the achievement of the company's goals. Their vision is to work as a consulting group that is the focal point for African Americans that will unify, support and empower others to grow and reach their ultimate potential.

The Cinergy Women's Network

The mission of the Women's Network is first, to motivate and support all women. Additionally, the group aims to heighten awareness about women's issues in order to remove barriers and be recognized as a valued force within the company.

The Hispanic Heritage Network

The mission of the Hispanic Heritage Network is to promote and preserve the Hispanic culture while helping Cinergy achieve its goals of leading a workforce that is truly balanced and a reflection of the people we serve. With this effort, we will lead in energizing the social, cultural and economic development of our community. The network's vision is to help Cinergy shape its future by improving its services, communications and creating a dynamic relationship with the growing Hispanic/Latino community. As Cinergy becomes part of this community, we will attract new talent who exhibit the drive, professional capabilities and desire to become part of the Cinergy family.

Strategic Plan and Diversity Leadership

How does the firm's leadership communicate the importance of diversity to everyone at the firm?

Cinergy's diversity performance initiative and its importance are communicated on Cinergy.com and on the company's intranet. Annually, each business unit president and/or executive vice presidents issue a communication expressing their continual support of this initiative. They also outline the continuing diversity education and awareness threshold requirement.

Who has primary responsibility for leading diversity initiatives at your firm?

Suzane Bradley— General Manger, Inclusion Strategies

Does your firm currently have a diversity committee?

Yes

If yes, please describe how the committee is structured, how often it meets, etc.

The company has a number of diversity teams and steering committees along with the Corporate Council for Diversity Leadership (CCDL). The CCDL is scheduled to meet monthly with the purpose of supporting the Inclusion Strategies function with strategy design and implementation by advocating corporate responsibility, cultivating and generating ideas, and evaluating and enhancing processes to achieve results.

If yes, does the committee's representation include one or more members of the firm's management/executive committee (or the equivalent)?

Yes

Please describe the committee.

Two officers from the CEO's management team serve on the CCDL. The council has 19 members and includes employees from across the organization, at different levels of the organization, including employees represented by some of our unions and other senior management employees.

Does the committee and/or diversity leader establish and set goals or objectives consistent with management's priorities?

Yes. The corporate diversity strategy is aligned with Cinergy's strategy to balance the needs of our stakeholders, improve all of our operations and grow the business.

Has the firm undertaken a formal or informal diversity program or set of initiatives aimed at increasing the diversity of the firm?

Yes, formal. In 2002, Cinergy rolled out its Balanced Workforce Initiative as part of our overall inclusion strategy to reemphasize its commitment to provide opportunities at all levels of the company to men and women of all races/ethnicities and to traditionally underrepresented groups. Ultimately, our goal is to have a workforce more reflective of the communities in which we live and serve.

How often does the firm's management review the firm's diversity progress/results?

Quarterly. In 2003, an Executive Oversight Committee chaired by Cinergy's CEO, Jim Rogers, and comprised of his Executive Vice Presidents was created to lead and influence some key aspects of our diversity strategies with primary focus on the balanced workforce and supplier diversity outcomes.

How is the firm's diversity committee and/or firm management held accountable for achieving results?

For 2005, the executive leadership team has diversity goals tied to their incentive pay. These goals have been communicated to their respective business unit leadership and management employees will be accountable for the results.

The Stats

DEMOGRAPHIC PROFILE	TOTAL IN THE U.S.		TOTAL OUTSIDE THE U.S		TOTAL WORLDWIDE	
	2004	2003	2004	2003	2004	2003
Number of employees	7,473	7,306	N/A	N/A	7,473	7,306
Revenues	$4.637 billion	$4.371 billion	$51 million	$45 million	$4.688 billion	$4.416 billion

Retention and Professional Development

How do 2004 minority and female attrition rates generally compare to those experienced in the prior year period?

About the same as in prior years

Please identify the specific steps you are taking to reduce the attrition rate of minority and women employees.

• Develop and/or support internal employee affinity groups (e.g., minority or women networks within the firm)
• Increase/review compensation relative to competition
• Increase/improve current work/life programs
• Succession plan includes emphasis on diversity
• Work with minority and women employees to develop career advancement plans
• Review work assignments and hours billed to key client matters to make sure minority and women employees are not being excluded
• Strengthen mentoring program for all employees, including minorities and women
• Professional skills development program, including minority and women employees

Diversity Mission Statement

To create an inclusive, performance based environment where no individual or group of individuals is advantaged or disadvantaged because of race, cultural background, gender, age, physical ability, geographic origin, sexual orientation, religion, tenure or any other diversity classification, and where each person is valued and challenged to reach their full potential and held accountable to contribute to the growth of Cinergy.

The Employer Says

As a company, Cinergy is faced with a significant turnover challenge over the next five to seven years, so it is incumbent upon us to access all available talent pools to attract the best people. We are building our external talent pipelines through internship and co-op programs, the MBA Navigator program, which may be expanded to include other graduate degrees, and we have employed some unique strategies to reach out to the minority community for recruiting candidates for our line apprentice programs. These actions demonstrate a commitment to doing things differently to achieve desired results in all of our staffing and recruiting activities.

We are continually looking at ways to identify and develop the talent within our organization through our annual succession planning process, the Management Development Associates (MDA) program for employees at the manager level, and through a newly developed Emerging Leaders program to be implemented later this year for employees at or below the supervisory level.

In addition to our management development and succession planning processes, the company offers additional career development tools and training, development courses through Cinergy's Virtual Academy, a formal mentoring program, and tuition reimbursement.

Cinergy has had a diversity performance initiative in place for 10 years. The cornerstone of our diversity education and awareness program is Journey Toward Inclusion (JTI) a one-day workshop dealing with the more visible dimensions of diversity. With JTI as a building block, employees are expected to meet an annual diversity threshold requirement to encourage and support continuous, meaningful diversity education and the application of related skills.

Under the direction of the Inclusion Strategies department, our Corporate Council for Diversity Leadership supports the development and implementation of Cinergy's corporate diversity strategic plan. Each business unit has a diversity steering committee, and there are several departmental diversity teams that address issues at the department and work group level. Along with the employee network groups and other strategic partners, the company has built quite an infrastructure to support its commitment to diversity. We also work hard to ensure fair and equitable employment practices through Cinergy's equal employment opportunity and affirmative action programs.

Over the last two years, an Executive Oversight Committee for Diversity has been monitoring progress toward providing opportunities for men and women of all races and ethnicities at all levels of the organization – with particular emphasis on middle and senior management. The Committee is chaired by the CEO and is comprised of our most senior executives. It meets quarterly.

Cinergy aspires to be the energy company preferred by each of its stakeholders, which includes employees. In March of this year, the Department of Labor awarded Cinergy Corp. with the highly coveted Secretary of Labor's Opportunity Award for 2004. This award represents the ultimate compliment to Cinergy's leadership and those employees dedicated to creating an inclusive, performance based environment. We are also honored to have been named one of the "100 Best Companies for Working Mothers" for eight consecutive years by *Working Mother* magazine. Although there is more work to be done, we believe we are on a pathway to success.

Diversity

is a source of strength for our people and our businesses.

At Citigroup, we have worked hard to create a workplace with an emphasis on inclusion, innovation and merit, rooted in our shared values and respect for our colleagues and the millions of people we serve. We aspire to be a company where the best people want to work; a company dedicated to empowering individuals and families around the world; and a company that provides opportunity for all.

An Equal Opportunity Employer M/F/D/V | careers.citigroup.com

citigroup

Citigroup Inc.

399 Park Avenue
New York, NY 10043
(800) 285-3000
Fax: (212) 793-3946
oncampus.Citigroup.com

Locations (worldwide)
Multiple

Diversity Leadership
Ana Duarte McCarthy, Director, Global
Workforce Diversity & College Relations

Employment Contact
Andrea Mason, Director of External
Partnerships, Global Workforce Diversity
One Court Square/9th Floor/Zone 9
Long Island City, NY 11120
masona@citigroup.com

Recruiting

Please list the schools/types of schools at which you recruit.

• Ivy League schools
• Other private schools
• Public state schools
• Historically Black Colleges and Universities (HBCUs)
• Hispanic Serving Institutions (HSIs)

Do you have any special outreach efforts that are directed to encourage minority students to consider your firm?

• Hold a reception for minority students
• Participate in/host minority student job fair(s)
• Sponsor minority student association events
• Firm's employees participate on career panels at school
• Outreach to leadership of minority student organizations
• Scholarships or intern/fellowships for minority students

What activities does the firm undertake to attract minority and women employees?

• Partner programs with women and minority associations
• Conferences: NBMBAA, NSHMBA, CGSM, NAWMBA, Reaching Out MBA
• Seek referrals from other employees
• Utilize online job services

Internships and Co-ops

INROADS

Deadline for application: Set by INROADS
Number of interns in the program in summer 2004 (internship) or 2004 (co-op): 69
Pay: $12 – $18 per hour
Length of the program: 10 weeks
Percentage of interns/co-ops in the program who receive offers of full-time employment: 60%
Web site for internship/co-op information: oncampus.Citigroup.com

Though not standard practice, interns are sometimes able to rotate to different functions within a particular business. Interns are hired into various departments in our Global Consumer Group and Corporate and Investment Banking businesses.

Scholarships

Citigroup/INROADS Scholarship

Deadline for application for the scholarship program: Administered by INROADS/NYC
Scholarship award amount: 4 at $2,500 yearly
Web site or other contact information for scholarship: INROADS/NYC

The eligibility for this scholarship is set by INROADS/NYC.

Affinity Groups/Employee Networks

African Heritage Network, Asian Heritage Network, Hispanic Heritage Network, Pride (focused on the LGBT community), Women's Network, Working Parents' Network

Employee networks are employee-initiated and employee-led groups open to all Citigroup employees in the country in which they are formed. Employee networks support the diversity and business initiatives of the organization and provide employees with an opportunity to share common experiences and build awareness of diverse cultures and communities within Citigroup.

Entry-Level Programs/Full-Time Opportunities

Retail Distribution Group Management Associate Program

Length of program: Two years
Geographic location(s) of program: New York, NY

Please describe the training/training component of this program: Two-year rotation through various Retail Banking functions

Global Transaction Services Analyst Program

Length of program: Two years
Geographic location(s) of program: New York, NY

Please describe the training/training component of this program: The program offers an initial six-week "boot camp" style training period where participants will gain in-depth training in accounting, credit/risk and financial analysis.

Strategic Plan and Diversity Leadership

How does the firm's leadership communicate the importance of diversity to everyone at the firm?

• Company intranet (www.citigroup.net/diversity)
• E-mail
• Newsletter
• Diversity Annual Report
• Employee Cultural Heritage Month Program

Who has primary responsibility for leading diversity initiatives at your firm?

Ana Duarte-McCarthy – Director, Global Workforce Diversity & College Relations

Does your firm currently have a diversity committee?

Yes

If yes, does the committee's representation include one or more members of the firm's management/executive committee (or the equivalent)?

Yes

Does the committee and/or diversity leader establish and set goals or objectives consistent with management's priorities?

Yes

Has the firm undertaken a formal or informal diversity program or set of initiatives aimed at increasing the diversity of the firm?

Yes, formal

How often does the firm's management review the firm's diversity progress/results?

Quarterly

The Stats

Employees: 300,000 (2004, worldwide)
Revenue: $86.190 billion (2004, worldwide)
Revenue: $77.442 billion (2003, worldwide)

Retention and Professional Development

Please identify the specific steps you are taking to reduce the attrition rate of minority and women employees.

• Develop and support internal employee affinity groups (e.g., minority or women networks within the firm)
• Succession plan includes emphasis on diversity
• Strengthen mentoring program for all employees, including minorities and women
• Professional skills development program, including minority and women employees

Diversity Mission Statement

Every day, everywhere that we do business, we strive to foster an environment where the unique backgrounds of our employees are respected and valued. Part of our focus on attracting and developing talent means creating a company where people feel they can fully contribute. The diversity of our people and their perspectives, their awareness and understanding of one another and our recruiting and mentoring programs – which emphasize diversity – help create an environment that works for us all.

The Employer Says

Citigroup's diversity strategy is based on four components-to be the employer of choice, service provider of choice, business partner of choice and neighbor of choice. We have taken concrete steps to inform our 300,000 employees about our diversity strategy. Our senior managers developed diversity plans and reviewed progress against these plans every quarter. We continue to embed mentoring programs to support career development, strengthen our employee network program and develop our products and services for an increasingly diverse customer base. We also partner with diversity organizations to identify and hire diverse talent – and we have seen positive results.

Embedding the principles of diversity and inclusion in everything we do is essential to Citigroup's goal to be the most respected global financial service company.

Clorox Company, The

1221 Broadway
Oakland, CA 94612
Phone: (510) 271-7332
Fax: (510) 271-6593
www.thecloroxcompany.com

Locations (worldwide)

Headquarters in Oakland, California; various global locations

Recruiting

Please list the schools/types of schools at which you recruit.

• Ivy League schools
• Public state schools

Do you have any special outreach efforts that are directed to encourage minority students to consider your firm?

Conferences: NSHMBA, SWE

What activities does the firm undertake to attract minority and women employees?

Partner programs with women and minority associations
Conferences: NSHMBA, SWE, NABA
Seek referrals from other employees

Do you use executive recruiting/search firms to seek to identify new diversity hires?

Yes

Internships and Co-ops

INROADS

Deadline for application: April for summer internship
Number of interns in the program in summer 2004 (INROADS): 4
Number of interns in the program in summer 2005 (INROADS): 11
Pay: $14-$18 per hour depending on level
Length of the program: 8-12 weeks

The Clorox Company offers three different internship programs:

There are 8-10 interns hired for Marketing, 8-10 hired for Research and Development and 10-12 INROADS interns hired for various other functions (i.e. Human Resources, Product Supply, Information Services and Finance and Accounting). Interns work closely with full-time professionals on a variety of projects. Marketing looks for Associate Marketing Managers and Associate Marketing Intelligence Managers for interns. To intern in Marketing, a business administration degree with a marketing focus and other marketing internships are pluses. Other qualifications include: demonstrated outstanding leadership/results orientation skills, and strong analytical/problem solving abilities.

Research and Development looks for Process Core Technology, Corporate Packaging and Consumer Applied Technology interns. To intern with Research and Development, students must have completed their junior year with a minimum 3.0 GPA. Recommended majors include a bachelor of science in either Packaging Sciences Engineering or Chemical Engineering. INROADS interns must have a cumulative GPA of 2.8 or better as a sophomore or junior at a four-year school with at least two summers remaining prior to graduation. Prefer degrees in: Business, Engineering, Information and Computer Sciences, Sales and Marketing.

Affinity Groups/Employee Networks

Affinity groups for Hispanics, Asians, African Americans, Women, and GLBT are to be created this fiscal year.

Strategic Plan and Diversity Leadership

How does the firm's leadership communicate the importance of diversity to everyone at the firm?

Web site, newsletters, meetings, Diversity and Inclusion Task Force

Who has primary responsibility for leading diversity initiatives at your firm?

Bill Ingham, Director, Talent Acquisition and Diversity

Does your firm currently have a diversity committee?

Yes.

• Steering Committee – 3 members of Executive Committee meet semi-annually
• Diversity and Inclusion Task Force – 25 cross functional leaders meet quarterly

If yes, does the committee's representation include one or more members of the firm's management/executive committee (or the equivalent)?

Yes

Does the committee and/or diversity leader establish and set goals or objectives consistent with management's priorities?

Yes, business and organizational effectiveness goals

Has the firm undertaken a formal or informal diversity program or set of initiatives aimed at increasing the diversity of the firm?

Yes, formal

How often does the firm's management review the firm's diversity progress/results?

Quarterly

How is the firm's diversity committee and/or firm management held accountable for achieving results?

It is tied to their compensation.

Retention and Professional Development

How do 2004 minority and female attrition rates generally compare to those experienced in the prior year period?

About the same as in prior years

Please identify the specific steps you are taking to reduce the attrition rate of minority and women employees.

• Develop and/or support internal employee affinity groups (e.g., minority or women networks within the firm)
• Increase/improve current work/life programs
• Succession plan includes emphasis on diversity
• Work with minority and women employees to develop career advancement plans
• Strengthen mentoring program for all employees, including minorities and women
• Professional skills development program, including minority and women employees

Columbia St. Mary's Health System

Locations (worldwide)
City of Milwaukee, Ozaukee County, Glendale

Diversity Leadership
Cynthia R. Stewart, Director, Diversity Resources & Language Services
4425 N. Port Washington Road
Glendale, WI 53212
Phone: (414) 326-2661
Fax: (414) 291-1427
E-mail: CStewart@Columbia-stmarys.org

Recruiting

Please list the schools/types of schools at which you recruit.

• Public state schools
• Hispanic Serving Institutions (HSIs)

Do you have any special outreach efforts that are directed to encourage minority students to consider your firm?

• Advertise in minority student association publication(s)
• Scholarships or intern/fellowships for minority students

What activities does the firm undertake to attract minority and women employees?

• Partner programs with women and minority associations
• Participate at minority job fairs

Do you use executive recruiting/search firms to seek to identify new diversity hires?

Yes

If yes, list all women- and/or minority-owned executive search/recruiting firms to which the firm paid a fee for placement servces in the past 12 months:

• Used for executive positions. Agency name unknown.

Internships and Co-ops

High School CNA Training Program

Deadline for application: April each year

Number of interns in the program in summer 2004 (internship) or 2004 (co-op): 7

Pay: $6-$7 per hour training rate

Length of the program: 30-36 weeks

Percentage of interns/co-ops in the program who receive offers of full-time employment: None – the interns go on to post-secondary education

To participate, students must be in school co-op program, write a 100-word essay and complete the CNA Training program. They are then placed on nursing units for 10-15 weeks per school year.

INROADS

Number of interns in the program in summer 2004 (internship) or 2004 (co-op): 12

Length of the program: 10 weeks annually

Percentage of interns/co-ops in the program who receive offers of full-time employment: For current year, 100% for graduating interns

College students are placed within the organization in areas related to their field of study and given project work and management or supervisory training to advance skills. Upon graduation the goal is to place them in a professional or leadership position for which they will need little training due to their in-house experience.

Scholarships

Estil Strawn Scholarship Program for employees

Deadline for application for the scholarship program: May 15, 2005

Scholarship award amount: $2,000 for entire scholarship

Web site or other contact information for scholarship: Only open to company employees

To apply, you must: be an employee in good standing; be studying in a field that would fit within a health care environment; and have successfully completed an application process including interview.

Black Nurses Association Scholarship

Deadline for application for the scholarship program: Varies

Scholarship award amount: Varies, $3,000-$5,000

Web site or other contact information for scholarship: The scholarship is given through the Black Nurses Association. Applicants should be nursing students in good standing.

Entry-Level Programs/Full-Time Opportunities

A succession management program is being developed

Strategic Plan and Diversity Leadership

How does the firm's leadership communicate the importance of diversity to everyone at the firm?

E-mails, leadership meetings, education sessions for staff and leadership, Diversity Scorecard, newsletter

Who has primary responsibility for leading diversity initiatives at your firm?

Director of Diversity

Does your firm currently have a diversity committee?

Yes

If yes, please describe how the committee is structured, how often it meets, etc.

The committee meets monthly. Four committees report to the council and they meet as necessary, usually one or more times per month. The council is made up of individuals from all levels of the organization, including executive leadership. The council is headed by an executive leader.

If yes, does the committee's representation include one or more members of the firm's management/executive committee (or the equivalent)?

Yes

Please describe the committee.

Four executives are on the committee who spent approximately 30+ hours furthering the diversity initiative. There are 13 members on the council and we meet monthly.

Does the committee and/or diversity leader establish and set goals or objectives consistent with management's priorities?

Yes

Has the firm undertaken a formal or informal diversity program or set of initiatives aimed at increasing the diversity of the firm?

Yes, formal. We have a diversity scorecard to measure progress.

How often does the firm's management review the firm's diversity progress/results?

Twice a year

How is the firm's diversity committee and/or firm management held accountable for achieving results?

Some goals are tied to management bonuses.

The Stats

Employees: 5,600 (2004, U.S.)

21% minorities in U.S.
83.9% female
60% female executives
7% minority

Retention and Professional Development

How do 2004 minority and female attrition rates generally compare to those experienced in the prior year period?

Lower than in prior years

Please identify the specific steps you are taking to reduce the attrition rate of minority and women employees.

• Increase/review compensation relative to competition
• Increase/improve current work/life programs
• Succession plan includes emphasis on diversity
• Strengthen mentoring program for all employees, including minorities and women

Diversity Mission Statement

The Columbia Saint Mary's Diversity Resources Council promotes the unique perspectives provided by distinctions of age, culture, ethnicity, family status, gender, physical/cognitive ability, race, religion, sexual orientation and socio-economic status.

The Council exists to support the overall vision and mission of CSM by advocating an inclusive environment that both respects and leverages the rich diversity of our employees, physicians, patients and surrounding community.

Our purpose is:

• To identify strategies and accountabilities related to diversity for CSM
• To educate the organization on how diversity is integral to achieving our mission
• To provide educational opportunities to continuously build cultural competence at all levels
• To strengthen the organization through valuing and promoting a diverse workforces

The Employer Says

The organization has a position dedicated to targeting youth at the high school and college ages to provide coaching, mentoring, internships etc. The goal is to increase the interest in health care and to provide growth opportunities for students.

Our Scorecard is designed to build accountability across the organization and at all levels.

We have a strong Language Services program with much emphasis on education and service to populations with limited or no English speaking abilities. We are also working to build programs or processes to hire more bilingual staff in positions at all levels in the organization and to utilize the skills of bilingual employees who have the skills necessary to serve as interpreters and translators.

We maintain affiliations and programs with community organizations to build community strength. We also own several clinics (medical and dental) that provide outreach to uninsured and underinsured persons and the homeless.

Comcast

1500 Market St.
Philadelphia, PA 19102-2148
Phone: (215) 665-1700
Fax: (215) 981-7790
www.comcast.com

The Employer Says

Programs that promote diversity

The leadership programs that Comcast has implemented have been a key driver in our succession planning efforts. Several years ago, as we looked at our workforce and the trend toward consolidation of the industry, we recognized the need to develop a plan to "grow our own" in order to meet our talent needs, foster retention and ensure diversity in the management levels of the company. In an industry which has not been historically diverse in either gender or race, we wanted to create a method of training high potential talent and positioning them to move up through the ranks of senior management. Although we have opted not to restrict participation in any programs to a particular race or gender, a focus on diversity is woven into the selection process and we have been able to create a highly diverse group of graduates. Now, we look first to the graduates of our programs as we staff key roles.

Comcast is strongly committed to fostering a diverse, inclusive work environment. This commitment is reinforced in a variety of ways. One of the Comcast core values is diversity, and this is reinforced constantly as part of the overall Comcast Credo, our Corporate Promise and our Company Touchstones. We draw and analyze data on a regular basis to examine trends in recruitment, career development and retention. We are also an affirmative action employer, which allows us to analyze current data and set goals in each market to increase diversity in hiring and promotions. Goals have been set to mirror the overall market availability, and we dedicate efforts to ensuring that our sourcing, interviewing and succession planning practices support the ability to meet these goals.

In the last few years, Comcast has established two committees as part of its commitment to diversity.

The first committee is the **Diversity Council**. The council is responsible for meeting quarterly and reviewing the company's overall progress in terms of 1) employee diversity, 2) diversity programming, and 3) supplier diversity. The council takes a critical look at progress in these three areas of the business and discusses and outlines means of holding executives in all markets accountable for reaching certain milestones.

The following executives serve on this council:

- David L. Cohen, EVP, Comcast Corporation
- Stephen B. Burke, Chief Operating Officer, Comcast Corporation and President, Comcast Cable Communications, LLC
- Charisse R. Lillie, VP of Human Resources, Comcast Corporation and SVP, Human Resources, Comcast Cable Communications
- Karen Buchholz, VP of Administration, Comcast Corporation

• Payne Brown, VP of Outreach Strategies, Comcast Corporation
• Matt Bond, EVP of Programming, Comcast Cable Communications
• Amy Banse, Executive Vice President, Comcast Corporation
• Filemon Lopez, Regional Senior VP of Operations (Miami), Comcast Cable Communications
• D'Arcy Rudnay, VP of Corporate Communications , Comcast Corporation
• Charles Thurston, President , Comcast Advertising Sales, Comcast Cable Communications
• Dave Watson, Executive VP of Marketing and Customer Service, Comcast Cable Communications
• Joe Waz, VP External Affairs, Comcast Corporation

The second committee committed to diversity in the workplace is the **Diversity Communications Committee.** The mission of this committee is to identify field best practices as it relates to diversity in programming, suppliers and among employees. This group meets quarterly to share with each other progress being made in local markets relative to our outreach efforts. Another important responsibility for this group is to identify internal talent worthy of nomination for various industry publications and awards. It is important to note that Comcast does not "put itself out there" relative to bragging about its own. One of the tasks of this committee is to identify the diverse talent in the workforce and look for opportunities to showcase this talent through publications, panel discussions, speaking engagements and industry awards.

The following people serve on this committee:

• Suzanne Amarant, Public Relations Manager, Comcast Cable Communications
• Payne Brown, VP of Outreach Strategies, Comcast Corporation
• Mary Beth Casey, Manager of Employee Communications, Comcast Corporation
• Erica Eusebio, Communications Manager, Comcast Cable Communications
• Klay Fennel, VP of Government Affairs, Comcast Cable Communications
• Ana Gabriel, VP of Communications and Public Affairs, Comcast Corporation
• Susan Gonzales, Senior Director of Communications, Comcast Cable Communications
• Marc Goodman, Public Relations Manager, Comcast Cable Communications
• Deborah Grossman, Director of Supplier Diversity, Comcast Cable Communications
• Earle Jones, VP of National Affairs, Comcast Cable Communications
• Patricia Keenan, VP of Communications, Comcast Cable Communications
• Liza Merida, Director of International Communications, Comcast Cable Communications
• Elizabeth Morrison, Manager of Employee Communications, Comcast Cable Communications
• Melanie Penna, VP of Human Resources, Comcast Cable Communications
• Mary Pennington, Director of Recruiting, Comcast Cable Communications
• Patricia Rockenwagner, VP of Communications, Comcast Cable Communications
• Colleen Rooney, Senior Director Employee Communications, Comcast Corporation
• Melissa Volin, Manager of Corporate Communications, Comcast Corporation

In addition to our many HR efforts aimed at increasing diversity in our workforce, Comcast has a robust supplier diversity program.

Our program encompasses the following vendor categories:

> • Small Businesses
> • Small Disadvantaged Businesses
> • Minority Owned Businesses
> • Women Owned Businesses
> • Veteran Owned Businesses
> • Service Disabled Veteran Owned Businesses
> • HubZone Businesses

We believe strongly in providing equal opportunity to all vendors. We provide special assistance and mentoring to small and multicultural business owners in their pursuit of Comcast business.

In addition to educating our supplier base, we realize it is equally important to educate our employees about our commitment so that they can take the necessary steps to ensure that we are successful as a company. Since 2003, we have traveled across the country to train key decision makers on our supplier diversity mission. This training has been extremely effective in getting our employees involved in the program and in their communities. In 2004, we were able to increase our percent of spending with diversity businesses by 22% versus a year ago.

Our commitment to our multicultural business community has been acknowledged through several awards and recognitions:

• Comcast was ranked as one of the top 50 corporations for multicultural business opportunities by DiversityBusiness.com, the largest organization of women and minority-owned businesses throughout the United States with more than 27,000 members. Also known as the Div50, the honor recognizes the top 50 corporate buyers of diversity products and services throughout the country. Over 350,000 women and minority-owned businesses (Blacks, Hispanics, Asians, Native Indian and other minority groups) had the opportunity to vote in the 2004 online election based on such factors as the volume, consistency and quality of business opportunities granted to women and minority-owned companies. In Comcast's first year on the list, it is ranked number 37 out of the 50 corporations recognized.

• Comcast was named one of the Top 10 Companies for Supplier Diversity by DiversityInc Magazine, and listed among the 25 Notable Companies for Diversity. In the survey's fifth year, it remains the only in-depth analysis of corporate diversity, compiling a substantial and valid metrics that assesses diversity success nationally. DiversityInc's Top 50 Companies for Diversity honors the top 50 out of the 203 participating companies, dedicated to diversity in four main categories: human capital, CEO commitment, corporate communications and supplier diversity. The 200+ question survey is also the basis for subsequent top 10 lists, including the Top 10 Companies for Supplier Diversity. In Comcast's first year participating in the survey, it is listed among the 25 Notable Companies for Diversity, and ranked number seven in the list of the top 10 companies recognized for supplier diversity.

• Comcast was presented with the Done Deals Award from the Women's Business Development Council of PA-NJ-DE on April 13, 2005. The award recognizes the Council member who has the highest number of actual deals and the highest amount of spend with the WBEC PA/NJ/DE WBENC certified women business enterprises for 2004.

• While we are very proud of our accomplishments, we know that there is still more to do to be among the best-in-class. To ensure continuous improvement, we implemented a Supplier Diversity Scorecard across all of our divisions beginning in January, 2005. This scorecard benchmarks past performance, actual year-to-date performance and goal achievement. Our divisions each sets goals and are being monitored to ensure they meet or exceed those goals.

ConAgra Foods

1 ConAgra Dr.
Omaha, NE 68102-5001
Phone: (402) 595-4000
Fax: (402) 595-4707
www.conagrafoods.com

Diversity Leadership
Staffing Support Team, College Recruiting

Employment Contact
One ConAgra Drive 1-252
Omaha, NE 68102
Phone: (402) 595.4000
Fax: (402) 595.4707

Recruiting

Please list the schools/types of schools at which you recruit.

• Other private schools: too numerous to list
• Public state schools: too numerous to list
• Historically Black Colleges and Universities (HBCUs): Xavier New Orleans, NCA&T, Howard
• Hispanic Serving Institutions (HSIs): UTEP

Do you have any special outreach efforts that are directed to encourage minority students to consider your firm?

• Conferences: Black MBA, Hispanic MBA, NHBA, Women's MBA, INROADS, MANRRS, Urban League, etc
• Participate in/host minority student job fair(s)
• Sponsor minority student association events
• Firm's employees participate on career panels at school
• Outreach to leadership of minority student organizations
• Scholarships or intern/fellowships for minority students

What activities does the firm undertake to attract minority and women employees?

• Partner programs with women and minority associations
• Conferences: see above
• Participate at minority job fairs
• Seek referrals from other employees
• Utilize online job services

Internships and Co-ops

INROADS

Deadline for application: April
Pay: Varies

Length of the program: Varies

Web site for internship/co-op information: www.conagrafoods.com

Strategic Plan and Diversity Leadership

Who has primary responsibility for leading diversity initiatives at your firm?

Vivian Ayuso, Diversity Director

Does your firm currently have a diversity committee?

Yes

If yes, does the committee's representation include one or more members of the firm's management/executive committee (or the equivalent)?

Yes

Does the committee and/or diversity leader establish and set goals or objectives consistent with management's priorities?

Yes

Has the firm undertaken a formal or informal diversity program or set of initiatives aimed at increasing the diversity of the firm?

Yes, formal

The Stats

Employees: 40,000 (2004, worldwide)
Revenue: $12 billion (2004, worldwide)

Retention and Professional Development

How do 2004 minority and female attrition rates generally compare to those experienced in the prior year period?

About the same as in prior years

Please identify the specific steps you are taking to reduce the attrition rate of minority and women employees.

• Develop and/or support internal employee affinity groups (e.g., minority or women networks within the firm)
• Increase/review compensation relative to competition
• Increase/improve current work/life programs
• Succession plan includes emphasis on diversity
• Strengthen mentoring program for all employees, including minorities and women
• Professional skills development program, including minority and women employees

Consolidated Edison Company of New York, Inc.

4 Irving Place
New York, NY 10003
Phone: (212) 460-4600
Fax: (212) 477-2536
Toll Free: (800) 752-6633
www.coned.com

Diversity Leadership
Contact Person: Matteo Dobrini, Senior Analyst
Joan Jacobs, Director, Equal Employment
Opportunity Affairs (EEOA)

Employment Contact
Diversity Campus Recruiting Team Leader
Crystal Wilson-Jackson, Section Manager,
Recruitment
4 Irving Place
New York, NY 10003
Phone: (212) 460-4434
Fax: (212) 677-5524

Recruiting

Please list the schools/types of schools at which you recruit.

- *Ivy League schools:* Columbia University, Cornell University, University of Pennsylvania
- *Other private schools:* Boston University, Clark Atlanta University, Cooper Union, Drexel University, Fordham University, Lafayette College, Lehigh University, Manhattan College, Marist College, New York Institute of Technology, New York University, Pace University, Polytechnic University, Rensselaer Polytechnic Institute, Stevens Institute of Technology, St. John's University
- *Public state schools:* Baruch College, City College of New York, Florida A&M University, Morgan State University, N e w Jersey Institute of Technology, Rutgers University, SUNY Albany, SUNY Maritime, University of Buffalo
- *Historically Black Colleges and Universities (HBCUs):* Clark Atlanta University, Florida A&M University, Morgan State University
- *Hispanic Serving Institutions (HSIs):* City College of New York

Do you have any special outreach efforts that are directed to encourage minority students to consider your firm?

- Conferences: American Association of Blacks in Energy (AABE), ASPIRA (Latino Youth), Asian American Business
- Development Center (AABDC), African American Female Executives (AAFE), Asian Women in Business (AWIB); One Hundred Black Men, Inc.
- Advertise in minority student association publication(s)
- Participate in/host minority student job fair(s)
- Sponsor minority student association events
- Firm's employees participate on career panels at school
- Outreach to leadership of minority student organizations
- Scholarships or intern/fellowships for minority students

What activities does the firm undertake to attract minority and women employees?

- Partner programs with women and minority associations: NEW, AABE, Society of Women Engineers, Society of Hispanic Professional Engineers
- Participate at minority job fairs
- Seek referrals from other employees

• Utilize online job services

Do you use executive recruiting/search firms to seek to identify new diversity hires?

Yes

If yes, list all women- and/or minority-owned executive search/recruiting firms to which the firm paid a fee for placement services in the past 12 months:

Buckner & Associate, Regional Alliance for Small Contractors' Clearinghouse

Internships and Co-ops

High School Weekly Co-op Program

Number of interns in the program in summer 2004 (co-op): 11
Web site for internship/co-op information: www.coned.com

Con Edison continues to provide New York City high school students with a variety of work experiences that add another dimension to the technical skills they learn in the classroom. Through the High School Weekly Co-op program, students benefit from career development information, teamwork experiences and skills development.

In 2004, 11 students, including six minorities (54.5 percent) and three women (27.3 percent), were participants. Eight of the co-op students were employed by Brooklyn/Queens Electric Operations and held positions that were engineering-/computer-related, and three held manual labor positions at the Hudson Avenue Generating Station. In the past five years, 78 students have participated in the program, of whom 51 (65.4 percent) were minorities, and 12 (15.4 percent) were women.

Co-op Intern Program

Number of interns in the program in summer 2004 (internship) or 2004 (co-op): 32
Web site for internship/co-op information: www.coned.com

The Co-op Intern program invites college students, many of whom had previously worked for the company as summer interns, to supplement their studies with hands-on work during the school year.

In 2004, of this program's 32 participants, 16 were minorities (50.0 percent), and four were women (12.5 percent). In the past five years, 239 students have participated in the program, including 138 minorities (57.7 percent) and 70 women (29.3 percent).

Summer Intern Program

Number of interns in the program in summer 2004 (internship): 56
Web site for internship/co-op information: www.coned.com

Con Edison's Summer Intern Program provides high school and college students with work experiences that help them bring textbook knowledge to real-world settings and gain an understanding of the way we work at Con Edison. With this program, Con Edison identifies students who demonstrate high energy, strong intellect, and a genuine thirst for learning, and who, upon graduation from college, may qualify as candidates for the company's Growth Opportunities for Leadership Development (GOLD) program. Students must be involved in the study of engineering, environmental science or business, such as accounting or finance.

In 2004, 56 interns participated in the program; 32 were minorities (57.1 percent), and 21 were women (37.5 percent). This year, the program attained the second-highest percentage (57.1 percent) of minorities in the last five years. Since 2000, 52.8 percent of all participants were minorities, and 36.6 percent were women.

Scholarships

Con Edison Scholarship Program

Deadline for application for the scholarship program: November 12
Scholarship award amount: $2,500 per student for 10 students – for entire scholarship
Web site or other contact information for scholarship: for Con Edison employees only – internal website

The Scholarship & Recognition Program, a nonprofit organization, administers this program.

Thurgood Marshall Scholarship Fund (TMSF)

Scholarship award amount: $10,000 per student for 2 students – for entire scholarship

The TMSF is the only national organization that awards four-year merit scholarships, programmatic and capacity building support to 45 Historically Black Public Colleges and Universities and the students who attend them. Con Edison supports this fund and the two scholarships are named for Con Edison and are for minority students majoring in the physical sciences and/or engineering.

The United Negro College Fund (UNCF)

Scholarship award amount: $5,000 per student for 3 students – for entire scholarship

The UNCF is the nation's oldest and most successful higher education assistance organization. The Con Edison Scholarship is awarded to students who are majoring in the fields of accounting, computer science, electrical, mechanical or nuclear engineering. This program fosters long-term relationships among the corporation, the students and the participating institutions. It increases student interest in the corporation and ultimately enlarges the pool of prospective minority employees.

The Hundred Year Association of New York

Scholarship award amount: $3,000 per student for 2 students – for entire scholarship

This program offers scholarships to the sons and daughters of career city employees. Con Edison has participated in this program since 1994. The selection committee receives 150 applications from diverse high school seniors each year and selections are based on scholastic achievement, leadership, commitment and community service.

CUNY Program for the Retention of Engineering Students (PRES)

This program was established in 1987 to provide academic support and guidance to underrepresented minorities and women in the engineering field, thereby reducing attrition. PRES currently serves more than 550 students and continues to effectively increase the performance of minority engineering students. Con Edison supports this program with an annual grant of $10,000.

Affinity Groups/Employee Networks

American Association of Blacks in Energy (AABE)

AABE is a national association of energy professionals founded and dedicated to ensure the input of African Americans and other minorities into the discussions and developments of energy policies regulations, R&D technologies and environmental issues.
aabe-nymac.org/home.html

Improve Continuously Committee (ICC)

This newly formed Con Edison group represents Lesbians, Gays, Bisexual and Transgender (LGBT) employees. ICC meets on a monthly basis to discuss providing opportunities for employee networks and mentoring. They also raise diversity awareness, share experiences and promote personal and professional growth.

Entry-Level Programs/Full-Time Opportunities

Growth Opportunities for Leadership Development (GOLD)

Length of program: 18 months
Geographic location(s) of program: New York

Please describe the training/training component of this program: This program develops high-caliber college graduates for positions of increasing responsibility and leadership within the company during the course of an 18-month period. Through a series of practical, rotational job assignments, mentoring and senior-management guidance, GOLD program participants tackle challenging supervisory and project-based jobs that provide valuable work experience and insight into Con Edison's practices and operations. Upon successful completion of the program, participants are poised to advance into Con Edison's management ranks. In the past four years, we have hired 51 GOLD associates who had previously participated in the Co-op and/or Summer Intern Programs.

The program continues to be successful in recruiting and retaining minorities and women. In 2004, it enabled 38 college graduates, 20 of whom were minorities (52.6 percent) and 16 of whom were women (42.1 percent), to begin careers at Con Edison. In the past five years, 232 GOLD associates have participated in the program, including 127 minorities (54.7 percent) and 84 women (36.2 percent).

Over the past five years, 76.7 percent of our GOLD program employees have remained with the company. Significantly, 76.4 percent of the minority participants and 78.6 percent of the women participants are continuing their careers at Con Edison. Such retention rates are solid signs of a successful program.

Tools for Employees Advancing into Management (TEAM)

Length of program: Approximately 12 months
Geographic location(s) of program: New York

Please describe the training/training component of this program: The TEAM Program is a developmental experience designed to provide recently promoted union employees with the tools necessary to make a successful transition into a management role. The program's goal is to develop the participants into quality supervisors or individual contributors.

Tuition Aid Program

Length of program: As long as the employee is going to college
Geographic location(s) of program: New York

Please describe the training/training component of this program: The Tuition Aid program continues to be a noteworthy feature of Con Edison's benefit package. The program offers reimbursement to eligible employees who pursue courses or programs that maintain or improve their present career skills. Upon the successful completion of a degree, the employee is provided with up to 100 percent reimbursement of tuition costs.

In 2004, 381 employees participated in the program; more than half of the participants were minorities, and 26.5 percent were women. Sixty-one employees received college degrees through this program in 2004; and in the previous four years, 310 employees received their degrees through this program.

Strategic Plan and Diversity Leadership

How does the firm's leadership communicate the importance of diversity to everyone at the firm?

Con Edison's commitment to diversity is reaffirmed in the Chairman's annual message that is mailed to every employee in the company. Following is that message:

Chairman's Message

TO: All Employees
FROM: Eugene R. McGrath, Chairman of the Board
DATE: June 30, 2005
SUBJECT: Reaffirmation of Our Commitment to Equal Employment Opportunity and Affirmative Action

At Con Edison, we have long supported the principles of Equal Employment Opportunity and Affirmative Action. At a time when rapid change has become a constant in our lives, we acknowledge and reaffirm that these enduring values are integral to the foundation of our society, our workplaces, and our communities. Con Edison's commitment to these principles is reflected in our diverse workforce, which is one of our greatest strengths.

We recognize that the men and women of Con Edison are the company's most valuable resource, and our company's success depends on how effectively we develop and utilize this valuable resource. In today's competitive environment, we must encourage and nurture the talent of the diverse individuals who come to Con Edison as productive and creative members of our workforce. Therefore, we remain dedicated to maintaining an environment that is free of discrimination and a workplace where all employees are afforded the opportunity to develop, perform, and advance to their maximum potential without regard to race, color, religion, gender, age, national origin, marital status, sexual orientation, citizenship, or disability; nor will such decisions be made based on Vietnam-Era, special disabled, and/or other qualified veteran status.

Our commitment to these principles is set forth in further detail in Corporate Policy Statement 500-4 (EEO Policy), 500-12 (Employment of Individuals with Disabilities and Veterans' Policy), and 500-14 (Sexual Harassment Policy), which complement our Standards of Business Conduct. I encourage you to reread these policies, as it is every employee's job to do their share in maintaining a workplace that is free of discrimination, harassment, and retaliation. Fulfilling this obligation means that we must promptly report any such behavior to the Corporate EEOA office, a supervisor with immediate or higher authority, or your Human Resource representative. You may also report violations using the EEO complaint line, 212-460.1065, or the complaint form on the EEO website (intranet/eeo). All complaints will be promptly investigated, and employees who are found to have violated our EEO polices are subject to discipline, up to and including termination.

Con Edison vigorously promotes and stands behind its EEO policies. Industry analysts have consistently recognized us for an outstanding EEO/diversity record. Sustaining and enhancing that record will help us attract and retain good employees, provide the best service to our customers, and achieve our full potential as a responsible and competitive company.

In addition to the Chairman's message, Con Edison sends out occasional e-mails to remind employees about the importance of diversity to all of us. We also post diversity messages on our elevator screens and bulletin boards at all our company locations. Finally, we encourage all employees to visit our internal EEOA website, which contains information regarding the importance of diversity.

Who has primary responsibility for leading diversity initiatives at your firm?

Joan Jacobs, Director, Equal Employment Opportunity Affairs (EEOA)

Does your firm currently have a diversity committee?

No

Does the diversity leader establish and set goals or objectives consistent with management's priorities?

Yes

Has the firm undertaken a formal or informal diversity program or set of initiatives aimed at increasing the diversity of the firm?

Yes, formal

How often does the firm's management review the firm's diversity progress/results?

Monthly

How is the firm's diversity firm management held accountable for achieving results?

It is reflected in the diversity director's performance review.

The Stats

DEMOGRAPHIC PROFILE	TOTAL IN THE U.S.		TOTAL OUTSIDE THE U.S		TOTAL WORLDWIDE	
	2004	2003	2004	2003	2004	2003
Number of employees	12,672	12,604	0	0	12,672	12,604
Revenues	$8 billion	$8.2 billion	0	0	$8 billion	$8.2 billion

Retention and Professional Development

How do 2004 minority and female attrition rates generally compare to those experienced in the prior year period?

About the same as in prior years

Please identify the specific steps you are taking to reduce the attrition rate of minority and women employees.

• Succession plan includes emphasis on diversity
• Work with minority and women employees to develop career advancement plans
• Strengthen mentoring program for all employees, including minorities and women
• Professional skills development program, including minority and women employees

Diversity Mission Statement

As our industry and our workforce continue to evolve in the new marketplace, we face challenges in maintaining and expanding our role as an industry leader and an employer of choice. To that end, our diverse workforce will continue to be one of our greatest strengths.

Con Edison has a longstanding commitment to the principles of equal employment opportunity and affirmative action, not just because it is a good business practice, but also because it is the right thing to do. Indeed, our company's success is tied to how effectively we develop and maximize the potential of our most valuable resources – the men and women of Con Edison.

At Con Edison, employment and personnel decisions, including hiring, job assignments, promotions and compensation are based on ability and merit, without regard for race, color, religion, gender, age, national origin, disability, marital status, sexual orientation, citizenship or military service status. In today's business world, workplace diversity and business accomplishment go hand in hand and we regard Con Edison's commitment to diversity as a key element in our company's ongoing success.

Our Equal Employment Opportunity (EEO) policies set forth our commitment to these principles. Maintaining a workplace free of discrimination is an integral part of each employee's job. Each of us must contribute to a safe, productive and harmonious work environment, and we must respect every individual's dignity and well-being.

Our compliance with these policies is one of our most effective means of attracting and retaining highly qualified employees, providing the best service to our customers, and achieving our full potential as a responsible, concerned and competitive company.

The Employer Says

The company's recruitment office continued to strengthen its relationship with Nontraditional Employment for Women (NEW), an organization that works to train and secure employment for women in trades. In 2004, The Con Edison Learning Center, the size of a small community college, is a place where skilled, professional instructors conduct courses in leadership and management development and in highly specialized fields ranging from electric systems to environmental compliance. The center provided hands-on training for 118 women enrolled with NEW, who learned basic electricity, carpentry, plumbing and math, and who were provided with an introduction to transmission and distribution systems. Since 2000, Con Edison has recruited 28 women from NEW, of whom 19 are still employed by the company. Of those, 16 hold the title of general utility worker, two are customer field representatives and one is a customer service representative. As hiring opportunities arise, NEW graduates will continue to be considered for employment opportunities.

In 2004, the recruitment office re-established a partnership with Access for Women, a program sponsored by the New York City College of Technology. Access for Women serves women preparing for two-year and four-year degrees in such nontraditional technical fields as construction, building trades and engineering technologies. Graduates of the program will be considered for employment opportunities.

Con Edison participated in several job fairs in 2004 that enabled us to meet a diverse pool of qualified potential applicants. These included the Careerbuilder Diversity Career Fair, sponsored by MSN Latino; iVillage; and BlackAmericaweb, held at the Metropolitan Pavilion in New York City, as well as the New York City Department of Education Alternative School Job Fair; the New York State Department of Labor and NYC Human Resources Administration Job Fair; and Careers and the Disabled Magazine Job Fair. In addition, Con Edison attended career fairs held at colleges sponsored by organizations that advocate for diversity, including the Society of Women Engineers, at Cornell University; the National Society of Black Engineers, at Drexel University; the National Society of Black Engineers and the Society of Hispanic Professional Engineers, at Rensselaer Polytechnic Institute; and the Professional Advancement of Black Chemists and Chemical Engineers, at Florida A&M University. Con Edison also participated in career fairs at historically black universities, including Atlanta University, Florida A & M University and Morgan State University.

In 2004, Con Edison placed various print ads in ethnic newspapers, including El Diario, African Abroad, Chinese World and Sing Tao.

Additional information regarding entry-level and full-time opportunities: Con Edison offers a variety of programs geared to assist all employees, including minorities and women, in mastering their job functions, advancing their careers and furthering their education. Classes and presentations are held at Con Edison's Learning Center, a multimillion-dollar facility, devoted to providing employees with practical training and personal development courses.

Whether it is training new customer service representatives or upgrading the skills of field workers, The Learning Center staff works closely with operating departments to develop training programs that enable us to maintain our system, run more effective operations, improve customer service and nurture employee leadership skills. Courses are provided in electric, gas and steam systems; customer operations; environment, health and safety information technology; and leadership. Additionally, Strategic Issues Seminars are designed to help employees gain the leadership skills necessary to run the Con Edison of tomorrow. These seminars are held frequently and cover a wide-range of topics. Con Edison is also a corporate member of the Institute for Management Studies and the American Management Association, where employees can find classes and seminars covering many different topics. The company also provides Web-based, self-study programs that employees are able to take at their convenience. The programs offered at The Learning Center are available to all employees and are particularly useful to individuals who may need to advance their skill level or want to try a new career path.

Con Edison has received the following corporate and individual awards in the past three years

2004

- *Fortune* magazine's "50 Best Companies for Minorities"
- *Hispanic* magazine's Corporate 100 List
- "The *LATINA Style* Top 50"
- *DiversityInc*'s "Top 50 Companies for Diversity"
- Asian American Business Development Center's "Outstanding 50 Asian Americans in Business"
- Leadership Institute for African American Female Executives
- Top 10 Queens Women in Business
- *The Network Journal* magazine's "25 Influential Black Women in Business"

2003

- *Fortune* magazine's "50 Best Companies for Minorities"
- "The *LATINA Style* Top 50"
- *Hispanic* magazine's "Corporate 100"
- Westchester County Press Award – for our commitment to hiring minorities and women
- Women's Enterprise Development Center Award
- American Society of Mechanical Engineers "Charles T. Main Gold Medal"
- YWCA's Academy of Women Achievers
- YMCA's Black Achievers program

2002

- *Fortune* magazine's "50 Best Companies for Minorities"
- "The *LATINA Style* Top 50"
- *ExecutiveFEMALE* magazine's "Top 25 Companies for Executive Women"
- National Puerto Rican Forum's "Amigo de NPRF Award"
- New York/New Jersey Minority Purchasing Council's "Regional Corporation of the Year"
- Brooklyn Council of the Boy Scouts of America "Women of Achievement Award"
- YWCA's Academy of Women Achievers
- YMCA's Black Achievers program
- Career Communications Group, Inc. Women of Color in Technology Award, "Rising Star in Technology"
- Career Communications Group, Inc. Women of Color in Technology Award, "Technology All-Star"

The following are organizations with diversity initiative programs that received Con Edison support in 2004

100 Hispanic Women, Inc.; Abyssinian Development Corporation; African American Men of Westchester; African Voices Communications, Inc.; Agudath Israel of America; American Association of Blacks in Energy ; American Civil Rights Education Services; Asian American Business Development Center; Asian American Federation of New York; Asian American Legal Defense and Education Fund; Asian Americans for Equality, Inc.; Asian Professional Extension, Inc.; Asian Women in Business; Asociación Puertorriqueña & Hermanos, Inc.; ASPIRA of New York, Inc.; Associated Black Charities; Association of Minority Enterprises of New York; AYUDA for the Arts; Ballet Hispanico of New York; Barnard College; Brooklyn Chinese-American Association, Inc.; Caribbean American Chamber of Commerce and Industry, Inc; Casita Maria, Inc.; Catalyst; Centro de Estudios Puertorriqueños; Chinese-American Planning Council, Inc.; Coalition of Asian Pacific Americans; Committee for Hispanic Children and Families, Inc.; Congressional Black Caucus Foundation, Inc.; Council of Jewish Organizations of Flatbush, Inc.; Dominican American National Roundtable; Dominican Foundation; Dominican Women's Development Center, Inc.; El Carnaval del Boulevard; El Museo del Barrio; Foundation for Ethnic Understanding, Inc.; Girls Incorporated of New York City; Girl Scout Council of Greater New York, Inc; GRADS Foundation, Inc; Hispanic Federation of New York City, Inc.; Hispanic Women Leaders of Westchester, Inc. ; Hong Kong Dragon Boat Festival in New York, Inc.; Institute for the Puerto Rican/Hispanic Elderly; Instituto Arte Teatral Internacional, Inc.; International Agency for Minority Artist Affairs, Inc.; Jewish Children's Museum; Jewish Community Relations Council of New York, Inc.; Jewish Museum; Korean-American Counseling Center, Inc.; Latino Civic Association, Inc.; Latino Commission on AIDS; Latino Gerontological Center; Latino Job Service Employer Committee; League of Women Voters of the City of New York; League of Women Voters of Westchester; Lewis H. Latimer Fund, Inc.; Martin Luther

King Jr. Concert Series, Inc.; Metropolitan Black Bar Association; Metropolitan Jewish Geriatric Foundation; Museum of Chinese in the Americas; Musica de Camara, Inc.; NAACP; NAACP ACT-SO Coalition of NYC Branches; NAACP Legal Defense and Education Fund; National Action Council for Minorities in Engineering; National Association for Female Executives Women's Foundation; National Association of Hispanic Journalists; National Council of Jewish Women, Inc.; National Hispanic Business Group; National Puerto Rican Forum, Inc; National Urban Fellows, Inc.; New York Coalition of 100 Black Women; New York State Assembly/Senate Puerto Rican/Hispanic Task Force; New York State Association of Black and Puerto Rican Legislators, Inc.; New York State Federation of Hispanic Chambers of Commerce; New York Women's Agenda; Northern Manhattan Coalition for Economic Development; One Hundred Black Men, Inc.; Organization of Chinese Americans – Westchester & Hudson Valley Chapter; Professional Women in Construction; Puerto Rican Bar Association Scholarship Fund, Inc.; Puerto Rican Family Institute, Inc.; Puerto Rican Legal Defense and Education Fund; Puerto Rican Traveling Theatre Company; Redhawk Indian Arts Council; Repertorio Español; Russian Ethnic Bilingual Educational and Cultural Association; San Juan Fiesta/Archdiocese of NY – Office of Hispanic Affairs; Sociedad Puertorriqueña de Queens, Inc.; Society of Hispanic Professional Engineers; Society of the Educational Arts, Inc./SEA; Teatro Circulo, Ltd; Thalia Spanish Theatre, Inc.; Tomchei Torah Chaim Birnbaum; Trey Whitfield Foundation Inc; United Negro College Fund; University of the West Indies; West Indian-American Day Carnival Association, Inc.; Wien House (YWHA); Women in Communications and Energy; Women In Need, Inc.; Women's City Club of New York, Inc.; Women's League of Science and Medicine, Inc.; Women's Research and Education Fund; Yeshiva University Museum; YWCA

173

Convergys Corporation

201 E. 4th St.
Cincinnati, OH 45202
Phone: (513) 723-7000
Fax: (513) 421-8624
Toll Free: (800) 344-3000
www.convergys.com/turnyourfutureon

Locations (worldwide)
Cincinnati, OH (headquarters); other
offices throughout the U.S. and the world

Diversity Leadership
Anthony Jones, Diversity Director
Diversity Campus Recruiting Team Leader:
Rebecca Face, College Relations Director

Employment Contact
Rebecca Face, College Relations Director
201 East 4th Street
Cincinnati, OH 45201
Phone: (513) 784-5501
E-mail: rebecca.face@Convergys.com

Recruiting

Please list the schools/types of schools at which you recruit.

• Ivy League schools
• Other private schools
• Public state schools
• Historically Black Colleges and Universities (HBCUs)
• Hispanic Serving Institutions (HSIs)

See below for specific schools at which we recruit:
• Bowling Green State University
• Brigham Young University
• Carnegie Mellon University
• Florida A&M
• Florida International University
• Florida State University
• Georgia State University
• Georgia Tech
• Miami University of Ohio
• Northern Kentucky University
• Ohio State University
• Ohio University
• Purdue University
• Rochester Institute of Technology
• Stanford University
• Tulane
• University of Central Florida
• University of Cincinnati
• University of Dayton
• University of Florida
• University of Georgia
• University of Kentucky

- University of Michigan
- University of North Florida
- University of Utah
- Weber State University
- Xavier University
- Yale University

Do you have any special outreach efforts that are directed to encourage minority students to consider your firm?

- Hold a reception for minority students
- Conferences
- Advertise in minority student association publication(s)
- Participate in/host minority student job fair(s)
- Sponsor minority student association events
- Firm's employees participate on career panels at school
- Outreach to leadership of minority student organizations
- Scholarships or intern/fellowships for minority students
- **Other:** Host a Women in Technology Conference; sit on affiliate boards (BDPA, for example)

What activities does the firm undertake to attract minority and women employees?

- Partner programs with women and minority associations
- Conferences
- Participate at minority job fairs
- Seek referrals from other employees
- Utilize online job services
- Other: Host a Women in Technology Conference

Internships and Co-ops

Convergys Internships in various Resource Units

Deadline for application: March 15th

Number of interns in the program in summer 2004 (internship) or 2004 (co-op): 60

Pay: $9-$18 per hour

Length of the program: 12 weeks

Percentage of interns/co-ops in the program who receive offers of full-time employment: 70%

Web site for internship/co-op information: www.convergys.com/turnyourfutureon

Convergys supports full-time summer internships and part-time year round internships in various locations, with Jacksonville, Florida, Orlando, Florida, Cincinnati, Ohi, and Itasca, Illinois being the primary locations of hiring activity.

We focus on IT/IS, accounting/finance, business, marketing and HR as disciplines of choice for the majority of our college hiring (full-time or interns).

We support the INROADS program as a national account.

Scholarships

Scholarships are offered at the following schools through the university scholarship program – do not contact Convergys. We also offer scholarships to selected INROADS interns throughout Convergys.

- Xavier University
- Ohio State
- Carnegie Mellon
- University of Cincinatti
- University of Michigan
- University of Central Florida
- University of Illinois
- University of Utah
- Brigham Young
- Miami of Ohio
- Bowling Green
- Purdue
- Florida State University
- Florida A&M University
- Georgia Tech

Affinity Groups/Employee Networks

Global Women's Network

Convergys has a global network for women that meets quarterly and various local site chapters that meet monthly or quarterly.

Entry-Level Programs/Full-Time Opportunities

Management Training Program

Length of program: 12 – 15 months
Geographic location(s) of program: US and Canada

Please describe the training/training component of this program: Management Trainees participate in hands-on experiential learning in multiple business unit programs from the Agent level to the Senior Operations manager. They also spend time in Resource Units such as Human Resources, Facilities and Operations Support. The workplace setting is complemented by additional contact center-related courses of study.

Strategic Plan and Diversity Leadership

How does the firm's leadership communicate the importance of diversity to everyone at the firm?

Company Corporate Communications, Organizational Development, Community Action Teams, Office of Diversity communications – e-mail, company intranet, desk-drops, Web

Who has primary responsibility for leading diversity initiatives at your firm?

Office of Diversity (Anthony Jones – Director of Diversity)

Does your firm currently have a diversity committee?

Yes.

• Diversity Steering Committee – comprised of most senior officers (CEO, CFO, etc.) and meets annually
• Business Unit Diversity Council – comprised of representatives from the business unit and chaired by business unit leader. Meets once per month.
• Corporate Diversity Council – comprised of representatives from corporate, chaired by Senior VP, Human Resources. Meets once per month.

If yes, does the committee's representation include one or more members of the firm's management/executive committee (or the equivalent)?

Yes

Does the committee and/or diversity leader establish and set goals or objectives consistent with management's priorities?

Yes

Has the firm undertaken a formal or informal diversity program or set of initiatives aimed at increasing the diversity of the firm?

Yes, formal

The Stats

Employees: 66,000 (2004, worldwide)
Employees: 50,000 (2003, worldwide)
Revenue: $2.5 billion (2004, worldwide)
Revenue: $2.3 billion (2003, worldwide)

Diversity Mission Statement

Diversity Principles

Through Convergys' diversity initiatives, we will establish and maintain an environment that:

• Values individual differences
• Fosters consistent, mutual respect and open communication of ideas
• Attracts, develops, supports, and retains a diverse workforce with the ability to compete in the global market
• Increases our competitive advantage by leveraging the knowledge, skills and unique talents of our employees
• Enhances career opportunities for all employees by working to develop each employee to his or her full potential
• Provides a richer, more fertile climate for creative thinking and innovation
• Is recognized by employees, clients and the community as a fair and rewarding place to work.

The Employer Says

For diversity, Convergys takes an all-company, all-employee approach. From the CEO and his direct reports, to the customer service agents on the phone, we all have responsibilities and accountabilities to ourselves, our teams, our clients and their customers. Our Office of Diversity is aligned with our business units' objectives as they pertain to client satisfaction and employee satisfaction. The office continually partners with our executives to maintain maximum alignment with business unit initiatives. Our approach is internal education, awareness and programs of choice, and our external message is clear and concise: "Diversity at Convergys is viewed as a continuous process. Cultivating a systemic approach to diversity ensures that we look at our employees, systems, policies, practices, and behaviors to capitalize on our success. Our unique differences are the lifeline of our company."

Credit Suisse First Boston

11 Madison Avenue
New York, NY 10010
Phone: 212-538-2594
Fax: 212-538-2594
Web site address for diversity:
www.csfb.com

Diversity Leadership
Tanji Dewberry, Assistant Vice President (also
Diversity Campus Recruiting Team Leader)
E-mail: tanji.dewberry@csfb.com

Recruiting

Please list the schools/types of schools at which you recruit.

• Ivy League schools
• Public state schools
• Private schools
• Historically Black Colleges and Universities (HBCUs)
• Hispanic Serving Institutions (HSIs)
• Other predominantly minority and/or women's colleges

Do you have any special outreach efforts that are directed to encourage minority students to consider your firm?

• Hold a reception for minority students
• Conferences
• Advertise in minority student association publication: National Association of Black Accountants newsletter, Howard School of Business newspaper
• Participate in/host minority student job fairs
• Sponsor minority student association events
• Firm's professionals participate on career panels at school
• Outreach to leadership of minority student organizations
• Scholarships or intern/fellowships for minority students

What activities does the firm undertake to attract women and minorities?

• Partner programs with women and minority business associations
• Conferences
• Participate at minority job fairs
• Seek referrals from other professionals
• Utilize online job services
• Market jobs to alumni networks of educational nonprofits

Do you use executive recruiting/search firms to seek to identify new diversity hires?

Yes

Internships

Summer Analyst - Corporate Investment Banking

Web site for information on all internships: www.csfb.com/standout
Deadline for application for the internship: December
Length of the program: 10 weeks

Our 10-week Summer Analyst Program for rising college seniors gives you outstanding exposure to business and the financial services industry.

Whether you're working alongside a full-time analyst or staffed as the only analyst on a deal team, our summer program gives you the tools you'll need to jump-start your career in finance and investment banking. Responsibilities may include analyzing companies using financial modeling and valuation techniques, examining the impact of a transaction on a client's capital structure and analyzing the consequences of a merger or acquisition.

Summer analysts will be placed directly into an industry or product group – in 2004, 100% of summer analysts received their first or second choice of groups. As a summer program participant, you will have the opportunity to work on deals in your group, gaining hands-on experience and working on all aspects of advising and transacting business for our clients. Summer analysts are formally reviewed at the mid and end points of the summer, and offers are made on the last day of the program, enabling you to return to school with a full-time position secured.

Summer analyst opportunities are available in New York, Chicago, Houston, Toronto, Los Angeles, Palo Alto and San Francisco. Our U.S. regional breadth offers unique opportunities to execute transactions from conception to close, which differentiates CSFB from our competitors.

Training: You'll attend a brief company orientation and a 7-day training program and then start work in your group for the summer, receiving further training while on the job.

Your learning experience will continue through the summer speaker series, where you'll hear from senior employees across the divisions. In addition, you'll participate in networking events and firm-wide events that will help ensure that you are exposed to all the areas within the bank and understand the big picture of a global investment bank. You'll also enjoy interacting with the other summer analysts and full-time employees at a variety of social events throughout the summer. To help you determine your strengths and plan your career, summer analysts are matched with junior and senior mentors within Investment Banking, who provide advice and guidance throughout the summer.

Summer Analyst - Fixed Income or Equity Sales & Trading

Deadline for application for the internship: December
Length of the program: 10 weeks

The CSFB Securities Division offers two separate, 10-week summer programs – one in Equity Sales and Trading and one in Fixed Income Sales and Trading. If chosen for a first-round interview, students will interview for BOTH the Equity sales and trading and the Fixed Income sales and trading programs – please only drop your resume once for these programs. Second round interviews are held separately and will be Equity specific or Fixed Income specific. This will be determined based on your first round interviews. In both programs, you'll spend one week in training, followed by three separate three-week rotations on either Fixed Income or Equity desks.

• Sales Rotation – You'll spend three weeks working within one sales product area. In Equity, this rotation will give you the chance to work with the Coverage Sales, Portfolio Sales, International Sales, Convertible Sales or Derivative sales teams. In Fixed Income, you'll work with the Corporate, Structured Products, Interest Rates, Global Foreign Exchange, Emerging Markets, CDO Group or Derivatives sales teams.

• Trading Rotation – You'll spend three weeks working within one trading product area. In Fixed Income, these groups include the Corporate, Structured Products, Interest Rates, Global Foreign Exchange, Emerging Markets or Interest Rate

Products trading teams. In Equity, it will include the Cash Trading, Derivative Trading, Program Trading, International Sales Trading and Exchange Traded Funds teams.

• Sales or Trading Rotation – You'll spend your final three weeks on one of the above-mentioned sales or trading desks in either Fixed Income or Equity.

These programs are a great way to become familiar to the Sales and Trading arena, as well as the overall investment process, gaining a broad and varied view of several potential career paths.

Training and content: Both programs provide summer analysts with the foundation necessary for a successful summer experience. They begin with an intense one-week training period in New York where all summer analysts participate in a capital markets overview, several desk overviews and a library tour. You'll be trained on Bloomberg and learn CSFB technology systems and databases. You'll tour the NYSE, and you'll meet with traders and salespeople from all of the various products.

After your first week of training, you'll hit the ground running, working to support a variety of desks within Fixed Income or Equity. Your learning experience will continue through the summer speaker series, where you'll hear from senior employees across the divisions. In addition, you'll participate in networking events, community service, and firm-wide events that will help ensure that you are exposed to all the areas within the bank and understand the big picture of a global investment bank.

To help you determine your strengths and plan your career, summer analysts are matched with junior and senior mentors within your program's division, who provide advice and guidance throughout the summer. You'll also enjoy networking with the other summer analysts and full time employees at a variety of social events throughout the summer.

Equity Research – Summer Analyst

Deadline for application for the internship: December
Length of the program: 10 weeks

If you are a dynamic undergraduate looking for an intense and valuable introduction to the Equity Research arena, the Equity Research Summer Analyst Program may be for you. By working with one of our top-ranked Senior Research Analysts, you will gain an in-depth understanding of company analysis as well as the overall investment process. You will also have exposure to other divisions at CSFB, including CSFB's global sales force, equity traders and institutional clients.

After joining one of our outstanding research teams, you may work on projects involving financial analysis and investigative research. Equity Research summer analysts also have the opportunity to learn financial modeling and forecasting skills and to help produce research reports. In addition to your day-to-day responsibilities, you will be assigned an industry-specific project to work on throughout the summer. You will also be responsible for presenting on a stock as part of our summer stock pitch.

Training: The Equity Research Summer Training program begins with an intense one-week training period in New York where summer analysts participate in a capital markets overview, accounting review, and a research product overview. You will be trained on Bloomberg and learn CSFB technology systems and databases. You will tour the NYSE, and you'll meet with traders and salespeople from all of the various products.

Your learning experience will continue through the summer speaker series, where you will hear from senior management across the divisions. In addition, you will participate in networking events, community service and firm-wide events that will help ensure that you are exposed to all the areas within the bank.

To help you determine your strengths and plan your career, summer analysts are matched with a buddy and a mentor within Equity Research, who provide advice and guidance throughout the summer.

Summer Analyst – Asset Finance

Deadline for application for the internship: December
Length of the program: 10 weeks

Asset Finance Summer Analysts are investment bankers within the Fixed Income Division ("FID"). As a member of the Asset Finance Group, you will work within a team to help develop funding strategies for our clients. You'll also act as a liaison between our clients and the capital markets division, and execute transactions backed by a variety of asset classes, including: auto loans, credit card receivables, home equity loans, manufactured housing loans and student loans. Our clients cover many different industries and range from specialty finance firms to Fortune 500 companies.

During the 10-week program, summer analysts will have the opportunity to participate in all aspects of transaction execution: working with the client, performing due diligence, communicating with the FID trading floor, and managing the accountants, rating agencies and attorneys. They will also help perform any cash flow or financial analyses involved in completing the transaction. Finally, summer analysts will support the ongoing effort to build and strengthen client relationships by preparing marketing materials to pitch the ABS product to new clients as well as presenting new ideas to current clients. Summer analyst positions are located in New York.

Training and Content: The Fixed Income Dedicated Summer Program begins with an intense one-week training period in New York where summer analysts participate in a capital markets overview, a bond math review, and a library tour. You'll be trained on Bloomberg and learn CSFB technology systems and databases. You'll tour the NYSE, and you'll meet with traders and salespeople from all of the various products.

Your learning experience will continue through the summer speaker series, where you'll hear from senior employees across the divisions. In addition, you'll participate in networking events, a community service project, and firm-wide events that will help ensure that you are exposed to all the areas within the bank and understand the big picture of a global investment bank.

To help you determine your strengths and plan your career, summer analysts are matched with junior and senior mentors within Fixed Income, who provide advice and guidance throughout the summer.

Summer Analyst - Leveraged Finance Research

Deadline for application for the internship: December
Length of the program: 10 weeks

Join our top-ranked Fixed Income Research department as a part of the Leveraged Finance Portfolio Strategy Team. Responsibilities will include:

- Generating, analyzing and interpreting data related to the leveraged finance markets from a portfolio strategy, or macroscopic, perspective. Interface with buy-side clients, salespeople, traders and bankers to assist with the interpretation of market data related to the high yield, leveraged loan, structured product, (i.e. CDOs) and credit derivative markets.
- Coordinating with a seven-person team to produce insightful analysis and research reports on topics such as event risk, defaults, performance, Western European high yield, leveraged loans and CDOs.
- Conducting portfolio analytics for high yield mutual fund managers, assisting in industry and sector position recommendations and determining optimal asset allocations in forecasting market environments.

Training and content: The Fixed Income Research program provides summer analysts with the foundation necessary for a successful summer experience. It begins with an intense one-week training period in New York where summer analysts participate in a capital markets overview, a bond math review, and a library tour. You'll be trained on Bloomberg and learn CSFB technology systems and databases. You'll tour the NYSE, and you'll meet with traders and salespeople from all of the various products.

After your first week of training, you'll hit the ground running, working to support a variety of desks within the Fixed Income Division. Your learning experience will continue through the summer speaker series, where you'll hear from senior employees across the divisions. In addition, you'll participate in networking events, community service, and firm-wide events that will help ensure that you are exposed to all the areas within the bank and understand the big picture of a global investment bank.

To help you determine your strengths and plan your career, summer analysts are matched with junior and senior mentors within Fixed Income, who provide advice and guidance throughout the summer. You'll also enjoy networking with the other summer analysts and full-time employees at a variety of social events throughout the summer.

Summer Analyst – Fixed Income Research

Deadline for application for the internship: December
Length of the program: 10 weeks

This summer you can join our top-ranked Fixed Income Research department as a Fixed Income Research Summer Analyst. By working with one of our widely respected Senior Research Analysts in Emerging Markets, Structured Products, Leveraged Finance or Credit Research, you'll become knowledgeable about a research group and learn the fundamentals of research analysis. You will also gain exposure to other divisions of CSFB including our sales force, fixed income traders, investment bankers and institutional clients.

Training and content: The Fixed Income Research program provides summer analysts with the foundation necessary for a successful summer experience. It begins with an intense one-week training period in New York where summer analysts participate in a capital markets overview, a bond math review and a library tour. You'll be trained on Bloomberg and learn CSFB technology systems and databases. You'll tour the NYSE, and you'll meet with traders and salespeople from all of the various products.

After your first week of training, you'll hit the ground running, working to support a variety of desks within the Fixed Income Division. Your learning experience will continue through the summer speaker series, where you'll hear from senior employees across the divisions. In addition, you'll participate in networking events, community service, and firm-wide events that will help ensure that you are exposed to all the areas within the bank and understand the big picture of a global investment bank.

To help you determine your strengths and plan your career, summer analysts are matched with junior and senior mentors within Fixed Income, who provide advice and guidance throughout the summer. You'll also enjoy networking with the other summer analysts and full-time employees at a variety of social events throughout the summer.

Summer Analyst – Real Estate Finance and Securitization

Deadline for application for the internship: December
Length of the program: 10 weeks

The Real Estate Finance & Securitization group's (REFS's) main product areas fall into the broad categories of real estate and real estate-related financial products — commercial mortgage-backed securities, for example. This group has a balance sheet of over $8 billion and operates in a principal capacity as well as providing investment banking services to corporate clients, institutions and publicly traded real estate companies.

REFS is organized into several operating teams:

• Origination Group – Organized on a geographic basis in both the New York and Los Angeles offices, origination teams invest in debt and equity and combination financing for office, industrial, retail, hotel and multifamily, single tenant and other property types. Loans can be made for "whole loan" sale, securitization or balance sheet purposes.
• Investment Banking – Provides advisory services for companies and institutions regarding their real estate activities. The work involves sale mandates, securitization, mergers and acquisitions, and other transactions.
• Structured Finance – Focuses on securitization transactions and other "financially engineered" exits for REFS's investments.
• Trading – Encompasses several units involving whole loans, commercial mortgage-backed securities (CMBS) and derivatives.

As a Summer Analyst, you will develop your understanding of the field by working on a variety of transactions. Summer analyst positions are located in New York.

Training and Content

The Fixed Income Dedicated Summer Program begins with an intense one-week training period in New York where summer analysts participate in a capital markets overview, a bond math review, and a library tour. You'll be trained on Bloomberg and learn CSFB technology systems and databases. You'll tour the NYSE, and you'll meet with traders and salespeople from all of the various products.

Your learning experience will continue through the summer speaker series, where you'll hear from senior employees across the divisions. In addition, you'll participate in networking events, a community service project, and firm-wide events that will help ensure that you are exposed to all the areas within the bank and understand the big picture of a global investment bank.

To help you determine your strengths and plan your career, summer analysts are matched with junior and senior mentors within Fixed Income, who provide advice and guidance throughout the summer.

Scholarships

Douglas L. Paul Award for Achievement

Scholarship award amount: $5,000

CSFB will offer $5,000 scholarships to a number of college sophomores of African, Latino, and Native American descent. Recipients of the scholarships will be selected based on their academic excellence, leadership abilities, and interest in the financial services industry. In addition to monetary resources, students who receive the scholarship will have the opportunity to participate in our Wall Street Summer Immersion Program in New York. This unique 10-week placement provides students with an educational opportunity to learn about the various areas of an investment bank, with rotations in Equities, Fixed Income and Investment Banking.

Affinity Groups/Employee Networks

The Open Network in the Americas and Europe highlights an inclusive work culture in which lesbian, gay, bisexual and transgender (LGBT) employees can advance and succeed. Open Network members regularly assist in LGBT recruitment efforts and organize fundraising for local organizations serving the LGBT community. Speakers at Open Network events have included members of the U.S. Congress, actors and the world's leading experts on issues facing the LGBT community in the workplace.

CSFB America's Women's Network (AWN) helps create a supportive workplace where women can achieve their full potential. Activities include informal mentoring, networking events and presentations by internal and external women executives on topics including strategies for career planning and negotiating office politics. AWN also assist in recruitment efforts, sponsor fundraising events and host regular speaker series.

The Multicultural Resources Network (MRN) in the Americas and Europe is a forum where employees with various ethnic backgrounds and experiences can work together to develop professionally. MRN special events have included guest speakers, receptions, art exhibits, fundraisers and even cooking and dancing demonstrations showcasing the cultural heritage of our global community. MRN members are active in the firm's recruitment efforts and volunteer with a number of community organizations.

The Parents' Networks in the Americas and Europe provide information and support for current and expectant working parents, caregivers and their families. Along with guest speakers, the Networks host monthly "Bring Your Own Lunch" meetings to discuss topics of interest parents can use in child-rearing.

Entry-Level Programs/Full-Time Opportunities

Analyst – Corporate Investment Banking

Length of program: 2 years
Geographic locations of program: Full-time analyst opportunities may be available in our offices throughout North America including in New York, Chicago, Houston, Toronto, Los Angeles, Palo Alto and San Francisco.

Please describe any other educational components of this program: Students are provided with mentors.

As a first-year analyst, you will receive intensive classroom training for seven weeks in New York, as part of a Investment Banking Training Program. Components of this training will include: an orientation to the firm, basics of accounting, corporate finance, financial modeling and valuation techniques, training on the firm's technology systems and the firm's database capabilities. You will learn key concepts integral to the career of an analyst and participate in a week long deal training seminar modeled after a real life scenario. The program also includes a variety of social events to facilitate networking among your peers and colleagues. In addition to our formal program, CSFB relies on on-the-job experience and continuous training to further develop an Analyst's skills and knowledge.

Equities Research Associate

Length of program: Ongoing
Geographic locations of program: While most of our positions are in New York, we may have opportunities in our other offices in North America, including in San Francisco, Boston, Chicago and Houston.

As a first-year analyst you will receive intensive classroom training for six weeks in New York, as part of a Global Securities Training Program. Components of this training will include: an orientation to the firm, a financial math "boot camp," a buy-side class and capital markets overview, an accounting class, a valuation class, an overview of global debt and equity markets and instruments, an introduction to the sales, trading and research groups, and training in presentation skills and computer systems and applications. You'll also sit for the series 7 and 63 exams, and in certain instances the series 3 and 55. You will learn key concepts in sales and trading and participate in portfolio management simulations and trading games. At our many social and networking events, you'll make business contacts from around the globe. You will be paired with a buddy and mentor to make sure you have a smooth transition into the world of Equity Research.

Our stellar program is focused on continuous training and development, and we offer our Research Associates monthly skill-building workshops, best practices lunches, in-house CFA and GMAT training, accounting and writing workshops, and participation in the Mock Call Program. You must pass the Series 7 and 63 exams and are strongly encouraged to sit for all three levels of the CFA exam. Strong performers will be considered for promotion to Associate Analyst at the end of their third year.

Equities Sales & Trading

Length of program: Ongoing
Geographic location of program: New York

The Equity Analyst Program provides the foundation necessary for a successful career. Components of your training will include: an orientation to the firm, a financial math and accounting "boot camp," a buy-side class and capital markets overview, an accounting class, a valuation class, an overview of global debt and equity markets and instruments, an introduction to the sales, trading, research and structuring groups, and training in presentation skills and computer systems and applications.

You'll also sit for the series 7 and 63 exams, and in certain instances the series 3 and series 55. You will learn key concepts in sales and trading and participate in portfolio management trading games. At our many social and networking events, you'll make business contacts from around the globe. You'll also be paired with a mentor to make sure you have a smooth transition into the world of Equities.

Fixed Income Sales & Trading

Length of program: Ongoing
Geographic location of program: New York

As a first-year Analyst, you will receive intensive classroom training for 11 weeks in New York, as part of a Global Securities Training Program. The Fixed Income Sales and Trading program provides Analysts with the foundation necessary for a successful career. Components of your training will include: an orientation to the Firm, a financial math "boot camp," a buy-side class and capital markets overview, an accounting class, a valuation class, an overview of global debt and equity markets and instruments, an introduction to the sales, trading, research and structuring groups, and training in presentation skills and computer systems and applications.

You'll also sit for the series 7 and 63 exams, and in certain instances the series 3. You will learn key concepts in sales and trading and participate in portfolio management trading games. At our many social and networking events, you'll make business contacts from around the globe. You'll also be paired with a mentor to make sure you have a smooth transition into the world of Fixed Income.

Analyst: Asset Finance

Length of program: Ongoing
Geographic location of program: New York

Asset Finance Analysts are investment bankers within the Fixed Income Division ("FID"). The financial structuring team focuses on developing and designing securitization structures for clients ranging from banks and insurance companies to consumer finance companies. The assets we focus on are consumer and commercial loans and leases, including automobile loans, credit card receivables, home equity loans, manufactured housing loans, student loans, equipment leases. Our team also structures and markets transactions indexed to esoteric risks including credit derivatives, regulatory assets and insurance payments

Training and Content: As a first-year Analyst, you will receive intensive classroom training for 11 weeks in New York, as part of a Global Securities Training Program. Components of this training will include: an orientation to the firm, a financial math "boot camp," a buy-side class and capital markets overview, an accounting class, a valuation class, an overview of global debt and equity markets and instruments, an introduction to the sales, trading, research and structuring groups, and training in presentation skills and computer systems and applications. You'll also sit for the series 7 and 63 exams, and in certain instances the series 3. You will learn key concepts in sales and trading and participate in portfolio management trading games. At our many social and networking events, you'll make business contacts from around the globe. You'll also be paired with a mentor to make sure you have a smooth transition into the world of Fixed Income.

Qualifications: Must be a degree candidate from a four-year college or university. Credit Suisse First Boston is noted for the diversity of its employees, but seeks candidates with a common set of abilities – highly motivated, a quantitative aptitude (statistics, math, econometrics or engineering background a plus) and computer/spread sheet literacy are essential. We are seeking candidates who possess strong problem solving abilities. While the focus of the financial structuring group is primarily analytical and quantitative, it is imperative that candidate have the ability to communicate technical concepts to a wide variety of individuals and can work effectively in a team environment. Strength in verbal and written communication, and computer literacy is essential to all that we do. We look for intelligent, driven and hardworking students with consistent leadership involvement in school activities and athletics, and proven interest in the financial sector arena.

Analyst: Fixed Income Leveraged Finance Research

Length of program: Ongoing
Geographic location of program: New York

Join our top-ranked Fixed Income Research department as a part of the Leveraged Finance Portfolio Strategy Team. Responsibilities will include:

- Generating, analyzing and interpreting data related to the leveraged finance markets from a portfolio strategy, or macroscopic, perspective. Interface with buy-side clients, salespeople, traders and bankers to assist with the interpretation of market data related to the high yield, leveraged loan, structured product, (i.e. CDOs) and credit derivative markets.
- Coordinating with a seven-person team to produce insightful analysis and research reports on topics such as event risk, defaults, performance, Western European high yield, leveraged loans and CDOs.
- Conducting portfolio analytics for high yield mutual fund managers, assisting in industry and sector position recommendations and determining optimal asset allocations in forecasting market environments.

Training and Content: As a first-year analyst, you will receive intensive classroom training for 11 weeks in New York, as part of a Global Securities Training Program. Components of this training will include: an orientation to the firm, a financial math "boot camp," a buy-side class and capital markets overview, an accounting class, a valuation class, an overview of global debt and equity markets and instruments, an introduction to the sales, trading, research and structuring groups, and training in presentation skills and computer systems and applications. You'll also sit for the series 7 and 63 exams, and in certain instances the series 3. You will learn key concepts in sales and trading and participate in portfolio management trading games. At our many social and networking events, you'll make business contacts from around the globe. You'll also be paired with a mentor to make sure you have a smooth transition into the world of Fixed Income.

Qualifications: Must be a degree candidate from a four-year college or university. Credit Suisse First Boston is noted for the diversity of its employees, but seeks candidates with a common set of abilities – highly motivated, and creative individuals who have demonstrated academic achievement, specifically in finance, marketing, and accounting courses and have the ability to work independently and as a member of a team. Strength in verbal and written communication, and computer literacy is essential to all that we do. We look for intelligent, driven and hardworking students with consistent leadership involvement in school activities and athletics, and proven interest in the financial sector arena. We look for a background in business, quantitative or economic related fields of work or study, strong quantitative, research, writing and communication skills, and a basic understanding of capital markets and statistics.

Analyst: Real Estate Finance & Securitization

Length of program: Ongoing
Geographic location of program: New York

The Real Estate Finance & Securitization (REFS) group's main product areas fall into the broad categories of real estate and real estate-related financial products — commercial mortgage-backed securities, for example. This group has a balance sheet of over $8 billion and operates in a principal capacity on an international basis, as well as providing investment banking services to corporate clients, institutions and publicly traded real estate companies.

REFS is organized into several operating teams:

- Origination Group – Organized on a geographic basis in both the New York and Los Angeles offices, origination teams invest in debt and equity and combination financing for office, industrial, retail, hotel and multifamily, single tenant and other property types. Loans can be made for "whole loan" sale, securitization or balance sheet purposes.

- Investment Banking – Provides advisory services for companies and institutions regarding their real estate activities. The work involves sale mandates, securitization, mergers and acquisitions, and other transactions.

- Structured Finance – Focuses on securitization transactions and other "financially engineered" exits for REFS' investments.

- Trading – Encompasses several units involving whole loans, commercial mortgage-backed securities (CMBS) and derivatives.

- International – A new venture responsible for CSFB's real estate investments and loans in both Japan and non-Japan Asia, through two investment vehicles. A separate London-based group handles investments in Western Europe.

As a new Analyst, you'll thoroughly develop your understanding of the field by first working as a generalist on a variety of transactions, and then developing your knowledge of specific products. After three years, high-performing Analysts may be eligible for our "Fast Track" program, allowing them to be promoted directly to Associate.

Training and content: As a first-year analyst, you will receive intensive classroom training for 11 weeks in New York, as part of a Global Securities Training Program. Components of this training will include: an orientation to the firm, a financial math "boot camp," a buy-side class and capital markets overview, an accounting class, a valuation class, an overview of global debt and equity markets and instruments, an introduction to the sales, trading, research and structuring groups, and training in presentation skills and computer systems and applications. You'll also sit for the series 7 and 63 exams, and in certain instances the series 3. You will learn key concepts in sales and trading and participate in portfolio management trading games. At our many social and networking events, you'll make business contacts from around the globe. You'll also be paired with a mentor to make sure you have a smooth transition into the world of Fixed Income.

Qualifications: Must be a degree candidate from a four-year college or university. Credit Suisse First Boston is noted for the diversity of its employees, but seeks candidates with a common set of abilities – highly motivated, and creative individuals who have demonstrated academic achievement, specifically in finance, marketing, and accounting courses and have the ability to work independently and as a member of a team. Strength in verbal and written communication, and computer literacy is essential to all that we do. We look for intelligent, driven and hardworking students with consistent leadership involvement in school activities and athletics, and proven interest in the financial sector arena.

Analyst: Asset Finance Structuring

> *Length of program:* Ongoing
> *Geographic location of program:* New York

We are seeking a Technical Analyst for the Asset Finance Group, who will be responsible for collateral analysis in the origination of asset-backed securities and in M&A activity related to consumer finance and loan portfolios. The Asset Finance Group focuses on the securitization of consumer and commercial loans and leases, including automobile loans, credit card receivables, home equity loans, manufactured housing loans, student loans, equipment leases and similar assets. It also structures and markets transactions indexed to esoteric risks including credit derivatives, regulatory assets and insurance payments.

As a Technical Analyst, you will interact closely with small deal teams and apply your technical skills in an intense and demanding environment. Responsibilities include working with issuers, rating agencies and accounting firms. The final product appears in marketing material delivered to investors. You will have significant interaction with other members of a deal team and our clients. You can expect to work on 20 to 25 transactions per year. The position provides an opportunity to develop your skills in a challenging environment.

Training and content: As a first-year analyst, you will receive intensive classroom training for 11 weeks in New York, as part of a Global Securities Training Program. Components of this training will include: an orientation to the firm, a financial math "boot camp," a buy-side class and capital markets overview, an accounting class, a valuation class, an overview of global debt and equity markets and instruments, an introduction to the sales, trading, research and structuring groups, and training in presentation skills and computer systems and applications. You'll also sit for the series 7 and 63 exams, and in certain instances the series 3. You will learn key concepts in sales and trading and participate in portfolio management trading games. At our many social and networking events, you'll make business contacts from around the globe. You'll also be paired with a mentor to make sure you have a smooth transition into the world of Fixed Income.

Qualifications: Must be a degree candidate from a four-year college or university. Credit Suisse First Boston is noted for the diversity of its employees, but seeks candidates with a common set of abilities – highly motivated, a quantitative aptitude (statistics, math, econometrics or engineering background a plus) and computer/spread sheet literacy are essential. We are seeking candidates who possess strong problem solving abilities. While the focus of the financial structuring group is primarily analytical and quantitative, it is imperative that candidate have the ability to communicate technical concepts to a wide variety of individuals and can work effectively in a team environment. Strength in verbal and written communication, and computer literacy is essential to all that we do. We look for intelligent, driven and hardworking students with consistent leadership involvement in school activities and athletics, and proven interest in the financial sector arena.

Application: All interested candidates MUST send their resume and cover letter to securities.recruiting@csfb.com by March 1st for consideration.

Analyst: Fixed Income Research

Length of program: Ongoing
Geographic location of program: New York

Join our top-ranked Fixed Income Research department as a Fixed Income Research Analyst. By working with one of our widely respected Senior Research Analysts in Emerging Markets, Structured Products, Leveraged Finance, or Credit Research, you'll become knowledgeable about a research group and learn the fundamentals of research analysis. You will also gain exposure to other divisions of CSFB including: our sales force, fixed income traders, investment bankers and institutional clients.

Training and content: As a first-year analyst, you will receive intensive classroom training for 11 weeks in New York, as part of a Global Securities Training Program. Components of this training will include: an orientation to the firm, a financial math "boot camp," a buy-side class and capital markets overview, an accounting class, a valuation class, an overview of global debt and equity markets and instruments, an introduction to the sales, trading, research and structuring groups, and training in presentation skills and computer systems and applications. You'll also sit for the series 7 and 63 exams, and in certain instances the series 3. You will learn key concepts in sales and trading and participate in portfolio management trading games. At our many social and networking events, you'll make business contacts from around the globe. You'll also be paired with a mentor to make sure you have a smooth transition into the world of Fixed Income.

Qualifications: Must be a degree candidate from a four-year college or university. Credit Suisse First Boston is noted for the diversity of its employees, but seeks candidates with a common set of abilities – highly motivated, and creative individuals who have demonstrated academic achievement, specifically in finance, marketing and accounting courses and have the ability to work independently and as a member of a team. Strength in verbal and written communication, and computer literacy is essential to all that we do. We look for intelligent, driven and hardworking students with consistent leadership involvement in school activities and athletics, and proven interest in the financial sector arena. We look for a background in business, quantitative or economic related fields of work or study, strong quantitative, research, writing and communication skills, and a basic understanding of capital markets and statistics. Some language skills are required for certain research groups.

Strategic Plan and Diversity Leadership

How does the firm's leadership communicate the importance of diversity to everyone at the firm?

CSFB utilizes a variety of communication methods to convey the importance of diversity including newsletters, marketing brochures, e-mail memorandums, meetings and a web site on the company intranet.

Who has primary responsibility for leading overall diversity initiatives at your firm?

Angie Casciato, Global Head of Diversity and Inclusion

Who has primary responsibility for diversity recruiting initiatives at your firm, if different from?

Tanji Dewberry, Assistant Vice President – for campus recruiting

Does your firm currently have a diversity committee?

Yes

If yes, does the committee's representation include one or more members of the firm's management/executive committee (or the equivalent)?

Yes

Please describe the committee.

> **Total senior managers on committee:** 26
> **Number of diversity meetings annually:** 6

Does the committee(s) and/or diversity leader establish and set goals or objectives consistent with management's priorities?

Yes

Has the firm undertaken a formal or informal diversity program or set of initiatives aimed at increasing the diversity of the firm?

Yes, formal

How often does the firm's management review the firm's diversity progress/results?

Quarterly

Diversity Mission Statement

CSFB's Global Inclusion and Diversity mission is to create an inclusive culture whereby:

- employees' differences are valued and leveraged for the benefit of the business
- employees are able to realize their full potential
- employees are treated with dignity and respect

The Employer Says

CSFB is dedicated to attracting, developing and retaining the best people in our industry. We bring together individuals of different genders, races, ages, nationalities, religions, sexual orientations and disabilities to create a world-class team of financial service professionals.

At the core of CSFB's philosophy of inclusion is the firm's Global Dignity at Work Policy – a set of conduct guidelines that apply to all employees worldwide. This policy ensures that diversity, inclusiveness and dignity in the workplace are everyone's responsibility. These enduring values are part of the very fabric of our business. They shape the way we hire, develop, and promote employees, and they guide us in the way we treat one another.

CSX Transportation

500 Water St., 15th Fl.
Jacksonville, FL 32202
Phone: 904-359-3100
Fax: 904-359-2459
www.CSX.com

Locations (worldwide)

CSX is the largest railroad in the Eastern U.S. We operate east of the Mississippi River with 10 Operating Divisions in Jacksonville, FL (headquarters city, as well); Atlanta; Florence, SC; Nashville, TN; Louisville, KY; Chicago; Cleveland; Baltimore; Huntington, WV; and Albany, NY.

Diversity Leadership

Susan O. Hamilton, AVP-Diversity & EEOC
500 Water Street
Jacksonville, FL 32202
Phone: (904) 366-4092
Fax: (904) 359-3728
E-mail: Susan_Hamilton@csx.com

Recruiting

Please list the schools/types of schools at which you recruit.

We recruit at approximately 25 different colleges and universities, including several historically black schools, and have a booth every year at both the National Black and National Hispanic MBA expositions.

Do you have any special outreach efforts that are directed to encourage minority students to consider your firm?

• Hold a reception for minority students
• Conferences
• Advertise in minority student association publication(s)
• Participate in/host minority student job fair(s)
• Firm's employees participate on career panels at school
• Outreach to leadership of minority student organizations
• Scholarships or intern/fellowships for minority students

What activities does the firm undertake to attract minority and women employees?

• Partner programs with women and minority associations
• Conferences
• Participate at minority job fairs
• Seek referrals from other employees
• Utilize online job services

Do you use executive recruiting/search firms to seek to identify new diversity hires?

Yes

Internships and Co-ops

Deadline for application: April

Number of interns in the program: Summer 2005, 25 (half are repeat interns from last year)

Pay: There is a base rate of pay that varies by department

Length of the program: 8 to 12 weeks, depending on return dates for school

Percentage of interns/co-ops in the program who receive offers of full-time employment: We have hired 17 interns permanently the past three years (however, some interns hired are from other programs and half our interns are still in school).

Affinity Groups/Employee Networks

Name(s) of affinity group(s)

• African American
• Hispanic
• Working Parents
• Employees Caring for Elderly Parents
• Young Professionals
• Military
• Gay/Lesbian
• Women's Network

All groups meet monthly and use the diversity web site on the CSX Employee Gateway.

Entry-Level Programs/Full-Time Opportunities

Management Training Program

Length of program: Two meeting times during the year, January/July and July/December

Geographic location(s) of program: Headquarters-based with some travel to field locations

Please describe the training/training component of this program: Rotations through the company with orientations periodically

Please describe any other educational components of this program: Open to graduates, MBA graduates and successful internal candidates.

Our corporate tuition reimbursement program is available to all management employees, not just new hires.

Strategic Plan and Diversity Leadership

How does the firm's leadership communicate the importance of diversity to everyone at the firm?

The CEO and his five direct reports have diversity goals in their overall performance management program. Diversity goals cascade within their organizations. Diversity is one of our core competencies.

Who has primary responsibility for leading diversity initiatives at your firm?

Susan Hamilton, Senior Vice President, AVP-Diversity and EEOC, reporting to Senior Vice President Bob Haulter, who reports to CEO

Does your firm currently have a diversity committee?

Yes. Global Diversity Council meets monthly, and there are 15 satellite diversity councils – they are within most operating divisions.

If yes, does the committee's representation include one or more members of the firm's management/executive committee (or the equivalent)?

Yes

Please describe the committee.

There are 60 members, each spending a minimum of two to five hours per month. Total executives on the committee:
• 1 Senior Vice President
• 1 Vice President
• 3 Division Managers
• 1 State Vice President
• 3 Assistant Vice Presidents

Does the committee and/or diversity leader establish and set goals or objectives consistent with management's priorities?

Yes. These priorities are included in the diversity leader's performance management goals.

Has the firm undertaken a formal or informal diversity program or set of initiatives aimed at increasing the diversity of the firm?

Yes, formal

How often does the firm's management review the firm's diversity progress/results?

Quarterly

How is the firm's diversity committee and/or firm management held accountable for achieving results?

1. We report periodically to the board of directors
2. We have shared performance goals
3. Shared competencies

The Stats

Employees: 34,000 (2004, U.S.)
Revenue: $8 billion (2004, U.S.)

Retention and Professional Development

How do 2004 minority and female attrition rates generally compare to those experienced in the prior year period?

About the same as in prior years

Please identify the specific steps you are taking to reduce the attrition rate of minority and women employees.

• Develop and/or support internal employee affinity groups (e.g., minority or women networks within the firm)
• Increase/review compensation relative to competition
• Increase/improve current work/life programs
• Adopt dispute resolution process
• Succession plan includes emphasis on diversity
• Work with minority and women employees to develop career advancement plans
• Review work assignments and hours billed to key client matters to make sure minority and women employees are not being excluded
• Strengthen mentoring program for all employees, including minorities and women
• Professional skills development program, including minority and women employees
• Other: Expanding our formal coaching/mentoring program to various field locations

Diversity Mission Statement

To embrace and value the differences of all CSX employees while blending them into one team.

DaimlerChrysler Corporation

1000 Chrysler Dr.
Auburn Hills, MI 48326-2766
Phone: (248) 576-5741
Fax: (248) 576-4742
www.daimlerchrysler.com

The Employer Says

DaimlerChrysler Corporation (DCC), also known as the Chrysler Group, is a North American-based unit of DaimlerChrysler AG. At the Chrysler Group, we design, manufacture and sell vehicles under the Chrysler, Jeep® and Dodge brand names. Through our fourth brand, Mopar®, we offer original equipment and performance quality parts.

The Chrysler Group's strategy is to grow product leadership by constantly building innovative and segment-defining vehicles and to continue to improve operating performance by leveraging the technology, purchasing and production synergies made possible by DaimlerChrysler's global reach.

DaimlerChrysler is committed to fostering an inclusive work environment where all employees are treated with dignity and respect. Our company policies and standards of conduct reinforce this commitment. In doing so, we recognize the value that diverse perspectives bring to business success in enabling innovation and robust decision making.

As stated in our corporate diversity statement and through the leadership commitment to diversity, DaimlerChrysler Corporation is proud of and committed to our diversity initiatives that create and maintain an inclusive work environment that encourages and values teamwork. One of the greatest strengths of our company is its diversity. We value our employees for their different talents, backgrounds, cultures and experiences and lifestyles, and strive to achieve the diversity in our workplace that reflects the diversity of our customers and the community in which we do business. Further, we are committed to encouraging diversity among our dealers, suppliers and partners throughout the business enterprise.

As such, DaimlerChrysler Corporation has a Diversity Council consisting of the company's top management which provides leadership on corporate actions and programs fostering diversity. Furthermore, DaimlerChrysler supports a rich community of diverse employee resource groups that are initiated and chartered by employees. These self-organized groups provide support and networking opportunities such as mentoring, working in the community, career development and assisting in other activities that promote cultural awareness.

Additionally, DaimlerChrysler offers a number of programs that help employees to better balance their work and personal lives. Some examples of these programs include a resource and referral program, discounted child-care and home services providers, a no-cost employee assistance program and flexible work arrangements.

From our cadres of diverse designers, engineers and staff to the men and women on the factory floor to our network of dealers and suppliers, we're dedicated to creating the best cars and trucks possible. To find out about more about DaimlerChrysler and career opportunities throughout its facilities, visit us at www.careers.chrysler-group.com.

Daymon Worldwide

700 Fairfield Ave
Stamford, CT 06902
(203) 352-7500
www.daymon.com

Locations (worldwide)

Mexico, South Africa, New Zealand,
Japan, Hong Kong, South Korea,
Malaysia, Singapore, China, Indonesia,
Taiwan, England, 30+ states in the US

Diversity Leadership

Clint Sollenberger, Director of Talent
Management
700 Fairfield Ave.
Stamford, CT 06902
Phone: (203) 352-7500
Fax: (203) 352-7947

Recruiting

Please list the schools/types of schools at which you recruit.

• Ivy League schools
• Other private schools
• Historically Black Colleges and Universities (HBCUs)

Do you have any special outreach efforts that are directed to encourage minority students to consider your firm?

• Scholarships or intern/fellowships for minority students

What activities does the firm undertake to attract minority and women employees?

• Partner programs with women and minority associations

Do you use executive recruiting/search firms to seek to identify new diversity hires?

No

Internships and Co-ops

INROADS

Deadline for application: March/April
Number of interns in the program in summer 2004 (internship) or 2004 (co-op): 16
Length of the program: 8-12 weeks (average)
Percentage of interns/co-ops in the program who receive offers of full-time employment: 75% – 100% (depending on performance and fit)

The goal of Daymon's Internship Program is to expose interns to as much of the business as possible and to help them find an area that piques their interest. The internship positions are project-based and can be found in our field locations, HR, Finance, IT and many other departments in the organization including the executive branch. Candidates for our program must possess the fol-

lowing competencies to be successful in this role: strategic agility, a drive for results, priority setting, interpersonal savvy, customer focus, business acumen, informing and personal learning.

Entry-Level Programs/Full-Time Opportunities

Management Development Program

> *Length of program:* 1 year
> *Geographic location(s) of program:* Throughout the country

Please describe the training/training component of this program: Three-month rotations in different areas of the business

Strategic Plan and Diversity Leadership

How does the firm's leadership communicate the importance of diversity to everyone at the firm?

• Communication with Senior Management to incorporate into business objectives
• Regular articles in company's daily online news publication and quarterly newsletter
• Company-wide quarterly conference calls
• New associate orientations

Who has primary responsibility for leading diversity initiatives at your firm?

Kelly Bruce, General Manager

Does your firm currently have a diversity committee?

Yes. The Council is comprised of a Chair, a Vice Chair, a Vice President Liaison, 13 Members and numerous Project Participants throughout the company. The Executive Sponsors of the Council are the company's President and Human Resources Vice President. Currently, the Council Members are located in three countries, and so meetings are held via conference call once per month. Subcommittees are formed for each project, and those teams meet on a calendar determined by each Project Lead. Projects are defined and then the appropriate research is conducted to provide a recommendation to the company with regard to the specific initiative. The Executive Sponsors review the recommendations and present them to the officer group for consideration.

If yes, does the committee's representation include one or more members of the firm's management/executive committee (or the equivalent)?

Yes

Please describe the committee.

> **Total executives on the committee:** Four. (Two executive sponsors, one VP liaison, and one member who is a VP.)

Does the committee and/or diversity leader establish and set goals or objectives consistent with management's priorities?

Yes

Has the firm undertaken a formal or informal diversity program or set of initiatives aimed at increasing the diversity of the firm?

Yes, formal – Diversity Metrics or Measures

How often does the firm's management review the firm's diversity progress/results?

Quarterly

The Stats

Employees: 1,558 (2004, U.S.)
Employees: 1,380 (2003, U.S.)
Employees: 11,000 (2004, worldwide)
Employees: 10,000 (2003, worldwide)

Retention and Professional Development

How do 2004 minority and female attrition rates generally compare to those experienced in the prior year period?

Higher than in prior years

Please identify the specific steps you are taking to reduce the attrition rate of minority and women employees.

• Succession plan includes emphasis on diversity
• Strengthen mentoring program for all employees, including minorities and women
• Professional skills development program, including minority and women employees

Diversity Mission Statement

Daymon Worldwide is a global company working in diverse markets and with diverse customers. Our company's motto of "Noble, Profitable and Fun" states our first value as being noble. Our company's greatest asset has always been – and will always be – our associates. Continuing to respect and support the diversity of our associates will increase the value of our company and will always be our greatest opportunity for growth as a business and as individuals. Our commitment to our associates and principals also extends to the communities where we conduct business. We strive to be a responsible and contributing member.

Duke Energy

526 S. Church St
Charlotte, NC 28202-1803
(704) 594-6200
Fax: (704) 382-3814
www.duke-energy.com/careers/welcome/

Locations (worldwide)
North and South America

Diversity Leadership
Linda D. Thomas, Workforce Diversity
Consultant

Employment Contact
Regeana Phillips
400 South Church Street
Charlotte, NC 28201
Phone: (704) 382-6841
Fax: (704) 382-0922
E-mail: riphilli@duke-energy.com

Recruiting

Please list the schools/types of schools at which you recruit.

• Ivy League schools
• Other private schools
• Public state schools
• Historically Black Colleges and Universities (HBCUs)

Do you have any special outreach efforts that are directed to encourage minority students to consider your firm?

• Hold a reception for minority students
• Conferences: In prior years, we have participated in the Black and Hispanic MBA conferences, National Society of Black
  Engineers and National Black Accountants conferences.
• Advertise in minority student association publication(s) We have participated in the past.
• Participate in/host minority student job fair(s)
• Sponsor minority student association events
• Outreach to leadership of minority student organizations
• Scholarships or intern/fellowships for minority students

What activities does the firm undertake to attract minority and women employees?

• Participate at minority job fairs
• Seek referrals from other employees
• Utilize online job services

At Duke Realty Corporation,

we recognize the value of respect and inclusiveness. We promote the understanding and appreciation of our differences as well as our similarities. We strive to attract, retain and develop the best and brightest Associates.

It's not just good business—
it's business that does good.

800.875.3366   **Duke** REALTY CORPORATION   www.dukerealty.com

Duke Realty Corporation

600 E. 96th St., Ste. 100
Indianapolis, IN 46240
Phone: (317) 808-6000
Fax: (317) 808-6794
Toll Free: (800) 875-3366
www.dukerealty.com

Locations (worldwide)

Corporate Headquarters – Indianapolis.
Other markets in Cincinnati, Columbus,
Cleveland, St. Louis, Nashville, Chicago,
Minneapolis, Atlanta, Raleigh, Dallas,
Tampa, Orlando and Weston

Employment Contact

Amanda Cummings, Employment Specialist
Jenny E. Bean, Senior Manager, Human
Resources

600 E. 96th Street, Suite 100
Indianapolis, IN 46240
Phone: (317) 808-6124
Fax: (317) 808-6764
E-mail: jenny.bean@dukerealty.com

Recruiting

Please list the schools/types of schools at which you recruit.

- *Private schools:* Spelman, Clark Atlanta, Morehouse, Vanderbilt
- *Public state schools:* Indiana University, Purdue University, Indiana-Purdue University (IUPUI), Georgia Tech, Florida State, Georgia State, Emory
- *Historically Black Colleges and Universities (HBCUs):* Spelman, Clark Atlanta, Morehouse

Do you have any special outreach efforts that are directed to encourage minority students to consider your firm?

- Hold a reception for minority students
- Conferences: AUC Job Fair
- Advertise in minority student association publication(s)
- Participate in/host minority student job fairs
- Firm's associates participate on career panels at school

What activities does the firm undertake to attract minority and women employees?

- Partner programs with women and minority associations
- Conferences: AUC, Black Expo, Career Forum for minorities and women
- Participate at minority job fairs
- Seek referrals from other associates
- Utilize online job services and other media outlets – iHispano
- Participants in Project REAP
- Participants in INROADS in Indianapolis, Chicago and Atlanta

Internships and Co-ops

The Duke Realty Internship Program (INROADS and Non-INROADS) Summer Program

Number of interns in the program: 21 Interns (9 INROADS and 12 Non-INROADS)

Pay: $12-$16/hour for 12 weeks

Percentage of interns/co-ops in the program who receive offers of full-time employment: We have a conversion rate of 95% +

Web site for internship/co-op information: www.Dukerealty.com

The Duke Internship Program is designed to be a multi-summer internship program with the ultimate goal of hiring the intern into a full-time position upon graduation. The intern will have 1-4 summers of in-house training with us prior to being offered a full-time position. During these summers, the intern will learn about our Company culture, delivery system and the long term benefits of employment at Duke, with the expectation that their contributions and productivity are successively higher each summer.

PROJECT REAP (Real Estate Associate Program)

Length of program: 12-month program

Number of interns in the program: 1 Associate a year

Pay: $40-$45k per year

Percentage of interns/co-ops in the program who receive offers of full-time employment: Conversion rate of 100%

Web site for internship/co-op information: www.REAP.ORG

REAP is an industry-backed, market driven program with a 5 year track record. REAP finds, trains, and places talented dedicated minority professionals with leading commercial real estate firms. The internship is for 12 months with the goal of converting the interns into full-time associates.

Entry-Level Programs/Full-Time Opportunities

Duke has two formal training programs available to interns and associates:

Career Development Training: Duke offers a variety of career development training courses to support associates in developing their work skills. Courses are available for interns and associates in all of our markets. Typical courses include:
• Personality Types in the Workplace
• Communication between the Genders
• Dealing with difficult people
• Effective Interviewing
• Stress Management
• More

ElementK: Computer-based training is available for all interns and associates. This online training solution provides training for select Microsoft products, sexual harassment and diversity training.

In addition, associates participate in departmental training.

Strategic Plan and Diversity Leadership

How does the firm's leadership communicate the importance of diversity to everyone at the firm?

Quarterly associate conference calls, company newsletters, annual performance reviews, including the CEO's annual review, e-mails, financial support for diversity council and other sponsored diversity activities, career development courses, quarterly diversity training activities and a diversity CD that new hires must review during their first few months at Duke.

Who has primary responsibility for leading diversity initiatives at your firm?

Denny Oklak – CEO and President and his Executive Team

Does your firm currently have a diversity committee?

Yes

Please describe the committee.

It is the mission of the Duke Realty Corporation Diversity Council to educate, increase awareness and be advocates for diversity at Duke. The Diversity Council will lead the company in recognizing the value of respect and inclusiveness, will foster Duke's core values and will promote the understanding and appreciation of our differences and similarities. In so doing, we strive to develop and nurture a strong, diverse workforce in order to produce exceptional customer satisfaction and shareholder value.

The Diversity Council is made up of 24 associates from every level (entry to Executive) and from each of our 14 locations nationwide. The Diversity Council meets two to three times per year in person and via conference calls every other month.

The Diversity Council also provides diversity training to over 1100 associates on a quarterly basis.

If yes, does the committee's representation include one or more members of the firm's management/executive committee (or the equivalent)?

Yes. There are 6 Executive/Management associates on the Diversity Council. Over 150 hours/year were spent on furthering the diversity initiatives.

Does the committee and/or diversity leader establish and set goals or objectives consistent with management's priorities?

Yes. Annually, corporate goals are set for management. These goals include increasing minority hires and decreasing minority turnover. Throughout the last few years, diversity was put on associates reviews, a minority vendor program was rolled out and associate satisfaction was measured with several questions pertaining to diversity at Duke. In addition, each intern has a Career Development Plan in place.

Has the firm undertaken a formal or informal diversity program or set of initiatives aimed at increasing the diversity of the firm?

Yes, formal. Our Diversity Council was created to assist the company in furthering its diversity goals and initiatives. One major accomplishment that the council achieved was to propose to Duke's management committee that they add a diversity component on all associate performance review forms.

How often does the firm's management review the firm's diversity progress/results?

Quarterly

How is the firm's diversity committee and/or firm management held accountable for achieving results?

It is on both the CEO's performance review and all employee performance reviews.

The Stats

Employees: 1,078 (2004, U.S.)
Employees: 1,031 (2003, U.S.)
Revenue: $7.7 billion (2004, U.S.)
Revenue: $8.4 billion (2003, U.S.)

Duke's population includes 6.7% minorities, 35% women and 65% men. Currently, our Executive and Management team consists of 2% women.

Retention and Professional Development

How do 2004 minority and female attrition rates generally compare to those experienced in the prior year period?

About the same as in prior years

Please identify the specific steps you are taking to reduce the attrition rate of minority and women employees.

• Increase/review compensation relative to competition
• Increase/review/improve current work/life programs
• Succession plan includes emphasis on diversity
• Strengthen mentoring program for all associates, including minorities and women
• Professional skills development program, including minority and women associates
• Associate Opinion Survey – including diversity questions

Diversity Mission Statement

Company Statement and Diversity Council Statement

Diversity is an important strategic issue at Duke Realty Corporation involving our associates, our customers and our shareholders. As our work force and customer base continues to become more diverse, our challenge is to understand and value our individual differences and similarities and those of our customers and prospective customers. Our behaviors and actions must demonstrate and confirm our respect for each other and each other's contributions.

Diversity involves developing organizational processes that are inclusionary rather than exclusionary, and which create an environment for company contributions by everyone.

Our expectation is that by responding in a positive and proactive way to these diversity issues, we will be better prepared for our long-term future through continued commitment of our associates, ongoing and successful relationships with existing and potential customers and continued investment from existing and prospective shareholders.

The company, recognizing the very broad nature of the term "diversity," offers the following examples of the many dimensions of diversity:

• Age and experience
• Culture (individual, group, global)
• Economic status
• Education and training
• Gender and sexual orientation
• Marital and family status
• Personal style
• Disabilities

• Race, nationality and ethnicity
• Religion
• Veteran and active armed service status

To reinforce this commitment in our daily work, all company activities, policies, practices and procedures are to be carried out in accordance with this policy. Each associate is personally responsible and accountable for ensuring that her/his actions and behaviors reflect this policy.

In addition to our Company Diversity Statement, our Diversity Council also has a mission statement.

It is the mission of the Duke Realty Corporation Diversity Council to educate, increase awareness and be advocates for diversity at Duke. The Diversity Council will lead the company in recognizing the value of respect and inclusiveness, will foster Duke's core values and will promote the understanding and appreciation of our differences and similarities. In so doing, we strive to develop and nurture a strong, diverse workforce in order to produce exceptional customer satisfaction and shareholder value.

The Employer Says

Duke's commitment to diversity in the workplace is paramount to the company's ability to attract and retain associates. The Duke Diversity Council was created to cultivate an environment in which all associates feel valued and have the opportunity to grow. This environment of inclusiveness helps make Duke an attractive culture for today's best and brightest.

To be able to attract and retain minority associates, the company offers a variety of diverse benefits. Here are just a few:

Adoption
Any full-time Associate with at least 90 days' service receives ten days' paid leave upon adopting a child. Duke offers an Adoption Assistance Plan, which will reimburse any full-time associates with at least six months of service, for certain qualifying adoption expenses up to $7,500 per adoption.

EAP
Duke realizes that in today's world, balancing work and home can be a real test of an associates time and energy. All associates and their immediate family, including spouses and dependent children, are immediately eligible to participate in Duke's Employee Assistance Program (EAP) and Work Life Benefit. The EAP is a free benefit, which provides con fidential consultation and short-term counseling for most of the problems that can hinder happiness and effectiveness at work and home. Examples include, but are not limited to: marital difficulties, financial or legal problems, parenting concerns and other stress-related issues. Prenatal kits, child safety kits and eldercare kits are also available at no cost.

Tuition Reimbursement
Duke reimburses associates (with at least six months of service) for 100% of the cost of tuition, registration fees and books to a maximum of $3,000 per year. Many Duke Associates have been able to achieve their goal of receiving a degree with the aid of the Tuition Reimbursement Program since Duke started offering it in 1998.

Health Insurance for PT Associates
Duke offers medical coverage to any part-time associate who has had at least three consecutive years of prior full-time service. In addition, there are additional paid benefits for part-time associates.

Employer Assisted Housing
The Employer Assisted Housing Program helps Duke associates realize the dream of home ownership. Any associate with at least six months' service and an annual salary of $57,000 or less (excluding bonus) may receive up to a $3,000 forgivable loan to use toward the purchase of their first home. Duke has been able to assist 70 associates with the purchase of their first home since the program began in 2001.

Career Resource Library
The Duke Human Resources Department maintains the Career Resource Library, which contains many different resources for Duke associates to use when situations, needs or interests arise.

Currently, the library contains over 300 different resources, some of which are the most popular titles in business today. Topics such as leadership, diversity, personal growth, time management & organization, business writing, communication and career development are available, as well as many others. Duke has also just added 'How to Speak Spanish' CDs to the library for associates to use.

Community Days

All associates receive two paid community days each year for use in volunteering in charitable community activities. 287 Associates at Duke utilized at least one Community Day in 2004. Volunteer activities have been performed for the following organizations:

• United Way
• Habitat for Humanity
• Big Brothers Big Sisters
• Cancer Socity
• Juvenile Diebetes Foundation
• Race for the Cure
• Arthritis Foundation

Duke is committed to diversity and we show our commitment in various ways. Whether it's volunteer support or financial support, diversity at Duke is making a difference.

Over the last several years, Duke associates have received various honors in appreciation for their commitment. Associates were honored for the following awards:

INROADS is the name of the program where the below awards were won.
• Board member of the year – three years in a row
• Business Coordinator of the year – two years
• Business Advisor of the year
• Highest Conversion Rate
• Rainmaker of the year – two years
• Finalist for Mayor's Diversity Award

Duke also supports various diverse organizations/associations. The following is a list of some of the organizations we support and participate in:

• INROADS in three cities
• Project REAP
• Asian Alliance
• Regional Black MBA
• CREW – Commercial Real Estate for Women

Along with the various honors, Duke contributes associate's time and company funding for various organizations and associations. Here is a small list:

• United Way in all 14 of our markets
• Big Brother/Big Sisters
• Habitat for Humanity
• American Cancer Society
• American Diabetes Association

DuPont Company

1007 Market Street
Wilmington, DE 19898
Phone: (302) 774-1000
Fax: (302) 999-4399
www1.dupont.com/dupontglobal/corp/careers/index.html

Diversity Leadership

Sandra Lewis, Manager, Diversity and WorkLife
Cary M. Sudler, EEO Officer
Phone: (302) 892-5664
E-mail: Cary.M.Sudler@usa.dupont.com

Employment Contact

Karen Machol Piraino, Manager, Talent Acquisition, U.S. Region
1007 Market Street
D6038
Wilmington, DE 19898
Phone: (302) 774-5977
Fax: (302) 773-4745
E-mail: Karen.N.Piraino@usa.dupont.com

Recruiting

Please list the schools/types of schools at which you recruit.

2004 – 2005 DuPont School List and Category

- *Ivy League schools:* Columbia University; Dartmouth Tuck College of Business; Harvard University; Princeton University; University of Pennsylvania; Yale University
- *Other private schools:* Brigham Young University; California Institute of Technology; Carnegie Mellon University; Columbia University – Business School; Duke University – Fuqua School of Business; Emory University; Fairleigh Dickinson University; LaSalle University; MIT; Northwestern University; Northwestern University – Kellogg Sch of Mgmt; Rice University; Stanford University; Swarthmore College; Tulane University; University of Chicago; University of Chicago – Graduate Sch of Business; University of Notre Dame; University of Pennsylvania – Wharton School of Business; University of Rochester; Vanderbilt University; Villanova University; Wake Forest University; Wake Forest University – Babcock Sch of Mgmt; Yale University – School of Management
- *Public state schools:* North Carolina State; Ohio State University; Pennsylvania State University; Purdue University; Rowan University; Rutgers University; San Diego State University; Southwest Missouri State University; Temple University; Texas A&M – College Station; Texas Tech; UMass Amherst; University of Akron; University of California – Berkeley; Drexel University; University of California – Davis; niversity of California – Irvine; University of California - Los Angeles; University of California – San Diego; University of California – Santa Barbara; University of Central Florida; University of Delaware; University of Florida; University of Houston; University of Maryland – Baltimore County; University of Idaho; University of Illinois; University of Maryland – College Park; University of Michigan; University of Texas – Austin – Engineering; Arizona State University; University of Virginia; Clemson University; University of Virginia – Darden School of Business; Georgia Tech ; University of Wisconsin – Madison (Engineering); Indiana University – Kelley School of Business; Virginia Tech University; Louisiana State University; West Virginia University; Michigan State University; Western Washington University; University of North Carolina; University of Minnesota; University of North Carolina Kenan-Flagler Business School; University of Oklahoma; University of Pittsburgh; University of Tennessee; University of Texas – Austin – Business; Montana State University; New Mexico State University • Historically Black Colleges and Universities (HBCUs)**:** North Carolina A&T; Tuskegee University
- *Hispanic Serving Institutions (HSIs):* University of Puerto Rico

• Other predominantly minority and/or women's colleges: Bryn Mawr College

Do you have any special outreach efforts that are directed to encourage minority students to consider your firm?

• Hold a reception for minority students
• Conferences: SWE, NSBE, SHPE, AISES, NSHMBA, NOBCCHE, Consortium, NABA, WEPAN
• Advertise in minority student association publication(s)
• Participate in/host minority student job fair(s)
• Sponsor minority student association events
• Firm's employees participate on career panels at school
• Outreach to leadership of minority student organizations
• Scholarships or intern/fellowships for minority students: GEM, NACME

What activities does the firm undertake to attract minority and women employees?

• Partner programs with women and minority associations
• Conferences: see above
• Participate at minority job fairs
• Seek referrals from other employees
• Utilize online job services

Internships and Co-ops

Engineering Co-op/Intern Program

Deadline for application: Ongoing posting on the Web. We have three main terms (spring, summer and fall).
Combined total co-op/interns: 150
Pay: Pay is competitive, based on student's education level and degree.
Length of the program: We offer terms of varying length, based on business need and student availability during the school year. Some students work the 12-16 weeks in the summer. We also have students who work six-month terms (spring/summer or summer/fall)
Percentage of interns/co-ops in the program who receive offers of full-time employment: About 50%
Web site for internship/co-op information: www1.dupont.com/dupontglobal/corp/careers/univ_internships.html

Our co-op/internship program is a key part of DuPont's engineer recruiting strategy. The program provides an excellent pool of motivated, diverse and well-prepared employees for DuPont. Assignments are located throughout the U.S. Minimum qualifications:

• Legal right to work in the United States without restrictions
• Attending an ABET accredited ENGINEERING school
• 3.3 minimum GPA preferred (3.0 as absolute minimum)
• Completed freshman year
• Prior work or volunteer experience
• Demonstrated leadership capability

Sourcing & Logistics Co-op Program

Deadline for application: Recruit throughout the year based on need. There are two sessions for co-ops: May/June – December and January – June.

Number of co-ops in the program: 12-24 at any given time

Pay: Pay is competitive, based on student's education level and degree.

Length of the program: Approximately 6 months/ 24 weeks

Percentage of interns/co-ops in the program who receive offers of full-time employment: Approximately 50%

Web site for internship/co-op information: www1.dupont.com/dupontglobal/corp/careers/univ_internships.html

The Sourcing & Logistics Co-op Program is a key part of our recruiting strategy. The program provides an excellent pool of motivated, diverse and well-prepared employees for DuPont. Assignments are located in Wilmington, Delaware. Minimum qualifications:

- Currently enrolled as a full-time, undergraduate student at an accredited college or university
- BA/BS candidates: a specific major is not relevant although some preference will be given to candidates studying supply chain management, logistics, engineering, operations management, transportation or business administration
- Only those candidates who are able to complete the entire assignment will be considered.
- Minimum GPA 2.8
- Ability to relocate to Wilmington, Delaware for the duration of the Co-Op/Internship program.
- Legal right to work in the United States without restrictions

In addition to these requirements, candidates must possess the following qualifications:

- *Business knowledge:* Ability to learn about DuPont's various businesses and their unique purchasing agreements
- *Computer skills:* Experience with MS Office (WORD, Excel, Access, PowerPoint). Candidates must be able to work with the Internet and learn internal DuPont systems and tools.
- *Resourcefulness:* The ability to identify leveraging opportunities (the advantage of having businesses buy supplies and services collectively versus individually).
- *Implementation:* The ability to handle multiple priority assignments, as well as the ability to work independently with minimal supervision.
- *Networking skills:* The ability to network with different internal and external groups and contacts and be capable of working in a team environment.

Scholarships

We no longer give scholarships directly, however, we provide funding through third parties (e.g. NACME, UNCF).

Affinity Groups/Employee Networks

Corporate Black Employees Network (CBEN)

This network aims to link the individual-site networks into a unified network so that we build a strong, united community ready to address issues and challenges to ensure that we can contribute to our fullest potential in the work environment and achieve business success. This network:

- Recognizes, strengthens and supports all Black networks throughout the corporation
- Creates an atmosphere of nurturing and mentoring for all Black employees
- Allows CBEN to partner with DuPont leadership in addressing issues affecting Black employees
- Communicates information to all Black employees in a timely manner

- Encourages two-way communications among networks (sharing of best practices)

• Provides a more cohesive, concentrated and formalized effort to shape organizational decisions
• Seeks alignment and agreement to identify and implement initiatives affecting the greater whole
• Helps the corporate leadership understand issues affecting Black employees
• Serves as an agent for positive change within the DuPont Corporation, wholly owned subsidiaries and associated joint ventures.

DuPont Women's Network (DWN)

Our mission is to foster development of DuPont women (and DuPont as a whole) through the leveraging of tools and ideas, to enable retention and personal and business growth, and to improve the capability of the corporate intellectual asset base.

Hispanic Network (HISNET)

The mission of the Hispanic Network is to promote an environment across the corporation that empowers Hispanics to perform at their maximum potential and that recognizes and values the contribution of Hispanic employees.

The Hispanic Network will work toward accomplishing the following goals:

• Inclusion of Hispanics in all aspects of the businesses
• Empowerment of all Hispanics to contribute, learn, grow and advance
• Recognition of Hispanic employees for their accomplishments and contributions
• Fair and respectful treatment of Hispanic employees
• A corporate work environment that welcomes and supports Hispanic employees

DuPont Asian Group (DPAG)

• To promote a corporate environment that fully values and maximizes contributions of Asian-Americans
• To encourage and support DuPont Asian-Americans in achieving business success and personal growth

Bisexuals, Gays, Lesbians, Transgendered and Allies at DuPont Network (BGLAD)

Web site: www.dupontbglad.com/

BGLAD's mission is to help DuPont attract, utilize, and retain talented bisexual, gay, lesbian, and transgendered people by:

• Using its collective power to eliminate homophobia and heterosexism within DuPont businesses
• Serving as a resource regarding bisexual, gay, lesbian and transgender issues, and as a point of contact between DuPont and the community at large
• Partnering with Human Resources to address mental, emotional and physical health issues and to help design compen sation and benefit plans accordingly
• Providing opportunities to discuss and advance issues, to expand the network and increase the visibility of its members
• Ensuring a safe, healthy and supportive environment in the workplace that empowers bisexual, gay, lesbian and transgendered employees to be open and authentic about themselves
• Partnering with DuPont businesses to identify and capitalize on the bisexual, gay, lesbian and transgendered market

DuPont Part-Time Network (DPTEN)

The Global DuPont Part-time Employees Network exists to provide a community of support and information for all DuPont employees and businesses currently in or considering part-time roles. Our members are global, both men and women, working both full and part-time schedules.

DPTEN exists to maximize DuPont employee professional contribution, maximize personal life balance satisfaction and maximize DuPont sustainable business results through valued employees.

Our Purpose:

• To establish a community for full-service DuPont employees working part-time or any interested supportive DuPont employee working full time
• To provide a voice from this diverse work group
• To define the benefit/value of the part-time employee

There are both corporately sponsored and site-sponsored affinity networks within DuPont. Corporately sponsored networks receive funding support for initiatives and activities that are driven through DuPont Corporate Headquarters. However, site and business units maintain autonomy in their support of local networks.

The networks conduct bi-annual conferences. BGLAD, DPAG and HISNET included marketing segments during their last conference. Some networks conducted marketing surveys and used the information gathered to conduct sessions where conference participants helped business marketing managers identify opportunities for businesses covering automotive paints and refinishes, Corian® and Zodiaq® surfaces and SolaeTM products. The CBEN network identified an opportunity that provided future opportunity for the Crop Protection business and CBEN collected funds during its last conference to help villagers in underdeveloped countries.

Entry-Level Programs/Full-Time Opportunities

Field Engineering Program

Length of program: 4 years minimum (2 assignment minimum)
Geographic location(s) of program: U.S.-based program – locations throughout country

Please describe the training/training component of this program: Series of rotational assignments providing developmental experience in roles such as engineering, business, operations leadership, sales/marketing, R&D and Six Sigma. The program places a strong emphasis on career development via tools, training & coaching throughout the year. Required participation in annual development meeting that offers: training (soft & hard skills), presentations on business initiatives & programs, networking opportunities (with peers, technical leaders & management) and exposure to senior leadership via keynote presentation(s). Six Sigma training required.

Please describe any other educational components of this program: Tuition reimbursement supported via corporate program. Support for professional engineering society conferences & educational opportunities.

Web site: www1.dupont.com/dupontglobal/corp/careers/univ_fieldprograms_engineering.html

Finance Field Program

Length of program: 2-3 rotational assignments in 4-6 years
Geographic location(s) of program: United States

Please describe the training/training component of this program: Training would be aimed at providing:
• 3 diverse work experiences
• DuPont Finance University Courses – Ethics, DuPont Accounting, Internal Controls, etc.

Please describe any other educational components of this program: Support of certifications such as CPA, CIA and continuing education

Marketing Leadership Development Program

Length of program: 3 years

Geographic location(s) of program: Start in Wilmington, DE (for U.S. hires) and rotate within U.S. and potentially to one of our global markets

Please describe the training/training component of this program: The program is a development program comprised of many elements that could be considered training. For example, we have developed a Performance Assessment process unique to the program to ensure that our participants get the feedback they need to develop into potential business leaders.

With regard to formal training, we have scheduled formal training, which includes:

• Six Sigma training in the first year
• LEAD II training (middle manager training in DuPont) the second year
• At each of our semi-annual meetings we include topical training. Examples include: Myers-Briggs, "Strengthfinders," "The first 90 Days," etc.

Please describe any other educational components of this program: We offer tuition assistance to those foreign students whom we localize outside the U.S. Additionally, DuPont offers tuition reimbursement for pre-approved and agreed upon educational development opportunities.

Web site: www1.dupont.com/dupontglobal/corp/careers/univ_fieldprograms_marketing.html

DuPont Corporate IT Field Program

Length of program: Field Members are required to complete 3-5 assignments from 18-30 months in length. On average, members are part of the program for 6-8 years.

Geographic location(s) of program: Primarily within the contiguous states where DuPont is located, including Wilmington, DE

Please describe the training/training component of this program:
• Basic training and orientation for new employees
• DuPont Targeted Development Discussion Training
• Other training and education is based upon developmental gaps identified for each assignment

Please describe any other educational components of this program: For qualified candidates; there is tuition reimbursement program.

Web site: www1.dupont.com/dupontglobal/corp/careers/paths_infotech.html

DuPont Human Resources Field Program

Length of program: Based upon the series of rotational development assignments designed for the individual, a participant may be associated with the program from 3 to 5 years.

Geographic location(s) of program: The program is focused within the United States. The rotational design entails relocation to DuPont sites throughout the U.S. and corporate headquarters located in Wilmington, DE. Participants gain global business experience and an understanding of human resources policies and strategies associated with a global workforce. Opportunities to work on global teams and interact with employees around the world are provided to participants.

Please describe the training/training component of this program: The DuPont Human Resources Field Program provides participants with early-career development opportunities through a series of rotational assignments. Each rotational assignment is designed to give the individuals the opportunity to foster their skills in a variety of HR functional areas. Upon completion of the program, individuals will have a strong foundation on which to build an exciting career as an HR leader at DuPont. Program benefits include:

• Exposure to many of the businesses within the DuPont portfolio
• Extensive contact with senior level HR and business leaders across the company
• A support network of fellow program participants that will be beneficial to the individual throughout their career
• Meaningful assignments designed to engage individual development goals and career objectives
• Bi-annual development workshops created specifically for program participants

Please describe any other educational components of this program: Individual development is the foundation upon which the Human Resources Field Program is founded. The program has a listing of training programs that each individual is required to attend. Six Sigma training and certification is also required. Bi-annual development workshops designed specifically for program participants are also held. Individual development/training is identified through personal Targeted Development Plans. As with all employees at DuPont, program participants may participate in our Assistance for Lifelong Learning (tuition refund) program.

Strategic Plan and Diversity Leadership

Who has primary responsibility for leading diversity initiatives at your firm? Name of person and his/her title:

Willie C. Martin, Vice-President for Diversity and WorkLife
Sandra Lewis, Manager, Diversity and WorkLife

How often does the firm's management review the firm's diversity progress/results?

Ongoing reviews vary according to drivers/processes

How is the firm's diversity committee and/or firm management held accountable for achieving results?

Management is held accountable for achieving results in several different ways including the annual assignment of critical operating tasks and as part of managers' normal performance. Managers are held accountable by leadership, which reviews succession plans at every level of the organization. The CEO and a representative from the diversity area review succession plans for directors and all levels above. DuPont's corporately sponsored affinity networks hold conferences bi-annually. The conferences are a forum for employees to meet, review past performance and set new expectations for the coming years. During these conferences, leadership is also held directly accountable by employees.

The Stats

DEMOGRAPHIC PROFILE	TOTAL IN THE U.S.		TOTAL OUTSIDE THE U.S		TOTAL WORLDWIDE	
	2004	2003	2004	2003	2004	2003
Number of employees	12,199	12,891	34,000	53,000	60,000	81,000
Revenues	N/A	N/A	N/A	N/A	$27.3 billion	N/A

Retention and Professional Development

Please identify the specific steps you are taking to reduce the attrition rate of minority and women employees.

• Develop and/or support internal employee affinity groups (e.g., minority or women networks within the firm)
• Increase/review compensation relative to competition
• Increase/improve current work/life programs
• Adopt dispute resolution process
• Succession plan includes emphasis on diversity
• Work with minority and women employees to develop career advancement plans
• Review work assignments and hours billed to key client matters to make sure minority and women employees are not being excluded
• Strengthen mentoring program for all employees, including minorities and women
• Professional skills development program, including minority and women employees

Diversity Mission Statement

To foster an inclusive environment in a way that unleashes the potential of people and enables winning businesses to deliver significant shareholder value.

The Employer Says

DuPont believes in the power of our networks (affinity groups) and the role they play in helping employees realize their full potential and achieve business success. The six corporately sponsored networks (i.e., Corporate Black Employees Network (CBEN), DuPont Women's Network (DWN), Hispanic Network (HISNET), DuPont Asian Group (DPAG), Bisexual, Gay, Lesbian, Transgendered and Allies in DuPont Network (BGLAD), and the DuPont Part-Time Network (DPTEN) are critical to the success of the DuPont diversity strategic imperatives. The networks assist in recruiting, retention, representation, community relations, marketing and communications initiatives. They serve as sounding boards for the organization and are partners in helping DuPont achieve its diversity vision by improving performance feedback, employee development and retention and marketing strategies to diverse customers. The networks provide a diverse perspective and, in some cases, drive company policy. Additionally, they are role models of an inclusive organization, as all networks are open to anyone who wants to join in support of their objectives.

The networks are helping DuPont gain a global competitive advantage. For example, the DuPont Asian Network hosted a "Glimpse of Asia/Business Expo" during Asian Heritage Month, 2004 to build cultural awareness as DuPont moves into emerging markets. The exposition was so successful that the Hispanic Network soon followed with an exposition as well. These events are examples of how diverse groups of employees have contributed to business success by helping leadership understand that as DuPont moves into new markets, and subsequently, cultures, the appreciation for diversity within the business context is key to success.

Beginning as early as 1985, the results of several work/life surveys determined work balance issues were not only a concern for women, but also for men as well. DuPont concluded that work/life balance was a "mainstream business issue". Other work/life surveys have helped us gather information to implement programs that assist employees in becoming more productive. Follow-up surveys proved a direct correlation between work/life supports and happy, healthy employees. Feedback indicated that those employees that had used our work/life programs or knew about our work/life programs felt more supported and less stressed. It also indicated that employees were more productive and more likely to go the "extra mile" for the company's success.

Our current work/life offerings are:

• Paid Adoption Leave
• Adoption Assistance
• Dependent Care Spending Accounts

- Dependent Care Reimbursement for overnight travel
- Family Leave
- Flexible Work Practices
- Just In Time Care (back up dependent care program)
- LifeWorks (Resource and Referral Service)
- WorkLife Committees/Teams

Awards and Recognition (involving treatment of people)

The National Association for Female Executives (NAFE) named DuPont one of the "Top 30 Companies for Executive Women."

- DuPont was honored as one of the "100 Best Companies for Working Mothers" in the United States by *Working Mother* magazine.
- DuPont India was named one of India's top 25 employers by the 'Best Employers in India' 2004 survey released by Hewitt Associates.
- DuPont Argentina was named a "Best Place to Work" in the "2004 Great Place to Work" survey.
- DuPont Mexico was named a "Best Company to Work For", in a survey published by the Mexican business magazine *EXPANSION* and The Great Place To Work Institute®.
- DuPont was named one of the 30 Best Employers in Belgium for 2004.
- DuPont was one of 11 companies named a "Best Corporate Citizen" in China.
- DuPont Hong Kong was named a "Caring Company" by The Hong Kong Council of Social Service in honor of its donations and community service activities.

Dynegy Inc

1000 Louisiana St., Ste. 5800
Houston, TX 77002
Phone: (713) 507-6400
Toll Free: (877) 396-3499
www.dynegy.com

The Employer Says

Dynegy Inc. provides electricity, natural gas and natural gas liquids to markets and customers throughout the United States. Through its energy businesses, Power Generation and Natural Gas Liquids, the company owns and operates a diverse portfolio of assets. The company also strives to achieve diversity in its human capital assets, recognizing that diversity encompasses a great many factors such as ethnicity/race, gender, sexual orientation, language, religion, work status and social and economic status. One of the company's goals is to promote and maintain an inclusive environment free from discrimination.

Erie Insurance Group

100 Erie Insurance Place
Erie, PA 16530-0001
Phone: (814) 870-2000
Fax: (814) 870-3126
Toll Free: (800) 458-0811
www.erieinsurance.com

Locations (worldwide)

Illinois, Indiana, Maryland, North Carolina, New York, Ohio, Pennsylvania, Tennessee, Virginia, Wisconsin, West Virginia, Washington, D.C.

Diversity Leadership

Ann K. Scott, Vice President - Employment
100 Erie Insurance Place
Erie, PA 16530
Phone: (814) 870-2000
Fax: (814) 461-2694
E-mail: Ann.Scott@ErieInsurance.com

Recruiting

Please list the schools/types of schools at which you recruit.

• Private schools
• Public state schools:
• Historically Black Colleges and Universities (HBCUs)

We recruit at the following schools: Penn State University (University Park), Penn State Behrend (Erie), Gannon University, Edinboro University of PA, Allegheny College, University of Pittsburgh, Ohio State University, Slippery Rock University, Clarion University, Indiana University of PA, Thiel College, Westminster College, Robert Morris College, Howard University, Central State University, Cheyney University of PA, Mercyhurst College

Do you have any special outreach efforts that are directed to encourage minority students to consider your firm?

• Hold a reception for minority students
• Participate in/host minority student job fair(s)
• Firm's employees participate on career panels at school
• Outreach to leadership of minority student organizations

What activities does the firm undertake to attract minority and women employees?

• Seek referrals from other employees
• Utilize online job services
• Other: Sponsorship of diverse community organizations and events
• Other: Seek referrals from diverse community organizations

Internships and Co-ops

Future Focus – Actuarial & IT Internship Program

Deadline for application: March
Number of interns in the program in summer 2004 (internship) or 2004 (co-op): 27
Pay: Varies according to the work performed - generally between $11 and $16 per hour
Length of the program: Varies according to student schedule and department need; most are full-time May-August; opportunities may exist to continue part-time through the school year for local students
Percentage of interns/co-ops in the program who receive offers of full-time employment: 45%
Web site for internship/co-op information: www.erieinsurance.com

The Erie Insurance Group Future Focus internship is available to students whose permanent residence is within approximately 250 miles of ERIE's Home Office or who would like to begin a career in the Erie, PA community. Applications are accepted from students who are completing their sophomore or junior year. Qualifications include a major in IT or Computer Science for the IT internship, and in math or actuarial science for the Actuarial internship. A minimum GPA of 3.0 is also required. For an IT internship, completion of the first class in COBOL is preferred. For an Actuarial internship, passing at least one actuarial exam is preferred. Several interns are hired each year for this paid internship program. Relocation assistance is available if needed.

About the Special Features

The internship includes orientation to the company and the insurance industry through -

• A variety of challenging assignments in a stimulating work environment
• A personal mentor
• A welcome event for the interns and their mentors and supervisors
• Educational programs and round table lunches with company management
• Planned social events and opportunities for a wide variety of recreational activities will round out the interns' experience in Pennsylvania's scenic city on the lake

How to Apply

Contact Melissa DiGiacomo, Employment Specialist
Employment Department
Erie Insurance Group
100 Erie Insurance Place
Erie, PA 16530
Phone: (814) 870-4035
Fax: (814) 461-2893
E-mail: Melissa.DiGiacomo@ErieInsurance.com

Entry-Level Programs/Full-Time Opportunities

Erie University Claims Adjuster Training Program

Length of program: 4 months
Geographic location(s) of program: Erie Insurance field claims office service territories; locations vary according to the needs of the company at the time of the training class

ERIE University is an exciting, dynamic training program that prepares bright, independent, hard working candidates for careers in insurance claims. Training consists of a combination of fieldwork at the branch of initial hire, and travel to our state-of-the art facility in Erie, Pa for classroom training in an intense, supportive learning environment. Training lasts for approximately four

months and covers a variety of topics such as: overview of the insurance industry and Erie Insurance; ERIE's service philosophy & standards; ERIE's product lines; claims, marketing, underwriting and other functions and procedures; field/home office inter-actions; product and policy information; and other related topics.

Trainees attend classes taught by insurance experts both on company time and after hours. They also independently complete a variety of assigned projects and handle claims hands-on in the field. Trainees are also assigned a mentor who is a senior claims representative. Insurance training through the Insurance Institute of America is also included.

The ERIE University program leads to a career path in insurance that could eventually lead to management opportunities. Adjusters start in the position of Claims Adjuster I. With experience and additional education, they may advance to Claims Adjuster II and III. Then to Claims Examiner, Claims Supervisor, Claims Manager, etc.

Requirements include:

Bachelor's degree, any major, with some work experience beyond graduation. Willingness to enroll in extensive training and commit to the challenging and rewarding career of claims adjusting. Enthusiasm about locating in a territory according to the company's needs. Insurance knowledge is not required.

Before entering ERIE University, candidates must commit to locating in an assigned territory as determined by the company's needs. Assigned territories will be in areas that report to the hiring office. For example, our Indianapolis Branch serves the entire southern portion of the state of Indiana from Illinois east to Ohio and from the Kentucky border north to approximately Lafayette and Muncie. Our Rochester Branch serves the entire state of New York. Candidates should be enthusiastic about relocating any-where within their branch's service area.

A valid drivers license, good driving record, and acceptable credit history are required — Motor Vehicle, Credit, and Criminal his-tory reports will be ordered. College degrees will also be verified.

Good communication, interpersonal, analytical and organizational skills are required, along with independence and self-motiva-tion.

Strategic Plan and Diversity Leadership

How does the firm's leadership communicate the importance of diversity to everyone at the firm?

Our commitment to diversity is incorporated into all of our communications both internally and externally. Our message of equal professional service is incorporated into all of our management and employee training.

Who has primary responsibility for leading diversity initiatives at your firm?

Michael Krahe, Executive Vice President, Leadership & Development

Does your firm currently have a diversity committee?

No

Does the committee and/or diversity leader establish and set goals or objectives consistent with management's priorities?

Yes

Has the firm undertaken a formal or informal diversity program or set of initiatives aimed at increasing the diversity of the firm?

Yes, informal

The Stats

Employees: 4,432 (2004, U.S.)
Employees: 4,330 (2003, U.S.)
Total Operating Revenue: $1.123 billion (2004, U.S.)
Total Operating Revenue: $1,049 billion (2003, U.S.)

(Erie Insurance Group has U.S. operations only)

Retention and Professional Development

How do 2004 minority and female attrition rates generally compare to those experienced in the prior year period?

About the same as in prior years

Please identify the specific steps you are taking to reduce the attrition rate of minority and women employees.

• Strengthen mentoring program for all employees, including minorities and women
• Professional skills development program, including minority and women employees

Fannie Mae

3900 Wisconsin Ave., NW
Washington, DC 20016-2892
Phone: (202) 752-7000
Fax: (202) 752-3868
www.fanniemae.com/careers

Locations (worldwide)

Washington, D.C., Atlanta, Philadelphia, Chicago, Dallas, Pasadena, plus 54 partnership offices across the U.S.

Diversity Leadership

Emmanuel Bailey, VP, Chief Diversity Officer
Phil Hendrickson, Diversity Sourcing Manager

Employment Contact

Mary Tennyson, Campus Recruiter
Fannie Mae
3900 Wisconsin Avenue, NW
Washington, D.C. 20016
Phone: (202) 752-3900

Recruiting

Please list the schools/types of schools at which you recruit.

• Ivy League schools
• Public state schools:
• Historically Black Colleges and Universities (HBCUs)
• Hispanic Serving Institutions (HSIs)

Do you have any special outreach efforts that are directed to encourage minority students to consider your firm?

• Conferences: NSHMBA, NBMBA
• Participate in/host minority student job fair(s)
• Firm's employees participate on career panels at school
• Scholarships or intern/fellowships for minority students

What activities does the firm undertake to attract minority and women employees?

• Conferences
• Participate at minority job fairs
• Seek referrals from other employees
• Utilize online job services

Do you use executive recruiting/search firms to seek to identify new diversity hires?

Yes

Internships and Co-ops

Virginia High Tech Internship Program

Deadline for application: June 1, each year
Number of interns in the program in summer 2004 (internship) or 2004 (co-op): 5
Pay: Hourly rate based upon year in school
Length of the program: 10 weeks
Percentage of interns/co-ops in the program who receive offers of full-time employment: 10-20%

To apply, please e-mail campus_recruiting@fanniemae.com

MBA Internship and Scholarship

Deadline for application: Feb. 15
Number of interns in the program in summer 2004 (internship) or 2004 (co-op): 1 MBA
Length of the program: 10 weeks
Percentage of interns/co-ops in the program who receive offers of full-time employment: 100%

D.C. Public High School Program

Deadline for application: June 1
Number of interns in the program in summer 2004 (internship) or 2004 (co-op): 10
Pay: Minimum wage
Length of the program: 8 weeks
Percentage of interns/co-ops in the program who receive offers of full-time employment: None; it is for work experience in corporate.

Scholarships

MBA Scholarship

Deadline for application for the scholarship program: Feb. 15
Scholarship award amount: $2K

Seeking MBA intern interested in housing finance and minority home ownership; 1st year MBA with strong finance skills; strong academic performance; recommendation from professor and personal recommendation.

Affinity Groups/Employee Networks

Fannie Mae has several affinity groups all intended to foster a culture in which employees recognize and appreciate the diversity of their coworkers; the groups are employee led and are encouraged to raise any issues and concerns to leadership. The groups include:

- African American
- Asian
- Catholic
- Parents with children with special needs

- Christian
- Hispanic
- Jewish
- Lesbian, Gay and Transgender
- Muslim
- Single Parent
- US Military Service
- Women

Each group determines its meeting times and each group must submit a proposed charter and mission statement to be recognized as an Employee Networking Group.

Entry-Level Programs/Full-Time Opportunities

For the following section, please repeat this template as necessary if you have more than one full-time, entry-level program, training program or management/leadership program at your organization.

Analyst Program

> *Length of program:* 24 months
> *Geographic location(s) of program:* Primarily D.C. or Bethesda, MD

Please describe the training/training component of this program: 2-3 weeks at start of program

Internal Audit

> *Length of program:* Full-time opportunities
> *Geographic location(s) of program:* Washington, D.C.

Controllers

> *Length of program:* Full-time opportunities
> *Geographic location(s) of program:* Washington, D.C.

Strategic Plan and Diversity Leadership

How does the firm's leadership communicate the importance of diversity to everyone at the firm?

We have an Office of Diversity and they are responsible for many programs that promote a diverse work environment. Fannie Mae is very committed to the minority home ownership challenges and our business is providing liquidity to the mortgage finance market so that more lenders can offer loans to potential home buyers. We set minority home ownership goals each year. Every employee of Fannie Mae appreciates and contributes to that mission every day in the work they do.

Who has primary responsibility for leading diversity initiatives at your firm?

Emmanuel Bailey, VP and Chief Diversity Officer

Does your firm currently have a diversity committee?

Yes

If yes, does the committee's representation include one or more members of the firm's management/executive committee (or the equivalent)?

Yes

Does the committee and/or diversity leader establish and set goals or objectives consistent with management's priorities?

Yes. Diversity is one of ten core commitments essential to our success.

Has the firm undertaken a formal or informal diversity program or set of initiatives aimed at increasing the diversity of the firm?

Yes, formal. We have an Office of Diversity whose primary mission is to foster a diverse culture and environment through policies, programs, thought leadership and partnerships. Our recruiting efforts are very focused on diversity efforts and we partner with many constituents both internally and externally to be successful in attracting a diverse workforce to Fannie Mae.

How often does the firm's management review the firm's diversity progress/results?

Quarterly

The Stats

Employees: 5,300 (2004, U.S.)

Retention and Professional Development

How do 2004 minority and female attrition rates generally compare to those experienced in the prior year period?

About the same as in prior years

Please identify the specific steps you are taking to reduce the attrition rate of minority and women employees.

• Develop and/or support internal employee affinity groups (e.g., minority or women networks within the firm)
• Increase/improve current work/life programs
• Strengthen mentoring program for all employees, including minorities and women
• Professional skills development program, including minority and women employees
• Other: training class on diversity

Diversity Mission Statement

As a corporation, Fannie Mae is guided by a set of values that permeates the way we conduct our business. Honesty, integrity and respect for others must be central to everything we do. Just as they are at the core of the way we do business, these values are permanent.

In keeping with these values, our corporate philosophy on diversity is based on respect for one another and recognition that each person brings his or her own unique attributes to the corporation. We are committed to providing equal opportunity for all employees to reach their full potential; it is a fundamental value, and it makes good business sense. Fannie Mae will be most successful in meeting its public mission and our corporate goals when we fully capitalize on the skills, talents and potential of all our employees.

Fannie Mae's approach to diversity is based on a two-tiered business rationale driven by our mission to tear down barriers, lower costs and increase the opportunities for home ownership and rental housing for all Americans. By this we mean that we designed

the program to create opportunities for all employees internally, which in turn empowers employees to create opportunities for all Americans externally. The reason we do this is simple: it makes good business sense, because it enables us to fulfill our mission. We must reflect the diversity of the society we serve in order to understand and address their home-buying needs.

FedEx

942 S. Shady Grove Rd.
Memphis, TN 38120
Phone: (901) 818-7500
Fax: (901) 395-2000
www.fedex.com

Diversity Leadership

Thelma Person, Manager, Human Resources
3660 Hacks Cross Road, Building F, 3rd floor.
Memphis, TN 38125
Phone: (901) 434-6242
Fax: (901) 434-6374
E-mail: Thelma.person-savage@fedex.com

Recruiting

Please list the schools/types of schools at which you recruit.

• Ivy League schools
• Other private schools
• Public state schools
• Historically Black Colleges and Universities (HBCUs)

Do you have any special outreach efforts that are directed to encourage minority students to consider your firm?

• Advertise in minority student association publication(s)
• Sponsor minority student association events
• Firm's employees participate on career panels at school
• Outreach to leadership of minority student organizations
• Scholarships or intern/fellowships for minority students

What activities does the firm undertake to attract minority and women employees?

• Partner programs with women and minority associations
• Participate at minority job fairs
• Seek referrals from other employees
• Utilize online job services

Do you use executive recruiting/search firms to seek to identify new diversity hires?

No

Internships and Co-ops

FedEx Express

Deadline for application: None

Number of interns in the program in summer 2004 (internship): 39 total

Pay: $2,700 month

Length of the program: 10-12 weeks

Percentage of interns/co-ops in the program who receive offers of full-time employment: 10 %

Departments that hire interns include: Finance, Legal, Air Operations, IT, Engineering, Latin American /International and Customer service. Participants must be in undergraduate or graduate school.

Affinity Groups/Employee Networks

Name(s) of affinity group(s)

• Asia
• African American
• Hispanic
• Women

Strategic Plan and Diversity Leadership

How does the firm's leadership communicate the importance of diversity to everyone at the firm?

E -mails, web site, quarterly diversity newsletter, forums for affinity groups, meetings, etc.

Who has primary responsibility for leading diversity initiatives at your firm?

Linda Carter, Manager, Affirmative Action & Diversity

Does your firm currently have a diversity committee?

Yes. The Diversity Committee is made up of 12 vice presidents from different divisions at FedEx, and they meet quarterly.

If yes, does the committee's representation include one or more members of the firm's management/executive committee (or the equivalent)?

Yes

Total executives on the committee: 12 vice presidents

Does the committee and/or diversity leader establish and set goals or objectives consistent with management's priorities?

Yes

Has the firm undertaken a formal or informal diversity program or set of initiatives aimed at increasing the diversity of the firm?

Yes, formal. Goals and strategies of the VP Diversity Council:

1. Develop strategies that attract, promote and retain diverse talent at all levels of the corporation
2. Create the best work environment for diverse groups through programs, services and benefits enhancements

3. Educate and raise awareness about diversity at FedEx

4. Support the use of diverse suppliers

5. Promote FedEx as a neighbor and employer of choice by enhancing its image through community outreach programs and internal and external communication strategies

6. Support the development and implementation of marketing strategies aimed at diverse customers

7. Develop corporate diversity strategies, programs and goals and ensure that the corporation accomplishes its diversity objectives

How often does the firm's management review the firm's diversity progress/results?

Quarterly

Retention and Professional Development

How do 2004 minority and female attrition rates generally compare to those experienced in the prior year period?

About the same as in prior years

Please identify the specific steps you are taking to reduce the attrition rate of minority and women employees.

• Develop and/or support internal employee affinity groups (e.g., minority or women networks within the firm)
• Increase/review compensation relative to competition
• Increase/improve current work/life programs

Diversity Mission Statement

Our diverse workforce, supplier base and supporting culture enable FedEx to better serve our customers and compete more effectively in the global marketplace. We value the contributions and perspectives of all employees regardless of race, gender, culture, religion, age, nationality, disability or sexual orientation. We will strive in our workplace practices to deal with our employees, customers and suppliers in a fair and ethical manner.

The Employer Says

We continue to be viewed as innovators and trendsetters in the business world and are often asked to share our progressive systems, programs and philosophies that have earned us our reputation as an Employer of Choice. FedEx has earned recognition as one of the World's Most Admired Companies (*Fortune* magazine). Other national awards include:

• 50 Best Companies for Minorities to Work – *Fortune* magazine
• The 100 Best Companies to Work for in America – *Fortune* magazine
• 100 Best Companies for Working Mothers – *Working Mother* magazine
• 50 Best Companies in America for Asians, Blacks, & Hispanics – *Fortune* magazine
• 20 Better Places to Work – *Mother Jones* magazine
• Outstanding Corporate Support Award – National Minority Business Council
• Award for Excellence in Corporate Community Services – Points of Light Foundation
• The Top 100 Companies Providing the Most Opportunities for Hispanics – *Hispanic* magazine
• Diversity 100 Recognition Award – *Next Step* magazine

Fidelity Investments

82 Devonshire St
Boston, MA 02109
Phone: (617) 563-7000
www.fidelity.com/jobs

Locations (worldwide)

Fidelity is headquartered in Boston, with eight regional centers in the U.S. & Canada and investor centers in more than 91 U.S. cities. International sites include: Canada, Hong Kong, Japan, France, India, U.K., Germany and Ireland

Fidelity Investments

Fidelity Investments is one of the most trusted providers of financial services and investment resources that helps individuals and institutions meet their financial objectives. Fidelity offers investment management, retirement planning, brokerage, and human resources and benefits outsourcing services. Over the course of building an industry-leading, worldwide business, we have become known for our integrity, commitment to continuous improvement, state-of-the-art technology, and peerless customer service. Fidelity offers market-competitive compensation and a comprehensive benefits package including health, insurance, and retirement, as well as a variety of work life programs.

Learn about our opportunities:
www.fidelity.com/jobs

Recruiting

Please list the schools/types of schools at which you recruit.

• Ivy League schools
• Other private schools
• Public state schools
• Other predominantly minority and/or women's colleges

Do you have any special outreach efforts that are directed to encourage minority students to consider your firm?

• Advertise in minority student association publication(s)
• Firm's employees participate on career panels at school

What activities does the firm undertake to attract minority and women employees?

• Partner programs with women and minority associations
• Participate at minority job fairs
• Seek referrals from other employees
• Utilize online job services

Do you use executive recruiting/search firms to seek to identify new diversity hires?

No

Internships and Co-ops

Fidelity Intern program

Deadline for application: April

Number of interns in the program in summer 2004 (internship) or 2004 (co-op): 400 interns and co-ops company wide

Length of the program: 12 weeks

2004 percentage of interns/co-ops in the program who receive offers of full-time employment: 30%

Web site for internship/co-op information: www.fidelity.com/jobs

The Stats

Employees: 30,000 (2004, U.S.)

Employees: 3,000 (2004, outside U.S.)

Fifth Third Bank

38 Fountain Square Plaza
Cincinnati, OH 45263
Phone: (513) 579-5300
Toll Free: (800) 972-3030
www.53.com (Fifth Third Bank is developing a new college recruiting website)

Locations
Ohio, Indiana, Illinois, Kentucky,
Tennessee, Florida, Michican, Indiana,
West Virginia

Diversity Leadership
Vickie Mc Mullen, Campus Relations Leader
38 Fountain Square Plaza
Cincinnati, OH 45263
Phone: (513) 534-6264
Fax: (513) 534-8621
E-mail: Vickie.McMullen@53.com

Recruiting

Please list the schools/types of schools at which you recruit.

- *Private schools:* Xavier University (Ohio) and University of Dayton
- *Public state schools:* University of Cincinnati, Ohio State University, Northern Kentucky University, Michigan State University, University of Illinois, Miami University of Ohio, Case Western Reserve University and other regional universities.
- *Historically Black Colleges and Universities (HBCUs):* Wilberforce University

Fifth Third Bank is currently reviewing its target schools and considering adding additional historically black colleges and universities to our campus recruiting efforts.

Do you have any special outreach efforts that are directed to encourage minority students to consider your firm?

- Receptions for minority students
- *Conferences:* National Black MBA, National Society of Hispanic MBAs
- Sponsor minority student association events
- Firm's employees participate on career panels at universities
- Other: Contributes funds to minority scholarship programs
- Other: Participate in the INROADS program

What activities does the firm undertake to attract minority and women employees?

- Partner programs with women and minority professional associations
- Attends minority job fairs
- Seeks referrals from other employees
- Utilize online job services

Do you use executive recruiting/search firms to seek to identify new diversity hires?

Yes

If yes, list all women- and/or minority-owned executive search/recruiting firms to which the firm paid a fee for placement services in the past 12 months:

We use majority-owned firms, but demand diverse slates of candidates.

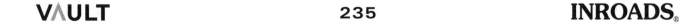

Internships and Co-ops

Deadline for applications to internship/co-op program: We follow campus deadlines for applications for co-ops and interns.

Number of interns in the program in summer 2004 (internship) or 2004 (co-op): 10 total

Pay: $12.00 – $14.00 an hour

Length of the program: 8 weeks

Percentage of interns/co-ops in the program who receive offers of full-time employment: 60%

A College Recruiting website is being developed which will provide internship/co-op information.

Co-op and internship opportunities currently exist in: Audit, Operations, IT, Finance, Tax, the Commercial Division and the Asset Management Group.

Applicants must have a GPA of 3.0 or above and a major in Accounting, Finance, IT, Business Administration or Marketing. For the Operations internship, a specialization in Operations is desired. Additional desired characteristics include strong analytical skills, ability to work in a team environment, good pc skills and good oral and written communication skills.

Affinity Groups/Employee Networks

Women's Network (Cincinnati, Cleveland, Columbus, Toledo, Detroit); African American Network (Cleveland, Chicago and Detroit); Hispanic Network (Chicago)

The Affinity Groups' purpose is to act as support networks, and to encourage and provide opportunities for professional development through mentors, seminars and networking. Meetings are held once a month.

Entry-Level Programs/Full-Time Opportunities

IT Leadership Program, Operatons Associate Program, Retail Associate Program, Commercial Associate Program, EFT Associate Program

Length of program: Varies from 6-18 months

Geographic location(s) of program: Most 5/3rd Bank locations (the exception being the Operations Associates Program and the IT Leadership Program - in Cincinnati only)

Please describe the training/training component of this program: Business practices, operations and procedures in each department rotation; acquiring the knowledge and skills and experience required for assuming a permanent role. All programs provide classroom and on-the-job training.

Please describe any other educational components of this program: Fifth Third Bank offers classroom and on-line professional development courses for knowledge and skill development.

Tuition reimbursement is offered as a benefit for all employees.

Strategic Plan and Diversity Leadership

How does the firm's leadership communicate the importance of diversity to everyone at the firm?

Diversity web site, company newsletters, Diversity Board

Who has primary responsibility for leading diversity initiatives at your firm?

Ann Lazarus-Barnes, VP and Director of Diversity

Does your firm currently have a diversity committee?

Yes. The Board meets on a bi-monthly basis and is divided into four key committees.

If yes, does the committee's representation include one or more members of the firm's management/executive committee (or the equivalent)?

Yes

Please describe the committee.

   Total executives on the committee: 10

Does the committee and/or diversity leader establish and set goals or objectives consistent with management's priorities?

Yes. The purpose of the Board is to insure strategic success on diversity priorities.

Has the firm undertaken a formal or informal diversity program or set of initiatives aimed at increasing the diversity of the firm?

Yes, formal

How often does the firm's management review the firm's diversity progress/results?

Quarterly

How is the firm's diversity committee and/or firm management held accountable for achieving results?

Each EVP and affiliate president is responsible for achieving success as laid out by the Diversity Plan.

The Stats

Employees: 21,027 (2004, U.S.)
Employees: 20,211 (2003, U.S.)
Revenue: $1.525 billion (2004, U.S.)
Revenue: $1,665 billion (2003, U.S.)

Retention and Professional Development

How do 2004 minority and female attrition rates generally compare to those experienced in the prior year period?

About the same as in prior years

Please identify the specific steps you are taking to reduce the attrition rate of minority and women employees.

• Develop and/or support internal employee affinity groups (e.g., minority or women networks within the firm)
• Increase/review compensation relative to competition
• Increase/improve current work/life programs
• Succession plan includes emphasis on diversity
• Work with minority and women employees to develop career advancement plans

Diversity Mission Statement

Fifth Third Bank has a strong commitment to respect each individual and value every employee's personal contribution to the business. At Fifth Third Bank, we create an environment where everyone can be fully engaged, leaving no one out. We value diversity as an asset and will provide an environment where all individuals can maximize their potential for development.

The Employer Says

All affiliates and lines of business have diversity plans. These plans have clear and measurable goals and focus on key initiatives to support long-term results, particularly in the key areas of recruitment, retention, advancement and promotion. Each line of business and affiliate has its own plan so that there is a common level of expectation and performance.

FPL Group

700 Universe Blvd.
P.O. Box 14000
Juno Beach, FL 33408
Phone: (561) 694-4000
Fax: (561) 694-4620
www.fpl.com

Locations (worldwide)
Various cities in Florida and other cities in the U.S.

Diversity Leadership
Yolanda Cornell, Manager of EEO and Diversity

Employment Contact
Courtney Greenwell, College Recruiter
700 Universe Blvd HRR/JB
Juno Beach, FL 33408
Phone: (561) 694-6211
Fax: (561) 694-4669
E-mail: Courtney_Greenwell@fpl.com

Recruiting

Please list the schools/types of schools at which you recruit.

• Ivy League schools
• Other private schools
• Public state schools
• Historically Black Colleges and Universities (HBCUs)

Do you have any special outreach efforts that are directed to encourage minority students to consider your firm?

• Conferences: SWE, NSBE, NSHMBA, NSBMBA
• Sponsor minority student association events

What activities does the firm undertake to attract minority and women employees?

• Conferences (see above)
• Seek referrals from other employees

Do you use executive recruiting/search firms to seek to identify new diversity hires?

No

Internships and Co-ops

Internship Program

Number of interns in the program in summer 2004 (internship) or 2004 (co-op): 94
Pay: $870-$1,672 bi-weekly
Length of the program: Approximately 12 weeks
Web site for internship/co-op information: www.fpl.com

Interns are hired throughout the company in various different business units. Approximately 90% of the interns are in the engineering field. Qualifications usually entail working towards a relevant degree in the area of the internship, and successful completion of a screening interview.

Entry-Level Programs/Full-Time Opportunities

Full-time New Hires

Geographic location(s) of program: Various cities in Southeast Florida

Please describe the training/training component of this program: On-the-job training

Please describe any other educational components of this program: The company provides tuition reimbursement for graduate and undergraduate degrees.

Strategic Plan and Diversity Leadership

Who has primary responsibility for leading diversity initiatives at your firm?

Yolanda Cornell Manager of EEO and Diversity

Does the committee and/or diversity leader establish and set goals or objectives consistent with management's priorities?

Yes

Has the firm undertaken a formal or informal diversity program or set of initiatives aimed at increasing the diversity of the firm?

Yes, formal. We have a team of diversity professionals whose main goal is to concentrate on minority recruiting and meet the guidelines of hiring minorities.

The Stats

Employees: 14,805 (2004, U.S.)
Revenue: $10.522 billion (2004, U.S.)
Revenue: $9,630 billion (2003, U.S.)

Retention and Professional Development

How do 2004 minority and female attrition rates generally compare to those experienced in the prior year period?

About the same as in prior years

Please identify the specific steps you are taking to reduce the attrition rate of minority and women employees.

• Increase/improve current work/life programs
• Succession plan includes emphasis on diversity
• Work with minority and women employees to develop career advancement plans
• Professional skills development program, including minority and women employees

Diversity Mission Statement

We will foster an inclusive business environment that values and leverages the diverse talents, perspectives and ideas of all employees.

find out what's blowing in the wind

If 20 of GE's wind turbines were used to replace the same amount of energy generated in the U.S. through traditional sources, greenhouse gas emissions could be reduced by an amount equal to taking nearly 27,000 cars off the road in the U.S. We call this ecomagination. At GE we invite you to find your answer to ecomagination through a career in engineering, finance, manufacturing, sales and marketing, human resources, or information technology.

ecomagination℠
to learn more visit us at gecareers.com
an equal opportunity employer

GE imagination at work

A diversified technology, financial services, media company.

GE

3135 Easton Tpke.
Fairfield, CT 06828-0001
Phone (203) 373-2211
Fax: (203) 373-3131
gecareers.com

Locations (worldwide)
100 countries

Employment Contact
Shari Hubert, Manager, Campus Recruiting
Steve Canale, Manager Recruiting & Staffing
Services
3135 Easton Turnpike
Fairfield, CT 06828
Phone: (203) 373-2246
Fax: (203) 373-3292
E-mail: steve.canale@ge.com

Recruiting

Please list the schools/types of schools at which you recruit.

• Ivy League schools
• Other private schools
• Public state schools
• Historically Black Colleges and Universities (HBCUs)
• Hispanic Serving Institutions (HSIs)
• Other predominantly minority and/or women's colleges

GE actively recruits at 38 Focused Schools in the U.S. and hires approximately 1000 undergrad, masters and Ph.D students each year in the U.S., and nearly an equal number outside the U.S. Every year, GE businesses have hires from over 100 U.S. colleges with 60% coming from the 38 Focused Schools.

Do you have any special outreach efforts that are directed to encourage minority students to consider your firm?

• Hold a reception for minority students
• Conferences: NSBE, SHPE, NBMBA NSHMBA, SWE, INROADS, Consortium, DISCO
• Advertise in minority student association publication(s)
• Participate in/host minority student job fair(s)
• Sponsor minority student association events
• Firm's employees participate on career panels at school
• Outreach to leadership of minority student organizations
• Scholarships or intern/fellowships for minority students
• Other: Jackie Robinson Foundation, NACME

What activities does the firm undertake to attract minority and women employees?

• Partner programs with women and minority associations
• Conferences: NSBE, SHPE, NBMBA NSHMBA, SWE, INROADS, Consortium, DISCO
• Participate at minority job fairs
• Seek referrals from other employees
• Utilize online job services

• Other: GE is a founding member of many of the organizations listed above. GE actively strives to recruit the best and brightest college students from all ethnic backgrounds.

Do you use executive recruiting/search firms to seek to identify new diversity hires?

No, not for entry level college and MBA recruiting

Internships and Co-ops

GE Early Identification (EID)

Deadline for application: Typically April/May

Number of interns in the program in summer 2005 (internship) or 2005 (co-op): 2400

Pay: varies by degree and college year

Length of the program: Typically 10-12 weeks

Percentage of interns/co-ops in the program who receive offers of full-time employment: 50% of those eligible

Web site for internship/co-op information: gecareers.com

GPA minimum 3.0 (cumulative). Looking for bright students with demonstrated academic success, leadership skills and a willingness to learn and grow professionally.

Scholarships

All scholarship inquiries should be directed to the GE Foundation. The Foundation provides scholarships to NSBE, Jackie Robinson, SWE, NBMBA and Consortium scholars, to name a few.

Affinity Groups/Employee Networks

African American Forum (AAF), Hispanic Forum, Asian Pacific Forum, Women's Network

The purpose of all affinity groups is to provide an organization that can provide coaching, networking and career advancement opportunities to its membership.

Entry-Level Programs/Full-Time Opportunities

• Financial Management Program (FMP)
• Edison Engineering Development Program (EEDP)
• Operations Management Leadership Program (OMLP)
• Information Management Leadership Program IMLP)
• Human Resources Leadership Program (HRLP)
• Experienced Commercial Leadership Program (ECLP)

Length of programs: All are 2 years

Geographic location(s) of program: U.S. and global

Please describe the training/training component of this program: All programs consist of formal classroom training within the function and leadership and six sigma quality training. Training is also complimented by on-line training courses. There are typically four job rotations while in the program.

Please describe any other educational components of this program: All employees are eligible for tuition reimbursement for studies in fields related to their positions.

Strategic Plan and Diversity Leadership

How does the firm's leadership communicate the importance of diversity to everyone at the firm?

E-mails, web site, newsletters, meetings, etc.

Who has primary responsibility for leading diversity initiatives at your firm?

Deb Elam, Manager, Global Employer of Choice

Does your firm currently have a diversity committee?

Diversity is reviewed annually at all levels during GE's formal HR refer process referred to as "Session C."

The Stats

DEMOGRAPHIC PROFILE	TOTAL IN THE U.S.		TOTAL OUTSIDE THE U.S		TOTAL WORLDWIDE	
	2004	2003	2004	2003	2004	2003
Number of employees	168,000	N/A	145,000	N/A	313,000	N/A
Revenues	$86 billion	N/A	$70 billion	N/A	$156 billion	N/A

Retention and Professional Development

How do 2004 minority and female attrition rates generally compare to those experienced in the prior year period?

About the same as in prior years

Please identify the specific steps you are taking to reduce the attrition rate of minority and women employees.

Other: The most important thing that GE does to retain all top talent is to provide them challenging and rewarding work. In addition, GE provides the tools and networks that give all employees an equal opportunity to grow and advance their careers.

Diversity Mission Statement

Diversity & Inclusiveness

As a global company with operations in more than 100 countries, diversity isn't merely a noble idea – it's the reflection of our business. Every day GE works to ensure that all employees, no matter where they are located in the world and no matter where they come from, have an opportunity to contribute and succeed. Encompassed in that goal are promoting traditional ideas of diversity including ethnicity, race and gender, while at the same time exploring more contemporary concepts like inclusiveness.

We track diverse representation at all levels of the organization – by business, by geography and by function. We have robust reviews with the leadership of the company to show us where progress is being made, to glean best practices and where we have work to do, so that we can intensify efforts. Metrics are critical in setting goals and achieving results.

While GE has made progress, significant efforts continue to improve the representation of women, U.S. Minorities and Non-U.S. citizens in leadership roles in the company. In 2004, 33% of company officers and 40% of senior executives were diverse (women, U.S. minorities, and non U.S. citizens) versus 22% of company officers and 29% of senior executives in 2000. Nearly one quarter of GE's leadership is outside the U.S.

One of the key mechanisms for facilitating dialogue and progress in our diversity efforts is GE's Affinity Networks: The African American Forum, The Asian Pacific American Forum, The Hispanic Forum, The Women's Network and The Native American Forum. These Affinity Networks play a critical role in attracting, developing, engaging and retaining employees at all levels across the company. These networks work in close partnership with Chairman and CEO Jeff Immelt, business leaders and the human resources team to continually uncover ways to improve in this area and opportunities for growth. These range from mentoring employees for professional growth to engaging customers for business growth. One powerful example of the impact the Affinity Networks have is in GE's philanthropic work in Africa. This initiative was a direct result of the Chairman's involvement with The African American Forum and a collective desire to make a difference in Africa.

Building off of the success of GE's Affinity Networks, employees in Japan were inspired to launch the "Barrier Free Network" in October 2004. This group aims to improve the mutual understanding between employees with disabilities and their colleagues by increasing awareness of key issues and their impact. This is one of the first employee groups for the disabled ever formed in a major company in Japan.

This group will work to ensure that disabled employees have the same access to opportunity and the ability to reach their highest potential within the company. The group has launched a web site that details different types of disabilities and awareness activities developed by the network. The group has also started a sign language session with 20 participants who are learning the language for the first time.

Another facet of the GE diversity strategy is a commitment to diversity of its supply base. The company's Supplier Diversity program started more than 25 years ago and focuses on the development and inclusion of all capable suppliers.

The Employer Says

2004 Awards:

- Catalyst Award for efforts to advance women leaders within GE
- Executive Leadership Council Corporate Award for leadership in advancing diversity in corporate America
- *Working Mother* magazine "100 Best Companies for Working Mothers" 2003, 2004
- Best Place to Work EU (Multiple Locations; China, Ireland, Czech Republic, Spain, etc.)
- Diversity Inc – Top 10 Best Companies for Asian Americans
- *Woman Engineer* – #1 Company
- World's Most Respected Company – *Financial Times*
- Global Most Admired Company – *Fortune* magazine
- Top 50 Technology Companies – *Scientific American*

Gillette Company, The

Prudential Tower Building
Boston, MA 02199
Phone: (617) 421-7000
Fax: (617) 421-7123
www.gillette.com/careers

Locations (worldwide)
Manufacturing operations at 31 facilities in 14 countries - 54 subsidiaries

Diversity Leadership
Dawn Frazier-Bohnert, VP, Workforce Diversity & Inclusion
Phone: (617) 421-7994
Fax: (617) 421-8581
E-mail: Dawn_Frazier-Bohnert@gillette.com

Employment Contact
Andrea Kwiatkowski, Manager, Talent Acquisition
Prudential Tower Building
800 Boylston Street
Boston, MA 02199
Phone: (617) 421-9525

Recruiting

Please list the schools/types of schools at which you recruit.

• Private schools
• Public state schools
• Historically Black Colleges and Universities (HBCUs)

Undergraduate:

• Babson College
• Northeastern University
• Bentley College
• Ohio State University
• Boston College
• University of Mass.-Amherst
• MIT
• Worcester Polytechnical Institute
• NC A&T State University

Do you have any special outreach efforts that are directed to encourage minority students to consider your firm?

• Participate in/host minority student job fair(s)
• Sponsor minority student association events
• Firm's employees participate on career panels at school
• Scholarships or intern/fellowships for minority students

What activities does the firm undertake to attract minority and women employees?

• Partner programs with women and minority associations
• Conferences   Please list
• Participate at minority job fairs
• Seek referrals from other employees

• Utilize online job services
• Conferences: National Black MBA Association; National Sales Network; National Society of Hispanic MBAs; Society of Women Engineers; Consortium for Graduate Study; National Society of Black Engineers; National Association of Black Accountants; Delta Sigma Theta Sorority; National Organization of Black Chemists & Engineers; Association of Latino Professionals in Finance & Accounting

Do you use executive recruiting/search firms to seek to identify new diversity hires?

Yes

Internships and Co-ops

Although Gillette hires co-ops from other schools, it has a formal relationship with Northeastern University (5-year program).

Deadline for application: March/April for June-December Co-op/Intern hires; September/October for January-June Co-op hires

Number of interns/co-ops in the program in summer: Approximately 220 (including summer students and students from January -December)

Pay: Salary varies depending on the student's academic standing; weekly pay period

Length of the program: 6 months for co-ops; 8-12 weeks for summer interns

Percentage of interns/co-ops in the program who receive offers of full-time employment: varies

Web site for internship/co-op information: www.gillette.com/careers

Undergraduate students are hired across all business functions, e.g., finance, accounting, manufacturing, supply chain and engineering.

Undergraduate and MBA Internships

Deadline for application: March/April - undergraduate interns; January - MBA interns

Number of interns in the program: Undergraduate - 20-25; MBA - 10

Pay: Undergraduate -salary varies depending on the student's academic standing; weekly pay period; MBA: varies according to business function; monthly pay period

Length of the program: Undergraduate - 8-12 weeks; MBA - 10 weeks - 4 months

Percentage of interns/co-ops in the program who receive offers of full-time employment: Varies

Web site for internship/co-op information: www.gillette.com/careers

Undergraduate students are hired across all business functions, e.g., finance, accounting, manufacturing, supply chain and engineering. MBA interns are hired for marketing and finance.

Scholarships

The Gillette Scholars Program

Deadline for application for the scholarship program: June 1, annually

Scholarship award amount: Varies according to eligibility criteria; paid annually

Scholarship program is available to designated schools. Candidates must be pursuing their bachelor's degree and must be in their 1st or 2nd year of academic study. Applications are reviewed by the University Relations Committee, and finalists are selected based on business need and strength of application. Recipients are from designated schools.

National Merit Scholarship Program

Deadline for application for the scholarship program: January 20
Scholarship award amount: Varies according to eligibility criteria; paid annually

Scholarships are available only to employees' children who meet eligibility criteria.

Affinity Groups/Employee Networks

African Origin Network

The mission of this group is to provide a support system that will help to attract, retain and develop employees of African origin at all levels thereby maximizing their contributions to the Gillette Co. and the community. Monthly meetings are held with advisory board and leaders.

Strategic Plan and Diversity Leadership

How does the firm's leadership communicate the importance of diversity to everyone at the firm?

Workforce Diversity & Inclusion web site, Management Forum, Newsletter, Inclusion Leadership Speaker Series, Publication of the "Business Case for Global Workforce Diversity & Inclusion." Training programs include Managing Inclusion, Exploring Inclusion, Efficacy for Women and Preventing Workplace Harassment. Established an online Mentoring Toolkit.

Who has primary responsibility for leading diversity initiatives at your firm?

Dawn Frazier-Bohnert, VP, Workforce Diversity & Inclusion

Does your firm currently have a diversity committee?

Yes. The Gillette Steering committee was formed in July, 2001. The Committee is headed by Jim Kilts, CEO, and includes other members of his senior management team Together, they guide current initiatives to underscore the importance of diversity.

If yes, does the committee's representation include one or more members of the firm's management/executive committee (or the equivalent)?

Yes

How many employees are on the committee, and how often does the committee convene in furtherance of the firm's diversity initiatives?

Total executives on the committee: 8. The committee meets quarterly.

Does the committee and/or diversity leader establish and set goals or objectives consistent with management's priorities?

Yes

Has the firm undertaken a formal or informal diversity program or set of initiatives aimed at increasing the diversity of the firm?

Yes, formal

How often does the firm's management review the firm's diversity progress/results?

Quarterly

How is the firm's diversity committee and/or firm management held accountable for achieving results?

Managers are responsible for establishing diversity objectives/scorecard. Results are measured and recorded within their Performance Development Plan.

The Stats

DEMOGRAPHIC PROFILE	TOTAL IN THE U.S.		TOTAL OUTSIDE THE U.S		TOTAL WORLDWIDE	
	2004	2003	2004	2003	2004	2003
Number of employees	7,715	8,820	21,525	20,580	28,700	29,400
Revenues	$3.966 billion	$3.708 billion	$6.511 billion	$5.544 billion	$10.477 billion	$9.252 billion

Retention and Professional Development

How do 2004 minority and female attrition rates generally compare to those experienced in the prior year period?

Lower than in prior years

Please identify the specific steps you are taking to reduce the attrition rate of minority and women employees.

• Develop and/or support internal employee affinity groups (e.g., minority or women networks within the firm)
• Increase/review compensation relative to competition
• Succession plan includes emphasis on diversity
• Professional skills development program, including minority and women employees
• Other: Established an Efficacy for Women program and Inclusion Leadership Series in 2005

Diversity Mission Statement

At The Gillette Company, we believe a business environment that respects individual differences makes good business sense. Our Mission states the following:

"We strive to ensure that Gillette is an outstanding place to work by establishing an inclusive environment that encourages and enables our diverse workforce to fully contribute to, and participate in, the business success."

The Employer Says

Below is a section from our Business Case for Global Workforce Diversity & Inclusion brochure that further explains our commitment to diversity.

"Diversity is not a problem that needs to be solved. Nor is it a program that has a beginning and an end. Diversity is an ongoing strategic imperative, driven by the powerful market forces of competition, demography and globalization, and as critical to our company as product development, marketing and distribution. Diversity presents an opportunity and a strength to be leveraged, embraced, celebrated, encouraged and managed by everyone who works for Gillette and shares in our company's success.

How we deal with our increasing diversity will ultimately define us as an employer. How we thrive in the future may well be influenced not only by our policies of inclusion, but also by a real internal shift towards acceptance of all aspects of diversity as a competitive advantage and a source of innovation.

The power of Gillette's strengths - its superior products, innovative technology, iconic brands, global reach and leading market shares - has made our company a true world-class organization and a formidable competitor around the world. We have faced, and met, the ongoing challenges of ever-changing market forces to create some of the most useful and innovative products ever invented.

By creating an inclusive, flexible and diverse workforce, we can unleash the fullest potential of every associate. That combination of strength and potential gives Gillette an advantage that no competitor can match."

In addition, Gillette has been recognized in New England as an industry leader by the New England Minority Supplier Development Council (NEMSDC). The New England Minority Supplier Development Council is a Regional Council affiliated with the National Minority Supplier Development Council (NMSDC). Composed of over 100 Corporate Members and 350 supplier members, the council creates direct links between corporate America and minority businesses in New England.

In both 2003 and 2004, we were named the "NEMSDC Corporation of the Year" to acknowledge the strides Gillette has made in our Supplier Diversity Program within the New England business community. Additionally, in 2004, we were honored to receive the "NEMSDC President's Award" to recognize our exemplary work in sourcing diverse suppliers in our Temporary Labor Sourcing Project. This business was ultimately awarded to Total Technical Services, Inc.

Goldman, Sachs & Co.

85 Broad St.
New York, NY 10004
Phone: (212) 902-1000
Fax: (212) 902-3000
www.gs.com

Locations (worldwide)

(45 Locations) Atlanta, Auckland, Bangalore, Bangkok, Beijing, Boston, Buenos Aires, Calgary, Chicago, Dallas, Dublin, Frankfurt, Geneva, George Town, Hong Kong, Houston, Jersey City, Johannesburg, London, Los Angeles, Madrid, Melbourne, Mexico City, Miami, Milan, Moscow, New York, Paris, Philadelphia, Princeton, Salt Lake City, San Francisco, Sao Paulo, Seattle, Seoul, Shanghai, Singapore,Stockholm, Sydney, Taipei, Tampa, Tokyo, Toronto, Washington D.C., Zurich

Diversity Leadership

Contact Person: Martin Rodriguez, Associate Melinda Wolfe, Managing Director, Global Head of Global Leadership and Diversity; Diversity Campus Recruiting

Employment Contact

Team Leader: Lance LaVergne, Vice President, Head of Americas FirmwideDiversityRecruiting@gs.com

Diversity web site:
www.gs.com/our_firm/our_culture/global_leadership_and_diversity/index.html

Recruiting

Please list the schools/types of schools at which you recruit.

- *Ivy League schools:* Harvard University, Princeton University, University of Pennsylvania, Columbia University, Brown University, Dartmouth College, Yale University, Cornell University
- *Public state schools:* University of Illinois, University of Indiana, University of California-Los Angeles, University of California-Berkeley, University of Michigan, University of Virginia, University of Texas, Rutgers University, City University of New York-Baruch College
- *Private schools:* Stanford, New York University, University of Chicago, Northwestern, Duke University, Georgetown University, Massachusetts Institute of Technology, Boston College, Williams College, Villanova University, St. John's University, Pace University, University of Notre Dame, Middlebury College, Carnegie Mellon University, Florida International University, University of Southern California, Florida International University
- *Historically Black Colleges and Universities (HBCUs):* Howard University, Morehouse College, Spelman College, Florida A&M University
- *Women's colleges:* Barnard College, Wellesley College, Smith College, Mt. Holyoke College

Do you have any special outreach efforts that are directed to encourage minority students to consider your firm?

- Host receptions for minority students
- Conferences
- Host and sponsor various student club conferences at schools from which we recruit
- Advertise in minority student association publications
- Participate in/host minority student job fairs
- Sponsor minority student association events

• Firm's professionals participate on career panels at school
• Outreach to leadership of minority student organizations
• Scholarships or intern/fellowships for minority students
• Other: Sponsors and supporters of Robert Toigo Foundation, Consortium for
• Graduate Study in Management, Forte Foundation, Management Leadership for Tomorrow, National Hispanic Business Association
• Other: Host workshops for graduate and undergraduate students through programs such as undergraduate and MBA camps

What activities does the firm undertake to attract minority and women employees?

• Partner programs with women and minority banking associations
• Conferences: National Black MBA (NBMBAA), National Society of Hispanic MBAs (NSHMBA), National Society of Black Engineers (NSBE), Society of Hispanic Engineers (SHPE), National Association of Black Accountants (NABA), Association of Latin Professionals in Finance and Accounting (ALPFA), Hispanic Alliance for Career Enhancement (HACE), Consortium for Graduate Study in Management (CGSM), Society of Women Engineers (SWE)
• Participate at minority job fairs
• Seek referrals from other professionals

Do you use executive recruiting/search firms to seek to identify new diversity hires?

Yes

Internships and Co-ops

Summer Analyst Program

> *Deadline for application for the internship:* Winter 2005 (though it varies from school to School)
> *Number of interns in the program in summer 2004:* 915 (worldwide)
> *Length of the program:* 10 weeks
> *Program web site:* www.gs.com/careers

Summer Analysts join a 10 week comprehensive program, where they are given the opportunity to learn critical business skills, while gaining fundamental experience in their respective divisions. Goldman Sachs seeks highly motivated candidates who have demonstrated outstanding achievements in academic and extracurricular activities. We are looking for self-motivated team players who have excellent organizational and communication skills. While a background in finance or accounting is not required, candidates should have an interest in business and financial markets.

The following divisions hire summer analysts:

• Equities
• Fixed Income
• Currency & Commodities
• Financing Group
• Finance (includes Controllers, Credit & Corporate Treasury and Firmwide Risk)
• Global Investment Research
• Human Capital Management
• Investment Banking/Corporate Finance
• Investment Management-Asset Management
• Investment Management-Private Wealth Management
• Global Compliance

• Legal & Management Controls
• Merchant Banking/Private Equity
• Operations (includes CorporateServices and Global Operations)
• Technology

Please visit our web site for specific divisional overviews at: www.gs.com.

Scholarships

Scholarship for Excellence

> *Deadline for application for the scholarship program:* December, 2005
> *Scholarship award amount:* $5,000 – sophomores, with an opportunity to be considered for an additional $7,500 in their junior year; $7,500 – juniors
> *Web site:* www.gs.com/careers/about_goldman_sachs/diversity/internships_scholarships/index.html

Other contact information for scholarship:

Contact: Cindy Joseph
cindy.joseph@gs.com
Phone: 917-343-8562

The Goldman Sachs Scholarship for Excellence Program was established in 1994 and is an integral part of our diversity recruiting effort, helping to attract undergraduate students of Black, Hispanic and Native American heritage to careers at Goldman Sachs. Students of all majors and disciplines are encouraged to apply.

Recipients of the scholarship will receive:

• Sophomores – $5,000 scholarship to cover tuition and fees, and
• Upon successful completion of summer internship, an opportunity to receive an additional award and an offer to return for a second summer internship
• Juniors – $7,500 scholarship to cover tuition and fees, and an internship as a summer analyst in which the scholarship recipient will gain insight into the financial services industry, the firm and our unique culture; a coach/mentor that will help ensure a successful summer experience; and exposure to senior level managers and participation in firm-wide networking opportunities

Eligibility:

The following are criteria we consider when selecting our scholarship recipients:
• Enrollment at one of our recruiting schools as a current sophomore or junior
• Black, Hispanic or Native American heritage
• Minimum cumulative grade point average of 3.4 or above on a 4.0 scale
• Interest in the financial services industry
• Community involvement – service to campus and community
• Demonstrated leadership and teamwork capabilities

Affinity Groups/Employee Networks

Firmwide Black Network

Names of affinity group leaders: Tom Mattox, Gregg Gonsalves

The mission of the Goldman Sachs Firmwide Black Network is to enhance professional development and advancement opportunities for Black employees and to support recruitment and retention. The FBN also engages and advises senior business managers regarding the firm's diversity strategy and issues of importance to the firm's Black community.

The Goldman Sachs Firmwide Black Network ("FBN") was formally launched in October, 2001 to enrich the professional lives of Black employees and to assist the firm in identifying and addressing issues of importance to the firm's Black community. The

FBN presents programs focusing on strategies and skills to catalyze professional advancement, and it sponsors events to promote awareness and understanding of the relationships between public policy and business challenges in the financial services industry. The FBN partners with senior leaders of the firm's businesses and diversity efforts to develop initiatives and sponsor activities that augment the firm's commitment to strengthen the franchise through its people. With a diverse workforce becoming increasingly more important in the firm's ability to continue to compete effectively in a global environment, the FBN represents a critical resource in supporting the firm's business principles and objectives.

Firmwide Hispanic/Latin Network (FHLN)

Name of affinity group leader: Marina Roesler

The mission of the Goldman Sachs Firmwide Hispanic/Latin Network will be to focus on recruitment, retention, promotion, development and advocacy for the Goldman Sachs Hispanic/Latin community. This organization is dedicated to inspiring the Hispanic/Latin community to actively participate in leadership development and community service. It will foster an inclusive business climate that leverages the unique talents, perspectives and experiences of the group. The network will create a sense of community and cultural awareness among the Hispanics/Latinos and the broader population of the firm. We will create a work environment that enables people to do their best work by establishing informal networks, mentoring, mobility and communication.

Asian Professionals Network (APN)

Name of affinity group leader: Jacqueline Liau

The mission of the Asian Professionals Network ("APN") is to act as a bridge in the firm for the recruitment, retention, development and promotion of Asian professionals. The organization serves as a channel to shares ideas, raise awareness and create a sense of collaboration and community among Asian professionals. It provides a forum to promote the diverse achievements and contributions of Asian professionals to the firm. The network also works to enhance the Goldman experience for Asian professionals by implementing programs that will foster greater interaction with the broader community. The APN aims to energize, amplify and empower Asian professionals to make greater contributions to the firm and to the outside community.

Gay and Lesbian Network

Names of affinity group leaders: Robert Barry, Arden Hoffman

As part of Goldman Sachs' commitment to diversity, the Gay and Lesbian Network's mission is to advocate a work environment that respects, welcomes and supports lesbian, gay, bisexual and transgender professionals, and empowers them to perform to their fullest potential and contribute to the greater goals of the firm.

The organization works to increase the visibility of openly lesbian, gay, bisexual and transgender (LGBT) employees at Goldman Sachs, and to foster greater inclusion within the greater Goldman Sachs community. It provides a global, supportive, profession-

al network that promotes mentoring and a sense of community. It also advocates on diversit issues related to sexual orientation and gender identity within the firm, and serves as an information resource to management on LGBT issues.

Firmwide Women's Network

Name of affinity group leader: Luciana Miranda

The Firmwide Women's Network mission is to recruit, retain and develop women professionals at Goldman Sachs, and to increase their representation at senior levels.

Entry-Level Programs/Full-Time Opportunities

Full-time Analyst Program

Length of program: Average of 2-3 years
Geographic location(s) of program: Opportunities are available at several of our global offices.

Most analysts join two-to-three year formal training programs. The main purpose of these programs is to help our analysts learn critical business skills while gaining fundamental skills in their respective divisions. Goldman Sachs seeks highly motivated candidates who have demonstrated outstanding achievements in academic and extracurricular activities.

We are looking for self-motivated team players who have excellent organizational and communication skills. While a background in finance or accounting is not required, candidates should have an interest in business and financial markets.

Goldman Sachs hires full-time analysts for the following divisions:

- Equities
- Fixed Income
- Currency & Commodities
- Financing Group
- Finance (includes Controllers, Credit & Corporate Treasury and Firmwide Risk)
- Global Investment Research
- Human Capital Management,
- Investment Banking/Corporate Finance
- Investment Management-Asset Management
- Investment Management-Private Wealth Management
- Global Compliance
- Legal & Management Controls
- Merchant Banking/Private Equity
- Operations (includes Corporate Services and Global Operations)
- Technology.

Please visit our web site for specific divisional overviews at: www.gs.com.

Strategic Plan and Diversity Leadership

How does the firm's leadership communicate the importance of diversity to everyone at the firm?

E-mails, web site, meetings, workshops, newsletters and town halls

Who has primary responsibility for leading diversity initiatives at your firm?

Melinda Wolfe, Managing Director, Global Head of Global Leadership and Diversity

Does your firm currently have a diversity committee?

Yes

If yes, does the committee's representation include one or more members of the firm's management/executive committee (or the equivalent)?

Yes

If yes, how many executives are on the committee, and in 2004, what was the total number of hours collectively spent by the committee in furtherance of the firm's diversity initiatives? How many employees are on the committee, and how often does the committee convene in furtherance of the firm's diversity initiatives?

• *Total senior managers on committee:* 21
• *Number of diversity meetings annually:* Quarterly

Does the committee and/or diversity leader establish and set goals or objectives consistent with management's priorities?

Yes

Has the firm undertaken a formal or informal diversity program or set of initiatives aimed at increasing the diversity of the firm?

Yes, formal

How often does the firm's management review the firm's diversity progress/results?

Quarterly

How is the firm's diversity committee and/or firm management held accountable for achieving results?

Senior management reports to the Board of Directors annually on the state of the firm's diversity initiatives.

Diversity Mission Statement

Goldman Sachs aims to be the employer, advisor and investment of choice by attractingand retaining the best and most diverse talent. Through our leadership and diversity efforts, including the affinity network program, we work to provide a supportive and

inclusive environment where all individuals, regardless of gender, race, ethnicity, nationalorigin, sexual orientation, gender identity, disability or other classification can maximize their full potential, which in turn leads to strengthening the firm's position as a leader in the industry.

To manage diversity well, we have to manage people well. We realize that successful formal processes have a particularly positive influence on women, historically underrepresented groups and non-U.S. nationals. The Office of Global Leadership and Diversity reinforces our culture of meritocracy by advancing leadership and management skills, and integrating diversity considerations into our key business and people processes, such as recruiting, training, career development and other retention strategies.

We leverage FOUR CATALYSTS to affect change:

• LEADERSHIP COMMITMENT
• EDUCATION & TRAINING
• COMMUNICATION & INVOLVEMENT
• MEASUREMENT & ACCOUNTABILITY

The Employer Says

At Goldman Sachs we recognize that having a diverse workforce encourages increased creativity and innovation. This is crucial to improved performance and continued business success. To that end, we are committed to creating an environment that values diversity and promotes inclusion. Goldman Sachs recruits individuals from diverse cultures and backgrounds. The result is a wealth of talent and creativity where exceptional individuals work together to provide a world-class service to a broad spectrum of corporate, government, institutional and private clients.

In our search for outstanding individuals we partner with organizations promoting diversity. Through our work with INROADS, Sponsors for Educational Opportunity, the Jackie Robinson Foundation, the Forte Foundation, the Employers Forum on Disability and others, we increase our commitment to recruiting women, students from ethnic minorities and those with disabilities. Further, we have initiated and manage a number of programs designed to increase awareness of the firm and our industry. These programs allow us to offer academic scholarships, educational opportunities, summer internships and full-time positions to many outstanding students. Not of all of these students have a finance or business background; we actively seek candidates from a broad array of academic disciplines and concentrations such as liberal arts, applied math, sciences and engineering, in order to reach a wide spectrum of strong candidates.

We invite to take a closer look at our firm and learn more about the different programs and opportunities available to you.

www.gs.com/careers

Hallmark Cards, Inc.

2501 McGee St.
Kansas City, MO 64108
Phone: (816) 274-5111
Fax: (816) 274-5061
Toll Free: (800) 425-5627
www.hallmark.com

Diversity Leadership
Vickie Harris, Corporate Diversity Director

Employment Contact
Dawn Harp, Corporate Staffing Manager
 P.O. Box 419580
Kansas City, MO 64141
Phone: (816) 274-5111
E-mail: hcorp01@hallmark.com

Recruiting

Please list the schools/types of schools at which you recruit.

• Public state schools

Do you have any special outreach efforts that are directed to encourage minority students to consider your firm?

• Participate in/host minority student job fair(s)
• Sponsor minority student association events
• Firm's employees participate on career panels at school
• Outreach to leadership of minority student organizations
• Scholarships or intern/fellowships for minority students

What activities does the firm undertake to attract minority and women employees?

• Partner programs with women and minority associations
• Conferences.   NSBE, SWE, Black MBA, Hispanic MBA
• Participate at minority job fairs
• Seek referrals from other employees
• Utilize online job services

Do you use executive recruiting/search firms to seek to identify new diversity hires?

No

Internships and Co-ops

Summer Internship (in Finance, Operations, Marketing, Creative)

Deadline for application: January for all but Creative, which does not have a deadline
Number of interns in the program in summer 2004: 25
Pay: Depending on year in school, $12.50-$17.50 per hour

Length of the program: 12 weeks

Percentage of interns/co-ops in the program who receive offers of full-time employment: approximately 90%

Web site for internship/co-op information: www.hallmark.com

Our program includes rich assignments, many networking opportunities and social events for the interns. We search for interns for our Marketing, Finance, Operations and Creative divisions. The qualifications are that the student be obtaining a degree within the area of discipline appropriate to the division. Typically we look for students entering their senior year.

Affinity Groups/Employee Networks

HAAL: Hallmark African American Leadership

Mission is to ensure there is value for cultural differences and that those differences add value to the company by identifying solutions concerning: education and awareness; recruitment, development and retention of African-Americans; product development and retail for African-Americans; and maintaining community alliances with organizations who have similar business interests to Hallmark.

HEART: Hispanic Education Awareness Resource Team

Mission is to enable our company to reach Hispanic consumers and to educate employees on Hispanic culture. Additionally, HEART focuses on the retention, recruitment and development of Hispanic employees, and leveraging the Hispanic culture, traditions and opportunities through local community involvement.

HERE: Hallmark Employees Reaching Equality

Mission is to provides Hallmark's gay, lesbian, bisexual and transgendered (GLBT) employees with a support network, as well as a forum to work with management and peers on education and awareness of issues that affect them.

Strategic Plan and Diversity Leadership

Who has primary responsibility for leading diversity initiatives at your firm?

Vickie Harris, Corporate Diversity Director

Does your firm currently have a diversity committee?

Yes. The Corporate Diversity Council (CDC) is made up of senior leaders from across Hallmark. They set the diversity strategy for the company and ensure that this strategy is executed both at corporate and division levels.

If yes, does the committee's representation include one or more members of the firm's management/executive committee (or the equivalent)?

Yes

Please describe the committee.

There are 12 executives and two employees on the committee and they spent an estimated 1170 hours collectively on CDC related initiatives in 2004. They meet bi-monthly.

Does the committee and/or diversity leader establish and set goals or objectives consistent with management's priorities?

Yes. The strategy uses "Marketplace," "Workplace" and "Workforce" as the framework for setting goals and objectives which naturally fit with the priorities of the business and with HR. Also, since the CDC is comprised of business leaders, they are instrumental in ensuring that the objectives are aligned with the business goals.

Has the firm undertaken a formal or informal diversity program or set of initiatives aimed at increasing the diversity of the firm?

Yes, formal. We a) attend at least four diversity recruiting conferences every year, b) have division diversity councils who often make increasing the diversity of their division a key goal, c) do targeted development, such as using Inroads interns, and d) have awareness programs for all employees.

How often does the firm's management review the firm's diversity progress/results?

Quarterly

How is the firm's diversity committee and/or firm management held accountable for achieving results?

They are held accountable via their annual performance reviews.

Retention and Professional Development

How do 2004 minority and female attrition rates generally compare to those experienced in the prior year period?

About the same as in prior years

Please identify the specific steps you are taking to reduce the attrition rate of minority and women employees.

- Develop and/or support internal employee affinity groups (e.g., minority or women networks within the firm)
- Increase/improve current work/life programs
- Adopt dispute resolution process
- Succession plan includes emphasis on diversity
- Work with minority and women employees to develop career advancement plans
- Professional skills development program, including minority and women employees

Diversity Mission Statement

Hallmark's goal is to create an environment that fully taps the potential of all individuals in pursuit of corporate objectives. We strive to accomplish this by:

- Developing a critical mass of change agents throughout the company who value diversity and will assist in driving a change process
- Offering programs that build awareness regarding diversity and the business success that results from effectively man aging diversity
- Developing and supporting systems, processes and programs that serve to eliminate artificial barriers, which prevent individuals from achieving full potential
- Sustaining a positive image as a company that values diversity

A family of hospitals.
For families everywhere.

The HCA Family has been providing quality healthcare since 1968. Today we are a national leader in innovative healthcare technology, providing Patient Safety initiatives which are helping to improve the future of healthcare for families across the country. Our HCA family includes 190 hospitals and more than 180,000 dedicated employees, all working together to provide the best in healthcare. It's an ongoing commitment to families, renewed daily by our family.

HCA
Hospital Corporation of America℠

HCA, Hospital Corporation of America

One Park Plaza
Nashville, TN 37203
Phone: (615) 344-9551
Fax: (615) 344-2555
http://www.hcahealthcare.com/CustomPa
ge.asp?guidCustomContentID=9DA0908
2-0E2D-4238-B8F3-FF663D4BD372

Locations (worldwide)
U.S. (in 23 states)
England and Switzerland

Diversity Leadership
Kim Sharp, VP, Diversity and HR
Communications

Employment Contact
Candy Burlason
AVP, Recruiting
One Park Plaza
Nashville, TN 37203
Phone: (615) 344-9551
Fax: (615) 344-2555
E-mail: executive.recruiting@hcahealthcare.com

Recruiting

Please list the schools/types of schools at which you recruit.

• Private schools
• Public state schools
• Historically Black Colleges and Universities (HBCUs): Howard & Spelman some years
• Other predominantly minority and/or women's colleges

Do you have any special outreach efforts that are directed to encourage minority students to consider your firm?

• Participate in/host minority student job fair(s): Participate in local job fairs
• Sponsor minority student association events: INROADS
• Firm's employees participate on career panels at school
• Outreach to leadership of minority student organizations: INROADS and at HBCUs
• Other: HCA Community Outreach/Foundation has a scholarship program for the children of employees.

What activities does the firm undertake to attract minority and women employees?

• Participate at minority job fairs: Nashville Urban League Fair, NBMBAA, NASSE, NAHSE, NSHMBA, NABA, National Urban League Fair, MED Week
• Seek referrals from other employees
• Utilize online job services
• Other: INROADS

Do you use executive recruiting/search firms to seek to identify new diversity hires?

Yes

If yes, list all women- and/or minority-owned executive search/recruiting firms to which the firm paid a fee for placement services in the past 12 months:

We use Computer Professional Inc., usually on a contract-to-hire basis.

Internships and Co-ops

Diversity Business & Inclusion Program

Deadline for application: April

Number of interns in the program in summer 2004 (internship) or 2004 (co-op): 3

Length of the program: 10 – 12 weeks

Supply chain group – minority internship program (no official name)

Deadline for application: May 1

Number of interns in the program in summer 2004 (internship) or 2004 (co-op): Had 9 interns in the summer, 4 of which continued into the year

Pay: Paid by the hour—amount not available

Length of the program: Throughout the year

Percentage of interns/co-ops in the program who receive offers of full-time employment: About 20-30%

We are looking for students who have strong potential for being hired, not just those looking for a part-time job. We're making an investment in finding candidates who would be good additions to the HCA workforce. Interns are usually juniors or seniors, 18 years or older, with a 3.0 or better GPA. We will also hire those students who were previously awarded scholarships.

Scholarships

HCA Cares Scholarship Program

Deadline for application for the scholarship program: Rolling

Scholarship award amount: $5000-$12000 per year

Web site or other contact information for scholarship: www.hcacares.com

Philip R. Patton Healthcare Scholarship

Deadline for application for the scholarship program: January each year

Scholarship award amount: $1,000

Web site or other contact information for scholarship: www.hosa.org

Entry-Level Programs/Full-Time Opportunities

COO Development Program

Length of program: 2-4 years

Geographic location(s) of program: Nationwide

The COO Development Program is a full-time position reporting to the program director, but placed at selected hospitals with selected mentors. As the name implies, it is a development program designed to prepare participants to take the role of Chief Operating Officer (COO) at an HCA facility.

The majority of the training takes place in the hospital as a result of the work and projects assigned. In addition to the training received at the hospital, associates (i.e. program participants) are required to attend quarterly seminars. These seminars vary in content (planning/CAMS, budget, leadership, patient safety and quality, physician relations), but are designed to aid in their development for the role of COO.

The COO Development Program requires attendance at The American College of Healthcare Executives annual meeting. This is an opportunity for continuing education for all program participants. The program covers the cost of membership and attendance. Other continuing education opportunities are encouraged and the cost is covered on a case-by-case basis.

Strategic Plan and Diversity Leadership

How does the firm's leadership communicate the importance of diversity to everyone at the firm?

E-mails, newsletters, company-wide magazine, meetings

Who has primary responsibility for leading diversity initiatives at your firm?

Kim Sharp – VP, Diversity and HR Communications
Jack Bovender, our CEO, is our Chief Diversity Officer.

Does your firm currently have a diversity committee?

Yes. The committee is structured cross-functionally to operations and corporate. The committee meets periodically with frequent communications between meetings.

If yes, does the committee's representation include one or more members of the firm's management/executive committee (or the equivalent)?

Yes

Does the committee and/or diversity leader establish and set goals or objectives consistent with management's priorities?

Yes

Has the firm undertaken a formal or informal diversity program or set of initiatives aimed at increasing the diversity of the firm?

Yes, formal

How often does the firm's management review the firm's diversity progress/results?

• Annually, at the Board level
• Periodic – other management

How is the firm's diversity committee and/or firm management held accountable for achieving results?

Performance-based financial incentives

Diversity Mission Statement

At HCA, we will foster a culture of inclusion and diversity across all areas of our company which embraces and enriches our workforce, physicians, patients, partners and communities.

The Employer Says

HCA is a company that is committed to the care and improvement of human life. In recognition of this commitment, we strive to deliver high quality, cost-effective healthcare in the communities we serve. Because caring for people is at the very core of who we are, caring about the unique individual in a culturally inclusive environment is a natural progression. With this in mind, we want to improve cultural competence in order to enable us to identify and eliminate real and perceived barriers attributed to race, gender, ethnicity, religion, age, disability, sexual orientation and other areas of difference.

Diversity is a business imperative at HCA because of the communities we serve and because of the talented professionals that we wish to attract to our workforce. Our hospitals, surgery centers and affiliates are serving communities that are changing daily and growing into a truly multicultural mix of people. Our affiliates and hospitals want to be the place selected when the people in our communities need care, and we want to have the best staff of professionals there to serve their needs. For the patient, our workplace is one where patient-focused cultural competence enables us to provide safe quality care. For the worker or employee, our workplace is one where people and their unique talents are genuinely recognized, valued, celebrated and fully utilized to benefit our corporate community and affiliates. To further that work culture, we instill reward, incentive and accountability systems that support our belief in diversity.

To ensure the maximum effectiveness of our diversity efforts, we have executive leadership support, which includes our Corporate CEO as the Chief Diversity Officer. In our hospitals, the Hospital CEOs serves as the Chief Diversity Officers and as such are accountable for making diversity and cultural competency a priority in their hospital community and with their affiliates.

HCA is a company that has the privilege of having many opportunities to practice diversity due to the nature of our business. Caring about people is what we are all about and caring about the uniqueness that each person brings is what we strive for in our diversity mission.

The following lists the names of minority associations with which HCA has relationships:

• Access Services of Mid TN/Technology Access Center
• ACE Mentor Program of TN, Inc.
• African Leadership
• Ailey II (Links)
• American Association of Refugee and Immigrant Women
• Association for Hispanic Healthcare Executives
• Brightstone, Inc.
• Business Women's Network/Diversity Best Practices
• Catalyst Diversity, Inc.
• Center for Independent Living of Mid TN
• Community Health Center
• Conexion Americas
• Congress of Racial Equality
• Creating an Environment of Success
• Education for Equal Opportunity Group
• Faith Family Medical Clinic
• Girl Scouts of the USA
• Greater Nashville Black Chamber of Commerce
• Institute for Diversity in Health Management
• Matthew Walker Clinic CHC
• MED Week

- Meharry-Venderbilt Alliance Foundation
- Mental Health Association of Mid TN
- Nashville Minority Business Development Center
- National Association for the Advancement of Colored People (NAACP)
- National Association of Latino Elected Officials
- National Black Chamber of Commerce
- National Black MBA Association
- National Conference for Community and Justice
- National Hispanic Chamber of Commerce on Health
- National Hispanic Leadership Institute
- National Minority Business Association
- National Minority Contractors Association
- National Society of Hispanic MBAs
- National Supplier Development Council,
- National Urban League
- Progress, Inc.
- Safety Net Consortium
- Salama Urban Ministries
- Siloam Family Health Clinic
- Sisters for Sisters
- Tennessee Hispanic Chamber of Commerce
- Tennessee Minority Supplier Development Council
- The 100 Black Men
- Time to Rise
- U.S Hispanic Chamber of Commerce.
- United Negro College Fund
- Urban League
- Women in Business National Council

HCA also has additional relationships in those states where they do business

Hershey Company, The

100 Crystal A Dr.
Hershey, PA 17033-0810
Phone: 717-534-6799
Fax: 717-534-6760
Toll Free: 800-539-0261
www.hersheys.com

Diversity Leadership
Diane Crawford, Manager of Diversity & Inclusion

Employment Contact
Andre Goodlett, Senior Director of Diversity & Inclusion
100 Crystal A Drive
Harrisburg, PA 17110
Phone: (717) 508-3886
Fax: (717) 534-8053

Recruiting

Please list the schools/types of schools at which you recruit.

• Ivy League schools
• Public state schools
• Historically Black Colleges and Universities (HBCUs)
• Hispanic Serving Institutions (HSIs)

Do you have any special outreach efforts that are directed to encourage minority students to consider your firm?

• Firm's employees participate on career panels at school
• Scholarships or intern/fellowships for minority students

What activities does the firm undertake to attract minority and women employees?

• Partner programs with women and minority associations
• Participate at minority job fairs
• Seek referrals from other employees
• Utilize online job services

Do you use executive recruiting/search firms to seek to identify new diversity hires?

Yes

Internships and Co-ops

(HIPP) Hershey's Intern Professional Program

Deadline for application: Ongoing all year

Number of interns in the program in summer 2004 (internship) or 2004 (co-op): 59 interns and 14 co-ops

Pay: Ranges from $11.75 - $21.60 per hour, depending on major and year in school

Length of the program: Typically 12, though possibly longer, depending on a student's availability and department needs.

Percentage of interns/co-ops in the program who receive offers of full-time employment: Companywide the figure is less than 10%; In the Sales Department it's 20%+

Web site for internship/co-op information: www.hersheys.com

Typically Engineering, Sales, Human Resources and Finance have the majority of undergrad interns/co-ops.

Hershey's Inter Professional Programs (HIPP) formally began in 1978. Over the years, HIPP has grown to become a critical element in Hershey's strategic recruiting and hiring plans. The program provides students with opportunities to develop and apply their skills in a challenging, exciting and industry -leading corporate environment. Many interns have moved right into great jobs with Hershey's upon graduation. Future job offers have also been extended to some interns before returning to school to finish their senior year!

Scholarships

Hershey Scholar Program

Deadline for application for the scholarship program: February 15

Scholarship award amount: $500-$3,000 - Paid in two equal installments on August 15 and December 30

Scholarships are available only for children of employees

UNCF/Hershey Scholar Program

Deadline for application for the scholarship program: April 30

Scholarship award amount: $5,000

Scholarships are only available to minority Pennsylvania residents attending one of UNCF's 38 member colleges, or one of 14 institutions under the Pennsylvania state system of higher education.

Affinity Groups/Employee Networks

Women's Council

The Women's Council is in its infancy stage. We are currently conducting focus group sessions with female employees at all levels of the organization to identify the issues relative to the female workforce. The group will also focus on networking, mentoring, education and developmental opportunities.

Entry-Level Programs/Full-Time Opportunities

Building Organizational Excellence

Length of program: 4 days
Geographic location(s) of program: Hershey, PA

Please describe the training/training component of this program: The program gives an overview of company heritage, organizational departments/functions, diversity, human relations, as well as a performance overview.

The Role of the Hershey Leader

Length of program: 2 Days
Geographic location(s) of program: Hershey, PA

Please describe the training/training component of this program: Leadership training, Diversity overview, HR Overview

Strategic Plan and Diversity Leadership

How does the firm's leadership communicate the importance of diversity to everyone at the firm?

The Hershey Company has a dedicated diversity web site with a cultural calendar to help educate and share diversity related information. In addition, the Public Relations Department sends out monthly e-mails to employees highlighting diversity events and activities that are both internal and external.

Who has primary responsibility for leading diversity initiatives at your firm?

Andre Goodlett, Senior Director of Diversity & Inclusion

Does your firm currently have a diversity committee?

Yes. The committee is structured into five sub-teams which align with the organization's overall strategic goals: culture and community, recruitment & retention, marketing initiative, communication and education. The groups meet monthly, the Team Leads meet monthly and the full council meets quarterly.

If yes, does the committee's representation include one or more members of the firm's management/executive committee (or the equivalent)?

Yes

Please describe the committee.

There are two executive members. There are approximately 80 hours devoted to diversity initiatives. The full council consist of 31members and they convene as a full council four times a year.

Does the committee and/or diversity leader establish and set goals or objectives consistent with management's priorities?

Yes

Has the firm undertaken a formal or informal diversity program or set of initiatives aimed at increasing the diversity of the firm?

Yes, formal

How often does the firm's management review the firm's diversity progress/results?

Quarterly

The Stats

DEMOGRAPHIC PROFILE	TOTAL IN THE U.S.		TOTAL OUTSIDE THE U.S		TOTAL WORLDWIDE	
	2004	2003	2004	2003	2004	2003
Number of employees	11,251	N/A	2,490	N/A	13,741	N/A
Revenues	$3.997 billion	$3.814 billion	$431.936 million	$358.452 million	$4.429 billion	$4.173 billion

Retention and Professional Development

How do 2004 minority and female attrition rates generally compare to those experienced in the prior year period?

Lower than in prior years

Please identify the specific steps you are taking to reduce the attrition rate of minority and women employees.

• Develop and/or support internal employee affinity groups (e.g., minority or women networks within the firm)
• Increase/review compensation relative to competition
• Increase/improve current work/life programs
• Succession plan includes emphasis on diversity
• Work with minority and women employees to develop career advancement plans

Diversity Mission Statement

At The Hershey Company, diversity is a key ingredient in making us one of the finest companies in the world. We value the differences that make each individual, supplier, community, customer and consumer unique. Our success is a product of our ability to recognize, understand and incorporate those differences into everything we do. Hershey's strength and future success lie in its diversity - the diversity of thought, management styles, experience and abilities that only can come from bringing together people with different backgrounds and different ways of seeing the world. Hershey's approach to diversity emphasizes four areas: Customer and Consumer Alignment, Employee Involvement and Support, Supplier Diversity and Community Involvement.

Additional Information

Hershey's Initiatives

Customer and Consumer Alignment – Hershey has significant opportunity in a diverse U.S. marketplace with an estimated ethnic buying power of $1 trillion. Hershey's multifaceted partnership with Latina superstar Thalia and acquisition of Mexican candy company Grupo Lorena and its top brand, Pelon Pelo Rico, are significant steps in reaching these consumers. Hershey has introduced a new line of co-branded, Latin-inspired candies to build an awareness of a preference for its brands with this fast growing, dynamic population.

Employee Involvement and Support – Reaching out to employees through various diversity councils, affinity groups, continuous diversity education and internal cultural awareness campaigns are all vehicles through which The Hershey Company demonstrates its commitment to diversity.

Supplier Diversity – One of the most important aspects of our business is our interaction with our suppliers. Like our employees, our suppliers make our success possible. Maintaining a diverse network of suppliers makes us a more efficient company while contributing to the economic development of the communities in which we live and work. Our approach is to partner nationally and locally with organizations to identify diverse suppliers. We also aim to open up opportunities at all levels and in all categories of spending to certified diversity suppliers and, in areas where the diversity supplier is limited, to mentor promising minority and women businesses.

Community Involvement — The Hershey Company has a long history of community leadership. Central to who we are as a company is our belief in making a difference in the lives of youth. We demonstrate our commitment through our participation with The Milton Hershey School, UNCF scholarships and the Hershey Youth Track and Field program. We also believe in the value of maintaining strong relationships with diversity focused organizations nationally and locally. We partner nationally with organizations like NAACP, La Raza and the United Way and in the Hershey, PA area with organizations like the Urban League, Y Black Achievers and JR Achievement.

Humana Inc.

The Humana Bldg.
500 W. Main St.
Louisville, KY 40202
Phone: (502) 580-1000
Fax: (502) 580-3677
Toll Free: (800) 486-2620
http://www.humana.com

The Employer Says

Diversity Strategy

At Humana we are committed to embracing diversity as a core value. Our corporate strategic focus is on growth, innovation and meeting the needs of our consumers. We recognize that diversity is a business imperative. Diversity serves as a catalyst for increasing employee engagement, promoting creative thinking and building business partners.

For this reason our diversity strategy focuses on the workplace, marketplace and the community. Our goal, in each of these areas, is for Humana to become the employer, health solution and community partner for choice.

Building talent at Humana is essnetial to achieving this goal. Therefore,. we are using INROADS and other internship/professional development programs to infuse diverse talent into our workforce. This past summer Humana had more than 50 interns working throughout the company, and we expect the number to grow. Our hope is that many of these interns will go on to be full-time associates. We believe that having the right talent in place at all levels of our organization will drive Humana's business success.

IBM ibm.com/diversity

ON DEMAND VISION

IBM proudly supports diversity. Coming together behind one clear vision is the essence of On Demand Business. By combining industry experience, business insight and executional know-how, we can help your organization drive a new standard of productivity, efficiency and innovation. It's an on demand world. Be an On DemandBusiness. For more information visit **ibm.com**/ondemand

IBM Corporation

New Orchard Rd.
Armonk, NY 10504
Phone: (914) 499-1900
Fax: (914) 765-7382
Toll Free: (800) 426-4968
www.ibm.com/careers

Locations (worldwide)
170 locations in North America, South America, Asia Pacific, Europe, Middle East, and Africa

Diversity Leadership
Bill Lawrence, Senior Diversity Program Manager

Employment Contact
Margaret Ashida, Director, University Talent Programs

Recruiting

Please list the schools/types of schools at which you recruit.

- Ivy League schools
- Other private schools
- Public state schools
- Historically Black Colleges and Universities (HBCUs)
- Hispanic Serving Institutions (HSIs)
- Native American Tribal Universities
- Other predominantly minority and/or women's colleges

Do you have any special outreach efforts that are directed to encourage minority students to consider your firm?

- Hold a reception for minority students
- Conferences: American Indian Science and Engineering Society (AISES), Grace Hopper Conference for Women in Computing. HENAAC, National Association of Asian American Professionals (NAAAP), National Association of Women MBA (NAWM-BA), National Black MBA Association (NBMBAA), National Society of Black Engineers (NSBE), National Society of Hispanic MBAs (NSHMBA), Reaching Out, Society of Hispanic Professional Engineers (SHPE), Society of Mexican American Engineers and Scientists (MAES), Society of Women Engineers (SWE), Women In Technology International (WITI)
- Advertise in minority student association publication(s)
- Participate in/host minority student job fair(s)
- Sponsor minority student association events
- Firm's employees participate on career panels at school
- Outreach to leadership of minority student organizations
- Scholarships or intern/fellowships for minority students
- INROADS, National GEM Consortium, National Action Council for Minorities in Engineering (NACME), Sponsors for Educational Opportunity (SEO), Project View, Project Able and Entry Point (focused on People with Disabilities)

URL: www.ibm.com/employment/us, Click on University, then Diversity Recruitment Programs

What activities does the firm undertake to attract minority and women employees?

- Partner programs with women and minority associations

- Conferences: American Indian Science and Engineering Society (AISES), Grace Hopper Conference for Women in Computing. HENAAC, National Association of Asian American Professionals (NAAAP), National Association of Women MBA (NAWM-BA), National Black MBA Association (NBMBAA), National Society of Black Engineers (NSBE), National Society of Hispanic MBAs (NSHMBA), Reaching Out, Society of Hispanic Professional Engineers (SHPE), Society of Mexican American Engineers and Scientists (MAES), Society of Women Engineers (SWE), Women In Technology International (WITI)
- Participate at minority job fairs
- Seek referrals from other employees
- Utilize online job services
- INROADS, National GEM Consortium, National Action Council for Minorities in Engineering (NACME), Sponsors for Educational Opportunity (SEO), Project View, Project Able and Entry Point (focused on People with Disabilities)

URL: http://www.ibm.com/employment/us, Click on University, then Diversity Recruitment Programs

Do you use executive recruiting/search firms to seek to identify new diversity hires?

Yes

Internships and Co-ops

Employment Pathways for Interns and Co-ops (EPIC)

> *Deadline for application:* Applications accepted year round
> *Pay:* Competitive with industry
> *Length of the program:* Internships are typically 10-14 weeks, co-ops are typically 6 or 7 months
> *Web site for internship/co-op information:* www.ibm.com/careers

A student employment assignment at IBM gives you real-world experience that offers you a competitive edge when you enter the workforce. Student employment assignments provide you the opportunity to become familiar with IBM's organization, work style and corporate culture. Co-op and internship programs are an important recruiting channel for IBM because they help management identify high-potential prospective employees. Participating students are often considered for a long-term commitment of regular employment. Our philosophy is recruit once, hire twice.

As an IBM intern or co-op, you will be assigned to a paid technical or non-technical position related to your major or career goals.

Extreme Blue

> *Deadline for application:* Applications accepted year round
> *Pay:* Competitive with industry
> *Length of the program:* Typically 10-14 weeks
> *Web site for internship/co-op information:* www.ibm.com/extremeblue

The Extreme Blue™ internship program-IBM's incubator for talent, technology, and business innovation-challenges project teams of technical and MBA interns (along with their technical and business mentors) to start something BIG by developing new high-growth businesses.

Scholarships

IBM-INROADS Scholarship

Scholarship award amount: $1500 tuition scholarship (one time scholarship) - several scholarships awarded

Web site or other contact information for scholarship: Available to INROADS interns at IBM only

The IBM-INROADS Scholarship provides $1500 tuition scholarships to IBM INROADS interns who have demonstrated both academic and professional excellence.

Affinity Groups/Employee Networks

Over 172 affinity networking groups globally. Global Affinity Groups at IBM:

- Asian
- Black
- Gay, Lesbian, Bisexual, Transgender (GLBT)
- Hispanic / Latino
- Men
- Native American
- People with Disabilities
- Women

Diversity Network Groups consist of employees who voluntarily come together with the ultimate goal of enhancing the success of IBM's business objectives by helping their members become more effective in the workplace through:

- Meeting and teaming
- Networking
- Mentoring and coaching
- Community outreach
- Social, cultural, and educational events
- Developing professional skills
- Enhancing recruitment and welcoming

Entry-Level Programs/Full-Time Opportunities

International Business Machines Corporation, headquartered in Armonk, N.Y., is the world's largest information technology (IT) company. While we are the IT leader, the solutions and services we deliver to our clients span all major industries, including financial services, healthcare, government, automotive, telecommunications and education, among others. It is the breadth of our portfolio – across hardware, software, services, consulting, research, financing and technology – that uniquely separates IBM from other companies. We have a rich history of driving innovations that help our clients transform themselves into On Demand businesses through our professional solutions, services and consulting businesses. IBM has a diverse and talented workforce that conducts business in 170 countries.

For more information about IBM career opportunities including our business areas and geographic locations, please visit www.ibm.com/careers.

Strategic Plan and Diversity Leadership

How does the firm's leadership communicate the importance of diversity to everyone at the firm?

The importance of diversity is communicated at all levels in IBM via electronic communications, meetings and training.

Who has primary responsibility for leading diversity initiatives at your firm?

Ted Childs, Vice President, Global Workforce Diversity

Does your firm currently have a diversity committee?

Yes, a global diversity council governs over 70 local diversity councils around the world. Additionally, there are executive task forces for eight constituencies - Asian, Black, Gay, Lesbian, Bisexual, Transgender (GLBT), Hispanic/Latino, Men, Native American, People with Disabilities, and Women

If yes, please describe how the committee is structured, how often it meets, etc.

Diversity Councils are located at multiple IBM based locations worldwide. Executive task forces are structured in a way that "immerses executive sponsors in the specific challenges faced by the employee constituency groups" and focuses on tactical issues. [Reference: Thomas, David A. Diversity as Strategy. Harvard Business Review, September 2004; Reprint R0409G]

If yes, does the committee's representation include one or more members of the firm's management/executive committee (or the equivalent)? Yes

Does the committee and/or diversity leader establish and set goals or objectives consistent with management's priorities? Yes

Has the firm undertaken a formal or informal diversity program or set of initiatives aimed at increasing the diversity of the firm? Yes, formal

How often does the firm's management review the firm's diversity progress/results? Annually

How is the firm's diversity committee and/or firm management held accountable for achieving results?

Through the annual Chairmans' review, senior level executives report on year to year progress.

The Stats

Employees: Approximately 329,000 worldwide (140,000 in the U.S.) in 2004
Approximately 319,000 worldwide (141,000 in the U.S.) in 2003

Total Revenue: $96.3 billion (2004), $89.1 billion (2003)

Source: www.ibm.com/investor/financials/index.phtml

Employment data for U.S. locations, 2004								
Area	Total	Men	Women	All Minorities	Black	Asian	Hispanic	Native American
Officials/Mgrs	17,494	12,515	4,979	2,775	1,018	1,078	573	106
Professionals	60,353	40,385	19,968	15,175	4,569	7,658	2,620	328
Technicians	11,992	10,615	1,377	2,551	1,044	664	757	86
Marketing	39,699	28,658	11,041	9,713	2,814	5,234	1,454	211
Office/Clerical	6,747	2,234	4,513	2,372	1,548	281	465	78
Craft Workers	1,338	843	495	208	95	63	44	6
Operatives	2,276	1,449	827	460	187	179	87	7
Totals	139,899	96,699	43,200	33,254	11,275	15,157	6,000	822

Source: www-306.ibm.com/employment/us/diverse/employment_data.shtml

Retention and Professional Development

Please identify the specific steps you are taking to reduce the attrition rate of minority and women employees.

- Develop and/or support internal employee affinity groups (e.g., minority or women networks within the firm)
- Increase/review compensation relative to competition
- Increase/improve current work/life programs
- Adopt dispute resolution process
- Succession plan includes emphasis on diversity
- Work with minority and women employees to develop career advancement plans
- Strengthen mentoring program for all employees, including minorities and women
- Professional skills development program, including minority and women employees

Diversity Mission Statement

IBM leaders, in every generation, have believed that an inclusive workplace is right for the company, no matter what the prevailing views of the day represented. That kind of leadership didn't just happen - it is a natural companion to our shared beliefs and values. Diversity and the concept of workforce inclusion are key factors in helping define how we do business.

"Diversity policies lie as close to IBM's core as they have throughout our heritage," says Sam Palmisano, IBM chairman and CEO. "Today we're building a workforce in keeping with the global, diverse marketplace, to better serve our customers and capture a greater share of the on demand opportunity."

The Employer Says

Project View is IBM's award-winning diversity recruitment program that offers Black, Hispanic/Latino, Native American, Asian, Women, and people with disabilities, the chance to be considered for IBM career opportunities nationally. Travel, meals, and lodging are included in this unique one and a half day visit. Only IBM makes a job search this much fun! Selection is based on work experience, skills, and overall academic achievement. This program is open to students receiving a BA, BS, MS or PhD.

Project View is open to US Citizens or nationals; permanent residents, refugees, asylees or those authorized to work under the amnesty provisions of the US immigration law.

Multicultural People in Technology (MPIT) is a multicultural IBM employee initiative the focuses on

• Support the growth, development, advancement, and recognition of IBM's current multicultural technical talent
• Attract and recruit technical multicultural talent to IBM
• Encourage more multicultural youths (K-12) to pursue education and careers in science and technology

Currently, MPIT manages internal and external programs that address these needs in six multicultural constituencies: Asian, Black, Gay/Lesbian/Bisexual/Transgender, Hispanic/Latino, Native American and People with Disabilities

EXploring Interests in Technology and Engineering (EXCITE) Camps are an extension of IBM's commitment to reach groups that are under-represented in the technical workforce and to train and recruit individuals from those constituencies for technical careers. Through its EXITE Camps, IBM identifies 12- and 13-year-old girls with an interest or proficiency in math and science and prepares them to fill the technical pipeline by introducing them to the potential of technology as well as the fun and exciting things they can do with it right now, and exposing them to women who have successful technology careers.

Nearly 2,000 IBM volunteers, female and male, will participate in the EXITE Camps, developing, coordinating and overseeing such activities as web page design, computer chip design, laser optics, animation, robotics and working with computer hardware and software. The volunteers will also introduce the girls to a variety of IBM technologies including TryScience.org, an award-winning web site designed to make learning science more fun for kids. In addition, they will serve as e-mentors, corresponding with participants during the school year via email, providing tutoring and encouraging the students to further pursue their interests in math, science and technology.

MentorNet is a not-for-profit educational organization focused on furthering women's progress in engineering and science fields through the use of an E-mentoring network. MentorNet matches protégés from various colleges and universities with mentors from industry and academia. IBM is a strategic partner of MentorNet, and IBMers comprise the program's largest source of professional mentors.

285

small-company environment

big-company impact®

Who says you have to choose?

At Johnson & Johnson companies we celebrate and promote small-company environments that support the needs of individuals and teams. Our decentralized, adaptive organization has grown to become the world's most broadly based health care company. Through more than 200 companies, selling products in over 175 countries, we bring real, in-depth solutions to nearly every corner of global health care.

Look deeper at the Johnson & Johnson Family of Companies.

find more
www.jnj.com/careers

Johnson & Johnson
Family of Companies

small-company environment
big-company impact

Johnson & Johnson

1 Johnson & Johnson Plaza
New Brunswick, NJ 08933
Phone: (732) 524-0400
Fax: (732) 524-3300
www.jnj.com/careers

The Stats
Employees: 110,900
Total revenues: $47.3 billion

Diversity Leadership
Caridad Arroyo, Manager, Diversity Outreach
501 George St.
New Brunswick, NJ 08901
Phone: (732) 524-1958
Fax: (732) 524-2587
E-mail: carroy1@corus.jnj.com

Recruiting

Please list the schools/types of schools at which you recruit.

• Ivy League schools
• Other private schools
• Public state schools
• Historically Black Colleges and Universities (HBCUs)
• Hispanic Serving Institutions (HSIs)

Do you have any special outreach efforts that are directed to encourage minority students to consider your firm?

• Hold receptions for minority students
• Conferences: National Society of Black Engineers, Society of Hispanic Professional engineers, CGSM, GEM, National Society of Hispanic MBA, NBMBAA, Reaching Out, Disco, MBA Diversity Forum
• Advertise in minority student association publication(s)
• Participate in/host minority student job fair(s)
• Sponsor minority student association events
• Firm's employees participate on career panels at school
• Outreach to leadership of minority student organizations
• Scholarships or intern/fellowships for minority students

What activities does the firm undertake to attract minority and women employees?

• Partner programs with women and minority associations: HACU, HACE and many others
• Conferences (support and attendance): SWE chapter level, National Society of Black Engineers, Society of Hispanic Professional engineers, CGSM, GEM, National Society of Hispanic MBA, NBMBAA, Reaching Out, Disco, MBA Diversity Forum
• Participate at minority job fairs
• Seek referrals from other employees
• Utilize online job services
• Advertising

Internships and Co-ops

We have over 1000 interns yearly and 90+ INROADers

Length of the program: Varies based on the student schedule, program

Percentage of interns/co-ops in the program who receive offers of full-time employment: 60% INROADS, the other programs are run by the operating companies - decentralized recruitment.

Scholarships

HBCU and HIS scholarships, NSBE, SHPE, Penn State

Scholarship award amount: Varies

Affinity Groups/Employee Networks

- (AALC) African American Leadership Council
- (CAAJJ) Community of Asian Associates at Johnson & Johnson
- (GLOBAL) Gay & Lesbian Organization for Business and Leadership
- (HOLA) Hispanic Organization for Leadership and Achievement
- (HONOR) Help our Neighbors with our Resources
- (SAPNA) South Asian Professional Network & Association
- (WLI) Women's Leadership Initiative

Entry-Level Programs/Full-Time Opportunities

Finance Leadership Dev. Program, IM Leadership Dev. Program, Engineering/Operations Leadership Dev. HRLDP, Marketing Leadership Dev. Program

Length of program: 2 years

Geographic location(s) of program: Across the U.S. and Puerto Rico

Strategic Plan and Diversity Leadership

How does the firm's leadership communicate the importance of diversity to everyone at the firm?

Office of Diversity, Diversity Minute Webinar, in-house conferences, e-mails, newsletters, web sites and meetings.

Who has primary responsibility for leading diversity initiatives at your firm?

Office of Diversity, VP Frank Bolden

Does your firm currently have a diversity committee?

Yes

If yes, does the committee's representation include one or more members of the firm's management/executive committee (or the equivalent)?

Yes

Does the committee and/or diversity leader establish and set goals or objectives consistent with management's priorities?

Yes

Has the firm undertaken a formal or informal diversity program or set of initiatives aimed at increasing the diversity of the firm?

Yes, formal and informal.

Retention and Professional Development

How do 2004 minority and female attrition rates generally compare to those experienced in the prior year period?

About the same as in prior years

Please identify the specific steps you are taking to reduce the attrition rate of minority and women employees.

• Develop and/or support internal employee affinity groups (e.g., minority or women networks within the firm)
• Increase/review compensation relative to competition
• Increase/improve current work/life programs
• Adopt dispute resolution process
• Work with minority and women employees on career development and advancement plans (done across the board for all employees)
• Strengthen mentoring program for all employees, including minorities and women
• Professional skills development program, including minority and women employees

Diversity Mission Statement

Johnson & Johnson's Credo sets forth our responsibilities to our employees. It recognizes their dignity and merit, their individuality and the requirement for equal opportunity in employment, development and advancement for those qualified. From these principles, modified over the years, Johnson & Johnson has fostered and encouraged the development of a diverse workforce - a workforce for the future. While we can point with pride to a commitment to diversity deeply rooted in our value system, we recognize that our employees, customers and communities, then, were far different from those of today. However, our commitment to these core stakeholders as they have evolved and as Johnson & Johnson has evolved is as strong as ever. Today's customers and employees come from all over the world and represent different ages, cultures, genders, races and physical capabilities. Through their life experiences, they provide a diversity of thought and perspective that must be reflected in our corporate culture.

To achieve this vision, we must build a workforce that is increasingly skilled, diverse, motivated and committed to dynamic leadership. This workforce should reflect our diverse customer base and be knowledgeable of the markets we serve. Being the Employer of Choice in a dynamic global enviroment means embracing the differences and similarities of all our employees and prospective employees. It also means the execution of innovative diversity and marketing initiatives to ensure our ability to recruit, develop, retain and promote exceptional talent from an array of backgrounds and geographies, while continuing our pursuit of excellence. Our goal is to ensure our ability to meet the demands of a changing world with a vision worthy of our values and our commitment to be the leader in health care across the globe. When we achieve our vision, diversity becomes one of our most important competitive advantages.

Kellogg's

1 Kellogg Sq.
Battle Creek, MI 49016-3599
Phone: (269) 961-2000
Fax: (269) 961-2871
Toll Free: (800) 962-1413
www.kellogg.com/careers

Locations (worldwide)
N. America, Latin America, Europe, Asia
Pacific

Diversity Leadership
VeLois Bowers, VP Diversity & Inclusion

Employment Contact
Byron Foster
One Kellogg Square
Kalamazoo, MI 49016

Recruiting

Please list the schools/types of schools at which you recruit.

• *Public state schools:* Western Michigan University, DePaul Univ., Michigan State Univ.,UTEP, UCLA, Indiana Univ.
• *Historically Black Colleges and Universities (HBCUs):* Lincoln Univ. (MO.), Central State Univ., Clark Atlanta Univ., Howard Univ., Morgan State Univ., Chicago State Univ.,Alabama A&M, Univ. of Arkansas-Pine Bluff, Hampton Univ., Wilberforce Univ.
• *Hispanic Serving Institutions (HSIs):* Texas A&M

Do you have any special outreach efforts that are directed to encourage minority students to consider your firm?

• Host a reception for minority students
• Conferences
• Participate in/host minority student job fair(s)
• Sponsor minority student association events
• Outreach to leadership of minority student organizations
• Scholarships or intern/fellowships for minority students

What activities does the firm undertake to attract minority and women employees?

• Partner programs with women and minority associations
• Conferences: NSBE, Consortium, NBMBAA, NABA, NSHMBA, ALPHA, SHPE, SWE, NSN, NAWMBA
• Participate at minority job fairs
• Seek referrals from other employees
• Utilize online job services
• Network with diversity organizations

Do you use executive recruiting/search firms to seek to identify new diversity hires?

Yes

Internships and Co-ops

The internship programs are in several Kellogg business groups and are typically recruited for during the academic year. Most of the internships are during the summer, following the close of the academic year. The internships consist of undergraduate and graduate students

> *Number of interns in the program in summer 2004 (internship):* 26
> *Length of the program:* 12
> *Percentage of interns/co-ops in the program who receive offers of full-time employment:* 75%
> *Web site for internship/co-op information:* Kellogg.com/careers

The internships are designed as developmental tools which are meaningful projects providing a bridge to full time positions following graduation. The quality of work and successful project completion are among the key factors to determine if intern will receive an offer of employment.

Scholarships

Kellogg's Corporate Citizen Fund (KCCF) has provided funding for scholarship programs that are weighted to selection of diverse students, including the following:

• Carson's Scholars Fund – $25,000 to support the Carson's Scholars Fund offered to Battle Creek Public School students
• Consortium for Graduate Study in Management – $15,000 to support Millenium Campaign for Educational Excellence
• Hispanic College Fund – $10,000
• Hispanic Scholarship Fund – $6,000
• MESAB - $10,000 scholarship support for Medical Education for South African Blacks
• National Association for Black Accountants (NABA) – $6,000
• Women's Grocer Association – $1,000

Affinity Groups/Employee Networks

Kellogg Employee Resource Groups offer opportunities for employees who are connected by some common dimension of diversity to come together to build relationships; identify and generate potential solutions to real or perceived barriers that interfere their ability to realize their full potential; and to create opportunities to aid Kellogg Company in driving positive business results.

Women of Kellogg (WOK)

This community is dedicated to the personal & professional growth and development of the women within Kellogg Company. They join together to project a common voice for the shared experiences, perceptions, and needs of women in the Kellogg workplace and to help members reach their full potential.

> **Meets:** Monthly
> **Web site:** www.kelloggs.com

Kellogg African American Resource Group (KAARG):

This group contributes to company objectives by ensuring the professional development of its members, and serving as a resource to positively influence the Kellogg environment. They provide career development strategies and activities, advise company leadership as appropriate, and actively drive retention.

> **Meets:** Monthly
> **Web site:** www.kelloggs.com

Kellogg Young Professionals

This group provides professional and social networking opportunities for young employees (30 years and under) to assist in their acclimation & development within the company. Professional development opportunities focused on enhancing the understanding of Kellogg Operations while providing both macro- and micro-level learning.

> **Meets:** Monthly
> **Web site:** www.kelloggs.com

New: (2005 developmental phase)

- Hispanic Employee Resource Group
- Multicultural Employee Resource Group (KMERG)

Entry-Level Programs/Full-Time Opportunities/Training Programs

Global Learning & Development opportunities (25 workshops offered in 2005)

Strategic Plan and Diversity Leadership

Who has primary responsibility for leading diversity initiatives at your firm?

VeLois Bowers, Vice President Diversity & Inclusion

Does your firm currently have a diversity committee?

No

Does the committee and/or diversity leader establish and set goals or objectives consistent with management's priorities?

Yes

Has the firm undertaken a formal or informal diversity program or set of initiatives aimed at increasing the diversity of the firm?

Yes, formal

How often does the firm's management review the firm's diversity progress/results?

Quarterly

How is the firm's diversity committee and/or firm management held accountable for achieving results?

At the core of Kellogg's diversity and inclusion initiative is accountability. That is the essence and strongest component of the initiative. Performance measures were added to the evaluations of all people managers around the initiative. The success of the initiative became one of several factors that played a part in performance evaluations, promotions & bonuses.

Human resources and people managers knew that the Executive Management Council (EMC) was reviewing the overall diversity and inclusion plan quarterly. A standing agenda item for the EMC was the number of women and minorities who are being prepared for positions of increasing responsibility in the company.

A Diversity Scorecard was designed to allow the company to see its progress on the initiative. It had measurable objectives for hiring, retention and promotion of women and minorities. The Scorecard kept track of company sponsored training of women

and minorities, demographics, affirmative action deficiencies, and women and minority underutilization. On a quarterly basis, managers were given their scorecard to determine their progress.

The Stats

DEMOGRAPHIC PROFILE	TOTAL IN THE U.S.		TOTAL OUTSIDE THE U.S		TOTAL WORLDWIDE	
	2004	2003	2004	2003	2004	2003
Number of employees	15,983	16,585	9,189	8,665	25,171	25,250
Revenues	$6.369 billion	$5.954 billion	$3.244 billion	$2.857 billion	$9.613 billion	$8.811 billion

Retention and Professional Development

How do 2004 minority and female attrition rates generally compare to those experienced in the prior year period?

Lower than in prior years

Please identify the specific steps you are taking to reduce the attrition rate of minority and women employees. (It is suggested that you elaborate on this issue in the final question of this survey.)

• Develop and/or support internal employee affinity groups (e.g., minority or women networks within the firm)
• Increase/review compensation relative to competition
• Increase/improve current work/life programs
• Succession plan includes emphasis on diversity
• Work with minority and women employees to develop career advancement plans
• Strengthen mentoring program for all employees, including minorities and women
• Professional skills development program, including minority and women employees

Diversity Mission Statement

Valuing Diversity

At Kellogg Company, we're dedicated to the things that set us apart and make us better. With different backgrounds, cultures and experiences, everyone brings something valuable to our team. We thrive on the diverse talents of our employees, and we expect all of our team members to show dignity and respect to those talents. There's always a better idea just around the corner and, with support, creative thoughts become brilliant working solutions. At Kellogg Company, it's all about being yourself, being accepted, and being successful.

The Employer Says

People are our most important asset.

Kellogg Diversity and Inclusion Strategy focuses on four key strategic areas:

• Build accountability for diversity and inclusion throughout the organization
• Recruit, retain and develop talented people
• Drive understanding, education and awareness
• Create the environment

Companies are constantly in flux as to who is responsible for making sure that the people of the organization are developed, trained and motivated to give their best for the success of the company. The question is continually being asked as to who is accountable for providing skill-building experiences so that employees are always learning and continually creating innovative products. At Kellogg, the world's leading producer of cereal and a leading producer of convenience foods, the answer is its strategy. Accountability: Everyone, Every Level. Every management level and every people manager within the organization must have measurable accountabilities which help to ensure that Kellogg attracts, retains and promotes people from the broad range of backgrounds that comprise the diverse global marketplace it serves.

Such accountability is broad in its scope. But the creation of the K Values, made it reasonable to believe that the company could embrace and support such an initiative. The K Values, six guiding Kellogg values, encompass the way the company runs its business and builds relationships with its employees.

The K Values are:

• We act with integrity and show respect
• We are all accountable
• We are passionate about our business, our brands, and our food
• We have the humility and hunger to learn
• We strive for simplicity
• We love success

The key value underpinning the diversity and inclusion initiative is "We act with integrity and show respect." This K Values call of everyone in the company to show respect and value all individuals for their diverse backgrounds, experience, styles, approaches and ideas. And, it requires every member of the organization to listen to others.

Everyone who manages people at Kellogg has measurable performance requirements around the initiative. But, three groups in particular are accountable for ensuring the integration of the initiative within the company. They are:

• The Executive Management Committee (EMC)
• Human Resource Professionals
• The company's people managers

The specific tasks and deliverables for each group differ, but each has accountabilities in the four key strategic focuses of the Diversity and Inclusion Strategy:

• Build accountability for diversity and inclusion throughout the organization
• Recruit, retain and develop talented people
• Drive understanding, education and awareness
• Create the environment

Three programs help to ensure that the key accountabilities are driven throughout the organization:

• Kellogg's Performance Management Review
• The Diversity and Inclusion Scorecard
• Managing Inclusion Training

Knight Ridder

50 W. San Fernando St., Ste. 1500
San Jose, CA 95113
Phone: (408) 938-7700
Fax: (408) 938-7766
www.kri.com/career/

Locations (worldwide)

Knight Ridder is the nation's second-largest newspaper publisher, with products in print and online. The company publishes 31 daily newspapers in 28 U.S. markets, with a readership of 9.0 million daily and 12.7 million Sunday. Knight Ridder also has investments in a variety of Internet and technology companies and two newsprint companies. The company's Internet operation, Knight Ridder Digital, develops and manages the company's online properties. It is the founder and operator of Real Cities (www.RealCities.com), the largest national network of city and regional Web sites in more than 110 U.S. markets. Knight Ridder and Knight Ridder Digital are headquartered in San Jose, Calif.

Diversity Leadership

Larry Olmstead, Vice President/Staff development and Diversity

Employment Contact

Gail Yoshimoto Shih, Director of Employment/Chief Talent Wizard
50 W. San Fernando St., Suite 1500
San Jose, California 95113
Phone: (408) 938-7768
Fax: (408) 938-0205
E-mail: goshih@knightridder.com

Recruiting

Please list the schools/types of schools at which you recruit.

- *Ivy League schools:* Harvard, Stanford, Princeton, Columbia, MIT, Kellogg, Wharton
- *Other private schools:* Temple University, NYU, Emerson, Northwestern, Norte Dame, Duke, Univ. of Miami, TCU, USC
- *Public state schools:* University of VA, University of MD, University of SC, University of NC, NC State, San Jose State, University of MO, University of MN, Michigan State, University of Michigan, University of TX (Arlington), University of MS, University of AL, Penn State, University of Southern IL, University of KY, UCLA, Historically Black Colleges and Universities
- *(HBCUs):* Spelman, Florida A & M University, Howard University, Morehouse, Tennese State, Hampton University, Fisk University, Prairie View
- *Hispanic Serving Institutions (HSIs):* University of Southern Calif., Cal State Fullerton, University of TX (Austin),San Jose State
- *Native American Tribal Universities:* Haskell Indian Nations University (KS)
- *Other predominantly minority and/or women's colleges:* Spelman

Do you have any special outreach efforts that are directed to encourage minority students to consider your firm?

- Hold a reception for minority students
- Conferences: CNBAM

- Advertise in minority student association publication(s): Black Collegian
- Participate in/host minority student job fair(s)
- Sponsor minority student association events
- Firm's employees participate on career panels at school
- Outreach to leadership of minority student organizations
- Scholarships or intern/fellowships for minority students

What activities does the firm undertake to attract minority and women employees?

- Partner programs with women and minority associations - Underwriting and sponsoring for various programs for NABJ, NAHJ, AAJA, NAJA, NLGJA, UNITY, CNBAM, AAF
- Conferences: American Advertising Federation (AAF) Most Promising Minorities Program, AAF Mosaic Program, CNBAM, HBCU Newspaper Conference, Society of Professional Journalists Regional Conferences, American Copy Editors Society, CCNMA, Howard University Jobs Fair, Spirit of Diversity Jobs Fair, ASNE Job fair for Minorities
- Participate at minority job fairs - NABJ, NAHJ, AAJA, NAJA, NLGJA, UNITY, ACES
- Seek referrals from other employees - employee referral program pays $500
- Utilize online job services - CareerBuilder
- Workplace awards

Do you use executive recruiting/search firms to seek to identify new diversity hires?

Yes

If yes, list all women- and/or minority-owned executive search/recruiting firms to which the firm paid a fee for placement services in the past 12 months:

NIWA, Inc., Financial Staffing Group

Scholarships

Knight Ridder Scholars Programs

This is a four-year program offered to graduating high school seniors residing in areas served by Knight Ridder properties. Each property sets up a scholarship committee, solicits applications each fall from area high schools, selects students from that pool of candidates and recommends them to corporate for consideration for a national scholarship. Local winners are usually given a small scholarship by the local property and offered an internship at that property, regardless of whether they win a national scholarship. The national winners, there will be five in 2001, are awarded $40,000 in cash assistance for college, four 12-week internships paid by corporate. If winners accept, they must also agree to work for Knight Ridder for at least a year upon graduation, starting at the Knight Ridder property that sponsored them (another KR property if the sponsoring one is no longer affiliated). The first year's pay and FTE are carried by corporate.

Knight Ridder HBCU Scholars Program

This is a two-year scholarship aimed at students attending specific historically black colleges and universities (Spelman, Florida A & M University, Howard University). Up to four scholarships worth $10,000 each are awarded each year. Spelman is for journalism. FAMU is for printing arts/production management. Howard is for advertising sales and marketing. Candidates are recommended by the schools or themselves and are selected each spring after interviews and an assessment of their interest in newspapering. In addition to scholarship assistance, winners are awarded a corporate paid 12-week internship and are required to work for Knight Ridder for at least a year upon graduation, if offered a job. In cases where candidates are not chosen from one of these schools, a minority student focusing on business for another school (and usually in our intern pool of promising talent) may be considered.

Knight Ridder Summer Intern Program for Minorities

This program provides 10 weeks of funding to local properties to support training opportunities for students and recent graduates of color. While most internships are in the summer, increasingly internships are at various times of the year. Each fall, papers apply to the corporate Office of Diversity for intern funding. Allocations are generally made by early December.

Knight Ridder Native American Internship Program

This 12-week internship program is aimed at boosting the ranks of Native Americans at our papers. Five papers are involved in this program each year. They are Wichita, Saint Paul, Grand Forks, Aberdeen and Duluth.

Knight Ridder Specialty Program

Known historically as the "two-year program," the Specialty Program is a one-year program for people of color who have completed college or some part thereof and/or may be changing careers. The specialty is that they are trained in specific fields in which people of color are underrepresented (arts criticism, graphic arts, religion writing, medicine). The interns (there are six each year) work at one of four papers for one year and are paid at that paper's entry level employee rate. The training papers are Philadelphia Inquirer (1), Detroit Free Press (1), San Jose Mercury News (1)and Miami Herald (1). Candidates are selected by the participating papers around December of each year based on applications from prospects and recommendations from other KR papers. Generally, the specialty interns start in June of each year. The Office of Diversity covers compensation and carries the FTE. The local property provides one off-site development experience during the year and evaluates the intern with the idea in mind of recommending employment at the training paper or another Knight Ridder paper.

Knight Ridder Rotating Internship Program

Formerly the "CapCities" Rotating Internship Program, this is a one-year newsroom opportunity for early career journalists. It consists of four-month tours of duty at three papers in the program for each of the seven interns selected. Housing is provided. Local utilities are paid. The intern receives a small stipend. Sripends and FTE's are covered by the Office of Diversity. Prospects need to apply by December 1 of each year to a participating paper or the Office of Diversity. They are selected by late January and start work in June. Rotations are assigned for the full year, although interns can be hired out after their second tour of duty. Participating papers include Kansas City, Belleville, Contra Costa, Fort Worth and Saint Paul.

For more information, kindly refer to our website: http://www.kri.com/career/internships.html

Entry-Level Programs/Full-Time Opportunities

All Knight Ridder professional development programs work hard to maintain a diverse pool of participants. Development of our people is a core company value. Recognized as an industry leader, Knight Ridder is frequently cited for state-of-the-art training and unique learning opportunities. These range from learning new skills in the classroom and on the Web to broadened responsibility on the job to cross training to partial tuition reimbursement for completing a degree program. Some programs are sponsored by Knight Ridder and delivered regionally or at the corporate headquarters. Many more are developed and delivered locally by the newspapers and online operations, some in partnership with local universities and colleges. These include but are not limited to:

Executive development programs – Circulation Management Development, Newsroom Management Development and Advertising Management Development, Finance Management Development - are two-year-long development programs to prepare successor candidates and high-potential leaders to assume greater responsibility. Participants earn about company strategy, resource allocation and leadership from Knight Ridder executives and experts in their functional areas. The goal is for the most successful to advance to greater responsibility within two to three years.

The Executive Academy, designed for top executives, is an intensive exploration of critical issues of strategic importance. Participants are chosen in consultation with corporate senior management.

The Emerging Leaders Program is a one-year program that deepens bench strength by providing coaching and feedback to a diverse group of high-potential frontline supervisors to help develop them for fruitful careers.

Project Benchstrength pairs a top executive with a promising leader to mentor, coach and learn from each other.

Assigning Editor Seminars and Writer's Workshops focus on developing skills in newsrooms. Strategic Solutions for Customer Results prepares sales managers and account executives to ask the right questions and devise solutions that fit customer needs.

Strategic Plan and Diversity Leadership

How does the firm's leadership communicate the importance of diversity to everyone at the firm?

These diversity goals are communicated to all our employees, online as well as in print, through KR News, our company internal newsletter, our website (http://www.kri.com/career/diversity.html), company meetings (formalized through ReachUp), our annual report. The diversity mission is also showcased during our orientation sessions for new employees.

Who has primary responsibility for leading diversity initiatives at your firm?

Larry Olmstead, Vice President/ Staff development and Diversity

Does your firm currently have a diversity committee?

No

Does the committee and/or diversity leader establish and set goals or objectives consistent with management's priorities?

Yes

Has the firm undertaken a formal or informal diversity program or set of initiatives aimed at increasing the diversity of the firm?

Yes, formal. Each year, all executives who participate in our annual bonus plan have as a prominent goal advancement of women and minorities - "Knight Ridder will increase the number of people ready now to succeed division directors, and ensure that the successor group is more diverse than the existing division director and above group." In addition, the MBO Journalism goal includes a tenet called "People Like Me," to encourage coverage of all parts of our communities, so readers will see themselves reflected in our pages. This underscores the importance our company places in understanding the different needs and interests of our diverse markets and the importance of developing content to address those needs and interests.

Diversity is identified as one of the leadership competencies by which Knight Ridder managers are evaluated. It is specifically noted under "Builds Relationships," "Builds and Maintains a High-Performance Workforce," and "Showing Understanding of People."

Through ReachUP, a companywide performance management system, employees and managers work together to understand business needs and create individual performance plans aligned with company goals. Diversity is a prominent annual goal. Managers meet regularly with staffers to set expectations, share feedback, coach and review progress.

A Leadership Development Review is conducted each year at every company to assess the depth of available leadership talent and to evaluate the potential and progress of people preparing for or currently in upper management positions. Individual development plans are created. This ensures that qualified candidates are ready when senior-level job openings occur. We track minority and female progress through this annual LDR program.

How often does the firm's management review the firm's diversity progress/results?

Quarterly

How is the firm's diversity committee and/or firm management held accountable for achieving results?

These diversity goals as they relate to our annual bonus plans are also tracked/incented at our local newspapers and at corporate. Management compensation is rigorously tied to achievement of these diversity and journalism goals.

The Stats

DEMOGRAPHIC PROFILE	TOTAL IN THE U.S.		TOTAL OUTSIDE THE U.S		TOTAL WORLDWIDE	
	2004	2003	2004	2003	2004	2003
Number of employees	19,057	19,648	0	0	19,057	19,648
Revenues	$3.014 billion	$2.945 billion	0	0	$3.014 billion	$2.945 billion

Retention and Professional Development

How do 2004 minority and female attrition rates generally compare to those experienced in the prior year period?

About the same as in prior years

Please identify the specific steps you are taking to reduce the attrition rate of minority and women employees.

• Increase/review compensation relative to competition
• Increase/improve current work/life programs
• Succession plan includes emphasis on diversity
• Work with minority and women employees to develop career advancement plans
• Review work assignments and hours billed to key client matters to make sure minority and women employees are not being excluded
• Strengthen mentoring program for all employees, including minorities and women
• Professional skills development program, including minority and women employees

All Knight Ridder professional development programs work hard to maintain a diverse pool of participants.

Knight Ridder newspapers are active participants in national fellowships and training programs at prestigious academic institutions. Selected journalists are supported with fellowships at Harvard, Stanford, Columbia, and the University of Michigan while others might attend programs at the Maynard Institute, Northwestern University Media Management Center, the Knight Center for Specialized Reporting, the National Institute for Computer-Assisted Reporting, and Poynter Institute for Media Studies. Nearly every year, Knight Ridder is represented in the nation's most prestigious fellowships, including the Nieman Scholars, the National Endowment for the Humanities fellowship at The University of Michigan and the Stanford Executive Program.

Depending on career goals and progress, employees might attend other programs where Knight Ridder is actively represented, including:

• Editing Program for Minority Journalists
• Northwestern University Newspaper Management Center Training Program
• Albert E. Fitzpatrick Leadership Development Institute
• Robert C. Maynard Institute for Journalism Education
• Harvard Advanced Management Program
• American Press Institute

• National Association of Minority Media Executives events

Diversity Mission Statement

Knight Ridder's diversity philosophy is as simple as its motto: *"Diversity. No excuses."*

"We will reflect the diversity of the audiences we serve, including viewpoints and cultures, in our content and in our workforces."

"We promise to help you develop, to show you respect, to reward you fairly, to provide a workplace in which individual differences are valued."

Chairman and CEO Tony Ridder speaks often and passionately on the subject. As 2003-2004 chairman of the Newspaper Association of American (NAA), he reminded his colleagues: *"Only diversity of thought and background and origin enables us to genuinely reflect our heterogeneous readership. Only diversity of customer relationships enables us to tap the true business potential of our burgeoning ethnic population. Diversity within our ranks is so clearly the right thing to do that argument to the contrary goes nowhere."*

For more information on our diversity programs and initiatives, kindly refer to our website: www.kri.com/career/diversity.html

The Employer Says

Knight Ridder has the industry's most diverse corporate executive team. Of the company's 23 officers, 26 percent are minorities and 30 percent are women.

Knight Ridder has doubled its number of minority executive editors and managing editors since 2001. Women hold the top news-room post in 15 of our 29 daily newspapers and are serving as interim editor in three more. Our newsrooms also compare well. Minority representation in Knight Ridder newsrooms is 21.0% compared with 12.9% for the industry. Minorities comprise 23.4% of Knight Ridder newsroom supervisors; the industry figure is 10.5%, according to the American Society of Newspaper Editors.

The company is committed to developing future leaders of the business. Its four-year Minority Scholars Program has produced 17 current full-time KR employees, with four more scheduled to go to work this fall. The one-year Minority Internship Program has a retention rate of more than 70 percent, helping to keep diverse talent flowing into the newsrooms. Knight Ridder underwrites 45 minority summer interns each year at its newspapers, which use their own funds to hire many more.

Knight Ridder newspapers take pride in public-service journalism and encourage its executives and employees to take an active role in a broad and diverse spectrum of community service activities and organizations. Following are a few of the workplace awards where Knight Ridder has been honored.

2005
Knight Ridder made *DiversityInc*'s 2005 Top 50 Companies for Diversity list. Companies were evaluated in four key areas: CEO commitment; human capital; corporate communications (internal and external); and supplier diversity. Knight Ridder also ranked eighth in the magazine's list of Top 10 Companies for Executive Women.

2005
Knight Ridder will be recognized by *Essence* maga zine as a Great Place to Work in its May 2005 issue for the kinds of programs, training and progressive management goals that help African-American women advance in the workplace. Companies were assessed on organizational commitment to diversity, representation in management ranks, career development and mentoring, management-leadership training, recent hiring of black women, networking and support groups, work-life balance, compensation, community involvement and support, acceptance and respect for diverse styles, and supplier relationships.

2005
Black Collegian ranked Knight Ridder as one of the Top 100 Employers in 2005. In creating this list, *The Black Collegian*, a career and self-development magazine for African-American students, surveyed major employers in industry, government and business on their projected number of hires from college recruiting efforts.

2005

The National Association for Female Executives (NAFE) named Knight Ridder to its Top 30 Companies for Executive Women, a ranking based on the number of women who hold senior executive positions, are top earners, serve on a company's board, and hold profit-and-loss responsibility in senior level positions. The list appears annually in NAFE's February magazine.

2005, 2004

LATINA Style magazine named Knight Ridder to the LATINA Style 50 2004, its annual list of the top 50 companies for Hispanic professional women. Knight Ridder was chosen from among 600 companies evaluated on their representation of Latinas in the workforce and among top decision-makers and wage earners. KR also was cited for its mentoring programs, alternative work arrangements and recruitment practices.

2005, 2004

Professional Business Women of California (PBWC)'s Pacesetter Award, which goes to the top Bay Area, Calif., companies that support the advancement of women in the workplace. The PBWC Pacesetter Award winners were selected from the largest public companies from nine Bay Area counties that promote women into the highest ranks of their organizations and encourage women to take leadership roles on an ongoing basis.

2004, 2002 & 1999

Fortune magazine list of the 50 Best Companies for Minorities. *Fortune* included Knight Ridder as the only media company after a review of the diversity of the work force, Board and top-level managers. In 2004, Knight Ridder's work force was composed of more than 29 percent people of color. In 2003, more than 30 percent of Knight Ridder new hires were people of color. Knight Ridder has doubled the number of minorities in top editor jobs since 2002, continually striving to make newsrooms more reflective of the communities on which they report.

1996

The Catalyst Award for comprehensive initiatives to advance women through the corporate ranks. Catalyst, the nonprofit research and advisory organization, working to advance women in business and the professions, honors innovative approaches with proven results taken by companies to address the recruitment, development and advancement of all managerial women, including women of color.

KPMG LLP

345 Park Ave.
New York, NY 10154-0102
Phone: 212-758-9700
Fax: 212-758-9819
www.kpmgcareers.com

Locations (worldwide)
94 U.S. offices

Diversity Leadership
Contact Person: Kara Keszkowski, Senior Associate, Workplace Solutions/HR Communications

Employment Contact
Jennifer Neal - Diversity Recruiting Manager
3 Chestnut Ridge Road
Montvale, NJ 07645
Phone: (201) 307-7362
Fax: (201) 505-6100
E-mail: jmneal@kpmg.com

Recruiting

Please list the schools/types of schools at which you recruit.

• *Private schools:* KPMG maintains recruiting relationships with well over 100 colleges and universities across the United States - both private and public institutions
• *Historically Black Colleges and Universities (HBCUs):* Howard University, Hampton University, Florida A&M, University, North Carolina A&T State University, Clark Atlanta University

Do you have any special outreach efforts that are directed to encourage minority students to consider your firm?

• Hold a reception for minority students
• Conferences: National Association of Black Accountants (NABA), Association of Latino Professionals in Finance and Accounting (ALPFA), Hispanic Student Business Association (HSBA)
• Advertise in minority student association publication(s)
• Sponsor minority student association events
• Firm's employees participate on career panels at school
• Outreach to leadership of minority student organizations
• Scholarships or intern/fellowships for minority students
• Other: Host Case Study Competitions

What activities does the firm undertake to attract minority and women employees?

• Conferences: National Association of Black Accountants, Association of Latino Professionals in Finance and Accounting, Hispanic Business Student Association, INROADS, American Society of Women Accountants.
• Participate at minority job fairs
• Seek referrals from other employees
• Utilize online job services (Diversity Inc, NABA, ALPFA)
• KPMG advertises in a variety of mainstream print and electronic media.. Examples include, *Hispanic* magazine, *DiversityInc.* magazine, *FORTUNE* magazine - Best Companies for Minorities, *Working Mother* magazine, American Society of Women Accountant, *The Advocate,* Transition Assistance Online (taonline.com), goldsea.com, Gay Financial Network.

Do you use executive recruiting/search firms to seek to identify new diversity hires?

Yes. KPMG does use executive search firms that focus on minority and women professionals.

Internships and Co-ops

INROADS

Deadline for application: May

Number of interns in the program in summer 2004 (internship) or 2004 (co-op): 55

Pay: Varies

Length of the program: 8 weeks

Percentage of interns/co-ops in the program who receive offers of full-time employment: Of our 2004 INROADS interns, 100% of those eligible to receive a full time offer received one.

Web site for internship/co-op information: www.INROADS.org

KPMG is a member of INROADS, a program that places minority students in intern positions in our offices throughout the country. Through this program we are able to offer internships at an early stage, i.e., prior to entering college and for as long as four years, compared with the traditional one-year internship beginning the summer before graduation. In 2004 we had nearly 60 such interns at KPMG. In 2004 , full-time positions were offered to approximately 90 percent of the interns In addition, six KPMG professionals serve as INROADS board members in their respective cities.

Scholarships

Frank Ross/KPMG Scholarship

Deadline for application for the scholarship program: April

Scholarship award amount: $2,500 (4)

Web site or other contact information for scholarship: Awarded through NABA

We provide (4) $2,500 Scholarships during the National NABA convention. The students are chosen by NABA based on the criteria and weightings below.

• GPA: 40%
• Financial Need: 20%
• Essay: 15%
• Leadership: 15%
• Working for Education Funds: 10%
• Total: 100%

Affinity Groups/Employee Networks

KPMG's business structure is unique in that a significant number of our 18,200 employees and 1,600 partners spend a large portion of their time at client sites. As a result of this industry-wide reality, senior leadership depends on office leaders (office managing partners and engagement partners) to help keep partners and employees apprised of ongoing events related to technical and functional development and community opportunities. To the same degree, office leaders channel national messages to their office, which includes raising diversity awareness. KPMG's affinity groups are initiated by our professionals and implemented at the local office level. There are typically two partner (firm leadership) champions that help manage the group, which enhances our efforts to keep partners and employees connected with leadership. Depending on the office, affinity groups tend to meet on a monthly basis. The firm's national diversity team also lends support when necessary to help ensure the group is progressing.

The following affinity groups exist in KPMG offices across the country.

• African-American network

- Latino network
- Asian-Pacific Islander network
- Filipino network
- Gay, Lesbian, Bisexual and Transgender (GLBT) network
- Diversity Councils, which encompass African-American, Asian-American and Latino professionals
- KPMG's Network of Women (KNOW)

Affinity groups at KPMG have funds allotted to their cause in the office's budget, which is managed by the Office Managing Partner. Following are examples of successful networking events:

- KNOW in Silicon Valley hosted a women partner panel to discuss career development, their career path, and work and family balance.
- KPMG's GLBT network in San Francisco hosted the local chapter Out & Equal breakfast and panel discussion to support our GLBT professionals.

Women's Initiatives

For the past several years, women have comprised at least one half of all of KPMG's new hires and represent a significant portion of the firm's potential talent. To help advance the personal and professional goals of our women, KPMG formed the Women's Advisory Board (WAB) in 2003.

Members of the WAB meet for a full day in different offices around the country every other month and hold conference calls on alternate months. WAB members attend KPMG's Network of Women (KNOW) events in the city in which the bimonthly meetings take place. WAB members also meet with the firm's Area leadership to discuss its mission and progress and how leadership can assist the WAB. Ongoing progress around women's initiatives is communicated through virtual meetings and KPMG Today messages. One of the highlights of WAB is its support of the expansion of KNOW to 36 chapters. Another positive result attributed to WAB is the large number of women professionals who participated in KPMG's management and/or leadership training programs. The numbers more than doubled compared with last year.

KNOW has more than doubled its presence over the past year. KNOW began in Atlanta, Chicago

and Dallas over a year ago and has proven to be a successful venue for women to network, establish relationships and enhance their careers on a professional and personal level. Due to the success of the three networks and the support of firm leadership, KNOW has expanded to 36 chapters across the country. Office Managing Partners play an

integral role in the implementation and progress of the KNOW chapter. There are typically two partner (firm leadership) champions that help manage the group, which enhances our efforts to keep partners and employees connected with leadership. KNOW chapters typically meet on a monthly basis.

Entry-Level Programs/Full-Time Opportunities/Training Programs

Professional Training and Development

Training is available to entry-level employees and availability continues throughout each individual's career through learning opportunities to audit, tax and advisory professionals to keep each individual technically current in their accounting discipline and fully prepared to apply their auditing and accounting knowledge to the particular industry context relevant to the clients they serve. Complementary learning opportunities are available to increase skill in client relationship management, collaboration, leadership, and other personal effectiveness skills. All told, partner and employee training averages 72 hours per person annually, which significantly exceeds the National State Boards of Accountancy (NASBA) annual and triennial requirements.

KPMG has also enhanced the curriculum available to our Client Service Support (CSS) staff to better enable their individual skills development and career success within KPMG and beyond. Areas of training include: business writing and making effective presentations; building effective relationships with colleagues and clients; problem solving and decision making; leading and mobilizing teams; performance management; project management; and self-management of one's career. The overall management of learning and development is carried out by the Firm's Center for Learning and Development (CLD). The central budget managed by the CLD exceeds $50 million annually. The CLD is staffed with a team of experienced, dedicated professionals who are the

backbone of KPMG's education and training environment. Their efforts are complemented by the contributions of hundreds of Audit, Tax and Advisory professionals who are drawn in to develop and deliver the comprehensive curriculum that is available to employees of the firm.

KLEARN LIVE!: Key to the Firm's blended learning approach is KLEARN LIVE!, a Centra-Software based, virtual-classroom that delivers training in an efficient, non-intrusive way. Individuals simply log in for the training they need. Instructors and subject matter experts lead training sessions from anywhere, using slides, multimedia, whiteboards, questions, chats and other training tools. KLEARN LIVE! is a vital part of our overall training with more than 4,000 participant/sessions occurring per month, positioning KPMG at the forefront of enterprise-wide use of this technology.

Respect and Dignity Training: KPMG's Web-based training course entitled, Respect and Dignity, was designed for KPMG's diverse multi-cultural partners and employee population to clarify what constitutes appropriate behavior in the workplace, reinforcing an environment of respect and dignity.

Diversity Training: KPMG Web-based training course entitled Diversity encourages a culture of mutual respect as the cornerstone of its work environment.

Local Professional and Personal Development Opportunities

KPMG Communities: KPMG Communities are small groups of individuals who meet periodically, communicate office and firm initiatives, mentor employees, solicit constructive feedback and generally give people a sense of belonging.

Partner Breakfast/Lunch Program This event provides junior professionals an opportunity to interact and connect with upper management in a relaxed setting. The open forum encourages individuals to discuss succession plans with leaders.

Total BEST (Balance, Excellence, Service, Truth): This program is designed to help employees develop and enjoy work/life effectiveness.

Senior Manager Development Sessions: This effort provides senior managers with an opportunity to build skills that support the firm's three strategic priorities.

It also provides senior managers with a means to express feedback to their local leadership. Some local examples of events and activities are career pathing; a C-class presentation skill course; and a trip to a leading client, including a training session.

Lunch and Learn Sessions: In an effort to educate our people on work/life effectiveness, Lunch and Learn, provides an informational forum on topics that can impact the personal lives of employees and help address the life needs of various groups within our community.

Health Fairs: Designed to increase awareness of wellness with easy access to wellness information and vendors. Some offices provide interested individuals with access to glucose, blood pressure and cholesterol testing.

Strategic Plan and Diversity Leadership

How does the firm's leadership communicate the importance of diversity to everyone at the firm?

KPMG's business structure is unique in that a majority of our 18,200 employees and 1,600 partners spend a large portion of their time at client sites. As a result of this industry-wide reality, senior leadership depends on office leaders (office managing partners and engagement partners) to help keep partners and employees apprised of ongoing events related to technical and functional development and community opportunities. With that said, communication is a critical component of the firm's strategic people priority, in other words, to be a great place for advancing the careers of our people in a rewarding environment.

KPMG's leadership teams use a variety of communication methods to help foster a supportive and inclusive work environment. National monthly celebrations, industry diversity trends, messages on values, affinity group and networking events are highlighted through the traditional means of email, memo and intranet, and by innovative methods such as Town Hall Meetings and Webcasts. KPMG Today, the firm's Outlook-delivered daily update on news and events both internal and external to the firm, delivers information in "real-time" and the Diversity section provides information on diversity celebrations, minority profession-

al profiles, and sponsorship events. The firm's magazine, KPMGLife, is an opportunity for not only our professionals but also their family and friends to read about various aspects of KPMG and its partners and employees.

Who has primary responsibility for leading diversity initiatives at your firm?

Clyde Jones, National Director, Diversity and EEO/AAP

Does your firm currently have a diversity committee?

Yes

If yes, please describe how the committee is structured, how often it meets, etc.

National Diversity Committee: As part of the firm's national Human Resources structure, KPMG's Diversity team, led by Clyde Jones, National Director, Diversity and his staff help drive the firm's diversity strategy while maintaining and strengthening business relationships with external diverse professional networks, affinity groups and the business community. KPMG's national Diversity team typically meets on a monthly basis. Clyde and his team also work closely with KPMG's recruiting teams (campus and experience hire) to promote KPMG's commitment to diversity among prospective employees.

Local Diversity Committees: KPMG's professionals, with the support of local office leadership, implement diversity "committees" on the local office level, in the form of networks, affinity groups and diversity councils. Local office leadership often gets involved in raising diversity awareness in various ways such as supporting minority and women networks, encouraging diversity month celebrations, etc.

Diversity "committees" at KPMG are designed to support the firm's diversity strategy on a local basis both internally and in the marketplace.

Meeting schedules vary by office location.

In general, the firm asks that these groups to work towards achieving some/all of the following aspirations.

• To support KPMG's values and diversity policy and teams.
• To sponsor and support social, networking and mentoring activities.
• To help enhance recruitment and retention of minority and women professionals at KPMG.
• To provide resources to professional development and peer support.
• To continue to serve our communities through the firm's national community service program, Involve or as a network.
• To act as a liaison between KPMG and the business community.

Has the firm undertaken a formal or informal diversity program or set of initiatives aimed at increasing the diversity of the firm?

Yes, formal. For years, KPMG has had a formal diversity statement, which captures the firm's commitment to achieving an even more inclusive workplace. KPMG's diversity strategy is also reflected in our value system, and all of our partners and employees are expected to live out the firm's values. This diversity statement is located on the firm's Diversity Web site via the Intranet, recruiting materials and KPMG's external Web site, www.us.kpmg.com.

As an equal opportunity employer, our goal is to treat everyone fairly regardless of race, color, creed, religion, age, gender, national origin, citizenship status, marital status, sexual orientation, disability, veteran status, or other category protected by federal, state, or local law.

Our Vision: Our aim is to make enhancements to the firm's work environment by valuing our differences and including them in what we do.

Our values support it. Our clients value it. And our success depends on it. By valuing our differences, we continue to build upon our individual, team, and firm strengths, which are vital in helping us to continue to stand apart from our competition.

Our Mission: Maintaining a work environment that embraces diversity - of our people, their ideas and lifestyles, professional insights and personal perspectives - is vital for KPMG to stand apart from other audit, tax and advisory services firms and as an employer of choice. Our aim is to make a difference by valuing our differences.

Our Strategy: By leveraging, valuing, and encouraging diversities of thought, perspective and approach to create an open and inclusive work environment where both business and personal objectives/growth can be met through:

• Awareness: Promote KPMG's strategy and commitment to diversity/inclusion internally and externally.
• Recruitment: Recruit, retain, and promote the best and the brightest.
• Education: Provide orientation into KPMG through consistent and ongoing messaging around our culture of values, competencies and our diversity strategy, including networking, mentoring, and career development.

Memberships: KPMG is a member of the American Institute of Certified Public Accountants (AICPA), where Clyde Jones, National Director, Diversity and EEO/AAP, sits on the Minorities Initiative Committee, a group that is focused on increasing the number of minorities in the accounting profession. This is an appointed position and Mr. Jones is in the first year of a three-year term. The committee meets quarterly and subgroups operate throughout the year. Mr. Jones serves on the academic support and outreach committee, which involves providing scholarships to minority students, as well as the leadership development committee, which is responsible for developing curriculum and identifying speakers for the committee's national leadership conference.

Recruiting: Our campus recruiting team is actively involved in recruiting at Historically Black Colleges and Universities (HBCUs) and participates at the NABA student chapter level on a regional basis. They also participate in numerous career fairs held by minority organizations.

Our interest in increasing our presence on HBCUs campuses is exemplified by our participation in the Howard 21st Century Advantage Program for the past three years. Through the program we've worked closely with groups of 20 students each year and have provided mentoring on a one-to-one basis from minority employees at KPMG.

Supplier Diversity Program: The firm actively seeks to promote participation of minority-owned, women-owned, Veteran-owned, and Special disabled veteran owned businesses in our purchasing supplier process. Equal opportunity is given to minority-owned, women-owned, Veteran-owned, and Special disabled veteran owned businesses to join our supplier base by competing and participating in the purchasing process, subject to established purchasing policies and procedures.

Diversity Training: Web-based training entitled, Treating People with Respect and Dignity, was developed and designed to reaffirm expected behaviors in our work environment and to more closely examine our long-standing policy of nondiscrimination in an effort to reinforce expected behaviors. The training also reinforces the notion that treating everyone with respect makes good business sense and should be incorporated into our every-day interactions with our colleagues.

Equal Employment Opportunity: KPMG has a long-standing policy of providing equal opportunity for all applicants and employees regardless of their race, color, creed, religion, age, gender, national origin, citizenship status, marital status, sexual orientation, disability, veteran status, or other category protected by federal, state, or local law.

This policy extends to recruiting, recruitment advertising and other communications media, hiring, rates of pay and other compensation, benefits, overtime, promotions, transfers, demotions, layoffs or terminations, recalls, disciplinary action and all other terms, conditions, or privileges of employment.

KPMG Foundation: KPMG Foundation is the creator, cofounder, and administrator of The PhD Project, an ambitious diversity program to address increasing the representation of minority Americans in business, higher education, and the corporate workforce. A landmark effort, The PhD Project aims to put more minorities on business school faculties, with the goal of attracting more minority students and creating greater diversity among future business students.

In December 1994, The PhD Project, with additional funding from academia and leading corporations, held a conference to bring together 266 potential minority doctoral candidates with current doctoral students, business school faculty, deans, and heads of doctoral programs for a two-day conference. Less than one year after the first PhD Project conference, the nation's business schools reported a 42 percent one-year increase in the number of African-Americans, Hispanic-Americans, and Native Americans entering doctoral programs in business. Half of those newly created Ph.D. students were individuals who had been reached by The PhD Project. Now in its eleventh year, The PhD Project has increased the number of minority business professors from 294 in 1994 to 751 in 2005. For more information visit www.phdproject.org.

• PhD Project Statistics 45 of the 266 individuals who attended The PhD Project conference in 1994 began a doctoral program the following year; 62 percent of them were women. Of the 45, 19 have finished the doctoral program and are currently teaching at a university; 13 are women.

• Since 1994, 10,027 individuals have submitted an application for the annual November conference, of which 4,584 were selected and 4,233 have attended.
• Of the 4,233 past conference attendees, 374 started a business doctoral program, of which 109 have finished the doctoral program and currently teaching at a university, 58 of that new faculty are women.

PhD Project Doctoral Students Associations: In August 1994, KPMG Foundation formed the first African-American Accounting Doctoral Students Association (AADSA), now known as The PhD Project Accounting Doctoral Students Association. Since 1994, the Foundation has expanded the associations to include finance, information systems, management, and marketing students, and membership has been extended to Hispanic-Americans and Native Americans. The PhD Project Doctoral Students Associations (DSAs) help sustain a high level of commitment and sense of connection among minority students in business through networking, joint research opportunities, peer support, and mentoring. As a result, 92 percent of DSA members have completed or are continuing in their doctoral programs, compared with 70 percent among doctoral candidates generally. AACSB International reports that 60.5 percent of those who earn businessdoctorates are in teaching positions. For The PhD Project, that number is an astounding 99 percent.

Minority Doctoral Scholarship Program: The KPMG Foundation invested $7 million to establish a Minority Doctoral Scholarship Program, open to African-American, Hispanic-American, and Native-American accounting doctoral students (scholarships were also awarded to information systems doctoral students from 1997-2002). This program annually awards nearly $600,000 in scholarships. This is in addition to the teaching and research assistantship and waiver of tuition and fees normally provided by doctoral-granting institutions. To date, 50 percent of the minority doctoral scholarships have been awarded to women, and 100% percent of the Foundation's minority accounting doctoral scholarships awarded to women in 2003 was renewed in 2004.

Historically Black Colleges and Universities Accreditation Program: KPMG Foundation instituted a grant program to assist Historically Black Colleges and Universities (HBCUs) in the AACSB International accreditation process for university business schools to ensure continuous improvement. When this program started in 1994, only five HBCUs held AACSB accreditation. Today, nine more are accredited, and all received KPMG funding. Ten HBCUs are in the accreditation candidacy process, all of which are being funded by KPMG Foundation.

How often does the firm's management review the firm's diversity progress/results?

Annually

The Stats

Employees: 18,200 (2004, U.S.)
Revenue: $4.1 billion (2004, U.S.)

Retention and Professional Development

How do 2004 minority and female attrition rates generally compare to those experienced in the prior year period?

Lower than in prior years

Please identify the specific steps you are taking to reduce the attrition rate of minority and women employees.

• Develop and/or support internal employee affinity groups (e.g., minority or women networks within the firm)
• Increase/review compensation relative to competition
• Increase/improve current work/life programs
• Professional skills development programs

Diversity Mission Statement

Foster a work environment that is inclusive and embraces diversity of our people, their ideas and lifestyles, professional insights, and personal perspectives. This is vital for KPMG to stand apart from other audit, tax, and advisory services firms and as an employer of choice.

The Employer Says

KPMG is committed to diversity. We embrace diversity and encourage our partners and employees to share their views and lifestyles, thereby broadening everyone's awareness of differences and hopefully creating an inclusive environment free of discrimination. The varied backgrounds and experiences of our professionals are crucial to understanding and meeting our clients' needs in an increasingly diverse marketplace.

Diversity is a critical component to being an employer of choice, and one of KPMG's genuine strengths. People are KPMG's most important asset and the driving force behind its success. The firm invests heavily to provide its workforce with a supportive and inclusive environment that is built on the firm's standards and values. These help create the trust, support and openness necessary for successful people and, in turn, a successful firm.

KPMG's Values

KPMG's values define our culture and our commitment to the highest principles of personal and professional conduct. They represent how we relate to each other, what we expect from our clients, and what our clients and the marketplace should expect from us. As such, they will continue to be at the heart of how we operate as a firm.

The following is a list of KPMG seven values:

- We lead by example - We, as firms and individuals, act in a manner that exemplifies what we expect of each other and our clients, and what our clients should expect of us.
- We work together - Forging relationships across diverse teams, cultures, functions and practices to enhance team and business results.
- We respect the individual - We respect all individuals for their diversity, who they are and what they bring as individuals and as team members for the benefit of our clients and the firm.
- We seek the facts and provide insight - We listen to and proactively challenge different points of view in order to arrive at the right judgments.
- We are open and honest in our communication - We encourage timely, clear and constructive two-way communication.
- We are committed to our communities - We, as individuals and teams, use our time and resources to support our local communities.
- Above all, we act with integrity - We are professional first and foremost, take pride in being part of KPMG, and are committed to objectivity, quality and service of the highest standards.

External Diversity Outreach

A key part of the firm's diversity strategy is to raise awareness externally of KPMG's commitment to being an inclusive workplace KPMG supports PINK magazine, the nation's first and only national magazine exclusively for women in business. This venture presents an additional opportunity to help further recruit talented women into the firm while supporting the development of our women professionals.

KPMG is a corporate sponsor of the National Association of Black Accountants (NABA) and Association of Latino Professionals in Finance and Accounting (ALPFA) national conventions. Over the years, KPMG has selected approximately 1,500 of our African-American and Latino professionals to attend the conference..

Among KPMG's sponsored events are the regional and national case study competitions. The premise of the case study competition is to engage students in high level and complex accounting problems, both independently and as a team. The cases developed by KPMG are based on realistic accounting, finance and business issues. Each team is asked to work together to identify the relevant issues, research the problems and present a solution to the case. A panel of judges comprised of KPMG professionals and NABA and ALPFA respectively, select the top team on the overall quality of their presentation, including identification of rele-

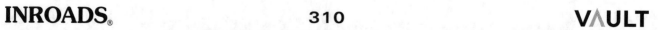

vant accounting, finance and business issues and recommended solution. Throughout the competition students have the opportunity to network with KPMG professionals and vice versa.

The firm has sponsored many minority organizations over the years. KPMG's ongoing commitment to support external affinity associations continues to grow with this year's combined contributions totaling nearly $50K to the following groups:

• Out & Equal American Indian Business Leaders
• Hispanic Alliance for Career Enhancement
• National Association of Asian American Professionals
• Urban Financial Services Coalition

Diversity Recognitions in 2004/2005

KPMG demonstrates our commitment to diversity in the marketplace. The firm has been recognized for our commitment to our minority and women professionals.

• Abilities, Inc./NBDC at the National Center for Disability Services - "Making the Difference Award" (2004)
• Companies That Care Honor Roll (2004, 2005)
• *Diversity Inc.* magazine's Top 10 Companies for Asian Americans (2004)
• *Diversity Inc.* magazine's Top 10 Companies for Executive Women (2004)
• *Diversity Inc.* magazine 20 Noteworthy Companies List (2004)
• *Hispanic* magazine's Corporate 100 "Best Places to Work for Latinos" (2004, 2005)
• *The Black Collegian* magazine's "Top 100 Employers" (2004)
• *Working Mother* magazine "100 Best Companies" (2004)

The materials contained within this document provide a general overview of some of KPMG's programs, practices, and policies. It is important to remember that individual situations do and will vary. Further, the programs, policies, and practices described generally herein do change from time to time, and we reserve the right to make such changes and/or discontinue any of them at any time and for any reason, subject to applicable federal, state, and/or local laws.

Lehman Brothers

745 Seventh Ave.
New York, NY 10019
Phone: (212) 526-7000
Fax: (212) 526-8766
Toll Free: (800) 666-2388
www.lehman.com/careers

Locations (worldwide)
America, Europe, Asia

Diversity Leadership
Anne Erni, Managing Director, Chief Diversity Officer

Diversity Campus Recruiting Team Leader
Deirdre O'Donnell, Senior Vice President, Global Head of Diversity Recruiting

Lateral Recruiting Team Leader
Erica Irish Brown, Senior Vice President

Recruiting

Please list the schools/types of schools at which you recruit.

- *Ivy League schools:* Harvard (AN/AS), Yale (AN/AS), Princeton (AN), Cornell (AN/AS), Columbia (AN/AS), Brown (AN), Penn (AN/AS), Dartmouth (AN/AS)
- *Public state schools:* UCLA(AN/AS), UT-Austin (AN/AS), UMichigan (AS), UNC (AS), UVA (AN/AS)
- *Private schools:* Amherst, Northwestern (AN/AS), Stanford (AN/AS), Williams, Duke (AN/AS), Georgetown, Johns Hopkins, NYU (AN/AS), Wesleyan, MIT (AN/AS), UChicago (AS)
- *Historically Black Colleges and Universities (HBCUs):* Morehouse, Spelman
- *Women's colleges:* Wellesley, Smith, Mt. Holyoke, Bryn Mawr, Barnard

In addition to the schools listed above, Lehman Brothers hires many students from other schools through its targeted recruiting program, which focuses on reaching out to strong candidates from universities across the country into our analyst programs.

Do you have any special outreach efforts that are directed to encourage minority students to consider your firm?

- Hold a reception for minority students
- Conferences: NBMBAA, NSHMBA, Reaching Out Conference, MBA Jumpstart, SHPE, NSBE
- Advertise in minority student association publication(s)
- Participate in/host minority student job fair(s)
- Sponsor minority student association events
- Firm's professionals participate on career panels at school
- Outreach to leadership of minority student organizations
- Scholarships or intern/fellowships for minority students
- Other: Resume and Interview Skills Workshops

Internships and Co-ops

Equities & Fixed Income Summer Analyst Program

Pay: Competitive
Length of the program: 10 weeks
Program web site: www.lehman.com\careers

The 10-week summer analyst program provides college juniors with an internship position in one of the Fixed Income Sales, Trading, Origination or Research areas, and in one of the Equity Sales, Trading or Research areas. Analysts are assigned mentors to provide guidance throughout the summer. Weekly workshops and seminars are provided to expose interns to all areas of the firm.

The divisions look upon the summer analyst program as a primary source for hiring full-time analysts. Accordingly, those who are interested in full-time employment are strongly encouraged to apply to the summer program.

Investment Banking Summer Analyst

Pay: Competitive
Length of the program: 10 weeks
Program web site: www.lehman.com\careers

The summer analyst program provides students in the summer prior to their senior year with a chance to evaluate the working environment and career opportunities at Lehman Brothers.

The summer program begins with one week of training followed by nine weeks working in an industry, product or geographic group. Analysts are given hands-on opportunities to work as full members of client teams on a variety of transactions. They are exposed to everything a first-year analyst would experience. Each summer analyst is assigned a senior and junior mentor to help guide him or her through their experience at Lehman Brothers. Summer analysts are provided with detailed feedback midway through and at the end of the 10-week program. They enjoy extensive contact with the firm's professionals at all levels through group events and informal functions. This invaluable experience prepares many of the summer analysts for permanent job offers in the Investment Banking Division.

The division looks upon the summer analyst program as a primary source for hiring full-time analysts. Accordingly, those who are interested in full-time employment are strongly encouraged to apply to the summer program.

Finance Summer Analyst Program

Pay: Competitive
Length of the program: 10 weeks
Program web site: www.lehman.com\careers

Summer analysts work in the Finance Division for 10 weeks. The Finance Division offers opportunities to summer analysts in all of its major departments. These include Financial Control and Analysis, Treasury and Tax. Precise positions are determined based on business needs at the time of hire. For the most part, summer analyst positions are based on analyst program rotations, which in turn reflect entry-level positions for high potential employees. Summer analysts work with senior managers on a daily basis. The summer analyst program also provides training to include an introductory course in global capital markets, internal faculty courses, online PC training and a weekly seminar on the different departments within the Finance Division. Summer analysts will also be asked to give weekly presentations on their work content, as well as give a group presentation at the end of the summer. Since the division looks upon the summer analyst program as a primary source for hiring full-time analysts, those who are interested in full-time employment are strongly encouraged to apply to the program.

Operations Summer Analyst Program

Pay: Competitive
Length of the program: 10 weeks
Program web site: www.lehman.com\careers

Summer analysts are assigned to a specific business area within the Operations Division for the duration of the 10-week program. To ensure analysts receive overall exposure to the division, they are provided with a comprehensive curriculum to supplement their on-the-job experience. This curriculum includes weekly management-led overviews, presentations by internal and external experts on various financial products and market topics, and tours of the various exchanges and the Federal Reserve Bank.

The Operations Division utilizes the summer analyst program as the primary recruitment source for the full-time analyst program. Individuals who are interested in pursuing a career in the Operations Division upon graduation are strongly encouraged to apply for this program during their junior year.

Information Technology Summer Analyst Program

Pay: Competitive
Length of the program: 10 weeks
Program web site: www.lehman.com\careers

The Information Technology Division offers a 10-week work experience program to computer science, computer/electrical engineering and information systems students entering their senior year (students in other majors with a strong technical background will also be considered).

IT summer analysts gain valuable experience and knowledge while meeting new people and learning new skills. Training and a weekly speaker series featuring the Chief Information Officer and senior IT professionals provide exposure to senior management and the business of Wall Street. In addition, the summer program can provide an opening to a full-time position and a meaningful long-term career with the firm.

Investment Management Summer Analyst Program

Pay: Competitive
Length of the program: 10 weeks
Program web site: www.lehman.com\careers

The summer analyst program provides students in the summer prior to their senior year a chance to evaluate the working environment at Lehman Brothers.

The summer analyst program is a 10-week program where each participant is provided with the chance to work in one or two different business areas. Summer analysts are given hands-on opportunities to work as full team members and are exposed to the typical work flow of a first-year analyst.

Summer analysts are provided with detailed feedback midway through and at the end of the 10-week program. They enjoy extensive contact with the firm's professionals at all levels through group events and informal functions. This invaluable experience prepares many of the summer analysts for permanent job offers in the Investment Management Division. The Investment Management Division looks upon the summer analyst program as a primary source for hiring full-time analysts. Accordingly, those who are interested in full-time employment are strongly encouraged to apply to the summer program.

Affinity Groups/Employee Networks

Lehman Brothers' diversity initiative is aimed at attracting the best people and providing a culture and work environment that helps maximize the productivity and growth potential of each employee. Additionally, we recognize that having a diverse workforce encourages increased creativity and innovation, which are crucial drivers for continued business success. To help achieve our diversity goals, the firm endorses employee networks.

In the U.S., Europe and Asia there is active participation in one or more of the following networks:

• Lehman Brothers Asian Network (LBAN)
• Lehman Brothers Gay & Lesbian Network (LBGLN)
• Lehman Employees of African Descent (LEAD)
• The Latin American Council (TLAC)
• Women's Initiatives Leading Lehman (WILL)
• Disability Working Forum

Entry-Level Programs/Full-Time Opportunities

Equities & Fixed Income Analyst Program

> *Length of program:* Two to three years
> *Geographic location(s) of program:* New York

The two- to three-year program begins in New York with several weeks of classroom training in which all Sales, Trading & Research Training (START) analysts participate.

The training consists of an orientation to the firm and a comprehensive capital markets course covering a variety of topics, including stock and bond analysis as well as an overview of all the major capital markets instruments and businesses. Analysts gain exposure to many aspects of the firm through a series of business presentations, lectures and interactive projects. Additionally, analysts receive training for the Series 7 and Series 63 licensing exams.

At the completion of the training program, generalist analysts will begin a rotation process through our Equities and Fixed Income Divisions. Analysts will have the opportunity to explore various areas and roles, and will have the ability to state their placement preferences following these intensive interactions. Placement decisions are made by the glob- al heads of both the Equities and Fixed Income Divisions at the end of the rotation process and are based on the overall business needs and analyst preferences.

Investment Banking Analyst Program

> *Length of program:* Two to three years
> *Geographic location(s) of program:* New York, Los Angeles, Menlo Park, Chicago, Houston

All analysts begin their two- to three-year program with a four-week training program in New York. This training introduces them to the firm and its team-oriented approach and reinforces the skills that they will apply as investment bankers.

Classroom training during the first four weeks includes technical skills training in accounting, computer modeling and financial valuation techniques. The incoming analysts also participate in small teams on projects which provide them with a better understanding of the firm's capabilities and enable them to develop a global network of peers.

Following the classroom training, analysts return to their region of hire and join one of the firm's industry, product or regionally-focused groups. This placement is based on the particular interest of the analyst and on the firm's needs. Each analyst participates as a fully contributing member of selected project teams, working with bankers at all levels on diverse assignments.

Investment Management Analyst Program

Length of program: Two to three years
Geographic location(s) of program: New York

The two- to three-year analyst program begins with an orientation to the firm and classroom training. The training program includes a comprehensive capital markets course that covers a variety of topics, including stock and bond analysis as well as an overview of the major capital markets instruments and businesses. During this training program, our analysts will gain exposure to many aspects of the firm through a series of business presentations, lectures and interactive projects. Following the capital markets module, our analysts receive in-depth training on our Investment Management Division's platform, products and capabilities. In addition, analysts will receive training for the Series 7 and Series 63 registration exams.

Investment Management Division analysts will have the opportunity to sample jobs in our different functional areas such as: Investments & Research, Client Development & Marketing and New Product Development & Strategy. Permanent placement decisions are made based on the overall business needs and analyst preferences.

Operations Analyst Program

Length of program: Two years
Geographic location(s) of program: New York, New Jersey

The two-year program begins with a three-day orientation hosted by the senior managementof the Operations Division. At the conclusion of the orientation, analysts are placed throughout the division based on business needs.

Analysts receive comprehensive on-the-job training, which is supplemented with web-based and instructor-led programs. After one year of successful performance within their initial placement, analysts are eligible to explore available opportunities within the division.

Finance Analyst Program

Length of program: Two years
Geographic location(s) of program: New York

The Finance analyst program is a two-year rotational program. Analysts undertake three successive eight-month rotations in various departments of the Finance Division, including Financial Control and Analysis, Treasury and Tax. The rotational structure of the program exposes analysts to a broad range of functions and departments within the Finance Division and allows them to gain experience with capital markets products and to build financial skills. As a result, the program allows analysts to develop their interests as theyare prepared for careers in management roles.

Information Technology Analyst Program

Geographic location(s) of program: New York

The Technology Development Program is an intensive four-month training program that includes technical training, financial markets instruction, professional development and leadership skills guidance and a speaker series led by senior management in the IT Division.

The interview process and subsequent job placements are made based on the individual's background, skills, experience and interest. Technical training is then customized based on the individual's placement.

INROADS®

Strategic Plan and Diversity Leadership

How does the firm's leadership communicate the importance of diversity to everyone at the firm?

Leadership communication related to diversity utilizes all avenues available within the firm, including Divisional Town Hall meetings, e-mails to all employees from senior leaders, postings to the firm's intranet (known as LehmanLive), the Lehman Daily News (a broadcast email to highlight news impacting the entire firm), event invitations, periodic Diversity Newsletters, Recruiting Updates, brochures and posters in elevators and floor lobbies.

Who has primary responsibility for leading diversity initiatives at your firm?

Anne Erni, Managing Director and Chief Diversity Officer

Does your firm currently have a diversity committee?

No. The firm does not currently have a corporate-wide diversity council; however, there are regional and divisional councils chaired by their respective business leaders. The following committees are currently active: European Regional Diversity Committee, Equities ivisional Diversity Committee and Operations Divisional Diversity Committee.

If yes, how many executives are on the committee, and in 2004, what was the total number of hours collectively spent by the committee in furtherance of the firm's diversity initiatives?

There are approximately 15 to 18 members in each of the regional and divisional diversity councils, all of whom are Senior Vice Presidents or Managing Directors. Total senior managers on cthe ommittee: 48. Number of diversity meetings annually: The councils meet on average 8 to 10 times during the year.

Does the committee and/or diversity leader establish and set goals or objectives consistent with management's priorities?

Yes

Has the firm undertaken a formal or informal diversity program or set of initiatives aimed at increasing the diversity of the firm?

Yes, formal

How often does the firm's management review the firm's diversity progress/results?

Twice a year

How is the firm's diversity committee and/or firm management held accountable for achieving results?

Lehman Brothers holds all management, including those at the top of the organization, accountable for diversity. Each business division is responsible for developing an annual diversity plan which addresses their particular opportunities and defines measurable action steps for achieving results. Regional CEOs and the firm's president review the diversity plans. To the extent a division is successful in achieving their diversity goals, they are rewarded with an additional pool of incentive compensation to allocate to employees who have made a significant contribution to the divisional diversity effort. Our performance management system incorporates criteria on diversity practices for all employees.

Diversity Mission Statement

Chairman and Chief Executive Officer, Richard S. Fuld, Jr. has made the following statement with regard to diversity and inclusion: "At Lehman Brothers, diversity is an integral part of our vision and a business imperative. We define diversity as valuing differences in thought and perspective. Our goal is to integrate diversity into every aspect of our business - from dealing with our clients to managing our workforce.

Our continued success rests in our ability to be the firm of choice for the very best people from the widest available pools of talent. To this end, we are dedicating significant time and resources to promote a diverse and inclusive workplace.

- Our employee networks in the U.S. and Europe are committed to enriching our "One Firm" culture and to fostering an inclusive environment for all employees.
- Global, regional and divisional diversity councils are in place, expanding and working proactively to enhance and implement our diversity plans.
- Lehman Brothers supports a range of global sponsorships that promote diversity.

The strength of Lehman Brothers' culture has helped us to achieve wonderful success.

Both our culture and our success depend on the quality and breadth of the people who are part of our firm. It is critical that our organization continue the momentum to broaden the representation of our employees - to ensure that diversity of thought and perspective is brought to our clients. At Lehman Brothers, we see diversity as good business practice."

The Employer Says

At Lehman Brothers we are committed to attracting, retaining and developing the best people from the broadest backgrounds, and to nurturing our inclusive culture that fosters employee development and contributes to our commercial success. Each of our employees comes from a unique background, each brings a diverse perspective to the firm based on his or her variety of life experiences. This variety of thought and perspective is of intrinsic value to us in our talent evaluation process.

To assist in the retention and development of our people, we emphasize tools such as networking opportunities, mentoring programs, employee and management education and training, and corporate citizenship.

Following are a sample of our employee programs:

- Employee Networks in all geographic regions open to all employees
- Over 500 employees act as mentors in one of over 20 mentoring programs
- Over 10,000 employees have taken part in our Awareness Training program, with more slated before the end of the year
- The firm and its networks partnered with over 70 diversity related community organizations in 2004, either through financial or volunteer sponsorship.

These include:

- Student organizations: SEO, Robert A. Toigo, Posse, Capital Chances, Opportunity Now
- Community organizations: Robin Hood, Harlem's Children Zone, Girl Scouts
- Professional organizations: New York Women's Foundation, National Association of Asian Professionals, The Hispanic Federation, The Twenty First Century Foundation Life Balance

Investment Banking is characterized by fast-paced, demanding work environments; however, Lehman is highly committed to fostering a culture that supports and respects our employees' need to balance the complex and sometimes competing demands of their careers and personal lives.

Our enhanced policies and benefits reflect our commitment to this culture; resources are dedicated specifically to ensuring we maintain best practices.

Our most recent policy enhancements took place in 2004, and included:

- An extra week of paid vacation for nearly all employees
- Implementation of firm-sponsored flexible work arrangements including reduced or compressed work week, flextime, and telecommuting or flexspace for employees with conducive roles
- Introduction of a partially-paid sabbatical for tenured employees
- Increased subsidies for adoption, additional time off for elder care, bereavement and secondary care givers after child birth or adoption.

All these policies reinforce the value we place on contributions and results versus face time.

Career mobility is also emphasized through the firm's support of internal transfers; managers are encouraged to fill staffing vacancies through the transfer or promotion of current employees of the firm, whenever possible.

Recognition of our Efforts

- Selected achievements in 2004:
- Opportunity Now Focus Group Award for strategy and commitment to diversity and inclusion in the U.K.
- 100% on the Human Rights Campaign's Corporate Equality Index for the past two years
- America's largest gay, lesbian, bisexual and transgender organization
- Top 40 "Ideal Diversity Employers" in the *Black Collegian*/Universum campus survey (both M.B.A. and undergraduate students)
- "Dr. Antonia Pantoja Corporate Leadership Award" by Aspira of New York for leadership and support of Hispanic youth

Thank you so much for you interest in Lehman Brothers. We are proud of our commitment to diversity and inclusion, and wish you good fortune in your career aspirations.

321

Liberty Mutual Group

175 Berkeley St.
Boston, MA 02116
Phone: (617) 357-9500
Fax: (617) 350-7648
www.libertymutual.com/careers

Locations (worldwide)
Corporate headquarters - Boston, MA;
900 locations worldwide

Campus Recruiting Team Leader
Ann Nowak, Manager of College Relations

Employment Contact
175 Berkeley St
Boston, MA 02129
Phone: (617) 357-9500
Fax: (617) 574-5616
E-mail: campus.recruiting@libertymutual.com

Recruiting

Please list the schools/types of schools at which you recruit.

Liberty Mutual visits campuses throughout the US including HBCUs, and HSIs, as well as private and public institutions of higher education. If we are not on a particular campus we welcome resumes through our website.

Do you have any special outreach efforts that are directed to encourage minority students to consider your firm?

• Liberty Mutual is eager to meet minority students on the campuses we visit and will participate in activities, association meetings and job fairs. Scholarship opportunities are also available through the Hispanic Scholarship Fund and the United Negro College Fund as well as to students at Morehouse College and Howard University..
• Hold a reception for minority students
• Conferences
• Advertise in minority student association publication(s)
• Sponsor minority student association events
• Firm's employees participate on career panels at school
• Outreach to leadership of minority student organizations
• Scholarships or intern/fellowships for minority students

What activities does the firm undertake to attract minority and women employees?

• Partner programs with women and minority associations
• Participate at minority job fairs
• Utilize online job services

Internships and Co-ops

Liberty Mutual Internship Program

Deadline for application: Early spring semester

Number of interns in the program in summer 2004 (internship) or 2004 (co-op): 250

Pay: Competitive

Length of the program: 10-12 weeks

Percentage of interns/co-ops in the program who receive offers of full-time employment: 85%

Web site for internship/co-op information: www.libertymutual.com/campus

Liberty Mutual will hire approximately 250 undergraduate interns each summer and approximately 25-30 MBA level interns. Approximately half of these undergraduate interns will come from the INROADS program. Pay is competitive and positions are throughout the US. Internships are based on business needs so interns work in a variety of functional areas throughout organization including traditional business jobs; accounting, finance, IT and HR. Positions also exist in the functional areas specific to the insurance industry; claims, underwriting, sales, loss prevention and actuarial. During the summer interns participate in training programs to learn about the business of insurance as well as the organization. Undergraduate rising seniors have the opportunity to visit the Boston headquarters and meet with Senior Executives and interview for positions. Development plans are developed for each student so that returning interns see a progression through a job family. MBA interns will meet with Senior Executives to gain a perspective on strategic initiatives.

Scholarships

Target School Scholarship Program

(Liberty Mutual has a scholarship program at a number of our targeted campuses including Morehouse and Howard)

Deadline for application for the scholarship program: Spring of sophomore year

Scholarship award amount: Varies by school

Web site or other contact information for scholarship: www.libertymutual.com/campus

UNCF

Deadline for application for the scholarship program: See website for details

Web site or other contact information for scholarship: www.uncf.org

HSF

Deadline for application for the scholarship program: See website for details

Web site or other contact information for scholarship: www.hsf.net

FIHE

Deadline for application for the scholarship program: See website for details

Web site or other contact information for scholarship: www.FIHE.org

Scholarships are given to juniors with competitive GPAs and interested recipients are encouraged to intern at Liberty Mutual prior to their senior year. Scholarships are renewed to eligible seniors.

Entry-Level Programs/Full-Time Opportunities

Fellowship in Finance and Accounting (FIFA)

Length of program: 2 years (three 8 month assignments within the Corporate Finance and Accounting and Strategic Business Units)
Geographic location(s) of program: Boston

Please describe the training/training component of this program: Training opportunities include a 2-week Employee Orientation, Professional Development, On-the -job training and Technical Training programs.

Foundations for Sales Success

Length of program: 4-12 months
Geographic location(s) of program: Field based

Please describe the training/training component of this program: Includes technical classroom training and field experience

Technical Development Program (TDP)

Length of program: 3-5 years
Geographic location(s) of program: Portsmouth, Wausau (some opportunity for rotations in Indianapolis)

Please describe the training/training component of this program: Three phases of your development include a classroom orientation, a business assignment, technical immersion as well as up to 4 Information Systems Rotations

Corporate Real Estate Rotational Program

Length of program: 18-24 months
Geographic location(s) of program: Boston, MA

Please describe the training/training component of this program: Within rotations, on-the-job training will develop participants skills. Rotations include: Strategic planning, budget preparation and monitoring of office relocation projects within Corporate Real Estate, Tenant Services, and Procurement

HRDP - Human Resource Development Program

Length of program: 18-24 months
Geographic location(s) of program: Boston

Please describe the training/training component of this program: Individual rotations included all areas of HR, benefits, HR systems, and compensation within the corporate and business groups

Strategic Plan and Diversity Leadership

Has the firm undertaken a formal or informal diversity program or set of initiatives aimed at increasing the diversity of the firm?

Yes, informal. Our strategy is based on inclusion and managed within the business groups.

How often does the firm's management review the firm's diversity progress/results?

Quarterly

How is the firm's diversity committee and/or firm management held accountable for achieving results?

Attraction and retention of diverse talent pool

The Stats

Employees: 38,000 (2004, worldwide)
Revenue: $19.6 billion in consolidated revenue (2004, worldwide)

Retention and Professional Development

How do 2004 minority and female attrition rates generally compare to those experienced in the prior year period?

About the same as in prior years

The Employer Says

Liberty Mutual has a strong promote-from-within philosophy, therefore it is critical that we bring strong talent into the organization from college campuses. This initiative includes working with diversity associations on campus, INROADS, professional associations including NBMBAA, NSHMBA, ALPFA, NABA, the Consortium, NAACP and Urban League among others. Our recruiting on campus includes visits to HBCUs.

Inclusion is critical to our success. By tapping all available pools of talent, we will better serve the needs of our customers in the communities we serve and want to serve. An inclusive company also treats people with dignity and respect and provides the opportunity to grow and succeed based on ability, performance and aspirations.

Liz Claiborne, Inc.

1441 Broadway
New York, NY 10018
Phone: 212-354-4900
Fax: 212-626-3416
www.lizclaiborneinc.com

Locations (worldwide)

North Bergen, NJ; New York, NY;
Atlanta, GA; Dallas, TX; Los Angeles, CA;
Arleta, CA; Commerce, CA; Vernon, CA;
Wakefield, MA;
Ontario, Canada; Amsterdam, The
Netherlands; Montreal, Quebec, Canada;
Voorschoten, The Netherlands; Hong
Kong; Jakarta, Indonesia; Manila,
Philippines; Huxquilucan, Mexico;
Shanghai, China; Madrid, Spain; Sri
Lanka; Taiwan
Distribution Center Locations: North
Bergen, NJ; Lincoln, RI; Mt. Pocono, PA;
Santa Fe Springs, CA; Dayton, NJ;
Breinigsville, PA; West Chester, OH;
Vernon, CA; Ontario, Canada; Montreal,
Canada

Employment Contact

Marla Schwartz, College Relations
1441 Broadway, 20th Floor
New York, NY 10018
Phone: (212) 626-5447
Fax: (212) 626-5527
E-mail: marla_Schwartz@liz.com

Recruitment of Interns, Co-ops & Entry-level College Graduate Hires

Please list the schools/types of schools at which you recruit.

• Ivy League schools
• Other private schools
• Public state schools
• Historically Black Colleges and Universities (HBCUs)
• Other predominantly minority and/or women's colleges

Do you have any special outreach efforts that are directed to encourage minority students to consider your firm?

• Advertise in minority student association publication(s)
• Participate in/host minority student job fair(s)
• Firm's employees participate on career panels at school
• Scholarships or intern/fellowships for minority students

What activities does the firm undertake to attract minority and women employees?

• Partner programs with women and minority associations
• Participate at minority job fairs
• Seek referrals from other employees

• Utilize online job services
• Black Retail Association Group (BRAG) and INROADS

Do you use executive recruiting/search firms to seek to identify new diversity hires?
No

Internships and Co-ops

Liz Claiborne Inc. Summer Internship Program

Number of interns in the program in summer 2004 (internship) or 2004 (co-op): 70 Students (65 Undergraduate, 5 MBAs)

Pay: Undergraduate: $10/hr. IT/IS Undergraduate: $12-$15/hr. MBA: $1500/ 10 Weeks

Percentage of interns/co-ops in the program who receive offers of full-time employment: Of the ones we identify as stand-outs, we hire at least 50% depending on business needs (head count)

Web site for internship/co-op information: www.lizclaiborneinc.com

The Summer Internship program starts in mid-June and runs through mid-August for 10 weeks. We offer internships in the following areas: Design, Merchandising/Planning, Production/Manufacturing, Sales, Finance, Information Systems, Human Resources and Legal.

Each intern is also given a summer project that will take 6-8 weeks to complete. The summer project will create a hands-on experience for each intern to gain better exposure to the area in which they have been placed.

The Summer Internship Program also provides exposure to different areas of the company as the intern is completing their assignments. There are weekly activities that include brown bag lunches, field trips and other activities for the interns to interact with each other as well as gain more exposure to other areas of the organization.

Affinity Groups/Employee Networks

We do not currently have any affinity groups, although every intern is paired with a mentor/buddy to help them with the transition into Liz Claiborne Inc. and our corporate environment.

Entry-Level Programs/Full-Time Opportunities

Finance Management Training Program and Accounting Management Program. Both are a four-month rotation through our Finance and Accounting Divisions. Once the rotation is completed a full-time opportunity is identified.

Through our **Organizational Development Department** an extensive list of training programs and classes for Liz Claiborne associates are offered.

Classes included are: Civil Treatment® for Employees, Civil Treatment® for Managers, ValuEthics™ Basic Retail Math, Presentation Skills for Designers, Presentation Skills for Sales Associates, Business Simulation, Business Writing 1, Business Writing 2, Coaching & Counseling for the Experienced Manager, Dale Carnegie, Executive Presentation Skills, Focus - Time Management, Frontline Leadership, Management Effectiveness, Positive Power & Influence Skills, The Accounting Game, The Finance Game. Also, see below for Attraction, Retention, Professional and Leadership Developmen

Strategic Plan and Diversity Leadership

How does the firm's leadership communicate the importance of diversity to everyone at the firm?

Our diversity and inclusion efforts are our CEO's number one non-financial initiative. There is constant discussion and reminders of the importance of expanding our diversity and inclusion efforts at all levels. Our CEO's Diversity and Inclusion statement is featured on our Intranet.

Who has primary responsibility for leading diversity initiatives at your firm?

Dennis Butler, Vice President of Associate Relations

It is a company-wide effort and initiative, so every manager, executive, etc is committed to its growth.

Does your firm currently have a diversity committee?

Yes

If yes, please describe how the committee is structured, how often it meets, etc.

Currently, the diversity committee includes an Executive VP, a Group President, the Senior VP HR, The VP, Associate Relations and A Director, HR.. We are currently in the process of identifying 10-15 additional members at VP level or higher from a cross section of our organization.

If yes, does the committee's representation include one or more members of the firm's management/executive committee (or the equivalent)?

Yes

Please describe the committee.

Currently, the Committee is meeting monthly.

Does the committee and/or diversity leader establish and set goals or objectives consistent with management's priorities?

The most senior member of the committee (EVP, GP, and SVP) have non-financial objectives relative to increasing and valuing the diversity of our workforce.

Has the firm undertaken a formal or informal diversity program or set of initiatives aimed at increasing the diversity of the firm?

Yes, informal. As a Federal contractor, we are and affirmative action employer with written AAPs that are reviewed and updated annually. Where underutilization exists, specific formal goals are set.

Additionally, we recognize that having a diverse workforce that reflects the diversity of our marketplace makes good business sense. Accordingly, we are actively working to increase awareness and the valuing of diversity.

How often does the firm's management review the firm's diversity progress/results?

Quarterly

How is the firm's diversity committee and/or firm management held accountable for achieving results?

Key executive non-financial objectives reflect inclusion goals.

The Stats

Employees: 9,374 (2004, U.S.)
Employees: 8,741 (2003, U.S.)
Employees: 14,000 (2004, worldwide)
Employees: 13,000 (2003, worldwide)
Revenue: $4.6 billion (2004, worldwide)

Company overall - U.S.

• 76% female
• 36% minority

Executives

• 60% female leadership council
• 9% min leadership council
• 40% female exec council

Retention and Professional Development

How do 2004 minority and female attrition rates generally compare to those experienced in the prior year period?

About the same as in prior years

Please identify the specific steps you are taking to reduce the attrition rate of minority and women employees.

• Increase/review compensation relative to competition
• Increase/improve current work/life programs
• Succession plan includes emphasis on diversity
• Work with minority and women employees to develop career advancement plans
• Strengthen mentoring program for all employees, including minorities and women
• Professional skills development program, including minority and women employees

Attraction, Retention, Professional and Leadership Development:

The survival of any organization depends on the attraction, retention and development of quality associates. The stewardship review and talent management process provide the opportunity to review the performance of key executives and other high potential associates. HR generalists and executives meet on a regular basis (formally and informally) to discuss cross-functional, promotional and other developmental opportunities for high-potentials. During this process, we make a conscious effort to identify minorities as candidates for these opportunities. By recognizing these outstanding performers, we are able to strategically develop and create a diverse pipeline for the future leadership of Liz Claiborne.

In addition to many internal and external training/leadership development courses offered, following are programs we have established to enhance the developmental opportunities, retention and promotability of all associates. In implementing these programs, specific attention is given to assuring that the current and future leadership of our organization appropriately reflects the diversity of the labor pool and marketplace.

This year, we introduced the "Leader Studio". This three-phase program includes an experiential learning opportunity and on-the-job practice using concepts of adult learning styles, and generational influences which can be effectively applied to managing a diverse workforce. As part of the learning, participants visit the Civil Rights Museum in Memphis, TN. This event enhances their appreciation of peoples' differences by encouraging them to better understand the experiences of those who were involved in the Civil Rights movement.

We have increased funding and support for associates' participation in networking conferences specific to Women of Color. This year, the Working Mother Women of Color Conference (NY, NY), the Hispanic Women's Conference (Phoenix, AZ) and the NAFE Conference (NY, NY) were attended by female associates of various ethnic backgrounds and at all levels.

Additionally, we have implemented the following:

• **Senior Executive Stewardship Reviews:** Annually, the Chairman/CEO and Human Resources, meet with each of the Division Presidents and Corporate Department Senior Vice Presidents to discuss their direct reports and any high potential associates that should be considered part of our strategic succession planning process. Developmental needs and opportunities are discussed as part of this process. The process also helps uncover and address skill gaps and to surface any other real or perceived barriers that may be blocking the advancement or development of associates. As part of this process, the Chairman specifically charges his executive team with assessing their recruiting, retention and development strategies to be sure they adequately address the needs of our diverse workforce and marketplace.

• **Organizational Reviews:** Annually, each division and corporate department in partnership with Human Resources, reviews their organization to identify High Potentials/Promotables, Performers/Technical Experts and any Non-Performers. Managers discuss their subordinates with their supervisors to ensure that appropriate development plans exist and are being executed. This process follows the setting of individual performance and development plans by associates and their managers.

• **Talent Management:** As an expansion and enhancement of the existing Organizational Review process, the Talent Management process was developed. All Human Resources Generalists, Recruiters and Organizational Development leadership meet formally several times throughout the year to review the internal talent pool in great detail. The group discusses career paths, strengths, development needs and explores any existing and future, new and/or cross-functional opportunities for each High Potential/Potential High Potential employees (approx 500 of whom are women). The opportunity to share information regarding top and emerging talent – our future leaders – results in more efficient and timely promotion of internal movement and development. As part of process we annually conduct all-day Talent Management Summits.

Diversity Mission Statement

From our CEO:
February 7, 2005
To: All Liz Claiborne Associates
Subject: Diversity & Inclusion

The creation of a diverse portfolio has been a cornerstone of our strategy. Multiple brands that are sold in multiple channels and geographies and that touch multiple consumer demographics have generated an enviable record of consistent performance and growth. In order to be successful in this environment, we must be innovative, responsive, dynamic and adaptable to the demands of a global marketplace. While it is our consistency of execution that creates our competitive advantage, it is our ability to understand and translate the distinct differences of our consumers, brands and channels of distribution that distinguishes us.

We are a global corporation and take pride in a culture of achievement and excellence. Among our standards of excellence is the consistent goal to create a workplace in which our behaviors, practices and policies promote respect, opportunity and advancement for all our associates. A key to these standards in our culture is inclusion.

Inclusion reflects the diversity of backgrounds, experiences and outlooks our associates bring to the workplace. More importantly, inclusion focuses on behaviors and actions that reflect our value for diversity in our workplaces, communities and markets.

In our workplace, inclusion must be embodied in everything we do and be a vital part of our cultural fabric from ideas, concepts and processes to training, development, mentoring and our day-to-day relationships. Inclusion will allow us to attract and retain the best talent.

In our communities and the workforce from which we draw our associates, inclusion must be evident in our recruiting outreach and community involvement.

In our marketplace, inclusion is visible in our suppliers and in our sales and marketing initiatives.

Most of all, inclusion is a shared responsibility. My senior executives and I have a responsibility as leaders of our company to demonstrate a visible commitment to fostering an environment of inclusion. As associates of this company, we all have a responsibility to model behaviors that honor and celebrate the unique contributions and perspectives our associates bring to this work we share.

Great companies accelerate the pace of change and push beyond the status quo to uncover new ideas, concepts and opportunities. Great companies fuel that acceleration by increasing inclusion initiatives and renewing the values and beliefs that guide their actions.

We are a great company that I believe can be greater. Embracing differences, leading change through innovation, committing to common goals, valuing integrity in everything we do and engaging the minds and energies of each and every associate - these will enable us to realize that greatness.

Paul R. Charron

The Employer Says

We are a visionary and progressive company that actively supports the advancement of qualified minorities and women. We have a workforce that mirrors the diversity of our marketplace. Women and minorities are well represented throughout all levels of the company.

CEO commitment to inclusion has resulted in the establishment of a Diversity Steering Committee and the communication of the CEO's Inclusion Statement to all associates. We have increased representation of Latinas across the Company. Additionally, key executive non-financial objectives reflect inclusion goals, our intern program has successfully targeted and recruited more minorities, and we have expanded funding to support associate attendance at conferences for Latinas and other Women of Color.

Our programs give associates the opportunity to focus on professional development while balancing their work and family needs. We offer a very generous paid time-off program, Alternative Work Arrangements, Summer Hours, steep clothing discounts and more. Additionally, our "traditional" benefits are very competitive, including healthcare, Employee Assistance Programs, 401K matching, tuition reimbursement, gym membership discounts (including an on-site facility).

The focus of the Liz Claiborne's Foundation on women's issues and efforts of our Corporate initiatives relative to domestic violence, help women, including minorities, achieve their life goals for safety, professional achievement and family.

We continue to develop strategic approaches for creating a more inclusive culture in which behaviors, values and practices promote respect, representation, career development and success across all forms of diversity. Our culture, which empowers associates to achieve their full potential, attracts and retains loyal, dedicated, promotable associates, including women and minorities.

Lockheed Martin Corporation

6801 Rockledge Dr.
Bethesda, MD 20817-1877
Phone: (301) 897-6000
Fax: (301) 897-6704
www.lockheedmartin.com/careers

Locations (worldwide)

Major sites in Philadelphia, PA area; Washington, DC area; Marietta, GA; Orlando, FL area; Dallas/Fort Worth, TX area; Denver, CO area; Palmdale, CA; San Jose/Bay, CA area as well as many other national and international sites.

Diversity Leadership

Shantella Carr, Vice President for Diversity and Equal Opportunity Programs
6801 Rockledge Drive
Bethesda, MD 20817

Employment Contact

Leslie L. Chappell, Senior Manager, University Relations

Recruitment of Interns, Co-ops and Entry-level College Graduate Hires

Please list the schools/types of schools at which you recruit.

- Ivy League schools
- Other private schools
- Public state schools
- Historically Black Colleges and Universities (HBCUs)
- Hispanic Serving Institutions (HSIs)
- Other predominantly minority and/or women's colleges

Do you have any special outreach efforts that are directed to encourage minority students to consider your firm?

- Hold a reception for minority students
- *Conferences:* HACU, HENAAC, NSBE, SWE, SHPE, AISES, MAES, NAMEPA, BEY
- *Advertise in minority student association publication(s): Minority Engineer, Women Engineer*
- Participate in/host minority student job fair(s)
- Sponsor minority student association events
- Firm's employees participate on career panels at school
- Outreach to leadership of minority student organizations
- Scholarships or intern/fellowships for minority students
- Internship/Co-op opportunities, workshops, special speakers, mentors

What activities does the firm undertake to attract minority and women employees?

- Partner programs with women and minority associations
- *Conferences:* HACU, HENAAC, NSBE, SWE, SHPE, AISES, MAES, NAMEPA
- Participate at minority job fairs
- Seek referrals from other employees

• Utilize online job services

Do you use executive recruiting/search firms to seek to identify new diversity hires?

Yes

Internships and Co-ops

Ongoing

Number of interns in the program in summer 2004 (internship) or 2004 (co-op): 1,464
Pay: Varies by academic level, major and geographic location
Length of the program: Typically, 9-11 weeks
Web site for internship/co-op information: www.lockheedmartin.com/careers

Lockheed Martin seeks students at all academic levels in the following majors: Aeronautical Engineering, Computer Engineering, Computer Science, Electrical Engineering, Mechanical Engineering and Systems Engineering. We also have limited opportunities in Finance, Human Resources, Accounting and Business.

Scholarships

Lockheed Martin participates in the following scholarship programs aimed at women and minority students, please see their websites for details on deadlines, amounts and eligibility requirements:

• American Indian College Fund -Tribunal Scholarships: www.collegefund.org/
• American Indian Science and Engineering Society: http://aises.org/highered/scholarships/
• Hispanic Association of Colleges & Universities - HACU Scholarships: https://scholarships.hacu.net/applications/applicants/
• Hispanic Scholarship Fund: www.hsf.net/scholarships.php
• League of Latin American Citizens Scholars - LULAC: www.chci.org/chciyouth/scholarship/listofscholarships.htm
• Mexican-American Engineering Society (MAES) Scholarship: www.maes-natl.org/index.php?module=ContentExpress&func=display&ceid=237&meid=241
• National Society of Black Engineers Corporate Scholarships: www.nsbe.org/programs/nsbescholarships.php
• Society of Women Engineers Scholarship: www.swe.org/stellent/idcplg?IdcService=SS_GET_PAGE&nodeId=9&ssSourceNodeId=5
• Society of Hispanic Professional Engineers Foundation (Scholarships): www.shpe.org/index.php/docs/239
• Lockheed Martin also offers many scholarships for diversity students that are administered directly by the schools with whom we partner, most are in engineering. These scholarships have a wide range of eligibility requirements, deadlines and award amounts.

Entry-Level Programs/Full-Time Opportunities

Leadership Development Program (LDP) (various specialties)

Length of program: Two years of rotational assignments
Geographic location(s) of program: Nationwide

Please describe the training/training component of this program: Employees receive week-long training each summer and periodic communications throughout the year. Most large worksites have dedicated LDP managers who help guide the employees.

Please describe any other educational components of this program: Tuition reimbursement is provided so that employees in this program can pursue a masters degree. In some cases, paid time off is provided in order to attend classes or to study for examinations. In some cases, flexible work schedules can be arranged so that the employee can attend day classes if necessary.

Strategic Plan and Diversity Leadership

How does the firm's leadership communicate the importance of diversity to everyone at the firm?

Who has primary responsibility for leading diversity initiatives at your firm?

Shantella Carr, Vice President for Diversity and Equal Opportunity Programs

Does your firm currently have a diversity committee?

Yes

If yes, please describe how the committee is structured, how often it meets, etc.

Our Executive Diversity Council (EDC) is chaired by our Chairman, President and CEO, Robert J Stevens and vice-chaired by our CFO, Chris Kubasik. The members consist of 26 of the top leaders of the corporation, including Executive Vice Presidents, Operating Business Unit Presidents, the Chief Information Officer (CIO) and Senior Vice President of Human Resources. The EDC serves as an advisory function to our executive management council. It is their vision and strategy that is driven down through out the corporate via the diversity councils at our business units.

If yes, does the committee's representation include one or more members of the firm's management/executive committee (or the equivalent)?

Yes

Please describe the committee.

The EDC spends approximately 1,000 hours amongst the 26 members furthering Lockheed Martin's diversity initiatives. There are approximately 36 business unit diversity councils. It is difficult to calculate how many hours they spend furthering the diversity initiatives, due to the large number of members in this diversity community.

Does the committee and/or diversity leader establish and set goals or objectives consistent with management's priorities?

Yes. We have aligned our business processes with our people management process to ensure our goals & objectives are consistent with management's priorities.

Has the firm undertaken a formal or informal diversity program or set of initiatives aimed at increasing the diversity of the firm?

Yes, formal. Lockheed Martin views diversity in a broad sense of the term that goes beyond race and gender. While those are two aspects of our view on how we define diversity, we look at things like educational background, geographic location, personal style, etc. Our efforts at creating a more inclusive environment focuses on all aspects of diversity. When we talk about increasing the number of women and minorities, we use the term increasing representation. Our approach to increasing representation is maintaining a positive compliance posture, as defined by the affirmative action regulations to address underutilization.

How often does the firm's management review the firm's diversity progress/results?

Quarterly

How is the firm's diversity committee and/or firm management held accountable for achieving results?

We have put an assessment process in place to measure the performance of a business unit in the area of diversity inclusion. The assessment process takes employee opinion, as well as the kinds of processes and practices in place to foster inclusion. The busi-

ness unit receives a numeric score associated with the assessment and BU leaders are held accountable for results through their incentive compensation plan.

The Stats

Employees: 130,000 (2004, worldwide)
Revenue: $35.5 billion (2004, worldwide)

Of our total workforce: 24% are female and 20% are minorities.

Retention and Professional Development

How do 2004 minority and female attrition rates generally compare to those experienced in the prior year period?

Lower than in prior years

Please identify the specific steps you are taking to reduce the attrition rate of minority and women employees.

• Develop and/or support internal employee affinity groups (e.g., minority or women networks within the firm) at some locations and with our company executive leadership
• Increase/review compensation relative to competition for all employees
• Increase/improve current work/life programs alternative work schedule, telecommuting, flexible work schedules, etc.
• Adopt dispute resolution process corporate policy statement to address dispute resolution
• Succession plan includes emphasis on diversity
• Work with minority and women employees to develop career advancement plans Review work assignments and hours billed to key client matters to make sure minority and women employees are not being excluded

Diversity Mission Statement

Lockheed Martin is committed to creating one company, one team, all inclusive, where diversity contributes to mission success. Diversity at Lockheed Martin is an inclusive team that values and leverages each person's individuality.

Additional Information

At Lockheed Martin, we recognize that diversity is not just a short-term trend. It is a business imperative. Our long-term success depends on a commitment to diversity. We have to leverage the individuality of each employee as a competitive advantage by , eliminating barriers to inclusiveness. Diversity is about creating an environment that welcomes, respects and develops our individual differences as a competitive strength. It begins with our core values of Ethics, Excellence, "Can-Do" Attitude, Integrity, People and Teamwork. It extends to every activity involved in attracting and retaining a talented workforce that reflects the diversity of our customers, suppliers and our world.

There's a difference between stating our commitment to diversity and living it. We are dedicated to a process that listens to the voices of our employees and partners to help shape our course. It is through this process that we set goals and develop a strategy that will hold us accountable for making Lockheed Martin a place of "institutionalized inclusion."

Our approach to diversity is analogous to our work as system integrators. Each element, each subsystem must do its job, but function as part of a larger, integrated whole, which together achieve astounding results. The whole is definitely stronger than its individual parts. In similar fashion, Lockheed Martin is made stronger by the combined efforts of each employee and each operating business unit working as one team.

The Lockheed Martin team is naturally diverse – encompassing 130,000 people with a wide variety of skills, backgrounds, perspectives and lifestyles. We draw from this tremendous source of talent to forge a great company – one team that is committed to the success of our customers on projects of profound significance to our world.

As a world-class advanced technology leader, we must continually reach out to new and different points of view to succeed in the global marketplace. This means we must have an environment that attracts the best people with the biggest dreams and the highest standards – and give them the support and encouragement they need to reach their full potential. It also keeps us focused on assuring the widest possible circle of suppliers with whom we do business.

Diversity must be more than words. Having an inclusive environment really demands an engagement process that starts at the top – in my office – and extends throughout the Corporation to each and every employee and stakeholder in this enterprise. We share in this commitment as a team because it is right for people and right for business.

That's what diversity is all about for Lockheed Martin and the people and institutions we serve. Diversity is a journey, and we are on this journey together.

TO BUILD BEAUTY, WE NEED TALENT.

"A DIVERSE WORKFORCE ENHANCES OUR CREATIVITY AND OUR UNDERSTANDING OF CONSUMERS AND ALLOWS US TO DEVELOP AND MARKET HIGHLY RELEVANT PRODUCTS."
JEAN-PAUL AGON, PRESIDENT AND CEO L'ORÉAL USA

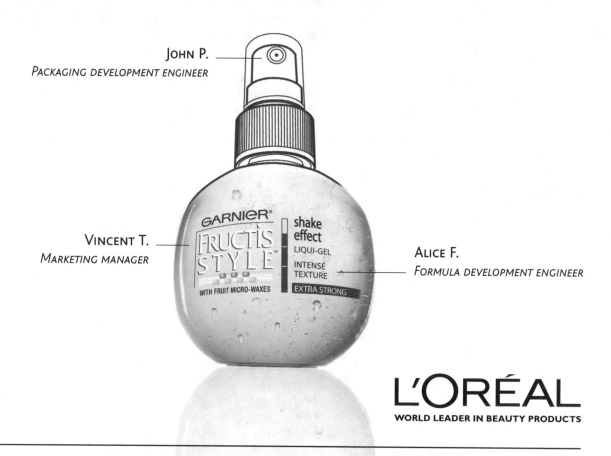

JOHN P.
PACKAGING DEVELOPMENT ENGINEER

VINCENT T.
MARKETING MANAGER

ALICE F.
FORMULA DEVELOPMENT ENGINEER

L'ORÉAL
WORLD LEADER IN BEAUTY PRODUCTS

JOIN US. WITH $4 BILLION IN ANNUAL SALES AND ACCOLADES THAT INCLUDE THE DIVERSITY BEST PRACTICES 2004 GLOBAL LEADERSHIP AWARD, L'ORÉAL USA IS A PLACE WHERE YOUR UNIQUE TALENTS CAN LEAD THE WAY TO A GREAT CAREER.

L'ORÉAL USA MANAGEMENT DEVELOPMENT PROGRAM
MARKETING ▪ SALES ▪ FINANCE ▪ INFORMATION SYSTEMS ▪ LOGISTICS ▪ MANUFACTURING ▪ RESEARCH & DEVELOPMENT

IF YOU ARE AN IMAGINATIVE AND RESULTS-FOCUSED GRADUATING SENIOR WITH AN ENTREPRENEURIAL SPIRIT AND COMMITMENT TO EXCELLENCE, THEN L'ORÉAL USA MAY HAVE THE OPPORTUNITY FOR YOU. UPON ENTERING OUR ROTATIONAL TRAINING PROGRAM, YOU WILL BECOME AN INTEGRAL PART OF OUR TEAM, WITH CONCRETE RESPONSIBILITY FROM DAY ONE. YOU WILL WORK ALONGSIDE TOP PROFESSIONALS WHO SHAPE THE INDUSTRY, CONTRIBUTING TO THE CREATION OF IDEAS AND THE PROCESSES THAT TURN THOSE IDEAS INTO REALITIES. IN ADDITION TO PROFESSIONAL DEVELOPMENT TRAINING HELD AT OUR MANAGEMENT DEVELOPMENT CENTER, WE OFFER COMPETITIVE COMPENSATION AND BENEFITS. LEARN MORE ABOUT THIS EXCITING FULL-TIME OPPORTUNITY, AS WELL AS INTERNSHIP OPPORTUNITIES, AND APPLY AT **WWW.LOREALUSA.COM**. EQUAL OPPORTUNITY EMPLOYER.

L'Oréal USA

575 Fifth Ave.
New York, NY 10017
Phone: (212) 818-1500
Fax: (212) 984-4999
http://lorealusa.com/careers

Diversity Leadership
Edward Bullock, Chief Diversity Officer
575 Fifth Avenue
New York, NY 10017

Recruiting

Please list the schools/types of schools at which you recruit.

• Ivy League schools
• Other private schools
• Historically Black Colleges and Universities (HBCUs)
• Hispanic Serving Institutions (HSIs)
• Other predominantly minority and/or women's colleges

Do you have any special outreach efforts that are directed to encourage minority students to consider your firm?

• Hold a reception for minority students
• Conferences: NBMBAA, NSHMBA
• Advertise in minority student association publication(s) such as The Black Collegian and Carambau
• Participate in/host minority student job fair(s)
• Sponsor minority student association events
• Firm's employees participate on career panels at school
• Outreach to leadership of minority student organizations
• Scholarships or intern/fellowships for minority students

What activities does the firm undertake to attract minority and women employees?

• Partner programs with women and minority associations
• Conferences: NBMBA, NSHMBA, Reaching Out
• Participate at minority job fairs
• Seek referrals from other employees
• Utilize online job services

Internships and Co-ops

L'Oreal Summer Internship Program

Marketing, Sales, Finance, Accounting, Information Systems, Logistics, Manufacturing, Research & Development or Human Resources

Deadline for application: Rolling application, but most offers are finalized by April 1st

Number of interns in the program in summer 2005: 46 Undergraduate Interns

Pay: Competitive

Length of the program: 10-12 weeks (varies by intern's academic calendar)

Web site for internship/co-op information: www.lorealusa.com

L'Oréal USA offers a formal internship program consisting of three main elements (1) the day to day functional job assignment, (2) a business related project to be completed and presented to management and (3) Educational and Professional Development sessions. The individual job assignments will vary with department needs, but you will get a chance to release your creativity and gain a new view to the world's leading beauty company.

Entry-Level Programs/Full-Time Opportunities

Management Development Program

Marketing, Sales, Finance, Information Systems, Manufacturing or Research & Development

Length of program: 2 years for Undergraduates; 1 year for MBAs

Geographic location(s) of program: Specific to the division and function

The Management Development Program is designed for students graduating with a bachelor's degree who want to pursue a career in Marketing, Sales, Finance, Information Systems, Logistics, Manufacturing or Research & Development. L'Oréal USA's management development program has been designed to develop our future leaders.

As part of the L'Oréal USA management development program, students are placed into one of the channels of trade at L'Oréal USA - Consumer Products, Luxury Products, Professional Products or Active Cosmetics or one of our Corporate functions i.e. Finance, Accounting, Manufacturing or Research & Development. The program is designed to give you the opportunity to gain exposure and hone your skills through hands-on assignments. It puts a strong emphasis on professional development through formal training held at our Management Development Center and individual check-points with members of the HR community. L'Oréal USA takes a 3-pronged approach to the program whereby successful candidates will experience a period of integration, participate in training rotationals, and ultimately be placed in an entry level management position.

Strategic Plan and Diversity Leadership

How does the firm's leadership communicate the importance of diversity to everyone at the firm?

The President of the company presents diversity communication annually in the Corporate Newsletter and through Executive Leadership Meetings with divisions for L'Oréal.

A diversity video featuring Lindsay Owen-Jones, Chairman & CEO of L'Oréal has been created to convey the L'Oréal Diversity philosophy. This video is featured at all orientations and leadership programs.

Who has primary responsibility for leading diversity initiatives at your firm?

President & CEO Lauren Attal – supported by the Office of Diversity

Does your firm currently have a diversity committee?

Yes

Does the committee and/or diversity leader establish and set goals or objectives consistent with management's priorities?

Yes

Has the firm undertaken a formal or informal diversity program or set of initiatives aimed at increasing the diversity of the firm?

Yes, formal. Four programs that provide Employee Orientation, Management to Leadership, Global Executive Leadership as well as mandatory Diversity Training for all employees.

How often does the firm's management review the firm's diversity progress/results?

Quarterly

The Stats

DEMOGRAPHIC PROFILE	TOTAL IN THE U.S.		TOTAL OUTSIDE THE U.S		TOTAL WORLDWIDE	
	2004	2003	2004	2003	2004	2003
Number of employees	7,629	7,884	43,274	42,241	50,903	50,125
Revenues	€3.280 billion	€3.318 billion	€10.939 billion	€10.385 billion	€14.219 billion	€13.704 billion

Retention and Professional Development

Please identify the specific steps you are taking to reduce the attrition rate of minority and women employees.

• Increase/improve current work/life programs
• Succession plan includes emphasis on diversity

The Employer Says

L'Oréal is dedicated to serving all expressions of beauty and well being, which it seeks to make accessible to women and men all over the world.

We believe our approach to diversity and inclusion must stand on a firm foundation of respect for the individual as stated in our L'Oréal Code of Business Ethics.

We embrace the philosophy of "first being diverse from within" and in order to become more diverse from within, we have established the Office of Diversity reporting to the President & CEO of L'Oréal USA and supporting global initiatives. This position will insure our steady progress toward a more inclusive and innovative organization.

Our Definition of Diversity

Diversity is the mosaic of people who bring a variety of backgrounds, styles, perspectives, values, beliefs and differences as assets to the groups and organizations with which they interact.

Our Thoughts on Diversity

The strength of L'Oréal USA lies in the diversity of its workforce. Our ability to embrace and respect various cultures, ethnicities and age groups as well as different values, ideals and points of view are critical to our success. Our openness to a variety of perspectives resonates throughout the company and is an integral part of achieving and advancing our common goals: to maintain our reputation for excellence and to bring to the marketplace a portfolio of diverse products that meet the beauty needs of all individuals.

At L'Oréal we manage diversity by giving value and respect to our employees, our consumers and our business partners as core ingredients in the formula for our success. We respect the talents, creativity and diversity they bring to our entire brand portfolio. We are committed to the recruitment, retention and development of a diverse workforce without regard to gender, ethnicity, religion, disabilities or sexual orientation.

    – Edward W. Bullock, VP Diversity, L'Oréal USA

Lucent Technologies

600 Mountain Ave.
Murray Hill, NJ 07974
Phone: (908) 582-8500
Fax: (908) 508-2576
Toll Free: (888) 458-2368
www.lucent.com/careers

Employment Contact
Ethel Batten, Vice President of Talent
Management, responsible for areas that
include Recruiting, Staffing, Policy, Equal
Opportunity, Affirmative Action and Diversity
600 Mountain Avenue
Murray Hill, New Jersey 07974
Phone: (908) 582-8500
Fax: (908) 508-2576

Recruiting

Please list the schools/types of schools at which you recruit.

- *Ivy League schools:* Harvard, University of Pennsylvania, Columbia and Cornell
- *Other private schools:* Purdue, Stanford, Massachusetts Institute of Technology, Seton Hall, Stevens Institute of Technology, Babson College, St Peters College, Boston College, Emory University, Northwestern, University of Chicago, Duke
- *Public state schools:* Rutgers, University of Illinois, Penn State University, Boston University, University of Georgia, New Jersey Institute of Technology, Ohio State University and University of Illinois-Chicago
- *Historically Black Colleges and Universities (HBCUs):* Howard University and Tennessee State University

Do you have any special outreach efforts that are directed to encourage minority students to consider your firm?

- Conferences
- Participate in/host minority student job fair(s)
- Outreach to leadership of minority student organizations
- Scholarships or intern/fellowships for minority students

What activities does the firm undertake to attract minority and women employees?

- Conferences
- Participate at minority job fairs
- Seek referrals from other employees
- Utilize online job services

Do you use executive recruiting/search firms to seek to identify new diversity hires?

Yes

Internships and Co-ops

Summer Internship Program

Deadline for application: January 31
Number of interns in the program in summer 2004 (internship) or 2004 (co-op): 181
Pay: Depends on year, degree and experience
Length of the program: 10 weeks
Web site for internship/co-op information: www.lucent.com/work/collegerecruitment.html

Lucent's Summer Internship Program provides valuable work experience within a corporate environment to outstanding college students ranging from first year through the masters level, PhD levels and college faculty members.

The objective of the program is to provide summer employment with positive work/training experience, identify and track potential regular full-time employees and establish "goodwill ambassadors" for Lucent on campuses. Interns receive project-focused assignments and challenging objectives consistent with their career goals. Interns also are assigned a mentor in addition to their supervisor/coach.

Interns receive a broad orientation to Lucent, the specific business unit and the individual work group to which they will be contributing. Developmental opportunities may include meetings with corporate executives, various educational workshops, business unit information exchanges, networking events and facility tours.

All offers for our summer internship program will be extended by April 15th. Submit your resume by January 31st, however we will accept resumes after this date. Please see the instructions below for submitting your resume.

To participate in Lucent's Early Career Identification Programs, you must meet the following criteria:

GPA: Overall GPA of 3.0/4.0 or above.

Citizenship: U.S. citizen, permanent or conditional permanent resident, temporary resident, asylee or refugee. We will accept students on F-1 or J-1 Visas.

Student Status: Full-time students will be considered from any four or five year, accredited U.S. college or university. Students must be enrolled to return as a full time student following the internship.

Majors: Accounting, Behavior Science, Business Administration, Chemical Engineering, Chemistry, Computer Engineering, Computer Science, Economics, Electrical Engineering, Engineering Mechanics, Finance, Industrial Engineering, Journalism, Management, Manufacturing Engineering, Mathematics, Mechanical Engineering, Operations Research, Physics, Public Relations, Sales/Marketing, Statistics, Systems Engineering and Telecommunications.

Principal U.S. locations: North & Central New Jersey, Naperville IL, Columbus OH, North Andover & Westford, MA, Alpharetta, GA, Hunt Valley, MD, Cary, NC, Miramar, FL, Alameda, CA, Denver area, CO.

Network Solutions AMPS/PCS Co-op Program

Number of interns in the program in summer 2004 (internship) or 2004 (co-op): 8
Length of the program: 26 weeks

Bell Labs Graduate Research Fellowship Program

Deadline for application: January 14
Web site for internship/co-op information: www.lucent.com/news/foundation/blgrfp/

The Bell Labs Graduate Research Fellowship Program is designed to increase the number of minorities and women in the fields of science, math, engineering and technology. A Bell Labs Graduate Research Fellowship is a wonderful opportunity to help outstanding minorities and women enhance their knowledge and to pursue a PH.D. degree in science and engineering.

Fellowships are awarded to women and members of a minority group currently underrepresented in the sciences* who are U.S. citizens, permanent residents or non-residents here on an F1 student visa. The program is primarily directed to graduating college seniors, but applications from first-year graduate students will be considered. Ten (10) fellowships are awarded each year.

Candidates are selected on the basis of scholastic attainment in their fields of specialization, and other evidence of their ability and potential as research scientists. Students must be pursuing full-time doctorial studies in the following disciplines:

A distinctive feature of the program is the opportunity for fellowship participants to gain firsthand research and development experience, through on-site activities at Lucent Technologies Bell Labs, under the guidance of research scientists and engineers. Each participant is expected to spend the first summer working with their mentor at Bell Labs on a research project in their area of interest. Fellowship participants are encouraged to continue their association with their mentors during the following academic year and throughout their graduate studies.

Scholarships

Lucent's Graduate Research Fellowship Program, sponsored by the Lucent Foundation, works to increase the numbers of women and under-represented minority groups in the fields of science and engineering. Each year, ten fellowships are awarded to outstanding scholars who are working toward doctoral degrees in disciplines such as chemistry, physics and engineering.

Children of Lucent employees can apply for scholarships of $6,500 for each academic year of full-time study. The money can be used for tuition, books, academic fees, and room and board. The scholarship can be renewed each year for no more than three years or until a degree is earned, whichever comes first.

Lucent is a national sponsor of the INROADS program.

Through the Lucent Foundation, Lucent supports Project GRAD (Graduation Really Achieves Dreams), which works with students at Malcolm X Shabazz High School and the K-8 schools in Newark, N.J., to raise student achievement in reading, writing and math, with the intention of increasing the number of high-school graduates and college students.

In December 2004, The Lucent Foundation announced a two-year extension of the Global Fund for Youth Development that will benefit young people in 14 countries. The next phase of this program — funded through a $2.8 million grant — will assist young people and teachers in Argentina, Australia, Brazil, China, Germany, India, Korea, Mexico, Netherlands, the Philippines, Poland, Russia, Spain, and Venezuela.

Affinity Groups/Employee Networks

Lucent actively supports and encourages its Employee Business Partner (EBP) Groups; individual organizations that offer programs to address the needs of different ethnic and social groups.

Lucent's EBP groups are an important part of our culture, and help advance the professional and personal growth of all employees through networking forums, career development programs and community service.

Lucent's Employee Business Partner Groups are:

• 4A — Asian-Pacific American Association for Advancement at Lucent Technologies
• ABLE — Alliance of Black Lucent Technologies Employees
• EQUAL — Lesbian, Bisexual, Gay and Transgendered Employees of Lucent Technologies
• HISPA — Hispanic Association of Lucent Technologies Employees
• IDEAL — Individuals with Disabilities Enabling Advocacy Link at Lucent Technologies
• LUNA — United Native Americans of Lucent Technologies
• WILL — Women in Leadership at Lucent Technologies

To provide guidance and support to these groups while they continue this work, several Lucent leaders have been named EBP Advisors, and work closely with each EBP group on a rotating basis.

Entry-Level Programs/Full-Time Opportunities

Under Lucent's Tuition Assistance Program, employees are eligible for $7,000 per year for undergraduate and other education and $9,000 per year for graduate education. The purpose of this program is to broaden employees' knowledge, keep them current with business and technology changes, enhance their abilities and help them meet the competitive challenges of a global business.

Finance Leadership Development Program

Length of program: 38-month program

FLDP candidates are recruited and interviewed each year between Sept. 1 and March 15. From March 15 through Sept. 1, resumes are collected but are not reviewed until after Sept. 1. Each FLDP class starts in mid-June.

The FLDP is a rigorous 38-month program in finance that combines real-time on-the-job developmental experiences with graduate school-level education. The program provides a strong combination of technical and strategic skill development. Participants rotate into a new job assignment every 12 months. At the same time, participants engage in selected financial and leadership development sessions specifically designed to provide both academic theory and practical application. Upon successful completion of the program, graduates are placed into key developmental financial positions where they will enjoy responsibility, decision-making accountability and visibility.

The criteria that must be met to be considered a candidate for the FLDP are:

• Recent College Graduates or persons with less than five years work experience
• A Bachelors Business Degree with at least three semesters of Accounting, three semesters of Finance-related courses and three semesters of Economics related courses
• A G.P.A. of 3.5 or better
• Demonstrate exemplary leadership attributes

Supply Chain Network MBA Leadership Development Program

Length of program: 36 months

SCN LDP candidates are recruited and interviewed each year between September 1st and March 15th. Resumes for both full time and summer intern positions are gathered during this time frame. From March 15th through September 1st resumes are collected but not reviewed until after September 1st.

The Leadership Development Program sponsored by Supply Chain Networks (SCN) originates, and is supported, by the entire SCN Senior Leadership team. The program is focused on developing future global leaders while engaging them in challenging projects critical to Lucent's future. The LDP is a rigorous 36-month program consisting of 3-4 rotations, approximately 12 months in duration. The summer intern component consists of a 10-week work assignment, which may lead to future full time opportunities. Each position offers a wide range of responsibilities and business opportunities for the new hire and the LDP executive mentoring program enhances this growth.

Supply Chain Networks provides Lucent with all supplier and supply chain engineering and management, manufacturing, logistics, and distribution functions for global provisioning from end to end. SCN LDP is seeking advanced level degree graduates to work on projects that focus on the following areas: General Management, Business development/Strategy, Supply Chain Management, Demand Management, Product Design Chain, Operations, Customer Facing, Order Fulfillment, Supplier Management, Provisioning/Manufacturing, to name a few.

Qualifications/experience criteria

• Minimum of five years post bachelor degree full time work experience, with previous overseas work assignment(s) desirable.
• Must have the right to work in the US on a permanent/full time basis.
• Undergraduate degree in Engineering or Business/Finance desirable.
• Proficiency in two or more languages preferred and/or willingness to acquire a second language skill.

• Demonstration of leadership characteristics and/or experience, change agent, thinks strategically, results oriented, proven high level of performance.
• Demonstrated ability to work in a global environment as well as experience doing business in a different culture.

If you meet Lucent's criteria and are interested in applying for an SCN Leadership Development Program position, please submit your resume online: www.lucent.com/hireme.

Lucent's leaders have placed a top priority on the continued development of our talent. To address this, a comprehensive program talent management program, "Developing Great Talent" (DGT), is being launched to ensure all managers at Lucent understand the critical role they play in identifying, acquiring, developing and retaining great talent.

Lucent's mentoring program, Leading Lucent's Future, is being revamped. This program works to accelerate Lucent's performance through increased contributions of rising leaders and build a diverse group of future leaders.

Strategic Plan and Diversity Leadership

How does the firm's leadership communicate the importance of diversity to everyone at the firm?

• Lucent's Chairman & CEO released a diversity statement.
• Each of the leaders released a diversity statement along with a memo stressing the importance of diversity. This message was deployed throughout their organizations.
• Articles in LT Today (Lucent's daily electronic newsletter)
• Agenda item on the leaders' team meetings.
• Diversity web page
• Employee Business Partner Groups

Who has primary responsibility for leading diversity initiatives at your firm?

Ethel Batten/Global Diversity Officer

Does your firm currently have a diversity committee?

Yes

If yes, please describe how the committee is structured, how often it meets, etc.

• The committee is comprised of representation both nationally and internationally. There is representation from all business segments and corporate centers as well as levels. The committee meets on a bi-monthly basis.
• The primary responsibility of the committee is to align business objectives with diversity priorities, translating the priorities of the senior management committee into realities for the business segments.
• The committee also tracks the progress of Lucent's 5-year diversity strategy and serves as a voice of the people on an ongoing basis.

If yes, does the committee's representation include one or more members of the firm's management/executive committee (or the equivalent)?

Yes

Please describe the committee.

• There are 4 executives on the committee.
• There are a total of 43 employees on the committee.
• The committee convenes on a bi-monthly basis (6 times/year).

Does the committee and/or diversity leader establish and set goals or objectives consistent with management's priorities?

Yes

Has the firm undertaken a formal or informal diversity program or set of initiatives aimed at increasing the diversity of the firm?

Yes, formal

How often does the firm's management review the firm's diversity progress/results?

Quarterly

How is the firm's diversity committee and/or firm management held accountable for achieving results?

Diversity measurements/objectives are included in the committee's scorecard. They are annually assessed during performance management.

Diversity Mission Statement

"We achieve our shared purpose by embracing the full richness of our people's differences. We believe the diversity of our people enriches our work experience and is the source of our innovation and our competitive advantage. We adhere to Lucent's core values and treat everyone with dignity and deepest respect."

Additional Information

Diversity is an important part of Lucent's heritage. We have always valued and remain strongly committed to diversity through our corporate culture, recruiting and development programs.

Diverse people and ideas are vital to our corporate culture, to our success as a global business and to our ability to attract and retain talented employees.

Over the last few years, Lucent has faced a changing telecom industry and a challenging market. Our company has had to adjust to this new reality. Our workforce has been affected, but our commitment to diversity as a business imperative has not.

At Lucent, we work to respect each other, acknowledge others' ideas and appreciate what makes us distinct as individuals. Respecting our differences is an integral part of our culture and values, and it shows.

Lucent has a strong set of core values, which is clearly evident in our internal and external Web sites, as well as in Business Guideposts. Business Guideposts is Lucent's code of conduct, which all employees are required to read and certify online. Business Guideposts describes Lucent's standards for ethical business behavior and addresses a wide range of business and personnel issues.

In April 2004, part of Lucent's ongoing Ethics and Compliance Training Program, the next course in our Web-based training platform was rolled out. "Preventing Workplace Harassment" was mandatory for all employees at all levels. This course reinforces our commitment to providing a work environment that is free from discrimination.

People with different backgrounds, experiences and cultures bring very different perspectives to Lucent and enrich the quality of our performance for our customers. The debate and discussion, the creativity, innovations and the diversity of ideas that diverse perspectives generate are essential for any successful global company.

Lucent formed a Global Diversity Council to build on diversity efforts already in place, as well as expand our focus on diversity. This council, which has the commitment and participation of our top business leaders, will work to evaluate current programs and suggest ways to further endorse diversity efforts. In addition to the Global Diversity Council, there are a number of diversity councils on the business unit level.

Lucent has always been and continues to be a strong advocate for supplier diversity. This is a critical requirement for Lucent and our key customers. To be a leading player in the global market, the whole team needs to be diverse, and our suppliers and business partners are a critical part of the team working to meet our customers' expectations. We also work hard to incorporate diversity suppliers into the business and work to strengthen our relationships with them.

AT&T was the first Fortune 500 to add sexual preference to its EO/AA policy in 1974 and the first company to have a Gay and Lesbian affinity group. In 1999, Lucent continued its trend setting legacy by adding "gender identity, characteristics and expressions" to the EO/AA policy. Lucent was the first company to include that language in their policy.

Marriott International, Inc.

1 Marriott Drive
Washington, D.C. 20058
Phone: (301) 380-3000
Fax: (301) 380-3969
www.marriott.com/careers

Contact Person:
Stephen O'Connor, Vice President, University Relations & Property Staffing

Diversity Leadership:
Maruiel Perkins Chavis, Vice President, Workforce Effectiveness and Diversity Talent Management
1 Marriott Drive
Washington, D.C. 20058
Phone: (301) 380-8960
Fax: (301) 380-4202

Recruiting

What activities does the firm undertake to attract minority and women employees?

Marriott maintains a strong commitment to national recruitment advertising, with placements in such publications as *Black Collegian*, *Black Enterprise*, *Black MBA*, *Careers and the Disabled*, *DiversityInc*, *Hispanic Business* and *Working Mother*.

Our strategic relationships with dozens of affinity organizations and media outlets help us get the word out that minorities and women have a great future at Marriott – as associates, vendors, franchisees, and guests. Examples include the National Association of Black Accountants, the National Black MBA Association, the National Society of Minority Hoteliers, the Organization of Chinese-Americans, National Council of La Raza, the Women Business Enterprise Council, National Hispanic Corporate Council, the U.S. Hispanic Chamber of Commerce, the NAACP, and the National Urban League.

Scholarships

Marriott is actively involved in the Emerging Markets Program of the International Franchise Association. The company contributes monetary, in-kind and management executive talent resources to IFA, and has partnered with the association to launch a Minority Entrepreneurs Scholarship program.

Contact information for scholars:

Mr. John Reynolds, President
IFA Educational Foundation
1350 New York Ave NW
Suite 900
Washington DC NW 200005
202-662-0764
johnr@franchise.org

Strategic Plan and Diversity Leadership

Does your firm currently have a diversity committee?

The Marriott Board of Directors has established a subcommittee on diversity which meets regularly to set significant goals and monitor progress at every level of the corporation.

Has the firm undertaken a formal or informal diversity program or set of initiatives aimed at increasing the diversity of the firm?

Six regional Diversity Councils drive our corporate diversity message home in the field with implementation of diveristy related initiatives to include strategic partnerships, targeted recruitment campaigns, leadership development programs, internships, conferences and other outreach to women and minorities.

The Stats

Our commitment to diversity begins at home. Marriott's 133,000 associates hail from dozens of nations, speak more than 50 languages and work under the Marriott banner in 66 countries and territories around the world. Fifty-eight percent of our associates are minorities and 54 percent are women, many of whom take advantage of the company's professional development programs to move up and map out long-term careers with the company.

• Nearly 3,000 of Marriott's current managers began their careers with Marriott in hourly positions. Currently, 55.7 percent of the company's supervisors – the first step toward achieving a management post – are minorities.

• During 2004, of the new managers hired, 23 percent were minorities and 47 percent were women.

Diversity Mission Statement

At Marriott International, diversity is more than a goal…it's our business. From our global workforce and vendors, to our franchisees, our customers and communities, we thrive on the differences that give our company its strength and competitive edge. In the process, we've set the standard for the entire hospitality industry. And it shows:

• *DiversityInc* ranked Marriott #12 on its list of "Top 50 Companies for Diversity." Marriott was the only lodging company on the list. (April 2005)

• Marriott was recognized as one of the Top 50 Companies for Supplier Diversity by *Hispanic Trends* magazine (Jan/Feb 2005 issue)

• National Society of Minorities in Hospitality presented Marriott International with its first ever "Corporate Lifetime Commitment Award" as a result of our work and support of the association.

• In Oct. 2004, John W. Marriott, III co-chaired the 2004 National Minority Supplier Development Council Conference. The conference, which drew more than 6400 attendees, represents the nation's largest convergence of minority suppliers and corporate purchasing organizations

• The National Urban League awarded David M. Sampson, senior vice president, diversity initiatives, and Priscilla J. Hollman, vice president, diversity relations, the prestigious Donald H. McGannon Award for their commitment to ideals and beliefs in equal opportunity.

• Black Data Processing Associates (BDPA) and WorkplaceDiversity.com have awarded Marriott International, Inc. their "Best Companies for Blacks in Technology Award."

• *Essence* magazine named Marriott as one of the publication's "Best Companies for Black Women."

• *Hispanic* magazine's "Corporate 100" recognizes Marriott International as one of the 100 "Best Places to Work for Latinos"

- Marriott was ranked in the top ten U.S. Companies for diversity in the "Best of the Best" Corporate Awards for Diversity & Women by Diversity Best Practices and Business Women's Network.

- The NAACP has ranked Marriott #1 in its Lodging Industry Report six out of the past seven years.

- *Latina Style* magazine has named Marriott to its list of "The 50 Best Companies for Latinas to Work for in the U.S." the sixth year in a row.

- J.W. Marriott, Jr. received the Jackie Robinson Foundation's 2004 ROBIE Award for Achievement in Industry for the company's commitment to diversity. The foundation recognized Marriott for the company's success in employment and supplier diversity.

- *Working Mother* magazine has listed Marriott among its "100 Best Companies for Working Mothers" for 14 years.

- *Fortune* magazine recognized Marriott as one of the "100 Best Companies to Work For" for the last seven consecutive years.

The Employer Says

Our stakeholders know we're serious about diversity

Marriott International's stakeholders know that our commitment to diversity can be summed up in one word: absolute.

- Marriott Chairman and CEO J.W. Marriott, Jr., sits on the Board of Trustees of the National Urban League.

- In February 2003, J.W. Marriott, Jr. was awarded the Lifetime Achievement Award by the Hospitality Industry Diversity Institute for his commitment to recognizing and including women, minorities and people with disabilities in the hospitality industry.

Suppliers and vendors: A world of opportunity at Marriott

Every big company begins as a small business. Marriott did… back in 1927. We've never forgotten the opportunities that others gave us to succeed. Today, we proudly continue the tradition by reaching out to a whole new generation of entrepreneurs.

- In 2004, we exceeded our own goal of spending seven percent of our annual purchasing dollars with minority- and women-owned suppliers. We have established a new goal of spending $1 billion over the next five years with diverse suppliers.

- In 2004, through our companywide supplier diversity program, Marriott purchased and facilitated spending of more than $260 million in goods and services from more than 10,000 minority- and women-owned businesses.

- Marriott retains the mutual fund management services of Ariel Capital Management LLC – a premier African-American owned investment management company – to administer the company's profit-sharing retirement savings plan.

In 2004, Marriott spent more than $1 million with Land-Ron, a Hispanic-owned architecture and construction contractor. Asian-American owned company Tronex recently signed a $1.4 million annual contract to supply latex gloves to Marriott. Our company expects to save more than $200,000 annually with our new supplier..

Minority franchisees and owners grow with us

As Marriott pursues its growth plan and continues to expand, we want diverse partners and stakeholders to grow and prosper alongside us.

- Our Minority ownership Initiative helps us attract and develop relationships with quality-minded minority and female owners and franchisees, and support them through every step of the development process. Today, 15 percent of franchise units are owned by minorities.

- As of year-end 2004, more than 270 Marriott hotels are owned, operated or under development by women or ethnic minorities.

- Marriott is actively involved in the Emerging Markets Program of the International Franchise Association. The company contributes monetary, in-kind and management executive talent resources to IFA, and has partnered with the association to launch a Minority Entrepreneurs Scholarship program.

Four Fires LLC, a financial consortium composed of four Native American tribes, has teamed up with Marriott in a first-of-its-kind partnership to build a 13-story Residence Inn in downtown Washington, D.C., near the Smithsonian's new National Museum of the American Indian, which is slated to open in late 2004.

Mirroring our stakeholders and our communities

We won't be satisfied until every aspect of our business reflects the rich diversity of the people and communities who touch Marriott's world.

Our strategic relationships with dozens of affinity organizations and media outlets help us get the word out that minorities and women have a great future at Marriott – as associates, vendors, franchisees, and guests. Examples include the National Association of Black Accountants, the National Black MBA Association, the National Society of Minority Hoteliers, the Organization of Chinese-Americans, National Council of La Raza, the Women Business Enterprise Council, National Hispanic Corporate Council, the U.S. Hispanic Chamber of Commerce, the NAACP, and the National Urban League.

For more information about...

- **External Diversity Initiatives:** Dave Sampson, Senior Vice President, Diversity Initiatives, at (301) 380-3046 or Priscilla Hollman at (301) 380-1223.
- **Supplier Diversity:** Louise Rosamont at (301) 380-5889.
- **University Relations & Recruiting:** Stephen O'Connor at www.steve.oconnor@marriott.com
- **Media inquiries:** Corporate Communications at (301) 380-7770.

Marshall and Ilsley Corporation

770 N. Water St.
Milwaukee, WI 53202 (Map)
Phone: (414) 765-7700
Fax: (414) 298-2921
www.micorp.com

Diversity Leadership

Walt A. Buckhanan, Vice President, Corporate
Diversity/Inclusion Manager
770 N Water St
Milwaukee, WI 53202
Phone: (414) 765-7771
Fax: (414) 765-7514
E-mail: Walt.Buckhanan@micorp.com

Recruiting

Please list the schools/types of schools at which you recruit.

• Private schools:
• Public state schools:

Do you have any special outreach efforts that are directed to encourage minority students to consider your firm?

• *Conferences:* Black MBA and NEON
• Participate in/host minority student job fair(s)
• Sponsor minority student association events
• Firm's employees participate on career panels at school

What activities does the firm undertake to attract minority and women employees?

• Partner programs with women and minority associations
• *Conferences:* Black MBA, NEON, M&I Milwaukee and You
• Participate at minority job fairs
• Seek referrals from other employees
• Utilize online job services

Do you use executive recruiting/search firms to seek to identify new diversity hires?
Yes

Internships and Co-ops

INROADS

Deadline for application: February 28th
Number of interns in the program in summer 2004 (internship) or 2004 (co-op): 8
Pay: TBD (Based on experience and grade level)
Length of the program: 12 weeks

Percentage of interns/co-ops in the program who receive offers of full-time employment: 100%

Web site for internship/co-op information: WWW.MICORP.COM

Jr. Associate Program

Deadline for application: February 28th

Number of interns in the program in summer 2004 (internship) or 2004 (co-op): 27

Pay: TBD (Based on experience and Grade level)

Length of the program: 12 weeks

Percentage of interns/co-ops in the program who receive offers of full-time employment: 80%

Web site for internship/co-op information: WWW.MICORP.COM

Each Manager develops a job description on an annual basis.

Affinity Groups/Employee Networks

We are in the process of developing criteria for employee resource groups.

Entry-Level Programs/Full-Time Opportunities

Financial Sales Program

Length of program: 7-12 months

Geographic location(s) of program: Arizona, Minnesota, Missouri and Wisconsin

Treasury Management Sales Program

Length of program: 7-12 months

Geographic location(s) of program: Arizona, Minnesota, Missouri and Wisconsin

Corporate Banking Program

Length of program: 7-12 months

Geographic location(s) of program: Arizona, Minnesota, Missouri and Wisconsin

Trust Operations Program

Length of program: 7-12 months

Geographic location(s) of program: Arizona, Minnesota, Missouri and Wisconsin

Audit Analysis Program

Length of program: 7-12 months

Geographic location(s) of program: Arizona, Minnesota, Missouri and Wisconsin

Strategic Plan and Diversity Leadership

How does the firm's leadership communicate the importance of diversity to everyone at the firm?

Corporate newsletter, emails, meetings and training.

Who has primary responsibility for leading diversity initiatives at your firm?

Walt A. Buckhanan, V.P. Corporate Diversity/Inclusion Manager

Does your firm currently have a diversity committee?

Yes

If yes, please describe how the committee is structured, how often it meets, etc.

It is made up of business line managers representing key area's of responsibilities.

If yes, does the committee's representation include one or more members of the firm's management/executive committee (or the equivalent)?

Yes

If yes, how many executives are on the committee, and in 2004, what was the total number of hours collectively spent by the committee in furtherance of the firm's diversity initiatives?

How many employees are on the committee, and how often does the committee convene in furtherance of the firm's diversity initiatives?

Our diversity council make up is apprised of: (1) Executive Sponsor (The CEO) (9) Business Line Managers. The Council meets quarterly

Does the committee and/or diversity leader establish and set goals or objectives consistent with management's priorities?

Yes

Has the firm undertaken a formal or informal diversity program or set of initiatives aimed at increasing the diversity of the firm?

Yes, formal

How often does the firm's management review the firm's diversity progress/results?

Quarterly

The Stats

Employees: 12,660 (2004, U.S.)
Employees: 12,113 (2003, U.S.)

Retention and Professional Development

How do 2004 minority and female attrition rates generally compare to those experienced in the prior year period?

About the same as in prior years

Please identify the specific steps you are taking to reduce the attrition rate of minority and women employees.

• Increase/review compensation relative to competition
• Succession plan includes emphasis on diversity
• Work with minority and women employees to develop career advancement plans
• Strengthen mentoring program for all employees, including minorities and women

Diversity Mission Statement

Marshall & Ilsley Corporation is committed to a diverse workforce that reflects the communities we serve. We value our employees' talents and support a work environment that is inclusive and respectful.

Mattel, Inc.

333 Continental Blvd.
El Segundo, CA 90245-5012
Phone: (310) 252-2000
Fax: (310) 252-2180
www.mattel.com

Locations (worldwide)
With worldwide headquarters in El Segundo, California, Mattel employs more than 25,000 people in 36 countries and sells products in more than 150 nations throughout the world.

Diversity Leadership
Graciela Meibar, VP Global Diversity

Employment Contact
Teresa Newcomb, Corporate Staffing
333 Continental Blvd.
El Segundo, CA 90245
Phone: (310) 252-2000
Fax: (310) 252-2180
E-mail: teresa.newcomb@mattel.com

Recruiting

Please list the schools/types of schools at which you recruit.

• Historically Black Colleges and Universities (HBCUs)
• Hispanic Serving Institutions (HSIs)

Do you have any special outreach efforts that are directed to encourage minority students to consider your firm?

• Conferences: NSHMBA and NBMBAA
• Firm's employees participate on career panels at school

What activities does the firm undertake to attract minority and women employees?

• Partner programs with women and minority associations
• Conferences: NSHMBA and NBMBAA
• Seek referrals from other employees

Do you use executive recruiting/search firms to seek to identify new diversity hires?

No

Internships and Co-ops

INROADS and Magic Johnson Foundation

Deadline for application: April
Number of interns in the program in summer 2004 (internship) or 2004 (co-op): INROADS 15, MJF 3
Pay: $12/hr
Length of the program: 10-12 weeks
Percentage of interns/co-ops in the program who receive offers of full-time employment: 67%

Scholarships

Only for employees' children

Affinity Groups/Employee Networks

None at this time; starting a women's network

Strategic Plan and Diversity Leadership

How does the firm's leadership communicate the importance of diversity to everyone at the firm?

E-mails and newsletters

Who has primary responsibility for leading diversity initiatives at your firm?

Graciela Meibar, VP Global Diversity

Does your firm currently have a diversity committee?

No

Does the committee and/or diversity leader establish and set goals or objectives consistent with management's priorities?

Yes

Has the firm undertaken a formal or informal diversity program or set of initiatives aimed at increasing the diversity of the firm?

Yes, informal

How often does the firm's management review the firm's diversity progress/results?

Quarterly

The Stats

Employees: 5,000 (2004, U.S.)
Employees: 20,000 (2004, outside the U.S.)
Employees: 25,000 (2004, worldwide)
Employees: 5,000 (2003, U.S.)
Employees: 20,000 (2003, outside the U.S.)
Employees: 25,000 (2003, worldwide)
Revenue: $5.1 Billion (2004, worldwide)
Revenue: $4.96 Billion (2003, worldwide)

Retention and Professional Development

How do 2004 minority and female attrition rates generally compare to those experienced in the prior year period?

About the same as in prior years

Please identify the specific steps you are taking to reduce the attrition rate of minority and women employees.

• Develop and/or support internal employee affinity groups (e.g., minority or women networks within the firm)

• Strengthen mentoring program for all employees, including minorities and women

• Professional skills development program, including minority and women employees

The Employer Says

Diversity is a strategic business plan imperative to Mattel, Inc. As we get closer to our consumers, we will become more successful. The best way to do so is by having a work force that reflects our worldwide consumers.

McDonald's Corporation

McDonald's Plaza
Oak Brook, IL 60523
Phone: (630) 623-3000
Fax: (630) 623-5004
www.mcdonalds.com

Locations (worldwide)
Oak Brook, IL - Headquarters

Diversity Leadership
Pat Harris, Chief Diversity Officer

Employment Contact:
Kim Smutny, Coordinator
2111 McDonald's Drive, Dept. 147
Oak Brook, IL 60523
Phone: (630) 623-4833
Fax: (630) 623-7232
E-mail: kim.smutny@mcd.com

Recruiting

What activities does the firm undertake to attract minority and women employees?

• Partner programs with women and minority associations
• Conferences: NAACP, NUL, NCLR, NAAAP, WFF, HACU, LULAC, JASC, NBMBA, ALPFA, Bennett College for Women
• Seek referrals from other employees

Do you use executive recruiting/search firms to seek to identify new diversity hires?

No

Scholarships

RMHC/African American Future Achievers Scholarship Program

Commitment to education

The RMHC/African-American Future Achievers Scholarship program is a program of Ronald McDonald House Charities global office and its U.S. Chapters. It is one of several RMHC scholarships designed to assist specific students who face a widening education gap. The goal of this RMHC program is to provide scholarships to graduating high school seniors who may need an extra hand getting in and staying in college. Studies show that the more difficult it is for a student to get into college, the less likely they are to graduate. Funding from RMHC can sometimes make the difference between attending and not attending the college of someone's choice. During the 2003-2004 RMHC/African-American Future Achievers program, over $1.3 million was awarded in scholarships

The RMHC/Future Achievers Scholarship program provides financial support to students who are committed to pursuing post-secondary education in their chosen field at an accredited institution. The RMHC/Future Achievers program recognizes young peoples' education accomplishments, their potential and their commitment to serve the community. Local Chapters of RMHC operate the program in their respective geographic areas with support from the global office of RMHC, local McDonald's restaurants and other businesses and organizations in the community.

Scholarship information and eligibility

To apply for a RMHC/Future Achievers scholarship, students must...

- have at least one parent of African-American origin;
- be eligible to enroll in and attend a two-year or four-year accredited college with a full course of study;
- attend college in the U.S.; and,
- reside in a participating local Chapter's geographic area.

Scholarships are generally a minimum of $1,000 and are designated for graduating high school seniors, although some local programs may award different scholarship amounts.

Scholarship recipients are selected based on:

- academic achievement;
- financial need;
- community involvement; and,
- personal qualities and strengths as portrayed in a required essay.

Recipients must enroll in and attend an accredited institution in the academic year after their selection and provide verification of enrollment. Scholarship funds are paid directly to the schools and no funds will be dispersed to students directly.

Additional eligibility information and instructions are provided on the scholarship application.

Scholarship applications

The deadline for the 2004-2005 academic year was February 15, 2005. Please check back in the Fall of 2005 for an applications for the 2005-2006 program.

RMHC/ASIA (Asian Students Increasing Achievement) Scholarship Program

Commitment to education

The RMHC/ASIA Scholarship program is a program of Ronald McDonald House Charities global office and its U.S. Chapters. It is one of several RMHC scholarships designed to assist specific students who face a widening education gap. The goal of this RMHC program is to provide scholarships to graduating high school seniors who may need an extra hand getting in and staying in college. Studies show that the more difficult it is for a student to get into college, the less likely they are to graduate. Funding from RMHC can sometimes make the difference between attending and not attending the college of someone's choice. During the 2003-2004 RMHC/ASIA program, over $600,000 was awarded in scholarships.

The RMHC/ASIA Scholarship program provides financial support to students who are committed to pursuing post-secondary education in their chosen field at an accredited institution. The RMHC/ASIA program recognizes young peoples' education accomplishments, their potential and their commitment to serve the community. Local Chapters of RMHC operate the program in their respective geographic areas with support from the global office of RMHC, local McDonald's restaurants and other businesses and organizations in the community.

Scholarship information and eligibility

To apply for a RMHC/ASIA scholarship, students must...

- have at least one parent of Asian-Pacific origin (any major Asian-American, Southeast Asian, South Asian or Pacific-Islander group);
- be eligible to enroll in and attend a two-year or four-year accredited college with a full course of study;
- attend college in the U.S.; and,
- reside in a participating local Chapter's geographic area.

Scholarships are generally a minimum of $1,000 and are designated for graduating high school seniors, although some local programs may award different scholarship amounts.

Scholarship recipients are selected based on:

• academic achievement;
• financial need;
• community involvement; and,
• personal qualities and strengths as portrayed in a required essay.

Recipients must enroll in and attend an accredited institution in the academic year after their selection and provide verification of enrollment. Scholarship funds are paid directly to the schools and no funds will be dispersed to students directly.

Additional eligibility information and instructions are provided on the scholarship application.

Scholarship applications

The deadline for the 2004-2005 academic year was February 15, 2005. Please check back in the Fall of 2005 for an applications for the 2005-2006 program.

RMHC/HACER (Hispanic American Commitment to Educational Resources) Scholarship Program

Commitment to education

The RMHC/HACER Scholarship program is a program of Ronald McDonald House Charities global office and its U.S. Chapters. It is one of several RMHC scholarships designed to assist specific students who face a widening education gap. The goal of this RMHC program is to provide scholarships to graduating high school seniors who may need an extra hand getting in and staying in college. Studies show that the more difficult it is for a student to get into college, the less likely they are to graduate. Funding from RMHC can sometimes make the difference between attending and not attending the college of someone's choice. During the 2003-2004 RMHC/HACER program, more than $2 million was awarded in scholarships.

The RMHC/HACER Scholarship program provides financial support to students who are committed to pursuing post-secondary education in their chosen field at an accredited institution. The RMHC/HACER program recognizes young peoples' education accomplishments, their potential and their commitment to serve the community. Local Chapters of RMHC operate the program in their respective geographic areas with support from the global office of RMHC, local McDonald's restaurants and other businesses and organizations in the community.

History of the program

As a former educator, McDonald's franchisee Richard Castro from El Paso, TX, was keenly aware of the alarming number of Hispanic students who dropped out of high school in his hometown and across the country. Driven by his commitment to give back, Castro acted to change the situation by leading the effort to create a scholarship program that would serve as encouragement for young Hispanics to complete high school and continue their education.

Castro rallied his fellow McDonald's franchisees and McDonald's Corporation and secured the support of Ronald McDonald House Charities to establish the RMHC/HACER program in 1985. An initial fund of $97,000 served to launch the program, providing $1,000 awards to high school seniors in various communities. Today, the RMHC/HACER Scholarship Program has become the largest high school-to-college scholarship program for Hispanic students and a nationally-recognized program.

Scholarship information and eligibility

To apply for a RMHC/HACER scholarship, students must…

• have at least one parent of Hispanic origin;
• be eligible to enroll in and attend a two-year or four-year accredited college with a full course of study;
• attend college in the U.S.; and,
• reside in a participating local Chapter's geographic area.

Scholarships are generally a minimum of $1,000 and are designated for graduating high school seniors, although some local programs may award different scholarship amounts.

Scholarship recipients are selected based on:

• academic achievement;
• financial need;
• community involvement; and,
• personal qualities and strengths as portrayed in a required essay.

Recipients must enroll in and attend an accredited institution in the academic year after their selection and provide verification of enrollment. Scholarship funds are paid directly to the schools and no funds will be dispersed to students directly.

Additional eligibility information and instructions are provided on the scholarship application.

Scholarship applications

The deadline for the 2004-2005 academic year was February 15, 2005. Please check back in the Fall of 2005 for an applications for the 2005-2006 program.

Scholarship Web Site

www.rmhc.org/mission/scholarships/index.html

Affinity Groups/Employee Networks

Asian Employee Network, McDonald's African American Employee Network, Hispanic Employee Network, Hispanic Leadership Council, Women's Leadership Network

An employee network is an interconnected or interrelated group of (voluntary) people that act as a resource, support base and advocate for the employees they represent. In addition, they often serve to provide a sense of community among participants. They should be grass-roots in origin, and not mandated by the company. However, they should have visible support from management. Employee networks serve many purposes. They act as a support base; provide information, education, and advice and counsel for both the employees and for the company.

Entry-Level Programs/Full-Time Opportunities

LAMP

Length of program: 12 months
Geographic location(s) of program: U.S.

The purpose of the Leadership at McDonald's Program (LAMP) is to accelerate the development of high potential leaders in a way that drives results, shapes organizational culture and builds leadership depth.

Development focuses on leveraging on-the-job experiences, while providing appropriate skills that can be applied and practiced in each participant's day-to-day job. It will also focus on developing the leadership abilities of each participant. The framework that will be used to guide leadership development is based upon three leadership challenges: leading oneself, leading high performance teams and leading the organization.

Strategic Plan and Diversity Leadership

How does the firm's leadership communicate the importance of diversity to everyone at the firm?

Who has primary responsibility for leading diversity initiatives at your firm?

Pat Harris, Chief Diversity Officer

Does your firm currently have a diversity committee?

Yes - We have a Diversity Council.

If yes, please describe how the committee is structured, how often it meets, etc.

The Council was started in 2004 under the direction of the CEO of McDonald's USA. With a focus on diversity and inclusion the Council participants represent diversity thought leaders throughout our Corporation.

If yes, does the committee's representation include one or more members of the firm's management/executive committee (or the equivalent)?

Yes

Please describe the committee.

There are 5 executives on the council. There are an additional 28 employees on the council and the meet on a quarterly basis.

Does the committee and/or diversity leader establish and set goals or objectives consistent with management's priorities?

Yes

Has the firm undertaken a formal or informal diversity program or set of initiatives aimed at increasing the diversity of the firm?

Yes, formal

How often does the firm's management review the firm's diversity progress/results?

Twice a year

The Stats

Employees: 102,391 (2004, U.S.)
Employees: 100,863 (2003, U.S.)
Revenue: $19.065 billion (2004, U.S.)
Revenue: $17,140 billion (2003, U.S.)

Retention and Professional Development

How do 2004 minority and female attrition rates generally compare to those experienced in the prior year period?

About the same as in prior years

Please identify the specific steps you are taking to reduce the attrition rate of minority and women employees.

• Develop and/or support internal employee affinity groups (e.g., minority or women networks within the firm)
• Succession plan includes emphasis on diversity
• Strengthen mentoring program for all employees, including minorities and women

Diversity Mission Statement

Ensure our employees, owner/operators and suppliers reflect and represent the diverse population McDonald's serves around the world. Harness the multi-faced qualities of our diversity - individual and group differences among our people - as a combined complimentary force to run great restaurants.

The Employer Says

Diversity - It's Everybody's Business

It is our belief that diversity is a shared accountability across the U.S. business.

The Diversity Initiatives Department provides the strategic direction for diversity. This department is charged with developing the internal framework to integrate diversity into business strategies. This framework is delivered through consulting with the Divisions and Home Office Departments to ensure the alignment of diversity initiatives with the Plan to Win key business strategies. The Diversity Initiatives Department serves as brand ambassadors with external organizations to strengthen and optimize McDonald's national partnerships with diverse community, political and educational organizations.

In the spirit of "Diversity - It's Everybody's Business" partnerships across the U.S Field and the U.S. Corporate Departments, diversity has become a part of the fabric of the organization. These partnerships have positioned core diversity strategies to leverage our current strengths and to develop actionable initiatives for areas of diversity development.

Medtronic, Inc.

710 Medtronic Pkwy. NE
Minneapolis, MN 55432-5604
Phone: (763) 514-4000
Fax: (763) 514-4879
www.medtronic.com

Diversity Leadership
Leondias Butcher, Workplace Inclusion Officer
710 Medtronic Parkway
Minneapolis, MN 55432
Phone: (763) 505-2854
Fax: (763) 505-2892
E-mail: leondias.butcher@medtronic.com

Recruiting

Please list the schools/types of schools at which you recruit.

• Ivy League schools
• Other private schools
• Public state schools
• Historically Black Colleges and Universities (HBCUs)
• Other predominantly minority and/or women's colleges

Do you have any special outreach efforts that are directed to encourage minority students to consider your firm?

• Hold a reception for minority students
• Conferences: SWE, AISES, SHPE, NSBE, NBMBA, NSHMBA, NSN
• Advertise in minority student association publication(s)
• Participate in/host minority student job fair(s)
• Sponsor minority student association events
• Firm's employees participate on career panels at school
• Outreach to leadership of minority student organizations
• Scholarships or intern/fellowships for minority students

What activities does the firm undertake to attract minority and women employees?

• Partner programs with women and minority associations
• Participate at minority job fairs
• Seek referrals from other employees
• Utilize online job services
• Other, please specify - Minorities Placement Agencies

Do you use executive recruiting/search firms to seek to identify new diversity hires?

Yes

Internships and Co-ops

Number of interns in the program in summer 2004 (internship) or 2004 (co-op): 150
Length of the program: 12 weeks
Percentage of interns/co-ops in the program who receive offers of full-time employment: 80%
Web site for internship/co-op information: Medtronic.com/Career

Scholarships

Medtronic Scholar

Affinity Groups/Employee Networks

Name of affinity groups: FOCUS, MWC, MECCA, MTA, MLCN, ABLE, MARG, CERG, EXCEL

Strategic Plan and Diversity Leadership

How does the firm's leadership communicate the importance of diversity to everyone at the firm?

Via e-mails, meetings, website

Who has primary responsibility for leading diversity initiatives at your firm?

Art Collins - CEO

Does your firm currently have a diversity committee?

Yes

Has the firm undertaken a formal or informal diversity program or set of initiatives aimed at increasing the diversity of the firm?

Yes, formal

How often does the firm's management review the firm's diversity progress/results?

Quarterly

Diversity Mission Statement

Medtronic's Inclusion Vision Statement

Medtronic seeks to create a culture of inclusion that leverages the benefits of a diverse workforce in fulfilling the needs of our customers, patients, health care providers, suppliers and other constituents while increasing our shareholder value.

Diversity includes many characteristics that may be visible such as race, gender and age, and it also includes less obvious characteristics like personality style, ethnicity, ability, education, religion, job function, life experience, life style, sexual orientation and family situation that make us all similar to and different from one another.

Monsanto

800 N. Lindbergh Blvd.
St. Louis, MO 63167
Phone: (314) 694-1000
Fax: (314) 694-8394
www.monsanto.com

Diversity Leadership
John Nesbitt, Director, Employment Marketing
& College Recruiting
Claire P.Simmons, College Recruiting

Employment Contact
800 No. Lindbergh Blvd
St. Louis, MO 63167

Recruiting

Please list the schools/types of schools at which you recruit.

• Private schools
• Public state schools
• Historically Black Colleges and Universities (HBCUs)

Do you have any special outreach efforts that are directed to encourage minority students to consider your firm?

• Conferences: HACE, MANRRS
• Advertise in minority student association publication(s)
• Firm's employees participate on career panels at school

What activities does the firm undertake to attract minority and women employees?

• Conferences: MANRRS, HACE, BDPA, LULAC
• Participate at minority job fairs

Internships and Co-ops

IT Co-op Program & Internships

Deadline for application: Ongoing
Number of interns in the program in summer 2004 (internship) or 2004 (co-op): 140 combined
Pay: Based on completed year in school; pay is every 2 weeks
Length of the program: IT Co-op 6 months/ Interns 10-12 weeks
Percentage of interns/co-ops in the program who receive offers of full-time employment: Varies
Web site for internship/co-op information: www.monsanto.com
College recruiting: Co-ops (fall and winter) and interns (summer)

The Monsanto Intern Program

This program offers college students on-the-job experience through paid temporary, full-time positions. Participants gain valuable professional experience and develop an insider's understanding of how Monsanto operates. Students typically participate in the Intern Program during their summer semester break. Interns generally work forty hours per week and assignments may vary in length from 10 to 12 weeks during the summer. Internships are for students who wish to explore a career at Monsanto. If you are interested, we encourage you to respond online.

Children of employees can be considered for internships, but must go through the same selection process as all other candidates. If selected, children may not work in any direct or indirect reporting relationship to their parent.

Program requirements

You must be currently enrolled as a full-time student in a Bachelor's, Master's or Ph.D. degree program at an accredited university or be a post-doc. In most cases, you must have completed at least the freshman year. Preferred candidates should have:

- Demonstrated leadership, communication and business acumen
- One of the following majors: accounting, finance, human resources, law, information systems, agronomy, animal science, agricultural business, plant breeding, plant physiology, genetic engineering, chemical engineering, biological sciences, botany, chemistry, or other agricultural-oriented major.
- Interns could be assigned to work in one of the following functional areas: Engineering, Operations, Research & Development, Finance/Accounting, Sales, Animal Ag, Manufacturing/Seed Operations, Technology and Supply Chain.

Selection

Selection is based on student credentials, behavioral-based interview results and the matching of student's skills to available openings.

Program details

- Dates: The Intern Program typically begins in May and continues through August. We usually fill positions by mid-February.
- Locations: We have opportunities located throughout North America and Hawaii. Our headquarters are located in St. Louis, MO.

Logistics

- Transportation - Students are primarily responsible for securing their own transportation to and from the work-site on a daily basis. Monsanto is able to provide information to students regarding carpools, rental cars and public transportation.
- Travel Lump Sum - The Travel Lump Sum provision of the program provides a relocating student with a pre-determined dollar amount based upon the mileage traveled round trip between the city in which the school is located and the city in which the work site is located.

Why you should consider a Monsanto Internship for the summer!

- Networking. You'll interact with senior executives at a variety of meetings and receptions, and interact with each other at First Day Welcome, volunteer activities and social events.
- Professional Developmentt. Your work will be measurable and realistic and allow you to stretch your ability. To give you practice interacting with managers and demonstrating your business acumen, you may be chosen to present a summary of your project work to managers and peers at the end of your internship.
- Guidance. At the start of the summer, we'll help you develop a career development plan, and you'll receive a mid-point and end-of-summer performance evaluation. We'll also pair you with a mentor on an individual basis.
- Compensation. Internship compensation is very competitive.

Affinity Groups/Employee Networks

African Americans in Monsanto; Hispanic Network and Asian Network

The Stats

Employees: 6,317 (as of 5/31/2004, U.S.)
Employees: 6,690 (as of 5/31/2003, U.S.)
Employees: 6,288 (as of 5/31/2004, outside U.S.)
Employees: 6,517 (as of 5/31/2003, outside U.S.)
Employees: 12,605 (as of 5/31/2004, worldwide)
Employees: 13,207 as of 5/31/2003, worldwide)
Revenue (Net Sales): $5.457 billion (2004, worldwide)
Revenue (Net Sales): $4,910 (2003, worldwide)

Diversity Mission Statement

To build an inclusive and diverse organization, which values and engages all of our people's talents and perspectives. To leverage our diversity to achieve outstanding business success overall, and to ensure the growth and acceptance of biotechnology.

This commitment has launched a number of actions. In addition, the importance of diversity is also reflected in our external Pledge under the heading of Respect.

Specifically, we will respect the religious, cultural and ethical concerns of people throughout the world. We will act with integrity, courage, respect, candor, honesty, humility, and consistency. We will place our highest priority on the safety of our employees, the communities where we operate, our customers, consumers, and the environment.

The Employer Says

At Monsanto, we believe diversity is a business imperative. We have created a culture that reinforces diversity. As part of Monsanto's on-going Create a Winning Environment initiative, all employees are encouraged to recognize, appreciate and leverage diversity. People managers and employees alike are trained to look for and appreciate the unique value that each individual brings to work and strive to create a more inclusive environment where everyone can contribute what they can to the collective goals of the organization.

To foster a highly inclusive environment for all, the company offers several different training experiences that range from basic diversity awareness to advanced relationship skills for people managers. In addition, each employee is expected to set at least one DPR goal related to how they will create a more inclusive work environment. Our innovative staffing process seeks to provide a slate of diverse candidates for available positions.

We fundamentally believe that diversity leads to outstanding business success. Our commitment is driven by an urgency to create a Monsanto that better reflects the skills and perspectives required for continued global success.

Some creative examples of our diversity efforts are listed below.

• The Global Diversity Website
• Quarterly featured employee called "Who Am I"
• Town Halls
• Demonstration by African dancers to increase cultural awareness
• Visibility for Network Leads to update organization on activities
• Viewing of CBT's created by employees on local diversity issues

- Pledge report
- Examples of fostering participation and collaboration
- Diversity Fairs
- Networking and sharing
- Poster sessions on what's happening around the world
- Speaker series
- Leadership skills for Asian Pacific Professionals
- Dale Carnegie Training
- Language lessons
- French and Spanish classes offered by employees

Nationwide

1 Nationwide Plaza
Columbus, OH 43215-2220
Phone: (614) 249-7111
Fax: (614) 249-7705
Toll Free: (800) 882-2822
www.nationwide.com/careers/index.htm

Locations (worldwide)

All 50 U.S. states, District of Columbia,
Virgin Islands, Asia, Europe and Latin
America

Diversity Leadership

Candace Barnhardt, AVP, Organizational
Effectiveness Practice

Employment Contact

One Nationwide Plaza 1-01-20
Columbus, Ohio 43215

Recruiting

Please list the schools/types of schools at which you recruit.

• Ivy League schools
• Other private schools
• Public state schools
• Historically Black Colleges and Universities (HBCUs)

Do you have any special outreach efforts that are directed to encourage minority students to consider your firm?

• Hold a reception for minority students
• Advertise in minority student association publication(s)
• Participate in/host minority student job fair(s)
• Sponsor minority student association events
• Firm's employees participate on career panels at school
• Outreach to leadership of minority student organizations
• Scholarships or intern/fellowships for minority students

What activities does the firm undertake to attract minority and women employees?

• Conferences.
• NAACP
• NABA (National Association of Black Accountants)
• National Urban League Conference
• NBMBAA Conference (National Black MBA Association)
• NSHMBA (National Society of Hispanic MBAs)
• NAAAP (National Association of Asian American Professionals)
• Participate at minority job fairs
• Utilize online job services

Do you use executive recruiting/search firms to seek to identify new diversity hires?

No

Internships and Co-ops

Tom Joyner/Nationwide, "On Your Side" internship program

Deadline for application: February 28
Number of interns in the program in summer 2004 (internship) or 2004 (co-op): 20 interns
Pay: Range $10-$15 per hour
Length of the program: 10 weeks
Web site for internship/co-op information: /www.nationwide.com/careers/colrecruiting/undergrad.htm

INROADS

Number of interns in the program in summer 2004 (internship) or 2004 (co-op): 10 interns
Pay: $10-$15 per hour
Length of the program: 12 weeks
Web site for internship/co-op information: www.nationwide.com/careers/colrecruiting/undergrad.htm

Leader Development Institute (LDI) graduate level internship program

Deadline for application: Driven by manager's request (no later than May). Students can post their resume for internship opportunities year round.
Number of interns in the program in summer 2004 (internship) or 2004 (co-op): 12 interns
Pay: $20-$25 per hour
Length of the program: 12 weeks
Percentage of interns/co-ops in the program who receive offers of full-time employment: 2004 - 8 of 12 students rec'd an offer
Web site for internship/co-op information: www.nationwide.com/careers/colrecruiting/grad.htm

Interns Today...Leaders Tomorrow (Corporate Internship Program)

Deadline for application: Driven by manager's request (usually no later than May). Students can post their resume for internship opportunities year round.
Number of interns in the program in summer 2004 (internship) or 2004 (co-op): 168 (includes Tom Joyner, INROADS and LDI programs)
Pay: $10-$25 per hour
Length of the program: 10 - 12 weeks
Percentage of interns/co-ops in the program who receive offers of full-time employment: 40%
Web site for internship/co-op information: www.nationwide.com/careers/colrecruiting/index.htm

Interns are placed in various business units across Nationwide. Placement stems from our managers request. Once they've identified a hiring strategy University Relations works to identify and recruit the best and brightest for that area. Qualified candidates should have at least a 3.0 GPA, status as rising junior or senior, solid academic achievement, strong oral and written communication skills, involvement in various student organizations, prior internship experience (preferred but not a must). Each business unit identifies projects and assignments for their intern.

Our Tom Joyner program requires same qualifications with one addition. Student must be enrolled at a Historically Black College or University.

Qualification for our graduate level internship program - LDI consist of: completion of first year at an accredited MBA program, at least three years work experience, competitive academic performance, coursework concentration in Finance, Marketing, Business or Information Technology. Features of the LDI program include a variety of activities to enhance learning.

Scholarships

Tom Joyner/Nationwide, "On Your Side" Scholarship
(Directly related to the internship program mentioned above.)

Deadline for application for the scholarship program: February
Scholarship award amount: Entire scholarship up to $2500, based on unmet financial need
Web site or other contact information for scholarship: www.nationwide.com/careers/colrecruiting/undergrad.htm

Only interns selected to participate in the Tom Joyner/Nationwide, "On Your Side" internship program are eligible. The scholarship amount is up to $2500 and is based on the student's unmet financial need.

Affinity Groups/Employee Networks

Asian Awareness Network

This group works to network and create awareness and understanding of the Asian cultures within Nationwide through business, social and multi-cultural activities.

Pride Gay & Lesbian Club

This club meets to network on social, service and cultural activities. In addition, the group provides support and other resources for members who seek to improve their relationship with friends or family members who are gay or lesbian.

Raising Interest in Spanish Awareness (RISA)

This group is for those interested in building a more inclusive environment through education, social and business networking. The members participate in a variety of activities including: mentoring Hispanic students, child car seat inspections, job fairs, Latino Festival, and educational and cultural events.

Umoja Network

The mission of the Umoja Network is to recognize, celebrate, educate and raise awareness of the African Amercian contribution. The group promotes a message of inclusion and shares knowledge about topics that are important to success in the workplace and as members of the larger community.

Entry-Level Programs/Full-Time Opportunities

Financial Leadership Rotation Program (FLRP)

Length of program: 2 years
Geographic location(s) of program: Columbus, OH

Please describe the training/training component of this program: Tailored Orientation (2-weeks), Mentoring Partnerships, Project Assignments, Coaching and Feedback, Professional Networking, Recognition through Placement

Nationwide Financial Leader Development Program (NFLDP)

> *Length of program:* 12 months
> *Geographic location(s) of program:* Columbus, OH

Please describe the training/training component of this program: Components include but are not limited to: Coaching Sessions, Team Building, Presentation Skills, Surveys/Assessments, 360 Feedback, Mentoring

Strategic Plan and Diversity Leadership

Who has primary responsibility for leading diversity initiatives at your firm?

Candance Barnhardt, Associate Vice President, Organizational Effectiveness Practice

Does your firm currently have a diversity committee?

Yes

North Carolina Office of State Personnel

116 West Jones Street, 1331
Mail Service Center,
Raleigh, NC 27699-1331
Main Office Number (919) 733-3182
www.osp.state.nc.us

Diversity Leadership
Contact Person: Nellie Riley, Human Resources, Managing Partner

Employment Contact
Charlene Shabazz, HR Partner
116 West Jones Street
Raleigh, NC 27603
Phone: (919) 733-0205
Fax: (919) 733-0653
E-mail: Charlene.Shabazz@ncmail.net

Recruiting

Please list the schools/types of schools at which you recruit.

• Public state schools
• Historically Black Colleges and Universities (HBCUs)
• Other predominantly minority and/or women's colleges

Do you have any special outreach efforts that are directed to encourage minority students to consider your firm?

• Participate in/host minority student job fair(s)
• Outreach to leadership of minority student organizations
• Scholarships or intern/fellowships for minority students

What activities does the firm undertake to attract minority and women employees?

• Partner programs with women and minority associations
• Participate at minority job fairs
• Seek referrals from other employees

Do you use executive recruiting/search firms to seek to identify new diversity hires?

No

Internships and Co-ops

Model Cooperative Education

Deadline for application: Varies by semester
Number of interns in the program in summer 2004 (internship) or 2004 (co-op): 22
Pay: The budget is $69,600.00 for the entire program
Length of the program: 12 weeks
Percentage of interns/co-ops in the program who receive offers of full-time employment: 3%

Qualifications for the Model Cooperative Education Program for the state: at least a 2.00 grade point average, majoring in area that is specified on the position announcement, a resident of North Carolina.

Summer Assistance Department of Transportation

Deadline for application: Varies by semester: April 1st each year
Number of interns in the program in summer 2004 (internship) or 2004 (co-op): 100
Pay: The budget is $75,000.00 for the entire program
Length of the program: 12 weeks
Percentage of interns/co-ops in the program who receive offers of full-time employment: 60%
Web site for internship/co-op information: www.NC DOT.org

This program is for students majoring in Civil Engineering. Must have at least a 2.5 grade point average and 21 semester hours.

Affinity Groups/Employee Networks

No specific names but affinity groups/ networks have been established for African American males and females. Opportunities to network and career development are the reasons the groups have been established.

Entry-Level Programs/Full-Time Opportunities

DOT Assistance Program

Length of program: 18 months
Geographic location(s) of program: Statewide

Please describe the training/training component of this program: New engineers rotate assignments throughout the department.

Please describe any other educational components of this program: Tuition reimbursement, career development assistance with Professional Engineering license.

Strategic Plan and Diversity Leadership

How does the firm's leadership communicate the importance of diversity to everyone at the firm?

E-mails, newsletters, Diversity Council meetings. Diversity is a part of the mission statement for the Office of State Personnel- the Headquarters for the State personnel system that has approximately 88,000 employees subject to the State Personnel Act.

Who has primary responsibility for leading diversity initiatives at your firm?

Nellie Riley-HR Managing Partner-EEO and diversity expert for the state

Does your firm currently have a diversity committee?

Yes

If yes, please describe how the committee is structured, how often it meets, etc.

The Council includes representatives from all demographic groups (women, Veterans, American Indians, Hispanics, African Americans, the disabled and the State's Historically Underutilized Businesses) as well as the director of the NC Human Relations Commission.

If yes, does the committee's representation include one or more members of the firm's management/executive committee (or the equivalent)?

Yes

Please describe the committee.

The Council convenes once a month for two hours. There are 13 committee members. Total executives on the committee: 3.

Does the committee and/or diversity leader establish and set goals or objectives consistent with management's priorities?

Yes. The Office of State Personnel's mission statement includes attracting and retaining a diverse workforce.

Has the firm undertaken a formal or informal diversity program or set of initiatives aimed at increasing the diversity of the firm?

Yes, formal. Special Emphasis Project for African American Males, females, the disabled, older workers and people of color.

How often does the firm's management review the firm's diversity progress/results?

Annually.

How is the firm's diversity committee and/or firm management held accountable for achieving results?

Through the work plans.

The Stats

Employees: 88,000 (2004, U.S.)

Retention and Professional Development

How do 2004 minority and female attrition rates generally compare to those experienced in the prior year period?

Higher than in prior years

Please identify the specific steps you are taking to reduce the attrition rate of minority and women employees.

• Develop and/or support internal employee affinity groups (e.g., minority or women networks within the firm)

• Increase/improve current work/life programs

• Work with minority and women employees to develop career advancement plans

• Strengthen mentoring program for all employees, including minorities and women

• Professional skills development program, including minority and women employees.

• All of the initiatives are being undertaken in the Special Emphasis Project

The Employer Says

The State of North Carolina is committed to diversity through several means which include: A requirement that all new managers and supervisors attend the Equal Employment Opportunity Institute within their first year of appointment; an Executive Order that requires that all occupational categories reflect the diversity of the State; Statewide Diversity Council that was organized by the Office of State Personnel, a specific project- entitled Special Emphasis that focuses on the needs of all demographic groups (women, African American males, older workers, the disabled, people of color and white male inclusion).

NOT ON
MY WATCH.

HOMELAND SECURITY.
IT'S STAYING ONE STEP AHEAD OF THE ENEMY.

**WE COMB THE DATA. RUN POSSIBLE SCENARIOS.
BECAUSE ANTICIPATING A THREAT MEANS WE CAN STOP IT.**

Developing advanced surveillance systems. Providing leading-edge
infrastructure protection. The latest modeling and simulation
facilities. Northrop Grumman is committed to making sure America
is a step ahead of terrorism. It's a career defining challenge where
only the best and the brightest will succeed. Making it perfect for
someone like you.

Achievement never ends.

For current opportunities, please visit our website:
careers.northropgrumman.com

NORTHROP GRUMMAN
DEFINING THE FUTURE™

careers.northropgrumman.com

Northrop Grumman

1840 Century Park East
Los Angeles, CA 90067-2199
Phone: (310) 553-6262
Fax: (310) 553-2076
www.northropgrumman.com

Recruiting

Please list the schools/types of schools at which you recruit.

• Ivy League schools
• Other private schools
• Public state schools
• Historically Black Colleges and Universities (HBCUs)
• Hispanic Serving Institutions (HSIs)
• Native American Tribal Universities
• Other predominantly minority and/or women's colleges

Do you have any special outreach efforts that are directed to encourage minority students to consider your firm?

• Hold a reception for minority students
• *Conferences:* SHPE, NSBE, HENAAC, SWE
• Advertise in minority student association publication(s)
• Participate in/host minority student job fair(s)
• Sponsor minority student association events
• Firm's employees participate on career panels at school
• Outreach to leadership of minority student organizations
• Scholarships or intern/fellowships for minority students
• UNCF, INROADS, United Negro College Fund; provide speakers for minority targeted luncheons & banquets, workshops

What activities does the firm undertake to attract minority and women employees?

• Partner programs with women and minority associations
• *Conferences:* SHPE, AISE, NSBE HENAAC, SWE
• Participate at minority job fairs
• Seek referrals from other employees
• Utilize online job services
• Host/sponsor regional diversity organization monthly meetings

Do you use executive recruiting/search firms to seek to identify new diversity hires?

Yes

Internships and Co-ops

NASA-SHARP & CAMS CA. ACADEMY MATH & SCIENCE, MONSTER DIVERSITY LEADERSHIP PROGRAM

Deadline for application: Varies
Number of interns in the program in summer 2004 (internship) or 2004 (co-op): 632 interns & 128 co-ops
Pay: Varies by location
Length of the program: Flexible to meet student's needs
Percentage of interns/co-ops in the program who receive offers of full-time employment: Varies by business area
Web site for internship/co-op information: DEFINING THE FUTURE.COM

Typically a 3.0 GPA and sophomore status from an accredited college or university is required. Requirements may vary by business unit.

Scholarships

UNCF/NG Diversity Scholarship, HIP Scholarship; Diversity ENS. Scholarship Program

Affinity Groups/Employee Networks

WINGS; Women's Networking Group, Community Practice

Entry-Level Programs/Full-Time Opportunities

Engineering & Business Prof. Dev. Programs (ES); Leadership Training Prog.

Length of program: 15 months
Geographic location(s) of program: Baltimore, MD

Please describe the training/training component of this program: Rotational assignments supported by internal & external coursework
Please describe any other educational components of this program (i.e., tuition reimbursement): Tuition reimbursement; mentoring programs

Strategic Plan and Diversity Leadership

Does your firm currently have a diversity committee?

Yes

Does the committee and/or diversity leader establish and set goals or objectives consistent with management's priorities?

Yes

Has the firm undertaken a formal or informal diversity program or set of initiatives aimed at increasing the diversity of the firm?

Yes, formal

The Stats

Employees: 120,000 (2004, U.S.)
Revenue: $29.853 billion (2004, U.S.)
Revenues: $26.396 billion (2003, U.S.)

Retention and Professional Development

Please identify the specific steps you are taking to reduce the attrition rate of minority and women employees.

• Support to local chapters of minority organizations such as SHPE, WSBE, etc.

Looking for an internship that offers more?

INTERNSHIPS   CAREERS   PERSONAL PLANNING   BUSINESS PLANNING

Learn more. Grow more. Explore more. An internship with the Northwestern Mutual Financial Network allows you to learn about our financial products and share what you know with our clients. Find out more. www.internship.nmfn.com

Northwestern Mutual
FINANCIAL NETWORK®
The Quiet Company.®

Northwestern Mutual Financial Network, The

720 East Wisconsin Avenue,
Milwaukee, Wisconsin 53202-4797
Phone: (414) 271-1444.
www.careers.nmfn.com
www.internship.nmfn.com

Locations (worldwide)
350 locations nationwide

Recruiting

Please list the schools/types of schools at which you recruit.

• Private schools
• Public state schools
• Historically Black Colleges and Universities (HBCUs)
• Hispanic Serving Institutions (HSIs)
• Other predominantly minority and/or women's colleges

Do you have any special outreach efforts that are directed to encourage minority students to consider your firm?

• Advertise in minority student association publication(s): Black Collegian magazine, local ads by many nationwide net work offices.
• Participate in/host minority student job fair(s): Career Conferences of America - Career Forum for Women and Minorities, National Black MBA, National Hispanic MBA.
• Sponsor minority student association events: Many local offices participate in local events; national participation at National Black and Hispanic MBA associations.
• Scholarships or intern/fellowships for minority students: Many network offices offer scholarships at local colleges; however, scholarships do not require students to be financial representative interns or pursue the financial representative career.

What activities does the firm undertake to attract minority and women employees?

• *Partner programs with women and minority associations:*
  • NAACP
  • U.S. Hispanic Chamber of Commerce
  • Women in Insurance and Financial Services
  • Black Enterprise
  • INROADS
• *Conferences:*
  • Career Conferences of America - Career Forum for Women and Minorities
  • National Black MBA
  • National Hispanic MBA
  • NAACP
  • U.S. Hispanic Chamber of Commerce

- Women in Insurance and Financial Services
- Black Enterprise.
- Participate at minority job fairs
- Seek referrals from other employees
- Utilize online job services: Presence on affiliated diversity sites of Yahoo-HotJobs.com, CareerBuilder.com and Monster.com.

Internships and Co-ops

Financial Representative Internship Program*

> ***Deadline for application:*** Ongoing
> ***Number of interns in the program in summer 2004 (internship) or 2004 (co-op):*** 1000 yearly nationwide
> ***Pay:*** Performance-based
> ***Length of the program:*** Internships can span a summer or yearly period and can lead to full-time practice
> ***Percentage of interns/co-ops in the program who receive offers of full-time employment:*** 35%
> ***Web site for internship/co-op information:*** www.internship.nmfn.com

Financial representative interns with the Northwestern Mutual Financial Network have the same opportunities to build their careers as our full-time representatives. Like financial representatives, our interns provide expert guidance and innovative solutions for the planning needs of individuals and businesses in the areas of retirement planning, insurance and investment services, estate planning, business planning, education funding and employee benefits. They strive to understand their clients' goals in order to help develop financial solutions to meet them. Interns have the opportunity to begin developing their own practice, but they are not alone. Supported by our network of specialists, training programs and mentoring opportunities, our interns have access to the resources, products and assistance they need to help their clients and build their practices.

* Financial representatives and financial representative interns are independent contractors, and not employees of Northwestern Mutual.

Strategic Plan and Diversity Leadership

Has the firm undertaken a formal or informal diversity program or set of initiatives aimed at increasing the diversity of the firm?

Yes, formal. Northwestern Mutual has three strategic programs that focus on: increasing diversity in corporate positions, attracting diverse candidates to network offices nationwide and market development for women and minority clientele.

How often does the firm's management review the firm's diversity progress/results?

Quarterly

The Employer Says

Best known as one of the oldest insurance companies in the United States, Northwestern Mutual is the largest direct provider of individual life insurance in the U.S. Although the company has been offering insurance since 1857, today, through its subsidiaries, it also provides financial guidance, estate planning, trust services and a variety of investment products for its customers which are available through appropriately registered representatives and interns. With $124 billion in assets, the company was ranked No. 36 by assets in the 2004 Fortune 500. In March 2005, Fortune named Northwestern Mutual the "most admired life insurance company" for the 22nd straight year.

The Northwestern Mutual Financial Network is the marketing name for the sales and distribution arm of Northwestern Mutual. Together with the company, its subsidiaries and affiliates, the Network's 7,900 financial representatives nationwide distribute life insurance, annuities, mutual funds, long-term care insurance, disability income insurance and employee benefit services to the personal, group employee and executive markets. Among its affiliated companies are those that comprise the Russell Investment Group, which provide investment management and advisory services; Northwestern Mutual Investment Services, LLC (NMIS), the securities brokerage firm; and Northwestern Mutual Trust Company, a special purpose federal savings bank. A subsidiary, Northwestern Long Term Care Insurance Company, offers long-term care insurance.

Office Depot

2200 Old Germantown Rd.
Delray Beach, FL 33445
Phone: (561) 438-4800
Fax: (561) 438-4001
www.officedepot.com/links/jobs

Locations (worldwide)
Headquartered in Delray Beach, FL; world-wide locations

Diversity Leadership
Virgina Rebata, Vice President, Organizational Development

Employment Contact
Daniela Saladrigas, Recruiter
Jewell Crute, College Recruiter
2200 Old Germantown Road
Delray Beach, FL 33445
Phone: (561) 438-4800
Fax: (561) 438-8246
E-mail: collegerelations@officedepot.com

Recruiting

Please list the schools/types of schools at which you recruit.

• Ivy League schools
• Other private schools
• Public state schools
• Historically Black Colleges and Universities (HBCUs)

Do you have any special outreach efforts that are directed to encourage minority students to consider your firm?

• Sponsor minority student association events
• Firm's employees participate on career panels at school
• Outreach to leadership of minority student organizations
• Other: work with INROADS

What activities does the firm undertake to attract minority and women employees?

• Partner programs with women and minority associations
• Conferences: Office Depot Success Strategies for Business Women Conference
• Participate at minority job fairs
• Seek referrals from other employees
• Utilize online job services

Do you use executive recruiting/search firms to seek to identify new diversity hires?

No

Internships and Co-ops

Retail Management Internship Program

Deadline for application: March 15
Number of interns in the program in summer 2004 (internship): 55
Pay: $10-12 per hour
Length of the program: 10 weeks
Web site for internship/co-op information: www.officedepot.com/links/jobs

Corporate Internship Program
(Openings vary from year to year and often exist in IT, Marketing/Merchandising, HR, Finance/Accounting/Tax and others)

Deadline for application: March 15
Number of interns in the program in summer 2004 (internship): 39
Pay: $11-18 per hour
Length of the program: 12 weeks
Web site for internship/co-op information: www.officedepot.com/links/jobs

Office Depot offers several types of paid undergrad internship programs. The programs are highly structured and individualized. Our interns work on meaningful projects, contribute to business units and achieve amazing results. All interns own a project which they ultimately present to senior management. We strive to place successful interns as full-time Office Depot employees after graduation.

Our Retail Management Internship Program is offered at store locations throughout the country. It is designed to expose the intern to the day-to-day life of retail management. The program offers hands-on experience in a fun, fast-paced environment and helps build skills in management, customer service, time management, problem solving and relationship building that the intern can utilize in all future endeavors.

The Corporate Internship Program is based at our Corporate Headquarters in Delray Beach, Florida. Each intern is assigned to a specific division within the company and follows a curriculum created by the specific intern's manager. Opportunities vary from year to year and often exist in the following areas: Information Technology, E-Commerce, Merchandising/Replenishment, Marketing, Finance/Accounting/Tax, Internal Audit, Customer Relations and Human Resources.

Entry-Level Programs/Full-Time Opportunities

Onboarding Program

Length of program: One week
Geographic location(s) of program: Delray Beach, Florida

The one-week program to orient and acclimate new college hires into Office Depot consists of:

• Buddy Programs
• Exposure to executives
• Company History, Values & Culture
• Benefits
• Diversity and Ethics Workshops
• Systems Training

• Team Building Activities
• Transition to Work Discussion
• Store and Warehouse visits
• Touch Base Meetings/Feedback Surveys quarterly for up to 12 months after date of hire

Strategic Plan and Diversity Leadership

How does the firm's leadership communicate the importance of diversity to everyone at the firm?

Web sites, monthly calendars, corporate cultural celebrations, newsletters and e-mails

Who has primary responsibility for leading diversity initiatives at your firm?

Virginia Rebata, Vice President of Organizational Development and Diversity for Office Depot

Does your firm currently have a diversity committee?

Yes. The EVPs, VPs and Directors meet quarterly.

If yes, does the committee's representation include one or more members of the firm's management/executive committee (or the equivalent)?

Yes

Please describe the committee.

> **Total executives on the committee:** 7

Does the committee and/or diversity leader establish and set goals or objectives consistent with management's priorities?

Yes

Has the firm undertaken a formal or informal diversity program or set of initiatives aimed at increasing the diversity of the firm?

Yes, formal

How often does the firm's management review the firm's diversity progress/results?

Quarterly

How is the firm's diversity committee and/or firm management held accountable for achieving results?

We utilize a balance score card to measure all of our executives. The Diversity Committee is an integral part of that score card.

The Stats

Employees: 35,467 (2004, U.S.)
Employees: 33,671 (2003, U.S.)
Revenue: $10 billion (2004, U.S.)
Revenue: $9.7 billion (2003, U.S.)
Revenue: $3.6 billion (2004, outside U.S.)
Revenue: $2.7 billion (2003, outside U.S.)
Revenue: $13.6 billion (2004, worldwide)
Revenue: $12.4 billion (2003, worldwide)

Diversity Mission Statement

At Office Depot, we are committed to creating an inclusive environment where all people are valued and respected. Diversity is an important dimension of respect for the individual-one of our core values-and a key to our success in a global marketplace.

Remember dreaming about the perfect job?

At OSRAM SYLVANIA, our business is the creation of light. As a global lighting leader, our name has defined innovation in the industry. The power behind our vision is our people – a wealth of talented professionals. At the root of our global team is our Associate Development Program – an innovative two-year immersion program that places new associates in the center of our core business functions. Candidates are considered for one of five program tracks: engineering and manufacturing, finance, human resources, information technology, or marketing and sales. Upon completion of the program, successful associates qualify for positions throughout the company. We offer generous compensation and incomparable growth opportunities for luminous minds to excel. Visit www.sylvania.com or your career placement office for more information. We are an EOE.

Osram Sylvania

100 Endicott St.
Danvers, MA 01923 (Map)
Phone: (978) 777-1900
Fax: (978) 750-2152
www.sylvania.com

Locations (worldwide)
United States, Mexico and Canada

Diversity Leadership
Leah Weinberg, Manager of Diversity
Integration and the Associate Development
Program
100 Endicott Street
Danvers, MA 01923
Phone: (978) 750-2761
Fax: (978) 646-6534
E-mail: leah.weinberg@sylvania.com

Recruiting

Please list the schools/types of schools at which you recruit.

• *Ivy League schools:* Cornell
• *Other private schools:* Babson College, Bentley College, Boston College, Boston University, Brandeis University, Bucknell University, Endicott College, Gordon College, Merrimack College, McGill University, Suffolk University, and University of Notre Dame
• *Public state schools:* Bryant University, Georgia Institute of Technology, Massachusetts Institute of Technology, Northeastern University, Northshore Community College, Ohio State University, Pennsylvania State University, Rensselaer Polytechnic Institute, Salem State College, University of Florida-Gainesville, University of Illinois-Urbana Champaign, University of Kentucky, University of Massachusetts-Amherst, University of Massachusetts-Boston, University of Massachusetts-Lowell, University of Toronto, and Virginia Polytechnic Institute and State University
• *Historically Black Colleges and Universities (HBCUs):* Florida A&M University
• *Hispanic Serving Institutions (HSIs):* University of Texas-El Paso
• *Other predominantly minority and/or women's colleges:* Roxbury Community College and University of Monterrey

Do you have any special outreach efforts that are directed to encourage minority students to consider your firm?

• Participate in/host minority student job fair(s)
• Advertise in the Minority College Edition of Diversity/Careers in Engineering and Information Technology

What activities does the firm undertake to attract minority and women employees?

• Participate at minority job fairs
• Seek referrals from other employees
• Utilize online job services

Do you use executive recruiting/search firms to seek to identify new diversity hires?

Yes

Internships and Co-ops

OSRAM SYLVANIA Intern and Co-op Program

Deadline for application: Our program is year-round. We have intern and co-op positions available throughout the year; so resumes are accepted on a continuous basis. For our summer intern and co-op positions, applications are due by April 15.

Number of interns in the program in summer 2004 (internship) or 2004 (co-op): 49

Pay: $470-725 weekly

Length of the program: 12-52 weeks. This depends upon the Intern or Co-op's availability and the needs of the hiring manager.

Percentage of interns/co-ops in the program who receive offers of full-time employment: 14%

Web site for internship/co-op information: An external website for intern and co-op information is currently under development. Anyone interested in an intern or co-op position should send his/her resume to the Intern Coordinator at intern.coordinator@sylvania.com.

Opportunities within our Intern and Co-op Program are available in, but are not limited to, Engineering, Finance and Accounting, Human Resources, Information Technology and Marketing. Availability is based upon the company's needs at any given time.

Affinity Groups/Employee Networks

We presently have six affinity groups/networks in our organization: the African-American, Asian, Disabled, Gay, Lesbian, Bisexual &Transgender, Latino and Women's Networks. The Women's Network currently has two subgroups-the Sales & Marketing Women's Network and the Women In Science and Engineering (WISE) Network. Each of these groups embraces the unique characteristics of, supports and empowers the employees who compose our increasingly diverse workforce.

Entry-Level Programs/Full-Time Opportunities

Associate Development Program

Length of program: 24 months

Geographic location(s) of program: United States, Mexico, Canada, and Germany

Please describe the training/training component of this program: Associates are given three different assignments throughout the company. This rotational component provides both training in and exposure to various areas of our business.

There are formal training programs provided by our Human Resources Training and Development Department. For example, Process Quality Improvement (PQI) is our six-sigma approach to quality/process improvement. There is also a seminar held annually for the associates. This seminar provides additional training opportunities for the associates on a regular basis targeting professional skills development.

Please describe any other educational components of this program (i.e., tuition reimbursement): The mission of the Associate Development Program is to develop both the leadership skills and professional work ethics of the highest quality college graduates, while also providing access to positions of increasing responsibility within OSRAM SYLVANIA. All of this, in turn, works with the company-wide goal of leading OSRAM SYLVANIA to become the number one global lighting manufacturer in the world.

The Program is comprised of six disciplines:

1) Engineering

Engineering at OSRAM SYLVANIA is directly responsible for technological breakthroughs that have revolutionized the world of lighting and precision materials. The scope and diversity of Engineering at OSRAM SYLVANIA are as far-reaching as our achievements. As an Engineering Associate, you will be given assignments in the areas of Research and Development, Product Development, Process Engineering, Equipment Development, Materials Development or Testing and Analysis.

Assignments may include opportunities to:

• Assist in the transfer of technology from pilot stage to full-scale production
• Design and develop innovative processes that result in increased efficiency, quality and cost reduction
• Develop high speed automated assembly equipment
• Introduce new materials for use in lighting and other products

Academic requirements:

• BS or MS in Material Science Engineering, Electrical Engineering, Mechanical Engineering, Chemical Engineering or Ceramic Engineering

2) Finance

OSRAM SYLVANIA's position of leadership in the lighting technology industry and its vision for the future require the Financial Organization to play a key role through continuous improvement in measurement, analysis and resource allocation. Total quality and internal and external customer satisfaction are constant goals. As a Finance Associate, you will be given assignments with immediate exposure to our business.

Assignments are at the corporate, division and plant level and include diverse responsibilities in financial analysis, accounting and internal auditing such as:

• Coordinating and consolidating the development of an annual budget and analyzing results and variances
• Working closely with factory personnel to develop standards, identify cost reduction opportunities and prepare capital expenditure requests
• Developing an integrated reporting system which measures the profitability and key indicators of product lines within a division
• Analyzing historical and forecasted market price trends and recommending short and long term actions to enhance product profitability

Academic requirements:

• BS in Accounting, Business, Finance or Economics
• Minimum of 12 credit hours of accounting

3) Human Resources

With a work force of approximately 11,600 employees, OSRAM SYLVANIA believes its greatest strength is its employees. As a Human Resources Associate, you will apply your skills and academic training toward maximizing employee commitment, satisfaction, and productivity-stated goals of the OSRAM SYLVANIA Human Resources charter.

• Recruiting and selecting new employees whose education, skills and work philosophies match the organization's needs
• Implementing performance management programs that effectively motivate and provide rewards for results
• Developing labor strategies and participating in the resolution of labor negotiations, grievances, and arbitration
• Managing programs that facilitate employee involvement and team problem-solving processes

Academic requirements:

• BS, MS, or MBA in Human Resources Management or Industrial Relations

4) Information Technology

Information technology that provides accurate and timely data for all levels of a corporation is essential to compete in today's business environment. OSRAM SYLVANIA's Corporate Information Technology group is considered "leading edge" in its use of client server technology to ensure that marketing, sales, manufacturing, and financial personnel always have the right information at the right time. OSRAM SYLVANIA's Associate Development Program in Information Technology offers an unequaled opportunity to gain professional competency through real-world business exposure. As an Information Technology Associate, you will be given assignments that focus on different facets of the information technology function such as:

- Being part of the group which is the single point of contact for all OSRAM SYLVANIA business users for the resolution of information technology problems
- Participating as a member of a key information technology project or process team and having the opportunity to do programming, systems design, testing and implementation
- Implementing new technologies associated with network, server, or desktop design and analysis, including working with computer platforms, operating systems,and various network technologies

The program consists of three eight-month assignments rotated over a two-year period to encourage exploration and advance leadership, problem solving, decision-making, and other skills.

Academic requirements:

- BS in Computer Information Systems or related field

5) Manufacturing

The production of quality products using state of the art equipment, in an efficient, cost effective way is the cornerstone of success for a world class manufacturing organization. The OSRAM SYLVANIA Associate Development Program in manufacturing offers an unequaled opportunity to experience this highly technical field, as well as to give you professional competency through real-world business exposure. As a Manufacturing Associate, you will be given challenging opportunities to participate in, or lead, continuous improvement programs such as:

- Analyzing manufacturing processes, recommending and implementing changes to improve material and/or labor efficiencies
- Applying new systems and measurements such as Total Cycle TimeSM, First Pass Yield and ISO 9000 to existing processes to create a streamlined, consistent means of operating departments and business
- Participating in team activities to promote involvement, share ideas and gain the commitment of employees at all levels of the organization
- Supervising a department or work area with responsibility for meeting safety, quality, production, and cost targets

Academic requirements:

- BS or MS in Mechanical Engineering, Electrical Engineering, Material Science, Ceramic Engineering, or Chemical Engineering

6) Marketing and Sales

At OSRAM SYLVANIA, we value innovation not only in product development but also in our approach to the various markets that we serve. From large city skyscrapers to the living room, from rock concerts to the operating table, lighting is an essential part of daily life. As a Marketing/Sales Associate, you will be exposed to the realities of a competitive and rewarding marketplace. Assignments may include the following responsibilities:

- Market planning and research
- Product management
- Sales
- Advertising and promotion
- Training and education
- Competitive analysis
- Logistics and customer service

Academic Requirements:

• BS in Business or Marketing or BA in Liberal Arts

Benefits

While in the program, associates receive the same benefits as all other OSRAM SYLVANIA employees. We offer multiple medical and dental plans, along with a competitive, non-contributory pension program. **Here are some highlights:**

• Indemnity, PPO and HMO medical plans, two dental plans, and a vision plan
• A company match to individual 401(k) investments
• Generous company-paid life insurance benefits with options to buy additional life insurance for oneself, a spouse, and dependents at group rates
• Convenience, care, and income protection benefits including:
• Discounted auto and homeowner's insurance
• Short-term and long-term disability
• Optional long-term care insurance for themselves or a family member
• Physical fitness programs-on-site or through a reimbursement program

Many OSRAM SYLVANIA employees use our educational assistance/tuition reimbursement plan for themselves and our scholarship program for their children. We match employee gifts to schools at all grade levels, and distribute cash grants to organizations with whom our employees volunteer.

Relocation assistance is also available for associates who move more than 50 miles while in the program.

Strategic Plan and Diversity Leadership

How does the firm's leadership communicate the importance of diversity to everyone at the firm?

Letters from executives, emails, an internal diversity website, and diversity topics are communicated at quarterly meetings held by executives.

Who has primary responsibility for leading diversity initiatives at your firm?

Leah Weinberg, Manager of Diversity Integration and the Associate Development Program

Does your firm currently have a diversity committee?

Yes.

The Diversity Council was established by our company president in 2001 "to analyze the diversity situation at OSRAM SYLVANIA and to keep (management) attuned to changes that need to be made if the diversity initiative is to be successful, especially over the long term." The Council is comprised of 21 employees from various business units, one advisor, and one champion. The Council meets four times per year. The council has a chairperson, facilitator and an administrator elected by the council at large on an annual basis. It is organized into five committees focusing on Communications, Training, Recruitment and Retention, Employee Involvement and Metrics.

The goals established by the council are: to develop measurements of success for diversity at OSRAM SYLVANIA and monitor progress; provide management with suggestions for improving diversity at OSRAM SYLVANIA; communicate the benefits of diversity within the company; and provide employees with an avenue to voice their concerns or issues regarding diversity in our facilities without fear of repercussion.

If yes, does the committee's representation include one or more members of the firm's management/executive committee (or the equivalent)?

Yes

If yes, how many executives are on the committee, and in 2004, what was the total number of hours collectively spent by the committee in furtherance of the firm's diversity initiatives?

Two executives, and more than 1,500 hours.

Does the committee and/or diversity leader establish and set goals or objectives consistent with management's priorities?

Yes

Has the firm undertaken a formal or informal diversity program or set of initiatives aimed at increasing the diversity of the firm?

Yes, formal. The council has been tasked with identifying systems required to support diversity, identifying enablers and barriers to success, and making recommendations to management on direction and more specifically on programs and policies. The council has successfully recommended and implemented a mentoring program, a communication program, the start-up of an affinity group network, and others. These programs are designed to support diversity in both employee representation and customer support.

How often does the firm's management review the firm's diversity progress/results?

Quarterly

How is the firm's diversity committee and/or firm management held accountable for achieving results?

The Diversity Council is required to present progress to the Executive Committee each quarter. This includes a review of progress on programs and initiatives as well as making recommendations for future activities. The Manager of Diversity Integration is responsible for achieving the desired results.

The Stats

Total in North America 2004/2003

1. Number of employees: 9,000
2. Revenues: approximately EUR 1.6 billion

Total outside the U.S. 2004/2003

1. Number of employees: 39,200*
2. Revenues: $5.64 billion*

Total worldwide 2004/2003

1. Number of employees: 48,200*
2. Revenues: $7.77 billion*

*Includes OSRAM

Gender and Ethnicity

30.9% is female
69.1% male
9.9% is non-Caucasian
90.1% Caucasian

Retention and Professional Development

Please identify the specific steps you are taking to reduce the attrition rate of minority and women employees.

• Develop and/or support internal employee affinity groups (e.g., minority or women networks within the firm)
• Increase/review compensation relative to competition

- Increase/improve current work/life programs
- Adopt dispute resolution process
- Succession plan includes emphasis on diversity
- Work with minority and women employees to develop career advancement plans
- Strengthen mentoring program for all employees, including minorities and women
- Professional skills development program, including minority and women employees

Diversity Mission Statement

OSRAM SYLVANIA is committed to developing an increasingly diverse workforce with fair and open access to career opportunities. We cultivate an inclusive, supportive climate, thereby enabling us to better meet the needs of our employees and customers. We believe that variety of opinion, approach, perspective, and talent are the cornerstones of a strong, flexible, and competitive company.

The Employer Says

OSRAM SYLVANIA is committed to developing and retaining an increasingly diverse workforce. In the area of recruitment, we are developing a corporate commitment to programs that serve minority student populations, such as INROADS. We are seeking to develop strategic relationships and partnerships with colleges, universities, and professional organizations that have significant female and minority populations. With regard to retention, we are launching programs and strategies that will result in a more diverse and inclusive work environment. These programs include affinity groups and a mentoring program. Increased emphasis is being placed upon diversity in our succession planning. With hard work, careful planning, and execution, along with the powerful commitment of our management team, OSRAM SYLVANIA will become the type of environment where every talented individual will be proud to work.

Owens & Minor

4800 Cox Rd.
Glen Allen, VA 23060-6292
Phone: (804) 747-9794
Fax: (804) 270-7281
www.owens-minor.com

The Employer Says

At Owens & Minor our vision is to be a world class organization that builds its strength through the successful integration of the diverse cultures, backgrounds and experience of our teammates and business partners. Our inclusive environment enhances our efforts as we work to find solutions for our customers and supply chain partners. Each of our teammates, customers, suppliers, as well as the communities we serve has differing views. They trust that we take these views into account as we plan our business. In order for us to be the best we can be, we must clearly understand these diverse needs and perspectives. Strategically, this can be best accomplished by capitalizing on the value of a diverse workforce and supplier base.

We believe that the diversity of our teammates will help our company "deliver" the difference in this increasingly diverse market. At Owens & Minor we look toward our leadership team to:

• establish diversity as a key component of how we conduct business
• encourage all teammates to support Owens & Minor's diversity plan and diversity efforts
• measure the success of the team at achieving specific goals for hiring, developing, promoting, and retaining teammates in underrepresented or underutilized job groups and businesses.

It is our belief that diversity and business success go hand in hand.

PACIFICARE CAREERS: Envision. Innovate. Accomplish.

As one of the nation's leading consumer health organizations, PacifiCare seeks high achievers who believe, as we do, that "Caring is Good. Doing Something is Better.^{SM}"

We are a company of action, developing innovative health solutions that make a difference in people's lives, like our Consumer Health Initiatives for Asians, African-Americans and Latinos, designing products and services specifically tailored to meet the needs of the diverse communities we serve.

At PacifiCare, we also believe we are stronger because of our differences. We are actively seeking a diverse workforce of knowledge experts to create the future of health care. To begin on this extraordinary path, visit us online at www.pacificare.com and explore the many opportunities throughout PacifiCare's family of companies.

PacifiCare®

Caring is good. Doing something is better.^{SN}

PacifiCare Health Systems, Inc.

5995 Plaza Dr.
Cypress, CA 90630
Phone: (714) 952-1121
Fax: (714) 226-3581
www.pacificare.com/

Locations (worldwide)

Corporate headquarters in Cypress, CA, regional offices throughout California, Arizona, Texas, Colorado, Oklahoma, Nevada, Oregon, Washington, and in Green Bay, WI. Sales offices and other support centers nationwide.

Diversity Leadership

Kate Kanne, Vice President, Brand & Consumer Initiatives

Employment Contact

Sherri Bliss, Program Manager, Employment Branding, Talent Acquisition Department
5995 Plaza Drive
Cypress, CA 90630
Phone: (714) 952-1121
Fax: (714) 226-3787
E-mail: diversity@phs.com

Recruiting

Please list the schools/types of schools at which you recruit.

• *Private schools:* University of Southern California (USC), The Claremont Colleges, Azusa Pacific University
• *Public state schools:* California State Long Beach, San Diego and Fullerton; University of California Los Angeles, Santa Barbara, Irvine, Berkeley, and Santa Clara; University of Pennsylvania; University of Rochester; University of Colorado at Boulder

Do you have any special outreach efforts that are directed to encourage minority students to consider your firm?

• Participate in/host minority student job fair(s)
• Sponsor minority student association events
• Firm's employees participate on career panels at school

What activities does the firm undertake to attract minority and women employees?

• Partner programs with women and minority associations
• Conferences:
• Women of Color Town Hall
• C200 Annual conference for women entrepreneurs
• Participate at minority job fairs
• Seek referrals from other employees
• Utilize online job services

Do you use executive recruiting/search firms to seek to identify new diversity hires?

No

Internships and Co-ops

Actuarial Summer Internship Program

Deadline for application: March 31st annually

Number of interns in the program in summer 2004: 5

Pay: $13-15 per hour

Length of the program: 10 weeks

Percentage of interns/co-ops in the program who receive offers of full-time employment: Since inception in 1999, approximately 50% of the interns have been offered full-time positions.

Web site for internship/co-op information: www.pacificare.com, employment, college recruitment

The Actuarial Summer Internship Program (ASIP) at PacifiCare is a 10-week program from June to September, with flexible start and end dates depending on each intern's summer schedule. Interns will work 40 hours per week at either the Cypress or Santa Ana office in Orange County, California. Salary is competitive and will take into account any actuarial exams passed.

Interns will work on projects ranging from product pricing, provider contract analysis, reserves calculation to financial reporting. During the process, interns will go through various training programs to learn more about the managed care industry, PacifiCare's business models, and how to use database query language and Microsoft applications to perform actuarial calculations. Interns will also be guided through the examination preparation process in a full-time work setting, and study materials will be provided for the November exam sitting.

Qualifications:

• Working toward a bachelor's or master's degree in Mathematics, Statistics, Actuarial Science or other major with rel evant experience;

• At least junior standing with minimum 3.2 GPA;

• Strong computer, analytical and communication skills;

• Completion of one actuarial exam preferred; however, candidates with high GPA and analytical skill will be consid ered.

Scholarships

The scholarship program outlined below is for high school seniors going into college.

Latino Health Scholars Program

Deadline for application for the scholarship program: June 30th annually

Scholarship award amount: 70 $2,000 total scholarships and two $25,000 total scholarships available

Web site or other contact information for scholarship: www.pacificare.com , and www.pacificarelatino.com

PacifiCare introduced the PacifiCare Latino Health Scholars Program in 2003 to address the critical shortage of Spanish speakers in the educational pipeline for health professions. Under the program, PacifiCare offers annual scholarships of $2,000 each for bilingual, bicultural high school students interested in pursuing careers in the health care industry. In 2004, PacifiCare increased the number of scholarships available from 33 to 50, for a two-year total scholarship opportunity of $166,000. Through this program, PacifiCare hopes to reverse what is currently a widening gap between the Latino population and the number of bilingual and bicultural professionals in the health care field.

For 2005, PacifiCare is further expanding its Latino Health Scholars program to include – in addition to the 70 $2,000 scholarships the company will award this fall – two $25,000 scholarships for the most deserving bilingual and bicultural students dedicated to pursuing careers in health care. These two scholarships, entitled the PacifiCare Freedom Award, recognize outstanding individuals and organizations that have demonstrated tremendous sacrifice and commitment to make a positive difference in our communities. The award was inspired by the heroic actions of U.S. Marine Sgt. Rafael Peralta who was killed last November by enemy action in Iraq. Fighting alongside his fellow marines in Falluja, Peralta, wounded by gunshots, reached out for a grenade that was hurled by an insurgent and cradled it to his body to protect others from the blast. His heroism saved the lives of five of his fellow Marines.

Affinity Groups

Asian, Latino, African American, and Women's Resource Groups

PacifiCare's Asian, Latino, African-American, and Women's resource groups focus on specific target markets in several states. Leadership and meeting structure varies for each group. The resource groups receive guidance and strategic directions from a committee called the Diversity Leadership Team, which is a group of individuals selected by the Diversity Council to assist in the implementation of the diversity initiative across the regions.

Resource group members influence product design by participating in focus groups to provide employee perspectives on products and services for target market segments, participate in community health awareness programs, and help ensure our work environment addresses the needs of our diverse employees. For example, the Asian Resource Group members assisted the Customer Service department in interviewing customer service associates for the newly established Chinese Language Line. The Latino Resource Group represented the company in local health fairs targeting diabetes among Hispanics. In addition, resource groups coordinate seminars and other events to provide professional development opportunities for employees.

Diversity Champions Network

PacifiCare's first employee network was a virtual community called the Diversity Champions and currently numbers more than 700 employees of all backgrounds. These employees belong to the network because they have an interest in furthering PacifiCare's efforts to realize its strategic vision for diversity. Employees receive updates on diversity activities and initiatives, and are asked to provide feedback to assist PacifiCare in achieving its diversity goals. In addition, they also receive invitations to participate in community outreach, in seminars to promote professional development, and other diversity-related activities.

Entry-Level Programs/Full-Time Opportunities

Achieving Career Excellence (ACE) program for recent college graduates

> *Length of program:* 8 months
> *Geographic location(s) of program:* Cypress, CA

Please describe the training/training component of this program: The Achieving Career Excellence (ACE) Program in the California Customer Service Center, Cypress, California, is an 8-month program from June to February for recent college graduates to learn and grow in the healthcare industry. Candidates will rotate through all areas of Operations including Claims, Membership Accounting and Customer Service to learn critical processes and contribute in selected project work. An adjunct to the ACE program is an association with a mentor in a managerial or director position. The mentorship program will also assist in developing these Operations Trainees for future positions within the company. Candidates will apply for positions in Western Region Customer Service Center Operations at the end of program.

Please describe any other educational components of this program: A company-wide benefit at PacifiCare is $4,000 tuition reimbursement annually.

Qualifications:

- BA/BS Degree
- GPA of 3.0
- Desire to pursue a career in healthcare operations
- Highly motivated with exceptional communication, analytical, organizational, leadership and interpersonal skills
- Knowledge of Microsoft office suite

Strategic Plan and Diversity Leadership

How does the firm's leadership communicate the importance of diversity to everyone at the firm?

Senior Executives work with the Diversity Council to coordinate the communication efforts around diversity, using the theme of "Everyone Matters." There is an Intranet site dedicated to the diversity initiative, and an Internet site is planned for launch later this year. Diversity bulletin boards are present at several local offices. Members of the Diversity Council and regional Diversity Leadership Team frequently give presentations at all-employee forums, departmental staff meetings, and executive management meetings. In addition, the Council and our diverse Consumer Initiatives groups sponsor activities to celebrate ethnic holidays. For example, during the recent Lunar New Year, employees were encouraged to submit responses to questions related to the holiday's history and traditions for entry into a drawing. Employees and their children were also invited to participate in a coloring contest to celebrate the recent Martin Luther King, Jr. holiday. These types of activities further increase diversity awareness among PacifiCare employees.

Who has primary responsibility for leading diversity initiatives at your firm?

Joseph Konowiecki, Executive Vice President, Corporate Affairs and General Counsel

Does your firm currently have a diversity committee?

Yes

If yes, please describe how the committee is structured, how often it meets, etc.

PacifiCare has a formal Diversity Council to champion specific programs, develop measurable diversity goals and help keep PacifiCare focused on achieving those goals. The Diversity Council is a strategic committee, the main task of which is to implement PacifiCare's strategic vision for diversity. Members consist of individuals across functional areas who were appointed by executive management.

To assist in the implementation of the diversity initiative throughout the enterprise, the Diversity Council, along with executive management, selected several individuals to become a part of the Diversity Leadership Team in each state. Members consist of two to eight individuals per state, across functional areas and job levels. Leadership and meeting structure varies for each team. One of the important tasks for the teams is to provide guidance to resource/affinity groups in their efforts to provide tactical and hands-on support to key diversity initiatives. The Diversity Leadership Teams receive strategic direction from the Diversity Council and communicate with the Council on a regular basis.

If yes, does the committee's representation include one or more members of the firm's management/executive committee (or the equivalent)?

Yes

If yes, how many executives are on the committee, and in 2004, what was the total number of hours collectively spent by the committee in furtherance of the firm's diversity initiatives? How many employees are on the committee, and how often does the committee convene in furtherance of the firm's diversity initiatives?

Total executives on the committee: 3

The Diversity Council consists of 12 employees at the manager and above level. A bi-weekly 1-hour teleconference meeting is conducted on an ongoing basis to discuss progress and make strategic decisions. The Council also meets twice a year for an in-person summit. As mentioned in #2 above, the Diversity Leadership Team members assist the Council in its efforts to implement the diversity initiative across the regions. Thirty employees belong to the Diversity Leadership Team. Frequency of meeting among the Diversity Leadership Team members varies by state. All teams meet annually at the corporate headquarter for a summit.

Approximately 2,100 hours were spent collectively by the Diversity Council, and an additional 900 hours by the Diversity Leadership Team last year. Taking into account both efforts, PacifiCare spent approximately 3,000 hours last year in launching and managing the Strategic Diversity Initiative.

Does the committee and/or diversity leader establish and set goals or objectives consistent with management's priorities?

Yes. The Diversity Council receives strategic guidance from the executive sponsor who reports directly to the Chairman and CEO. The Council also meets once a year with the Office of the Chairman members, who are senior executives at the highest level in the company. At these meetings, progress is reviewed and goals are established.

Has the firm undertaken a formal or informal diversity program or set of initiatives aimed at increasing the diversity of the firm?

Yes, formal. To expand the pursuit of diversity in helping PacifiCare achieve its business goal, the Diversity Council developed the strategic vision for diversity. This vision guides everything related to the Strategic Diversity Initiative. The vision states that as a result of the diversity efforts, PacifiCare will be stronger in four specific and measurable ways:

- Membership growth: PacifiCare will experience an increase in profitable commercial and senior membership among diverse populations.
- Better health outcomes and reduced health care costs: PacifiCare will experience lower health care costs for its members in diverse populations.
- A representative employee population: PacifiCare's employee population will, to the extent possible, reflect the diverse populations in the markets where we do business.
- A culture that embraces diversity: It will be clear to everyone who works at PacifiCare or does business with us that PacifiCare embraces diversity.

Consistent with best practices research, the Diversity Council established employee networks in 2004 to implement the diversity initiative throughout the company. All activities conducted to further the initiative were guided by the above strategic visions for diversity. Details regarding the Diversity Leadership Team and the resource/affinity groups are included in earlier sections of this survey.

How often does the firm's management review the firm's diversity progress/results?

Once a year.

How is the firm's diversity committee and/or firm management held accountable for achieving results?

All members of the Diversity Council and the Diversity Leadership Team have a diversity goal as part of their formal performance planning and review process. In addition, specific departments such as Human Resources implemented specific metrics to measure diversity recruitment, retention, and other related initiatives. Efforts are underway to establish comprehensive and formal diversity metrics.

The Stats

Employees: 7,800 (2004, U.S.)
Employees: 7,200 (2003, U.S.)
Revenue: $12 billion (2004, U.S.)
Revenue: $11 billion (2004, U.S.)

In 2004, almost 44 percent of all exempt open positions were filled with ethnic minorities, creating an internal work force composed of 48 percent ethnic minorities, an increase of almost 12 percent from December 2003, including 29 percent of management positions. Women comprise 73 percent of our workforce, including 60 percent of management positions.

Retention and Professional Development

Please identify the specific steps you are taking to reduce the attrition rate of minority and women employees.

• Develop and/or support internal employee affinity groups (e.g., minority or women networks within the firm)
• Increase/review compensation relative to competition
• Increase/improve current work/life programs
• Work with minority and women employees to develop career advancement plans

Diversity Mission Statement

At PacifiCare, we seek a diverse workforce of knowledge experts to provide the best, most cost effective, products and services while improving the health of the diverse communities we serve.

The Employer Says

As one of the nation's leading consumer health organizations, PacifiCare values diversity as a business philosophy above and beyond standalone programs and events. We understand that our diverse customers are best served by knowledgeable employees who are sensitive to their needs. Our goal is to continuously improve our hiring, training and retention activities to develop a diverse work force of experts committed to creating innovative, culturally relevant health products, information portals and customer-service experiences that aim to alleviate discrepancies in access to and utilization of quality health care.

PacifiCare's Consumer Health Initiatives, which include African American, Asian American, Latino, and Women's Health Solutions represent PacifiCare's commitment to develop and enhance products and services specifically designed to address the unique health care needs of our diverse consumers and to help build stronger ties with diverse members and organizations, including physicians, brokers, employers and individual consumers. Consumer Health Initiatives goals include improving healthcare outcomes by creating culturally relevant educational portals on-line and outreach programs within the communities where we do business. For example, in 2004, PacifiCare's African American Health Solutions and LLuminari, Inc., a national health firm, co-sponsored a community health initiative in Los Angeles called "We Matter," delivering life-saving diabetes information, prevention techniques and teaching tools to African Americans, a group disproportionately affected by this deadly disease. Our Latino Health Solutions was recognized by the American Heart Association as a Health Honoree for the association's fourth annual Corazones Unidos (Hearts United) gala in recognition of the numerous health education materials we developed in Spanish. And, our Asian American Markets program participated in the San Fernando Chinese New Year celebration and 106th annual Golden Dragon Parade in Los Angeles, where we entered a float on parade day and maintained an exhibition booth for the entire Chinese New Year celebration.

In acknowledgement of our exemplary diversity efforts in 2004, we received tremendous recognition as an Employer of Choice:

• PacifiCare selected a Top Ten Company for Asian Americans by Asian Enterprise Magazine
• PacifiCare selected as one of the 50 best companies for Latinas by LATINA Style Magazine
• PacifiCare named to the Hispanic Magazine Corporate 100, an annual list recognizing companies nationwide that have raised the bar when it comes to employing, working with and serving the burgeoning Hispanic population."
• PacifiCare honored as Corporation of the Year by The Black Chamber of Commerce of Orange County for its efforts to improve the health of the diverse communities served by the managed-care insurance firm.
• PacifiCare recognized by Catalyst as being in the top 25 percent of companies for gender diversity in top management positions

The more opinions, ideas and perspectives a company can generate, the greater the chances for success. At Pearson Education, this is the guiding principle that has positioned us as the world's leading integrated education business.

Whether through our diverse publishing operations or our extensive online education resources, the world at Pearson reflects the world at large. Diverse, collaborative, and always exciting. We welcome anyone who feels that they can contribute to the continuing success of Pearson to apply and become part of our team.

Thank you to INROADS and all our Interns whose talents have contributed to the success of our business!

The world's leading educational publisher.
www.pearsoned.com

Pearson Education

1 Lake St.
Upper Saddle River, NJ 07458
Phone: (201) 236-7000
Fax: (201) 236-3290
www.pearsoned.com/careers

Locations (worldwide)

U.S.: Upper Saddle River (NJ) • New York
(NY), White Plains (NY) • Boston (MA),
Glenview & Champaign (IL) • San
Francisco • Parsippany (NJ) • Indianapolis •
Mesa (AZ) • Old Tappan (NJ) • Columbus
(OH) • Eagan & Bloomington (MN) •
Arlington (VA) • Iowa City (IA), Lawrence
(KS) • and others
International: Canada • South America •
Europe • India • Middle East • Africa,
Asia • Australia & New Zealand

Diversity Leadership

Christine Pfeiffer, Diversity Team Leader
Ryan Darlington, College Recruiting

Employment Contact

Anne Adamo, Manager, Employee Relations
One Lake Street
Upper Saddle River, NJ 07458
Phone: (201) 236-3419
Fax: (201) 236-3381
E-mail: anne.adamo@pearsoned.com

Recruiting

Please list the schools/types of schools at which you recruit.

• *Ivy League schools:* Princeton, Harvard, Yale
• *Other private schools:* Marist, William Patterson, Fairleigh Dickinson, St. Thomas Aquinas, Columbia, Vassar, NYU
• *Public state schools:* Rutgers, SUNY
• *Other predominantly minority and/or women's colleges:* Quinnipiac

Do you have any special outreach efforts that are directed to encourage minority students to consider your firm?

• Conferences: Monster Diversity Leadership Program
• Participate in/host minority student job fair(s)
• Sponsor minority student association events
• Firm's employees participate on career panels at school

What activities does the firm undertake to attract minority and women employees?

• Participate at minority job fairs
• Seek referrals from other employees
• Utilize online job services
• MonsterDiversity.com
• America's Job Bank.com

Do you use executive recruiting/search firms to seek to identify new diversity hires?

No

Internships and Co-ops

Pearson Intern Program

Deadline for application: March 1
Number of interns in the program in summer 2004 (internship) or 2004 (co-op): 100 at multiple locations throughout the US
Pay: varies
Length of the program: Minimum 8 weeks during June/July/August
Percentage of interns/co-ops in the program who receive offers of full-time employment: varies by position / location
Web site for internship/co-op information: www.pearsoned.com/careers

Establish and maintain a Summer College Intern Program that enables Pearson to recruit and train a diverse group of people for careers in publishing by providing students an opportunity to expand their theoretical knowledge, clarify their career goals and enhance opportunities for full time employment. Students will be placed in departments that suit their interests, as well as, their major course of study. The departmental structure includes corporate functions, editorial, marketing, sales, production, design, and human resources.

Entry-Level Programs/Full-Time Opportunities

General Accounting Program

Length of program: 2 years
Geographic location(s) of program: Upper Saddle River Facility

Please describe the training/training component of this program: Hands-on experience in 4 major accounting areas

Please describe any other educational components of this program(i.e., tuition reimbursement): Tuition reimbursement is offered, but as company policy, not just for this program

Strategic Plan and Diversity Leadership

Who has primary responsibility for leading diversity initiatives at your firm?

Christine Trum, Senior VP Human Resources

Does your firm currently have a diversity committee?

Yes

If yes, please describe how the committee is structured, how often it meets, etc.

Diversity Council meets Quarterly, includes Executive Management

If yes, does the committee's representation include one or more members of the firm's management/executive committee (or the equivalent)?

Yes

Total executives on the committee: 9

Does the committee and/or diversity leader establish and set goals or objectives consistent with management's priorities?

Yes

Has the firm undertaken a formal or informal diversity program or set of initiatives aimed at increasing the diversity of the firm?

Yes, formal. HR Diversity Team, Metrics, Internship Program, Training Initiatives

How often does the firm's management review the firm's diversity progress/results?

Quarterly

How is the firm's diversity committee and/or firm management held accountable for achieving results?

Diversity metrics and practices are reviewed by the Pearson plc Board each year. Goals are set and scrutinized annually.

The Stats

Employees, Pearson U.S: 16,000 (2004)
Employees, Pearson Education: 7,383 (2004)
Revenue, Pearson Education: $563 million (2004)

Retention and Professional Development

Please identify the specific steps you are taking to reduce the attrition rate of minority and women employees.

• Develop and/or support internal employee affinity groups (e.g., minority or women networks within the firm)
• Increase/improve current work/life programs
• Succession plan includes emphasis on diversity
• Strengthen mentoring program for all employees, including minorities and women
• Professional skills development program, including minority and women employees

Diversity Mission Statement

We want to be: (1) A diverse company – To attract the very best candidates, at all levels, regardless of race, gender, age, physical ability, religion or sexual orientation. We always try to hire the best person for the job, and to ensure that our candidate pool is diverse, and our hiring is non-discriminatory. (2) A fair company – To ensure that pay, retention, promotions and terminations are determined without regard to race, gender, age, physical ability, religion or sexual orientation. (3) A company which uses diversity to help achieve its commercial goals and targets new opportunities in growing markets.

The Employer Says

Pearson Education is the worldwide education business of Pearson plc, the international media group.

Educating 100 million people, Pearson Education is the global leader in integrated education publishing. With such renowned brands as Pearson Prentice Hall, Pearson Scott Foresman, Pearson Addison Wesley, Pearson Allyn & Bacon, Pearson NCS and many others, we provide quality content, assessment tools and educational services in all available media to a worldwide marketplace, spanning the learning curve from birth through college and beyond. With over a thousand textbook companion web

sites, interactive courseware and online professional learning; Pearson Education is the world's largest integrated education business. Internationally, we operate in 55 countries and 27 languages and have more global publishing than any other competitor.

As the world's leading integrated education business, we take great pride in a reputation that has been established by acquiring the top talent in our industry. We firmly believe that helping our employees succeed in the dizzying whirl of modern life makes good business sense and is critical to our maintaining our leadership position. Pearson continues to consistently attract and retain the best talent available in the marketplace.

In all we do, Pearson, and the people who work for it, aspire to be brave, imaginative and decent. Our people are our most important asset.

Pearson is a recipient of the following INROADS Awards: Bronze Corporate Spirit Award for leadership in fully making the INROADS mission a part of our daily work; Growth Award for significantly increasing the number of INROADS internships; and Business Advisor of the Year to our Corporate INROADS Liaison. We are also the recipient of the Garden State SHRM Best Practices in Diversity Award.

In addition, Pearson offers Work/Life programs including Flexible Work Arrangements, Tuition Assistance, Matching Gifts, Scholarship Program, Parental and Serious Illness in the Family Leave, Emergency Back-Up Childcare Services, Adoption Assistance, Community-Based Childcare, Resource and Referral Program, Employee Assistance Program, paid personal and sick days, paid holiday and vacation time, support groups, and Medical/Dental/Vision Benefits. Because of these programs, Pearson has been recognized as one of the 100 Best Companies for Working Mothers for five consecutive years.

Our outreach efforts in our local communities include: Jumpstart, the Pearson Teacher Fellowship, Day of Caring, Time to Read, and drives for food, back-to-school supplies, gifts for seniors, military packets, toys and blood. Pearson also provides support to AIDS Walk, Making Strides Against Breast Cancer, March of Dimes and American Cancer Society Daffodil Days.

Pearson offers a variety of employee training and education programs via classroom, audio, video and the Web.

www.pearsoned.com/careers – Pearson is an Equal Opportunity Employer.

Pitney Bowes

1 Elmcroft Rd.
Stamford, CT 06926-0700
Phone: (203) 356-5000
Fax: (203) 351-7336
Toll Free: (800) 672-6937
www.pb.com/careers

Locations (worldwide)
We have locations in 130 countries

Contact Person
Michael Holmes, Director, Strategic Talent
Management & Diversity Leadership

Diversity Leadership
Denise Rawles-Smith, Manager, Diversity
Christine Castellano, Diversity Specialist
1 Elmcroft Road, MSC 51-46
Stamford, Connecticut 06926
Phone: (203) 351-7910
Fax: (203) 348-1289
E-mail: denise.rawles@pb.com

Recruiting

Please list the schools/types of schools at which you recruit.

• *Private schools:* Columbia University, Rensselaer Polytechnic Institute (RPI), Rochester Institute Technology (RIT), Fairfield University
• *Public state schools:* University of Connecticut and the University of Waterloo

Do you have any special outreach efforts that are directed to encourage minority students to consider your firm?

We participate in the colleges' and universities' job fairs

What activities does the firm undertake to attract minority and women employees?

• Partner programs with women and minority associations
• Conferences: National Black MBA, National Society of Hispanic MBAs, National Society of Black Engineers, Society of Women Engineers
• Participate at minority job fairs: National Urban League, Diversity Career Fair and job fairs at National Black MBA, National Society of Hispanic MBAs, National Society of Black Engineers, Society of Women Engineers
• Seek referrals from other employees
• Utilize online job services
• We advertise our career opportunities in diverse publications such as Hispanic Business, DiversityInc., NSBE SWE, Asian Enterprise. We also participate in the INROADS internship process every year.

Do you use executive recruiting/search firms to seek to identify new diversity hires?

Yes

Internships and Co-ops

INROADS

> *Number of interns in the program in summer 2004 (internship) or 2004 (co-op):* 14 interns
> *Pay:* $12.50 to $16.00 per hour
> *Length of the program:* 12 weeks
> *Percentage of interns/co-ops in the program who receive offers of full-time* employment: 66%
> *Web site for internship/co-op information:* www.pb.com/careers

In response to our hiring requirements, INROADS screens and selects a slate of high potential talent for Pitney Bowes to interview at the annual INROADS Corporate Interview Day (CID). At the CID Pitney Bowes Human Resource professionals interview and select candidates with demonstrated academic achievement, leadership potential, and community involvement. Once an offer has been made, the Pitney Bowes Program Office works with various hiring departments to structure an assignment plan for each intern. Assignments are determined based on each individual's educational background and career goals, as well as the business needs of Pitney Bowes. Interns are matched with Pitney Bowes managers that demonstrate a strong mentoring track record and a need for entry-level personnel. Each intern is placed in a challenging work assignment with a manager that is committed to his or her career development. Performance and development discussions provide interns with a formal review of their work performance, academic progress and career goals. These discussions take place at the mid-point and at the end of the summer assignment.

Engineering Co-op/Intern

> *Deadline for application:* Varies on time of year
> *Number of interns in the program in summer 2004 (internship) or 2004 (co-op):* 42
> *Pay:* $17.00 to $26.00 per hour
> *Length of the program:* 3 to 6 months
> *Percentage of interns/co-ops in the program who receive offers of full-time* employment: 5%
> *Web site for internship/co-op information:* www.pb.com/careers

Most Pitney Bowes co-ops are headquartered in the Technology Center in Shelton, Connecticut, the heart of the company's R&D and product development efforts. The different project teams that co-ops are assigned to help In developing total solutions for improving the efficiency and effectiveness of business communications.

TechCenter project leaders hire co-ops on Engineering teams on a project-by-project basis, drawing from four functional groups:

- Mechanical/Electrical/Systems
- Software
- Product Usability and Design, and
- Technical Support/Operations

Co-ops find support for their career development on the functional side while working toward specific deadlines and output goals on their various product assignments.

Pitney Bowes' Advanced Concepts in Technology, a unit dedicated to capturing the advantages of technologies likely to emerge in the next ten years, also employs engineers on its research and development projects.

Entry-Level Programs/Full-Time Opportunities

Pitney Bowes TechCentral Professional Development Program (PDP)

Length of program: 3 year rotational program
Geographic location(s) of program: Connecticut

The Pitney Bowes TechCentral Professional Development Program (PDP) is a rotational program to develop Technical and Managerial leaders within our IT organization. The program offers challenging "real job" assignments based on individual's specific education, experience, development needs, and interests. It consists of two or three assignments over a three-year period, followed by a final placement. Throughout the three years, participants can expect to be provided with:

• Exposure to Business Leaders across Pitney Bowes
• Work assignments with challenge and learning opportunities
• Personal development coaching & feedback
• Opportunities to network with peers

The program approach is to hire extremely talented people, nurture their growth and give them opportunities to make an impact. We are working to identify great technical talent and to assist them in acquiring the unique skills and experiences they need to excel in their careers.

Pitney Bowes has a culture of continuous learning and encourages all employees to take advantage of training. Depending on the need, participants are provided with the foundation needed to increase responsibilities and develop as business contributors. The program staff provides additional feedback and coaching to program members. Each participant assignment presents opportunities to develop key competencies and advanced technical & business skills, gain exposure to Pitney Bowes' diverse Business Operations and interact with Senior Management.

Strategic Plan and Diversity Leadership

How does the firm's leadership communicate the importance of diversity to everyone at the firm?

We have developed a comprehensive Diversity Communications strategy to inform employees and our key audiences about our diversity initiatives and to develop strategic partnerships with key diverse communities and key organizations within those communities. We want to convey to them that Pitney Bowes is a company that values diversity and that we welcome them as employees/potential employees, customers, suppliers and stakeholders. We also use CEO voicemails, town hall meetings, intranet announcements, articles in internal publications, diversity forums and events, e-mail communications, diversity leadership councils, diversity marketing collateral and training to communicate the importance of diversity to our employees.

Who has primary responsibility for leading diversity initiatives at your firm?

Susan Johnson, Vice President, Strategic Talent Management & Diversity Leadership

Does your firm currently have a diversity committee?

No

Does the committee and/or diversity leader establish and set goals or objectives consistent with management's priorities?

Yes. Diversity governance is an enterprise wide initiative, which includes accountability to the CEO and Board level. The CEO receives detailed reports regarding diversity, LRP (Succession Planning), as well as performance assessments. In addition, Business Unit Presidents and their direct reports, including senior corporate staff, are held accountable for the success of diversity initiatives within their individual business units. Diversity is an objective of senior management and the Board of Directors and is enforced by tying compensation to successful completion of the diversity objective. The Diversity Strategic Planning process outlines goals for the company and places responsibility for meeting those goals in the hands of employees organized into

what is known as our Diversity Leadership Councils. Through these councils, we have diversity champions throughout all of Pitney Bowes who are actively engaged to help foster employee involvement.

Has the firm undertaken a formal or informal diversity program or set of initiatives aimed at increasing the diversity of the firm?

Yes, formal. The 2005 Diversity Strategy is a 3-pronged approach. It outlines initiatives that we feel are of strategic importance to the overall business objectives. The first element of the Diversity Strategy outlines initiatives from an enterprise level and explains the work that we are doing from a corporate perspective. As a business partner, we want to ensure that the work we are doing at the corporate level is aligned with the business units to help them achieve their Strategic Architecture objectives. We also want to ensure that we are providing assistance to help the business units improve their recruitment and retention efforts. One way to do this is to maximize the participation of our diversity events by collaborating with the lines of businesses.

The second element is what the lines of businesses plan to do to meet their Diversity Strategic Architecture. We want to ensure that we are aligning diversity initiatives with business unit needs. We want to ensure that the objectives are specific and obtainable and are asking each business unit to identify stretch objective(s). These discussions will also allow us to explore opportunities for partnering.

The third element is the initiatives within the HR functions and other staff groups. This will give the business units a sense of how we are aligned to achieve Pitney Bowes Diversity Metrics in the Strategic Architecture. These partnerships broaden the company's sourcing capabilities and provide business units with a recruitment link for staffing needs to help drive representation.

Through this collaborative effort we look at current representation and identify where the opportunities are. We can leverage the relationships within the business units, staffing groups and diversity partners to help provide a strong pipeline of diverse candidates. The Diversity Strategy gives us the ability to look across all business units and have a better understanding of their business needs and priorities related to diversity. This will also help us to identify best practices.

How often does the firm's management review the firm's diversity progress/results?

Twice a year

How is the firm's diversity committee and/or firm management held accountable for achieving results?

We have built Diverstiy metrics into our corporation's objectives through specific metrics. The CEO, SVP of HR and VP, Strategic Talent Management and Diversity Leadership have accountability to the Corporate Responsibility Committee (a subset of the Board of Directors). Each business leader is held accountable for furthering our diversity efforts. We have a Leadership Model that describes and holds Leaders accountable for their behaviors (Explicit and implicit). Managers are accountable for the development of their people and diversity is an objective of senior management and the Board of Directors and is enforced by tying compensation to successful completion of the diversity objective.

The Stats

DEMOGRAPHIC PROFILE	TOTAL IN THE U.S.		TOTAL OUTSIDE THE U.S		TOTAL WORLDWIDE	
	2004	2003	2004	2003	2004	2003
Number of employees	27,152	24,747	8,031	7,727	35,183	32,474
Revenues	$3.703 billion	$3.507 billion	$1.254 billion	$1.070 billion	$4.957 billion	$4.577 billion

Retention and Professional Development

Please identify the specific steps you are taking to reduce the attrition rate of minority and women employees.

• Develop and/or support internal employee affinity groups (e.g., minority or women networks within the firm)
• Increase/review compensation relative to competition
• Increase/improve current work/life programs
• Adopt dispute resolution process
• Succession plan includes emphasis on diversity
• Work with minority and women employees to develop career advancement plans
• Strengthen mentoring program for all employees, including minorities and women
• Professional skills development program, including minority and women employees

Diversity Mission Statement

Pitney Bowes does business in work places characterized by valuable diversity. We value, actively pursue, and leverage diversity in our employees, and through our relationships with customers, business partners and communities, because it is essential to innovation and growth. Pitney Bowes' commitment to diversity is also consistent with and further supports the company's values and practices.

The Employer Says

The focus on transformation and on talent and leadership lay the foundation for growth. We are improving our systems and processes to deliver greater value to our customers and employees. Diversity is the spirit of freedom expressed through individuality. At Pitney Bowes, we embrace that spirit. We value the unique contributions brought to our company by a diverse workforce. We respect ingenuity, innovation, and ideas that are the genius of humankind no matter what age, gender, religious belief, race, ethnicity, family circumstance, sexual orientation, physical or mental ability, or education. A diverse workforce will allow Pitney Bowes to strengthen the fabric of its workforce to respond quickly, efficiently and creatively to the needs of customers all over the globe. By maximizing the potential of every employee, by supporting the needs of the spectrum of businesses and communities that interact with the company, and by understanding and responding to the increasingly varied global marketplace, there is no limit to what Pitney Bowes can accomplish for our employees, customers, shareholders and business partners around the world.

To help advance women and minorities, Pitney Bowes has an initiative to augment its leadership and professional development programs into upper management. LEAD! is Pitney Bowes' multi-faceted, comprehensive initiative that provides managers with the training, tools and processes to enhance their leadership skills and to help them become successful.

Pitney Bowes also believes in providing its employees opportunities to advance in the company with the flexibility to manage their time between their careers and their life commitments. We offer programs such as flexible work arrangements, transportation programs, employee resources fairs, on-site amenities that includes fitness centers and medical clinics, an employee assistance program (EAP) and on-site financial education programs.

In addition, Pitney Bowes has a long and admirable history of corporate-wide commitment to minority and women-owned supplier development dating back to the 1960s. Pitney Bowes realized the need and importance of a full-time staff of Business Diversity professionals dedicated to creating and implementing various development programs and slates to increase procurement with M/WBEs and formalized its Business Diversity Development department in 1997. This department is also responsible for collecting, formulating, and distributing M/WBE purchase data to our many valued customers who require this type of specialized subcontracting reporting on a scheduled basis.

Diversity Recognition and Awards

- Pitney Bowes awarded the "Brillante Award" in the Corporate Award Category by the National Society of Hispanic MBAs – 2005
- Pitney Bowes ranked one of the "30 Best Companies for Diversity" by *Black Enterprise*
- Pitney Bowes recognized on Latin Business's 2005 Corporate Diversity Honor Roll – 2005
- Pitney Bowes ranked among DiversityInc.com's "Top 50 Companies for Diversity" – 2005, 2004, 2003, 2002, 2001; ranked the #1 Company for Diversity in 2004
- Pitney Bowes Australia has been awarded "Employer of Choice for Women" by the Equal Opportunity for Women in the Workplace Agency – 2004, 2003, 2002
- Pitney Bowes awarded "Corporate Partner of the Year" by the Connecticut Chapter of the National Society of Hispanic MBAs – 2005, 2001
- Pitney Bowes ranked among DIV2000.com's "America's Top Organizations for Multicultural Business Opportunities" – 2005, 2004, 2003, 2002, 2001
- Pitney Bowes ranked among Top 100 Companies for Hispanics by *Hispanic* magazine – 2005, 2004, 2003, 2002, 2001, 2000, 1999
- Pitney Bowes ranked among *Hispanic* magazine's "Top 50 Recruitment Programs" – 2005, 2004, 2003, 2002, 2001, 2000, 1999, 1998
- Pitney Bowes awarded the "Outstanding Corporate Supplier Diversity Award" by the National Minority Business Council – 2005
- Pitney Bowes named to *Asian Enterprise* magazine's "10 Best Companies for Asian Pacific Americans" – 2005, 2004, 2003, 2001, 2000
- Pitney Bowes ranked among *Fortune* magazine's "America's Best Companies for Minorities" – 2004, 2002, 2001, 2000, 1999, 1998
- Pitney Bowes ranked among DiversityInc.com's "Top Companies for Recruitment & Retention" – 2004, 2003, 2002; ranked the #1 Company for Recruitment & Retention in 2004
- Pitney Bowes ranked among DiversityInc.com's "Top 10 Companies for Latinos" – 2004, 2003
- Pitney Bowes ranked among "Best Employers for Workers 50 and Over" by AARP – 2004
- Pitney Bowes is rated in the 100 Best Corporate Citizens by *Business Ethics* magazine – 2004, 2003, 2002, 2001, 2000
- Pitney Bowes ranked among *Hispanic* magazine's "Top 25 Vendor Programs for Latinos" – 2004, 2003, 2002, 2001, 2000, 1999
- Pitney Bowes recognized as Employer of the Year by Project Equality – 2003
- Bowes recognized by the Small Business Administration for its support of the nation's small business community – 2003
- Pitney Bowes awarded Excellence in Diversity Award by *Savoy Professional* magazine – 2003
- Pitney Bowes awarded the "Amigo" award from ASPIRA of Connecticut – 2003
- Pitney Bowes recognized by *Latina Style* magazine in their national listing of the top 50 companies providing the best professional opportunities for Latinas – 2003, 2002, 2001, 2000, 1999, 1998
- Pitney Bowes awarded the "Lifeline" award by the National Conference of Black Mayors – 2003
- Nancy Armstrong, Pitney Bowes Senior Buyer, was awarded the "Buyer of the Year" award from the Connecticut Minority Supplier Development Council – 2003
- Pitney Bowes wins Board of Education and Services for the Blind 2002 Employer of the Year Award – 2002
- Keith Williamson ranked among *Fortune* magazine's "50 Most Powerful African American Executives" – 2002
- Pitney Bowes Management Services honored by the Legal Clinic for the Disabled – 2002
- Pitney Bowes received Dialogue on Diversity's "2001 Corporate Excellence Award" for fostering the growth of business enterprise among women
- Pitney Bowes ranked among "The Great Companies for Blacks" by *U.S. Black Engineer & IT* – 2001
- Pitney Bowes received the American Foundation for the Blind's "Helen Keller Achievement Award in Technology" – 2001
- Pitney Bowes named to *Next Step* magazine's "Diversity 100" list of the top 100 companies that embrace diversity – 2001, 2000, 1999, 1998
- Pitney Bowes recognized by *Working Woman* magazine's "Top 25 Public Companies for Executive Women" – 2001, 2000, 1999, 1998
- Pitney Bowes ranked by *Working Woman* magazine as one of the "Top 30 Firms Which Spend the Most Money with Diverse Suppliers" – 2001
- Pitney Bowes received "Supported Employer of the Year" award from The Kennedy Center, Inc. in recognition of outstanding commitment to and understanding of persons with disabilities – 2001

- Michael Critelli awarded Human Relations Award by the National Conference for Community and Justice (formerly known as the National Conference of Christians and Jews) – 2001
- Michael Critelli awarded the Heart of Gold Award from the Volunteer Center – 2001
- Pitney Bowes received Minority Corporate Council Association's "Diversity 2000 Award" as employer of choice for minority lawyers – 2000
- Pitney Bowes recognized by *Minority MBA* magazine as one of "The 10 Best Companies for Minority MBA's" – 2000, 1999, 1998
- Pitney Bowes received "Access 2000" Award from the American Foundation for the Blind in recognition of "technological innovations that improve workplace conditions for the blind" – 2000
- Pitney Bowes named among the "Top 50" employers for "achieving meaningful diversity within your company" by the readers of *Careers & The Disabled* magazine – 2000

PPG

1 PPG Place
Pittsburgh, PA 15272
Phone: (412) 434-3131
Fax: (412) 434-2011
www.ppg.com

Locations (worldwide)

Pittsburgh (corporate headquarters)

Diversity Leadership

Laura Randall, Manager, Diversity

Employment Contact

John Coyne, Manager, Corporate Recruiting
One PPG Place
Pittsburgh, PA 15272
Phone: (412) 434-2015
Fax: (412) 434-2011
E-mail: jpcoyne@ppg.com

Recruiting

Please list the schools/types of schools at which you recruit.

- Ivy League schools
- Other private schools
- Public state schools
- Historically Black Colleges and Universities (HBCUs): Hampton, NC A&T, Florida A&M
- Hispanic Serving Institutions (HSIs): Univ of Houston, Texas A&M

Do you have any special outreach efforts that are directed to encourage minority students to consider your firm?

- Hold a reception for minority students
- Conferences
- Advertise in minority student association publication(s)
- Participate in/host minority student job fair(s)
- Sponsor minority student association events
- Firm's employees participate on career panels at school
- Outreach to leadership of minority student organizations
- Scholarships or intern/fellowships for minority students

What activities does the firm undertake to attract minority and women employees?

- Partner programs with women and minority associations
- Conferences
- Participate at minority job fairs
- Seek referrals from other employees
- Utilize online job services

Do you use executive recruiting/search firms to seek to identify new diversity hires?

Yes

Internships and Co-ops

We have internship programs for Engineering, Chemists, Finance, IT and Marketing each summer. Pay varies by position and we attempt to offer full time employment if there is a fit and we have jobs.

Scholarships

We have a scholarship program available for each school at which we recruit.

Entry-Level Programs/Full-Time Opportunities

We hire full time graduates in various disciplines, technical and business. They are placed across the U.S. and have a variety of training programs.

Strategic Plan and Diversity Leadership

Who has primary responsibility for leading diversity initiatives at your firm?

Laura Randall

Does your firm currently have a diversity committee?

Yes

If yes, please describe how the committee is structured, how often it meets, etc.

Meet 4 times a year and it has all levels of employees on the committee.

If yes, does the committee's representation include one or more members of the firm's management/executive committee (or the equivalent)?

Yes

>   **Total executives on the committee:** 8

Does the committee and/or diversity leader establish and set goals or objectives consistent with management's priorities?

Yes

Has the firm undertaken a formal or informal diversity program or set of initiatives aimed at increasing the diversity of the firm?

Yes, formal

How often does the firm's management review the firm's diversity progress/results?

Quarterly

How is the firm's diversity committee and/or firm management held accountable for achieving results?

Reports to CEO and Board of Directors

The Stats

Employees: 32,000 (2004, worldwide)
Revenue: $8.5 billion (2004, worldwide)

Retention and Professional Development

How do 2004 minority and female attrition rates generally compare to those experienced in the prior year period?

Lower than in prior years

Please identify the specific steps you are taking to reduce the attrition rate of minority and women employees.

• Develop and/or support internal employee affinity groups (e.g., minority or women networks within the firm)
• Increase/improve current work/life programs
• Adopt dispute resolution process
• Succession plan includes emphasis on diversity
• Work with minority and women employees to develop career advancement plans
• Strengthen mentoring program for all employees, including minorities and women
• Professional skills development program, including minority and women employees

could you spend your life building someone else's career path?*

Giving students the opportunity to succeed opens doors not just for them, but for the future of business as well. Thank you INROADS.

*connectedthinking

PRICEWATERHOUSE COOPERS

PricewaterhouseCoopers

1177 Avenue of the Americas
New York, NY 10036
Phone: (646) 471-4000
Fax: (646) 471-3188
Apply at www.pwc.com/lookhere

Locations (worldwide)
Offices in 144 countries worldwide

Diversity Leadership
Rod Adams, Director of Diversity Recruiting

Recruiting

Please list the schools/types of schools at which you recruit.

- *Ivy League schools*
- *Private schools:* We recruit at over 200 private and public schools
- *Public state schools:* We recruit at over 200 private and public schools
- *Historically Black Colleges and Universities (HBCUs):* Howard University, Florida A&M University, Hampton University, Morgan State University, North Carolina A&T University, Atlanta University Center
- *Hispanic Serving Institutions (HSIs):* Florida International University

Do you have any special outreach efforts that are directed to encourage minority students to consider your firm?

- Host a leadership and scholarship program for diverse students
- Conferences
- Advertise in minority student association publication(s)
- Participate in/host minority student job fair(s)
- Sponsor minority student association events
- Firm's employees participate on career panels at school
- Outreach to leadership of minority student organizations
- Internships for minority students
- Other: Partner with universities to offer H.S. Programs to promote accounting awareness

What activities does the firm undertake to attract minority and women employees?

- Partner programs with women and minority associations
- Conferences: Association of Latino Professionals in Finance and Accounting Annual Conference, National Association of Black Accountants Annual Convention, National Black MBA Association Annual Convention , National Society of Hispanic MBAs Annual Conference, Working Mother magazine, WorkLife Congress, National Association of Black Accountants Regional Student Conferences, National Hispanic Business Association, PwC's Minorities in Business Leadership Conference, Monster Diversity Leadership Program
- Participate at minority job fairs
- Seek referrals from other employees
- Utilize online job services
- Advertise in National Publications

Internships

INROADS

Deadline for application: Need to apply during fall semester or early spring semester (winter quarter)
Number of interns in the program in summer 2004 (internship): 197
Pay: $2,200-$4,000/month
Length of the program: 8-10 weeks
Percentage of interns in the program who receive offers of full-time employment: 85%
Web site for internship information: www.pwc.com/lookhere

Rising Freshman, Sophomores & Juniors

In our eight-to-ten-week (may extend longer) summer program, PricewaterhouseCoopers interns get to experience first-hand the PwC values and culture. It is an internship involving multi-dimensional, integrated learning coupled with a practical paid work experience. Our interns will attend orientation and receive a laptop computer. They will be assigned to work in Internal Firm Services (IFS) group – Human Resources/Recruiting, Marketing, Learning & Education (may require travel), Finance, Diversity & WorkLife, Meeting & Event Services, Information Technology and/or Sales & Business Development. They will get exposure to our Lines of Service – Assurance, Tax and Advisory – through shadow days, interaction with assigned mentors and workshops. The internship experience will also include social events and community service activities. If successful, our interns will receive offers for client service internships.

Rising Seniors

In our eight-to-ten-week (may extend longer) summer program, PricewaterhouseCoopers interns get a taste of what it's like to work here full-time. It is an internship involving multi-dimensional, integrated learning coupled with a practical paid work experience. Interns attend orientation, off-site training and receive a laptop computer. As interns, they will function in client service roles in Advisory, Tax or Advisory. They will have responsibilities similar to a first-year associate on client engagement. They will be a part of a team of business advisors, serving diverse clients and developing optimal strategies for those clients. Interns will help advise our clients on solutions to the issues facing them and as a member of a client service team, they'll help offer clients a thorough understanding of current and emerging issues and the underlying business concerns. Interns will be challenged to think, stimulated to grow, and encouraged to contribute. If successful, our interns will receive full-time offers.

Externship and/or Leadership Programs

Deadline for application: Need to apply during fall semester or early spring semester (winter quarter)
Pay: None
Length of the program: 3 – 5 days
Percentage of interns in the program who receive offers of full-time employment: 70%
Web site for internship information: www.pwc.com/lookhere

Promoting a professional yet casual experience

• Multi-event innovative programs inspiring teamwork and leadership development
• Geared to bridge the gap between academic education and initial intern assignments
• Events may include:
• Client Shadowing
• Etiquette Dinners
• Social Activities

PwC Client Service Internship Program

Deadline for application: Need to apply during fall semester or early spring semester (winter quarter)
Number of interns in the program in summer 2004 (internship): 2000
Pay: $2,700-$4,000/month
Length of the program: 8-10 weeks
Percentage of interns/co-ops in the program who receive offers of full-time employment: 85%
Web site for internship information: www.pwc.com/lookhere

In our eight-to-ten week (may extend longer) summer program, PricewaterhouseCoopers interns get a taste of what it's like to work here full-time. It is an internship involving multi-dimensional, integrated learning coupled with a practical paid work experience. Interns attend orientation, off-site training and receive a laptop computer. As an intern they will function in a client service role in Advisory, Tax or Advisory. They will have responsibilities similar to a first year associate on client engagement. They will be a part of a team of business advisors, serving diverse clients and developing optimal strategies for those clients. Interns will help advise our clients on solutions to the issues facing them and as a member of a client service team, they'll help offer clients a thorough understanding of current and emerging issues and the underlying business concerns. Interns will be challenged to think, stimulated to grow and encouraged to contribute. If successful, our interns will receive full-time offers.

Scholarships

Minority Scholars Program

Deadline for application for the scholarship program: Application process runs from September through December.
Scholarship award amount: $ 3,000
Web site or other contact information for scholarship: www.pwc.com/minorityscholars

To achieve our business goals, PwC has a number of initiatives and programs that support its strategy to hire, retain and advance people of color. For PwC, diversity is a business imperative that will help it sustain its position as the U.S. professional services firm. Since 1990, PwC has awarded scholarships to some of the best and brightest African American, Hispanic/Latino and Native American students in the U.S. Our scholarship program includes:

• A $3,000 scholarship
• An invitation to our annual Minorities in Business Leadership Conference
• An opportunity to be considered for a winter or summer internship

Affinity Groups/Employee Networks

Diversity Circles and Women's Networking Circles

At PricewaterhouseCoopers LLP, we are committed to creating an inclusive culture where everyone can succeed in achieving their personal and professional goals. We recognize that networks are critical to career success. Networks provide access to information and new business leads, as well as support and guidance in achieve career goals. Research shows that exclusion from informal networks and limited access to mentors can be barriers to advancement. A key goal of "Circles," as we call our affinity groups, is to provide that connection.

Circle members receive valuable career advice, expand skills, increase their knowledge of the firm's businesses and share best practices – all within a community of talented women and our diverse staff. Circle members meet regularly to exchange ideas, analyze developmental issues and receive feedback and guidance as a group. They also advise and mentor each other as relationships develop.

Circle Goals

- To ignite and empower women and our diverse staff to achieve their personal and professional ambitions.
- To provide a sense of community and connectivity
- To create opportunities for networking and visibility
- To present opportunities for professional and personal development, and
- To provide role models and a mentoring environment.

Entry-Level Programs/Full-Time Opportunities

Full-time roles are available in all client service lines of business

Geographic location(s) of program: U.S.

Please describe the training component of this program: Each line of service has a specific entry-level training program. The duration of the program depends on the service line, Assurance, Tax or Advisory.

Please describe any other educational components of this program: Tuition reimbursement is available for all full -time PwC employees who qualify for the program

Strategic Plan and Diversity Leadership

How does the firm's leadership communicate the importance of diversity to everyone at the firm?

The U.S. firms' Senior Partner communicates the importance of diversity in his "Weekly Wrap" to our partners and his bi-monthly email to all employees. In addition our Chief Diversity Officer hosts webcasts and communicates through e-mails and PwC's newly launched diversity and worklife web site.

Who has primary responsibility for leading diversity initiatives at your firm?

Chris Simmons, Chief Diversity Officer

Does your firm currently have a diversity committee?

Yes

If yes, please describe how the committee is structured, how often it meets, etc.

Our National Diversity Council is comprised of two representatives from each of our 18 Diversity Circle affinity groups and holds quarterly conference calls and an annual national meeting.

If yes, does the committee's representation include one or more members of the firm's management/executive committee (or the equivalent)?

Yes, it includes four members of the firm's leadership team.

If yes, how many executives are on the committee? 4

Does the committee and/or diversity leader establish and set goals or objectives consistent with management's priorities?

Yes

Has the firm undertaken a formal or informal diversity program or set of initiatives aimed at increasing the diversity of the firm?

Yes, the firm has a formal program.

How often does the firm's management review the firm's diversity progress/results?

Monthly

The Stats

Number of partners and staff: More than 122,000 (FY 2004 worldwide)
Revenue: $16.3 billion (FY 2004 worldwide)

23.9% of all U.S. client service staff are minorities. In 2005, 31% of our campus new hires were minorities.

Retention and Professional Development

How do 2004 minority and female attrition rates generally compare to those experienced in the prior year period?

Lower than in prior years

Please identify the specific steps you are taking to reduce the attrition rate of minority and women employees.

• Develop and/or support internal employee affinity groups (e.g., diversity or women networks within the firm)
• Increase/improve current work/life programs
• Succession plan includes emphasis on diversity
• Work with minority and women employees to develop career advancement plans
• Review work assignments and hours billed to key client matters to ensure proportional representation on top client engagements
• Strengthen mentoring program for all employees, including minorities and women
• Professional skills development program for all employees, including minority and women employees

The Employer Says

"We must promote diversity and inclusion to attract and retain the best talent, to maintain meaningful client relationships and successfully interact with our clients who have diverse work forces."

- Dennis Nally, U.S. Firm Senior Partner

At PricewaterhouseCoopers LLP, we are committed to creating an inclusive culture where everyone can succeed in achieving their personal and professional goals. An inclusive culture enables us to embrace the richness of backgrounds and perspectives of our people and leverage their diverse talents to arrive at winning business solutions. At PwC, we know that an inclusive workplace is critical to the continued success of our firm.

In a period of time when many organizations may have reduced their budgets, our leadership has made significant investments in our diversity effort by providing resources to hire Diversity WorkLife Leaders in our major markets. Our Diversity WorkLife Leaders serve as "change agents" on the ground that collaborate with Office Managing Partners and HR Leaders to develop locally customized strategies to promote inclusion and dedicate all of their time and attention to developing diverse leaders, improving minority retention and improving flexibility for all.

Our story is one of commitment-from the Chairman's Office that sets national policy to the local offices where our client teams are on the ground working with our Diversity/WorkLife Leaders. We are committed to building a culture of equity and fairness, of integrity and excellence in everything we do. We demand the best of our people and they, in turn, demand the best from us. They demand that we demonstrate a visible commitment to diversity not just policy statements and programs, but tangibly through the actions of their leadership and peers-and visibly by the results.

We acknowledge that it is a journey, yet we are strengthened knowing that diversity is now embedded in everything we do as a firm-from recruiting to coaching and developing, from succession planning to winning clients. We know that the success of our firm depends entirely upon our people – and we can't afford not to invest in each and every one.

Procter & Gamble

1 Procter & Gamble Plaza
Cincinnati, OH 45202
Phone: (513) 983-1100
Fax: (513) 983-9369
pgjobs.pg.com

Locations (worldwide)

180 countries.
Main offices: Cincinnati – U.S., Kobe –
Japan, Geneva – Switzerland, Brussels –
Belgium, Caracas – Venezuela, Mexico
City – Mexico, San Juan – Puerto Rico,
Guangzhou – China

Diversity Leadership

Jorge Rivera, Manager Diversity Recruiting

Contact Person

Shaun Howard, Recruiting Specialist
2 P&G Plaza
Cincinnati, OH 45202
Phone: (513) 983-1100
E-mail: howard.sd.1@pg.com

Recruiting

Please list the schools/types of schools at which you recruit.

• Ivy League schools
• Other private schools
• Public state schools
• Historically Black Colleges and Universities (HBCUs)
• Hispanic Serving Institutions (HSIs)
• Native American Tribal Universities
• Other predominantly minority and/or women's colleges

Do you have any special outreach efforts that are directed to encourage minority students to consider your firm?

• Hold a reception for minority students
• Conferences
• Advertise in minority student association publication(s)
• Participate in/host minority student job fair(s)
• Sponsor minority student association events
• Firm's employees participate on career panels at school
• Outreach to leadership of minority student organizations
• Scholarships or intern/fellowships for minority students

What activities does the firm undertake to attract minority and women employees?

• Partner programs with women and minority associations
• Conferences: NSHBMA, SHPE, NSBE, NBMBAA, SWE, AISES, NAAAP, ADI, CGSM, COSD, NHBA
• Participate at minority job fairs
• Seek referrals from other employees

• Utilize online job services

Do you use executive recruiting/search firms to seek to identify new diversity hires?

Yes

If yes, list all women- and/or minority-owned executive search/recruiting firms to which the firm paid a fee for placement services in the past 12 months:

HACU

Internships and Co-ops

Corporate Internship Program (includes INROADS)

Deadline for application: Varies by discipline
Number of interns in the program in summer 2004 (internship) or 2004 (co-op): 339
Length of the program: 12 weeks
Percentage of interns/co-ops in the program who receive offers of full-time employment: 80%
Web site for internship/co-op information: pgjobs.pg.com

Scholarships

The P&G Fund

Deadline for application for the scholarship program: Varies
Web site or other contact information for scholarship: pg.com

Affinity Groups/Employee Networks

Hispanic (H) Leadership Team, African American (AA) Leadership Team, Asian or Pacific American (APA) Leadership Team, Native American (NAI) Leadership Team

These teams within P&G advise on recruiting, retention and development and provide mentorship. They meet once a month.

Strategic Plan and Diversity Leadership

How does the firm's leadership communicate the importance of diversity to everyone at the firm?

E-mails, web site, newsletters, meetings, presentations

Who has primary responsibility for leading diversity initiatives at your firm?

Every employee at P&G owns diversity

Does your firm currently have a diversity committee?

Yes

If yes, does the committee's representation include one or more members of the firm's management/executive committee (or the equivalent)?

Yes

Does the committee and/or diversity leader establish and set goals or objectives consistent with management's priorities?

Yes

How often does the firm's management review the firm's diversity progress/results?

Quarterly

How is the firm's diversity committee and/or firm management held accountable for achieving results?

Quarterly

The Stats

Employees: 100,000 (2004, worldwide)
Revenue: $58 billion (2004, worldwide)

Retention and Professional Development

How do 2004 minority and female attrition rates generally compare to those experienced in the prior year period?

Lower than in prior years

Please identify the specific steps you are taking to reduce the attrition rate of minority and women employees.

• Develop and/or support internal employee affinity groups (e.g., minority or women networks within the firm)
• Increase/review compensation relative to competition
• Increase/improve current work/life programs
• Adopt dispute resolution process
• Work with minority and women employees to develop career advancement plans
• Strengthen mentoring program for all employees, including minorities and women
• Professional skills development program, including minority and women employees

Protective Life Corporation

2801 Hwy. 280 South
Birmingham, AL 35223
Phone: (205) 268-1000
Fax: (205) 268-3196
Toll Free: 800-866-3555
www.protective.com

Locations

AL, CA, OH, IL, MO, MN, TN, KS

Diversity Leadership

Darcell Streeter, Manager, Opportunity at
Protective
POB 2606
Birmingham, AL 35202
Phone: (205) 268-3801
Fax: 205-268-7202
E-mail: darcell.streeter@protective. com

Recruiting

Please list the schools/types of schools at which you recruit.

• Private schools
• Public state schools
• Historically Black Colleges and Universities (HBCUs)

Do you have any special outreach efforts that are directed to encourage minority students to consider your firm?

• Advertise in minority student association publication(s)
• Participate in/host minority student job fair(s)
• Scholarships or intern/fellowships for minority students

Internships and Co-ops

Bridges – building the future of Protective

Number of interns in the program in summer 2004 (internship) or 2004 (co-op): 14
*Length of the program:*Ssummer program 10-12 weeks

Entry-Level Programs/Full-Time Opportunities

Managing Inclusion (managers)

A companion course to managing inclusion for non-managers including online learning and knowledge builders

Length of program: 4 hours, 2 hours, 1.5 hours
Geographic location(s) of program: All offices

Please describe the training/training component of this program: Provide managers with the right tools to put the full range of people in demanding positions where they acquire skills and knowledge that will make them indispensable assets to the high value economy.

Strategic Plan and Diversity Leadership

How does the firm's leadership communicate the importance of diversity to everyone at the firm?

Training, focus groups, workshop, employee communication, e-mails, summits

Who has primary responsibility for leading diversity initiatives at your firm?

Opportunity Council, managed by Darcell Streeter

Does your firm currently have a diversity committee?

Yes

If yes, please describe how the committee is structured, how often it meets, etc.

Twelve-member Opportunity Council. Council meets bi-monthly. The purpose of the council is to facilitate and complement Protective Life's commitment to inclusion and opportunity, provide recommendations for achieving wholesale Inclusion at Protective Life and identify barriers to Protective Life's quest to become a complete meritocracy.

If yes, does the committee's representation include one or more members of the firm's management/executive committee (or the equivalent)?

Yes

Please describe the committee.

The Council spent a total of about 300 hours in the furtherance of our initiative in 2004. There are two executives and three senior managers, four directors, two coordinators, one open seat

Does the committee and/or diversity leader establish and set goals or objectives consistent with management's priorities?

Yes

Has the firm undertaken a formal or informal diversity program or set of initiatives aimed at increasing the diversity of the firm?

Yes, formal

How often does the firm's management review the firm's diversity progress/results?

Bi-monthly

How is the firm's diversity committee and/or firm management held accountable for achieving results?

Behavioral evaluations, required training, personal development plans.

Diversity Mission Statement

Our purpose is to promote an environment in which opportunity for growth exists, by building roles and responsibilities so that everyone has the opportunity to grow based on performance and results. We want to provide the right balance of nurturing potential and opportunity (based on individual drive and results) to ensure everyone has the opportunity to reach their full potential. Our desire is to create an environment in which we celebrate differences and learn from each other's cultural backgrounds, experiences and beliefs. It is important that we value and reward good work ethics. As we strive toward our mission, we want everyone to understand that promoting opportunity applies to everyone, no matter who you are. We want to make sure that no barrier to advancement, real or perceived, exists at Protective Life Corporation.

The Employer Says

Guidance on Opportunity at Protective

At Protective, we are firmly committed to providing equal opportunity to all individuals, regardless of a person's gender, race, age, national origin, religion, sexual orientation or other matters not relevant to job performance or career advancement. We want our company to be a meritocracy, a place where talent, hard work, good results and commitment to our values are appreciated and rewarded. This commitment to a merit-based workplace is consistent with our values and critically important to our future success.

If our company is to be a place where all employees have an equal opportunity to reach their potential as employees and human beings, Protective people must believe that they have an equal opportunity to advance. If they do not, a barrier to this goal will exist, even if equal opportunity does in fact exist. We want to make sure that no such barrier, real or perceived, exists at Protective.

One of our company's core values is growth. By growth, we mean not only growth of our company, but also the personal growth and development of Protective people within the company. As our company grows, we must also make sure that we give all Protective people the opportunity for career and personal growth.

Another of our values is serving people. To fulfill this value, we must recognize that people see the world in many different ways and that our success as a company depends upon our ability to respond to the needs of the many different types of people we serve as customers. Thus, the fact that we have a varied and diverse employee group supports our commitment to serving people and can be a competitive advantage to the extent we derive from our people the capacity to better understand the diverse needs and points of view of our customers.

This is not to say that we favor advancing a less qualified individual over a more qualified individual. Rather, it is to say that we must create an environment in which all employees will be appreciated for their unique talents and contributions; will be encouraged to perform at their full potential; and will be rewarded for doing the best job possible of satisfying the needs of the diverse customer base that we serve.

To reach our full potential as a company, we must have a highly motivated, loyal and talented workforce. We simply cannot afford to lose any talented employee because of any factor not related to job performance. We want to be the "employer of choice" for the best and the brightest of the people available for employment wherever we do business.

For these reasons, we encourage and embrace variety and diversity in the workplace at all levels of this company. Adherence to these principles is the right thing to do, and it is clearly smart business.

PSEG

80 Park Plaza
Newark, NJ 07102
Phone: (973) 430-7000
Fax: (973) 623-5389
Toll Free: (800) 436-7734
www.pseg.com

Locations (worldwide)
Corporate headquarters in Newark, NJ.
Locations throughout NJ; limited facilities
in NY, CT.

Employment Contact
Chandra Ledford, Enterprise Outreach
Specialist
80 Park Plaza, T21D
Newark, NJ 07102
Phone: (973) 430-5257
Fax: (973) 623-5389
E-mail: chandra.ledford@pseg.com

Recruiting

Please list the schools/types of schools at which you recruit.

• Ivy League schools
• Other private schools
• Public state schools
• Historically Black Colleges and Universities (HBCUs)

Do you have any special outreach efforts that are directed to encourage minority students to consider your firm?

• Conferences
• Advertise in minority student association publication(s)
• Firm's employees participate on career panels at school
• Outreach to leadership of minority student organizations

What activities does the firm undertake to attract minority and women employees?

• Partner programs with women and minority associations
• Conferences
• Participate at minority job fairs
• Other: seek referrals from other employees
• Utilize online job services

Internships and Co-ops

Generation Engineer Program (3-year program)

Deadline for application: Summer/fall of each year

This program is for college graduates, not students, but the company interviews students during their senior year of school.

The successful candidate will be hired into an entry-level engineering position as a Generation Engineer. The new Generation Engineer will be involved in a three-year training and development program within the PSEG Fossil, LLC Organization. During this period, the Generation Engineer will be assigned to various power plant locations, with subsequent other rotational assignments, along with a variety of leadership development sessions and technical training. This broad experience will aid in developing the Generation Engineer's skills and knowledge of PSEG Fossil, LLC and PSEG Power, LLC.

The station assignments will allow the Generation Engineer to understand the operation and maintenance activities associated with a power generating station thru participation in selected operating and maintenance type activities. During this period, shift-work is required and overtime compensation is offered. Other assignments will enable the engineer to understand the various roles and responsibilities of the support organizations and the services they provide to the generating stations. Throughout the three-year development period, there will be opportunities to participate in specific leadership development programs, as well as other special training.

We are looking for college graduates with:

BS Degrees primarily in: Electrical Engineering (EE), Mechanical Engineering (ME), Civil Engineering (CE), and Chemical/Environmental Engineering with a GPA of 3.0 or higher. We are looking for individuals who are interested in a career at a major energy company in Power Generation, which includes Engineering, Operations and Maintenance applications. A valid Driver's License is also required.

Affinity Groups/Employee Networks

Adelante

Vision

To cultivate an environment where Hispanics/Latinos are recognized and represented at all levels throughout PSEG.

Mission

• To be a resource for PSEG employees at all levels who want to gain a greater understanding of, or contribute to, the Hispanic/Latino experience and perspective.

• To communicate the collective needs of PSEG Hispanic/Latino employees and the Hispanic/Latino community.

• To help PSEG leadership increase its awareness of the intellectual and technological capital provided by Hispanics/Latinos that support the successful performance and achievement of Adelante and PSEG goals.

Black Data Processing Associates

The New Jersey chapter of Black Data Processing Associates (NJ BDPA) was originally established in 1981 and was known as Northern New Jersey, one of the premier chapters of the National BDPA. Chapter membership rose to over 125 members and eventually experienced a decline that resulted in the chapter becoming inactive in 1998.

NJ BDPA proudly stands with over 40 active chapters of the National BDPA, which was founded in 1975, in Philadelphia and is currently headquartered in Washington D.C. In the tradition of the national organization, NJ BDPA is a non-profit, member-focused organization that exists to provide professional development programs and services to position its members at the forefront of the information technology industry.

NJ BDPA offers monthly program meetings, featuring special guest speakers who share their knowledge and professional experiences. NJ BDPA is in high gear preparing a selected group of young men and women for the National High School Computer Competition. Winners will be announced at the 23rd Annual Conference in Chicago.

American Association of Blacks in Energy (AABE)

Established over 20 years ago, AABE is a non-profit national organization comprised of energy professionals dedicated to ensuring the input of minorities in the discussion and development of energy policies, regulations, R&D technologies, entrepreneur opportunities and environmental issues in the United States. Today, there are 32 chapters in six geographic regions in the United States.

For more information on AABE visit the AABE web site.

Minority Interchange (MI)

Minority Interchange (MI) is a not-for-profit corporation that provides a forum for the development and nurturing of leadership ability and the promotion of career-enhancing skills and techniques. This goal is accomplished through education, employment, and networking opportunities. MI is run entirely by volunteers and membership is open to everyone. MI's tone is upbeat, motivational, and inspirational. To learn more about the Minority Interchange, please visit their national website at: www.mi-hq.org.

Women's Network

The PSEG Women's Network is an informal group that meets at lunchtime about eight times a year, with speakers from inside and outside of the company. Their mission is to be a forum to provide professional women at PSEG with career development insight and skills to aid in their success in both job satisfaction and advancement, as well as providing an environment that will foster collaborative mentoring and support

Strategic Plan and Diversity Leadership

Does your firm currently have a diversity committee?

Yes

If yes, please describe how the committee is structured, how often it meets, etc.

Structured as follows: EOG Diversity Steering Committee – PSEG Enterprise Diversity Council – Business Area Councils

If yes, does the committee's representation include one or more members of the firm's management/executive committee (or the equivalent)?

Yes

Retention and Professional Development

Please identify the specific steps you are taking to reduce the attrition rate of minority and women employees.

• Develop and/or support internal employee affinity groups (e.g., minority or women networks within the firm)
• Increase/improve current work/life programs
• Adopt dispute resolution process
• Strengthen mentoring program for all employees, including minorities and women
• Professional skills development program, including minority and women employees

Diversity Mission Statement

PSEG Diversity Vision

PSEG strives to be a company that truly values diversity and where all associates support each other, customers and vendors in ways that their unique characteristics become enablers of, rather than barriers to, corporate success and shareholder value.

Diversity is a value that is demonstrated through mutual respect and appreciation of the similarities and differences (such as age, culture, education, ethnicity, experience, gender, race, religion, sexual orientation, etc.) that make people unique. An environment where diversity is respected is one where – as individuals and united as members of teams – we can effectively apply all of our talents, skills and experiences in pursuit of achieving business objectives.

PSEG Diversity Commitment

- Foster strong leadership, dedication and support
- Attract and recruit from a diverse pool of candidates; focus on identifying and leveraging the most effective sources or qualified talent
- Create and sustain a respectful and inclusive environment and culture, to support retention of a diverse workforce
- Align diversity with human resources practices, including leadership development and training; integrate with business planning and operations
- Assure representation of the diversity of the company in internal and external communications

Qualcomm Incorporated

5775 Morehouse Dr.
San Diego, CA 92121-1714
Phone: (858) 587-1121
Fax: (858) 658-2100
www.qualcomm.com/careers

Locations (worldwide)
23 U.S. locations and 44 international
locations

Employment Contact
Lee Wills-Irvine, Manager, Staffing
5775 Morehouse Drive
San Diego, CA 92109
Phone: (858) 587-1121
Fax: (858) 658-2100

Recruiting

Please list the schools/types of schools at which you recruit.

We recruit from numerous schools and the ones that we visit vary from year to year. Since they change each year the schools listed below are representative of where we visit, but are not a complete list.

• Ivy League schools
• Private schools: Stanford; Carnegie Mellon; MIT; University of Southern California
• Public state schools: University of California, San Diego; San Diego State University; University of California, Los Angeles; Texas A&M; Univ-Wisconsin; UC Berkeley; Rensselaer Polytechnic Institute; North Carolina State, University Austin Texas; Rutgers; University of Cincinnati; Georgia Tech
• Historically Black Colleges and Universities (HBCUs): North Carolina State
• Hispanic Serving Institutions (HSIs): Cal Poly, CA

Do you have any special outreach efforts that are directed to encourage minority students to consider your firm?

• Hold a reception for minority students
• Conferences:
• MESA- Math Engineering and Science Achievement Annual Conference hosted on-site with three different Universities- SDSU
• UCSD and one Junior College
• Meet with diversity groups such as NSBE, SHPE, and SWE
• Participate in/host minority student job fair(s): UC Berkeley Diversity Career Fair; MIT Diversity Fair, USC CED (Center for Engineering Diversity); SDSU MEP (Minority Engineering Program)
• Sponsor minority student association events
• Firm's employees participate on career panels at school
• Outreach to leadership of minority student organizations
• Scholarships or intern/fellowships for minority students

What activities does the firm undertake to attract minority and women employees?

• Partner programs with women and minority associations
• Conferences: NSBE National Conference, SHPE National Conference, NSHMBA National Conference, NBMBAA National Conference, SWE National Conference, WITI Conference

• Participate at minority job fairs: NSBE Career Fair, SHPE Career Fair, SWE Career Fair, WITI and NBMBA career fair.

• Seek referrals from other emploees

• Utilize online job services

Do you use executive recruiting/search firms to seek to identify new diversity hires?

Yes

If yes, list all women- and/or minority-owned executive search/recruiting firms to which the firm paid a fee for placement services in the past 12 months:

Diverse Connections (www.diverseconnections.net)

Internships and Co-ops

Intern Program

We have numerous Internships available throughout the year. Each summer we hire between 200 and 300 interns. See below for a list of open Intern positions as of 06/28/2005

> *Deadline for application:* Continuing
>
> *Number of interns in the program in summer 2004 (internship) or 2004 (co-op):* Approximately 300
>
> *Pay:* Varies
>
> *Length of the program:* Varies- can last from a few months up to several years
>
> *Percentage of interns/co-ops in the program who receive offers of full-time* employment: Approximately 20-40%
>
> *Web site for internship/co-op information:* www.qualcomm.com/college

We accept resumes from students at the BS, MS and PhD level for internships. Preference is given to Junior class standing or higher with a minimum GPA of 3.0. Most of our openings are in the areas of hardware, software, systems and test engineering for technical majors in:

• Electrical Engineering
• Computer Engineering
• Computer Science

We have a limited number of business openings for majors in:

• Accounting
• Finance
• Information Technology

Intern Positions:

Interim-Intern; Intern – Gov't Relations; Intern – IT (Enterprise Apps.); Intern – IT (QA Test); Interim Intern – Interim Intern; Intern – Human resources; Seasonal Hire – ITSS; Interim Intern; Interim Intern – Interim Intern; Intern – Intern; Intern – Supply Management; Intern – Field Mktg; Intern – Bus. Dev.; Intern – Web Support;; Verification/Intergration Intern (audio); Intern – ASIC Product Engineering; Intern – Package Engineering; Intern – Systems SD;Interim Engineering Intern; Interim Engineering Intern; Engineering Intern – Customer Quality; Intern – Test Methodology/DFT; Intern – Chemical; Interim Engineering Intern – S – Interim Engineering Intern; Interim Engineering Intern – S – Interim Engineering Intern; Intern – QCT Digital ASIC Group (Summer); Intern – Wireless/Digital Communications (System Test); Digital Signal Processing Intern – 2005; Intern – System Integration & Test; Intern – CDMA-1X Perl Testing; Intern – S/W Development Tools; Intern – S/W Development Tools; Intern – MediaFLO Integration; Interim Engineering Intern; Intern – S/W Embedded Test; Intern – S/W Test; Intern -; Intern – S/W Embedded Test; Intern – SoC Design; Intern – Engineering (Systems); Interim Engineering Intern; Interim Engineering Intern; Interim Engineering Intern; Interim Engineering Intern; Interim Engineering Intern; Interim Engineering Intern; Intern – OFDM/System Test; Interim Engineering Intern; Intern – Yield Management Intern; Intern – Test Engineering; Intern – Product

& Test Engineering; Interim Engineering Intern; Systems Test, CDMA/HDR Data – Engineering Intern; Intern – ASIC System Test; Intern – gpsOne Automation; Intern – ASW; Intern – Realtime Protocols; Intern – Engineering (Sys Int & Test); Interim Engineering Intern – S – Interim Engineering Intern; QMT Intern-Panel Test; Interim Engineering Intern – S – Interim Engineering Intern; Intern – Test Automation; Interim Engineering Intern; Intern – ASW; Intern – Procurement; Intern – Software/Graphics; Interim Engineering Intern; Intern – Device Drivers; Intern – .NET Application Development Intern; Systems Test Intern; Workstudy Intern – Client Test; Workstudy Intern – API Ref. Guide; Workstudy Intern – Prov. Mobile Dev.; Workstudy Intern – BREW App's; Workstudy Intern – Prog. Mgmt; Workstudy Intern – BDS Dev; Workstudy Intern – BREW Apps Servers; Workstudy Intern – QChat Apps Servers; Intern – Test Automation; Intern – Wireless/Digital Communications (System Test); Intern – 3G Application Automation Development (Perl); Intern – 1x EVDO Data Services Software Development; Intern – Engineering (Firmware); Intern – Wireless/Digital Communications (System Test); Intern – Software/Application Test; Intern – UMTS Software Build/Applications; Intern – Hardware Integration Test Team – ASIC Systems Test; Intern – Hardware Integration Test Team – ASIC Systems Test; Product Development Engineers – Analog/Power Management IC s; Intern – Intern; Product Development Engineers – RF/Analog IC; SHPE; Intern – ASW; Intern – engineering (QMT); Interim Intern(Network Optimization & Planning); Software Engineer – DSP Firmware Developer; Interim Intern – Interim Intern; Engineering Intern; Hardware Engineering Intern; Hardware Engineering Intern; Summer Intern;

Scholarships

GEM (2 awarded per year)

Scholarship award amount: Full tuition for a two-year graduate program

"QUALCOMM Q Award of Excellence" (10 scholarships are awarded each year)

Scholarship award amount: $1,500/year

Affinity Groups/Employee Networks

SHPE-Society of Hispanic Engineers

QCSHPE was created in 1994 to provide Qualcomm management and Hispanic employees with a link to the community.

SHPE was selected as a parent organization because it has a national agenda that bridges corporations, universities, colleges, K-12 schools, and the local communities.

AFROAM-QUALCOMM

AFROAM-QUALCOMM started as an internal mailing list created for the dissemination of information by and for African-American employees at QUALCOMM, Incorporated. The mailing list has grown from an information outlet to an organization that has sponsored several special events here at QUALCOMM celebrating diversity and ethnicity.

Mission Statement: AFROAM's mission is to contribute to the success of QUALCOMM by recruiting qualified candidates, encouraging employees to further develop professional skills and cultural awareness, and promoting education and communication technologies in our communities.

LAMBDA – Gay, Lesbian, Bisexual Group

The group meets to socialize, celebrate and support each other through social gatherings, participation in community events, and daily conversation on our own internal mailing lists.

Entry-Level Programs/Full-Time Opportunities

Management Skills Training Program

Length of program: 4 days

Geographic location(s) of program: San Diego

Please describe the training/training component of this program: Designed to develop and enhance competencies as a manager, this program offers a valuable opportunity to add to management skills. Attendees will study key management topics. Through interactive discussions with other QUALCOMM managers, attendees will acquire new ideas, thoughts and suggestions which will improve your ability to handle your daily management challenges.

Please describe any other educational components of this program (i.e., tuition reimbursement): We also offer tuition reimbursement for those who are pursuing job related courses, or a course of study leading to a job related degree, and attending an approved university.

Strategic Plan and Diversity Leadership

How does the firm's leadership communicate the importance of diversity to everyone at the firm?

This is communicated to employees in many ways- through the companies intra net, the company newsletter, emails, financial support, and in many other ways. Global Inclusion is the catalyst for raising the consciousness about how diversity positively impacts all aspects of our business – employees, customers and communities. It is not a set of rules that gets filed and forgotten. It is a viable philosophy that reflects the global nature of QUALCOMM. In addition, we offer several diversity training and awareness classes including disability awareness.

Who has primary responsibility for leading diversity initiatives at your firm?

Lee Wills-Irvine, Staffing, Manager

Does your firm currently have a diversity committee?

No

Has the firm undertaken a formal or informal diversity program or set of initiatives aimed at increasing the diversity of the firm?

Yes, informal. We have undertaken many efforts to increase diversity at Qualcomm such as community involvement in minority and diversity organizations, as well as QUALCOMM's dedication to furthering math and science in schools and universities through its support of programs such as High Tech High and Workforce Generation. We also participate in many diversity focused career fairs and attend Universities with large minority populations in our recruitment efforts.

How often does the firm's management review the firm's diversity progress/results?

This is not a formal process but rather an on-going process that is continually examined and re-evaluated.

The Stats

Employees: 7,000 (2004, U.S.)*
Employees: 1,000 (2004, outside the U.S.)*
Employees: 8,000 (2004, worldwide)*

* Numbers are approximate.

Retention and Professional Development

How do 2004 minority and female attrition rates generally compare to those experienced in the prior year period?

About the same as in prior years

Please identify the specific steps you are taking to reduce the attrition rate of minority and women employees.

• Develop and/or support internal employee affinity groups (e.g., minority or women networks within the firm)
• Increase/review compensation relative to competition
• Increase/improve current work/life programs
• Adopt dispute resolution process
• Strengthen mentoring program for all employees, including minorities and women
• Professional skills development program, including minority and women employees

Diversity Mission Statement

We are a communications company that thrives on the ideas and perspective that are evident in a diverse and multinational workforce. Our teams are charged with energy that comes from different backgrounds coming together in a working environment that embraces creativity and open minds. Diversity plays an integral role in our global viewpoint and provides an atmosphere that fosters the kind of free-flow of ideas that has made us a technology leader. By communicating with people from diverse backgrounds and groups all over the world, we engage in a dialogue that drives the wireless communication's industry.

Our value of global inclusion is reflected in our employees, corporate culture, programs and activities throughout the world. We take this philosophy into our communities where we live and work by supporting initiatives that further opportunities for education, cultural enrichment and community needs. An active employee volunteer program fosters understanding by partnering with local community activities in a wide variety of opportunities. We also recognize the importance of future generation's and launched what we call the NEXT Generation Workforce Initiative to increase minority and women representation in the engineering, computer science, information technology and related fields.

Qwest Communications International Inc.

1801 California St.
Denver, CO 80202
Phone: (303) 992-1400
Fax: (303) 992-1724
Toll Free: (800) 899-7780
www.qwest.com/careers

Internships and Co-ops

Qwest has partnered with the INROADS organization to provide internships for minority youth across the nation for 20 years. The locations vary each year, as do the number and types of opportunities. For more information regarding INROADS please visit their website at www.inroads.org.

Affinity Groups/Employee Networks

Qwest has a number of employee diversity groups. These groups are comprised of current Qwest employees with a common interest in promoting the Qwest diversity philosophy. Qwest recognizes the following self governing groups:

• *ABTP (*Alliance of Black Telecommunications Professionals)
• Qwest Women
• *Voice of Many Feathers* (Native American)
• *SOMOS* (Qwest Hispanic Resource Network)
• *Qwest Friends* (Persons With Disabilities)
• *EAGLE* (Employee Association for Gays and Lesbians)
• Qwest Veterans
• *PAAN* (Pacific Asian American Network)

The focus of these groups includes:

• Act as a resource and/or mentor to their membership
• Provide a unique cultural perspective to Qwest on how to increase market share and improve performance
• Provide a link between Qwest and the diverse communities it serves

Qwest provides each resource group an operating budget, meeting space and an Intranet site for member communications. In addition, each resource group has an annual Qwest Foundation budget of $5,000 to be used for grants to community organizations recommended by the resource groups that meet Foundation guidelines. Activities of the resource groups are open to all Qwest employees and are publicized through the company's employee communications channels.

The Employer Says

Qwest Communications International Inc. (NYSE: Q) is a leading provider of voice, video and data services. The company's more than 40,000 employees are committed to the "Spirit of Service" and providing world-class services that exceed customers' expectations for quality, value and reliability. Whether you're a single household, a small business or a global corporation, from voice to data to video, Qwest has a solution just for you.

Diversity awareness is an important part of Qwest's values and has been incorporated into each management employee's annual objectives. Our business culture promotes mutual respect, acceptance, cooperation and productivity among employees who are diverse in age, color, race, national origin, veteran status, religion, gender, sexual orientation, ethnicity, marital or family status, disability and any other legally protected category.

Our diversity philosophy extends to our customers and states, "At Qwest, we embrace diversity in all aspects of the business. We meet competitive challenges by understanding and valuing all our existing and potential customers and the dedicated employees who meet their needs each day."

What makes Qwest's approach to the advancement of diversity in the workplace unique is that it is accomplished within the context of-not at the expense of-the company's overall corporate strategy.

For more information about Qwest please visit our website qwest.com. If you are interested in career opportunities available at Qwest, please visit our career website at qwest.com/careers.

Regions Financial Corporation

417 N. 20th St.
Birmingham, AL 35202
Phone: (205) 944-1300
Fax: (205) 326-7756
Toll Free: (800) 734-4667
www.regions.com

Locations

AL, TN, GA, MS, FL, SC, NC, KY, IL, LA,
AR, IN, TX, MO, IA

Contact Person

Demetruis Sullen, Recruiting Project Manager
Birmingham, AL
Phone: (334) 230-6662
E-mail: Demetruis.Sullen@Regions.com

Recruiting

Please list the schools/types of schools at which you recruit.

• Public state schools
• Historically Black Colleges and Universities (HBCUs)
• Hispanic Serving Institutions (HSIs)
• Native American Tribal Universities
• Other predominantly minority and/or women's colleges

Do you have any special outreach efforts that are directed to encourage minority students to consider your firm?

• Advertise in minority student association publication(s)
• Participate in/host minority student job fair(s)
• Outreach to leadership of minority student organizations
• Scholarships or intern/fellowships for minority students

What activities does the firm undertake to attract minority and women employees?

• Partner programs with women and minority associations
• Participate at minority job fairs
• Seek referrals from other employees
• Utilize online job services

Do you use executive recruiting/search firms to seek to identify new diversity hires?

No

Internships and Co-ops

INROADS

Number of interns in the program in summer 2004 (internship) or 2004 (co-op): 2
Length of the program: 12 weeks

Regions is in the process of developing a company-sponsored internship program. We do employ interns within our organization in various areas such as technology and finance in addition to placements with INROADS.

Scholarships

Regions Academic Achievement Scholorship Program

Scholarship award amount: Book and tuition scholarships are provided (ranging between $250-$1,000 per student)

Students with a 3.0 GPA at select universities within the Regions footprint are elegible to recieve book or tuition scholarships. Scholarships are awarded in the fall and spring

Entry-Level Programs/Full-Time Opportunities

Regions has a management trainee program. The trainee is responsible for mastering a detailed agenda of on-the-job skills for applicable department and job. Incumbent may be required to successfully complete a structured curriculum of training courses (self-paced and instructor-led) throughout first year as a trainee. Occasional travel may also be required.

Qualifications:

• Four-year college degree in Finance, Accounting, Banking, Business Administration or related degree or experience.
• Minimum GPA of 3.0/4.0
• Strong leadership skills.
• Excellent oral and presentation skills.
• Outstanding people skills.
• Experience in retail, sales, customer service, or business atmosphere preferred, but not necessary.

The Employer Says

The merger of REGIONS Financial Corporation and Union Planters Corporation created a regional force in the financial services industry. The new REGIONS Financial Corporation is one of the Top 15 financial services providers in the nation, with $84 billion in assets and a market capitalization of more than $15 billion as of September 30, 2004. Serving some five million customers across a 15-state geographic footprint in the South, Midwest and Texas, REGIONS is a full-service provider of retail and commercial banking, trust, securities brokerage, mortgage, and insurance products and services.

REGIONS, headquartered in Birmingham, Ala., opened a new chapter in its history as the new REGIONS when the formal completion of the merger with Tennessee-based Union Planters was announced in July 2004. The combination of these two companies, which both have been in business for 139 years, has created a new organization that draws on strong traditions of delivering superior customer service, focusing on the community and creating shareholder value.

Who has primary responsibility for leading diversity initiatives at your firm?

Arturo Corral, Director of Diversity

Does your firm currently have a diversity committee?

Yes

Please describe how the committee is structured, how often it meets, etc.:

We have a corporate committee that is structured by representation across business units with Human Resource Generalists and Specialists. This group meets on a monthly basis and is lead by the diversity team.

Does the committee's representation include one or more members of the firm's management/executive committee (or the equivalent)?

Yes, the committee includes a number of executives.

Please describe the committee

There are about 12 members total and the total time devoted (for all members), including planning, meeting and follow-up is approximately 10-20 hours per month.

Does the committee and/or diversity leader establish and set goals or objectives consistent with management's priorities?

Yes. The committee aligns its activities to goals and objectives of HR as well as the company's vision and mission.

Diversity Mission Statement

A Diversity Workforce is made up of individuals with a variety of backgrounds and ethnic make-up and experiences which translate into different perspectives.

Rockwell Collins

400 Collins Rd. NE
Cedar Rapids, IA 52498
Phone: (319) 295-1000
Fax: (319) 295-5429
www.rockwellcollins.com

Locations (worldwide)
105 U.S. locations

Contact Person
Patty Stephens, Manager, University Relations
400 Collins Road NE
Cedar Rapids, Iowa 52498
Phone: (319) 295-7415
Fax: (319) 295-9347
E-mail: pjstephe@rockwellcollins.com

Recruiting

Please list the schools/types of schools at which you recruit.

• *Private schools:* Rose Hulman Institute of Technology, LeTourneau University, Embry-Riddle Aeronautical University – Prescott/Daytona campus
• *Public state schools:* Iowa State University, University of Iowa, Northern Iowa University, South Dakota School of Mines and Technology, North Dakota State University, University of North Dakota, Michigan Tech University, Texas A&M, University of Illinois – Urbana/Champaign, University of Texas – Dallas, Purdue University, Florida Institute of Technology, University of Florida – Gainsville, University of California – Irvine, California Polytechnic University, Pomona
• *Historically Black Colleges and Universities (HBCUs):* North Carolina Agriculture and Technology

Do you have any special outreach efforts that are directed to encourage minority students to consider your firm?

• Hold a reception for minority students
• Conferences: Purdue Diversity weekend/career fair
• Advertise in minority student association publication(s)
• Participate in/host minority student job fair(s)
• Sponsor minority student association events
• Firm's employees participate on career panels at school
• Outreach to leadership of minority student organizations
• Scholarships or intern/fellowships for minority students

What activities does the firm undertake to attract minority and women employees?

• Partner programs with women and minority associations
• Conferences: SWE • NSBE • SHPE
• Participate at minority job fairs
• Seek referrals from other employees

Do you use executive recruiting/search firms to seek to identify new diversity hires?

No

Internships and Co-ops

Rockwell Collins Internship and Co-op Program

Deadline for application: Ongoing, request that students apply online.

Number of interns in the program in summer 2004 (internship) or 2004 (co-op): 200

Pay: Depends on # of credit hours completed for interns and # of sessions for the co-op program

Length of the program: Intern program – 12 weeks, Co-op Program – 3 work sessions that rotate with school session and total 12 months of work experience when complete.

Web site for internship/co-op information: www.rockwellcollins.com

Strategic Plan and Diversity Leadership

How does the firm's leadership communicate the importance of diversity to everyone at the firm?

• E-mail communication and leader/employee meetings
• Newsletters
• Videos
• Posters/signage

Who has primary responsibility for leading diversity initiatives at your firm?

Rod Dooley, Directory Corporate Diversity

Does your firm currently have a diversity committee?

Yes

If yes, please describe how the committee is structured, how often it meets, etc.

• Executive Diversity Council and the meeting frequency is monthly
• Diversity Planning Council and the meeting frequency is bi-monthly

If yes, does the committee's representation include one or more members of the firm's management/executive committee (or the equivalent)?

Yes

Please describe the committee

• **Total executives on the committee:** 11
• **Total hours spent:** 20 hours monthly

Does the committee and/or diversity leader establish and set goals or objectives consistent with management's priorities?

Yes

Has the firm undertaken a formal or informal diversity program or set of initiatives aimed at increasing the diversity of the firm?

Yes, formal

How is the firm's diversity committee and/or firm management held accountable for achieving results?

A monthly cadence review on diversity metrics.

The Stats

Employees: 15,000 (2004, U.S.)

Retention and Professional Development

Please identify the specific steps you are taking to reduce the attrition rate of minority and women employees.

• Develop and/or support internal employee affinity groups (e.g., minority or women networks within the firm)
• Increase/review compensation relative to competition
• Increase/improve current work/life programs
• Succession plan includes emphasis on diversity
• Work with minority and women employees to develop career advancement plans
• Strengthen mentoring program for all employees, including minorities and women
• Professional skills development program, including minority and women employees

Diversity Mission Statement

Valuing and leveraging differences to fuel innovations and build a stronger company.

RR Donnelley

111 S. Wacker Dr. Chicago, IL 60606-4301 Phone: (312) 326-8000 Fax: (312) 326-8543 www.rrdonnelley.com	**Contact Person:** Toyia K. Stewart, Diversity Program Manager 111 S. Wacker Chicago, Illinois 60606 Phone: (312) 326-8577 Fax: (312) 326-7660 E-mail: toyia.k.stewart@rrd.com

Recruiting

Please list the schools/types of schools at which you recruit.

• Private schools
• Historically Black Colleges and Universities (HBCUs)
• Other predominantly minority and/or women's colleges

Do you have any special outreach efforts that are directed to encourage minority students to consider your firm?

• Advertise in minority student association publication(s)
• Participate in/host minority student job fair(s)
• Firm's employees participate on career panels at school
• Outreach to leadership of minority student organizations
• Scholarships or intern/fellowships for minority students
• Sponsor professional development associations that would target graduate students, e.g., Black MBA, Executive Leadership Conference.

What activities does the firm undertake to attract minority and women employees?

• Partner programs with women and minority associations
• Conferences: INROADS • UNCF • Rainbow Push • Executive Leadership Council (mid-level managers) Symposium • Catalyst • Global Summit of Women • Empowering Women Network
• Participate at minority job fairs
• Seek referrals from other employees
• Utilize online job services
• RR Donnelley sponsors monthly and quarterly meetings for professional organizations.

Do you use executive recruiting/search firms to seek to identify new diversity hires?

Yes

Internships and Co-ops

INROADS and UNCF

Deadline for application: Spring
Pay: $1800-$2700 per month
Length of the program: 8 to 10 weeks

Diversity is a critical factor in RR Donnelley's business success. Through effective recruiting, we have the opportunity to make a significant difference and improve diversity in the organization.

These are the internship programs we partner with in our diversity recruiting efforts:

INROADS (Intern Program)

25 East Washington Avenue, Suite 801
Chicago, IL 60602
(312) 553-5000

www.inroads.org

The mission of INROADS is to develop and place talented minority youth in business and industry and prepare them for corporate and community leadership.

The United Negro College Fund (UNCF) Universities

8260 Willow Oaks, Corporate Drive
Fairfax, VA 22031
703-205-3400
www.uncf.org

The United Negro College Fund mission is to enhance the quality of education by providing financial assistance to deserving students, raising operating funds for member colleges and universities, and increasing access to technology for students and faculty at historically black colleges and universities (HBCUs). Since its inception in 1944, UNCF has grown to become the nation's oldest and most successful African American education assistance organization.

Scholarships

RR Donnelley contributes scholarship support by sponsoring external organizations like N'DIGO Foundation, UNCF, and PUSH Excel.

Affinity Groups/Employee Networks

RR Donnelley does not have affinity groups, but has site and regional active Inclusion Councils throughout the U.S.

Inclusion Councils at RR Donnelley strive to be a diverse representation of the employee population. They advocate for and promote and inclusive workforce by implementing programs, activities and education resources that address workplace culture, community partnerships, and marketplace relationships.

Entry-Level Programs/Full-Time Opportunities

Corporate Mentoring Program

Length of program: 1-3 years

Geographic location(s) of program: Domestic United States

Please describe the training/training component of this program: Protégés in program participate in various development opportunities, including inclusion training, personal career management, goal-setting, special projects, mentor assignment.

Strategic Plan and Diversity Leadership

How does the firm's leadership communicate the importance of diversity to everyone at the firm?

RR Donnelley promotes the importance of diversity through efforts of the Inclusion Councils, external/ internal website, online resource library, e-learning courses, management and sales training, CEO and executive commitment, community relations, and supplier diversity program.

Who has primary responsibility for leading diversity initiatives at your firm?

Damayanti Vasudevan, PH.D Vice President Diversity and Inclusion

Does your firm currently have a diversity committee?

No

Does the committee and/or diversity leader establish and set goals or objectives consistent with management's priorities?

Yes

Has the firm undertaken a formal or informal diversity program or set of initiatives aimed at increasing the diversity of the firm?

Yes, formal

How often does the firm's management review the firm's diversity progress/results?

Quarterly

How is the firm's diversity committee and/or firm management held accountable for achieving results?

RR Donnelley leaders are held accountable through MBO goals.

The Stats

Employees: 33,200 (2004, U.S.)

Employees: 9,200 (2004, outside the U.S.)

Employees: 42,400 (2004, worldwide)

Revenue: $7.2 billion (2004, worldwide)

Retention and Professional Development

How do 2004 minority and female attrition rates generally compare to those experienced in the prior year period?

About the same as in prior years

Please identify the specific steps you are taking to reduce the attrition rate of minority and women employees.

• Develop and/or support internal employee affinity groups – Inclusion Councils
• Increase/review compensation relative to competition- for all employees not just women & minorities
• Increase/improve current work/life programs
• Adopt dispute resolution process
• Succession plan includes emphasis on diversity
• Work with minority and women employees to develop career advancement plans
• Strengthen mentoring program for all employees, including minorities and women
• Professional skills development program, including minority and women employees

Diversity Mission Statement

RR Donnelley will build strong and lasting relationships with diverse partners in the workplace, marketplace and community. We will create a workplace in which behaviors, practices and policies promote respect, inclusion, utilization, career development and success across all forms of diversity.

The Employer Says

Diversity and Inclusion at RR Donnelley

To be a successful leader in the 21st century, our business practices must align with the changes in our world. The demographics of our business and workforce partners are changing rapidly, and we must stay ahead of the changes. This means we need to be diligent in ensuring that our workforce and business practices reflect the diversity and needs of the customers we serve around the world today and in the future.

Employment

RR Donnelley is building an inclusive workforce, through our employment practices, such as internal and external recruiting, hiring, employee development, evaluation, promotion and retention. This includes opportunities for training, development, recognition and advancement for all employees.

Workplace Quality

RR Donnelley is committed to providing an environment in which everyone can contribute fully, feel valued and respected, and are rewarded for their contributions to the company's goals.

RR Donnelley's policy on discrimination is simple: We do not tolerate it.

Each of us is responsible for pointing out actions that are inconsistent with our company's values. Through our Open Door policy, employees are encouraged to bring concerns, issues or complaints to any member of management, with the assurance that they will receive prompt, thorough attention without fear of retaliation. Our managers and supervisors are responsible for investigating complaints and taking prompt and appropriate disciplinary action if these standards are violated.

Every action we take-in everything we do every day-supports our goal of building a better workplace. Our Inclusion Councils engage employees at all levels to address diversity and inclusion issues and concerns. Our focus on shared responsibility and accountability is essential to our progress in diversity.

Through education and training on diversity and inclusion, we enable cultural change and integration of diverse talent.

Supplier Relationships

RR Donnelley is committed to building relationships with a variety of business partners.

Our supplier diversity program has been in place for more than 20 years. We seek out opportunities to conduct business with underutilized organizations, such as minority-owned and female-owned businesses.

We strive to identify and develop qualified underutilized suppliers, cultivating relationships with these businesses and monitoring our progress in these areas. In establishing these relationships, RR Donnelley contributes to the economic growth and development of diverse businesses.

Customers

In the dynamic world of business, we know our customers are changing.

Our increasingly diverse customers rely on us, on our insight and knowledge, to deliver the right solutions at the right time and at the right price. Meeting these expectations is a priority for RR Donnelley.

We continually assess our strategies, capabilities, practices and policies to ensure that we can serve all of our customers.

Community Involvement

RR Donnelley strives to be the neighbor of choice. We believe in being a good corporate citizen of society and of the communities in which we operate.

With programs focused on literacy, youth and families, our company has a long-standing tradition of supporting a wide range of organizations, many of which serve under-represented and non-traditional groups.

Russell Corporation

3330 Cumberland Blvd., Ste. 800
Atlanta, GA 30339
Phone: (678) 742-8000
Fax: (678) 742-8300
http://www.russellcorp.com

Locations (worldwide)
U.S., Honduras, Mexico, Asia, Japan, Continental Europe, United Kingdom, Canada and Australia.

Diversity Leadership
Kevin Clayton, VP, Diversity

Contact Person
Jackie Parker, Director, Diversity
3330 Cumberland Suite 800
Atlanta, Georgia 30339
Phone: (678) 742-8810
Fax: (256) 500-9064
E-mail: parkerjackie@russellcorp.com

Recruiting

Please list the schools/types of schools at which you recruit.

• Ivy League schools
• Historically Black Colleges and Universities (HBCUs)
• Hispanic Serving Institutions (HISs)

Do you have any special outreach efforts that are directed to encourage minority students to consider your firm?

• Hold a reception for minority students
• Firm's employees participate on career panels at school
• Scholarships or intern/fellowships for minority students

What activities does the firm undertake to attract minority and women employees?

• Partner programs with women and minority associations
• Participate at minority job fairs
• Seek referrals from other employees

Do you use executive recruiting/search firms to seek to identify new diversity hires?

Yes

If yes, list all women- and/or minority-owned executive search/recruiting firms to which the firm paid a fee for placement services in the past 12 months:

• Pathfinders, Inc.
• Diversity Search Inc.
• Staff Source
• First Pro
• Ingenium Partners, Inc.

Internships and Co-ops

Although Russell Corporation does not have a formal undergraduate internship program, we have been pleased to provide internship opportunities to both minority and non-minority undergraduate students from a variety of southeastern regional colleges and universities.

> **Number of interns in the program in summer 2004 (internship) or 2004 (co-op):** 4
> **Pay:** Hourly rate paid bi-monthly
> **Length of the program:** Typically 12 weeks
> **Percentage of interns/co-ops in the program who receive offers of full-time employment:** None, as these are full-time students returning to college.

Russell has had the pleasure of hosting summer undergraduate interns in our Finance, IT and Marketing departments. Students are channeled into appropriate departments based on their vocational interests/majors. They work closely with managers on a day-to-day basis to gain critical hands-on experience in a fast-paced corporate environment.

Affinity Groups/Employee Networks

- AHLC (African Heritage Leadership Council) – Atlanta
- AHLC (African Heritage Leadership Council) – Alexander City
- RLAHN (Russell Latin American Heritage Network) – Atlanta
- RWLN (Russell Women's Leadership Network) – Atlanta
- RWLN (Russell Women's Leadership Network) – Alexander City

The objective of the employee networks is to assist the company in identifying opportunities and issues that uniquely exist within these segments of the Russell employee population. They meet monthly on company time to address and manage these issues. There main goals are focused against 4 pillars: Workplace, Workforce, Community and Marketplace strategies.

Strategic Plan and Diversity Leadership

How does the firm's leadership communicate the importance of diversity to everyone at the firm?

Communication is done through monthly operating meetings, newsletters, e-mails and corporate web site.

Who has primary responsibility for leading diversity initiatives at your firm?

Kevin Clayton, VP of Diversity and Jackie Parker, Director of Diversity

Does your firm currently have a diversity committee?

Yes

If yes, please describe how the committee is structured, how often it meets, etc.

The team is comprised of Russell's most senior managers who meet on a quarterly basis. The purpose of the team is to remove barriers that may get in the way of the organization's diversity vision/goals.

If yes, does the committee's representation include one or more members of the firm's management/executive committee (or the equivalent)?

Yes

Does the committee and/or diversity leader establish and set goals or objectives consistent with management's priorities?

Yes

Has the firm undertaken a formal or informal diversity program or set of initiatives aimed at increasing the diversity of the firm?

Yes, formal

• To create awareness and confirm diversity as a business imperative.
• To increase the representation of women and minorities in mid to senior level professional and management positions.
• To integrate diversity into the Talent Management initiative and processes.
• To increase the use of women and minority owned enterprises as suppliers of products and services to SunTrust.
• To create management accountability for diversity.

How often does the firm's management review the firm's diversity progress/results?

Monthly

How is the firm's diversity committee and/or firm management held accountable for achieving results?

Accountability is tied to management's compensation through our SOP process.

The Stats

Total worldwide 2004

1. Number of Employees: approx.14,000
2. Revenues: approx. $1.3 billion

Ethnicity

	TOTAL	TOTAL US
Asian American	36	.6%
Asian Indian	7	.1%
Black	2,183	36.5%
Hispanic	468	7.8%
White	3,291	55%
Grand Total	5,985	

Gender

	TOTAL	TOTAL US
Female	3,028	50.6%
Male	2,957	49.4%
Grand Total	5,985	

Retention and Professional Development

How do 2004 minority and female attrition rates generally compare to those experienced in the prior year period?

About the same as in prior years

Please identify the specific steps you are taking to reduce the attrition rate of minority and women employees.

• Develop and/or support internal employee affinity groups (e.g., minority or women networks within the firm)
• Increase/review compensation relative to competition
• Succession plan includes emphasis on diversity
• Work with minority and women employees to develop career advancement plans

Diversity Vision Statement

To create a fair and equitable culture in which every member of the Global Russell Team reinforces our values and contributes to achieving our business goals.

The Employer Says

Russell also has a strong workplace diversity initiative with a goal of creating an environment where each employee is respected and valued, a place where people can celebrate his or her similarities and his or her differences. In today's competitive global marketplace, Russell feels its greatest strength is its people and that it needs all employees willing and able to contribute to move the company forward.

Our focus areas are:

• Workforce: To attract and retain superior talent
• Workplace: To foster and empowering culture that respects both differences and similarities
• Marketplace: To leverage our diversity to capitalize on unique revenue opportunities.
• Communities: To support the communities where we live and operate.

Ryder Systems, Inc.

11690 NW 105 Street
Miami, FL 33178-1103
Phone: (305) 500-3726
Fax: (305) 500-3203
www.ryder.com

Locations (worldwide)

Ryder provides leading-edge transportation, logistics, and supply chain management solutions worldwide. Ryder's product offerings range from full service leasing, commercial rental and programmed maintenance of vehicles to integrated services such as dedicated contract carriage and carrier management. Additionally, Ryder offers comprehensive supply chain solutions, consulting, lead logistics management services and e-Business solutions that support customers' entire supply chains, from inbound raw materials and parts through distribution and delivery of finished goods. Ryder serves customer needs throughout North America, in Latin America, Europe and Asia.

Diversity Leadership

Gerri Rocker, Group Director, Corporate Diversity & Work/Life Planning Department

Employment Contact

Toni Pruitt, Campus Recruiting Team Leader
11690 NW 105 Street
Miami, FL 33178
Phone: (305) 500-4492
Fax: (305) 500-5758
E-mail: Toni_Pruitt@Ryder.com

Recruiting

Please list the schools/types of schools at which you recruit.

• Ivy League schools
• Public state schools
• Historically Black Colleges and Universities (HBCUs)

Do you have any special outreach efforts that are directed to encourage minority students to consider your firm?

• Conferences: National Hispanic MBA • National Black MBA
• Scholarships or intern/fellowships for minority students

What activities does the firm undertake to attract minority and women employees?

• Conferences: National Hispanic MBA • National Black MBA
• Participate at minority job fairs
• Utilize online job services

Do you use executive recruiting/search firms to seek to identify new diversity hires?

Yes

Internships and Co-ops

INROADS

Number of interns in the program in summer 2004 (internship) or 2004 (co-op): 2 interns
Pay: $9.50 per hour
Length of the program: 11 weeks
Web site for internship/co-op information: Inroads.org

The INROADS internship program's mission is to develop and place talented minority youth in business and industry and prepare them for corporate and community leadership. INROADS seeks high performing African American, Hispanic and Native American Indian students for internship opportunities with some of the nation's largest companies. The INROADS Internship is typically a 10-12 week paid, summer program.

Interns are expected to maintain a 3.0 GPA or higher, they actively participate at the INROADS training and development sessions, attend monthly coaching sessions, and complete 40 hours of community service annually.

There are two interns actively participating in the program at Ryder. One of the interns is working in the Accounts Payable/Receivables department processing paperwork, monitoring invoices, and interpreting various reference reports. The other intern is assigned to the recruiting department assisting with various initiatives involving retention analysis and also working with the Relocation department reviewing various relocation cases for employees.

Scholarships

Detailed information provided at Ryder.com/scholarship

Ryder Rental Masters Scholarship

Employee scholarships are made possible through the personal contributions of the Ryder Rental Masters and matching company funds. Rental Masters are a select group of individuals who have distinguished themselves through their significant and steady contributions to the rental product lines. Applicants must be enrolled or have been accepted as a student in an accredited post-high school institution or higher learning (college, junior college, university, technical and/or trade school).

1st Place – $6,000, 2nd Place – $4,000, 3rd Place, $3,000

Ryder Roundtable

The Ryder Roundtable is an organization of select individuals who have obtained membership by demonstrating sales excellence. The purpose of the scholarship is to assist children of Ryder employees in furthering their education and accomplishing their ambitions. Applicants must be a member of the immediate family of a full-time Ryder employee who has been employed by Ryder for at least one year, a retired Ryder employee or of a deceased Ryder employee. Applicants must be enrolled or have been accepted as a student in an accredited post-high school institution of higher learning (junior college, college, university, technical, and/o trade school).

1st Place – $10,000, 2nd Place – $7,500, 3rd Place & 4th Place $5,000, 5th Place $2,500

Ryder Vehicle Team Excellence

Membership in Team Excellence symbolizes outstanding performance in the area of selling vehicles and stands as a goal for all employees involved with vehicle sales at Ryder. The purpose of the scholarship is to assist Vehicle Sales Employees, their children or immediate relatives in furthering their education. Applicants must be currently attending, enrolled in or applied to an accredited institution of higher learning (university, college, junior college, technical or trade school).

1st Place – $6,000, 2nd Place – $4,000, 3rd Place $2,000

Affinity Groups/Employee Networks

There are four company sanctioned groups:

• Ryder Administrative Professionals Association (APA)
• Ryder Black Employee Network (RBEN)
• Ryder Hispanic Network (RHN)
• Ryder's Women Management Association (WMA).

The overall mission of the Network groups is to provide professional growth for participants, provide education and awareness for employees and promote the company's mission, values and corporate goals.

Strategic Plan and Diversity Leadership

How does the firm's leadership communicate the importance of diversity to everyone at the firm?

• Mandatory Diversity education awareness training for all U.S. based employees, "The Inclusion Journey – Delivering on the Potential of a Diverse Workforce."
• Diversity Internet Site – Maintain information on the Ryder.com web page for Diversity. The site features highlights, best practices and facts/information to enhance communication and build awareness of diversity and work/life efforts for internal and external groups
• Cultural Recognition Events – Host a variety of multi-cultural events, i.e., Black History Month, Women's History Month, and Hispanic Heritage Month activities.
• "Diversity Spotlight," a series of articles written and communicated to employees that highlight various diversity topics. Information disseminated company-wide via Lotus Notes e-mail.
• Lunch & Learn Seminars – Develop and sponsor monthly seminars related to diversity & work/life issues, i.e., stress management, dealing with differences, consumer credit counseling, elder care, wellness etc.

Who has primary responsibility for leading diversity initiatives at your firm?

Gerri Rocker – Group Director, Corporate Diversity & Work/Life Planning

Does your firm currently have a diversity committee?

No, the organization does not have a committee; however, there is a department that is staffed to provide diversity & work/life resources company-wide.

The Stats

DEMOGRAPHIC PROFILE	TOTAL IN THE U.S.		TOTAL OUTSIDE THE U.S		TOTAL WORLDWIDE	
	2004	2003	2004	2003	2004	2003
Number of employees	20,386	20,788	5,914	5,912	26,300	26,700
Revenues	$4.2 billion	$3.9 billion	$920 million	$860 million	$5.2 billion	$4.8 billion

Retention and Professional Development

How do 2004 minority and female attrition rates generally compare to those experienced in the prior year period?

Lower than in prior years

Please identify the specific steps you are taking to reduce the attrition rate of minority and women employees.

• Develop and/or support internal employee affinity groups (e.g., minority or women networks within the firm)
• Increase/review compensation relative to competition
• Increase/improve current work/life programs
• Succession plan includes emphasis on diversity
• Professional skills development program, including minority and women employees

Diversity Mission Statement

Create a supportive environment which values individual differences and enables all employees to contribute their full potential in pursuit of business objectives".   The Diversity & Work/Life Department provides services company-wide and is responsible for building and sustaining an inclusive culture that recognizes, understands, values and utilizes the unique talents, contributions and perspectives of its diverse workforce to maximize employee/customer satisfaction and business profitability.

The Employer Says

Ryder realizes that many of the traditional jobs in the transportation and logistics industry are not ones that readily attract women and people of color. We know that our success is based on the commitment and contribution of all our employees. We are striving to ensure that every employee has the opportunity to fully participate, to grow professionally and to develop to his or her potential. Our diversity initiatives help ensure that we utilize our available pool of talent, develop women and people of color to their fullest potential and provide the company with a competitive advantage.

There are a variety of strategies and practices implemented to attract, retain, and promote a diverse employee base, including:

• Balance Scorecard program that tracks company-wide diversity measures linking to the business strategy
• Diversity education and awareness training for all U.S. employees
• Electronic staffing processes for internal and external candidates capitalizing on a diverse talent pool
• Community involvement in local initiatives, awareness campaigns, cultural observances and charitable activities and events

Ryder firmly believes it is important for the company to be involved in, and a contributor to, the communities in which it lives and works, and employees are encouraged to be involved in community activities. The company's support – both directly and through the Ryder Charitable Foundation, which is funded by company earnings – is focused in the areas of human needs, culture and education with increasing attention being given in recent years to education.

Our Chairman and Chief Executive Officer, Greg Swienton, has made a deep personal diversity commitment; he emphasizes "Diversity is an important dimension of respect for the individual – one of our core values – and a key to our success in the global marketplace. Changing times call for a dynamic, diverse, multi-disciplined workforce that embraces change, new ideas, and collaborative problem solving. That is the culture we are continually striving to instill here at Ryder."

The Ryland Group, Inc.

24025 Park Sorrento, Ste. 400
Calabasas, CA 91302
Phone: (818) 223-7500
Fax: (818) 223-7667
www.ryland.com/careers

Locations (worldwide)

Corporate: Calabasas, CA
Ryland Mortgage: Scottsdale, AZ and
Woodland Hills, CA
North Central: Baltimore, Chicago,
Cincinnati, Indianapolis, Minneapolis and
Washington, D.C., Austin, Dallas,
Houston and San Antonio
Southeast: Atlanta, Charleston, Charlotte,
Fort Myers, Greensboro, Greenville,
Jacksonville, Orlando and Tampa
West: California's Central Valley,
California's Inland Empire, Denver, Las
Vegas, Phoenix, Sacramento, San Diego
and the San Francisco Bay Area

Contact Person

Karen Ball, Recruiter
24025 Park Sorrento Suite 400
Calabasas, CA 91302
Phone: (818) 223.7523
Fax: (818) 223.7655
E-mail: kball@ryland.com

Recruiting

Please list the schools/types of schools at which you recruit.

• Private schools
• Public state schools

Do you have any special outreach efforts that are directed to encourage minority students to consider your firm?

• Participate in/host minority student job fair(s)
• Outreach to leadership of minority student organizations
• Work with leadership of university minority programs

What activities does the firm undertake to attract minority and women employees?

• Partner programs with women and minority associations
• Participate at minority job fairs
• Seek referrals from other employees
• Utilize online job services

Do you use executive recruiting/search firms to seek to identify new diversity hires?

No

Entry-Level Programs/Full-Time Opportunities

Ryland Mortgage Management Training Program

Geographic location(s) of program: Throughout our 27 markets, locations vary each year

Please describe the training/training component of this program: Ryland's Management Training Program is a company diversity initiative created to increase the number of women and ethnically diverse employees within our management team. By providing participants with a 360-degree view of the residential construction or mortgage industry, Ryland will create a strong pool of employees from which future leaders can emerge.

Ryland's 36 months of on-the-job training will expose you to all aspects of the residential construction or mortgage industry. Through each rotation, your mentor and performance evaluations will provide you on-going guidance and feedback to address your needs and interests.

Who We Are:

Ryland, a Fortune 500 company, is one of the nation's largest homebuilders and a leading mortgage-finance company. The Company currently operates in 27 markets across the country and has built more than 235,000 homes and financed more than 200,000 mortgages since its founding in 1967.

PHASE 1: FINANCIAL SERVICES OPERATIONS (1 year) – Located at the Ryland Operations Center in Scottsdale, AZ, participants gain exposure to mortgage loan origination, processing, underwriting, closing and delivery; title and escrow operations; and insurance operations. Participants will be enrolled in Mortgage Bankers' Association certification program courses.

PHASE 2: FINANCIAL SERVICES PRODUCTION (1 year) – Relocated to one of our high volume branches (see below for possible locations), participants gain exposure to loan and title production/origination, as well as insight into mortgage and builder operations.

PHASE 3: LEADERSHIP DEVELOPMENT ASSIGNMENT (1 year) – Returning to Scottsdale, AZ, participants are assigned to supervisory-level positions, and training focuses on the development of technical and management skills.

BRANCH OPERATIONS – Upon successful completion of the program, graduates will be relocated to a branch where they continue to participate in professional development plans aimed at fostering continued leadership development and career growth.

Locations

First and third rotations are in Scottsdale, AZ. Branch rotation(s) could be in: Atlanta, California, Charlotte, Indianapolis, Texas or Washington, DC area.

Qualifications

- Graduating senior or recent graduate from a four-year college
- Recent college graduates pursuing a master's degree are also eligible
- Major in finance, accounting, business or related field
- Strong academic record and verbal communication skills
- Solid customer service skills
- Previous supervisory management experience preferred, but not required
- Eligible to work in USA (sorry, no visa sponsorship available)
- Successfully pass pre-employment drug test and background check

Benefits

Medical, Dental, 401k, relocation assistance, vacation, life insurance, stock purchase plan, annual bonus, tuition reimbursement, health club reimbursement, home-buying bonus, mentoring, and training!

Ryland Homes Management Training Program

• **FIELD OPERATIONS (18 - 24 months)** – Gain experience in homebuilding production, land acquisition and development.

• **SALES AND MARKETING (6 months)** – Learn basic home-selling techniques and the fundamentals of mortgage financing while working in a Ryland community.

• **DIVISION ADMINISTRATION (6 - 12 months)** – Gain exposure to finance, purchasing and estimating while working in a division office.

Locations

North central
• Austin
• Baltimore
• Chicago,
• Cincinnati
• Dallas
• Houston
• Indianapolis
• Minneapolis
• San Antonio
• Washington, D.C.

Southeast
• Atlanta
• Charleston
• Charlotte
• Fort Myers
• Greensboro
• Greenville
• Jacksonville
• Orlando
• Tampa

West
• Bay Area
• Central Valley
• Denver
• Inland Empire
• Las Vegas
• Phoenix
• Sacramento
• San Diego

Qualifications

• Graduating senior or recent graduate from a four-year college
• Recent college graduates pursuing a master's degree are also eligible
• Major in construction, architecture, civil engineering, business or related field
• Strong academic record and verbal communication skills
• Valid driver's license
• Eligible to work in USA (sorry, no visa sponsorship available)
• Successfully pass pre-employment drug test and background check

Every year, most Ryland divisions hire a diverse participant in the Management Training Program. Candidates are invited to list their preferred geographic locations with the earliest applicants receiving priority.

Benefits

- Medical
- Dental
- 401k
- Auto-allowance
- Relocation assistance
- Vacation
- Life insurance
- Stock purchase plan
- Annual bonus
- Tuition reimbursement
- Health club reimbursement
- Home-buying bonus
- Mentoring
- Training

Strategic Plan and Diversity Leadership

How does the firm's leadership communicate the importance of diversity to everyone at the firm?

Intranet, internet, company newsletter

Safeway, Inc.

5918 Stoneridge Mall Rd.
Pleasanton, CA 94588-3229
www.safeway.com

Contact Person
Hieu Sweeney, Human Resources Representative

Diversity Leadership
Kim Farnham, Director, Human Resouces Planning

Recruiting

Please list the schools/types of schools at which you recruit.

- Ivy League schools
- Other private schools
- Public state schools
- Historically Black Colleges and Universities (HBCUs)
- Hispanic Serving Institutions (HSIs)

Do you have any special outreach efforts that are directed to encourage minority students to consider your firm?

- Hold a reception for minority students
- Advertise in minority student association publication(s)
- Participate in/host minority student job fair(s)
- Sponsor minority student association events
- Firm's employees participate on career panels at school
- Outreach to leadership of minority student organizations
- Scholarships or intern/fellowships for minority students

What activities does the firm undertake to attract minority and women employees?

- Partner programs with women and minority associations
- Conferences
- Participate at minority job fairs
- Seek referrals from other employees
- Utilize online job services

Do you use executive recruiting/search firms to seek to identify new diversity hires?

Yes

Internships and Co-ops

Safeway Inc Summer Internship Program

Deadline for application: Open

Number of interns in the program in summer 2004 (internship) or 2004 (co-op): No information for 2004, 2005 first year

Length of the program: 12 weeks

Percentage of interns/co-ops in the program who receive offers of full-time employment: Not yet tracked

Scholarships

Safeway offers undergraduate scholarships through DECA and graduate students from NSHMBA

Entry-Level Programs/Full-Time Opportunities/Training Programs

Marketing Trainee Program

Length of program: 3-9 months

Geographic location(s) of program: Pleasanton, CA

Please describe the training/training component of this program: 3-9 month training program in which trainees will be introduced to marketing functions including pricing, procurement and category management. After the successful completion of the trainee , you will be placed in one of three areas of marketing.

Strategic Plan and Diversity Leadership

How does the firm's leadership communicate the importance of diversity to everyone at the firm?

Statement from CEO, Training, Diversity Web site on intranet, Diversity Library, Cultural Heritage Videos

Who has primary responsibility for leading diversity initiatives at your firm?

Kim Farnham, Director, HR Planning

Does your firm currently have a diversity committee?

Yes

If yes, please describe how the committee is structured, how often it meets, etc.

13 Diversity Advisory Boards with over 150 members. One senior level board for all of Safeway, and 12 division boards. Individual Advisory Boards determine frequency of meetings. Range from every month to once a quarter.

If yes, does the committee's representation include one or more members of the firm's management/executive committee (or the equivalent)?

Yes

Does the committee and/or diversity leader establish and set goals or objectives consistent with management's priorities?

Yes

Has the firm undertaken a formal or informal diversity program or set of initiatives aimed at increasing the diversity of the firm?

Yes, formal

How often does the firm's management review the firm's diversity progress/results?

Quarterly

The Stats

Figures below represent employee numbers on 12/31/04 and on 12/31/03.

Employees: 151,043 (2004, U.S.)
Employees: 152,289 (2003, U.S.)
Employees: 23,453 (2004, outside U.S.)
Employees: 27,264 (2003, outside U.S.)
Employees: 174,496 (2004, worldwide)
Employees: 179,553 (2003, worldwide)

Demographic details

% Minorities: 26%
Number of minorities: 54,450
% Male: 50%
% Female: 50%
% Minorities: Officers and Managers: 28%
% Women: Officers and Managers: 42%

Retention and Professional Development

Please identify the specific steps you are taking to reduce the attrition rate of minority and women employees.

•Develop and/or support internal employee affinity groups (e.g., minority or women networks within the firm)
•Increase/review compensation relative to competition
•Increase/improve current work/life programs
•Succession plan includes emphasis on diversity
•Work with minority and women employees to develop career advancement plans
•Strengthen mentoring program for all employees, including minorities and women
•Professional skills development program, including minority and women employees

Diversity Mission Statement

Scope

This policy applies to all Safeway employees and applicants.

Policy

At Safeway, the diversity of our employees, customers, and the communities in which we operate is a key ingredient in our success.

• We value and celebrate the diversity of the men and women who make up our workforce.

• We respect the personal worth and unique contributions of each individual.

• We expect that each of us grant others the same respect, cooperation and fair treatment that we seek for ourselves.

Safeway supports equal employment opportunity in hiring, development and advancement for all qualified persons without regard to race, color, religion, age, gender, national origin, ancestry, physical or mental disability, veteran status, sexual orientation, or marital status. Safeway provides reasonable accommodations for applicants and employees with disabilities. We will not tolerate unlawful discrimination in any aspect of employment, nor will we tolerate harassment of any individual or group.

Every officer, manager, supervisor, and employee is expected to support and contribute to an environment that respects and values the diversity of our workforce and ensures the success of Safeway's equal employment opportunity commitment. Employees are encouraged to bring complaints and issues of concern to the company through their management or directly to the Human Resources Department. We take all complaints and concerns seriously, and will handle them promptly.

The principles described in this statement, while founded in state and federal laws, also reflect Safeway traditions and our beliefs that lie at the heart of everything we do.

Schering-Plough Corporation

2000 Galloping Hill Road
Kenilworth, New Jersey 07033-0530
(908) 298-4000
Fax:(908) 298-7653
www.schering-plough.com/careers

Locations (worldwide)

We have a presence in more than 100 countries in North America, Europe, Asia, Africa, Australia and Latin America.

Diversity Leadership

Eugene Tucker, Director, Equal Employment Opportunity and Diversity

2000 Galloping Hill Road
Kenilworth, New Jersey 07033
Phone: (908) 298-4144
Fax: (908) 298-3505
E-mail: eugene.tucker@spcorp.com

Recruiting

Please list the schools/types of schools at which you recruit.

• Ivy League schools
• Public state schools
• Historically Black Colleges and Universities (HBCUs)
• Hispanic Serving Institutions (HSIs)

Do you have any special outreach efforts that are directed to encourage minority students to consider your firm?

• Hold a reception for minority students
• Advertise in minority student association publication(s)
• Participate in/host minority student job fair(s)
• Sponsor minority student association events
• Firm's employees participate on career panels at school
• Outreach to leadership of minority student organizations
• Scholarships or intern/fellowships for minority students

What activities does the firm undertake to attract minority and women employees?

•Partner programs with women and minority associations
• Participate at minority job fairs

Do you use executive recruiting/search firms to seek to identify new diversity hires?

Yes

Internships and Co-ops

Inroads, Research, Manufacturing and Finance

Number of interns in the program in summer 2004 (internship) or 2004 (co-op): Due to organizational changes we did not sponsor internships in 2004.
Pay: Weekly; depends on the education major of the intern.

Length of the program: 11 weeks
Percentage of interns/co-ops in the program who receive offers of full-time employment: 5.0%
Web site for internship/co-op information: www.schering-plough.com/careers

Strategic Plan and Diversity Leadership

How does the firm's leadership communicate the importance of diversity to everyone at the firm?

Web site, news letter and meetings

Who has primary responsibility for leading diversity initiatives at your firm?

Paul Graves, Vice President Global Staffing and Diversity

Does your firm currently have a diversity committee?

No

Does the committee and/or diversity leader establish and set goals or objectives consistent with management's priorities?

Yes

Has the firm undertaken a formal or informal diversity program or set of initiatives aimed at increasing the diversity of the firm?

Yes, formal

How often does the firm's management review the firm's diversity progress/results?

Quarterly

How is the firm's diversity committee and/or firm management held accountable for achieving results?

Performance evaluation

The Stats

Employees: 12,000 (2004, U.S.)
Employees: 18,000 (2004, outside U.S.)
Employees: 30,000 (2004, worldwide)
Revenue: $8.27 billion (2004, worldwide)

Women represent 45.6%; men represent 54.4 of our U.S. population. There are a total of 10 Board Members. Women represent 20.0% and Minorities represent 20.0%. The management team consists of 35 members. 14.3% are women and 11.4% are minority.

Retention and Professional Development

How do 2004 minority and female attrition rates generally compare to those experienced in the prior year period?

About the same as in prior years

Please identify the specific steps you are taking to reduce the attrition rate of minority and women employees.

• Develop and/or support internal employee affinity groups (e.g., minority or women networks within the firm)
• Increase/review compensation relative to competition
• Increase/improve current work/life programs
• Succession plan includes emphasis on diversity
• Work with minority and women employees to develop career advancement plans
• Strengthen mentoring program for all employees, including minorities and women

Shell Oil Company

One Shell Plaza
910 Louisana St.
Houston, TX 77002
(713) 241-6161
Fax:(713) 241-4044
www.shell.com/careers

Contact Person
Julie A. Sacco, Attraction & Branding
Consultant
Diversity Leadership
Carmen Wright, Manager, Graduate Recruitment &
University Relations
910 Louisiana St. Houston, TX 77002

Recruiting

Please list the schools/types of schools at which you recruit.

• Private schools
• Public state schools
• Historically Black Colleges and Universities (HBCUs)
• Hispanic Serving Institutions (HSIs)

Do you have any special outreach efforts that are directed to encourage minority students to consider your firm?

•Hold a reception for minority students
•Conferences
•Advertise in minority student association publication(s)
•Participate in/host minority student job fair(s)
•Sponsor minority student association events
•Firm's employees participate on career panels at school
•Outreach to leadership of minority student organizations
•Scholarships or intern/fellowships for minority students

What activities does the firm undertake to attract minority and women employees?

• Partner programs with women and minority associations
• Conferences
• Participate at minority job fairs
• Seek referrals from other employees
• Utilize online job services

Do you use executive recruiting/search firms to seek to identify new diversity hires?

Yes

Internships and Co-ops

Shell Internship Program

Deadline for application: Year round, best availability October to March
Number of interns in the program in summer 2004 (internship) or 2004 (co-op): 147 interns
Length of the program: 10 to 12 weeks
Web site for internship/co-op information: www.shell.com/careers

Come and experience working with us

What's working life like at a world-class company? Could Shell be the place to start your career? If you're a talented and promising individual, you could get a taste of working with us during the summer.

A paid internship with Shell gives you real work responsibility and the chance to test your abilities on genuine business challenges.

To ensure that you get the maximum benefit from your experience with us, your internship will be tailored to your specific abilities and interests, and will be certain to provide you with an opportunity to prove yourself in a true business environment. The work experience also gives you the opportunity to find out whether you and Shell are right for each other.

A Great Opportunity

•See inside the energy industry
•Take part in real projects
•Try out business challenges
•Work with Shell employees or other students
•Get feedback from senior Shell managers
•Track the long-term results of your work

Throughout your time with us your performance will be assessed and you will receive structured feedback in order to further develop your skills, knowledge and business acumen.

We have a number of summer internship opportunities available for both technical and commercial students. Most take place during the summer in the U.S. However, as a global organization, there will be always be a number of international opportunities for exceptional candidates.

Scholarships

Shell Oil Company Technical Scholarship

Deadline for application for the scholarship program: December 31st
Scholarship award amount:

<u>Undergraduate</u> – $5,000 per year – (4-year renewable scholarship or until bachelor's degree requirements are completed, whichever occurs first.)
<u>Technical</u> – $2,500 total – (Payable over a two-year period)

Shell Oil Company offers scholarships to selected students pursuing two-year technical training in process technology or industrial instrumentation or a four-year college degree in engineering or geosciences at certain colleges as described herein. Scholarship recipients will be selected on a competitive basis by a selection committee and will be notified of their award in the early summer after the submission of their application.

To qualify you must:

Undergraduate Program

• Be a U.S. citizen or a permanent resident of the United States
• Be enrolled full-time and a sophomore, junior or senior in one of the institutions listed here
• Have a minimum 3.2 GPA, which must be maintained throughout your participation in the program
• Major in one of the following disciplines:
• Geology, geophysics or physics
• Chemical, civil, electrical, mechanical, petroleum, geological or geophysical engineering

Technical Training Program

• Be a U.S. citizen or a permanent resident of the United States
• Be enrolled full-time and have completed at least 12 semester hours in one of the community college technical schools listed here
• Have a minimum 3.0 GPA, which must be maintained throughout your participation in the program
• Major in Process Technology, Industrial Instrumentation or a related field to oil industry.

Affinity Groups/Employee Networks

• Network Next (Generation X Network)
• SAIL (Society Absent of Individual Limitations)
• SAPENG (Shell Asian Pacific Employee Network Group)
• SBNG (Shell Black Network Group)
• SHEN (Shell Hispanic Employee Network)
• WAVE (Women Adding Value Everywhere) (Women's Network)
• WIN (Women's Information Network) (Women's Network)
• SPAAN (Shell Progressive African American Network)

Strategic Plan and Diversity Leadership

Who has primary responsibility for leading diversity initiatives at your firm?

Director of Diversity

Does your firm currently have a diversity committee?

Yes

Has the firm undertaken a formal or informal diversity program or set of initiatives aimed at increasing the diversity of the firm?

Yes, formal

Smurfit-Stone Container

150 N. Michigan Ave.
Chicago, IL 60601
(312) 346-6600
Fax: (312) 580-2272
www.smurfit-stone.com

Diversity Leadership
Patty Olsen, Manager of Diversity and Talent Management
Wil Lewis, Corporate HR Manager – Recruiting Lead

Contact Person
Patty Olsen, Manager of Diversity and Talent Management
150 N. Michigan Avenue
Phone: (312) 580-4800
Fax: (312) 649-4332
E-mail: polsen@smurfit.com

Recruiting

Please list the schools/types of schools at which you recruit.

• Public state schools
• Historically Black Colleges and Universities (HBCUs)

Do you have any special outreach efforts that are directed to encourage minority students to consider your firm?

•Hold a reception for minority students
•Advertise in minority student association publication(s)
•Outreach to leadership of minority student organizations
•Scholarships or intern/fellowships for minority students

What activities does the firm undertake to attract minority and women employees?

• Partner programs with women and minority associations
• Participate at minority job fairs
• Seek referrals from other employees
• Utilize online job services

Do you use executive recruiting/search firms to seek to identify new diversity hires?

Yes

If yes, list all women- and/or minority-owned executive search/recruiting firms to which the firm paid a fee for placement services in the past 12 months:

Just began using in 2005.

Scholarships

Washington University Scholarship

Deadline for application for the scholarship program: January 2003
Scholarship award amount: $10,000/year

Scholarship given to a diverse student at Washington University based upon grades, other activities, and need. We are in the process of putting together a recommendation and a budget for scholarships to be distributed on campus in 2006.

Affinity Groups/Employee Networks

Women in Leadership

The team focuses on the recruitment, development and advancement of females within the organization. The team meets every other month and is working modifications to make more family friendly policies. They are also organizing networking/professional development events for professional females across the company. Two events are scheduled in Q3, 2005.

We are scheduled to form an African American team in Q4.

Entry-Level Programs/Full-Time Opportunities

Advanced Leadership Development

Length of program: Three phases of one week sessions
Geographic location(s) of program: St. Louis

Please describe the training/training component of this program:

• **Phase One:** Team Leadership – Sales & Marketing, Managerial Accounting, Leadership and Communications, Ethical Decision Making

• **Phase Two:** Strategic Business Unit Leadership – Competitive Strategy, Organization Strategy, Operating Strategy, Financial Strategy

• **Phase Three:** Corporate Leadership – Leading Organizational Change, Managing Organizational Change, Corporate Strategy, Corporate Finance

Please describe any other educational components of this program (i.e., tuition reimbursement):

Team with Washington University Faculty to deliver. All costs for room and board and training funded by Smurfit-Stone.

Strategic Plan and Diversity Leadership

How does the firm's leadership communicate the importance of diversity to everyone at the firm?

Our strategy is to infuse diversity as a piece in everything that we do. Diversity components are included in emails, speeches from CEO and key leadership, incorporation into meeting topics, company newsletters.

Who has primary responsibility for leading diversity initiatives at your firm?

Patty Olsen, Manager of Diversity and Talent Management with sponsorship from CEO and VP of HR

Does your firm currently have a diversity committee?

Yes

If yes, please describe how the committee is structured, how often it meets, etc

The committee is made up of key participants from the operating groups leadership (VP Level and HR Director) and others in Corporate (i.e. Communications, Legal, Supplier Diversity, Recruiting). The team was just recently reorganized in 2005 to ensure it was not simply an "HR Team" and truly a team that can impact change. The team is sponsored by the CEO and VP of HR who attend meetings periodically. The team meets every other month. Each of the operating units have also formed teams to drive the corporate strategy into the facilities.

If yes, does the committee's representation include one or more members of the firm's management/executive committee (or the equivalent)?

Yes

Please describe the committee.

The committee has a total of 15 people and was just reorganized in 2005 to include key executive leadership. In 2005 the team meets every other month and the members are also working to drive diversity into their operating units.

Total executives on the comittee: 7 VP Level Executives, 4 Director Level Executives

Does the committee and/or diversity leader establish and set goals or objectives consistent with management's priorities?

Yes

Has the firm undertaken a formal or informal diversity program or set of initiatives aimed at increasing the diversity of the firm?

Yes, formal. We have formed the Diversity Committee that is setting strategy for the Operating Units. We also have formed partnerships with professional organizations (i.e. NSHMBA) and are working with colleges with the intent of increasing the diversity representation in our hires. We are also working through Succession Planning and Performance Management to retain and promote diverse individuals particularly into the manager ranks.

How often does the firm's management review the firm's diversity progress/results?

Quarterly

How is the firm's diversity committee and/or firm management held accountable for achieving results?

The metrics are presented to the Executive Committee and Board of Directors each quarter. Diversity progress is incorporated into the HR Leadership and CEO's incentives and we are working on getting incorporated into all leadership's incentives in 2006.

The Stats

DEMOGRAPHIC PROFILE	TOTAL IN THE U.S.	
	2004	2003
Number of employees	35,000	38,000
Revenues	$8.3 billion	$7.7 billion

POPULATION	INDUSTRY	SSCC
White	76%	24%
Minority	70%	30%
Male	69%	83%
Female	31%	17%

Compared to industry we are competitive as it relates to minorities. We are currently working to increase our percentage of females.

Retention and Professional Development

How do 2004 minority and female attrition rates generally compare to those experienced in the prior year period?

About the same as in prior years

Please identify the specific steps you are taking to reduce the attrition rate of minority and women employees.

• Develop and/or support internal employee affinity groups (e.g., minority or women networks within the firm)
• Increase/review compensation relative to competition
• Increase/improve current work/life programs
• Succession plan includes emphasis on diversity
• Work with minority and women employees to develop career advancement plans
• Strengthen mentoring program for all employees, including minorities and women
• Professional skills development program, including minority and women employees

Diversity Mission Statement

To establish a company-wide culture that supports our CustomerONE philosophy and capitalizes on the differences and uniqueness of our employees.

The Employer Says

Activities in 2005

• Formation of diversity-related affinity groups (e.g. Women in Leadership)
• Creation of Division Diversity Teams to drive change into the Divisions and facilities
• Lunches/Dinners with CEO and high performing diverse groups of employees at facilities and at Corporate
• Pilot of New Hire Coaching Program
• Refinement of Career Pathing Model and continued emphasis on succession planning with tracking of diverse employees
• Incorporate diversity training into relevant existing training courses
• Creation of campus recruitment strategy
• Corporate Management Development Program
• Strong focus on Supplier Diversity – To achieve our goal of 5% of total applicable spend, we developed a progressive step-up plan that would increase our targeted growth goal over a five year period
• Measures provided quarterly to BOD
• Reengineering exit interview process to collect more accurate data on employees reasons for leaving – by Q3

Sodexho

9801 Washingtonian Blvd.
Gaithersburg, MD 20878
www.sodexhoUSA.com

Locations (worldwide)
Numerous – over 6,000 client locations
throughout the United States

Contact Person
John Lee, Director of College and External
Relations
200 Continental Drive, Suite 400
Newark, DE 19713
Phone: (302) 738-9500 ext. 5206
Fax: (302)738-5218
E-mail: john.lee@sodexhousa.com

Recruiting

Please list the schools/types of schools at which you recruit.

• *Ivy League schools:* Cornell
• *Other private schools:* J & W Providence, Villanova, Widener, Brigham Young University
• *Historically Black Colleges and Universities (HBCUs)*
• *Hispanic Serving Institutions (HSIs)*
• *Other predominantly minority and/or women's colleges:* Lexington College

We recruit at over 100 colleges, universities and Dietetic Internships.

Do you have any special outreach efforts that are directed to encourage minority students to consider your firm?

• Conferences: National Society of Minority Hospitality Students, HBCU Hospitality Management Consortium
• Advertise in minority student association publication(s)
• Participate in/host minority student job fair(s)
• Sponsor minority student association events
• Firm's employees participate on career panels at school
• Outreach to leadership of minority student organizations
• Scholarships or intern/fellowships for minority students

What activities does the firm undertake to attract minority and women employees?

• Partner programs with women and minority associations
• Conferences
• Participate at minority job fairs
• Seek referrals from other employees
• Utilize online job services
• Minority Trade Journals

Do you use executive recruiting/search firms to seek to identify new diversity hires?

Yes

Internships and Co-ops

HACU, NSMH

Deadline for application: March 9, 2005

Number of interns in the program in summer 2004 (internship) or 2004 (co-op): 17

Pay: $420/week

Length of the program: 10 weeks

Web site for internship/co-op information: www.sodexhoUSA.com

Interns are assigned to operating locations and complete a combination of our "Beginning Your Career" management training program, special projects and attend the BYC orientation.

Scholarships

HACU (as part of internship program); HIRE Scholarship co-sponsor via NSMH

Deadline for application for the scholarship program: March 9th, 2005

Scholarship award amount: Varies

Scholarship programs are through specific third party organizations.

Affinity Groups/Employee Networks

• African Leadership Forum (AALF)

• Sodexho Organization of Latinos (SOL)

• Women's Network Group (WING)

• Pan Asian Network Group (PANG)

• People Respecting Individual Diversity and Equality (PRIDE)

Information on Network (Affinity) Groups is available through our Home Page at www.sodexhousa.com

Meetings are variable based on regional and local chapters.

Entry-Level Programs/Full-Time Opportunities

"Beginning your Career"

Length of program: 90 days

Geographic location(s) of program: At individual location sites

Please describe the training/training component of this program: Sodexho University offers an in-depth management orientation process that includes a three-day orientation event (Beginning Your Career or BYC) combined with a self-study managerial skills program (Building Your Career-The First 90 Days). During the 3-day classroom experience, managers are introduced to Sodexho's culture and philosophies through eight workbooks from the "First 90 Days" kit.

Please describe any other educational components of this program (i.e., tuition reimbursement): Sodexho University offers many training programs (online and facilitated) as well as Accredited Degree Programs. Through Sodexho University, you have access to diverse learning opportunities specially designed to help you give your best to our clients and customers. Experts from each business line contributes to learning tools designed for you, the Sodexho employee. Flexible options include self-study, instructor-led classes and online learning.

Strategic Plan and Diversity Leadership

How does the firm's leadership communicate the importance of diversity to everyone at the firm?

E-mails, web site, newsletters, meetings.

Who has primary responsibility for leading diversity initiatives at your firm?

Rohini Anand, Chief Diversity Officer

Does your firm currently have a diversity committee?

Yes

Please describe how the committee is structured, how often it meets, etc.

There are Corporate and Divisional Diversity Councils. Structure and meeting schedules vary based on size and geography of the divisional councils.

Does the committee's representation include one or more members of the firm's management/executive committee (or the equivalent)?

Yes

> **Total executives on the committee:** Varies due to the fact that there are multiple councils

Does the committee and/or diversity leader establish and set goals or objectives consistent with management's priorities?

Yes

Has the firm undertaken a formal or informal diversity program or set of initiatives aimed at increasing the diversity of the firm?

Yes, formal. Our diversity programs are described at our website: www.sodexhousa.com

How often does the firm's management review the firm's diversity progress/results?

Monthly, Quarterly, Annually. There are multiple reporting venues used

How is the firm's diversity committee and/or firm management held accountable for achieving results?

Included in Performance Objectives

The Stats

Employees: 110,000 (2004, U.S.)
Revenue: $5.9 billion (2004, U.S.)

Retention and Professional Development

How do 2004 minority and female attrition rates generally compare to those experienced in the prior year period?

About the same as in prior years

Please identify the specific steps you are taking to reduce the attrition rate of minority and women employees.

• Develop and/or support internal employee affinity groups (e.g., minority or women networks within the firm)

• Increase/review compensation relative to competition

• Increase/improve current work/life programs

• Adopt dispute resolution process

• Succession plan includes emphasis on diversity

• Work with minority and women employees to develop career advancement plans

• Review work assignments and hours billed to key client matters to make sure minority and women employees are not being excluded

• Strengthen mentoring program for all employees, including minorities and women

• Professional skills development program, including minority and women employees

• Candidate Selection Review Panels

Diversity Mission Statement

We are committed to respecting, leveraging, and celebrating the diversity of our workforce, our clientele, and the communities in which we live, work, and serve.

The Employer Says

Diversity and inclusion is a strategic imperative at Sodexho. We measure our progress and report out our results on a quarterly basis along with our financial performance. Managers are held accountable for diversity results with a direct link to their incentive compensation. The use of an innovative scorecard provides managers with their progress.

Sodexho believes that workforce diversity is essential to the Company's growth and long-term success. By valuing and managing diversity at work, Sodexho can leverage the skills, knowledge, and abilities of all employees to increase employee, client, and customer satisfaction

Managing diversity at work is a process of inclusion; it is a means of achieving superior individual and group performance by recognizing and celebrating each employee's unique contribution toward meeting the Company's business objectives.

Sodexho believes that management's ability to respect and manage employee differences is essential to attracting diverse employees, and building diverse, high-performing work teams, which will allow us to more effectively serve our clients and enhance the Company's competitive advantage in the marketplace.

"At Sodexho we believe Diversity is a business imperative and ethical responsibility grounded in our values of Team Spirit, Service Spirit and Spirit of Progress. In our continuing efforts to attain a diversity mature organization, we understand the critical requirement to seek, leverage and respect the Diversity of our workforce, our clients and the communities in which we live, work and serve"

Richard Macedonia, President and CEO

We work together.

A network: a complex, interconnected group of people

The success of any company depends on its diverse network of employees. At Sprint, our employees come from different backgrounds, beliefs, lifestyles and abilities, allowing us to see the world from a fresh perspective and serve our customers in creative new ways. Recognizing and valuing differences enables us to create clear, simple communications solutions designed with you in mind.

The Sprint network of employees and suppliers is just as diverse as the people we serve. Better yet, we are the people we serve. We are calling you from down the street and sending you instant messages from across the nation. We are Sprint. And we are working together.

www.sprint.com

Together with NEXTEL

DiversityInc
top50
Companies
FOR DIVERSITY
2005

Sprint Nextel is proud to be an EEO/AA employer. We value diversity and offer a quality workplace.

Sprint

Sprint World Headquarters,
6200 Sprint Pkwy.
Overland Park, KS 66251
Phone: (800) 829-0965
Fax: (913) 523-8312
www.sprint.com/hr

Employment Contact:
Julio F. Suarez, Diversity Manager
6200 Sprint Parkway, KSOPHF0210-2A466
Overland Park, KS 66251
Phone: (913) 794-1468
Fax: (913) 523-2705
E-mail: Julio.F.Suarez@mail.sprint.com

Recruiting

Please list the schools/types of schools at which you recruit.

- *Public state schools:* Iowa State University; Kansas State University; Truman State University; University of Nebraska – Lincoln; University of Kansas; University of Maryland; University of Missouri – Columbia; University of Missouri – Kansas City; University of Missouri – Rolla; University of Virginia; Central Missouri State University; Florida A&M University; Florida State University; Northwest Missouri State University; Pittsburg State University; Purdue University; Southwest Missouri State University; University of Florida; Virginia Tech; Kansas City, MO Community Colleges
- *Historically Black Colleges and Universities (HBCUs)*

Do you have any special outreach efforts that are directed to encourage minority students to consider your firm?

- Hold a reception for minority students
- Conferences: Multicultural Student Success Conference, Alliance for Minority Engineering
- Advertise in minority student association publication(s)
- Participate in/host minority student job fair(s)
- Sponsor minority student association events
- Firm's employees participate on career panels at school
- Outreach to leadership of minority student organizations
- Scholarships or intern/fellowships for minority students

What activities does the firm undertake to attract minority and women employees?

- Partner programs with women and minority associations – INROADS, UNCF
- Conferences: NABA, NSBE, SHPE, SWE, NSHMBA, NBMBAA
- Participate at minority job fairs
- Seek referrals from other employees

Do you use executive recruiting/search firms to seek to identify new diversity hires?

No

Scholarships

Sprint Minority Engineering Scholarship Program

> *Deadline for application for the scholarship program:* April 1
>
> *Scholarship award amount:* Full scholarship
>
> *Web site or other contact information for scholarship:* www.kcmetro.edu/pubs/campusScholarshipLists.pdf

The Sprint Minority Engineering Scholarship Program is co-sponsored by the Kansas City Metropolitan Community Colleges, the University of Missouri-Rolla and Sprint to attract, encourage and support promising minority students wishing to enter the field of engineering or computer science.

UNCF/Sprint Scholars Program

> *Deadline for application for the scholarship program:* January 1
>
> *Scholarship award amount:* $5,000 annual award
>
> *Web site or other contact information for scholarship:* http://www.uncf.org

The UNCF/Sprint Scholars Program provides educational opportunities for African Americans, American Indians/Alaskan Natives, Asian Pacific Islander Americans and Hispanic American students who are U.S. Citizens.

Internships and Co-ops

Sprint Internship Program

> *Deadline for application:* Varies depending on campus interviews for fall and spring
>
> *Number of interns in the program in summer 2004 (internship) or 2004 (co-op):* 91 in internship
>
> *Pay:* $10-$22 hourly wage depending on school classification and prior intern experience
>
> *Length of the program:* 10 to 12 weeks
>
> *Percentage of interns/co-ops in the program who receive offers of full-time employment:* 60%
>
> *Web site for internship/co-op information:* www.sprint.com/hr/college_intern.html

The Internship Program is designed to enhance Sprint's recruitment efforts and reinforce the relationships developed through these efforts. The program objectives are to:

• promote meaningful assignments to enhance the student's learning
• provide Intern Program orientation materials to students and their supervisors
• coordinate opportunities for interaction with Sprint managers, executives and other interns
• enhance recruiting efforts with conversion to hire

Internships are 10-12 weeks in duration. During the internship, the intern learns about the company, the department functions and gains valuable work experience enhancing his or her educational goals. Sprint hires interns based on education and experience and business needs. They are placed in Business Sales, Consumer Sales, Finance, Information or Permanent Residents, through scholarships of up to $5,000 and paid summer internships at Sprint locations. The program accepts juniors majoring in Accounting, Business Administration, Economics, Finance, (Computer, Electrical, Industrial, Management) Engineering, Mathematics, Statistics and Management Information Systems.

Affinity Groups/Employee Networks

Diamond Network

The Diamond Network is an African American-focused affinity group whose mission is to aid Sprint in recruiting, retaining, developing and promoting African American employees. The vision of the Diamond Network is to be recognized as an organization that promotes inclusion and diversity as a competitive advantage for Sprint.

The goals of the Diamond Network are:

• Represent Sprint in recruitment activities
• Foster professional development
• Provide networking opportunities
• Promote diversity and inclusion

Enlace

Vision: The vision of Enlace is to be a Sprint resource for communicating, supporting and engaging the Hispanic community, employees and the Hispanic culture.

Mission: Enlace is committed to supporting the partnership with Sprint and the Hispanic Community. From community involvement, Hispanic cultural enrichment to employee development and market initiatives, Enlace is dedicated to promoting diversity.

Our Commitments:

• Community Involvement: To strengthen relationships and opportunities between Enlace and the Hispanic community
• Cultural Enrichment: To encourage the learning of and appreciation for Hispanic heritage and culture
• Employee Development: To encourage and promote self-development and career employment
• Market Initiative: To support Sprint initiatives that provide a competitive advantage for Hispanic marketing initiatives

The Alliance Council

Mission Statement: To create and maintain a company culture in which diversity is valued, respect for each other is practiced in spirit and deed and fairness in the application of policies and practices is achieved. Special emphasis is given to creating and maintaining positive changes within the culture of Sprint with respect to the professional growth and advancement of people of color, and to creating and maintaining a workforce that reflects the diversity of the customers and communities we serve.

Entry-Level Programs/Full-Time Opportunities

Leadership Development Program (LDP)

> *Length of program:* One year
> *Geographic location(s) of program:* Participants are located throughout Sprint locations in the U.S.A.

Please describe the training/training component of this program: The Leadership Development Program is aimed at four employee populations: the Senior Talent Pool, targeted future leaders, newly appointed leaders and in-place management. Participants learn about themselves via assessment surveys; they develop skills via on-the-job activities; they learn through assigned mentors; they work with an internal coach to further identify development areas; they attend satellite presentations on leadership topics presented by well-known leaders/authors.

New College Hire Development Program (NCHDP)

Length of program: Two years

Geographic location(s) of program: Participants are located throughout Sprint locations in the U.S.A

Please describe the training/training component of this program: The New College Hire Development Program (NCHDP) targets hires from college recruiting that are placed in entry-level exempt positions.

This program focuses on a development roadmap to help engage, acclimate and assimilate new college hires into Sprint and the Telecom industry during the first two years of employment. The program has four components: an orientation week, a core curriculum focused around the Sprint dimensions, a functional curriculum which is germane to the participant's area of entry (Marketing, IT, Engineering, Finance or Project Management), and tailored development opportunities such as job rotations and on-the-job training.

The Staff Associate Program (SAP)

Length of program: Three years

Geographic location(s) of program: Participants are located throughout Sprint locations in the U.S.A

Please describe the training/training component of this program: The Staff Associate Program develops Sprint's future leaders by hiring the best talent from premier business schools, accelerating their development through customized rotation paths and facilitating their exit from the program into positions of leadership within the company. The program has a continued commitment to as inclusion strategy by actively seeking diverse talent.

The Finance Management Development Program (FMDP)

Length of program: Three years

Geographic location(s) of program: Participants are located throughout Sprint locations in the U.S.A

Please describe the training/training component of this program: The Finance Management Development Program is an intensive three-year accelerated development program designed to develop well-rounded finance management professionals who play an integral part of making major business decisions. Participants in the FMDP build technical and leadership skills through personalized rotational assignments and special projects. This high-risk/high-rewards program challenges individuals to learn quickly and to make meaningful contributions to the company. Participants are paired with executive mentors and receive coaching and performance feedback throughout the program. Upon successful completion of the program, the participant is placed in a Finance leadership role.

Strategic Plan and Diversity Leadership

How does the firm's leadership communicate the importance of diversity to everyone at the firm?

Sprint communicates its commitment to diversity via e-mails, newsletters, training, web cast and executive presentations.

Who has primary responsibility for leading diversity initiatives at your firm?

David P. Thomas – Chief Diversity Officer

Does your firm currently have a diversity committee?

Yes. The Sprint Executive Diversity Council is composed of executives from our various business units and meets quarterly. The Council is chaired by our CEO, Gary Forsee, and co-chaired by the Chief Diversity Officer.

If yes, does the committee's representation include one or more members of the firm's management/executive committee (or the equivalent)?

Yes

Please describe the committee.

The Sprint Executive Diversity Council is made up of ten executives from our various business units. The council meets on a quarterly basis.

Does the committee and/or diversity leader establish and set goals or objectives consistent with management's priorities?

Yes

Has the firm undertaken a formal or informal diversity program or set of initiatives aimed at increasing the diversity of the firm?

Yes, formal

How often does the firm's management review the firm's diversity progress/results?

Quarterly

How is the firm's diversity committee and/or firm management held accountable for achieving results?

The success of the company's diversity and inclusion initiatives is part of the executive's performance review evaluation.

The Stats

DEMOGRAPHIC PROFILE	TOTAL IN THE U.S.		TOTAL OUTSIDE THE U.S		TOTAL WORLDWIDE	
	2004	2003	2004	2003	2004	2003
Number of employees	59,939	65,774	246	250	60,185	60,024
Revenues	N/A	N/A	N/A	N/A	$27.4 billion	$26.2 billion

Retention and Professional Development

How do 2004 minority and female attrition rates generally compare to those experienced in the prior year period?

Lower than in prior years

Please identify the specific steps you are taking to reduce the attrition rate of minority and women employees.

• Develop and/or support internal employee affinity groups (e.g., minority or women networks within the firm)
• Increase/improve current work/life programs
• Succession plan includes emphasis on diversity
• Strengthen mentoring program for all employees, including minorities and women
• Professional skills development program, including minority and women employees

Diversity Mission Statement

To foster a culture of inclusion in the Sprint community – resulting in tangible marketplace wins.

The Employer Says

To learn about Sprint's commitment to diversity and inclusion, please visit www.sprint.com/diversity

St. Paul Travelers

385 Washington St.
St. Paul, MN 55102
www.stpaultravelers.com

Diversity Leadership

Allison Keeton, Director College Relations
Laurie Buyniski, College Relations Consultant
One Tower Square
Hartford, CT 06183
Phone: (860) 954-2781
Fax: (860) 277-1970
E-mail: lebuynis@spt.com

Recruiting

Please list the schools/types of schools at which you recruit.

• Private schools
• Public state schools
• Historically Black Colleges and Universities (HBCUs)

Do you have any special outreach efforts that are directed to encourage minority students to consider your firm?

•Advertise in minority student association publication(s)
•Participate in/host minority student job fair(s)
•Sponsor minority student association events
•Firm's employees participate on career panels at school
•Outreach to leadership of minority student organizations
•Scholarships or intern/fellowships for minority students

What activities does the firm undertake to attract minority and women employees?

• Partner programs with women and minority associations
• Participate at minority job fairs
• Seek referrals from other employees
• Utilize online job services

Internships and Co-ops

Information Technology Leadership Development

Deadline for application: January
Number of interns in the program in summer 2004 (internship) or 2004 (co-op): 40 interns
Length of the program: 10 weeks
Percentage of interns/co-ops in the program who receive offers of full-time employment: 50%

Web site for internship/co-op information: http://www.stpaultravelers.com/careers/new_grads/interns/index.html

Actuarial Leadership Development Program Internship

Deadline for application: January

Number of interns in the program in summer 2004 (internship) or 2004 (co-op): 15 interns

Length of the program: 10 weeks

Percentage of interns/co-ops in the program who receive offers of full-time employment: 90%

Web site for internship/co-op information: http://www.stpaultravelers.com/careers/new_grads/interns/index.html

Financial Management Leadership Development Program Internship

Deadline for application: January

Number of interns in the program in summer 2004 (internship) or 2004 (co-op): 8 interns

Length of the program: 10 weeks

Percentage of interns/co-ops in the program who receive offers of full-time employment: 30%

Web site for internship/co-op information: http://www.stpaultravelers.com/careers/new_grads/interns/index.html

Personal Lines Product Management Internship Program

Deadline for application: January

Number of interns in the program in summer 2004 (internship) or 2004 (co-op): 10 interns

Length of the program: 10 weeks

Web site for internship/co-op information: http://www.stpaultravelers.com/careers/new_grads/interns/index.html

Investments Internship

Deadline for application: January

Number of interns in the program in summer 2004 (internship) or 2004 (co-op): 2 interns

Length of the program: 10 weeks

Web site for internship/co-op information: http://www.stpaultravelers.com/careers/new_grads/interns/index.html

INROADS Internship

Deadline for application: January

Number of interns in the program in summer 2004 (internship) or 2004 (co-op): 12 interns

Percentage of interns/co-ops in the program who receive offers of full-time employment: 40% (2 of 5 seniors)

Web site for internship/co-op information: http://www.stpaultravelers.com/careers/new_grads/interns/index.html

The St. Paul Travelers Summer Internship Programs provide college students with an excellent opportunity to gain firsthand experience. Our internship programs are designed to attract talented and motivated students who desire a career in actuarial, finance, information technology, or underwriting. Our opportunities extend beyond the work station. Beside our challenging assignments, St. Paul Travelers interns are busy with many activities within St. Paul Travelers as well within the Saint Paul, MN, and Hartford, CT communities.

Scholarships

Please describe the scholarship program, including basic requirements, eligibility, length of program and any other details you feel are relevant.

Basic requirements include overall GPA of 3.2 or above, majors in Actuarial Science, Finance, MIS, CS, Risk Management & Insurance, Economics (majors depend on the school), and ability to work in the US. The scholarship is a one-time award. For deadline and award amount, see school for details.

- Babson College
- Bentley College
- Bryant College
- Cal State-Fullerton
- Central Connecticut State University
- Hamilton College
- Howard University
- Lafayette
- Rensselaer Polytechnic Institute (RPI)
- St. Thomas
- SUNY – Albany
- SUNY -Geneseo
- SUNY – Stonybrook
- Temple
- University of CT
- University of GA
- University of Hartford
- UMASS
- University of MN
- University of Notre Dame
- Univ WI—Madison
- Williams College
- WPI

Entry-Level Programs/Full-Time Opportunities

Information Technology Leadership Development Program

Length of program: 3-5 years
Geographic location(s) of program: St. Paul, MN and Hartford, CT

ITLDP is a challenging, multi-faceted program designed to develop well-rounded, information systems leaders capable of mastering a dynamic business and technical environment. Each rotation increases in level of responsibility and complexity. Through the series of rotational assignments, participants receive in-depth exposure to information systems at St. Paul Travelers, while becoming familiar with the insurance and financial services industry. The program curriculum includes a study of insurance, various technical skills, and project management. In addition, seminars are held covering information resource management, strategic planning and effective leadership. The program curriculum is supplemented with specific training required by each rotation.

Actuarial Leadership Development Program

Length of program: 3 years
Geographic location(s) of program: St. Paul, MN and Hartford, CT

Please describe any other educational components of this program (i.e., tuition reimbursement): The St. Paul Travelers Actuarial Leadership Development Program (ALDP) focuses on building actuarial and business expertise and stimulating leadership development for individuals interested in pursuing an actuarial career in the insurance industry. Rotational work assignments give the ALDP participant an opportunity to experience the core actuarial functions across the various St. Paul Travelers business lines. Examples of rotational assignments include: Pricing/Product Development, Reserving, Business Planning and Research. In addition to the actuarial exam support and rotational work assignments, the ALDP offers a core Leadership Training Curriculum designed to give ALDP participants the tools necessary to achieve a leadership position in the organization. This curriculum includes seminars covering topics like management communications, information resource management, strategic planning, and effective leadership. The program curriculum is also supplemented with specific training required for each rotation.

Financial Management Leadership Development Program

Length of program: 3 years
Geographic location(s) of program: St. Paul, MN and Hartford, CT

Please describe any other educational components of this program (i.e., tuition reimbursement): The St. Paul Travelers Financial Management Leadership Development Program focuses on leadership development for individuals interested in pursuing a career in financial management within the property & casualty insurance industry. The FMLDP exposes you to senior management, whether it's during your rotation, at a business meeting, or during networking opportunities. As you work through your various rotations you will be in roles key to business function and will be leaned on by management to push yourself, for your continued learning, as well as to help the business succeed. Throughout all phases of the Financial Management Leadership Development Program you will receive both technical and leadership training. The leadership training consists of 1-3 day seminars/workshops on various topics, such as management communications, strategic planning and effective leadership. The program curriculum is also supplemented with specific technical training required for each rotation.

Personal Lines Product Management

Length of program: 1 year
Geographic location(s) of program: Hartford, CT

Please describe any other educational components of this program (i.e., tuition reimbursement): Based in Personal Lines headquarters in Hartford, CT, our Product Management organization operates in 11 regions across the country. Each team provides market, product and pricing analysis to rapidly deliver our products via increasingly sophisticated segmentation strategies. As a part of this program you will learn how to determine adequate pricing of products, analyze the marketplace first hand, as well as through competitor and industry data, quantify the impact of pricing and underwriting decisions, negotiate pricing decisions with various distribution channels, respond to state insurance department inquiries, build and monitor local agency strategy and performance, and facilitate peer development. The educational programs provided for participants of this program include technical training, interpersonal and management skills, business skills, project management and other skills training.

Environmental Claim Assistance Account Executive Program

Length of program: 12-14 weeks
Geographic location(s) of program: Baltimore, MD; Fairfax, VA; Indianapolis, IN; Dallas, TX; Hartford, CT; Denver, CO; Houston, TX

Please describe any other educational components of this program (i.e., tuition reimbursement): In this position, candidates work closely with our clients, brokers, and legal professionals to resolve coverage issues and settle high-risk environmental claims. Types of claims include asbestos, toxic chemicals, pharmaceutical products, hazardous waste and pollution. Formal paid training program which combines classroom and independent study. Practical training is designed to give trainees hands-on experience and confidence and is an integral part of our program. One-on-one mentoring provides for career guidance and sharp insights into current business and case law.

Underwriting Program

Length of program: 1 year
Geographic location(s) of program: National opportunities

Please describe any other educational components of this program (i.e., tuition reimbursement): The Underwriting Development Program's main goal is to attract students from a diverse background and prepare them for the role of a Commercial Lines Account Executive/Underwriter. The program is designed to develop a group of business leaders skilled in insurance underwriting, sales, marketing and product knowledge through a structured rotational program, coupled with training and mentoring. After being hired into a business unit, participants receive nine weeks of classroom training in our insurance operations office in Hartford, CT. They will then receive an additional three months of on the job training at their assigned locations followed by six months of a small assignment. To facilitate the learning process participants in the program will develop a mentoring relationship with individuals in senior management positions.

Bond Account Manager Trainee

Length of program: 6 months to one year
Geographic location(s) of program: National opportunities

Please describe any other educational components of this program (i.e., tuition reimbursement): Our Account Managers have a diverse role. Responsibilities include: sales and underwriting including evaluating exposures and negotiating terms and conditions, interaction with our independent agents and customers, and acting as a Marketing Representative to promote and expand Travelers' Bond business. Formal classroom training in our offices in Hartford, CT and practical training at one of our Field Offices will prepare you for this position. The training period is typically six months to one year. The combination of classroom and on-the-job training is designed to provide employees with the tools to develop leadership, sales, underwriting and management skills. Additionally, we encourage all of our employees to direct their own careers by taking initiative to identify opportunities that will help them succeed including tuition reimbursement.

Diversity Mission Statement

A diverse workforce builds positive relationships with our communities, customers, and investors. By incorporating diversity into the fabric of our business, we expand our business opportunities and contribute to the company's success.

St. Paul Travelers provides equal employment opportunity to all employees and applicants for employment free from unlawful discrimination based on race, color, religion, gender, age, national origin, disability, veteran status, marital status, sexual orientation or any other status or condition protected by local, state or federal law.

Staples, Inc.

500 Staples Drive
Framingham, MA 01072
www.staples.com

Contact Person
Michael Danubio, Manager of College
Relations and Technical Recruiting

Diversity Leadership
Doreen Nichols, Director of Associate Relations &
Diversity
500 Staples Drive
Framingham, MA 01702
Phone: (508) 253-5000
Fax: (508) 253-4227
E-mail: collegerecruiting@staples.com

Recruiting

Please list the schools/types of schools at which you recruit.

- *Ivy League schools:* Harvard, Dartmouth
- *Other private schools:* Northeastern, Babson, Bentley, Boston College, Boston University, Worcester Polytechnic Institute
- *Public state schools:* UMASS Amherst
- *Historically Black Colleges and Universities (HBCUs):* Morehouse, Spelman

Do you have any special outreach efforts that are directed to encourage minority students to consider your firm?

- Hold a reception for minority students
- Conferences: National Society of Hispanic MBAs (NSHMBA); National Black MBA Association (NBMBAA) ; Association of Latino Professionals in Finance and Accounting (ALPFA); National Association of Black Accountants (NABA); Monster Diversity Leadership Program
- Participate in/host minority student job fair(s)
- Outreach to leadership of minority student organizations
- Scholarships or intern/fellowships for minority students

What activities does the firm undertake to attract minority and women employees?

- Partner programs with women and minority associations
- Conferences: National Society of Hispanic MBAs (NSHMBA); National Black MBA Association (NBMBAA) ; Association of Latino Professionals in Finance and Accounting (ALPFA); National Association of Black Accountants (NABA)
- Participate at minority job fairs
- Seek referrals from other employees
- Utilize online job services

Do you use executive recruiting/search firms to seek to identify new diversity hires?

Yes

Internships and Co-ops

Deadline for application: March 31st; for co-ops, March 1st or October 1st

Number of interns in the program in summer 2004 (internship) or 2004 (co-op): 32 interns, 5 co-ops

Pay: $10-$12/hour interns; $13-$17/hour co-op

Length of the program: 12 weeks internship; 6 months co-op

Percentage of interns/co-ops in the program who receive offers of full-time employment: 25%

Web site for internship/co-op information: www.staplescampuscareers.com

We have interns in our home office in many different functional groups including merchandising, information systems, finance/accounting, marketing, strategy, public relations and media. Students must have a GPA of 3.0 and typically our opportunities are best suited for rising sophomores or above. In addition to the day-to-day responsibilities of the internship Staples interns are given the opportunity to participate in "lunch and learn" speaker series which gives the intern the opportunity to hear from and learn from senior level executives in the company. Past luncheons have focused on learning about Staples site usability, Staples Sports Marketing, and Staples Brands. We take the interns on a tour of one of our stores and they get to collectively have lunch and Q&A with the CEO. It is a great summer experience that is capped off with Intern Presentation Day – an opportunity for the interns to strut their stuff and give a presentation on what they did during their internship.

Scholarships

Staples participates with NSHMBA and ALPFA to give scholarships to minority students affiliated with those organizations. Students should contact www.nshmba.org or www.alpfa.org to learn more about how to qualify.

Entry-Level Programs/Full-Time Opportunities

Logistics Rotational Program

Length of program: 2 years

Geographic location(s) of program: Multiple U.S. locations

General format:

Each participant will be placed in one of the following positions for the described period of time:
• Supervisor-in-training – Fulfillment Center (12 months)
• Supervisor-in-training – Service Delivery Operation (6 months)
• Project Manager-in-training – Corporate office (6 months)

During each of the rotations, the associate will report to an Operations Manager who will be responsible for exposing the associate to all departments and functions of the location. Specified training plans for each piece of the rotation ensures both classroom and on the job learning. Also, each associate will be partnered with a mentor to provide guidance and direction throughout the entire two-year program.

Merchandise Training Program

Length of program: 18 months

Geographic location(s) of program: Framingham, MA

Store Assignment – 4 months

During the store assignment, you will be working out of one of our local Staples Superstores. The following components will make up the overall store assignment.

1. Orientation to the store, expectations, logistics, etc.
2. Participants will complete the following technical rotations using appropriate checklists through the Retail MIT program. (Approximately 12 weeks)

- Money Room
- Human Resources
- Business Services
- Sales and Service
- Service Desk / Front End
- Merchandising
- Retail Management
- Product Knowledge
- Receiving and Shipping

3. Take on normal workload (Approximately 10 weeks)
4. Distribution Center (2 weeks)

Inventory Management – 9 months

During this assignment, you will be placed in a modified inventory analyst position for one year and take on a normal workload. You will also be required to sign up for and attend various computer skills sessions including E3 and AS400 training. (Additionally materials have been provided in this binder with instructions on who to contact, what training is required, etc.) To supplement your on the job training, we have also designed the following workshops that will take place at various points throughout this 1 year assignment. You are required to attend all of the workshops listed below. (Additional details regarding specific dates and times will be sent to you at the beginning of this assignment)

- Time Management
- Retail & Replenishment Math
- Logistics
- Advertising & Marketing
- Store Presentation & Promo
- Catalog & Dot.com

Product Management – 5 months

During this assignment, you will be placed in a product specialist role for a minimum of one year and take on a normal workload. To supplement your on the job training, we have also designed the following workshops that will take place at various points throughout this 1 year assignment. You are required to attend all of the workshops listed below. (Additional details regarding specific dates and times will be sent to you at the beginning of this assignment)

- Pricing
- Negotiating
- Legal

Customer Service Rotation

> *Length of program:* 2 years
> *Geographic location(s) of program:* Kentucky; Englewood, NJ; Framingham, MA

General Format:

Each participant will be placed in one of the following positions for the described period of time:

- Manager-in-training – Kentucky Call Center (12 months)
- Manager-in-training – Rochester or Hackensack Call Center (6 months)
- Manager-in-training – Corporate office / Service Improvement Office (6 months)

During each of the rotations, the associate will report to a Manager who will be responsible for exposing the associate to all departments and functions of the location. Specified training plans for each piece of the rotation ensures both classroom and on the job learning. Also, each associate will be partnered with a mentor to provide guidance and direction throughout the entire two-year program.

Position Locations:

The locations are:

- Kentucky Call Center – Florence, Kentucky
- Rochester Call Center – Rochester, New York
- Hackensack Call Center – Hackensack, New Jersey
- Corporate Office – Framingham, Massachusetts

Strategic Plan and Diversity Leadership

How does the firm's leadership communicate the importance of diversity to everyone at the firm?

Diversity messages are interwoven within general corporate updates, either via sattelite broadcast, Staples News, or Internal Communications.

Who has primary responsibility for leading diversity initiatives at your firm?

Doreen Nichols, Director of Associate Relations and Diversity

Does your firm currently have a diversity committee?

No

Has the firm undertaken a formal or informal diversity program or set of initiatives aimed at increasing the diversity of the firm?

Yes, informal

How often does the firm's management review the firm's diversity progress/results?

Annually

How is the firm's diversity committee and/or firm management held accountable for achieving results?

Goals are set for the recruiting department and this is a component of each recruiters's performance appraisal.

The Stats

Employees: 65,000 (2004, worldwide)
Employees: 58,000 (2003, worldwide)
Revenue: $14.4 billion (2004, worldwide)
Revenue: $13.2 billion (2003, worldwide)

Retention and Professional Development

How do 2004 minority and female attrition rates generally compare to those experienced in the prior year period?

About the same as in prior years

Please identify the specific steps you are taking to reduce the attrition rate of minority and women employees.

Succession plan includes emphasis on diversity

Diversity Mission Statement

Reflecting the face of our customer through diversity is a commitment deeply embedded in Staples' corporate culture. We are dedicated to providing a work environment of inclusion and acceptance, and look for associates who will also embrace these values.

The Employer Says

To understand why diversity is so important to us, you don't have to look farther than your nearest Staples store. Our customers- whether they're shopping in our stores, online, or through Staples Contract or Business Delivery – are a mosaic of different cultures, ethnicities, genders, and ages. So it's not surprising that we strive for a workforce and a supplier network that reflect the diverse multicultural "face" of our customers.

Staples has been quietly building a workforce of diverse and talented associates, developing a network of diverse suppliers, and supporting diversity in our communities through the Staples Foundation for Learning. In recognition of our achievement in this area, *Diversity, Inc.* magazine named Staples one of the Top Ten companies for recruitment and retention of a diverse workforce in 2004.

We know there's much to do, but the results are starting to show. Our recent focus on diverse college recruitment initiatives and partnerships with professional organizations has been highly successful. Our supplier diversity program was the first in the industry to build a network of established regional Minority Women Business Enterprise (MWBE) partners, which allows customers to purchase directly from and be billed by diversity suppliers. In our local communities, we support diversity through the Staples Foundation for Learning, which provides job skills and educational opportunities for people of all backgrounds, with a special emphasis on disadvantaged youth.

At Staples, we are proud of our commitment to diversity and the great strides we've made toward achieving it. Our success is as multi-faceted as our associates and customers.

Starwood Hotels

777 Westchester Ave.
White Plains, NY 10604
www.starwoodhotels.com

Locations (worldwide)
Located in over 70 countries globally

Contact Person
Jeff Jones
Manager, Staffing & College Relations
Starwood Hotels & Resorts Worldwide
1111 Westchester Avenue
White Plains, NY 10604
Phone: (914) 640-8487
Fax: (914) 640-8373
jeff.jones@starwoodhotels.com

Recruiting

Please list the schools/types of schools at which you recruit.

• Ivy League schools
• Other private schools
• Public state schools
• Historically Black Colleges and Universities (HBCUs)

Do you have any special outreach efforts that are directed to encourage minority students to consider your firm?

• Conferences: NNBMBAA, NSHMBA, NSMH
• Advertise in minority student association publication(s)
• Sponsor minority student association events
• Participate in/host minority student job fair(s)
• Outreach to leadership of minority student organizations
• Scholarships or intern/fellowships for minority students

What activities does the firm undertake to attract minority and women employees?

• Partner programs with women and minority associations
• Conferences: OCA, NSMH, NSHMBA, NBMBAA, NAACP
• Participate at minority job fairs

Internships and Co-ops

INROADS

Number of interns in the program in summer 2004 (internship) or 2004 (co-op): 6 INROADS Interns
Pay: Varies by geographic placement
Length of the program: 10-12 weeks
Web site for internship/co-op information: www.starwoodcareers.com

Entry-Level Programs/Full-Time Opportunities

Management Training Program

Length of program: Three months

Geographic location(s) of program: Across U.S.

Please describe the training/training component of this program: Starwood's Management Training Program combines professional development, mentorships, and immersion into the service-oriented realm of hotel operations. Associates in this program will be poised for entry into management positions including Rooms, Food & Beverage, Sales, Revenue Management, Human Resources, Catering/Convention Services, Accounting and more. At the completion of a 12-week rotational program, each associate is placed in a position of responsibility at the same hotel where the training was completed.

The Employer Says

Starwood Hotels & Resorts is a global organization that is built on diversity. With six distinct brands – Westin, Sheraton, Four Points by Sheraton, St. Regis, The Luxury Collection and W Hotels – operating in over 80 countries, we maintain an associate and customer base as diverse as the world's population. Each brand's distinctive appeal affords us a unique position in the global marketplace that caters to travelers of all backgrounds and from almost every culture. Therefore, creating an environment of inclusion for our associates, guests and suppliers isn't just the right thing to do, it is the very core of our business.

Focusing on blending and mining the talents of our more than 110,000 associates from around the world and taking care of our guests who frequent our more than 750 Starwood properties is a commitment that begins at the top of our organization but is the shared responsibility of each associate. By creating national partnerships with associations focused on serving the needs and concerns of many types of visible and invisible differences – race, gender and sexual orientation, to name a few – we hope to have far reaching impact by making a difference in the markets in which we operate and for the people that encounter our organization.

In just our fifth year as a company, we have established a Diversity Council, made up of senior leaders in Starwood. Its role is to partner with other company leaders to drive the strategy forward with the support of a dedicated staff of change agents in our Office of Diversity and Inclusion.

Just as we approach other vital business imperatives, our Corporate Diversity Council has developed a strategy and multiyear plan for making accelerating change, particularly in the area of representation. As an organization, we're committed to setting the pace for the industry, raising the bar on how we deploy and develop associates – especially the 53% of our current associate population who are people of color – and, in the process understand how diversity yields business success. In 2002, we rolled out an inclusion-training program, beginning with senior management, which helps participants uncover their inner biases.

It takes time. We're committed to the task. Our associates must know that embracing diversity and learning how to mine different talents and opinions in a business like ours, improves our company, our product and all of us as individuals. Valuing individual differences is not new here; for years, we have offered domestic partner benefits for all of our associates without hesitation. Through inclusion training, we reinforce positive messages. By continuing to introduce metrics, like linking compensation to achieving diversity goals, and clarifying the diversity goals of each department, there is a shared understanding of how serious we are about making this an unconscious part of how we do business everyday, everywhere for everyone.

This is the Starwood way.

State Street

One Lincoln Street
Boston, MA 02111
(617) 786-3000
www.statestreet.com
(Click on "Careers," then "Job
Opportunities")

Locations (worldwide)
United States: California, Georgia, Illinois,
Massachusetts (Global HQ), Missouri,
New Jersey, New Hampshire, New York,
North Carolina
International: Austria, Australia, Belgium,
Canada, Cayman Islands, Chile, France,
Germany, Ireland, Italy, Japan,
Luxembourg, Netherlands, Singapore,
South Africa, South Korea, Switzerland,
Taiwan, Thailand, United Arab Emirates,
United Kingdom

Diversity Leadership
Maia Germain, College Relations and Diversity
Staffing Manager
State Street Financial Center,
One Lincoln Street
Boston, MA 02111
Phone: (617) 786-3000
E-mail: mgermain@statestreet.com

Recruiting

Please list the schools/types of schools at which you recruit.

• Ivy League schools
• Other private schools
• Public state schools
• Historically Black Colleges and Universities (HBCUs)
• Hispanic Serving Institutions (HSIs)
• Other predominantly minority and/or women's colleges

Do you have any special outreach efforts that are directed to encourage minority students to consider your firm?

• Participate in/host minority student job fair(s)
• Sponsor minority student association events
• Firm's employees participate on career panels at school
• Outreach to leadership of minority student organizations

What activities does the firm undertake to attract minority and women employees?

• Partner programs with women and minority associations
• Conferences
• Participate at minority job fairs
• Seek referrals from other employees, including affinity groups
• Utilize online job services

Do you use executive recruiting/search firms to seek to identify new diversity hires?

Yes

Internships and Co-ops

INROADS, PIC (Private Industry Council), Year Up, Internal program

Deadline for application: Open, depending on program

Number of interns in the program in summer 2004 (internship) or 2004 (co-op): Varies

Length of the program: Summer – 12 weeks, other depending on need

Web site for internship/co-op information: Currently under construction

Affinity Groups/Employee Networks

In the United States, State Street's ten employee affinity groups will play an active role in our company's commitment to inclusion. These groups include an Asian Professionals Group, Bible Study Group, Black Professionals Group, Chinese Affinity Group, Disability Awareness Alliance, Gay, Lesbian, Bi-Sexual and Transgender Group, Latin American Professional Network, Muslim Affinity Group, Working Parents Group and Professional Women's Network. Group members meet throughout the year to share ideas and experiences, mentor and network, and sponsor internal programs around national and international events like Black History Month, International Women's Day, Asian and Latin American Heritage Months and PRIDE. All of the affinity groups have the support of the corporation and are provided a discretionary budget to use in outreach, community service, membership promotion, etc. State Street affinity groups are publicized in employee communications, new employee orientation, meeting announcements and through the company's Intranet.

Entry-Level Programs/Full-Time Opportunities

Fund Accountant, Portfolio Accountant, Portfolio Administrator

Length of program: 2 weeks (each)

Geographic location(s) of program: Boston/Quincy, MA

Strategic Plan and Diversity Leadership

State Street's Global Inclusion Initiative brings together a team of employee opinion leaders from across the corporation representing myriad levels, cultural, professional and lifestyle backgrounds, geographic locations, and walks of life. The goal of the initiative is to provide all employees and managers with the tools, guidance and opportunity to perform to their potential and be valued, engaged and productive.

A Global Inclusion Steering Committee, comprised of representatives from State Street's senior leadership globally, leads the effort and is responsible for setting strategy and ultimately driving change centered on the work environment, gender/ethnicity and culture issues, internal mobility, management development and turnover management.

The Steering Committee is supported by three Global Inclusion Regional Groups, representing North America, Europe and the Asia/Pacific area, as well as five business unit implementation teams. These groups are actively working to complete recommendations on improving the quality of working life at the regional and corporate levels, currently focusing on management practices, recruitment and retention of a diverse work force, and improved communication effectiveness.

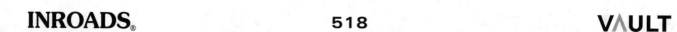

The Stats

DEMOGRAPHIC PROFILE	TOTAL IN THE U.S.		TOTAL OUTSIDE THE U.S		TOTAL WORLDWIDE	
	2004	2003	2004	2003	2004	2003
Number of employees	13,174	14,755	6,751	6,305	19,925	21,060
Revenues	$3.18 billion	$2.96 billion	$1.82 billion	$1.44 billion	$4.95 billion	$4.73 billion

Retention and Professional Development

Please identify the specific steps you are taking to reduce the attrition rate of minority and women employees.

• Develop and/or support internal employee affinity groups (e.g., minority or women networks within the firm)
• Increase/review compensation relative to competition
• Increase/improve current work/life programs
• Work with minority and women employees to develop career advancement plans
• Professional skills development program, including minority and women employees

Diversity Mission Statement

To be a place where all employees are engaged and valued

StorageTek

One StorageTek Dr.
Louisville, CO 80028-0001
Phone: (303) 673-5151
Fax: (303) 661-7637
Toll Free: (800) 877-9220
www.stortek.com

Diversity Leadership
Connie Fulmer, AA/EEO Specialist, Sr.
connie_fulmer@StorageTek.com

Employment Contact
Jennifer Gance, Mgr, Staffing Operations
One StorageTek Drive
Louisville, CO 80028
Phone: (303) 673-4837
Fax: (303) 661-2994
E-mail: jennifer_gance@StorageTek.com

Recruiting

Please list the schools/types of schools at which you recruit.

• *Ivy League schools:* Cornell
• *Other private schools:* Denver University, Kellogg
• *Public state schools:* Colorado University, Colorado State University, Colorado School of Mines
• *Historically Black Colleges and Universities (HBCUs):* Prairie View
• *Native American Tribal Universities:* Northeastern State
• *Other predominantly minority and/or women's colleges:* St. Mary's University

Do you have any special outreach efforts that are directed to encourage minority students to consider your firm?

• Sponsor minority student association events
• Firm's employees participate on career panels at school
• Outreach to leadership of minority student organizations
• Scholarships or intern/fellowships for minority students

What activities does the firm undertake to attract minority and women employees?
• Partner programs with women and minority associations
• Seek referrals from other employees
• Each alliance has a membership to its respective Chamber of Commerce and has members that volunteer in minority and/or women associations.

Do you use executive recruiting/search firms to seek to identify new diversity hires?
Yes

Internships and Co-ops

INROADS/Colorado, Inc.

Number of interns in the program in summer 2004 (internship) or 2004 (co-op): 6
Length of the program: 10 Weeks

Affinity Groups/Employee Networks

Asian Alliance

Asian Alliance is an all-inclusive network of professionals who are of Asian origin and others who are interested in the Asian cultures.

Black Global Alliance

Black Global Alliance provides an arena for all StorageTek employees who desire to address the specific concerns of StorageTek's African American and minority employees.

Éxito Latino Alliance

Éxito Latino Alliance is an inclusive professional affinity group committed to supporting, developing, and promoting success and networking in the Latino global community.

Intern Affinity Group

The Intern Affinity Group is committed to the development and support of the StorageTek interns as well as establishing the credibility of the intern contribution to the corporation.

Women's Alliance

Women's Alliance provides opportunities for professional and personal growth, support from female colleagues, and to attract and retain talented women at StorageTek

Entry-Level Programs/Full-Time Opportunities

Evolving Leaders

Length of program: 18 months
Geographic location(s) of program: Headquarters, Louisville, CO

Please describe the training/training component of this program: 18 months of continued class room instruction, events, networking

Strategic Plan and Diversity Leadership

How does the firm's leadership communicate the importance of diversity to everyone at the firm?

Emails, newsletters, diversity website, affinity group meetings

Who has primary responsibility for leading diversity initiatives at your firm?

E.J. Meier, Director, Corporate HR

Does your firm currently have a diversity committee?

Yes

If yes, please describe how the committee is structured, how often it meets, etc.

Each alliance has its own executive sponsor, funding, by-laws, officers, meeting times. The leads of each of these organizations meet monthly to discuss upcoming events, concerns and accomplishments.

If yes, does the committee's representation include one or more members of the firm's management/executive committee (or the equivalent)?

Yes. Each alliance has its own executive sponsor. The alliances report their accomplishments to those sponsors on a quarterly basis, with periodic reports to the executive management team.

Please describe the committee.

Some executive sponsors are more active with the alliance than others. Total numbers of collective hours has not been calculated. Each alliance has committees with volunteer employees, including employees from the U.S. field. Each committee has the responsibility to further the firm's diversity initiatives.

Does the committee and/or diversity leader establish and set goals or objectives consistent with management's priorities?

Yes. Executive management guides each alliance to perform to the corporation's goals and objectives. Each alliance has leadership awareness and education, recruitment and retention as part of its objective.

Has the firm undertaken a formal or informal diversity program or set of initiatives aimed at increasing the diversity of the firm?

Yes, formal

How often does the firm's management review the firm's diversity progress/results?

Quarterly

How is the firm's diversity committee and/or firm management held accountable for achieving results?

Management receives quarterly updates on hires and promotions. These become part of their performance management review. Each executive receives the roll up for their organization and the comparison of the organization to the corporate results.

The Stats

Employees: 3,975 (2004, U.S.)
Employees: 4,235 (2003, U.S.)
Revenue: $2.2 billion (2004, worldwide)
Revenue: $2.2 billion (2003, worldwide)

U.S. Executive Team

- Male – 84%
- Female – 16 %
- Minority – 16 %

U.S. 2004 – Exempt

- Male – 77%
- Female – 23 %
- Minority – 13 %

Retention and Professional Development

How do 2004 minority and female attrition rates generally compare to those experienced in the prior year period?

- Female – Higher than in prior years
- Minority – Lower than in prior years

Please identify the specific steps you are taking to reduce the attrition rate of minority and women employees.

- Develop and/or support internal employee affinity groups (e.g., minority or women networks within the firm)
- Increase/improve current work/life programs
- Work with minority and women employees to develop career advancement plans
- Strengthen mentoring program for all employees, including minorities and women
- Professional skills development program, including minority and women employees

Diversity Mission Statement

To support StorageTek's core values and business strategy by creating a corporate culture which attracts competent individuals, treats them with dignity, promotes their innovation and renewal, and values each individual's diversity. StorageTek is committed to Diversity as an integral part of its global business strategy

The Employer Says

StorageTek's business is making sure companies have the information they need to do their business. With over 30 years of expertise and the industry's most complete portfolio of products and services, StorageTek helps keep their information available and protected. With that in mind, StorageTek realizes that employees are its major asset and the diversity of employees produces better products and services.

StorageTek's community contributions have touched the lives of thousands of people and earned us many awards over the years. We're proud to have made a positive impact and will continue our commitment to enriching the community in the future. When employees contribute to the educational institution of their choice and/or volunteer their time, StorageTek contributes dollars to the institution or program.

Diversity is one of StorageTek's core values. It means accepting and valuing the uniqueness and similarities of all individuals-regardless of gender, race, age, sexual orientation, religion, national origin, veteran status and disability. These differences contribute to our company's strength and that of our customers. That's why we aggressively attract, recruit and retain top talent all over the world. We are committed to creating an environment of inclusion where employees feel valued, respected and empowered in the decisions that affect them. StorageTek's diversity strategy has a worldwide focus in four areas: Leadership, Awareness and Education, Recruitment, and Retention

Finding and developing young talent is one of the most important things we do at StorageTek. It's critical to the success of our company -always has been. That's why we support our employees' efforts to be successful in many ways. We've even created a handful of programs designed specifically for recent graduates. In return we ask for their best effort, best ideas and a desire to improve themselves as they help StorageTek reach new levels of success. The programs include: Evolving leaders; Rotational program; Associate Sales Executive program; and an Internship program.

Evolving leaders receive the training and skill development necessary to smoothly transition from the classroom to the workforce. Our program is benchmarked against similar programs developed by Fortune 500 companies and offers opportunities to: collaborate with executive team members, participate in leadership development courses, and build relationships through training and networking

In the Rotational program, employees receive insight into major areas of StorageTek's business operations. This program is designed to broaden your experience firsthand, deepen your understanding of the business, and make the most of your potential through: Exposure to multiple organizations like human resources, finance, marketing, operations and engineering, coaching from some of the best practitioners of their specific disciplines, and business and professional growth alignment.

Associate Sales Executive program trains employees how to be successful in sales. Through classroom and field training you will learn: networking skills, sales call techniques, negotiation/partnering, budget analysis, proposal writing and account territory management, marketing strategies, StorageTek's organizational structure, core values and competencies.

Through our internship program undergraduate and graduate students gain real-life business experience. This program also provides access to mentoring and networking opportunities through team building, social events, round tables, and executive dialogues.

In addition to being a great place to bank.... we're also a great place to work

Headquartered in Atlanta, Georgia, SunTrust operates an extensive distribution network primarily in Florida, Georgia, North Carolina, South Carolina, Tennessee, Maryland, Virginia and the District of Columbia - and also serves customers in selected markets nationally.

SunTrust is proud of its established partnership with INROADS, and provides internship opportunities throughout our footprint for talented minority students.

In addition, SunTrust was recently ranked as one of DiversityInc's "Top 50 Companies for Diversity" for 2005. Among the programs which contributed to SunTrust's inclusion on this list were:

• An active Corporate Diversity Council
• An aggressive Diversity recruiting strategy - resulting in a diverse workforce
• Work-life benefits
• Mentoring and leadership development programs for minorities
• Diversity training programs

SunTrust makes a significant investment in the training and development of its employees. Our comprehensive, professional internship and full-time Training Program positions provide a solid platform on which to build your career.

Visit us online at **suntrust.com** to learn more about our opportunities.

suntrust.com

SunTrust Bank

303 Peachtree St. NE
Atlanta, GA 30308
Phone: (404) 588-7711
Fax: (404) 588-8047
www.suntrust.com/careers

Locations (worldwide)
1,700 locations across the Southeast and
Mid-Atlantic regions

Diversity Leadership
Carolyn Cartwright
Director of Diversity
303 Peachtree Street
Atlanta, Georgia 30308

Recruiting

Please list the schools/types of schools at which you recruit.

- *Private schools:* Duke, Emory, Rollins College, University of Richmond, Vanderbilt, Wake Forest, and Washington & Lee
- *Public state schools:* Florida State, Georgia Tech, James Madison University, University of Central Florida, University of Florida, University of Georgia, University of Maryland, University of North Carolina-Chapel Hill, University of South Florida, University of Tennessee-Knoxville, University of Virginia, Virginia Commonwealth University, and Virginia Tech
- *Historically Black Colleges and Universities (HBCUs):* Florida A&M, Howard University, Spelman, and Tennessee State
- *Hispanic Serving Institutions (HSIs):* Florida International University and University of Miami

Do you have any special outreach efforts that are directed to encourage minority students to consider your firm?

- Hold a reception for minority students
- Conferences. Please list – Howard Financial Services Institute and Monster Diversity Leadership Program
- Participate in/host minority student job fair(s)
- Sponsor minority student association events
- Firm's employees participate on career panels at school
- Outreach to leadership of minority student organizations
- Participate in the Florida A&M Industry Cluster
- Participate in the SWEPT Program at Spelman
- Established an Executive Liaison Program where we have assigned SunTrust executives to each of our core HBCUs and HSIs

What activities does the firm undertake to attract minority and women employees?

- Partner programs with women and minority associations
- Conferences: Black Data Processing Associates, Monster Diversity Leadership Program, National Black MBA, National Society of Hispanic MBAs, Urban Financial Services Coalition, Women for Hire, and Women of Color Technology Awards Conference
- Participate at minority job fairs
- Seek referrals from other employees
- Utilize online job services
- Partnership with INROADS
- Send SunTrust representatives to facilitate sessions at the INROADS Leadership Development Institute events

Do you use executive recruiting/search firms to seek to identify new diversity hires?

No

Internships and Co-ops

In addition to the Internship Programs listed below, SunTrust also typically has intern opportunities in the following areas: Credit, Marketing, Strategic Sourcing, and Wealth & Investment Management. These internship opportunities vary each year, so be sure to check the Careers section of suntrust.com for a complete listing of our openings.

INROADS

Number of interns in the program in summer 2004 (internship) or 2004 (co-op): 20 in 2004 (24 in 2005)
Pay: Intern pay varies based on geographic location, department placement, and year in school
Length of the program: 10-12 weeks
Percentage of interns/co-ops in the program who receive offers of full-time employment: Approximately 70%
Web site for internship/co-op information: www.suntrust.com/careers

SunTrust typically places INROADS interns throughout the company's footprint, in the following lines of business: Commercial Banking, Commercial Real Estate, Mortgage Banking, Retail Banking, and Wealth & Investment Management. Interns generally spend from two to four summers with the organization learning analytical and/or sales skills through direct, hands-on participation. The summer experience includes some combination of client exposure, job-shadowing, and classroom training. In addition, all interns complete a summer project and presentation that reflects appropriate research and analysis for their particular function.

All INROADS interns are paired with a mentor and Human Resources local coordinator. They also participate in special programming activities throughout the summer, including a variety of professional development seminars. Rising seniors are invited to participate in SunTrust's INROADS Senior Summit. This two day event, which is held at our corporate headquarters in Atlanta, gives interns the opportunity to interact with senior management, gain exposure to our business strategies, and network with other fellow interns.

Qualifications: Varies by line of business and functional area.

Corporate and Investment Banking Internship Program

Number of interns in the program in summer 2004 (internship) or 2004 (co-op): 5
Pay: Intern pay varies based on geographic location, department placement, and year in school.
Length of the program: 10-12 weeks
Percentage of interns/co-ops in the program who receive offers of full-time employment: Approximately 60%
Web site for internship/co-op information: www.suntrust.com/careers

The Corporate and Investment Banking Internship Program, based in Atlanta, Georgia, is designed to provide exposure to a number of disciplines within Corporate and Investment Banking. Interns are assigned to a specific group to work on various analyses, modeling and underwriting assignments dealing with companies in excess of $250 million in annual revenues. Potential assignments include working within industry specialty groups, large corporate markets or debt capital markets. Interns will sharpen financial analysis skills, develop an understanding of corporate markets and clients, and build expertise in corporate finance and investment banking products through on-the-job training. To further enhance the experience, interns will participate in a structured mentor program. The overall goal of the program is for the intern to develop a solid understanding of our industry, our organization and our strategy. At the end of the summer, Interns will be considered for a full-time position in the Corporate and Investment Banking Analyst Program upon graduation.

Qualifications: Completed junior year of BA/BS degree; any major with at least one course in accounting; additional finance coursework preferred; overall GPA of 3.0 or above required; strong qualitative and quantitative analytical skills; strong sales orientation; solid leadership and interpersonal skills; effective oral and written communication skills.

Mortgage Internship Program

Number of interns in the program in summer 2004 (internship) or 2004 (co-op): 5

Pay: Intern pay varies based on geographic location, department placement, and year in school.

Length of the program: 10 weeks

Web site for internship/co-op information: www.suntrust.com/careers

The SunTrust Mortgage Internship Program, based in Richmond, Virginia, enables interns to provide project management support to various divisions within the SunTrust Mortgage line of business. Summer placements within SunTrust Mortgage typically include: Marketing, Finance, Customer Care, or Production Operations. Interns participate in project team meetings and perform related assignments. They also participate in the development and tracking of formal project plans and key milestones. Interns will have the opportunity to develop valuable relationships while working with project managers and other interns in the program. Scheduled seminars and training sessions will provide the interns with exposure to the various divisions within SunTrust Mortgage. In addition, all interns are assigned an experienced mentor.

Qualifications: Completed sophomore year of BA/BS degree – rising seniors preferred; any major – business majors strongly preferred; overall GPA of 2.8 or above required; solid interpersonal skills and customer service orientation; leadership experience and analytical aptitude; high motivation and ability to meet deadlines; strong computer skills to include: Microsoft Word, Excel, Internet Explorer, and PowerPoint

Affinity Groups/Employee Networks

We do not have formal affinity groups at SunTrust. However, we do have diversity site councils located across the enterprise in ten geographic markets. These diversity site councils have sub-committees that focus on certain dimensions of diversity (ie., women, GLBT, African Americans, Hispanics, Asians and People with Disabilities). These sub-committees focus on some of the same issues as affinity groups. Their purpose is to represent diversity in action at the local market level. Their activities include cultural celebrations, networking, recruiting new employees, mentoring, business development and community outreach. The councils meet at least once per quarter. They have market or regional websites where they can report their local information. Additionally, each site council has a page on the corporate website.

We also have two informal/unofficial affinity groups in place – a group that supports GLBT issues called Diversity Works, and an African American group called SunTrust League of Employees (SALE). Meeting frequency varies from monthly to quarterly. The groups focus on employee support, mentoring, community outreach, business development and recruiting.

Entry-Level Programs/Full-Time Opportunities

Commercial Banking Associate Program

Length of program: Approximately 11 months

Geographic location(s) of program: SunTrust Commercial Banking has offices throughout the company's footprint in Alabama, Florida, Georgia, Maryland, North Carolina, South Carolina, Tennessee, Virginia, and the District of Columbia.

The SunTrust Commercial Banking Line of Business focuses on providing comprehensive financial solutions, superior value and outstanding services to targeted companies throughout the SunTrust footprint. The majority of Commercial Banking clients are privately-held companies with annual revenues between $5-250 million. Commercial Banking Associates participate in an eleven-month training program that begins their progression towards a Relationship Manager position. The program focuses on three key areas – sales skills, analytical ability and product knowledge. Associates have the opportunity to build a professional network with their peers and Commercial Banking Managers throughout the SunTrust system by participating in centralized class-room training in Atlanta, Georgia. Associates also complete on-the-job training in their local banking units where they support Relationship Managers and Portfolio Specialists in financial statement analysis, industry research, and client call preparation

Qualifications: BA/BS required; Any major: Accounting, Finance or equivalent analytical coursework strongly preferred; over-all GPA of 2.8 or above required; interest in business and finance; strong sales orientation; solid interpersonal and communication skills; analytical aptitude.

Commercial Real Estate Associate Program

> *Length of program:* Approximately 11 months
> *Geographic location(s) of program:* SunTrust Commercial Real Estate has offices throughout the company's footprint in Alabama, Florida, Georgia, Maryland, North Carolina, South Carolina, Tennessee, Virginia, and the District of Columbia.

SunTrust Commercial Real Estate is a specialized, full-service banking group dedicated to providing financial solutions to com-mercial developers, real estate investors, national and local residential homebuilders, affordable housing groups, and real estate investment trusts. Commercial Real Estate clients are a combination of privately-held and publicly-traded companies ranging in size and complexity, and a number of them have market capitalization over $1 billion. Commercial Real Estate Associates par-ticipate in an 11-month program that begins their progression towards a Relationship Manager position. The program focuses on three key areas: sales skills, analytical ability, and product knowledge. Associates participate in centralized classroom training in Atlanta, Georgia and complete on-the-job assignments in the bank location where they were hired. Associates support Relationship Managers and Portfolio Specialists by analyzing companies, industries, markets and real estate projects, performing financial statement analysis, and reviewing the clients' current credit relationship with SunTrust.

Qualifications: BA/BS required; Any major: Accounting, Finance or equivalent analytical coursework strongly preferred; over-all GPA of 2.8 or above required; interest in business and finance; strong sales orientation; solid interpersonal and communication skills; analytical aptitude.

Corporate and Investment Banking Analyst Program

> *Length of program:* Approximately 12 months
> *Geographic location(s) of program:* Program is based in Atlanta, however potential rotation and placement opportuni-ties exist in Atlanta, Nashville, Orlando and Richmond.

Corporate and Investment Banking (CIB) offers clients, from corporations to institutions and public bodies, a wide array of finan-cial advisory services in addition to traditional banking products. Client Managers in CIB are organized along both industry and geographic lines. In all cases, their mission is to utilize their expertise, along with that of the various Product Specialists and Risk Managers, to deliver creative ideas and solutions to their clients. The CIB Analyst Training Program prepares Analysts to become Associates and eventually Client Managers or Product Specialists working with companies that typically have annual revenues greater than $250 million. The program, approximately twelve months in length, combines relevant classroom training in Atlanta with practical on-the-job rotations. Rotations and placement off the program will occur primarily in Atlanta, Orlando, Nashville or Richmond. Potential rotations include working within industry specialty groups, large corporate markets or debt capital mar-kets. Analysts will sharpen financial analysis skills, develop an understanding of corporate markets and clients, and build expert-ise in corporate finance and investment banking products.

Qualifications: BA/BS required; any major; minimum of two Accounting or Finance courses required; overall GPA of 3.0 or above required; strong qualitative and quantitative analytical skills; strong sales orientation; solid leadership and interpersonal skills; effective oral and written communication skills.

SunTrust Robinson Humphrey Equity Capital Markets Investment Banking Analyst Program

Length of program: 2 years
Geographic location(s) of program: Atlanta, Georgia

SunTrust Robinson Humphrey's Investment Banking Analyst Program is a two-year program designed to provide recent college graduates with an introduction to investment banking through an intensive learning experience. Analysts play integral roles on project teams by working closely with senior bankers on all aspects of investment banking transactions. During the first six months, analysts are encouraged to participate in transactions across a number of industries. Following this initial period, analysts focus on a particular industry, providing them the opportunity to develop industry and product knowledge and make significant contributions to transaction teams. The majority of analysts will be placed in Atlanta. SunTrust Robinson Humphrey also has satellite investment banking offices in Boston and Nashville.

Qualifications: BA/BS required; any major; accounting or finance coursework strongly preferred; high degree of academic and extracurricular achievement; interest in finance and investment banking; capability to commit a substantial amount of time and energy to the program; proven analytical ability and attention to detail; proven ability to work well with others; superior written and oral communication skills.

Strategic Plan and Diversity Leadership

How does the firm's leadership communicate the importance of diversity to everyone at the firm?

We have the following programs or tools for communicating information about diversity:

• New Employee Orientation Program
• Company website: www.suntrust.com
• Employee website
• Employee newsletter
• Annual Report on Diversity
• Diversity brochures
• Diversity commitment statements in Employee Handbook
• Collateral materials for marketing, benefits, & new hire orientation
• Diversity training

Who has primary responsibility for leading diversity initiatives at your firm?

Our Diversity Initiatives are led by Carolyn Cartwright, Senior Vice President

Does your firm currently have a diversity committee?

Yes

If yes, please describe how the committee is structured, how often it meets, etc.

We have a Corporate Diversity Council made up of twenty senior executives across the enterprise who are responsible for setting the strategic direction as thought leaders, monitoring activities and evaluating the overall effectiveness of the initiative. The Chairman/CEO and the President/COO co-chair the Corporate Diversity Council. The Corporate Council has sub-committees that serve as the working arms for moving ideas into action. The Corporate Council meets at least quarterly. The ten Diversity Site Councils (previously described in the Affinity Groups section) report to the Corporate Diversity Council.

If yes, does the committee's representation include one or more members of the firm's management/executive committee (or the equivalent)?

Yes

Total Executives on Committee:

20

Does the committee and/or diversity leader establish and set goals or objectives consistent with management's priorities?

Yes. diversity is a business imperative at SunTrust. It aligns and supports SunTrust's strategic intent. Specifically,

• We intend to be recognized as the leading provider of high value financial services to consumers, businesses and institutions within our designated geographies.
• Our success and financial market recognition will flow from our ability to enhance the economic well being of our customers, our shareholders, our people and our communities.

Our diversity mission and goals are tied to the mission, goals and values of the organization. The Corporate Diversity Council objectives are to:

• Confirm diversity as a business imperative in our workforce, marketplace and community.
• Convey management accountability for a diversity inclusive business environment.
• Maintain management accountability for increasing diversity representation.
• Create and sustain diversity awareness among all employees.
• Deliver diversity education and training.

Has the firm undertaken a formal or informal diversity program or set of initiatives aimed at increasing the diversity of the firm?

Yes, formal. Our diversity initiatives focus on the five previously stated diversity objectives. Some of the programs related to these objectives include an emerging and ethnic markets strategy, a development program for high potential people of color (POC) that is designed to accelerate the promotion rate of POC, the maintenance of a diversity representation scorecard, education and training for managers, a web-based training program for employees, and a diversity recruiting strategy.

How often does the firm's management review the firm's diversity progress/results?

Programmatic review of diversity events and strategies occurs at least quarterly and an annual evaluation is made on progress-to-date against goals. Goals are maintained or new ones established during annual planning meetings.

How is the firm's diversity committee and/or firm management held accountable for achieving results?

Managers are held accountable for their diversity representation scorecard results. The bank's performance appraisal system has a diversity performance factor. Additionally, diversity is one of the leadership elements of the Management Incentive Program.

The Stats

DEMOGRAPHIC PROFILE	TOTAL IN THE U.S.		TOTAL OUTSIDE THE U.S		TOTAL WORLDWIDE	
	2004	2003	2004	2003	2004	2003
Number of employees	33,156	27,578	0	0	33,156	27,578
Revenues	$6.348 billion	$5.688 billion	0	0	$6.348 billion	$5.688 billion

There are two women and two people of color on the SunTrust Board of Directors (Note: One female is also a person of color.) The SunTrust Management Committee's wish is for the operating committee of the company to have ten female members. Our workforce is made up of 70% females and 32% minorities. Women account for 62% of all promotions to executive, senior and middle management positions. Women make up 75% of entry-level managers. People of Color account for 13% of middle managers and senior professionals.

Retention and Professional Development

How do 2004 minority and female attrition rates generally compare to those experienced in the prior year period?

About the same as in prior years. Our turnover for women and people of color is about the same as it is for white males.

Please identify the specific steps you are taking to reduce the attrition rate of minority and women employees.

• Increase/review compensation relative to competition
• Increase/improve current work/life programs
• Adopt dispute resolution process
• Succession plan includes emphasis on diversity
• Work with minority and women employees to develop career advancement plans
• Review work assignments and hours billed to key client matters to make sure minority and women employees are not being excluded
• Strengthen mentoring program for all employees, including minorities and women
• Professional skills development program, including minority and women employees
• Diversity Training for managers and associates
• Employee Assistance Programs
• Tuition Reimbursement Program
• SunTrust University – SunTrust's Training and Development Division

Diversity Mission Statement

The SunTrust Diversity Statements:

Vision

To create an inclusive environment and culture at SunTrust that emphasizes respect and leverages diversity in our marketplace, workforce, workplace and communities so that we can beat our competition in making SunTrust a superior employer and financial services provider thus enhancing shareholder value.

Mission Statement

To be recognized as being among the best financial service providers in developing a diverse employee base that successfully meets the needs of our clients within our designated geographies.

The Employer Says

SunTrust has development programs in place that focus on providing exceptional work experiences and mentoring opportunities. We have both formal and informal mentoring throughout the organization. We have also established a Focused Leadership Development Program for minorities. The goal of the program is to accelerate the representation of ethnic minorities in key leadership and management positions. Fifteen participants were selected for a 2 year program which includes structured development activities, a business project, mentoring, coaching, 360 degree feedback and networking opportunities. It is a high level program to support SunTrust's talent management and diversity goals related to attracting, developing, promoting and retaining a diverse workforce.

We have targeted recruiting efforts which allow us to maintain strong relationships with minority colleges and organizations. Some of our college connections include Florida A&M, Howard, Spelman and Tennessee State University. A SunTrust executive, who acts as a corporate liaison, has been assigned to each of our core HBCUs and HSIs. Our hope is that their relationships with key faculty and staff will allow us to identify top talent from these institutions. We have also established a national partnership with INROADS.

To attract the best and brightest employees who reflect the diversity of our communities, we have established networks with key professional organizations, to include:

• Black Data Processing Associates
• National Association of Black Accountants
• National Black MBA Association
• National Society of Hispanic MBAs
• Urban Financial Services Coalition
• Women for Hire
• Women of Color

• SunTrust has achieved many successes through our Diversity Initiatives Program. Some of our accomplishments include:
• Ranked number 38 of 50 by *Diversityinc* magazine as one of the Best Places to Work for Minorities
• Presented the Corporate Award of the Year for support of diversity in the financial services industry
• 2004 Recipient of the New Freedom Initiative Award presented by the Dept of Labor, as an initiative of President Bush for employers with practices that address the needs of people with disabilities
• We placed in the top 100 of *Fortune* magazine's Best Places to Work for Minorities
• Awarded the best Diversity website by *Diversityinc* magazine
• Given a grade of 86 (out of 100) by the Human Rights Campaign for our programs for the GLBT community
• Ranked as one of the best places to work by *The Atlanta Tribune* and *The Atlanta Business Chronicle*

SunTrust is known as a good corporate citizen in the communities where we operate. We give time and financial support to organizations like:

• 100 Black Men
• Jack and Jill Organization
• Latin American Association
• Hispanic Chamber of Commerce
• Urban League
• Rainbow PUSH Coalition
• Asian American Chamber of Commerce
• Women in Finance
• M.L. King Centers
• Minority/Women Business Owners' Councils
• SCLC
• Asian American Heritage Foundation
• Human Rights Campaign
• YWCA
• Career Opportunities for Students with Disabilities

Synovus Financial Corp.

1000 5th Avenue
Columbus, Georgia 31901
Phone: (706) 644-0679
Fax: (706) 649-5793
www.synovus.com

Diversity Leadership
Audrey D. Hollingsworth, Senior Vice
President, Director, Diversity

Contact Person
Jeff Hart, Manager, Employment Services
1000 5th Avenue
Columbus, Georgia 31901
Phone: (706) 644-0679
Fax: (706) s649-5793
E-mail: jhart@synovus.com

Recruiting

Please list the schools/types of schools at which you recruit.

• Public state schools
• Historically Black Colleges and Universities (HBCUs)
• Other predominantly minority and/or women's colleges

Do you have any special outreach efforts that are directed to encourage minority students to consider your firm?

• Advertise in minority student association publication(s)
• Participate in/host minority student job fair(s)
• Sponsor minority student association events
• Firm's employees participate on career panels at school

What activities does the firm undertake to attract minority and women employees?

• Participate at minority job fairs
• Seek referrals from other employees
• Utilize online job services
• Targeted lunch sessions and on-site career day activities for minority students in the field of finance and banking

Do you use executive recruiting/search firms to seek to identify new diversity hires?

No

Internships and Co-ops

Synovus Internship/CO-OP Program

Deadline for application: Varies per position
Number of interns in the program in summer 2004 (internship) or 2004 (co-op): 11 interns and 1 co-op
Pay: $8.50-$10.00 per hour
Length of the program: 10-12 weeks
Percentage of interns/co-ops in the program who receive offers of full-time employment: 40%
Web site for internship/co-op information: www.synovus.com

The internship program encompasses several departments within our family of companies. It varies from year to year.

Scholarships

Jack Parker Scholarship Fund (internal scholarship program)

Deadline for application for the scholarship program: Applications for the Scholarship will be accepted each spring, with the award winners announced in the summer. Applications are reviewed and ranked by an independent, external Scholarship Selection Committee
Scholarship award amount: Number and size of the awards to be granted will be determined each year by the Board of Directors of The Jack B. Parker Foundation Inc., based on available funds. The most outstanding applicant is chosen to be The Jack Parker Scholar.

Our Company strives to assist the families of our team members through the Jack Parker Centennial Scholarship Program. The Jack Parker Scholarship Program was established in 1988, as a part of the commemoration of the 100th Anniversary of Columbus Bank and Trust Company. The Scholarship Program is managed by the Jack B. Parker Foundation, Inc., to award college or vocational institution scholarships to the children of Synovus family team members. The Scholarship Program and the foundation were named in memory of Jack B. Parker, whose career with our family of companies spanned 44 years. Jack's enthusiastic attitude, keen sense of duty and good heart were evident throughout his career. He served as resident historian, confidant and trainer for countless team members. Less well known was the role Jack played as an anonymous benefactor.

Children of current, retired or deceased employees are eligible to submit an application for the Scholarship Program.

Entry-Level Programs/Full-Time Opportunities

Management Associate Program

Length of program: Six to nine months
Geographic location(s) of program: Columbus, GA and several banks in the southeastern U.S.

Please describe the training/training component of this program: On-the-job training and classroom training encompassing several areas of retail and commercial banking.

Strategic Plan and Diversity Leadership

How does the firm's leadership communicate the importance of diversity to everyone at the firm?

Our Diversity Council and the President of our company provides planned communication throughout the year. We use a variety of communication vehicles and messages. The value of diversity to our organization is displayed on our company website to communicate our commitment to external sources. We use a formal print piece that is available for our CEO population to use during community or business meetings involving external audiences. Through our intranet (INSITE) we deliver bi-monthly articles to team members regarding various topics of interest on the subject of diversity. We also conduct an annual leadership presentation that includes progress results, goals and new year targets on diversity. Our Council meets semi-monthly to address issues of diversity, develop programmatic initiatives and prepare for focus groups session with team members.

Who has primary responsibility for leading diversity initiatives at your firm?

Audrey D. Hollingsworth, Senior Vice President, Director Diversity

Does your firm currently have a diversity committee?

Yes

If yes, please describe how the committee is structured, how often it meets, etc.

The Synovus Diversity Council is comprised of various senior/executive level corporate leaders from throughout the enterprise. The Council convenes semi-monthly quarterly to discuss goals, progress and additional efforts that can be made to further our commitment to diversity.

If yes, does the committee's representation include one or more members of the firm's management/executive committee (or the equivalent)?

Yes

Please describe the committee.

In 2004 there were 18 senior/executive leaders on the Synovus Advisory Council. The Council met at least six times per year for approximately 20 hours.

Does the committee and/or diversity leader establish and set goals or objectives consistent with management's priorities?

Yes. This year we established 3 major goals that aligned with our leadership priorities. Diversity training for all of our leaders; Targeted development plans for minorities and females; representation progress in the leadership tier

Has the firm undertaken a formal or informal diversity program or set of initiatives aimed at increasing the diversity of the firm?

Yes, formal. There are five areas that we use to measure and assess progress toward improving representation in our organization. Those areas are: Workforce, Leadership, Top Salaried, New Hires and Board of Directors (we are substituting Board of Directors for Termination results). We measure our progress against our community statistics, establish targets and measure progress. This year we will introduce a report card to assess individual company results

How often does the firm's management review the firm's diversity progress/results?

Quarterly

How is the firm's diversity committee and/or firm management held accountable for achieving results?

There is no formal accountability that is specifically directed at the Council, however, the Council holds itself accountable by publishing our goals to our team members and providing the team members with updates on progress toward our diversity goals. Essentially, our total workforce holds the Council accountable for delivering on the expectations that are established. It is about our credibility for doing what we say we will do.

The Stats

Employees: 11,904 (2004, U.S.)
Employees: 12,148 (2003, U.S.)
Revenue: $2.1 billion (2004, U.S.)
Revenue: $1.9 billion (2003, U.S.)

Retention and Professional Development

How do 2004 minority and female attrition rates generally compare to those experienced in the prior year period?

Lower than in prior years

Diversity Mission Statement

We are committed to creating an environment that appreciates individuality. And now, more than ever, we're renewing our commitment to diversity. We continue to recognize diversity as a broad collection of differences that encompasses many elements...beliefs, race, workstyles, age, education, ethnic origin, gender, ideas, physical ability, perspectives and more.

We believe that a wide "band of inclusion" helps to increase team member performance, empowerment, satisfaction, productivity, equity, creativity, respect, and fairness. Our focus on diversity will also position us to better promote diverse business partnerships, expand our customer base, attract and retain the top talent in the market, make the company a better place to work, better understand our diverse customers' unique needs, give customers and communities outstanding service and deliver greater value to our stakeholders. At Bank of Coweta, valuing and leveraging our differences is an essential part of our organization's success.

Our diversity strategy includes Education – discussing the benefits value and management of diversity. Representation – visible diversity at all levels of the organization. Business Partnerships – developing relationships with diverse business partners. Development – establishing mentoring and networking models that facilitate the continued growth and development of our team members. Work Place Practices – modifying our recruiting and hiring strategy to position us to compete for a diverse talent pool.

Diversity creates an environment where team members can contribute innovative ideas, seek challenge, assume leadership and continue to focus on and exceed business, professional and personal objectives. One approach toward individual success is to give people meaningful, challenging work and mentors to help them along the way.

Target

1000 Nicollet Mall
Minneapolis, MN 55403
(612) 304-6073
Fax: (612) 696-3731
http://target.com/targetcorp_group/careers
/index.jhtml

Locations (worldwide)

Target store headquarters is located in
Minneapolis, Minnesota, with regional
offices in Los Angeles, California; Dallas,
Texas; Minneapolis, Minnesota;
Richmond, Virginia; and Troy, Michigan.
Target has over 1330 store locations in
47 states, 23 distribution centers, and 3
import warehouses and has offices in
over 40 countries throughout the world to
support our global sourcing initiatives.

Employment

To learn more about career opportunities at
Target, please visit Target.com/careers.

Recruiting

Please list the schools/types of schools at which you recruit.

• Ivy League schools
• Other private schools
• Public state schools
• Historically Black Colleges and Universities (HBCUs)
• Hispanic Serving Institutions (HSIs)
• Other predominantly minority and/or women's colleges

Do you have any special outreach efforts that are directed to encourage minority students to consider your firm?

• Hold a reception for minority students
• Conferences: National Black MBA, National Society of Hispanic MBAs, Hispanic Alliance for Career Enhancement,
• National Hispanic Business Association, Monster Diversity Leadership Program, National Association of Asian American Professionals, National INROADS Alumni Association, Consortium for Graduate Study in Management
• Advertise in minority student association publication(s)
• Participate in/host minority student job fair(s)
• Sponsor minority student association events
• Firm's employees participate on career panels at school
• Outreach to leadership of minority student organizations
• Scholarships or intern/fellowships for minority students

What activities does the firm undertake to attract minority and women employees?

• Partner programs with women and minority associations

• Conferences. Please list-Same as above.
• Participate at minority job fairs
• Seek referrals from other employees
• Utilize online job services

Do you use executive recruiting/search firms to seek to identify new diversity hires?

No

Internships and Co-ops

Target Headquarters, Stores or Distribution Internship

Deadline for application: On campus interviews fall and spring

Number of interns in the program in summer 2004 (internship) or 2004 (co-op): approximately 1,000

Pay: Depends on position

Length of the program: 10-12 weeks

Percentage of interns/co-ops in the program who receive offers of full-time employment: 50%-general/80%-INROADS

Web site for internship/co-op information: Target.com/careers

Please describe the internship program or co-op, including departments hiring, intern/co-op responsibilities, qualifications for the program and any other details you feel are relevant.

• Asset Protection
• Distribution
• Finance/Accounting
• Human Resources
• Marketing/Advertising
• Merchandising
• Product Development & Design
• Property Development (Real Estate, Construction, Architecture, Engineering, Store Planning & Design, Building Services)
• Store Leadership
• Target Sourcing Services
• Target Technology Services
• Target.com – Merchandise Planning
• Target.com – Marketing

Responsibilities:

During our 10-week summer intern program you will play a significant role in analyzing/developing company strategies. We will train you by combining classroom training and on the job application. You'll be paired with a mentor who will guide you through the program and provide feedback along the way.

During the program, you will be assigned to a department and work hands-on with the team. Your responsibilities will include an analytical project to complete during your internship. You will be asked to present your results to your leadership group at the end of your internship program. You will also experience the daily activities of your assigned area.

You will learn about other areas of the company and get to know the other interns at various social events.

Qualifications:

• Undergrad: currently enrolled or accepted in a 4-year degree program with strong academic performance
• Demonstrated leadership and decision-making skills
• Team-oriented thinking
• Ability to communicate clearly and effectively

• Excellent problem-solving skills
• Strong planning and organizational skills
• Assertiveness and strong initiative

Scholarships

We fund undergraduate scholarships through general scholarship funds of the schools where we recruit. We also provide funding to the United Negro College Fund and the Hispanic Scholarship Fund.

Affinity Groups/Employee Networks

• African American Business Council
• Asian American Business Council
• GLBT Business Council
• Hispanic Business Council

Target's diversity business councils aim to create an inclusive environment and provide a forum to exchange information, share common interests, and establish mentoring relationships. Each business council is focused on helping team members grow professionally and has specific programs and objectives centered on retention and development.

Entry-Level Programs/Full-Time Opportunities

Team Leader In-Training (Distribution Centers), Business Analyst (HQ/Merchandising), Human Resouces In-Training (Distribution, HQ, and Stores), Executive Team Leader-In-Training (Stores), Target Technology Leadership Program(HQ)

Length of program: 12 week training program
Geographic location(s) of program: Nationally

Please describe the training/training component of this program: Get started with our extensive training program that involves classroom and on-the-job and a mentor who works with you throughout your training.

Please describe any other educational components of this program: Tuition reimbursement is available

Strategic Plan and Diversity Leadership

How does the firm's leadership communicate the importance of diversity to everyone at the firm?

Target uses all of the corporation's communication channels to share Diversity information including e-mails, web site, newsletters, posters, brochures, etc. Furthermore, Target annually administers an internal communication campaign centered on diversity awareness.

Who has primary responsibility for leading diversity initiatives at your firm?

Tamika Curry, Director of Diversity

Does your firm currently have a diversity committee?

Yes

If yes, please describe how the committee is structured, how often it meets, etc.

Target has a cross-functional Diversity Steering Committee chaired by a member of Senior Management. The committee meets monthly and is comprised of leaders from throughout the corporation. The objective of the committee is to provide direction, feedback, and guidance on Target's corporate diversity efforts.

If yes, does the committee's representation include one or more members of the firm's management/executive committee (or the equivalent)?

Yes

Please describe the committee

The committee meets monthly.
>   **Total executives on the committee:** 18
>   **Total employees on committee:** 22

Does the committee and/or diversity leader establish and set goals or objectives consistent with management's priorities?

Yes

Has the firm undertaken a formal or informal diversity program or set of initiatives aimed at increasing the diversity of the firm?

Yes, formal

How often does the firm's management review the firm's diversity progress/results?

Monthly

How are the firm's diversity committee and/or firm management held accountable for achieving results?

Management is required to report annually to the Target board of directors on its progress in achieving greater diversity of our workforce.

The Stats

Revenue: $46.839 billion (2004, worldwide)
Revenue: $42.025 billion (2003, worldwide)

Employees (2004, worldwide):
Totalt: 292,000
Minorities: 115,000
Female: 172,000

Employees (2003, worldwide)
Total: 274,000
Minorities: 104,000
Female: 161,000

* Revenue numbers reflect continuing operations
** Employee population outside of U.S. not material

Our long-standing commitment to equal opportunity has increased the diversity of our work force as reflected in our Equal Employment Opportunity (EEO) Report for 2004 (the most relevant portions of which follow).

Target percentage of all employees in the following job categories:		
	Female	Minority
Officials and managers	44%	22%
Professionals	56%	17%
Sales workers	64%	41%
All employees	59%	38%

Gender and ethnic diversity is reflected at the highest levels of the corporation, including Target's Board of Directors.

Diversity Mission Statement

OUR DIVERSITY STATEMENT

Target Is a Performance-Based Company with Equal Opportunities for All Who Perform

OUR COMMITMENT

We respect and value the individuality of all team members and guests. We know that valuing diversity makes good business sense and helps to ensure our future success.

OUR DEFINITION OF DIVERSITY

We define diversity as individuality. This individuality may include a wide spectrum of attributes like personal style, age, race, gender, ethnicity, sexual orientation, language, physical ability, religion, family, citizenship status, socio-economic circumstances, education and life experiences. To us, diversity is any attribute that makes an individual unique that does not interfere with effective job performance.

The Employer Says

Discrimination based upon race, color, religion, sex, age, national origin, disability, sexual orientation or other characteristics protected by law is not tolerated in our work place. In addition to prohibiting such discrimination, Target attempts to create an environment that recognizes the value of diversity and enhances the opportunity for success of all team members regardless of their differences.

The following are examples of initiatives within Target that are intended to promote diversity throughout our organization:

• Minority Recruitment – Employees of diverse backgrounds are sought by attending minority job fairs (National Black MBA Association, National Society of Hispanic MBA, Consortium for Graduate Study in Management, CareerFair.com minority career fairs, NAACP career fairs, Urban Job Expo), placing ads in minority media, posting jobs and looking for candidates on minority-focused web sites (IMDiversity, DiversityInc, HireDiversity and DiversityJobMarket), posting positions at schools and other public places with high minority populations, attending national meetings of minority organizations, and publishing and distributing recruitment literature emphasizing our commitment to diversity.

• Target also hires interns from INROADS at both the corporate and store level, and is a charter sponsor for the INROADS Retail Management Institute, aimed at attracting more students of color to retail careers.

• Target is a national leader in providing job opportunities for people with disabilities. Target participates in community-based training by seeking out agencies, school programs and government incentive programs in an effort to hire people with disabilities.

• Diversity Training – As part of our comprehensive leadership development program, Target provides diversity training that is intended to enhance awareness of diversity in the work place and to build skills necessary to promote that diversity and the benefits it offers.

• Diversity Team – Target has formed an internal Diversity Team that is solely dedicated to leveraging diversity throughout the organization. The team focuses on recruitment and retention, awareness and communication, and measurement, and works with business partners throughout the company to provide diversity guidance and drive change.

• Diversity Steering Committee – Target has a cross-functional committee designed to help the corporation build the best team possible. The committee, comprised of members from many levels and job positions, fosters support for diversity at all levels of the organization and helps develop programs to meet the needs of team members.

• Team Member Business Councils – Target sponsors a variety of team member business councils that create a network for people of similar backgrounds to facilitate professional development through peer support, mentoring, and coaching.

• Involvement and Partnerships – Target has partnerships with many diversity-focused organizations, including:

  • Project Equality
  • Diversity Best Practices
  • the National Black MBA Association Conference (NBMBAA),
  • the National Society of Hispanic MBAs (NSHMBA),
  • the National Minority Supplier Development Council (NMSDC),
  • the Women's Business Enterprise National Council (WBENC),
  • the NAACP,
  • the Urban League,
  • the United Negro College Fund (UNCF), and
  • the Hispanic College Fund (HCF).

Diversity has been one of the strengths of our company and will continue to be an important part of our business strategy as we expand into new and different markets. We are committed to promoting and reinforcing diversity throughout our company as we position our business for continued success in the 21st century.

Tech Data Corporation

5350 Tech Data Dr.
Clearwater, FL 33760
Phone: (727) 539-7429
Fax: (727) 538-7803
www.techdata.com/careers

Diversity Leadership
Amy Blake (campus recruiting) and Ed Krauss
(diversity team leader)

Employment Contact
Amy Blake, Manager, Employment
5301 Tech Data Drive
Clearwater, FL 33760
Phone: (727) 539-7429
Fax: (727) 539-7429

Recruiting

Please list the schools/types of schools at which you recruit.

• *Public state schools:* University of South Florida, University of Florida, Florida State, University of Tampa, Eckerd College, University of Central Florida
• *Historically Black Colleges and Universities (HBCUs):* Florida A&M University

Do you have any special outreach efforts that are directed to encourage minority students to consider your firm?

• Advertise in minority student association publication(s)
• Participate in/host minority student job fair(s)
• Scholarships or intern/fellowships for minority students
• InRoads internship program

What activities does the firm undertake to attract minority and women employees?

• Partner programs with women and minority associations
• Participate at minority job fairs
• Seek referrals from other employees
• Utilize online job services

Do you use executive recruiting/search firms to seek to identify new diversity hires?

Yes

Internships and Co-ops

INROADS

Deadline for application: Fall
Number of interns in the program in summer 2004 (internship): Three (3)
Pay: $10-12/hourly (full-time) – paid bi-weekly
Length of the program: 12 weeks
Percentage of interns/co-ops in the program who receive offers of full-time employment: 100%

Strategic Plan and Diversity Leadership

How does the firm's leadership communicate the importance of diversity to everyone at the firm?

E-mail, quarterly employee meetings, website, town hall meetings

Who has primary responsibility for leading diversity initiatives at your firm?

Ed Krauss, Sr. Manager, Employment Operations

Does your firm currently have a diversity committee?

Yes

If yes, please describe how the committee is structured, how often it meets, etc.

14 members meeting once a month

If yes, does the committee's representation include one or more members of the firm's management/executive committee (or the equivalent)?

Yes

Does the committee and/or diversity leader establish and set goals or objectives consistent with management's priorities?

Yes

Has the firm undertaken a formal or informal diversity program or set of initiatives aimed at increasing the diversity of the firm?

Yes, formal

How often does the firm's management review the firm's diversity progress/results?

Twice a year

The Stats

Employees: 2,500 (2004, U.S.)
Employees: 5,500 (2004, outside the U.S.)
Employees: 8,000+ (2004, worldwide)
Revenue: US $19.8 billion (2004, worldwide)

Retention and Professional Development

How do 2004 minority and female attrition rates generally compare to those experienced in the prior year period?

About the same as in prior years

Please identify the specific steps you are taking to reduce the attrition rate of minority and women employees.

• Increase/improve current work/life programs
• Succession plan includes emphasis on diversity
• Work with minority and women employees to develop career advancement plans
• Professional skills development program, including minority and women employees
• We also analyze exit interview data to identify opportunities for improvements and trends

Diversity Mission Statement

Diversity Statement

Tech Data's philosophy has always striven to place the greatest emphasis on the role of the individual within the company. That emphasis on the individual, at the same time, requires Tech Data to pay attention to the fact that each employee brings a wealth of different perspectives to the work environment. Tech Data and its employees needs to be respectful not only of those differences, but learn how to make difference, in itself, an additional value which can be incorporate into how others are treated and customers are approached.

The concept of meaningful sameness and meaningful difference is not a new one. Meaningful sameness is needed in order for people to operate within the context of a common set of standards and values for everyday operation. Employees also need to contribute meaningfully to the company in the performance of their jobs. Concurrently, Tech Data and its employees must respect and encourage meaningful difference, with the assumption that people from different perspectives provide vitality, creativity, new ideas, and growth.

Multiculturalism seeks to look at difference in the broadest parameters. Culture is often defined to include terms of race, gender, and national origin, and these specific indices are, of course, vital in shaping values. Additionally, culture also involves values derived from considerations relating to one's age, marital status, religion, sexual orientation, gender identity and/or expression, and disability. All of these factors, and more, shape an individual's value system, and all of these have actual potential value to Tech Data as a company.

Tech Data provides equal opportunity for all employees and applicants for employment regardless of race, color, creed, religion, national origin, sexual orientation, age, or sex. Similarly, Tech Data has stated that individuals with physical and mental limitations are evaluated on their ability to perform a specific job rather than on stereotypical assumptions about their disability, and that reasonable accommodations are made when appropriate. Tech Data continues to hold steadfast to this philosophy.

A policy limited to equal opportunity, however, is not sufficient to attract and retain members of historically underrepresented groups. While Tech Data has attracted an immensely talented workforce, the nets must be cast much more widely to attract available talent. The process Tech Data uses for that purpose is affirmative action; it is a means for Tech Data to achieve multiculturalism, i.e. the existence and valuing of difference. Tech Data's operating assumption is that talent is randomly distributed in all populations, and that Tech Data benefits by the participation of different groups in its workforce.

Affirmative action is a concept misunderstood by many. In many people's minds, it has meant lowered standards or preferential treatment. Tech Data's position is that we can behave affirmatively while retaining the highest standards, but that more energy, planning, and commitment must be committed to the inclusion of competitive talent from all segments of the population. That effort requires dedication, personal responsibility, and investment of resources. Tech Data needs to continue to find ways to encourage and support hiring managers to make the extra efforts needed to attract the best people.

Multiculturalism is crucial to Tech Data domestically within the United States and as a global corporation. Tech Data's future success in the United States depends heavily upon the ability to harness and include the vitality of the burgeoning minority populations, both as employees and customers. No one group will have majority status within ten years and demographic factors will have major implications for the workforce composition, as well as customers.

Globally, the world is getting smaller and Tech Data's presence internationally becomes more prominent every day. Tech Data has always sought local talent in order to compete effectively, and Tech Data needs to be open to and inclusive of ideas and values that originate outside the United States. Tech Data will continue to seek ways to incorporate different perspectives in global operations.

Managing multiculturalism is a critical part of success for any Twenty-First Century company and it is a challenge Tech Data is ready to pursue.

INVESTING IN TOMORROW'S LEADERS

Time Warner is proud to be a supporter of

Vault/INROADS Guide to Corporate Diversity Programs.

To explore opportunities with us, visit www.timewarner.com/careers

TimeWarner

  NEW LINE CINEMA   HBO TimeInc.

Time Warner Inc.

1 Time Warner Center
New York, NY 10019
(212) 484-8000
Fax: (212) 489-6183
www.timewarner.com

Locations (worldwide):
Corporate Headquarters, New York, NY

Contact Person
Caroline Taylor Ellerson, Senior Manager,
Recruitment Programs & Events
One Time Warner Center
New York, New York 10019
Phone: (212) 484-8611
E-mail: Caroline.Taylor.Ellerson@timewarner.com

Recruiting

Please list the schools/types of schools at which you recruit.

- *Ivy League schools:* Wharton, Harvard, Columbia
- *Other private schools:* NYU, Fordham, Stanford
- *Public state schools:* CUNY, Baruch, Georgia State, USC, UCLA
- *Historically Black Colleges and Universities (HBCUs):* NCA&T, Spelman, Morehouse, and Howard

Do you have any special outreach efforts that are directed to encourage minority students to consider your firm?

The company's broad diversity recruiting efforts are inclusive of minorities and include the following:

- Hold a reception for minority students
- Conferences: NSBE, NBMBAA, ALPFA, HACE, NABA, Women For Hire
- Participate in/host minority student job fair(s)
- Sponsor minority student association events
- Firm's employees participate on career panels at schools
- Outreach to leadership of minority student organizations
- Scholarships or intern/fellowships for minority students
- **Other:** Time Warner partners with a number of organizations in an effort to create inclusive candidate pools for open positions. These organizations include, but are not limited to, Posse, MLT, Emma Bowen Foundation, Torch, UNCF, HACU and Prep for Prep.

What activities does the firm undertake to attract minority and women employees?

The company's broad diversity recruiting efforts are inclusive of minority and women employees and include the following:

- Partner programs with women and minority associations
- Conferences: NSBE, NBMBAA, ALPFA, HACE, NABA, Women For Hire
- Participate at minority job fairs-
- Seek referrals from other employees
- Utilize online job services

Internships and Co-ops

The company's broad internship opportunities are inclusive of minority and women employees. Here is a listing of our major programs.

STARS summer internship program

STARS (Students Taking A Right Step) summer internship program provides selected students with mentors and development opportunities in the entertainment, news, media and telecommunications industry

> *Deadline for application:* March
> *Number of interns in the program in summer 2004 (internship) or 2004 (co-op):* 1000
> *Pay:* $8- $16 p/hr
> *Length of the program:* 10 weeks
> *Web site for internship/co-op information:* www.timewarner.com/careers
> *Locations:* New York- HBO, Time Inc, Time Warner & Time Warner Cable; Los Angeles- Warner Bros, The WB, Time Warner Cable, HBO & New Line Cinema. Atlanta- Turner. Dulles, VA- America Online.

AOL Summer Internship Program

Top students selected from 9 target universities.

> *Deadline for application:* April (end of month)
> *Number of interns in the program in summer 2004 (internship):* 150
> *Pay:* $9- $19 p/hr (grad students $25 – $38/hr)
> *Length of the program:* 12 weeks
> *Web site for internship/co-op information:* http://corp.aol.com/careers/campus.html
> *Locations:* Northern Virginia, California, New York, Ohio

HBO Internship Program

> *Deadline for application:* April 1st
> *Number of interns in the program in summer 2004 (internship):* 30
> *Pay:* $10 p/h
> *Length of the program:* 10-12 weeks
> *Web site for internship/co-op information:* www.hbo.com
> *Locations:* New York & Los Angeles

Time Warner Book Group Internship program

Undergraduate students particularly interested in Book Publishing.

> *Deadline for application:* May
> *Number of interns in the program in summer 2004 (internship):* 35
> *Pay:* $9- $10 p/hr
> *Length of the program:* 10 weeks
> *Web site for internship/co-op information:* www.bookjobs.com
> *Location:* New York

Editorial Internship Program

Rising seniors or students in-between graduate journalism school; rising juniors when nominated by school; acceptance by committee vote of application packet (300-word personal statement, resume, transcript, clips)

> *Deadline for application:* December
> *Number of interns in the program in summer 2004 (internship):* 50
> *Pay:* $350 per week plus housing stipend
> *Length of the program:* 9 weeks
> *Web site for internship/co-op information:* http://campusrecruiting.timeinc.com
> *Location:* New York

New Line Cinema Internship Program

Undergraduate students majoring in: Business, Communications & Film/TV.

> *Deadline for application:* August & December
> *Number of interns in the program:* 70
> *Pay:* Course Credit
> *Length of the program:* Academic Year
> *Web site for internship/co-op information:* www.newline.com
> *Locations:* New York and Los Angeles

Scholarships

United Negro College Fund

> *Deadline for application:* Deadline changes each year (but is around August-Sept)
> *Pay:* Amount $2,000-2,500 based on need per year beginning in sophomore year; renewable up to three years
> *Web site:* www.uncf.org

Hispanic Scholarship Fund

> *Deadline for application:* Deadline (has two application times on in the fall and one in the spring)
> *Pay:* Amount $2,500 based on need per year beginning in sophomore year
> *Web site:* www.hsf.org

Hispanic Association of Colleges and Universities

> *Deadline:* Summer
> *Pay:* Amount $2,000 based on need per year beginning in sophomore year
> *Web site:* www.hacu.org

Affinity Groups/Employee Networks

Affinity Groups have been established at Time Warner and many of its subsidiaries and affiliates based on the interests of the employee population at the particular business unit. These groups may include, but are not limited to, affinity groups for: African Americans; Asian Americans; Hispanic and Latino/as; Gay, Lesbian, Bisexual and Transgender; and Women.

Entry-Level Programs/Full-Time Opportunities

Time Inc. Logan Associates

Length of program: 12 months
Geographic location(s) of program: New York

Please describe the training/training component of this program: Full exposure to magazine publishing business.

Time Warner Cable - Marketing & Electrical Engineering Trainee Program

Length of program: 12 months
Geographic location(s) of program: Various Locations

Please describe the training/training component of this program: Exposure to the Cable Business

T3 Turner Trainee Team

Length of program: 11 months
Geographic location(s) of program: Atlanta, GA

Please describe the training/training component of this program: Exposure to the CNN/ Turner Business.

Warner Bros. Trainee Program

Length of program: 12 months
Geographic location(s) of program: Burbank, CA

Please describe the training/training component of this program: Exposure to media & entertainment business

Strategic Plan and Diversity Leadership

Who has primary responsibility for leading diversity initiatives at your firm?

Cindy Augustine, SVP, Talent Management

Does your firm currently have a diversity committee?

Yes

If yes, does the committee's representation include one or more members of the firm's management/executive committee (or the equivalent)?

Yes

Does the committee and/or diversity leader establish and set goals or objectives consistent with management's priorities?

Yes

Has the firm undertaken a formal or informal diversity program or set of initiatives aimed at increasing the diversity of the firm?

Yes, formal

The Stats

Employees: 69,117 (2004, U.S.)

Diversity Mission Statement

Fostering diversity is essential to our mission of becoming the world's most respected and valued company. From diversity comes a wide array of new ideas – and new ideas are what make our brands great. Embracing diversity not only helps us establish a competitive advantage in the markets we serve, but also is key to the goals of extending the benefits of the Information Age to all people and communities around the world. We have made a commitment to reflect diversity in every aspect of our business: in the way we hire, develop and promote; in the creative, journalistic and online content we produce; in the marketing of our products and services; in the suppliers with whom we do business; in the investments we make; and in the philanthropic causes we choose to support. At Time Warner Inc., we are building an inclusive workplace and a corporate culture that draws on the greatest range of people and perspectives – and we are committed to building our reputation as an employer of choice for women and minorities.

Tyco International, Inc.

9 Roszel Road
Princeton, NJ 08540
Phone: (609) 720-4200
Fax: (609) 720-4208
www.tyco.com

Diversity Leadership
Tracey Porter, University Relations, Manager
9 Roszel Road
Princeton, NJ 08540
Phone: (609) 806-2196
E-mail: tporter@tyco.com

Recruiting

Please list the schools/types of schools at which you recruit.

• Ivy League schools
• Public state schools
• Historically Black Colleges and Universities (HBCUs)

Do you have any special outreach efforts that are directed to encourage minority students to consider your firm?

• Hold a reception for minority students
• Conferences
• Participate in/host minority student job fair(s)
• Outreach to leadership of minority student organizations

What activities does the firm undertake to attract minority and women employees?

• Partner programs with women and minority associations
• Conferences
• Participate at minority job fairs
• Seek referrals from other employees

Do you use executive recruiting/search firms to seek to identify new diversity hires?

Yes

Internships and Co-ops

INROADS and the Lagrant Foundation Communication Internship Program

Deadline for application: Feb. 1st

Number of interns in the program in summer 2004 (internship) or 2004 (co-op): 50-75

Pay: Varies based on year in school

Length of the program: 10-12 weeks

Percentage of interns/co-ops in the program who receive offers of full-time employment: 35-40%

Web site for internship/co-op information: www.tyco.com

Please describe the internship program or co-op, including departments hiring, intern/co-op responsibilities, qualifications for the program and any other details you feel are relevant.

All functions. Undergraduate GPA 3.0 or better. Leadership and Analytical Skills

Entry-Level Programs/Full-Time Opportunities

IT, HR, and Supply Chain Rotational Programs

Length of program: 2 years

Geographic location(s) of program: National

Please describe the training/training component of this program: Job and classroom experience

Strategic Plan and Diversity Leadership

How does the firm's leadership communicate the importance of diversity to everyone at the firm?

E-mails, web site, newsletters, meetings

Who has primary responsibility for leading diversity initiatives at your firm?

V.P. of Diversity

Does your firm currently have a diversity committee?

Yes

If yes, does the committee's representation include one or more members of the firm's management/executive committee (or the equivalent)?

Yes

Does the committee and/or diversity leader establish and set goals or objectives consistent with management's priorities?

Yes

Has the firm undertaken a formal or informal diversity program or set of initiatives aimed at increasing the diversity of the firm?

Yes, formal

The Stats

Employees: 250,000 (2004, worldwide)
Revenue: $40 billion (2004, worldwide)

United Technologies Corporation

One Financial Plaza
Hartford, CT 06103
(860) 728-7000
Fax: (860) 728-7979
www.utc.com/careers

Locations (worldwide)

UTC is the parent company for the following companies: Carrier Corporation (HQ – Farmington, CT), Pratt and Whitney (HQ – East Hartford, CT), Hamilton Sundstrand (HQ – Windsor Locks, CT), Otis Elevator (HQ – Farmington, CT), Sikorsky Aircraft (HQ – Stratford, CT), UTC Power (HQ – South Windsor, CT), UTC Fire & Security (HQ – Farmington, CT). All companies have multiple international and domestic operations locations.

Diversity Leadership

Grace Figueredo, Director, Workforce Diversity
Phone: (860) 728-7810
Fax: (860) 998-8575
E-mail: grace.figueredo@utc.com

Contact Person

Joelle Hayes, Manager, Corporate Recruiting and Diversity Partnerships
One Financial Plaza, MS 504
Hartford, CT 06101
Phone: (860) 728-6516
Fax: (860) 660-9260
E-mail: joelle.hayes@utc.com

Recruiting

Please list the schools/types of schools at which you recruit.

- *Ivy League schools*: Cornell University
- *Other private schools:* Purdue University, Renssalaer Polytechnic Institute, MIT
- *Public state schools:* UCONN, GA Tech, University of Michigan, Penn State, University of Illinois – Champaign-Urbana
- *Historically Black Colleges and Universities (HBCUs):* Howard, North Carolina A&T State
- *Hispanic Serving Institutions (HSIs):* University of Puerto Rico – Mayaguez

Do you have any special outreach efforts that are directed to encourage minority students to consider your firm?

- Hold a reception for minority students
- Conferences: NSBE, SHPE-ETCC
- Participate in/host minority student job fair(s)
- Sponsor minority student association events
- Firm's employees participate on career panels at school
- Outreach to leadership of minority student organizations
- Scholarships or intern/fellowships for minority students

What activities does the firm undertake to attract minority and women employees?

- Partner programs with women and minority associations
- Conferences: NSBE (National and Regional), SWE, SHPE-ETCC
- Participate at minority job fairs
- Seek referrals from other employees
- Utilize online job services

• Career Services

Do you use executive recruiting/search firms to seek to identify new diversity hires?

Yes – mostly executives hires, some manager level hires

If yes, list all women – and/or minority-owned executive search/recruiting firms to which the firm paid a fee for placement services in the past 12 months:

Granville and Webb, Millette Granville, Principal. At one particular business unit, 30% of all search firms retained are women and minority owned.

Internships and Co-ops

INROADS is UTC's only internship program outside of its internal internship programs. Hamilton Sundstrand has an extremely robust co-op/experiential education program.

INROADS

Number of interns in the program in summer 2004 (internship) or 2004 (co-op): 182
Pay: Varies by major (technical/non technical) and classification
Length of the program: 10-12 weeks
Percentage of interns/co-ops in the program who receive offers of full-time employment: 75%
Web site for internship/co-op information: www.inroads.org

Scholarships

UTC INROADS Scholarship

Deadline for application for the scholarship program: July (varies each year)
Scholarship award amount: Varies – 2 awards at $3500; 2 at $2500, 2 at $1000, 5 at $500
Web site or other contact information for scholarship: Only for eligible returning INROADS interns employed by UTC

Affinity Groups

• African American Forum
• Hispanic Leadership Forum
• Women's Leadership Forum

UTC has established operating guidelines for affinity groups within the business units at UTC. Most of them meet on a monthly/quarterly basis. They have executive champions, who support/sponsor their activities and related events. The groups have charters, which support the overall diversity mission/vision of UTC. Most of the groups are focused on supporting the recruitment, development, advancement and retention of UTC's minority employees. They have websites that inform membership of their mission, upcoming events, resources, etc.

Entry-Level Programs/Full-Time Opportunities

- Financial Leadership Program – 24 months; Connecticut
- Information Technology Leadership Program – three 9-month rotations (27 months); Connecticut
- Pratt and Whitney Manufacturing Engineering Development Program – 24 months; Connecticut
- Hamilton Sundstrand HR Rotational Program – 24 months, various locations

Please describe any other educational components of this program: All full-time and part-time UTC employees are eligible for the Employee Scholar Program, which pays full tuition, fees and books towards degree study in any area.

Strategic Plan and Diversity Leadership

How does the firm's leadership communicate the importance of diversity to everyone at the firm?

UTC has a decentralized cascade-down approach to diversity. At the start of the year, each respective business unit sets key objectives; diversity is embedded into these. The senior leadership of each business unit utilizes various communication vehicles to share, monitor, and report on the progression of these objectives throughout the course of the year, (e.g. "roadmaps," scorecards, etc. are posted on websites, meetings, e-mail communiqués and town hall meetings are conducted to discuss the performance and results in these areas).

Who has primary responsibility for leading diversity initiatives at your firm?

Grace Figueredo, Director, Work Force Diversity. (In addition, each business unit has a diversity manager, who makes up the UTC Diversity Council).

Does your firm currently have a diversity committee?

No (however, some of the business units do have diversity committees that were formed at the grassroots level).

Has the firm undertaken a formal or informal diversity program or set of initiatives aimed at increasing the diversity of the firm?

Yes, formal. UTC has a decentralized cascade-down approach to diversity. At the start of the year, each respective business unit, sets goals regarding representation. In addition, we track, monitor and report on the associated activity, such as hiring, promotions, and attrition. Each business unit sets a strategic approach to addressing their opportunities; HR has the responsibility of partnering with line leaders to develop action and implementation plans. Every quarter at Operating Management Meetings, each of the business unit presidents presents a status update to the CEO and diversity performance/results are reported, reviewed and discussed.

How often does the firm's management review the firm's diversity progress/results?

Quarterly

How is the firm's diversity committee and/or firm management held accountable for achieving results?

As stated above, the UTC Diversity Progression metrics are reviewed at the quarterly OMM with the CEO. At the conclusion of each year, Executive Incentive Compensation is linked to their respective performance/results in all business deliverables, with diversity being one of the elements.

The Stats

Employees: 70,000 (2004, U.S.)
Employees: 135,000 (2004, outside the U.S.)
Employees: 205,000 (2004, worldwide)
Revenue: $27.9 billion (2004, U.S.)

• Executive Female Population: 14.9%
• Executive Minority Population: 12.8%
• Managerial Level Female Population: 13.1%
• Managerial Level Minority Population: 10.0%
• Professional Female Population: 22.1%
• Professional Minority Population: 13.8%

UTC Facts

• We employ 205,700 employees in 180 countries
• Our revenues for last year were $27.9 Billion
• We are the 49th largest company in the US
• We are headquartered in Hartford, CT
• We are truly global
• Over 55% of our employees are outside the US

• Our U.S. presence beyond Hartford, CT Metropolitan area is in:
  • Syracuse, NY, Athens, GA, Collierville, TN, Charlotte, NC – Carrier
  • Rockford, IL, San Diego, CA, Miramar, FL – Hamilton Sundstrand
  • West Palm Beach, FL – Sikorsky and Pratt & Whitney
  • Every major city – Otis
  • Many satellite sales and distributions offices – Otis and Carrier

Retention and Professional Development

How do 2004 minority and female attrition rates generally compare to those experienced in the prior year period?

Lower than in prior years. Our attrition rates were lower in the executive and professional arenas; however, in the managerial category our female and minority attrition rates were slightly higher.

Please identify the specific steps you are taking to reduce the attrition rate of minority and women employees.

Currently reviewing the Exit Interview Process across UTC to determine the qualitative reasons behind attrition, in order to proactively address turnover.

Diversity Mission Statement

UTC Diversity Vision

Our Diversity Vision is to create an environment that is one of the best places for people to work. It defines the value that is placed on the differences in the workforce and recognizes that diversity is key in broadening our experience and technical competency base to solve problems in our markets.

UTC Diversity Mission

To create an environment where all associates are encouraged to reach their fullest potential and where everyone values, accepts and respects the differences in our workforce.

The Employer Says

Since 1995, United Technologies Corporation has made significant progression in its diversity representation goals and has been recognized for numerous awards and honors regarding the area of diversity; most recently, the Brillante Award from NSHMBA (National Society of Hispanic MBAs), and the Black Torch Award from NSBE (National Society of Black Engineers).

UTC believes that innovation springs from knowledge, and is committed to supporting a highly educated work force. Currently, more than 13,000 employees participate in the UTC Employee Scholar Program, which provides pre-paid tuition and fees, time off to attend classes and study, and the award of UTC common stock upon graduation. The company encourages all employees to enroll in college classes to broaden their horizons, expand their thinking and sharpen their skills. Employees are free to explore their own interests, which need not be directly related to their work. The program is open to all UTC employees, and the response has been enthusiastic. Since the program's inception in 1996, UTC has invested more than $450 million in the Employee Scholar Program. Approximately 16,000 employees have received their degrees through the program. Retention among employees in the Employee Scholar program is greater than for those who are not.

In 2004, UTC granted $45,000 to fund scholarships for INROADS students to prepare them for positions of leadership in corporate America. UTC also supports several Historically Black Colleges and Universities such as North Carolina A&T, Howard University and Tuskegee.

In order to address employees' needs for resource and referral services, the Lifechoices program was established through the support of a consulting firm to provide employees with a variety of services including child and elder-care referral services, emergency dependent care referral services, fertility and adoption consulting services and a homework hotline. Last year, more than 15 percent of UTC's U.S. employees used the resources of Lifechoices. In addition, UTC earned recognition demonstrating efforts beyond organizational, cultural and demographic boundaries to achieve outstanding results in addressing employee needs with the Innovative Excellence Award from the AWLP (Alliance for Work/Life Progress).

UTC employees value the corporation's role in strengthening our communities through innovative and significant monetary contributions. Each year, UTC donates more than $16 million to organizations around the world that support community programs, the arts, education and the environment. This money is supplemented by the priceless contributions of time and effort made by thousands of employee volunteers. Each year, our employees spend more than 50,000 hours volunteering their time and expertise to their communities and nonprofit organizations. Like many companies, UTC matches the donations of their employees to nonprofit organizations. The company also recognizes and encourages volunteer activities by contributing to specific organizations to which employees donate a significant amount of their personal time. UTC is a leader in its support for Special Olympics. In 2004, UTC celebrated its 27th year of partnership with Special Olympics Connecticut. As a title sponsor of the state Summer Games, UTC supports Special Olympics Connecticut with more than 2,000 volunteers and $100,000 annually.

Our staff, faculty and students make a difference every day, and so can you!

SUNY Upstate Medical University is the regional academic medical center for professional education, biomedical research and patient care. It is one of four medical universities in the State University of New York system. With over 6,000 people on staff, we are one of Central New York's largest employers.

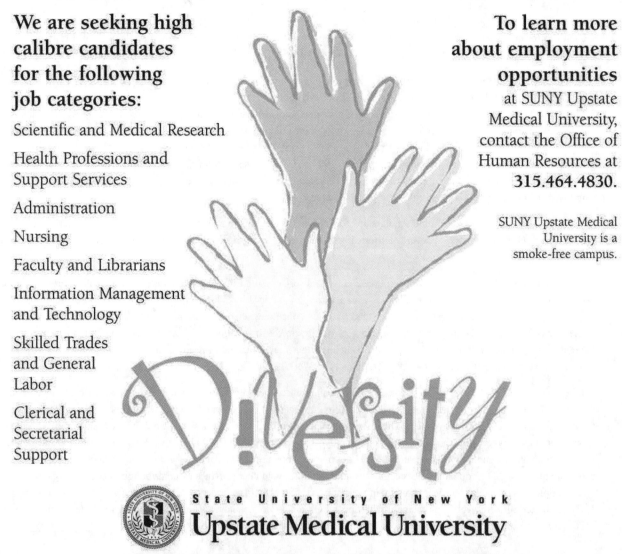

We are seeking high calibre candidates for the following job categories:

Scientific and Medical Research

Health Professions and Support Services

Administration

Nursing

Faculty and Librarians

Information Management and Technology

Skilled Trades and General Labor

Clerical and Secretarial Support

To learn more about employment opportunities at SUNY Upstate Medical University, contact the Office of Human Resources at **315.464.4830.**

SUNY Upstate Medical University is a smoke-free campus.

State University of New York
Upstate Medical University

SUNY Upstate Medical University/University Hospital is an AA/EEO/ADA employer **committed to excellence through diversity.**

Syracuse • New York
www.upstate.edu

University Hospital/(SUNY) Upstate Medical University

State University of New York
Upstate Medical University
750 East Adams Street
Syracuse, NY 13210-2375
(315) 464-5540
www.upstate.edu/hr
www.upstate.edu/prospective

Diversity Leadership
Maxine Thompson, Director, Office of Diversity &
Affirmative Action
Phone: (315) 464-5234
Fax: (315) 464-5232

Barbara Hamilton, Assistant Dean of
Multicultural Resources.(students)
Phone: (315) 464-5433
Fax: (315) 464-5431
E-mail: hamiltonb@upstate.edu

Contact Person

Edgar Johnson, Diversity Specialist, Office of Diversity & Affirmative Action
Phone: (315) 464-4924
E-mail: johnsone@upstate.edu

Recruiting

Please list the schools/types of schools at which you recruit.

• *Ivy League schools:* Cornell University
• *Other private schools:* LeMoyne College, Clarkson University, St. Lawrence University, Syracuse University
• *Public state schools:* State University of New York (SUNY)—SUNY Canton, SUNY Binghamton, SUNY IT Utica, SUNY Morrisville, SUNY Onondaga Community College, SUNY Cobleskill, SUNY Albany, SUNY Buffalo, SUNY Potsdam

Do you have any special outreach efforts that are directed to encourage minority students to consider your firm?

• Conferences: National Association of Minority Medical Educators (NAMME), American Association of Medical Colleges (AAMC), Other regional (Central New York) conferences/workshops
• Advertise in minority student association publication(s)
• Participate in/host minority student job fair(s)l
• Sponsor minority student association events
• Firm's employees participate on career panels at school
• Outreach to leadership of minority student organizations
• Scholarships or intern/fellowships for minority students
• Community Outreach to local agencies to include disabilities.

What activities does the firm undertake to attract minority and women employees?

• Partner programs with women and minority associations
• Participate at minority job fairs
• Seek referrals from other employees
• Utilize online job services

Do you use executive recruiting/search firms to seek to identify new diversity hires?

No

Internships and Co-ops

We have a variety clinical and non-clinical internships and co-ops opened to all (paid and unpaid) here at SUNY Upstate. Internships are coordinated and managed at the department level. As a major teaching hospital, individuals interested in internships should visit http://www.upstate.edu/hr/training/internship.shtml. Affiliation agreements must be established with the intern's college/university through our Contracts Division.

Additionally, we have established affiliation agreements with 2 HBCUs for Physical Therapy UNPAID internship opportunities at SUNY Upstate. Those schools are Howard University and University of Maryland Eastern Shore.
We are currently active participants of INROADS.

INROADS

Number of interns in the program in summer 2004 (internship) or 2004 (co-op): 1
Pay: $11-12/hr
Length of the program: 8–10 weeks
Percentage of interns/co-ops in the program who receive offers of full-time employment: Currently 0.
Web site for internship/co-op information: www.upstate.edu/hr/training/internship.shtml

Programs vary between departments

Scholarships

Empire State Minority Honors Scholarship

Scholarship award amount: Dollar amount commensurate with GPA. Maximum amount per student is $1,000 for entire scholarship
Web site or other contact information for scholarship: http://www.upstate.edu/currentstudents/finaid/

The New York State budget includes funds for SUNY to administer the Empire State Minority Honors Scholarship (ESMHS) Program for African American, Hispanic/Latino and Native American undergraduate students. Eligible students must be enrolled in a degree program either full- or part-time and have demonstrated high academic achievement. Scholarship applications will be sent to students with a 3.5 or better cumulative G.P.A. Recipients are not required to demonstrate financial need. However, to determine eligibility for other State and Federal financial aid, all recipients must complete the Free Application for Federal Student Aid (FAFSA).

Affinity Groups/Employee Networks

Staff and Faculty: Faculty/Staff Association for Diversity (FSAD)
Mission: Upstate employees formed the Faculty and Staff Association for Diversity to increase awareness of the contributions made by faculty and staff of color. This association, formed in 1997, is an initiative of the President's Diversity Enhancement Program, and meets monthly. FSAD assists in recruiting and retaining staff of color, and provide support services to staff of color, to include mentoring.

Students: The Office of Multicultural Resources serves as a resource for diverse students and is committed to supporting, enrolling, retaining and graduating historically underserved students.

Student Diversity and Affirmative Action Committee: The role of the Student Diversity and Affirmative Action (SDAA) Committee is to promote the education of the student body in matters related to Diversity and Affirmative Action. Members of the committee will work together with the faculty and administration to insure that students are given opportunities to expand their appreciation of the importance of cultural awareness and sensitivity throughout their medical training.

Other Affinity Groups include:

• Dean's Advisory Committee on Women's Issues
• Dean's Advisory Committee on Student Diversity
• American Medical Women's Association
• Asian Pacific American Medical Student Association
• Chinese Student Association
• The Christian Medical Fellowship
• Diversity in Allied Health Organization
• Jewish Medical Association
• Muslim Students' Association
• South Asian Medical Students Association

Entry-Level Programs/Full-Time Opportunities

Health Careers Opportunity Program for College Students (HCOP)

Length of program: Eight weeks summer program
Geographic location(s) of program: Syracuse, NY

Please describe the training/training component: This program is designed to prepare undergraduate college students for success in healthcare professions. An intensive 8 week summer program, students are exposed to academic courses, skills workshops, and field placements and/or research opportunities in a healthcare setting.

Please describe any other educational components of this program: A generous stipend is awarded upon successful completion of the program.

Strategic Plan and Diversity Leadership

How does the firm's leadership communicate the importance of diversity to everyone at the firm?

We utilize meetings, newsletters, websites, and mailings. We just recently mailed out to all employees our Diversity Commitment Statement endorsed by our President. The Diversity Commitment Statement will be prominently displayed in high traffic areas throughout the institution.

Who has primary responsibility for leading diversity initiatives at your firm?

Maxine Thompson, Director, Office of Diversity and Affirmative Action.

Does your firm currently have a diversity committee?

Yes – A Diversity Council was established in August 2004. This Council Reports to the President and the Executive Diversity Council which is comprised of the President, Associate VP for Human Resources, Director of Office of Diversity and Affirmative Action, and the Executive Vice President. And Dean of the College of Medicine.

If yes, please describe how the committee is structured, how often it meets, etc.

The Diversity Council is made up of 13 individuals from culturally diverse backgrounds. These individuals represent different areas of SUNY Upstate and most are in leadership roles to include executive roles. The council collects data and other information, make recommendations, craft new initiatives, help implement decisions, and monitor results. The committee meets on a monthly basis.

If yes, does the committee's representation include one or more members of the firm's management/executive committee (or the equivalent)?

Yes

Please describe the committee.

Combined, the Diversity Executive Council and the Diversity Council has 4 executives on the committee, and 12 employees. The Diversity Council meets monthly for about 2 hours PLUS outside meeting assignments (homework) are delegated to members, i.e., data collection. The Executive Diversity Council meets quarterly. Subcommittees are formed to assist and help with the furtherance of diversity initiatives. As such, it's difficult to calculate exact hours spent on diversity initiatives. However, as diversity is a priority here at SUNY Upstate and is currently in its infant stage, many, many hours are devoted to such tasks.

Total Executives on Committee: 4

Does the committee and/or diversity leader establish and set goals or objectives consistent with management's priorities?

Yes

Has the firm undertaken a formal or informal diversity program or set of initiatives aimed at increasing the diversity of the firm?

Yes, formal

How often does the firm's management review the firm's diversity progress/results?

Annually

How is the firm's diversity committee and/or firm management held accountable for achieving results?

Currently working on a strategic organizational plan which will be developed by the Diversity Council and will include outcomes through development and implementation of organizational competencies in terms of diversity integration into performance appraisals.

The Stats

Employees: 4,880 (2004, U.S.)
Employees: 4,727 (2003, U.S.)

Demographic Profile:		
SUNY Upstate:	**2004**	**2003**
Whites	3,991 (82%)	3899 (82%)
Blacks	448 (9%)	422 (9%)
Hispanics	69 (1%)	69 (1%)
Asians	344 (7%)	311 (7%)
Native Americans	28 (1%)	26 (1%)
Males	1,701 (35%)	1667 (35%)
Females	3,179 (65%)	3060 (65%)

Retention and Professional Development

How do 2004 minority and female attrition rates generally compare to those experienced in the prior year period?

• For SUNY Upstate minority employees the attrition rate was unchanged.

• For SUNY Upstate female employees the attrition rate was slightly higher in 2004 than in the prior year.

Please identify the specific steps you are taking to reduce the attrition rate of minority and women employees.

• Develop and/or support internal employee affinity groups (e.g., minority or women networks within the firm)

• Increase/improve current work/life programs

• Succession plan includes emphasis on diversity (Being Explored)

• Strengthen mentoring program for all employees, including minorities and women (Currently in Progress)

• Professional skills development program, including minority and women employees

Diversity Mission Statement

SUNY Upstate Medical University defines diversity as valuing the similarities and differences among individuals. This holistic approach encompasses various dimensions including the mind, body, spirit and physical environment of all who work, learn and receive care here.

In demonstrating how we value diversity, we practice fairness and equality in a manner that is consistent and that allows everyone to contribute and perform to their fullest potential. We identify and create leadership opportunities that recognize and maximize the skills, talents and abilities of a diverse workforce. We will ensure a safe, fair, supportive and inclusive environment for all at Upstate Medical University.

Recruiting, training and retaining a more diverse workforce is a business imperative of Upstate Medical University. As a major employer in Central New York, we benefit from a diverse workforce, obtaining new ideas and different perspectives, and positioning ourselves to successfully expand into a diverse community.

We recognize that achieving racial, ethnic and cultural diversity in the workforce is a critical component toward improving the delivery of culturally competent care to the community we serve, while addressing health care disparities.

Diversity is not only "the right thing to do" it is an essential and necessary step in improving the health care environment for all in the Central New York community.

Excellence through diversity positions us to successfully embrace all individuals within the community we serve

The Employer Says

It is the policy of the State University of New York (SUNY) Upstate Medical University to obtain a workforce that reflects the diverse communities in Central New York. To achieve this, SUNY Upstate has a Diversity Specialist/Recruiter whose job is dedicated to actively recruiting and interviewing prospective diverse employees. In addition, the institution abides by the guidelines of the State of New York regarding affirmative action employment policies that mandate equal consideration for all applicants for advertised positions.

SUNY Upstate Medical Center consists of the University Hospital and the Colleges of Medicine, Health Professions, Nursing and Graduate Studies. The institution is the largest employer in Central New York, an area populated by a wide variety of ethnic and racial groups. The Director of Diversity and Affirmative Action and the Diversity Council are responsible for initiating and leading all endeavors related to diversity. The Diversity Council, which reports directly to the President and to the Executive Diversity Council, was established in September 2004. It is comprised of thirteen staff and faculty members, a group of individuals representing a wide cross section of employees from a variety of professional and non-professional as well as various cultural and ethnic backgrounds. Responsibilities of the Council include: designing survey instruments, analyzing and collecting data from individuals and departments throughout the institution, making appropriate and timely recommendations to the President, and designing, implementing, monitoring and evaluating diversity initiatives.

In the relatively short time that it has been in existence, the Council has developed a Diversity Commitment Statement that was endorsed by the President and members of his cabinet (see XI, Diversity Mission Statement). This statement was mailed to every employee and is displayed prominently throughout the institution as well as plans to expand into off site clinics and health care facilities. Presently, in addition to planning the President's Seventh Diversity Forum, Council members are planning to participate in a three day training program in the fall of 2005 that will qualify them to conduct interviews requisite to the accurate assessment of our organization's cultural climate. Follow analysis of these data, the Council will make recommendations to the President regarding specific plans to achieve a more inclusive, nurturing climate.

The Diversity Council serves as the focal point for all employees, students, committees and groups that sponsor and promote events related to the appreciation of the diversity inherent within our institution and community. It includes: the Faculty /Staff Association For Diversity, the President's Committee for Diversity and Affirmative Action, the Student Diversity Committee, the Dean's Advisory Committee on Women's Issues, the Dean's Advisory Committee on Student Diversity, the Diversity Forum Planning Committee, the Health Career Opportunities Program as well as a variety of student interest groups organized to promote, study and gain an appreciation for individuals of various ethnic, religious and racial backgrounds and life style choices. Representatives from all of these groups report to the Council and rely upon its members for advice, guidance, support and integration of their programs in our quest to recruit and retain a diverse and inclusive workforce and student body.

UPS

55 Glenlake Pkwy., NE
Atlanta, GA 30328
Phone: (404) 828-6000
Fax: (404) 828-6562
www.ups.com

Locations (worldwide)

World headquarters in Atlanta, Georgia,
USA

Employment Contact

For information concerning employment
opportunities at UPS, please go to
www.upsjobs.com.
UPS is an equal opportunity employer.

The Stats

Employees: 328,000 (2004, U.S.)
Employees: 56,000 (2004, outside the U.S.)
Employees: 384,000 (2004, worldwide)
Revenue: $36.6 billion (2004, worldwide)

The Employer Says

Founded: August 28, 1907, in Seattle, Wash., USA
Chairman & CEO: Michael L. Eskew

UPS People

Diversity and UPS People

UPS's workforce is multicultural, multidimensional and reflective of the broad attributes of our global communities. In fact, each year since 1999, UPS has been consecutively ranked by FORTUNE® magazine as one of the "50 Best Companies for Minorities."

UPS understands that diversity encompasses more than ethnicity, gender and age. It's how employees think, the ideas they contribute and their general attitude toward work and life.

Diversity is encouraged by recognizing the value of people's different experiences, backgrounds and perspectives. Diversity is a valuable, core component of UPS because it brings a wider range of resources, skills and ideas to the business.

Long-standing company policies – such as employee ownership, equal opportunity, promotion from within and teamwork – have helped make UPS a preferred employer. Diversity impacts UPS's business from many perspectives, whether it's in meeting the needs of a diverse customer base, working with a diverse supplier network or gaining momentum from the varied contributions of our diverse workforce.

- African-Americans, Hispanics, Asian-Pacific Americans and other minorities make up 35 percent of the company's 317,000 employees in the United States.
- Minorities accounted for half of UPS's new employees in 2003.
- Women represent 27 percent of the U.S. management team and 21 percent of the overall workforce, holding jobs from package handlers, to drivers, to senior management and to the UPS Board of Directors.
- Among the company's 58,000 U.S. managers, minorities hold nearly 30 percent of those executive positions. Positions held include district managers, the UPS Management Committee and UPS's Board of Directors.

UPS Diversity Steering Council

- UPS expects diversity to be fostered and encouraged by every UPSer in their daily commitment to the company.
- UPS also has a Diversity Steering Council whose vision is to "ensure that workforce, customer and supplier diversity remain a visible core value that is integral to our business, our community relationships and The UPS Charter."
- The UPS Diversity Steering Council is co-chaired by Chairman and CEO Mike Eskew and Senior Vice President, Human Resources Lea Soupata. This cross-functional council consists of internal and external representatives.

Employer of Choice

- UPS is frequently recognized for its commitment to diversity. Since 1999, UPS has been consecutively ranked by *Fortune* magazine as one of 50 Best Companies for Minorities.
- UPS was profiled as a leader in Hispanic magazine's 13th annual Corporate 100 list, "a list of the top U.S. companies that excel in creating business and job opportunities for Hispanic Americans, as well as donating to philanthropies that target Latino communities."
- Since 2000, UPS has been consecutively named a top corporation for Women's Business Enterprises (WBEs) by the Women's Business Enterprise National Council (WBENC).
- UPS was honored with the coveted NAACP (National Association for the Advancement of Colored People) Corporate Citizen of the Year Award.
- UPS placed third in DiversityInc.com's Diversity Top 30 poll. The poll rates corporations on a range of criteria from employment and advancement of people of color to advertising in ethnic media.

Throughout our history at UPS, we've found that we grow by not only investing in our business but also in the communities where we live and work.

UPS does extensive work and partners with various organizations to improve social conditions that exist within the communities we serve. Below is a sample of the organizations UPS and UPS people partner with.

- 100 Black Men of America (100 BMOA)
- Family and Workplace Literacy Programs
- Hispanic Chamber of Commerce (HCC)
- INROADS
- National Association for the Advancement of Colored People (NAACP)
- NASCAR
- National Urban League (NUL)
- National Council of La Raza (NCLR)
- Native American Business Alliance (NABA)
- Organization of Chinese Americans (OCA)
- The National Newspapers Publishers Association (NNPA)
- Special Olympics
- Women's Business Enterprise National Council (WBENC)

Customers

UPS understands that customer diversity requires understanding the differences in cultural backgrounds and the unique needs of each customer.

Every day, more than 370,000 UPSers serve nearly 8 million customers in over 200 countries and territories worldwide. Because of its global impact, UPS has many unique opportunities to reach a broad range of diverse customers. UPS understands that diversity is essential as the company expands and finds ways to solve the individual needs of all customers.

Supplier Diversity

Formally launched in 1992, the UPS Supplier Diversity Program is committed to providing business opportunities to minority- and women-owned businesses.

UPS strives to have diversity among its business partners. In addition to developing strategic relationships with minority- and women-owned businesses, UPS encourages majority suppliers to support women- and minority-owned firms. We are committed to ensuring that our supplier diversity process strengthens the minority- and women-owned businesses that drive economic development in our communities.

More than 25,000 businesses across America are partners in the UPS supplier network.

US Airways

2345 Crystal Dr.
Arlington, VA 22227
Phone: (703) 872-7000
Fax: (703) 872-5134
www.usairways.com

Employment Contact

Debbie Shockley, Manager Diversity Programs
Headquarters
2345 Crystal Drive
Arlington, Virginia 22227
Phone: (703) 872.7000
Fax: (703) 872.5509

Recruiting

Please list the schools/types of schools at which you recruit.

• Ivy League schools
• Public state schools

Do you have any special outreach efforts that are directed to encourage minority students to consider your firm?

• Conferences: National Black MBA Conference

What activities does the firm undertake to attract minority and women employees?

• Participate at minority job fairs
• Seek referrals from other employees
• Utilize online job services

Do you use executive recruiting/search firms to seek to identify new diversity hires?

No

Internships and Co-ops

Preparing for Take-off Summer Internship Program
(Formerly Summer Minority Internship Program)

Deadline: April 1
Number of interns: 18
Pay: $10-$12 per hour (depending on school level and prior US Airways internship experience)
Web site: www.usairways.com

Affinity Groups/Employee Networks

Management Club

The US Airways Management Club is an organization that fosters cooperation, communication and understanding between all members of the corporate management team by providing opportunities for Education, Information and Interaction in a relaxed environment, which in turn stimulates personal and corporate growth.

CONTACT:
Lori Putnam
(412) 472-1448
Lori_Putnam@usairways.com

Minority Professional Association

MPA was organized in 1993 to provide an opportunity for management level African-American professionals to network and further their career development via a variety of seminars and workshops. Through the years, the scope of the organization has expanded to include all minority professionals at US Airways as identified by the Equal Employment Opportunity Commission. The MPA has hosted several annual conferences.

CONTACT:
Sheila Stokes-Langford
(703) 872-6194
Sheila_Stokes-Langford@usairways.com

Spectrum

Spectrum is a networking organization that is open to all gay, lesbian, bisexual, transgender and straight employees. This organization is our newest affinity group, organized in 2003. Spectrum is committed to promoting equality and recognition of sexual identity as it relates to the workplace through awareness, education and communication. Spectrum has conducted focus group meetings and membership drives in the corporate office and Philadelphia.

CONTACT:
spectrum@usairways.com

Professional Women's Group

PWG was organized in 2000 as a networking organization for professional women. The PWG works to recognize, develop and promote women in the company. One of the biggest successes of the organization is the creation of the Speaker Series, which provides an opportunity for our members to hear from and interact with successful women within and outside of US Airways.

CONTACT:
Kristen Showker
(703) 872.7673
Kristen_Showker@usairways.com

Strategic Plan and Diversity Leadership

Who has primary responsibility for leading diversity initiatives at your firm?

Debbie Shockley, Manager, Diversity Programs

Does your firm currently have a diversity committee?

Yes. The committee's structure is cross-divisional. They meet once a month.

If yes, does the committee's representation include one or more members of the firm's management/executive committee (or the equivalent)?

No

If yes, how many executives are on the committee, and in 2004, what was the total number of hours collectively spent by the committee in furtherance of the firm's diversity initiatives? How many employees are on the committee, and how often does the committee convene in furtherance of the firm's diversity initiatives?

15 Employees

Does the committee and/or diversity leader establish and set goals or objectives consistent with management's priorities?

Yes

Has the firm undertaken a formal or informal diversity program or set of initiatives aimed at increasing the diversity of the firm?

Yes, formal

How often does the firm's management review the firm's diversity progress/results?

Monthly

How is the firm's diversity committee and/or firm management held accountable for achieving results?

- Department Profile
- Recognized Accomplishments
- Partnerships

Demographic Profile and Retention and Professional Development

REPRESENTATION (2004)					
Category	TOTAL	FEM	MIN	FEM %	MIN %
01- ProfessionalsBlacks	8,401	990	636	11.80%	7.60%
02-All Others	17,290	9,360	3,403	54.10%	19.70%
Total	25,691	10,350	4,039	40.30%	15.70%

TURNOVER (2004)					
Category	TOTAL	FEM	MIN	FEM %	MIN %
01- ProfessionalsBlacks	8,401	990	636	11.80%	7.60%
02-All Others	17,290	9,360	3,403	54.10%	19.70%
Total	25,691	10,350	4,039	40.30%	15.70%

REPRESENTATION (2003)					
Category	TOTAL	FEM	MIN	FEM %	MIN %
01- ProfessionalsBlacks	9,424	1,108	652	11.80%	11.80%
02-All Others	19,130	10,311	3,502	53.90%	53.90%
Total	28,554	11,419	4,154	40.00%	40.00%

TURNOVER (2003)					
Category	TOTAL	FEM	MIN	FEM %	MIN %
01- ProfessionalsBlacks	1,319	139	104	10.50%	7.90%
02-All Others	3,599	2,140	741	59.50%	20.60%
Total	4,918	2,279	845	46.30%	17.20%

Diversity Mission Statement

Creating a culture that values diversity by maximizing and embracing the talents, skills, backgrounds, experiences and perspectives of all employees, thereby reflecting the diversity of customers served by US Airways.

Valero Energy Corporation

1 Valero Way
San Antonio, TX 78249-1112
Phone: (210) 345-2000
Fax: (210) 345-2646
Toll Free: (800) 531-7911
www.valero.com

Locations (worldwide)
Headquartered in San Antonio, TX

Contact Person
Ruth Pina, Staffing & Employee Services
Director

Diversity Leadership
Kim Griffin, Employment Services Manager
One Valero Way
San Antonio, TX 78249-1112
Phone: (210) 345-2028
Fax: (210) 345-2778
E-mail: kim.griffin@valero.com

Recruiting

Please list the schools/types of schools at which you recruit.

• Private schools
• Public state schools
• Hispanic Serving Institutions (HSIs)

Do you have any special outreach efforts that are directed to encourage minority students to consider your firm?

• Advertise in minority student association publication(s)
• Firm's employees participate on career panels at school

What activities does the firm undertake to attract minority and women employees?

• Partner programs with women and minority associations
• Seek referrals from other employees
• Utilize online job services

Do you use executive recruiting/search firms to seek to identify new diversity hires?

Yes

If yes, list all women- and/or minority-owned executive search/recruiting firms to which the firm paid a fee for placement services in the past 12 months:

Alpha Quality Services; Badon's Employment, Inc; Bullock Personnel; CAS Consulting Group, LLC; Channel Personnel Services; Energy Search Enterprises; Energy and Technical Associates, Inc.; FSC Technologies, LLC; Graves Recruiters for Professionals; Deacon Recruiting; SMR Consulting Services; L.V. Havlik and Associates, Inc.; L.K. Jordan and Associates; Lang Technology Services; J. Rawley Personnel Solutions, Inc.

Internships and Co-ops

Valero Internship Program

Deadline for application: Rolling

Number of interns in the program in summer 2004 (internship) or 2004 (co-op): 18 interns; 6 co-ops

Pay: $12.50/hr. for interns; $21.00/hr. for co-ops

Length of the program: Approximately 12 weeks

Percentage of interns/co-ops in the program who receive offers of full-time employment: 88%

Web site for internship/co-op information: valero.hrdpt.com/intern/

Scholarships

Since Valero began the scholarship program in 1981, the company has recognized outstanding children of all demographics including minority groups in support of their efforts to obtain a college education. Valero has awarded 265 scholarships totaling nearly $2 million.

In addition, for the past two years Valero has awarded scholarships to children of Aruban employees. Fourteen Aruba scholarships have been granted totaling $140,000.

Entry-Level Programs/Full-Time Opportunities

Listed below are the required courses for all employees, all supervisors/managers and all Sr. Managers and Directors.

All Employees

• Office Safety (CBT)
• Core Competency: Communicate Effectively
• Core Competency: Show Work Commitment
• Core Competency: Act with Integrity
• Core Competency: Value Diversity
• Harassment Free Workplace

All Supervisors and Managers

• The Leader's Role in Business Ethics
• What Do Great Manager's Do
• EPR: Prep for Success
• Harassment Free Workplace
• Communications: Interpersonal Relationships
• Communications: Listening and Non-Verbal
• Communications: Feedback
• Communications: Professional Business Writing
• Communications: Presentations

Note: The supervisor/manager is required to select one of the communication courses.

All Sr. Managers and Directors

• The Leader's Role in Business Ethics
• Situational Leadership Managers
• Harassment Free Workplace
• Dollars and Sense

Note: All courses listed are offered at different times during the year.

Strategic Plan and Diversity Leadership

How does the firm's leadership communicate the importance of diversity to everyone at the firm?

Valero has a comprehensive competency model that specifies the competencies required for success in positions throughout the organization. The model provides valuable information to employees regarding the areas most relevant to success in their current job and for jobs in which they might want to consider in the future. The model includes core competencies, such as Diversity, required for all Valero employees, core supervisor competencies for all Valero supervisors, and organization and contributor level competencies. These competencies are incorporated into many of the Valero Human Resources functions including behavioral interviewing, employee performance review, 360 assessment, training and development, career planning and the development library. Within this model, "Value Diversity" is defined as someone who shows and fosters respect and appreciation for each person whatever their background, race, age, gender, disability, values, lifestyle, perspectives, or interests; seeks to understand the worldview of others; see differences in people as opportunities for learning about and approaching things differently. Valuing diversity is being receptive to a wide range of people unlike oneself, according to any number of distinctions: national origin, physical ability, age, race, color, gender, class, native language, religion, sexual orientation, veteran status, professional experience, personal preferences, and work style.

These initiatives are a commitment to all employees and promote practices that demonstrate respect, trust and the value of each individual to ensure a pleasant work environment for all personnel. Valero demonstrates its fair treatment to all employees by providing everyone the opportunity to be considered for promotions through company-wide job postings. Diversity training is incorporated in "What Do Great Managers Do?", "Promises, Promises", "Sexual Harassment", Retail New Employee Orientation, Retail Assistant and Store Manager training and the AIM training for Retail Area Managers. These programs are provided for the purpose of maintaining a workplace that respects and dignifies each and every employee.

Who has primary responsibility for leading diversity initiatives at your firm?

Collective responsibility of HR group.

Does your firm currently have a diversity committee?

No

Has the firm undertaken a formal or informal diversity program or set of initiatives aimed at increasing the diversity of the firm?

Yes, informal

How often does the firm's management review the firm's diversity progress/results?

Annually

The Stats

The corporate office in San Antonio, Texas and operational sites throughout the United States are located in geographically diverse areas that enable the company to hire personnel of all demographics including minorities and females. As of July 2004, Valero employed a total of 15,685 individuals which included 40 percent minorities and 23 percent females. In addition, the CEO's lead-

ership team consists of five executives including one female. Valero generated $38 billion in revenues in 2003, and a record $55 billion in 2004.

Retention and Professional Development

How do 2004 minority and female attrition rates generally compare to those experienced in the prior year period?

In 2004 the company had a total of 9,644 terminations. Out of that total there were 4,310 minority terminations and 2,391 female terminations.

Please identify the specific steps you are taking to reduce the attrition rate of minority and women employees.

• Adopt dispute resolution process
• Succession plan includes emphasis on diversity
• Strengthen mentoring program for all employees, including minorities and women
• Professional skills development program, including minority and women employees

Valero is participating in Linkage conferences which target high potential employees as well as women and minorities. These conferences are pre-paid by the company and are made available to female managers and above. The sessions focus on diversity, women's issues in the workplace, and effective leadership strategies.

Valero has an Executive Development Program which was implemented in August of 2004. This program is comprised of a 3-day live simulation and feedback experience for current and emerging senior leaders throughout the organization. Graduate school incentives are also available to all employees. Costs for graduate school are reimbursed at a rate of 80% contingent upon sustaining a B average or above.

Valero strives to maximize retention of all managers within the organization including minority and female managers. This is accomplished through one-on-one coaching, training, on-line educational tools, HR Generalists services, Employee Performance Reviews, 360 Performance Reviews and on-going performance feedback. Valero believes that retention really begins during the selection and hiring process and puts a great deal of time and effort into maximizing the effectiveness of this process and thus minimizing efforts on the retention side. Through commitment to our Affirmative Action plans, minority targeted Succession Planning efforts and behavior based interviews and personality assessments, Valero's selection process very effectively supports the hiring of minority managers as well as on-going promotion of managers from within the minority talent pools.

Valero Wellness Program

This program provides opportunities for employees and their families to integrate healthy behaviors into all aspects of their life through an annual health assessment and numerous educational resources. Each year, Valero holds a Wellness Fair for all employees and their spouses at the corporate offices and at each refinery location. The fair provides an opportunity for the employee to schedule their wellness assessment and obtain valuable health and wellness information from some of the top health organizations in the community. The company pays 100% of the assessment expense for employees ($200 value) and offers the assessment for the employee's spouse at a reduced fee ($140). In addition, employees and their spouses have access to on-site fitness centers or fitness membership subsidies, which includes reimbursement for family memberships. A structured, physician monitored Weight Management Program and Disease Management Program are also available to employees at risk due to an illness or obesity. The Wellness Program also offers Weight Watchers At Work, Smoking Cessation, Lunch and Learn health-related sessions, monthly Fit Valero newsletter, Fit Valero Website, and monthly Vitality health magazine.

Wellness Center

A Wellness Center is available to all corporate employees at headquarters. The on-site personal care has saved employees time and money. The center provides prompt in-house access to excellent care for minor illnesses and injuries, as well as diagnostic tools and preventive care to identify and manage health risks. Valero provides these medical services free of charge to employees, with no insurance forms required. A doctor and nurse are available five days a week at varying times. In addition to the Wellness Center, Mother's Rooms and Sick Rooms are available at headquarters. As an additional service, employees also have access to an on-site massage therapist. A registered nurse is on site at all of the refinery locations.

LifeBalance Employee Assistance Program

Valero offers numerous programs and resources to provide employees with solutions to family and work-related issues. LifeBalance provides all employees and their immediate family members with a free, confidential employee assistance program that is available 24 hours a day, 7 days a week. LifeBalance is a one-stop resource that offers practical solutions, on-line resources, one-on-one consultations, and materials on a variety of personal, family and work issues. The program includes extensive on-line features, access to parenting and child care options, timesaving services (i.e., consumer resources, purchasing a car/home, repairs, etc.), and the opportunity to order free booklets, audio recordings and other self-help tools that can be mailed directly to the employee's home. If needed, employees and members of their immediate family may schedule up to 6 face-to-face sessions per problem with a local counselor at no charge.

SAFE Fund

In the event of an unusual emergency, employees experiencing a crisis are eligible to apply for assistance through the Valero Support Aid for Family Emergencies (SAFE) Fund. The process is confidential and the grant does not have to be repaid. During the past year, several employees received aid when their home was lost to fire. Many employees and their families also benefited from this fund when their homes were damaged due to heavy flooding in Texas and Louisiana. Others have received financial assistance for funeral expenses due to the loss of a loved one. Within 48 hours, employees received checks to help them with immediate needs.

Diversity Mission Statement

Valero has a comprehensive competency model that specifies the competencies required for success in positions throughout the organization. The model provides valuable information to employees regarding the areas most relevant to success in their current job and for jobs in which they might want to consider in the future. The model includes core competencies, such as Diversity, required for all Valero employees, core supervisor competencies for all Valero supervisors, and organization and contributor level competencies. These competencies are incorporated into many of the Valero Human Resources functions including behavioral interviewing, employee performance review, 360 assessment, training and development, career planning and the development library. Within this model, "Value Diversity" is defined as someone who shows and fosters respect and appreciation for each person whatever their background, race, age, gender disability, values, lifestyle, perspectives, or interests; seeks to understand the worldview of others; see differences in people as opportunities for learning about and approaching things differently. Valuing diversity is being receptive to a wide range of people unlike oneself, according to any number of distinctions: national origin, physical ability, age, race, color, gender, class, native language, religion, sexual orientation, veteran status, professional experience, personal preferences, and work style.

These initiatives are a commitment to all employees and promote practices that demonstrate respect, trust and the value of each individual to ensure a pleasant work environment for all personnel. Valero demonstrates its fair treatment to all employees by providing everyone the opportunity to be considered for promotions through company-wide job postings. Diversity training is incorporated in "What Do Great Managers Do?", "Promises, Promises", "Sexual Harassment", Retail New Employee Orientation, Retail Assistant and Store Manager training and the AIM training for Retail Area Managers. These programs are provided for the purpose of maintaining a workplace that respects and dignifies each and every employee.

The Employer Says

About Valero

Valero Energy Corporation is a Fortune 500 company based in San Antonio with approximately 20,000 employees and expected revenues of $55 billion.

One of the top U.S. refining companies, Valero has an extensive refining system with a throughput capacity of approximately 2.5 million barrels per day. The company's geographically diverse refining network stretches from Canada to the U.S. Gulf Coast and West Coast to the Caribbean.

In combination with its interest in Valero L.P., Valero has 4,800 miles of refined product and crude oil pipelines as well as refined product terminals and crude oil storage facilities, which complement its refining and marketing assets in the U.S. Southwest and Mid-continent regions.

A marketing leader, Valero has approximately 4,700 retail sites branded as Valero, Diamond Shamrock, Ultramar, Beacon and Total. The company markets on a retail and wholesale basis through a bulk and rack marketing network in 40 U.S. states, Canada, Latin America and the Caribbean region.

Valero has long been recognized throughout the industry as a leader in the production of premium, environmentally clean products, such as reformulated gasoline, California Air Resources Board (CARB) Phase II gasoline, low-sulfur diesel and oxygenates.

Caring and Sharing Spirit

One of the reasons for Valero's success is the special caring and sharing spirit that brings together employees from all levels and all departments – from the mail room to the board room – to help those in need and make our communities better places to live and work. Valero employees, old and new, show their spirit and give generously of their time and money to those who need it the most. We're proud of the significant contributions our employees make each year. Valero has had an unprecedented year for charitable giving and volunteering.

A few of the highlights include:

- Employees gave a record-breaking 200,000 hours of time to volunteer for everything from food drives and fund-raisers to community events and clean-up projects.
- Employees donated a record-breaking $9 million to the United Way when combined with the company match.
- Also as a result of the employees' efforts, the Valero Benefit for Children Golf Classic, which was held in conjunction with the PGA TOUR's Valero Texas Open, raised a record-breaking $4 million for charity . These proceeds were given to more than 100 children's charities in the communities where Valero has major operations.
- Through the sale of miracle balloons at our Diamond Shamrock stores, Valero raised more than $857,000 for 34 Children's Miracle Network hospitals located in communities where Valero has retail stores.
- And, Valero's annual "Shamrocks Against Dystrophy" campaign raised a record-breaking $1.2 million for the Muscular Dystrophy Association. To raise these much-needed funds, retail employees sold shamrocks at all company-operated U.S. stores.

Making a difference in the lives of others has been the foundation of Valero's success for more than 20 years. Despite the company's tremendous growth, Valero employees have remained committed to this caring philosophy.

Flex-Time Programs

To help employees balance family, home and work life issues, Valero offers several alternative work schedules. Valero offers a flexible work schedule by allowing employees to choose to work from 7 a.m. to 4 p.m., 7:30 a.m. to 4:30 p.m. or 8:30 a.m. to 5:30 p.m. as an option to the 8 a.m. to 5 p.m. schedule. At most of the facilities, the 9/80 work schedule is also offered, and allows for every other Friday as an off day, providing 26 extra days off a year. Additional alternative work schedules practiced at the refineries and logistics operations include:

- 4/10 (Employees work 4 10-hour days a week.)
- 5-2 12 hour rotating shift (Employees work 5 12-hour days one week, then 2 12-hour days the next week.)
- 4-3 12 hour rotating shift (Employees work 4 12-hour days one week, then 3 12-hour days the next week.)
- 4-4 12 hour rotating shift (Employees work 4 12-hour days and then have 4 days off.)

Awards and Recognition

Valero has received numerous honors and recognition including:

- Received the "2004 Spirit of America Award," the United Way's highest corporate honor given to one U.S. company each year. Since Valero received it in 1992, it is the second company to ever win the award twice.
- Added to the S&P 500 Index for being the "best of the best" among all of the public companies in the U.S. and a leader in the refining industry
- Moved up to #22 from #34 on this year's *Fortune* 500 ranking
- Recognized by *Fortune* magazine as #3 among large employers on the "100 Best Companies to Work for in America" list and received the Great Place To Work Institute's "Pride Award" in 2004
- Ranked 4th on *Forbes'* list of America's fastest-growing big companies (based on revenue growth)
- Captured the #1 spot on *Forbes* magazine's List of the 400 Best Big Companies in America (based on EPS and shareholder return)
- Received "Oil Company of the Year" at the 2004 Platts Global Energy Awards
- Recognized as One of the World's 100 Best-Managed Companies – *IndustryWeek* magazine
- Ranked among *Hispanic* magazine's "Corporate 100," in 2002, 2003 and 2004 for providing business and job opportunities for Hispanic Americans
- Recognized by the U.S. Department of Labor with the "Exemplary Voluntary Efforts" (EVE) Award for exemplary and innovative equal employment opportunity programs (one of just five companies honored in 2002)
- Received United Way's "Texans Helping Texans" Award in 2003, the United Way's Highest Statewide Award

Affirmative Action Program

Valero's Affirmative Action Program supports the company's diversity initiatives through the consistent and accurate administration of activities throughout the company's locations. The Corporate Human Resources Department works with a Human Resources representative from each location during the planning and preparation of their respective affirmative action plan. Activities include:

- Communication of goals to hiring supervisor when a job is posted
- Dissemination of quarterly reports to Human Resources Representatives at each location which include a summary of personnel activities and update on progress toward meeting their site's goals
- Presentations to the management team highlighting the company's yearly affirmative action activities and goals. (Annual presentations are conducted for Corporate Human Resources Managers, and in 2004, affirmative action presentations were delivered to the management teams at each of the 19 refinery locations.)
- Completion of internal audits of affirmative action procedures at randomly selected Valero locations
- Past recipient of the Department of Labor's prestigious Exemplary Voluntary Efforts (EVE) Award based on Valero's successful recruitment of minority and female college interns, high retention rate post graduation in professional positions at Valero, and notable progression into supervisory roles.

Names of Minority Associations which Valero Supports

- San Antonio Chamber of Commerce
- Hispanic Broadcasting
- Corpus Christi Hispanic Chamber
- Society of Hispanic Professionals
- National Hispanic Institute
- Farfield Hispanic Chamber of Commerce
- Hispanic Scholarship Fund
- Hispanic Association of Colleges and Universities
- La Prensa
- LULAC National Office
- Avance – Corpus Christi
- Guadalupe Cultural Arts Center

Verizon Communications

1095 Avenue of the Americas
New York, NY 10036
Phone: (212) 395-2121
Fax: (212) 869-3265
Toll Free: (800) 621-9900
www22.verizon.com/about/careers

Contact Person
Vicky Boston, Sr. Staff Consultant,
Workforce Diversity, Domestic Telecom
Human Resources

Diversity Leadership
Monice Sanders, Director, Workforce
Diversity, Domestic Telecom Human
Resources
1095 Avenue of the Americas
New York, NY   10036
Phone: (301) 236-1281
E-mail: monice.h.sanders@verizon.com

Recruiting

Please list the schools/types of schools at which you recruit.

• *Private schools:* Carnegie Mellon, Cornell, Devry, Georgia Tech, ITT Technical Institute, Purdue U, Rensselaer Polytechnic Institute, Rutgers, Stevens Institute of Technology
• *Public state schools:* City U of New York, U of Illinois-Urbana Champaign, U of Maryland-Baltimore & College Park, U of Massachusetts-Amherst, U of North Texas, U of Oklahoma, Texas A&M – College Station, U of California-Los Angeles, U of California-Riverside, U of South Florida, U of Southern California, U of Texas-Austin, U of Texas-Arlington
• *Historically Black Colleges and Universities (HBCUs):* Clark U, Florida A&M, Hampton U, Howard U, Morehouse, Morgan State U, Norfolk State U, North Carolina A&T, Spelman
• *Hispanic Serving Institutions (HSIs):* City U of New York colleges, U of Texas-San Antonio

Do you have any special outreach efforts that are directed to encourage minority students to consider your firm?

• Participate in/host minority student job fair(s)
• Sponsor minority student association events
• Firm's employees participate on career panels at school
• Outreach to leadership of minority student organizations

What activities does the firm undertake to attract minority and women employees?

• Partner programs with women and minority associations
• Conferences:
  • National Black MBA Association
  • Hispanic Business Student Association
  • Hispanic Engineer National Achievement Awards Conference
  • Society for Women Engineers
  • Society for Hispanic Professional Engineers
  • National Society of Black Engineers
  • American Indian Science & Engineering Society
  • National Society of Hispanic MBAs
  • Organization of Chinese Americans

• Participate at minority job fairs
• Seek referrals from other employees

Do you use executive recruiting/search firms to seek to identify new diversity hires?

No

Internships and Co-ops

Verizon Young Leaders Program

Deadline for application: Candidates are sent directly from the Hispanic Association of Colleges and Universities and the Hispanic College Fund
Number of interns in the program in summer 2004 (internship) or 2004 (co-op): 6
Pay: Varies depending on location and class level
Length of the program: 12 weeks

The Verizon Young Leaders program is a partnership with the Hispanic Association of Colleges and Universities and the Hispanic Scholarship Fund to increase the number of Hispanic summer interns at Verizon. In addition to the summer internship, each student is awarded a need based scholarship. The departments that hire will vary each summer and the responsibilities will be based on the needs of the business.

INROADS

Deadline for application: Candidates are sent directly from INROADS
Number of interns in the program in summer 2004 (internship) or 2004 (co-op): 9 internships
Pay: Varies depending on location and class level
Length of the program: Approximately 12 weeks; however, there may be an opportunity for internship(s) to extend throughout the year in a part-time position.
Percentage of interns/co-ops in the program who receive offers of full-time employment: 4.5%

Verizon has been a major participant and supporter of the INROADS Internship Program. Recruiting interns is integral to identifying talented, diverse candidates. A key to our company's long-term success is to identify challenging and mutually beneficial internship positions within Verizon each year. We are working to enhance the INROADS relationship and the number of interns we will employee for 2005 and going forward.

Scholarships

Verizon College Scholarships

Deadline for application for the scholarship program: Varies – Scholarships are awarded during the fall. Candidates are then selected during the spring or over the summer for the following school year by the colleges.
Scholarship award amount (2004): Scholarship amounts per school vary from $1,000 – $14,000
Web site or other contact information for scholarship: Candidates apply directly with the department for the school that was awarded the scholarship.

Scholarships are awarded to all of Verizon's targeted colleges and universities. They are awarded to students majoring in Engineering (Electrical, Mechanical, Industrial, Computer), Computer Science, Math or Business. The criteria for the scholarships are students must possess a minimum of a 3.0 GPA, must have a specific major and must be awarded to a student that is underrepresented in the field that Verizon is targeting.

Affinity Groups/Employee Networks

Our Employee Resource Groups (ERGs) are Verizon-supported and employee-run and organized affinity groups that promote personal and professional growth for employees with common interests. Through networking, mentoring, special initiatives, seminars and conferences, ERGs promote personal and professional growth of employees, enhance career advancement and provide a stronger sense of community within the company and externally. More than 10,000 employees are affiliated with our ten Employee Resource Groups.

- **Asian Pacific Employees for eXcellence (APEX)** aims to provide personal and professional development programs for its members. In addition, APEX strives to fulfill its social responsibilities by reaching out and supporting the communities in which they serve and increase cultural awareness and champion the corporation's response to issues facing the Asian-Pacific Islander community.

- **Consortium of Information and Telecommunications Executives (CITE®)** provides employee advocacy, issue awareness and professional development within Verizon. CITE serves as a resource for the African-American community at large. CITE makes a positive impact by hosting annual conferences, providing scholarships, implementing training and development programs and being actively involved in communities. Visit CITE's website at http://www.forcite.com to learn more about their history, initiatives, state chapters and upcoming events.

- **Disabilities Issues Awareness Leaders' (DIAL)** mission is to recognize the talents and develop the maximum potential of Verizon employees with disabilities. DIAL provides insight, recommendations, and support to individuals with disabilities and to Verizon, in keeping with the stated corporate commitment to universal design principles, the spirit of the Americans with Disability Act (ADA), and to managing diversity.

- **Gay, Lesbian, Bisexual, and Transgender Employees of Verizon and Their Allies' (GLOBE)** purpose is to address the needs and concerns of employees of Verizon who are Gay, Lesbian, Bisexual or Transgender or who have family, friends or colleagues who are Gay, Lesbian, Bisexual or Transgender, thereby creating a working environment in which each individual is treated with respect and dignity. For more information, visit GLOBE's website at http://globe-of-verizon.org.

- **The Hispanic Support Organization (HSO)** is the voice of the Hispanic employee who is committed to increasing opportunities for professional and personal development. HSO counsels and educates leaders to raise the awareness and increase responsiveness to issues affecting the Hispanic community within and outside Verizon Communications. To learn more about HSO, visit their website at http://www.hispanicsupportorganization.org.

- **The National Jewish Cultural Resource Group (NJCRG)** strives to create and maintain an environment in which members are encouraged to grow, participate, and contribute to the company's overall success. NJCRG provides a unique cultural perspective to Verizon on various issues, which will increase our competitive advantage with our changing customer base.

- **Native American People of Verizon (NAPV)** has a mission to support, educate and acknowledge, through cultural exchange, the historical and contemporary contributions of American Indians/Alaskan Natives; to enhance development, advancement, and recruitment of American Indians in Verizon; and support Verizon corporate values in our diverse workplace and community.

- **South-Asian Professionals Inspiring Cultural Enrichment (SPICE)** is committed to sharing the rich heritage of South Asian cultures, providing a forum for communication of common interests and goals, and strengthening the fabric of diversity throughout the corporation. Verizon serves a diverse customer base externally and hence a multicultural perspective internally can prove invaluable. SPICE seeks to provide and refine that perspective throughout Verizon with respect to the South-Asian community it serves.

- **Veterans Advisory Board of Verizon (VABVZ)** has a mission to provide to Senior Management, assistance, guidance and representation, regarding Veterans issues i.e., employment, health care, changes in health care as directed by the U.S. Veterans Administration, and legislation passed by U.S. Congress. These issues are of special interest to Verizon Veterans as dictated by the very nature, of the Veterans service to our country.

- **Women's Association of Verizon Employees (WAVE)** encourages an environment for learning new skills, addressing real 'women in the workplace' issues, networking and mentoring. Reaching out to women from associates through senior level executives in Verizon, WAVE works within the Consortium of Resource Groups to address issues such as child care, harassment in the workplace, and opportunities for advancement.

Entry-Level Programs/Full-Time Opportunities

The Company: Verizon is one of the world's leading providers of high-growth communications services. Verizon is a major wireline carrier, wireless service provider, directory supplier and leader in data networking. To win in the marketplace, Verizon needs top talent. We seek the best people (those with diverse experience, perspectives, knowledge, and backgrounds) and continue to provide the training they need to develop new or stronger skills, advance in the company, and achieve their goals, while contributing to Verizon's success.

The Benefits: Verizon provides an outstanding employee benefits package, including medical and dental plans, company-match 401(k) savings plan, life insurance, short- and long-term disability coverage, pension plan, personal lines of insurance, employee assistance program, domestic partner benefits, employee resource groups, flexible spending accounts and generous educational assistance program.

Contact Information: If you are interested in the following programs and meet the designated qualifications, contact your college placement office. For more information and to submit your resume online, please visit www.verizon.com/college. Verizon is an Equal Opportunity Employer and supports workforce diversity.

The Verizon Development Program – Marketing

This program provides a solid early career foundation to outstanding individuals who can address Verizon's marketing challenges, manage others, and ultimately assume leadership roles in one of Verizon's largest business units, Retail Markets. The focus of this program is Verizon consumer and business customer segments. The program is designed to provide broad exposure to Verizon's consumer and business-to-business marketing initiatives, complemented by customer contact experiences and the opportunity to supervise a team-an unbeatable formula for launching a successful career.

> *Length of program:* This two-year rotational program consists of two hands-on staff marketing assignments, each lasting about six months, plus a one-year assignment in a supervisory or customer contact role. The initial six-month assignments may involve any aspect of business-to-business or consumer marketing, including product management, product development, product launch, market analysis, promotional campaigns, distribution, and pricing.

> *Geographic location(s) of program:* Include, but not limited to: MA, NY, PA, MD, DC, VA, NC, FL, OH, IN, TX, CA, WA

Please describe the training/training component of this program: These assignments are typically based in a headquarters environment. Participants then transition from this headquarters exposure to the front line, where they may experience the dynamics of customer interaction and the challenges of supervising others. They gain both line and staff, headquarters and field perspectives, which will serve them well throughout their careers. Along the way, they are exposed to a broad array of telecommunications products and services-voice and data, network and hardware. At program completion, the career path typically leads to front-line management, with career progression to general marketing management in Verizon Retail Markets.

Please describe any other educational components of this program (i.e., tuition reimbursement): The program provides abundant training, with coursework in telecom technology, project management, presentation skills, leadership, supervision, customer relations, financial skills, and time management. Participants also attend Verizon Development Program Orientation. Orientation includes presentations by business leaders, team-building exercises, workshops, and social activities that provide opportunities to meet and network with peers.

Qualifications:

- BS in Marketing
- Excellent academic preparation and achievement with a minimum of 3.0/4.0 overall GPA
- Superior oral and written communications, leadership, analytical, and interpersonal skills
- Evidence of mature, flexible, and innovative approaches to work experiences
- Potential to assume supervisory responsibilities
- Willingness to relocate during the program experience
- Must have authorization to work permanently in the United States

Software/Systems Architect Development Program Verizon Information Technology (VZIT)

Length of program: The program format typically entails two rotational assignments, each lasting about six to nine months.

Geographic location(s) of program: Include, but not limited to, Dallas, TX; Tampa, FL; Boston, MA; and DC metro.

Please describe the training/training component of this program: The Verizon Software/Systems Architect Development Program (SSADP) provides innovative, technically sophisticated MS and PhD graduates the opportunity to immerse themselves in the dynamic environment of Verizon Information Technology (VZ-IT). Verizon IT represents the best of both worlds for technical professionals. We are a company that successfully takes advantage of the resources and security of a big corporation while maintaining a spirited and highly educated workforce. What this program offers you is the opportunity to make an impact on the future—to work within a financially stable but technologically creative environment.

You will be part of a brave new world, as the overarching Verizon IT goal is to become a technical innovator in developing and marketing information technology and eBusiness solutions. You can be part of this growth: contribute to it, develop and learn from it, establish your place in the industry, and refine your career as an IT professional.

Please describe any other educational components of this program: The Software/Systems Architect program is designed to perpetuate your academic success by developing well-rounded software engineers with a broad technology foundation, strong Verizon systems knowledge, and potential to ultimately assume technical leadership and/or general management roles at Verizon. These assignments provide exposure to different phases of the software development life cycle (i.e. requirements, design, development and testing), different technologies, and different sides of the Verizon business. SSADP Participants are also exposed to various facets of software design including, but not limited to: data (logical modeling, physical database, DBMS), applications (object modeling, systems development/ integration, high level object-oriented design) and infrastructure computing (networking platforms, operating systems and software). Technologies include Java, .Net, XML, J2EE, C#, and Web Services amongst others. These hands-on assignments enable you to gain valuable experience in the design and development of large-scale systems applications with mentorship from Verizon project leads.

Qualifications:

- MS/PhD in Computer Science, Electrical/Computer Engineering or related fields
- Excellent academic preparation and achievement with a minimum of 3.0/4.0 overall GPA
- Software design or development experience; experience with various platforms
- Exceptional analytical, interpersonal, teamwork, leadership and communications skills
- Willingness to relocate during the program experience

Verizon Finance Professional Development

Geographic location(s) of program: NY/NJ, Philadelphia, Boston, DC/MD/VA, Tampa, FL, Irving TX

Please describe the training/training component of this program: A comprehensive development program, which encompasses special orientation to Verizon and the Finance function; a personal development and training plan, with a targeted competency-based curriculum; access to extensive Verizon training opportunities via Verizon's NetLearn programs and access to the Verizon educational assistance program; ongoing performance feedback and coaching

Please describe any other educational components of this program (i.e., tuition reimbursement): Mentoring circle participation to encourage creating opportunities for collaborative learning experiences, exchanging ideas as a group, analyzing developmental issues, receiving feedback and guidance, providing ongoing support and a sense of community, developing a strong peer network

Developmental forums to include exposure to senior leadership, business issues and technology; skill assessment and creation of formal development/career plans; coming face-to-face with mentoring circles

Possible rotational assignment opportunities to help you gain knowledge and experience of other Finance disciplines, understand inter-relationship and dependence between the Finance organizations, develop and sharpen additional Finance skills and interests, demonstrate strengths and skill sets to other managers and supervisors

Qualifications:

Completion of degrees as follows:

- Most roles: BS/MBA in Finance/Accounting. Technical Financial Analysis roles; BS in MIS/IT/Computer Engineering.
- Verizon Capital Corp role: will also consider math, operations research and engineering majors.
- For all roles: Minimum 3.3/4.0 GPA preferred
- In-depth knowledge of MS Office products (knowledge of Hyperion for some positions)
- Superior organizational, analytical, critical thinking skills, communication and interpersonal skills
- Excellent quantitative skills; for some roles; outstanding modeling and operations research skills
- Able to work effectively under pressure to meet critical deadlines
- Must have authorization to work permanently in the United States

Verizon Finance & Accounting Full-Time/Internship Positions

Geographic location(s) of program: NY/NJ, PA, MA, DC, MD, VA, TX, FL

Please describe the training/training component of this program: Verizon financial and accounting roles provide excellent opportunities to apply your finance/accounting/technical background in a corporate finance setting.

Sample internships and full-time positions are in the areas of:

- **Consolidations** – Analyze subsidiary financial reports; prepare consolidated subsidiary financial statements
- **External Reporting** – Prepare and file periodic financial reports (Forms 10Q, 10-K); track, analyze impacts of SEC, GAAP developments
- **Staff Accounting** – Assist with monthly closing procedures, financial analyses, journal entries, account reconciliation; report results
- **Financial Performance and Assurance, Specialist-Business Development** – Evaluate business operations, financial projections, strategies, budgets and opportunities by developing financial models and conducting market/industry research
- **Line of Business Expenses** – Handle expense budgeting, planning and reporting for a Verizon line of business
- **Billing and Collections** – Handle billing for telecom industry customers, including adjustments, negotiations, settlements, documentation, tracking and accruals
- **Financial Planning & Analysis** – Develop and execute financial presentations, analysis and supporting documentation; support assigned business units
- **Financial Policies** – Assist with the operational implementation of new FASB and SEC accounting standards; support assigned business units, encompassing mergers and acquisitions, financial instruments, business combinations, etc.
- **Financial Reporting** – Prepare comparative financial data for quarterly earnings release; review trends, unusual items and variances to present a complete, accurate and balanced view of Verizon's financial performance to Wall Street analysts
- **Corporate Consolidations** – Review business unit data submissions for data integrity, including consistency, comparability and GAAP compliance; prepare, process inter-segment elimination activity and topside adjustments; perform inter-segment out-of-balance reviews and reconciliation; generate consolidated financial statement
- **Financial Planning & Analysis (Verizon Capital Corp)** – Provide pricing, valuation and transaction support of existing VCC portfolio, using sophisticated financial modeling and forecasting tools

• Technical Financial Analysis – Implement, maintain sophisticated support systems; conduct economic cost studies; make entry and exit decisions for product lines; perform ad hoc analyses and studies; develop models for policy makers and executives

Qualifications:

• Pursuing/completion of degrees as follows
  • Most roles: BS/MBA in Finance/Accounting
  • Technical Financial Analysis roles: BS in MIS/IT/Computer Engineering
  • Verizon Capital Corp role: will also consider math, operations research and engineering majors
  • For all roles: minimum 3.3/4.0 GPA preferred
• In-depth knowledge of MS Office products (knowledge of Hyperion for some positions)
• Superior organizational, analytical, critical thinking skills, communication and interpersonal skills
• Excellent quantitative skills; for some roles: outstanding modeling and operations research skills
• Able to work effectively under pressure to meet critical deadlines
• Must have authorization to work permanently in the United States

Full-Time Regular Positions Only:

The Professional Development: Members of the Verizon Finance team participate in special developmental and mentoring activities, including an orientation to Verizon and the Finance function.

Contact Information:

If you are interested and meet specified qualifications, please submit your resume to sandra.magwood@verizon.com; please reference "FT or Intern" in the "Subject" field of your email. For more information, please visit http://www.verizon.com/college. Verizon is an Equal Opportunity Employer and supports workforce diversity.

Strategic Plan and Diversity Leadership

How does the firm's leadership communicate the importance of diversity to everyone at the firm?

Advocacy for Verizon's diversity strategy incorporates various communications vehicles including corporate/line of business (LOB) specific intranet websites and diversity specific forums/meetings.

Examples include, but are not limited to:

• Verizon executives feature or incorporate diversity into their speeches and presentations to an internal employee audience and external groups.
• Verizon's Development and Leadership Initiative (DLI) Symposium provides the opportunity for Verizon's executives to articulate Verizon's Diversity Strategy and engage DLI participants in discussion.
• Employee Resource Group (ERG) events and activities, i.e., seminars, conferences, cultural celebrations, mentoring, etc., provides the opportunity to communicate Verizon's diversity strategy and it's commitment to having an aligned and integrated workplace where diversity is transparent, and where Verizon is an inclusive organization that leverages the diversity of employees, customers and suppliers for increased productivity, profitability and an enhanced reputation. Each of the 10 ERGs receive assistance in promoting their events and activities through the corporate email systems.
• HR Weekly, an online publication available through the Human Resources Communications webpage. In addition to an ongoing calendar of events, stories highlighting the ERG program are also featured. Weekly distribution to all employees utilized through the corporate email systems.
• The individual LOB and ERGs design and deploy intranet websites/webpages showcasing their support and commitment to Verizon's diversity strategy.

Who has primary responsibility for leading diversity initiatives at your firm?

Tracey Edwards, Vice President – Staffing and Diversity, Domestic Telecom – Human Resources, has the primary responsibility for the overall design, implementation and program management of various diversity initiatives within the Domestic Telecom Lines of Business in support of Verizon's Diversity strategy.

Does your firm currently have a diversity committee?

Yes

If yes, please describe how the committee is structured, how often it meets, etc.

Verizon strives for diversity at every level within the company from the top down. To make progress through diversity and to ensure that it remains an integral part of our business, each business unit across the company relies on its Diversity Councils to help them develop and implement customized diversity plans. Those plans are designed to meet the specific requirements of that business unit and help them execute the Verizon Diversity Strategy.

Each council chooses a chair. The chair can be anyone from a senior leader within a line of business, to a Human Resources Business Partner, to a member of the diversity council. Councils meet at least once a month via conference call and at least once a year in person to set goals and objectives, to strategize, and to implement the various diversity initiatives.

Each council is required to create and implement a diversity plan that includes diversity goals for their specific lines of business. Verizon's diversity goals include, but are not limited to:

• **Employee Development** – Encourage employees to take advantage of the specific leadership/management training classes available including the Affinity Workshops. Advocate continuous learning including enrollment in diversity training offered by Verizon through various mediums such as free on-line or classroom based diversity classes. Ensure all director level and above managers mentor lower level employees

• **Communication** – Ensure all employees have a clear understanding of Verizon's diversity strategy. Encourage employees to get involved with all diversity efforts and to let them know that the senior leaders stand behind diversity. Host diversity weeks, panel discussions, etc.

• **External Outreach and Partnerships** – Work within the communities Verizon serves to educate people on diversity, technology, humanitarian projects.

If yes, does the committee's representation include one or more members of the firm's management/executive committee (or the equivalent)?

Yes

Please describe the committee.

Executive representation and the number of employees on each committee vary by each LOB diversity council. Councils meet at least once a month via conference call and at least once a year in person to set goals and objectives, to strategize, and to implement the various diversity initiatives

> **Total executives on the committee:** Varies by LOB

Does the committee and/or diversity leader establish and set goals or objectives consistent with management's priorities?

Yes. Corporate Diversity sets the overall Verizon Diversity strategy, and Workforce Diversity provides the Councils with the Human Resources focus for the year (e.g. Employee Development for 2005). However, each LOB Council creates action plans and initiatives in support of those plans depending on the needs of their particular LOB. These plans are created with input for the LOB senior management team.

Has the firm undertaken a formal or informal diversity program or set of initiatives aimed at increasing the diversity of the firm?

Yes, formal. To ensure that diverse members of our multicultural work force are prepared for career advancement, we have established mentoring and leadership development programs, such as the Verizon Development and Leadership Initiative (DLI). The DLI provides tools that help participants identify professional goals and network with Verizon executives, while helping Verizon identify and develop a diverse pool of high-potential candidates.

The DLI and Verizon's employee development resources have strengthened Verizon's leadership team by developing high quality managers from diverse backgrounds who are prepared to assume new job assignments and additional responsibilities.

Verizon's mentoring initiative is critical to our strategy to win in the global marketplace and be the premier telecommunications company in the world. Mentoring helps drive this strategy because it fosters the development, growth and contributions of our most important asset – our people. Mentoring achieves this objective by leveraging informal work relationships, and enhancing the skills and capacity of our people to achieve their professional and personal objectives, while adding value to the business.

How often does the firm's management review the firm's diversity progress/results?

Quarterly

How is the firm's diversity committee and/or firm management held accountable for achieving results?

We have a commitment to diversity that stems from the top of the business. In addition to a leadership team that is becoming more and more diverse, we are also governed by a diverse Board of Directors representing a variety of industries and experiences.

Our management executives are held accountable for promoting diversity in their organizations and our Diversity Performance Incentive links our employment efforts to recruit, retain & develop a diverse population of employees to meet the needs of the diverse marketplace that we serve.

The Stats

Data as of 12/31/04

Gender and Ethnicity in the Ranks

Male
> Percent in Management positions: 57%
> Percent in Associate positions: 58%

Female
> Percent in Management positions: 43%
> Percent in Associate positions: 42%

Minorities
> Percent in Management positions: 30%
> Percent in Associate positions: 30%

* Excludes Verizon Wireless employees

Employees: 153,540 (2004, U.S.)*
Revenue: $42.2 billion (2004, U.S.)†
Revenue: $2 billion (2004, outside U.S.)††
Revenue: $44.2B (2004, worldwide)†††

† Includes Domestic Telecom and Information Services
†† Includes International
††† Includes Domestic Telecom, Information Services and International
*Excludes Verizon Wireless employees

Retention and Professional Development

How do 2004 minority and female attrition rates generally compare to those experienced in the prior year period?

Lower than in prior years

Please identify the specific steps you are taking to reduce the attrition rate of minority and women employees.

- Develop and/or support internal employee affinity groups (e.g., minority or women networks within the firm)
- Increase/review compensation relative to competition
- Succession plan includes emphasis on diversity
- Work with minority and women employees to develop career advancement plans
- Strengthen mentoring program for all employees, including minorities and women
- Professional skills development program, including minority and women employees
- Other: Increase/improve current work/life program

Diversity Mission Statement

Verizon is committed to maintaining an inclusive corporate culture that embraces and leverages the diversity of employees, customers and suppliers for increased productivity, profitability and an enhanced reputation. The culture of inclusion that defines our company will earn the trust of our employees and the diverse customers and communities we serve.

The Employer Says

Verizon is at the forefront of the transformation of the telecommunications industry and we remain committed to creating and fostering an inclusive culture that values the diversity of our employees. Competition in our industry is pervasive, and we recognize that in order to meet the ever changing and growing demands of our customers we must rely on the innovation and creativity that a diverse employee base provides. Verizon is proud of the broad range of products and services we offer and prouder still of our ability to foster, promote and preserve the diversity and human rights of our employees, customers and communities.

Awards and Recognition

Verizon has been recognized nationally for its commitment to diversity:

- *ESSENCE* magazine named Verizon to its list of 35 Great Places to Work. Verizon ranked as one of the magazine's top two companies for African-American women. (2005)
- *CAREERS & the disABLED* magazine named Verizon the Private-Sector Employer of the Year for its commitment to recruiting, hiring and advancing people with disabilities. (2005)
- *Fortune* magazine named Verizon to its list of The 50 Best Companies for Minorities. (2000 – 2004)
- Verizon ranked as top telecommunications company on *Fortune* magazine's list of 50 Most Admired Companies. (2004)
- *DiversityInc* named Verizon one of the Top 50 Companies for Diversity (2001-2005). Verizon was also named to the magazine's list of top companies for supplier diversity (2002 -2004), recruitment and retention (2002, 2004), African-Americans (2004), Hispanics (2004), Latinos (2004) and gay, lesbian, bi-sexual and transgender employees. (2004)
- *Latin Business* magazine named Verizon to its inaugural Corporate Diversity Honor Roll. (2004)
- The National Latina/o Lesbian, Gay, Bisexual and Transgender Organization (LLEGÓ) presented Verizon with its Plumed Warrior Premio Visionario (Visionary) Award for corporate commitment to diversity and workplace equality. (2004)
- Verizon earned the National Society of Black Engineers' Golden Torch Award for Corporate Community Service. (2004)
- The New York Urban League presented Verizon with its Champions of Diversity award. (2004)
- The Society of Hispanic Professional Engineers named Verizon Company of the Year. (2004)
- Verizon was named to the *LATINA Style* 50, top companies for Hispanic women to work for the United States. (2000/2001. Verizon named *LATINA Style* Company of the Year. (2003)
- The American Association of People with Disabilities presented Verizon with the 2003 Justice for All Award in recognition of the company's leadership in serving the needs of people with disabilities. (2003)
- The US Pan Asian American Chamber of Commerce named Verizon as its 2003 Corporation of the Year. (2003)
- The National Association of Female Executives named Verizon one of the Top 30 Companies for Female Executives. (2003)

• *Girlfriends* magazine listed Verizon among one of its Top Ten Lesbian Places to Work. (2002-2003)

• *Hispanic* magazine named Verizon to its Corporate 100 list for providing opportunities for Hispanics; as having one of the Top 25 Diversity Recruitment Programs; and as having one of the Top 25 Supplier Diversity Programs. (2000-2005)

Visteon Corporation

One Village Center
Van Buren Township, MI 48111
www.visteon.com/careers

Locations (worldwide)
Global in 19 countries

Diversity Leadership
Jennifer Karaskiewicz, Diversity Work/Life
Manager
One Village Center
Van Buren Township, MI 48111
Phone: (800) VISTEON

Recruiting

Please list the schools/types of schools at which you recruit.

• Public state schools
• Historically Black Colleges and Universities (HBCUs)

Do you have any special outreach efforts that are directed to encourage minority students to consider your firm?

• Hold a reception for minority students
• Participate in/host minority student job fair(s)
• Sponsor minority student association events
• Firm's employees participate on career panels at school

What activities does the firm undertake to attract minority and women employees?

• Partner programs with women and minority associations
• Seek referrals from other employees
• Utilize online job services

Do you use executive recruiting/search firms to seek to identify new diversity hires?

Yes, for experienced hires only

Internships and Co-ops

Visteon Internship Program

Deadline for application: October

Number of interns in the program in summer 2004 (internship) or 2004 (co-op): 100

Pay: Varies by discipline

Length of the program: Minimum 8 weeks

Percentage of interns/co-ops in the program who receive offers of full-time employment: 50-70%

Web site for internship/co-op information: www.visteon.com/careers

Affinity Groups/Employee Networks

- Visteon African Ancestry Network
- Women In Visteon
- Visteon Asian Indian Association
- Visteon Hispanic Network
- Gay, Lesbian, or Bisexual Employees
- Visteon Asian Pacific Employee Network
- Visteon Arab Resource Network

Each of our seven affinity groups are committed to advancing diversity initiatives at Visteon as well as providing support to their members in the areas of career development, education, and community outreach. Groups meet at varying schedules and leaders of all groups are regular members of the company's Executive Diversity Council

Entry-Level Programs/Full-Time Opportunities

Professional Development Program

Length of program: 3 to 4 years

Geographic location(s) of program: U.S. Locations

Please describe any other educational components of this program (i.e., tuition reimbursement): Tuition reimbursement for employees after 12 months of service, peer councils for events, volunteer activity, and program review.

Strategic Plan and Diversity Leadership

How does the firm's leadership communicate the importance of diversity to everyone at the firm?

E-mails, web site, newsletters, meetings, as well as monthly cultural celebrations, mandatory diversity training, and leadership support and involvement.

Who has primary responsibility for leading diversity initiatives at your firm?

Michael F. Johnston, CEO

Does your firm currently have a diversity committee?

Yes

If yes, please describe how the committee is structured, how often it meets, etc.

Representatives are our senior leadership committee, HR leaders, and presidents of each of the seven affinity groups. The group meets quarterly. The committee is chaired by the CEO.

If yes, does the committee's representation include one or more members of the firm's management/executive committee (or the equivalent)?

Yes

If yes, how many executives are on the committee?

Total executives on the committee: 10

Does the committee and/or diversity leader establish and set goals or objectives consistent with management's priorities?

Yes

Has the firm undertaken a formal or informal diversity program or set of initiatives aimed at increasing the diversity of the firm?

Yes, formal

How often does the firm's management review the firm's diversity progress/results?

Quarterly

How is the firm's diversity committee and/or firm management held accountable for achieving results?

Annually, during the talent review process with the group Vice Presidents

The Stats

Employees: 17,000 (2004, U.S.)
Employees: 55,000 (2004, outside U.S.)
Employees: 72,000 (2004, worldwide)

Global representation of women is above 20%, U.S. representation of minorities is above 25%

Retention and Professional Development

How do 2004 minority and female attrition rates generally compare to those experienced in the prior year period?

Higher than in prior years

Please identify the specific steps you are taking to reduce the attrition rate of minority and women employees.

• Develop and/or support internal employee affinity groups (e.g., minority or women networks within the firm
• Increase/improve current work/life programs
• Adopt dispute resolution process
• Succession plan includes emphasis on diversity
• Work with minority and women employees to develop career advancement plans
• Professional skills development program, including minority and women employees

Wachovia Corporation

1 Wachovia Center
Charlotte, NC 28288-0013
Phone: (704) 374-6565
Fax: (704) 374-3425
Toll Free: (800) 275-3862
www.wachovia.com

Diversity Leadership

Rosie Saez, SVP, Manager of Diversity
Integration
301 S. College Street
Charlotte, NC 28288

Recruiting

Please list the schools/types of schools at which you recruit.

- *Ivy League schools:* Harvard, Yale, Princeton
- *Other private schools:* Duke, Wake Forest University and others
- *Public state schools:* University of Connecticut, University of Virginia, University of Maryland, University of North Carolina, University of Texas, University of Florida and others
- *Historically Black Colleges and Universities (HBCUs):* Morehouse, Hampton, Spelman, Howard, Florida A & M
- *Hispanic Serving Institutions (HSIs):* Florida International University

Do you have any special outreach efforts that are directed to encourage minority students to consider your firm?

- Hold a reception for minority students
- Conferences: National Society of Hispanic MBAs; National Black MBA Association; NABA; NAACP; Women for Hire
- Participate in/host minority student job fair(s)
- Sponsor minority student association events
- Firm's employees participate on career panels at school
- Outreach to leadership of minority student organizations
- Scholarships or intern/fellowships for minority students

What activities does the firm undertake to attract minority and women employees?

- Partner programs with women and minority associations
- Conferences: same as above
- Participate at minority job fairs

• Seek referrals from other employees (Wachovia has a program called RAVE, for Refer Another Valuable Employee, which provides cash incentives for employees to make referrals.)
• Utilize online job services

Do you use executive recruiting/search firms to seek to identify new diversity hires?

Yes. (These are used mainly for mid-level to senior management level hiring.)

Internships and Co-ops

INROADS, HACU (sponsors the Hispanic National Internship Program)

Deadline for application: March 1
Number of interns in the program in summer 2004 (internship) or 2004 (co-op): 120 total for 2004 and 140 for 2005
Pay: from $12-$15 based on class year
Length of the program: 10 weeks
Percentage of interns/co-ops in the program who receive offers of full-time employment:oyment: Varies by line of business
Web site for internship/co-op information: www.wachovia.com/college

Scholarships

INROADS scholarship (for INROADS Interns), Harald Hanssen Scholarship (based out of the Georgia branch of Wachovia)

Scholarship award amount: between $1,000 and $5,000

Affinity Groups

Wachovia sponsors Employee Resource Networks (ERNs) based around the following identity groups: Black/African American, Asian, Native American, Hispanic/Latino/Latina, Gay & Lesbian, and Women. These groups meet regularly and actively support development for their members as well as the company's business strategy. Each ERN has website space on the corporate intranet.

Entry-Level Programs/Full-Time Opportunities

There are 14 entry-level associate programs in eight different lines of business. The specific positions vary every year, and are updated in August and again in January, depending on what our needs are. Please see www.wachovia.com/college for details.

Length of program: Varies from 6 weeks to 3-6 month rotations in various areas
Geographic location(s) of program: In every location within the Wachovia footprint

Strategic Plan and Diversity Leadership

How does the firm's leadership communicate the importance of diversity to everyone at the firm?

The company maintains a strong commitment to keeping employees informed about our commitment to diversity and our progress. We use multiple forms of media (e-mails, websites, newsletters, videos and meetings) to communicate with employees across our footprint. At least twice a year, our CEO, Ken Thompson sends a formal communication to all employees summarizing diversity progress and recognition. He also meets informally with employees across diverse identity groups and with the Employee Resource Networks. Each Line of Business head is also accountable for keeping his or her employees informed about diversity progress within the business unit.

Who has primary responsibility for leading diversity initiatives at your firm?

Ken Thompson, CEO

Does your firm currently have a diversity committee?

Yes, we have a 23 member Corporate Diversity Council that is headed by the CEO.

The Corporate Diversity Council is led by the CEO and the membership includes a diverse mix by race, gender, sexual orientation, business unit and level to ensure a synergy of perspectives in the development, guidance and review of corporate diversity strategies and progress. The council meets each quarter for a full day. There are 23 members on the council, four of which are permanent due to their functional responsibilities for diversity: the CEO, Director of HR, Manager of Diversity Integration and representation from Corporate Communications.

In addition, each business unit has a diversity council modeled after the corporate council with employees representing diverse identity groups. The business unit councils develop strategies and actions to support diversity progress in the line of business.

Does the committee's representation include one or more members of the firm's management/executive committee (or the equivalent)?

Yes, seven of the nine CEO direct reports sit on the council. All of the CEO's direct reports serve on the council at some point through the council membership rotation process.

Please describe the committee.

The company invests substantial time, money and resources to support its diversity commitment. It is impossible to calculate the hours invested given that the work cuts across all of our employee, customer and community segments.

> *Total executives on committee:* 20

Does the committee and/or diversity leader establish and set goals or objectives consistent with management's priorities?

Yes. We view language as critically important and have deliberately chosen to refer to our diversity work as a commitment rather than an initiative. Wachovia maintains a strategic plan for diversity composed of five core strategies and 17 actions that are implemented at the corporate and line of business levels. Each year, the Corporate Diversity Council holds an annual meeting in the first quarter to review progress and recommend specific actions that align with current needs and priorities.

Has the firm undertaken a formal or informal diversity program or set of initiatives aimed at increasing the diversity of the firm?

Yes, formal as part of our strategic plan for diversity. Additionally, while no specific targets are set, the CEO holds his direct reports accountable for increasing diversity in the highest valued jobs.

How often does the firm's management review the firm's diversity progress/results?

Quarterly and as needed.

How is the firm's diversity committee and/or firm management held accountable for achieving results?

The CEO holds diversity reviews with his direct reports each year to assess progress. Results are directly linked to the executives' incentive compensation.

The Stats

Employees: Over 95,000 (2004, worldwide)
$512 billion in assets under management

Retention and Professional Development

How do 2004 minority and female attrition rates generally compare to those experienced in the prior year period?
About the same as in prior years

Please identify the specific steps you are taking to reduce the attrition rate of minority and women employees.

• Develop and/or support internal employee affinity groups-Employee Resource Networks (e.g., minority or women networks within the firm)
• Succession plan includes emphasis on diversity
• Work with minority and women employees to develop career advancement plans
• Strengthen mentoring program for all employees, including minorities and women
• Professional skills development program, including minority and women employees
• Other: Enhance current work/life programs
• Other: Leaders pay attention to work and/or stretch assignments to ensure equitable treatment across diverse identity groups.
• Other: Dispute resolution process

Diversity Mission Statement

Diversity at Wachovia is a business imperative. Aligning with our customer base, engaging our communities and attracting and retaining talented individuals are critical to our success. We are committed to long-term positive culture change and seek to incorporate diversity into all aspects of our business. Every individual at Wachovia has an ongoing responsibility to advance diversity.

We are committed to being an inclusive company where all people are treated fairly, recognized for their individuality, promoted based on performance and encouraged to reach their full potential. We believe in recognizing, understanding, and respecting differences among all people. These differences include but are not limited to race, gender, sexual orientation, work/life status, ethnic origin, culture, spiritual beliefs and practices, age, level, physical/mental ability and veteran status.

The Employer Says

Diversity at Wachovia is established as a long-term culture change commitment to afford us the best opportunity to integrate diversity into all aspects of our business. By building awareness and acceptance of difference across race, gender, sexual orientation, age, level, etc. in our business practices, we build an organization that fully utilizes all of its human capital and has the best chance of becoming the employer of choice and a world-class organization.

Employer of Choice – Awards and Recognition

Wachovia is proud to be recognized by a number of publications and organizations for its ongoing commitment to a best-in-class diverse workforce. Here is a partial list of some recent awards Wachovia has won:

• *Working Mother* magazine named Wachovia one of the nation's Top 10 companies for working mothers as well as "Industry Leader" and "Best in Class" for family-friendly culture. The magazine selected Wachovia based on its programs and policies for child-care, leave for new parents, opportunities for women to advance, flexible work arrangements, work/life benefits such as elder care and other employee programs.

• *DiversityInc* magazine has honored Wachovia as one of the "Top 50 Companies for Diversity" in its annual survey. DiversityInc ranked the company based on its functional commitment to top diversity practices-employee networks, tying compensation to diversity initiatives-as well as commitment to philanthropic endeavors and to communicating its diversity message.

• *LATINA Style***'s** annual list of the best companies for Latinas ranks Wachovia among the top 50 to work for in the United States. The annual special edition survey, in its sixth year, surveyed more than 600 companies across the nation to tabulate its results.

• The *Black Collegian***'s** Top 100 Employers Survey included Wachovia among its major employers in industry, government, and business examined for hiring trends. The annual survey provides current information on where the jobs are, allowing graduating classes to focus their searches on employers actively hiring.

• For the third year in a row, Wachovia received the top score on the **NAACP's** annual Economic Reciprocity scorecard of financial services companies, this year with a grade of B.

• Wachovia scored a strong 86 out of 100 on the **Human Rights Campaign's 2005 Corporate Equality Index.**

• Wachovia was also recognized as an Outstanding Company for Black Women by *Essence* magazine.

Wells Fargo & Company

420 Montgomery St.
San Francisco, CA 94104
Phone: (800) 867-3557
http://www.wellsfargo.com/jobs

Locations (worldwide)

Wells Fargo is headquartered in San
Francisco and has offices in all 50 states

Diversity Leadership

Linda McConley, Diversity Manager
Lane Ceric, Corporate Recruitment Manager
420 Montgomery St.
San Francisco, CA 94104
Phone: (612) 667-0643
Fax: (612) 667-5353
E-mail: linda.k.mcconley@wellsfargo.com

Recruiting

Please list the schools/types of schools at which you recruit.

- *Historically Black Colleges and Universities (HBCUs):* Atlanta City Center Schools, Florida A&M
- *Native American Tribal Universities:* Through American Indian Business Leaders Conference

Do you have any special outreach efforts that are directed to encourage minority students to consider your firm?

- Hold a reception for minority students
- Conferences: American Indian Business Leaders, Graduate Women in Business, National Association of Black Accountants, National Black MBA Association, National Hispanic Business Association, National Society of Hispanic MBAs, Students in Free Enterprise, and various regional and campus student organizations
- Advertise in minority student association publication(s)
- Participate in/host minority student job fair(s)
- Sponsor minority student association events
- Firm's employees participate on career panels at school
- Outreach to leadership of minority student organizations
- Scholarships or intern/fellowships for minority students

What activities does the firm undertake to attract minority and women employees?

- Partner programs with women and minority associations
- Conferences: American Indian Business Leaders, Graduate Women in Business, National Association of Black Accountants, National Black MBA Association, National Hispanic Business Association, National Society of Hispanic MBAs, Students in Free Enterprise, and various regional and campus student organizations
- Participate at minority job fairs
- Seek referrals from other employees
- Utilize online job services

Do you use executive recruiting/search firms to seek to identify new diversity hires?

No

Internships and Co-ops

Corporate/Wholesale Banking Undergraduate Summer Analyst and MBA Summer Associate Program

Deadline for application: February 2006

Number of interns in the program in summer 2004 (internship) or 2004 (co-op): 57 undergraduates/11 MBAs

Pay: $3,500.00/month and $5,630.00/month

Length of the program: 10-12 weeks

Percentage of interns/co-ops in the program who receive offers of full-time employment: TBD. A complete roster of hires into the Class of 2005 will be available at the end of September.

Web site for internship information: http://www.wellsfargo.com/employment/undergraduates/summer/corporate

Corporate/Wholesale Banking Student Leadership Conference

Deadline for application: February 2006

Number of interns in the program in summer 2004 (internship) or 2004 (co-op): 25

Pay: $0.00/All costs are covered by Wells Fargo

Length of the program: 4 days

Percentage of interns/co-ops in the program who receive offers of full-time employment: TBD. These students are Freshman and Sophomores, so they will not be considered for full-time employment until September 2007 or 2008 start dates.

Web site for internship information: Not promoted via the Web. Applicants are invited to apply.

Internet Services Summer Intern Program

Deadline for application: March 2006

Number of interns in the program in summer 2004 (internship) or 2004 (co-op): 4 undergraduates/5 MBAs

Pay: $3,295.00/month and $4,470.00/month

Length of the program: 10-12 weeks

Percentage of interns/co-ops in the program who receive offers of full-time employment: TBD. A complete roster of hires into the Class of 2006 will be available at the end of September.

Web site for internship information: http://www.wellsfargo.com/employment/undergraduates/summer/internet

Scholarships

Hispanic Scholarship Fund (HSF)

Deadline for application for the scholarship program: October 2005

Scholarship award amount: 25 scholarships, $2500 per scholarship for each year up to 4 years

Web site or other contact information for scholarship: http://www.hsf.net/scholarships.php

Wells Fargo offers scholarship awards [as well as internships and future employment opportunities] to Latino students in partnership with the Hispanic Scholarship Fund (HSF).

Asian and Pacific Islander American Scholarship Fund (APIASF)

Scholarship award amount: $2,000

Web site or other contact information for scholarship: www.apiasf.org

Wells Fargo is one of several founding sponsors of the Asian and Pacific Islander American Scholarship Fund (APIASF). The scholarship is designed for college-bound students from underrepresented Asian and Pacific Islander communities interested in pursuing careers in banking and financial services.

Summer Search Foundation

Deadline for application for the scholarship program: Unknown, contact (415) 362-0500

Scholarship award amount: $5000 donation+compensation associated with participation in the intern programs detailed above

Web site or other contact information for scholarship: http://www.summersearch.org/about/s.php?P=home.html

The mission of Summer Search is to identify low-income high school youth who demonstrate resiliency in overcoming hardship and the desire to help others. Nurturing those qualities over time in students who have often been neglected allows them to become empowered future everyday leaders. Their ambitious mission is accomplished through a program that combines full scholarships to summer experiential education programs with intensive long-term mentoring. Summer Search currently works with 600 students a year in San Francisco, Boston, Napa-Sonoma, New York City and Seattle. Wells Fargo sponsors 3-5 interns per summer.

Students Rising Above (KRON Channel 4)

Deadline for application for the scholarship program: Mid-April 2006

Scholarship award amount: Compensation associated with participation in the intern programs detailed above

Web site or other contact information for scholarship: http://www.studentsrisingabove.org/

This scholarship was created by KRON 4 News reporter and anchor Wendy Tokuda for students living in dangerous or low income neighborhoods. Qualifications include: low income or living on government assistance; highly recommended by teachers, counselors or mentors; cannot already be receiving a 4 year scholarship; personal character; has overcome obstacles that are not of their own making; committed to earning a college degree; willing to talk about life experiences on camera; must live within 9 county Bay Area; 3.0+ GPA. Wells Fargo sponsors 3-5 interns per summer.

UC Berkeley SAGE Scholars Program

Deadline for application for the scholarship program: Varies annually

Scholarship award amount: $3800 administrative fee per scholar/per summer+compensation associated with participation in the intern programs detailed above

Web site or other contact information for scholarship: http://students.berkeley.edu/sagescholars/

UC Berkeley's SAGE (Student Achievement Guided by Experience) Scholars Program is an academically rigorous program that combines workplace experience with the professional skills needed to succeed in a competitive economy. SAGE works with highly motivated UC Berkeley's students from low income and diverse backgrounds. SAGE promotes quality professional leadership and career development training through internships, mentoring and education. Wells Fargo is on the Corporate Advisory Board for this organization, hired 1 SAGE Scholar in 2004, and 5 in 2005.

University of Texas, Austin Jumpstart Program

Deadline for application for the scholarship program: Varies annually

Scholarship award amount: Compensation associated with 3 years of pre-program employment+all tuition and fees associated with enrollment in the UT-Austin MBA program

A new program from The University of Texas at Austin's McCombs School of Business aims to meet that need by expanding the pool of top students who consider an MBA degree. The Jumpstart program targets undergraduate seniors who are academically qualified for a top-ranked MBA but lack the required work experience. Companies agree to provide the experience by hiring the students for three years. The McCombs School then offers candidates deferred admission to the MBA program based on the completion of their job commitment.

INROADS

Scholarship award amount: Administrative fee per intern/per summer+ compensation associated with participation in the intern programs detailed above

Affinity Groups/Employee Networks

Wells Fargo has 76 Team Member Resource Groups across the company. Networks are formed by individuals connected by a shared background, experience or other affinity. Any Wells Fargo team member can join an existing group or propose to start a new group. The mission: professional growth, education, community outreach, recruiting/retention, and customer insight. Current segments include:

- Arab
- African American (named CheckPoint)
- Asian/Pacific Islander (named Asian Connection)
- Team Members Dealing with Disabilities (named disAbilities Awareness)
- Hispanic/Latino (named Amigos)
- Native American (named Native Peoples)
- Persian (named Persian American Connection)
- GLBT (named PRIDE)

Entry-Level Programs/Full-Time Opportunities

Wells Fargo has several programs to attract and retain diverse team members to enhance our Diversity Objectives and provide management opportunities. Past experience has shown that many of these individuals quickly move up within the organization to leadership roles.

Participants in these programs, like all Wells Fargo team members, are eligible for tuition reimnursement.

Credit Management Training Program (MBA)

Length of program: 6 months

Geographic location of program: San Francisco

This program familiarizes participants with how Wells Fargo analyzes and evaluates credit situations. Associates work directly with corporate clients in building and strengthening relationships and recommending the necessary credit or other financial products to meet their needs.

Financial Analyst Program (BA/BS)

Length of program: 18-24 months
Geographic location of program: Major cities in California, Texas, and the Pacific Northwest, Chicago, Minneapolis, New York and other U.S. locations

Provide analytical and operational support to senior bankers during the deal making process, corporate meetings and presentations to senior managers. Formal training in accounting, corporate finance, treasury management and commercial credit.

Project Manager/Leadership Development Program (BA/BS)

Length of program: 12-18 months
Geographic location of program: San Francisco, St. Paul

Program under development is designed to train qualified diversity candidates for management roles in Corporate Banking support services.

Provides comprehensive exposure to the Wells Fargo Corporate/Wholesale businesses, in preparation for an individual contributor or management position within the business group.

Business Banking Associate Program (BA/BS)

Length of program: 12 months (two six-month rotations)
Geographic location of program: San Francisco, Sacramento, Concord, Boise, Minneapolis, San Antonio

Rotations include operations/customer service, finance/credit analysis, systems, mergers and acquisitions and human resources. Also includes formal training in technical, business and interpersonal skills.

Finance Associate Development Program (BA/BS)

Length of program: 12 months
Geographic location of program: San Francisco

Prepares recent graduates for a career in Finance through a combination of hands-on experience, classroom and Web-based training and peer interaction. Moves trainees through project teams in various Finance business lines, and one rotation in an unassociated Wells Fargo business line.

Internet Business Consultant Program (MBA)

Length of program: 12 months
Geographic location of program: San Francisco

Provides participants the opportunity to develop skill sets in the world of e-commerce and address key challenges in our business. Participants learn what makes an Internet business successful and contribute to that success.

Information Technology Associate (BS/BA/Masters)

Length of program: 12 months
Geographic location of program: San Francisco

Includes three project-based rotations over 12 months. The ITA program uses a combination of classroom training, computer based training, project team participation, peer interaction and working one-on-one with e-commerce technology professionals to prepare participants for their first assignment as an Internet Services IT professional.

Audit Rotational Training Program (BA/BS)

Length of program: 36 months
Geographic location of program: Des Moines, Minneapolis, Phoenix, San Francisco

A rotational program wherein individuals complete a formal training curriculum related to technical, business and behavioral skills while rotating among different audit groups.

Leadership Development Program (BA/BS)

Length of program: 12 months
Geographic location of program: Minneapolis, Phoenix, San Francisco

A rotational program providing exposure to a variety of functional enterprises within the Services Company. Participants may work in a retail store, a phone bank center, and/or in entry level operations and technology assignments. The will also receive guidance from the program mananager, a personal mentor and various assignment managers.

HR Leadership Program (MBA)

Length of program: 10-12 months
Geographic location of program: San Francisco

A program developing HR core competencies in recent MBAs. Participants work as consultants on projects in various Corporate HR business lines/lines of business.

"Class of" Program

Length of program: 6 months
Geographic location of program: Major cities nationwide

Trainees in the programs detailed above participate in Corporate Human Resource's Class of Program. The goal of this program is to offer participants exposure to the larger company, senior management, and each other, creating a sense of community and strong working relationships across business lines. The 6-month curriculum includes a 2-day executive exposure forum, networking opportunities with management and peers throughout the company and Webcasts on professional development and Wells Fargo's visions & values.

Strategic Plan and Diversity Leadership

How does the firm's leadership communicate the importance of diversity to everyone at the firm?

E-mail, internal and external web sites, newsletters, meetings, speeches, brochures, videos, training courses, phone announcements, letters from executives

Who has primary responsibility for leading diversity initiatives at your firm?

Linda McConley, Diversity Manager

Does your firm currently have a diversity committee?

Yes

If yes, please describe how the committee is structured, how often it meets, etc.

• 30 members representing each Wells Fargo business line (one Diversity Council representative per 5,000 team members)
• Meet six times per year (three face-to-face meetings, three teleconferences)

If yes, does the committee's representation include one or more members of the firm's management/executive committee (or the equivalent)?

Yes

Does the committee and/or diversity leader establish and set goals or objectives consistent with management's priorities?

Yes

Has the firm undertaken a formal or informal diversity program or set of initiatives aimed at increasing the diversity of the firm?

Yes, formal. Wells Fargo has a company-wide diversity platform called "Six Steps to Got Diversity." It includes six initiatives that the entire company is working on (executive involvement and accountability, recruiting and retention, diverse segment marketing, diverse community giving, supplier diversity, and communications.   We set goals and measure progress against these six things at the corporate level, and within each business line.

How often does the firm's management review the firm's diversity progress/results?

Twice a year.

How is the firm's diversity committee and/or firm management held accountable for achieving results?

Our Corporate Diversity Council reports directly to our Executive Management Committee twice each year. We discuss progress and action items within our Six Steps platform.

The Stats

Employees: 150,000 (2004, U.S.)

Employees: 140,000 (2003, U.S.)

Revenue: $30.1 billion (2004, U.S.)

- Percentage of U.S. minorities: 29.75%
- Percentage of male employees: 37.37%
- Percentage of female employees: 62.63%
- Percentage of minorities on executive team: 5.3%
- Percentage of women on executive team: 22.5%

Retention and Professional Development

How do 2004 minority and female attrition rates generally compare to those experienced in the prior year period?

About the same as in prior years

Please identify the specific steps you are taking to reduce the attrition rate of minority and women employees.

- Develop and/or support internal employee affinity groups (e.g., minority or women networks within the firm)
- Increase/improve current work/life programs
- Succession plan includes emphasis on diversity
- Work with minority and women employees to develop career advancement plans
- Strengthen mentoring program for all employees, including minorities and women
- Professional skills development program, including minority and women employees

Diversity Mission Statement

Wells Fargo team members should expect to work in an environment where each person feels valued for individual traits, skills and talents, and has the opportunity to fulfill ambitions and contribute to the success of the company.

The Employer Says

We know that making ourselves more diverse will make Wells Fargo a better company – and we're committed to doing that. Wells Fargo employs over 150,000 people – over 60% are women, and over 43% of new hires into Wells Fargo's professional development programs are diverse – and we offer many programs to help them manage their work and family responsibilities. We have over 75 Team Member Resource Groups (TMRGs) which provide team members with a common background – such as Latinas or African Americans – an opportunity to build connections, which is what diversity is all about.

Wells Fargo has a company-wide diversity platform called "Six Steps to Get Diversity." The Six Steps help guide and measure our success at hiring and retaining team members, serving customers and partnering with communities that are more diverse. Every Wells Fargo business line can set objectives and measure success against these six things:

- Our CEO and executive management team take responsibility for diversity and hold themselves and others accountable. Diversity is a part of Wells Fargo's Vision and Values. The corporate diversity council reports to the executive management team. Upper management references our diversity in internal and external, written and verbal communications.

• People from diverse backgrounds are in all levels of management. Managers are accountable for attracting diverse candidates and for developing and retaining a diverse leadership pipeline. Wells Fargo has a plan for increasing diversity among its upper management.

• We establish long-term relationships with diverse communities. Wells Fargo tailors products and services to diverse communities and communicates those products and services through targeted marketing and advertising.

• We contribute to the communities we work, live and do business in. Wells Fargo continues to foster a supplier-diversity program and diverse philanthropic and educational efforts.

• Diversity is present in all of our company communications. Diversity information and examples can be seen throughout corporate-wide, regional and business line communications and marketing materials (even if the word "diversity" isn't used). Diversity links are easily found on both Teamworks and wellsfargo.com.

• We are known as a diverse company. Job candidates, customers, vendors and shareholders seek Wells Fargo out because of its diverse reputation. Existing team members have avenues to voice their opinions on how inclusive Wells Fargo is. Wells Fargo earns credibility through national and community-based groups.

Never stop growing.

At Weyerhaeuser, we believe that to be the best forest products company in the world and global leader among all industries, we must hire and develop the best possible talent. That means creating an atmosphere where diversity is valued, achievements are recognized and people of all backgrounds and interests are encouraged to grow.

We are committed to our employees, their communities and the natural environment we are privileged to care for. At Weyerhaeuser, we don't just grow trees - we grow careers and lives, too.

▲ Weyerhaeuser
The future is growing™
weyerhaeuser.com/careers

Weyerhaeuser

33663 Weyerhaeuser Way South
Federal Way, WA 98063-9777
Phone: (253) 924-2345
Fax: (253) 924-2685
www.weyerhaeuser.com/careers

Diversity Leadership
Effenus Henderson, Director, Workforce
Representation & Diversity
Diversity Leadership
Darvi Mack, Diversity Manager
P.O. Box 9777
Federal Way, WA 98063-9777
Phone: (253) 924-2345
Fax: 253-924-4151

Recruiting

Please list the schools/types of schools at which you recruit.

We recruit from several of the following:
• Ivy League schools
• Other private schools
• Public state schools:
• Historically Black Colleges and Universities (HBCUs)
• Hispanic Serving Institutions (HSIs)
• Native American Tribal Universities

Do you have any special outreach efforts that are directed to encourage minority students to consider your firm?

• Hold a reception for minority students
• Conferences: National Black MBA, National Society Hispanic MBA, Society Women Engineers, INROADS, CATALYST, National Association Black Accountants, National Urban League Convention, Women in Construction, National Society of Black Engineers, National Association of Asian Professionals
• Advertise in minority student association publication(s)
• Participate in/host minority student job fair(s)
• Sponsor minority student association events
• Firm's employees participate on career panels at school
• Outreach to leadership of minority student organizations
• Scholarships or intern/fellowships for minority students

What activities does the firm undertake to attract minority and women employees?

• Partner programs with women and minority associations
• Conferences: National Black MBA, National Society Hispanic MBA, INROADS, Black Data Processing Association,
• Association Latino Professionals & Accountants; National Association Black Accountants, National Urban League Convention, Women in Construction, Society Women Engineers, CATALYST
• Participate at minority job fairs all major national Diversity job fairs as indicated: National Black MBA, National Society Hispanic MBA, Black Data Processing Association, Association Latino Professionals & Accountants; National Association Black Accountants, National Urban League Convention, Women in Construction, Society Women Engineers

• Seek referrals from other employees
• Utilize online job services

Do you use executive recruiting/search firms to seek to identify new diversity hires?

No

Internships and Co-ops

Weyerhaeuser/UNCF Corporate Scholars Program

Deadline for application: February 12th.
Number of interns in the program in summer 2004: 13 interns
Pay: $15.00/hour
Percentage of interns/co-ops in the program who receive offers of full-time employment:oyment: 95%
Web site for internship/co-op information: http://www.uncf.org/internships/internshipdetail.asp?Sch_ID=16607

Weyerhaeuser/UNCF Corporate Scholars Program was established to increase student interest in Weyerhaeuser and to expand the pool of prospective diverse employees. Sophomores and Juniors enrolled in participating schools in the areas of Forestry, Forest Product Sales and Marketing, Industrial/Manufacturing/Electrical Engineering and Operation Management & Supervision are eligible to apply.

Scholarships

Weyerhaeuser/UNCF Corporate Scholars Program

Deadline for application for the scholarship program: February 12th
Scholarship award amount: up to $10,000.00 for entire scholarship
Web site or other contact information for scholarship:
http://www.uncf.org/internships/internshipdetail.asp?Sch_ID=16607

The Weyerhaeuser/UNCF Corporate Scholars Program was established to increase student interest in Weyerhaeuser and to expand the pool of prospective diverse employees. Sophomores and Juniors enrolled in participating schools in the areas of Forestry, Forest Product Sales and Marketing, Industrial/Manufacturing/Electrical Engineering and Operation Management & Supervision are eligible to apply.

Affinity Groups/Employee Networks

WIA, GLBTE, BEST, Generation Next

All affinity groups serve as support for its membership and are committed to assisting the company in recruiting and retention of diverse employees, group professional development and fostering a respectful inclusive workplace.

Entry-Level Programs/Full-Time Opportunities

Managed Entry

> *Length of program:* Varies by program 18 months or longer
> *Geographic location(s) of program:* National

Please describe the training/training component of this program: Accounting, Engineering, Sales, Production, IT, HR

Please describe any other educational components of this program: All full-time employees are eligible for tuition reimbursement.

Strategic Plan and Diversity Leadership

How does the firm's leadership communicate the importance of diversity to everyone at the firm?

E-mails, company newsletters, business specific newsletters, web site, meetings, employee forums, training, brochures and via affinity groups/business networks.

Who has primary responsibility for leading diversity initiatives at your firm?

CEO & President – Steve R. Rogel

Does your firm currently have a diversity committee?

Yes

If yes, please describe how the committee is structured, how often it meets, etc.

We have several diversity committees including an all-executive level committee. Meets quarterly. Each business has a diversity committee.

If yes, does the committee's representation include one or more members of the firm's management/executive committee (or the equivalent)?

Yes

Please describe the committee.

Total executives on committee: 7 Executives, 1 Diversity Director; Meets quarterly; 50 hours spent in furtherance of the firm's diversity initiatives

Does the committee and/or diversity leader establish and set goals or objectives consistent with management's priorities?

Yes. The Executive Diversity Team sets the Diversity goals that align with business strategy.

Has the firm undertaken a formal or informal diversity program or set of initiatives aimed at increasing the diversity of the firm?

Yes, formal. The EDT has set 5 High Impact Action Areas aimed to increase diversity and retention of talent.

How often does the firm's management review the firm's diversity progress/results?

Quarterly

How is the firm's diversity committee and/or firm management held accountable for achieving results?

Accountability: 20% is linked to the Management Incentive Program Bonus Plan

The Stats

Employees: 42,349 (2004, U.S.)
Employees: 42,974 (2003, U.S.)
Revenue: $22.7 billion (2004, U.S.)
Revenue: $19.7 billion (2003, U.S.)

Retention and Professional Development

How do 2004 minority and female attrition rates generally compare to those experienced in the prior year period?

Lower than in prior years

Please identify the specific steps you are taking to reduce the attrition rate of minority and women employees.

• Develop and/or support internal employee affinity groups (e.g., minority or women networks within the firm)
• Increase/review compensation relative to competition
• Increase/improve current work/life programs
• Adopt dispute resolution process
• Succession plan includes emphasis on diversity
• Work with minority and women employees to develop career advancement plans
• Strengthen mentoring program for all employees, including minorities and women
• Professional skills development program, including minority and women employees

Diversity Mission Statement

We are an employer of choice with high-performing people who are treated with respect and work together in a safe and healthy workplace where diversity, development, teamwork and open communication are valued and recognized.

The Employer Says

We are a company that embraces diversity and fosters inclusion in the Weyerhaeuser Way. The Weyerhaeuser Way consists of a set of statements and principles that represent our aspirations and desired culture. At the operational level, they are reflected in our Roadmap for Success. Our values statements are further amplified by Weyerhaeuser's business conduct guidelines outlined in our code of ethics, Our Reputation: A Shared Responsibility.

Our Vision

The best forest products company in the world and a global leader among all industries

Our Mission

Produce superior returns for shareholders by focusing on our customers and working safely to:

• Grow and harvest trees.
• Manufacture and sell forest products.
• Build and sell homes.

Our Values

• Customers and suppliers. We listen to our customers and suppliers to improve our products and services to meet their present and future needs.

• People. We are an employer of choice with high-performing people who are treated with respect and work together in a safe and healthy workplace where diversity, development, teamwork and open communication are valued and recognized.

• Accountability. We expect superior performance and are accountable for our actions and results. Our leaders set clear goals and expectations, are supportive, and provide and seek frequent feedback.

• Citizenship. We support the communities where we do business, hold ourselves to the highest standards of ethical conduct and environmental responsibility, and communicate openly with Weyerhaeuser people and the public.

• Financial responsibility. We are prudent and effective in the use of the resources entrusted to us to create shareholder value.

Whirlpool Corporation

2000 N. M 63
Benton Harbor, MI 49022
Phone: (269) 923-5000
Fax: (269) 923-5443
www.whirlpoolcareers.com

Locations (worldwide)

Corporate Headquarters: Benton Harbor, Michigan

European Operations Center: Comerio, Italy

Regional Headquarters: Shanghai, PRC and Sao Paulo, Brazil

Additionally, Whirlpool has 50 manufacturing and technology centers around the world

Diversity Leadership

Chris Aisenbrey, Director, Global University Relations and Recruiting
2000 N. M-63
Benton Harbor, MI 49022
Phone: (269) 923-5000
Fax: (269) 923-2874

Recruiting

Please list the schools/types of schools at which you recruit.

• *Private schools:* University of Notre Dame, Harvard Business School
• *Public state schools:* University of Michigan, Michigan State University, Purdue University, Indiana University, Ohio State University, Western Michigan University, University of Florida, University of Miami, University of North Carolina, University of Georgia, University of Texas-Austin, Northern Illinois University, University of Arkansas, University of Arkansas-Fort Smith, Michigan Technology University

Do you have any special outreach efforts that are directed to encourage minority students to consider your firm?

Outreach to leadership of minority student organizations

What activities does the firm undertake to attract minority and women employees?

• Conferences: NSBE, SWE, NABA
• Utilize online job services

Do you use executive recruiting/search firms to seek to identify new diversity hires?

No

Internships and Co-ops

Deadline for application: January 2, 2006
Number of interns in the program in summer 2004 (internship) or 2004 (co-op): 57
Length of the program: 9-12 weeks
Percentage of interns/co-ops in the program who receive offers of full-time employment:oyment: 75%
Web site for internship/co-op information: www.whirlpoolcareers.com/campus

Internships are available in a many functional areas: Engineering, Accounting, Finance, Human Resources, Procurement,and Logistics.

Whirlpool's internship program provides real, hands-on work experience to give each intern a better understanding of the type of work they may perform as full-time employees. Whirlpool's internship program educates participants about the different areas of the company, its strategic objectives and the plans in place to achieve those objectives. The program also provides interns with an opportunity to experience the surrounding communities, develop lasting friendships with other interns, and get to know Whirlpool employees outside of the work environment. Finally, the program evaluates each intern's work performance, as well as allows him or her to evaluate whether Whirlpool Corporation would be a good fit for his or her full-time career aspirations.

Affinity Groups/Employee Networks

Whirlpool African American Network; Whirlpool Hispanic Network; Whirlpool Women's Network; Whirlpool Gay, Lesbian, Bi-sexual, and Transgender Network; Whirlpool Asian Network; and Whirlpool Native American Network.

Entry-Level Programs/Full-Time Opportunities

Real Whirled

Length of program: Seven weeks of intensive training
Geographic location(s) of program: Training conducted in Benton Harbor, MI Training program graduates then relocate to various locations throughout the United States.

Please describe the training/training component of this program: The Real Whirled program begins with a seven week intensive training program, both classroom and experiential. Participants live together in a house outfitted with Whirlpool and KitchenAid appliances for the entire training program.

The purpose of the program is to provide the participants with all the necessary information and skill development required for their new positions as market brand representatives. The classroom component of the training is focused on learning about the products sold by Whirlpool Corporation throughout the United States, as well as developing leadership, communication and selling skills. The experiential component of the program is centered around activities like job shadowing, mystery shopping and using the products in the house on a daily basis. It is common for Whirlpool's senior executives to join the class discussion and to come by the Real Whirled house for dinner during the training program. Once the initial seven weeks are over, the training continues through monthly webcasts, teleconferences and on occasion, regionally based face-to-face meetings.

Human Resource Leadership Development Program (HRLDP)

Length of program: Three years

Geographic location(s) of program: Primarily in Benton Harbor, MI. Additional assignments could be in any of Whirlpool's Manufacturing Divisions throughout the United States or around the world.

Please describe the training/training component of this program: The HRLDP is a three-year, three-rotation program that is designed to give the participants training and development through two avenues: on-the-job training and quarterly learning sessions.

First, the participants are assigned to a part of the company that has an open-staffing situation, and they are given the responsibilities and objectives attached to that role. The rotational assignments are not project-based jobs. Working for and directly with a senior HR manager/director, participants take what they learned during college and transform that knowledge into practical applications.

The second avenue for training is through quarterly learning sessions. Some of these sessions are focused specifically on HR topics, such as developments in the compensation system, to broader business skills, such as how to manage change. In addition to these learning opportunities and the feedback each HRLDP receives about their performance, HRLDPs also are assigned a senior HR leader as a mentor.

Whirlpool Technical Excellence Program (WTEP)

Length of program: Three years. Participants are assigned two six-month project assignments during their first year. The second year is based at the University of Michigan completing a masters degree in Engineering, and the third year is another series of two six-month assignments.

Geographic location(s) of program: The first and third year of the program can be in any of our technology and manufacturing sites in the United States (and in some cases around the world). Many of the assignments will be at our corporate headquarters in Benton Harbor, MI. The second year of the program is spent at the University of Michigan in Ann Arbor.

Please describe any other educational components of this program: Full-time enrollment in the University of Michigan's Masters of Engineering program.

Global Supply Chain Leadership Development Program (GSCLDP)

Length of program: Three years

Geographic location(s) of program: Primarily in Benton Harbor, MI, but could be at any of Whirlpool's manufacturing divisions throughout the United States.

Please describe the training/training component of this program: The GSCLPD is designed to develop Whirlpool's leadership capability in the areas of logistics, procurement and operations (manufacturing). During a series of one-year rotational assignments, program participants have the opportunity to learn about the three key areas of supply-based management at Whirlpool. Besides receiving on-the-job training, program participants also take part in learning programs designed to enhance their skills on a functional basis, as well as develop leadership skills. All program participants are assigned a mentor who is a senior leader in manufacturing, logistics or procurement.

Finance Leadership Development Program (FLPDP)

Geographic location(s) of program: Primarily in Benton Harbor, MI, but could be at any of Whirlpool's locations throughout the United States.

Please describe the training/training component of this program: The purpose of the Finance Leadership Development Program is to develop future leaders by leveraging the finance and accounting skills learned in college and supplementing that knowledge with opportunities to develop, learn and grow as leaders. All program participants take part in functional and cross-functional training to develop required skills and enhance their current skills.

The program has two different focuses. The first is for accounting majors who will join the Whirlpool Internal Audit and Internal Controls team. The second is for finance, accounting and economics majors who will provide financial analysis skills to the company.

Strategic Plan and Diversity Leadership

How does the firm's leadership communicate the importance of diversity to everyone at the firm?

We develop an annual communication plan that is part of the diversity council objectives. Primarily, we communicate through our global employee intranet portal, on our diversity web site, through our diversity networks' newsletters, through the annual diversity and inclusion meeting for managers and employees and at our annual diversity and inclusion summit.

Who has primary responsibility for leading diversity initiatives at your firm?

Angela Roseboro, corporate director, global diversity

Does your firm currently have a diversity committee?

Yes

If yes, please describe how the committee is structured, how often it meets, etc.:

Once a month

If yes, does the committee's representation include one or more members of the firm's management/executive committee (or the equivalent)?

Yes

If yes, how many executives are on the committee?

Nine

Does the committee and/or diversity leader establish and set goals or objectives consistent with management's priorities?

Yes. Each year the council reviews and measures objectives against plan. In addition, the January meeting focuses on setting objectives aligned with our strategic business issues.

Has the firm undertaken a formal or informal diversity program or set of initiatives aimed at increasing the diversity of the firm?

Yes, formal. Each region/function develops actions plans and goals for increasing representation at all levels of the organization, but particularly in the feeder groups and leadership ranks. Goals are part of an overall People Scorecard that is directly tied to compensation.

How often does the firm's management review the firm's diversity progress/results?

Quarterly

How is the firm's diversity committee and/or firm management held accountable for achieving results?

Each region/function develops actions plans and goals for increasing representation at all levels of the organization, but particularly in the feeder groups and leadership ranks. Goals are part of the an overall People Scorecard that is directly tied to compensation

The Stats

Total worldwide 2004/2003

1. Number of employees: 68,000/68,000
2. Revenues: 13.2 billion/12.2 billion

U.S. Total Employees – Minorities: 17%
U.S. Total Employees – Women: 40%

Retention and Professional Development

How do 2004 minority and female attrition rates generally compare to those experienced in the prior year period?

About the same as in prior years

Please identify the specific steps you are taking to reduce the attrition rate of minority and women employees.

• Develop and/or support internal employee affinity groups (e.g., minority or women networks within the firm)
• Increase/improve current work/life programs
• Strengthen mentoring program for all employees, including minorities and women

Diversity Mission Statement

To create a highly inclusive environment that promotes high levels of performance and discretionary effort

The Williams Companies

One Williams Center
Tulsa, OK 74172
Phone: (918) 573-2000
Phone: (800) 945-5426
www.williams.com/careers

Locations (worldwide)

Tulsa, OK (Corporate Headquarters);
Houston, TX (Regional); Salt Lake City,
UT (Regional); Denver, CO (Regional)

Diversity Leadership

Alison Anthony, Manager of Staffing,
Diversity & College Relations

Contact Person

Steve Beatie
One Williams Center
Tulsa, OK 74102
Phone: (918) 573-2200
Fax: (918) 573-7700

Recruiting

Please list the schools/types of schools at which you recruit.

- *Private schools:* University of Tulsa, University of Houston
- *Public state schools:* University of Oklahoma, Oklahoma State, Louisiana-Lafayette, Colorado School of Mines, University of Utah, Texas A&M, University of Texas, Texas State
- *Historically Black Colleges and Universities (HBCUs):* Florida A&M

Do you have any special outreach efforts that are directed to encourage minority students to consider your firm?

- Sponsor minority student association events
- Outreach to leadership of minority student organizations

Do you use executive recruiting/search firms to seek to identify new diversity hires?

No

Entry-Level Programs/Full-Time Opportunities

Rotational Program

Length of program: 2-3 years
Geographic location(s) of program: Houston; SLC

Please describe the training/training component of this program: Engineering OJT Rotations

Strategic Plan and Diversity Leadership

How does the firm's leadership communicate the importance of diversity to everyone at the firm?

Monthly highlights of diverse populations include e-mails, presentations, and a diversity intranet site

Who has primary responsibility for leading diversity initiatives at your firm?

Alison Anthony, Manager of Staffing, Diversity, and College Relations, although the primary responsibility rests with all of company leadership.

Does your firm currently have a diversity committee?

Yes

If yes, please describe how the committee is structured, how often it meets, etc.:

Meets quarterly, made of representatives across the organization

If yes, does the committee's representation include one or more members of the firm's management/executive committee (or the equivalent)?

Yes, the CEO is a member of the committee.

Does the committee and/or diversity leader establish and set goals or objectives consistent with management's priorities?

Yes

Has the firm undertaken a formal or informal diversity program or set of initiatives aimed at increasing the diversity of the firm?

Yes, informal

How often does the firm's management review the firm's diversity progress/results?

Quarterly and anually

The Stats

Employees: 3,600 (2003, U.S.)
Employees: 100 (2003, outside U.S.)
Employees: 3,700 (2003, worldwide)
Revenue: $12.3 billion (2003, worldwide)

Williams has a 14% minority rate and a 25% female rate in its workforce.

Retention and Professional Development

How do 2004 minority and female attrition rates generally compare to those experienced in the prior year period?

About the same as in prior years

Please identify the specific steps you are taking to reduce the attrition rate of minority and women employees.

• Develop and/or support internal employee affinity groups (e.g., minority or women networks within the firm)
• Increase/improve current work/life programs
• Succession plan includes emphasis on diversity

Diversity Mission Statement

At Williams, we foster an environment that attracts a high-performing, diverse workforce. All individuals are respected and valued for their contributions and have the opportunity to achieve their maximum potential.

Xcel Energy

800 Nicollet Mall
Minneapolis, MN 55402
Phone: (612) 330-5500
Fax: (612) 330-2900
www.xcelenergy.com

Locations (worldwide)
Minnesota, Wisconsin, North Dakota,
South Dakota, Michigan, Colorado, Texas,
New Mexico, Oklahoma, Kansas

Diversity Leadership
Mark Sauerbrey, Recruitment Consultant
414 Nicollet Mall
Minneapolis, MN 55401
Phone: (612) 330-5724
Fax: 612-330-7935
E-mail: mark.w.Sauerbrey@xcelenergy.com

Recruiting

Please list the schools/types of schools at which you recruit.

• Private schools
• Public state schools
• Hispanic Serving Institutions (HSIs)
• Other predominantly minority and/or women's colleges

Do you have any special outreach efforts that are directed to encourage minority students to consider your firm?

• Hold a reception for minority students
• Conferences
• Advertise in minority student association publication(s)
• Participate in/host minority student job fair(s)
• Sponsor minority student association events
• Firm's employees participate on career panels at school
• Outreach to leadership of minority student organizations

What activities does the firm undertake to attract minority and women employees?

• Partner programs with women and minority associations
• Conferences
• Participate at minority job fairs
• Utilize online job services

Do you use executive recruiting/search firms to seek to identify new diversity hires?

Yes

List all women- and/or minority-owned executive search/recruiting firms to which the firm paid a fee for placement services in the past 12 months:

Chandler Group

Internships and Co-ops

Engineering/Business internships are posted per business unit upon approval from hiring managers. The business units run corporation-wide and are open to all students per our EEO policy.

Deadline for application: Varies upon posting

Number of interns in the program in summer 2004 (internship) or 2004 (co-op): 37-40 internship opportunities; summer internships can lead to co-op

Pay: $13.00 to $21.00/hour

Percentage of interns/co-ops in the program who receive offers of full-time employment:oyment: 3-5% are hired to full-time positions, but they must apply as external candidates.

Web site for internship/co-op information: www.xcelenergy.com

Strategic Plan and Diversity Leadership

How does the firm's leadership communicate the importance of diversity to everyone at the firm?

E-mails, web site, newsletters, meetings.

Who has primary responsibility for leading diversity initiatives at your firm?

• Christine Cocchiarella – Director of Workforce Diversity
• Steve Boettcher – Director of Recruitment, Selection & Workforce Planning

Does your firm currently have a diversity committee?

No

Has the firm undertaken a formal or informal diversity program or set of initiatives aimed at increasing the diversity of the firm?

Yes, informal, aiming to inrease the number of women & minority applicants for 2005.

How often does the firm's management review the firm's diversity progress/results?

Monthly

The Stats

Employees: 10,650 (approximate, 2004, U.S.)
Revenue: $8.3 billion (2004, U.S.)

Retention and Professional Development

How do 2004 minority and female attrition rates generally compare to those experienced in the prior year period?

About the same as in prior years

Please identify the specific steps you are taking to reduce the attrition rate of minority and women employees.

• Develop and/or support internal employee affinity groups (e.g., minority or women networks within the firm)

• Increase/improve current work/life programs
• Succession plan includes emphasis on diversity
• Strengthen mentoring program for all employees, including minorities and women
• Professional skills development program, including minority and women employees

The Employer Says

One of Xcel Energy's core values is respecting all people. This ranks in importance with doing business in an ethical, honest manner, protecting our environment, working safely and serving our customers to the best of our ability.

When people believe that who they are and what they do is respected, morale and productivity go up. The end result is a workplace where people feel comfortable being who they are, regardless of their individual differences or personal characteristics.

A number of departments and sites will also go through a training program called "M.E.E.T. on Common Ground: Speaking Up for Respect in the Workplace."

Xerox Corporation

800 Long Ridge Rd.
Stamford, CT 06904
www.xerox.com

Locations (worldwide)
Stamford, CT (HQ)

Diversity Leadership
D. Garvin Byrd, Corporate HR, Manager of
College Programs
1700 Bayberry Court, Suite 200
Richmond, VA 23226
Phone: (804) 289-5493

Recruiting

Please list the schools/types of schools at which you recruit.

• Ivy League schools
• Other private schools
• Public state schools
• Historically Black Colleges and Universities (HBCUs)
• Hispanic Serving Institutions (HSIs)
• Native American Tribal Universities
• Other predominantly minority and/or women's colleges

Do you have any special outreach efforts that are directed to encourage minority students to consider your firm?

• Advertise in minority student association publication(s)
• Participate in/host minority student job fair(s)
• Sponsor minority student association events
• Firm's employees participate on career panels at school
• Outreach to leadership of minority student organizations
• Scholarships or intern/fellowships for minority students
• Brand ads in Diversity publications

What activities does the firm undertake to attract minority and women employees?

• Partner programs with women and minority associations
• Participate at minority job fairs
• Seek referrals from other employees
• Utilize online job services

Do you use executive recruiting/search firms to seek to identify new diversity hires?

No

Internships and Co-ops

Xerox College Experiential Learning Program

Deadline for application: March

Number of interns in the program in summer 2004 (internship) or 2004 (co-op): 171 Interns, 30 Co-ops

Pay: By week; Varies based on academic classification

Length of the program: Minimum 10 weeks

Percentage of interns/co-ops in the program who receive offers of full-time employment:oyment: 63% conversion rate

Web site for internship/co-op information: www.Xerox.com/employment

The internship / co-op program guidelines require the individual to be a full-time student enrolled in a college program leading to achievement of Bachelor's or higher level degree. Must be able to work a minimum of 10 weeks and carry a 3.0 or higher GPA.

Scholarships

Xerox Technical Minority Scholarship Program

Deadline for application for the scholarship program: September 15 of each year

Scholarship award amount: $1,000 to $10,000 once per each year award

Web site or other contact information for scholarship: www.Xerox.com/employment

Guidelines include: Applicant must be Asian , Black, Hispanic, or Native American ; must be enrolled in a four year technical degree program which, when completed, will result in applicant's obtaining a Bachelor's, Master's or PhD degree. Applicant must have a 3.0 GPA or higher.

Affinity Groups/Employee Networks

ACT – Asians Coming Together

Web site: http://www.asianscomingtogether.com/

Provides a voice and forum for education, professional development and interaction; to improve awareness and advocate equitable recognition and advancement opportunities for Asian employees within Xerox.

BWLC-Black Women Leadership Council

Web site: http://www.bwlc.com/

The Black Women's Leadership Council serves as a catalyst to advance professional development and address issues unique to Black women in the Xerox work place. The Black Women's Leadership Council forges partnerships with senior management that facilitate the hiring, retention and development of Black women, and satisfy business needs.

HAPA-The Association for Professional Advancement

Web site: http://www.hapa.org/

The HAPA National Leadership Council is the voice to Xerox management representing Xerox Hispanics and HAPA Chapters, promoting Hispanic objectives that enable increased Xerox business results

GALAXe-Pride at Work

Web site: http://www.galaxe.org/

Galaxe Pride At Work is a formal organization for Xerox employees who are or who support gay, lesbian, bisexual, or transgendered (GLBT) persons. Galaxe Pride At Work's mission is to offer support and visibility within Xerox and beyond to its members, and to provide an official point of contact between its membership and Xerox Corporation, as well as with other gay, lesbian, bisexual, and transgender organizations external to Xerox.

National Black Employee Association (NBEA)

Web site: http://www.nbea.net/

The National Black Employees Association (NBEA) is a national caucus group of African-American Xerox employees. Ten local caucus groups covering the continental United States make up the NBEA. The NBEA is devoted to the principle that professional abilities and talents are possessed by individuals and that these traits are not the exclusive traits of any one ethnic or racial group. NBEA supports all efforts to eliminate employment and promotion practices that tend to deny this fundamental principle.

TWA – The Women's Alliance

Web site: http://www.thewomensalliance.net/

The Women's Alliance (TWA) is a catalyst to increase communications and awareness of women at Xerox, enabling women to attain their personal goals. The vision of TWA is to see that the women of Xerox are recognized and valued by the Company for their significant contributions and leadership.

Entry-Level Programs/Full-Time Opportunities

VP Development Program

- Provides leadership development for "ready-now" and newly appointed VPs; content based on nine priority development objectives for VP candidates:
- Deliver more customer value
- Develop a powerful organizational vision and motivate their team to achieve it
- Explore a wide range of innovative options in the decision-making process
- Hire and retain the right people
- Make personal and organizational growth a priority
- Stay the course, walk the talk and maintain an optimistic outlook even in trying times
- Make the leap from a tactical to a strategic role
- Learn to prioritize more effectively
- Work for the benefit of the entire company

The Emerging Leader Program

This program provides leadership development opportunity for selected employees who have demonstrated the potential to move forward in the company. The program spans two years and involves four, 5-day face to-face participant meetings, and independent learning opportunities between meetings.

Tuition Assistance: Another important aspect of some employees' development and work/life balance is educational pursuits. If a Xerox employee or his/her dependent is planning to attend college, Xerox offers three programs to help finance this. The Tuition Aid Program supports an employee's professional development by reimbursing her/him for tuition and fees based upon successful completion of each course (up to $10,000 per year). The ConSern program offers employees the opportunity to apply for low-cost loans ranging from $2,000 to $20,000. The funds can be used for an accredited college or university, private secondary school or pre-approved proprietary or trade school. In addition, Xerox employees have access to an online university on our Intranet of more than 1,000 training courses, which they may pursue on their own or under the guidance of their manager – at no cost.

Strategic Plan and Diversity Leadership

How does the firm's leadership communicate the importance of diversity to everyone at the firm?

• Town Hall meetings with Senior managers
• Quarterly Reviews with Employee Caucus Group Leadership
• Internal and external Diversity website
• Electronic communication/ announcements to all employees
• See attached diversity brochure
• Electronic communication Web Board for employee stories

Who has primary responsibility for leading diversity initiatives at your firm?

Chief Diversity and Employee Advocacy Officer.

Does your firm currently have a diversity committee?

Yes

If yes, please describe how the committee is structured, how often it meets, etc.

Xerox Executive Diversity Council

Purpose: Serve as an executive leadership body and focus group for diversity and work environment initiatives and concerns. Represent the balanced needs and requirements of all employees.

Objectives: Focus efforts on the vital few i.e.,
• Work force representation
• Work environment
• Diverse Customer markets
• Review, recommend and advise on Xerox diversity practices
• Support organizational efforts to address the needs of a multicultural workforce

Council composition and operation:
• Members selected by the office of Corporate Diversity and Corporate VP of HR, and supported by the CEO
• Consist of 12 members
• Council meets two to three times per year

If yes, does the committee's representation include one or more members of the firm's management/executive committee (or the equivalent)?

Yes. Total executives on the committee: 6 Corporate Officers

Does the committee and/or diversity leader establish and set goals or objectives consistent with management's priorities?

Yes

Has the firm undertaken a formal or informal diversity program or set of initiatives aimed at increasing the diversity of the firm?

Yes, formal. In 1985, Xerox initiated its Balanced Work Force Strategy. The BWF program is intended to be a program of inclusion for all people. It is designed to achieve equitable representation with respect to race and gender at all levels, in all functions, in all disciplines, in all business divisions. All managers need to demonstrate appropriate diverse behaviors, and ensure that their human resource practices are fair and equitable. This strategy has been carefully designed to improve balances in representation in the Xerox work force and to ensure a balanced work force is maintained in the event of restructuring initiatives

Employee Caucus Groups

Primary mission:
- Employee Advocacy
- Self-Development
- Promoters of change
- Management interface on work environment

Corporate Champions Program

- Voice at corporate level for employee concerns
- Council's and advises Caucus leadership
- Serve as a communication linkage in regards to continuous improvement.

Succession Planning

- Focuses on all employees
- Ensures diverse supply of talent for key management positions.
- Help develops employees to meet their career objectives
- Assist in meeting the long-term business needs of the company

Minority/Female Vendor Program

- Demonstrates Xerox's commitment to purchasing products and supplies and services from qualified minority-owned and Women owned businesses.

Diversity Training

Two levels:
- Awareness: Introduces concepts, values and policies
- Skill Building: Leveraging Diversity to enhance performance and productivity
E-learning main delivery, limited trainer led sessions

Work Life Programs

- Dependent Care fund
- Alternative Work Schedules
- Life Cycle Assistance (Adoption Assistance, Mortgage Assistance & Partial Pay Replacement for FMLA Leaves)
- Child Care subsidy, Child Care Resource & Referral
- Employee Assistance Program
- Education Assistance
- A Matter of Choice (Benefits programs)
- Domestic Partner Benefits

How often does the firm's management review the firm's diversity progress/results?

Monthly, and Quarterly

Retention and Professional Development

How do 2004 minority and female attrition rates generally compare to those experienced in the prior year period?

Lower than in prior years

Please identify the specific steps you are taking to reduce the attrition rate of minority and women employees.

- Develop and/or support internal employee affinity groups (e.g., minority or women networks within the firm)
- Increase/review compensation relative to competition
- Increase/improve current work/life programs
- Succession plan includes emphasis on diversity
- Work with minority and women employees to develop career advancement plans
- Professional skills development program, including minority and women employees

The Employer Says

Vision:

Our vision is for everyone to treat each other with equality, dignity, and respect. As individuals on a team, each member can rely on others' strengths to build on team potential and company productivity.

Goal:

Our goal is to promote understanding and inclusion, and to raise awareness of behaviors surrounding all types of "isms", e.g. sexism, racism.

In support of this the company will:

- Leverage differences as a competitive advantage
- Develop leadership that values unique perspectives
- Embrace a framework which diverse work groups can consistently perform and improve their work.

YMCA of the USA

101 N. Wacker Dr.
Chicago, IL 60606
Phone: (312) 977-0031
Fax: (312) 977-9063
www.ymca.net

Diversity Leadership
Nicole Steels, Senior Human Resources
Generalist
101 N. Wacker Dr., Suite 1400
Chicago, IL 60606
Phone: (312) 977-0031
Fax: (312) 977-3542

Recruiting

What activities does the firm undertake to attract minority and women employees?

• Seek referrals from other employees
• Utilize online job services
• Other: Utilize minority job boards

Do you use executive recruiting/search firms to seek to identify new diversity hires?

Yes

If yes, list all women- and/or minority-owned executive search/recruiting firms to which the firm paid a fee for placement services in the past 12 months:

We make formal written requests to the each of recruiting and search firms whose services we use to seek out diverse candidates for our open positions.

Scholarships

F.M.M. Richardson Fund

Deadline for application for the scholarship program: Online applications are accepted year-round.
Scholarship award amount: $600 per person per academic year

This scholarship was established in 1971 through a bequest by F.M.M. Richardson, general secretary from 1929 to 1939 of the YMCA in Birmingham, AL. In accordance with his wishes, it assists black senior directors in obtaining training and education toward professional growth and greater upward mobility in the national movement. It also supports development projects at YMCAs serving black communities in the former "South Field" and throughout the Y system.

Applicants must be African American Certified Senior Directors of the YMCA.

William A. Hunton Fellowship Fund

Deadline for application for the scholarship program: The scholarship period is from July 1st to June 30th. Award monies will expire on July 1st of the following year.
Scholarship award amount: Scholarships are awarded based on need and availability, usually, but not necessarily, limited to $1000 per person per calendar year. Awards are disbursed on a reimbursement basis only.

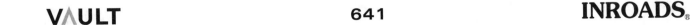

The purpose of the scholarship is to help African-American staff members complete the Staff Development Program of the YMCA of the USA: the scholarship can be awarded for training towards Director, Professional Director or Senior Director certification, or for college if the applicant has the Director or Professional Director certification.

William A. Hunton became the first full-time African-American director of a YMCA in 1888, when he joined the Colored Y of Norfolk, VA., as general secretary. He later joined the national YMCA staff as head of the Colored Works Department.

Eligibility criteria:

• Applicants must be African-American Exempt Staff members currently employed at a chartered YMCA.
• Awards will be made on the basis of need, with consideration given to the applicant's tenure, position and previous staff development training.
• Applicants must exhibit determination to continue their work with the YMCA.
• For college credit, the scholarship can be awarded only to those applicants who have completed YMCA training for Director Certification: Group Work, Volunteerism and Principles and Practices.

YMCA Minority Staff Scholarship Program

Deadline for application for the scholarship program: The scholarship period is from July 1st to June 30th. Award monies will expire on July 1st of the following year.

Scholarship award amount: Scholarships are awarded based on need and availability, usually, but not necessarily, limited to $1000 per person per calendar year. Awards are disbursed on a reimbursement basis only.

This program is sponsored by the YMCA of the USA. The purpose is twofold: to assist minority staff members to advance in the YMCA through training experiences that help them grow as YMCA professionals, and to assist them in completing their college education so they can embark on a professional YMCA career.

Eligibility criteria:

• Applicants must be active staff members of the YMCA: exempt or nonexempt, full-time or part-time.
• Applicants must be Hispanic/Latino, African American, Asian/Pacific Islander or Native American/Alaskan Native.
• Education and training events must be career related. They may be offered within or outside the YMCA.
• For education, scholarships are awarded only to those YMCA staff members who have taken some YMCA training towards achieving their YMCA Senior Director Certification.
• Applicants must exhibit determination to continue work with the YMCA.

Contact information for all scholarships

Jennifer Flannery
Scholarship Coordinator – YMCA University
YMCA of the USA
101 North Wacker Drive
Chicago, IL 60606
Toll Free: (800) 872-9622 x 8409
Direct: (312) 419-8409
Email: jennifer.flannery@ymca.net

Affinity Groups/Employee Networks

African American Alliance diversity group

The purpose of the group is to establish an alliance amongst African American staff at YMCA of the USA.

The goal is to develop an agenda that will identify strategies and solutions to create, enhance and promote opportunities for African American staff, both professionally and personally. The group also aims to work in establishing a more positive environment and working relationship within Y-USA.

SPEAK diversity group

Background and Justification: The YMCA of the USA SPEAK (Serving People with Equality, Acceptance and Kindness) Diversity Group was originally formed in 2002 to address Gay, Lesbian, Bisexual, Transgender and Questioning (GLBTQ) sexuality issues of Y-USA employees and to promote a work environment where all employees-regardless of sexual orientation-are treated equally.

Mission: Our mission is to connect, serve, and lead YMCAs in building a diverse culture of inclusion and respect-without discrimination, intimidation, or disparate treatment-especially for GLBTQ individuals within Y-USA and throughout the Movement.

Purpose: Our purpose is to educate national and local YMCA staff around GLBTQ issues, provide support, foster open discussion and create a welcoming environment for all employees.

Vision: We envision a workplace where sexual orientation plays no role in how an employee is treated, and where each employee feels welcome, important and respected based on his/her own merit, efforts and actions and not on perceptions, beliefs or stereotypes.

Strategic Plan and Diversity Leadership

How does the firm's leadership communicate the importance of diversity to everyone at the firm?

Our CEO takes the time to reinforce his support of our diversity initiatives at key speaking events, and in written communication to staff as part of our strategic plan. Additionally, our diversity group conducted staff focus groups and surveys specifically relating to diversity at YMCA of the USA, then released the results of the survey at a staff lunch presentation. Recently, the diversity group's strategic plan was distributed via our staff intranet along with an invitation for staff to participate in the group. The strategic plan was also discussed at the all-staff meeting.

Who has primary responsibility for leading diversity initiatives at your firm?

Ken Gladish, National Executive Director , and Sam Evans, Director of Movement Advancement

Does your firm currently have a diversity committee?

Yes. The group is set to meet at least once per month, but during the development of the strategic plan they have met approximately 3-4 times per month. The group is structured with a lead change agent for the group, one diversity consultant and the remaining staff members, who represent a cross-section of the organization in terms of position in the company, work location and different characteristics of diversity.

If yes, does the committee's representation include one or more members of the firm's management/executive committee (or the equivalent)?

Yes

If yes, how many executives are on the committee, and in 2004, what was the total number of hours collectively spent by the committee in furtherance of the firm's diversity initiatives? How many employees are on the committee, and how often does the committee convene in furtherance of the firm's diversity initiatives?

The committee has three executives who are involved with the group's goals and operations. The overall committee is made up of 13 individuals, with both Sam Evans serving as the primary change agent. In 2004, it is estimated that the group collectively spent approximately 150 hours to further the diversity initiative at YMCA of the USA.

Total Executives on Committee: 3

Does the committee and/or diversity leader establish and set goals or objectives consistent with management's priorities?

Yes

The diversity initiative is one of three primary initiatives for YMCA of the USA. Although the stated priority of the diversity initiative is directed towards making local YMCAs more diverse, we feel as though we need to serve as a model for local YMCA associations, and have given great attention to the issue of Diversity at YMCA of the USA.

Has the firm undertaken a formal or informal diversity program or set of initiatives aimed at increasing the diversity of the firm?

Yes, formal.

The YMCA of the USA is actively participating in the YMCA Diversity Initiative. The diversity initiative uses a six-step process for creating systemic change. Y-USA's vision for the diversity initiative is that the YMCA movement will be known for practicing inclusion by valuing the diversity of all people within its associations and the communities it serves. Through training and counsel, Y-USA helps YMCAs increase and support the cultural competence of their staff professionals, volunteers and members.

Diversity is the mosaic of people who bring a variety of backgrounds, styles, perspectives, beliefs and competencies as assets to the YMCA. By practicing inclusion, Ys not only address societal trends and remain relevant to their communities but also remain true to the YMCA mission, goals and values.

How often does the firm's management review the firm's diversity progress/results?

Annually. There will be a diversity team progress evaluation/review component built into the completed strategic plan.

How is the firm's diversity committee and/or firm management held accountable for achieving results?

YMCA of the USA sponsors the national diversity initiative, helping local YMCAs throughout the U.S.A and Canada to initiate their diversity initiatives. In this sense, we are held accountable by local YMCAs who expect us to lead them in diversity efforts.

Furthermore, the National Executive Director of YMCA of the USA has set out specific directives for his leadership team in regards to actions for their specific departments, and leadership team members are held accountable for achieving these goals as a part of the performance management process.

Additionally, YMCA of the USA has set an organizational performance goal stating that all staff must attend training in one of our three national initiatives, one of which is our diversity initiative. Thus far, over ½ of our staff have participated in this diversity training.

Finally, the diversity committee is presently finalizing the overall diversity strategic plan, and the plan will explicitly contain an accountability portion within it.

The Stats

Revenue: $79.684 million (2004, worldwide)
Revenue: $76.770 million (2003, worldwide)

Ethnicity

Asian Employees
2004 Percent of Total: 4
2003 Percent of Total: 3

Black Employees
2004 Percent of Total: 18
2003 Percent of Total: 18

Hispanic Employees – All Races
2004 Percent of Total: 5
2003 Percent of Total: 3

White Employees
2004 Percent of Total: 73
2003 Percent of Total: 75

Gender

Female Employees
2004 Percent of Total: 57
2003 Percent of Total: 58

Retention and Professional Development

How do 2004 minority and female attrition rates generally compare to those experienced in the prior year period?

About the same as in prior years

Please identify the specific steps you are taking to reduce the attrition rate of minority and women employees.

• Develop and/or support internal employee affinity groups (e.g., minority or women networks within the firm)
• Increase/improve current work/life programs
• Adopt dispute resolution process
• Professional skills development program, including minority and women employees

Diversity Mission Statement

Vision statements depict the ideal state of an organization 10 or more years in the future. Stated below is the vision for diversity and inclusion at YMCA of the USA. Imagine if we could truthfully and undeniably say this about ourselves here at Y-USA:

YMCA of the USA staff and leadership take pride in living our values of caring, honesty, respect and responsibility. We live out these values by fostering a culture in which we hold each other accountable for making diversity and inclusion integral to our plans, processes, decisions and actions. Together we create a trusting, exciting atmosphere that values the diversity, contribution, and talents of every individual, enabling all to reach their fullest potential. We do this to achieve our highest level of performance, resulting in exceptional leadership and service to YMCAs and the Movement.

Goals are the broad targets toward which an organization directs its efforts.

• The YMCA's mission is to build spirit, mind and body for all. Therefore we will value every staff member's diverse talents and help each other develop to our fullest potential.

• Because YMCA of the USA has a role in leading the movement, we will show our commitment to diversity and inclusion by moving forward with our own diversity plan and demonstrating daily policies and practices which fulfill that plan.

• In keeping with YMCA traditions-fun, fellowship, community and values-we will create a vibrant and trusting environment in which all staff feel that they are respected and that they belong.

• Diversity is an essential component of high-performing organizations, so we will build and maintain a diverse staff that reflects the YMCAs and communities we serve.

Strategies identify the course or path an organization will take-what it needs to do, to be, or to become-in order to attain its goals.

Strategies to achieve our vision and goals

• Culture: Create and nurture an environment of respect, trust and inclusion

• Access and development: Ensure equal access to opportunities and proactive development for all staff, so that we can utilize all staff to their full potential, increasing our capacity to serve YMCAs and the Movement.

• Dialogue practices: Actively engage principal stakeholders in meaningful dialogue before making decisions

• Leadership: Cultivate and reward leaders whose mindset, vision and behavior foster diversity and inclusion

• Accountability, evaluation and celebration: Engender ownership-responsibility, accountability and pride-in Y-USA's culture of inclusion

The Employer Says

History of the National Diversity Initiative – Continuing its Priority at the YMCA

Throughout its 154-year history, the YMCA has responded to the demands and shifts of a society being transformed with ever-growing communities in its quest to build strong kids, strong families and strong communities. A new era in fulfilling that mission arose in response to changing demographics and needs in communities served by YMCAs: a comprehensive diversity initiative for the YMCA of the USA was an 'idea whose time had come.' At the heart of this initiative is the voice of communities across the nation that expressed the need for the YMCA to remain significant, relevant and viable servant leaders to our communities and the families in them.

• In the late 1990s, the Urban Group began exploring ways that local associations could become more culturally competent and inclusive in their service areas. They formed a task force that assessed the cultures within YMCAs and brought back recommendations.

• Begun in 1999, the Task Force convened a team of twelve people that worked with Dr. Tina Rasmussen, the Y-USA's external diversity consultant, to create a diversity plan and process that could be implemented. Their goal was: "To support the YMCA mission by encouraging, facilitating and supporting increased cultural competence in YMCA individuals and organizations and achieving measurable progress on locally defined diversity goals."

The Y-USA's vision for diversity is:

The YMCA will be known for practicing inclusion by valuing the diversity of all people within our associations and the communities we serve.

The Task Force transitioned to a National Diversity Steering Committee comprised of CEOs, heads of leadership development networks (formerly termed "affinity groups"), national Y support staff, and the external consultant. Significant accomplishments have been made since the first YMCAs began their association-wide diversity initiatives in January 2000.

Principle accomplishments are:

• Championing a Diversity Initiative workshop, a two-and-a-half day institute was developed. This workshop guides CEOs, their association's change agents, staff and volunteers through the Six-Step Diversity Enhancement Process. More than 500 individuals representing more than 100 Associations (including YMCA of the USA) have graduated from this workshop with numerous Ys experiencing scorecard results as they implement the process;

• Diversity module added to Principles and Practices training series, ImpactPlus, Teens and other national and mission strategy trainings;

• The Y-USA created the Diversity Specialty Consultant position to guide the Initiative nationally and provide support to the YUSA internal diversity team (2002);

• Creation and preparation of a support network for Champions through the Designated Diversity Consultants (2003) and Diversity Initiative Advisory Team (July 2004);

- Inception of an interactive, innovative diversity website on the YMCA Exchange as of June 2004 where Ys can download tools and share program and other innovative strategies;

- Received and working collaboratively with other Y-USA staff seeking corporate and foundation funding support to sponsor aspects of implementation;

- Enjoyed the first issue of *Discovery Magazine* devoted specifically to the Diversity Initiative! (June 2004)

- Approximately 120 YMCAs have completed the initial workshop and are implementing the strategic model for ensuring that YMCAs serve all. Approximately 1000 YMCA staff, executives and board members have attended the workshop.

- A second level of workshop entitled, "Deepening the Diversity Initiative within Your YMCA" has been designed and launched in 2004 with tremendous results. In this two-day workshop, branch executives, other staff and volunteers become equipped to use the systemic change model in their every-day operations. To date, approximately ten such workshops have been conducted.

- In its 2005 summer issue, the Association of YMCA Professionals' publication, *Perspective* featured the National Diversity Initiative via its challenging theme, "Is the YMCA Truly for All?"

Yum! Brands, Inc.

1441 Gardiner Ln.
Louisville, KY 40213
www.yumcareers.com

Locations (worldwide)
Louisville, KY, Dallas, TX, Irvine, CA

Diversity Leadership
Richard-Abraham Rugnao, Public Affairs,
Manager, Global Diversity
1441 Gardiner Lane
Louisville, KY 40213
Phone: (502) 874-8300
Fax: (502) 874-8662

Recruiting

Please list the schools/types of schools at which you recruit.

• Ivy League schools
• Other private schools
• Public state schools
• Historically Black Colleges and Universities (HBCUs)
• Other predominantly minority and/or women's colleges:

Do you have any special outreach efforts that are directed to encourage minority students to consider your firm?

• Conferences: National Black/ Hispanic MBAs, INROADS
• Participate in/host minority student job fair(s)

What activities does the firm undertake to attract minority and women employees?

• Partner programs with women and minority associations
• Conferences: National Urban League, NAACP, NCLR, LULAC, OCA, INROADS
• Participate at minority job fairs
• Seek referrals from other employees
• Utilize online job services

Do you use executive recruiting/search firms to seek to identify new diversity hires?

No

Scholarships

• **Yum! Scholarship Program:** The Yum! Scholarship Program offers scholarship money to all U.S. based restaurant and Restaurant Support Center employees that have worked at the company for at least one year and average at least 20 hours per week. Yum awards the following: $2,500 for any field of study in a four-year or graduate program; $1,000 for any field of study

at a two-year or vocational-technical school; up to 10 "bonus" awards of $1,500 for students pursuing an approved food service/hospitality degree.

- In 2004, Yum! awarded more than $500,000 in scholarships for the Yum! Scholarship Program. Approximately 15 percent of the scholarships awarded went to African-American scholars.

- **KFC** – United Negro College Fund Scholars: As part of KFC's ongoing commitment to diversity and the development of its employees, KFC provides scholarships to eligible students attending UNCF schools. The KFC/UNCF Scholars Program is aimed towards employees who are entry-level college freshman pursuing degrees in Business Management, Computer Science or Liberal Arts.

- **Scholarships for Minorities:** Yum! Brands has a number of scholarships for minorities including the American Indian College Fund to increase the number of American Indian graduates, and similar programs for Hispanic, Asian and African-Americans.

- **Taco Bell – Glen Bell Scholarship Program:** Open to Taco Bell hourly employees, the program awards financial scholarships of up to $2,000 for accredited undergraduate, graduate and vocational-technical educations. In 2004, Taco Bell's Glen Bell awarded $100,000 in scholarships.

- **Language Class Reimbursement Program:** Hourly or salaried employees can receive up to $500 per year for language class tuition, books and materials.

- **Tuition Reimbursement Program:** The Company will reimburse full-time, salaried employees up to a maximum of $4,000 per calendar year for graduate and undergraduate courses.

Affinity Groups/Employee Networks

Pizza Hut has an African American, Hispanic, and Women's group. Each brand is exploring the development of their respective groups.

Strategic Plan and Diversity Leadership

How does the firm's leadership communicate the importance of diversity to everyone at the firm?

Yum! takes a comprehensive approach to communicating its diversity efforts. All means of internal and external communications are utilized.

Who has primary responsibility for leading diversity initiatives at your firm?

Terrian Barnes – Director, Global Diversity

Does your firm currently have a diversity committee?

No

Does the committee and/or diversity leader establish and set goals or objectives consistent with management's priorities?

Yes

Has the firm undertaken a formal or informal diversity program or set of initiatives aimed at increasing the diversity of the firm?

Yes, formal

How often does the firm's management review the firm's diversity progress/results?

Quarterly

The Stats

Employees: 130,000 (2004, U.S.)
Employees: 90,000 (2003, U.S.)
Employees: 220,000* (2004, worldwide)
Employees: 210,000* (2003, worldwide)
Revenue: $9.011 billion (2004, worldwide)
Revenue: $8,380 billion (2003, worldwide)

Includes only corporate employees – does not include employees of Yum! franchises

Retention and Professional Development

How do 2004 minority and female attrition rates generally compare to those experienced in the prior year period?

Higher than in prior years

Develop and/or support internal employee affinity groups (e.g., minority or women networks within the firm)

- Increase/review compensation relative to competition
- Increase/improve current work/life programs
- Adopt dispute resolution process
- Succession plan includes emphasis on diversity
- Work with minority and women employees to develop career advancement plans
- Strengthen mentoring program for all employees, including minorities and women
- Professional skills development program, including minority and women employees

Diversity Mission Statement

Diversity is not a strategy or a program at Yum! Brands. It's a shared commitment by all of us to uphold our founding truths and to live out our How We Work Together principles every day.

The Employer Says

Yum! Brands, Inc., with more than 33,000 restaurants in over 100 countries, is the parent to A&W Restaurants, KFC, Long John Silver's, Pizza Hut and Taco Bell. As the world's largest restaurant company and the third largest employer in the world with more than 850,000 employees around the globe, our continued success in the marketplace depends on creating an environment where all people are valued, appreciated, and have the opportunity to grow and learn. That is why we have built a global culture focused on respect and recognition.

Moreover, Yum! is committed to realizing the business benefits of driving diversity and inclusion by developing current and future business leaders, franchisees, and suppliers that reflect the changing demographics of our customers.

Making progress in diversity is a personal priority for our Chairman and CEO David Novak, and a business priority for our entire organization. David updates the system annually on the progress we are making to reflect the communities in which we operate. Everyone in the company – from our senior leadership team at the Restaurant Support Centers to our team members in the restaurants – is accountable for fostering an inclusive, diverse workplace culture.

"Yum! Brand's commitment to diversity helps drive all aspects of our business," says David C. Novak, Chairman and CEO, Yum! Brands, Inc. "It's important that our global culture is actively developing a workforce with a broad mix of backgrounds and viewpoints at all levels of management. Building on our diverse foundation at all of our brands gives us a competitive edge and helps drive Customer Mania."

For the past two years, Yum! Brands has been nationally recognized by a leading business magazine as one of the "50 Best Companies for Minorities," claiming the number-one spot for "managerial diversity." The magazine ranked Yum among the top ten companies having the highest percentage of African-American and Native American employees. In 2004, Yum! jumped 20 spots to place 15th out of 50 on the list.

In addition, Yum! also has been named the #1 company for Work/Life Balance in Louisville, one of the Best Places to Work in Kentucky and Pizza Hut has been named the #1 Best Place to Work in Dallas. We are very proud of these accomplishments because they reflect Yum's commitment to diversity and to making the company a great place to work.

Our goal for 2005 is to continue to embrace and strengthen our diversity effectiveness with customers, franchise partners, suppliers and the community, and to continue to build our talent pipeline with an even stronger emphasis on diversity.

Zurich American Insurance Company

www.zurichna.com

Locations (worldwide)
Complete listing on website

Diversity Leadership
- Bob Clawson, Vice President, Talent Management
- Lisa Montague, University Recruiting and Relations Officer

1400 American Lane
Schaumburg, IL 60196
Phone: (877) 847-6593
Fax: (847) 413-5206
E-mail: lisa.montague@zurichna.com

Recruiting

Please list the schools/types of schools at which you recruit.

- *Private schools:* Cornell University, Dartmouth College, Columbia University, Bradley University, Creighton University, Gannon University, Illinois Wesleyan University, Johns Hopkins University, Marquette University, Massachusetts Institute of Technology, New York University, Olivet College, Roosevelt University, St. John's University, St. Olaf College, Saint Mary's College, Saint Mary's University, Stanford University, Temple University, University of Notre Dame, University of Pennsylvania, University of Southern California

- *Public state schools:* Appalachian State University, Ball State University, California State University Sacramento, Columbia Southern University, Florida State University, Georgia State University, Grand Valley State University, Indiana State University, Illinois State University, Indiana State University, Middle Tennessee State University, Northern Illinois University, Purdue University, San Francisco State University, San Jose State University, University of Arizona, University of California at Berkeley, University of California at Davis, University of Central Arkansas, University of Delaware, University of Georgia, University of Hartford, University of Illinois at Chicago, University of Illinois Urbana Champaign, University of Michigan Ann Arbor, University of Mississippi, University of Nebraska, University of North Carolina, University of North Texas, University of South Carolina-Columbia, University of Texas at Austin, University of Wisconsin-Whitewater, University of Wisconsin-Madison

- *Historically Black Colleges and Universities (HBCUs):* Howard University, Morgan State

Do you have any special outreach efforts that are directed to encourage minority students to consider your firm?

- Participate in/host minority student job fair(s)
- Outreach to leadership of minority student organizations

What activities does the firm undertake to attract minority and women employees?

- Partner programs with women and minority associations
- Participate at minority job fairs
- Seek referrals from other employees
- Utilize online job services

Do you use executive recruiting/search firms to seek to identify new diversity hires?

Yes

List all women- and/or minority-owned executive search/recruiting firms to which the firm paid a fee for placement services in the past 12 months:

SL Enterprises, Career Advancement Consultants, Insurance Consultants, QuestPro, Pat Allen & Associates, The Marver Group, Pryor Associates, North Star International, National Search

Internships and Co-ops

Zurich Internship Program

Deadline for application: February 15th
Number of interns in the program in summer 2004 (internship) or 2004 (co-op): 70
Pay: $10-$25 per hour
Length of the program: 10-12 weeks
Web site for internship/co-op information: www.zurichna.com

The Internship Program seeks to provide participants with a strong understanding of and appreciation for the functional area that they are working in and how that functional area interacts with others in the organization, and an understanding of the framework of Zurich in North America.

Interns are recruited for the locations that have determined a need and have budgeted for the interns. The program is formalized and structured; it encompasses "real work" assignments. There are formalized program assessments as well as intern and mentor performance assessments throughout the summer. During the course of the summer program, the intern will assume the duties of the job as if it were a permanent position and will work alongside the talented professionals who actually hold these roles today.

The objective of the Internship Program is to prepare individuals for careers in their field of study. In the end, participants come away with a unique and well-rounded understanding of Zurich in North America – its products, its services, and its customers – a valuable set of skills and a chance to walk in the shoes of other professionals.

Zurich in North America provides interns with mentors during the summer program and has the complete commitment of senior management in recruitment and retention of talented college students.

The Internship Program looks for college sophomore and junior candidates who can demonstrate problem-solving skills in a customer-focused environment; a willingness to work hard and to learn; strong written and verbal communication skills; excellent time-management skills; flexibility; the ability to work independently; self-motivation; and a minimum cumulative grade point average of 3.0. Program is May to August only and unfortunately, we do not provide housing.

Entry-Level Programs/Full-Time Opportunities

Associate Program

Length of program: 11 months
Geographic location(s) of program: Nationwide travel, based out of Schaumburg, IL

Please describe the training/training component of this program: Rotation-based training in field offices combined with classroom training

Strategic Plan and Diversity Leadership

How does the firm's leadership communicate the importance of diversity to everyone at the firm?

Web site

Who has primary responsibility for leading diversity initiatives at your firm?

Bob Clawson, Vice President, Talent Management

Does your firm currently have a diversity committee?

No

Has the firm undertaken a formal or informal diversity program or set of initiatives aimed at increasing the diversity of the firm?

Yes, formal

How often does the firm's management review the firm's diversity progress/results?

Annually

The Stats

Employees: 9,011 (2004, U.S.)
Employees: 9,375 (2003, U.S.)

Minorities: 17%
Actual #: 1,642
Males: 41%
Females: 59%

Diversity Mission Statement

"We treat others with respect."

The Employer Says

• We are caring and respect the dignity of those we work with and those we serve
• We believe in equal opportunity, fair evaluations, and rewards based on performance and merit
• We value our gender, cultural, racial and other diversity
• We communicate professionally, even when we disagree

Zurich is committed to workforce diversity and acknowledging the many ways in which diversity issues are changing the world of business. As an organization, we strive to create an inclusive culture that understands and values the similarities and differences that exist among our managers, team members, customers and clients.

We want an environment where people who are diverse are recognized, feel valued, and can go as far as their talent and ambition allow. We want to create an inclusive culture that understands and values diversity in age, ethnic origin, gender, lifestyles, physical abilities, race, religious beliefs, sexual orientation, work background, and other perceived differences. We encourage, recognize and reward individuals to work together toward team, company and individual goals. We believe that by leveraging diversity as a competitive advantage we make our organization a better place to work.

About the Authors

About Vault

Vault is the leading media company for career information. The Vault Career Library includes 100+ titles for job seekers, professionals and researchers. Vault's team of industry-focused editors takes a journalistic approach in covering news, employment trends and specific employers in their industries. Vault annually surveys 10,000s of employees to bring readers the inside scoop on industries and specific employers.

Popular Vault career titles include

- The College Career Bible
- Vault Guide to the Top Internships
- Vault Career Guide to Consulting
- Vault Career Guide to Investment Banking
- Vault Career Guide to Media & Entertainment
- Vault Career Guide to Real Estate
- Vault Guide to Technology Careers
- Many more

For a full list of titles, go to www.vault.com

About INROADS

Since 1970, INROADS has provided leadership and support for the national effort to increase the representation of talented Black, Hispanic/Latino, and Native American Indian women and men in the private sector. The Fortune 500 companies and other organizations that support INROADS recognize that INROADS is a doorway for business – leading to the benefits of early access to the most talented ethnically diverse human capital before the competition.

In the past 34 years, INROADS has trained more than 40,000 high school and undergraduate students in leadership skills and business competencies. With a focus to improve access and build workforce diversity, INROADS provides a talent pipeline of high potential future executives to America's leading businesses by placing these professionally trained students in multi-year internships.

Alphabetical List of Underwriters

- Abercrombie & Fitch
- American Express Tax & Business Services
- American Family Insurance
- Aramark
- Bayer Crop Science
- Bristol Myers Squibb
- CIT
- Citigroup
- Computer Sciences Corporation
- Convergys Corporation
- Duke Realty Corporation
- Ernst & Young LLP
- Exelon Corporation
- Fifth Third Bank
- General Electric
- HCA
- IBM
- INROADS
- Liberty Mutual
- Limited Brands

- Lockheed Martin
- L'Oreal USA
- Northrop Grumman
- Northwestern Mutual
- Osram Sylvania
- Pacificare Health Systems
- Pearson
- PricewaterhouseCoopers
- Sprint
- SunTrust Banks
- SUNY Upstate
- Terex
- TXU
- Weyerhaeuser
- Xerox Corporation